Advances in Financial Risk Management

Advances in Financial Risk Management

Corporates, Intermediaries and Portfolios

Edited by

Jonathan A. Batten
Monash University, Melbourne, Australia

Peter MacKay
Hong Kong University of Science and Technology

and

Niklas Wagner
Department of Business and Economics, University of Passau, Germany

palgrave
macmillan

First published 2013 by
PALGRAVE MACMILLAN

Palgrave Macmillan in the UK is an imprint of Macmillan Publishers Limited, registered in England, company number 785998, of Houndmills, Basingstoke, Hampshire RG21 6XS.

Palgrave Macmillan in the US is a division of St Martin's Press LLC, 175 Fifth Avenue, New York, NY 10010.

Palgrave Macmillan is the global academic imprint of the above companies and has companies and representatives throughout the world.

Palgrave® and Macmillan® are registered trademarks in the United States, the United Kingdom, Europe and other countries

ISBN: 978–1–137–02508–1

This book is printed on paper suitable for recycling and made from fully managed and sustained forest sources. Logging, pulping and manufacturing processes are expected to conform to the environmental regulations of the country of origin.

A catalogue record for this book is available from the British Library.

A catalog record for this book is available from the Library of Congress.

Contents

Figures

Tables

Preface

Advances in Financial Risk Management: Corporates, Intermediaries and Portfolios includes seventeen chapters that provide the latest research on measuring, managing and pricing financial risk. Three very broad perspectives are considered. The volume comprises three parts: financial risk in non-financial corporations; in financial intermediaries such as banks, which importantly must comply with regulatory standards on measuring and managing risk; and finally within the context of a portfolio of securities of different credit quality and marketability.

Almost thirty years ago, Smith and Stulz (1985) established a theory to explain why some and not all value-maximizing corporations hedged financial risk, and of the risks hedged why some risks were hedged and others ignored. It is within this context that the first five chapters of this volume, compiled as Part I 'Corporate', should be considered.

I. Financial risk management in non-financial corporations

The first chapter, by Adam and Nain, shows how competition affects corporate hedging strategies. They investigate the foreign exchange rate exposures of a large sample of US firms and find that in more competitive industries fewer firms hedge. This phenomenon is driven by the presence of smaller firms, which are less likely to use derivatives. The key implications of their findings are that firms' hedging strategies are interdependent, and that equilibrium models are needed to better understand corporate risk management strategies.

The second chapter by Brown investigates the risk associated with the cashflow of corporate market investments. The context of this chapter is the observation that in recent years corporate liquidity has increased substantially and is positively correlated with firm-level cash-flow risk. Brown finds that market investment has a substantial impact on business cash-flow risk, while the effect of market-investment growth on cash-flow risk is robust to firm and year fixed effects.

The next chapter by Magee revisits the theme of how foreign currency hedging affects firm value. The author's initial findings are consistent with earlier research (for example, Mackay and Moeller, 2007) that foreign currency hedging is associated with an increase in firm value. Nonetheless, this finding ignores the possibility that firm value may affect foreign currency hedging. Once this possibility is addressed, the author finds that foreign currency hedging depends on past amounts of firm value and is therefore not strictly exogenous.

It is wellknown that employee and executive stock option programs affect equity repurchase decisions (for example, Bens et al., 2003). The fourth chapter by Rogers explores the possibility that repurchasing shares provides a pool of shares for option exercises and is therefore a corporate hedging strategy. Findings demonstrate a significant relation between repurchases and option grants after controlling for other rationales for repurchases and for other potential option variables. Consequently, the results are consistent with the hedging argument in that firms monetize the economic cost of a portion of their option grants during the year of grant.

The final chapter in this section asks the question of whether managers exhibit loss aversion in their risk management practices. Adam, Fernando and Golubeva investigate the gold mining industry and study how firms change their hedge positions in response to past changes in the gold price. The authors find that the response of gold managers is asymmetric: they decrease their hedge positions following past increases in the gold price, while they do not promptly increase their hedges following past gold price declines. This evidence suggests that corporate hedging strategies are affected by managerial behavioral biases and therefore cannot be predicted or explained simply with classical theory.

II. Financial risk management in financial intermediaries

Part II comprises six chapters (Chapters 6–11) that address financial risk management in the context of financial intermediaries. The broad context of this section is recent and proposed amendments to existing financial market regulation (especially the Basel III reforms) broadly aimed at providing a comprehensive set of reform measures to strengthen the regulation, supervision and risk management of the banking sector (BIS, 2011).

This section begins with a chapter by Battaglia and Mazzuca, which investigates the impact of asset securitization on bank liquidity risk. Banks have historically managed their asset-liability positions by securitizing – often the most illiquid – loans in their asset portfolios. In this chapter, the authors investigate the securitization practices of Italian firms over the period 2000–9, with the results proving that securitization has a positive effect on the liquidity of the originator banks (inverse relationship with the liquidity risk). Furthermore, the results also indicate that in the pre-crisis years (2000–6), the degree of securitization was the most important determinate to what happened in the subsequent period (2007–9). The authors argue that from the perspective of regulators, their results support the initiatives undertaken by the Basel Committee to define an international framework for liquidity risk and strengthen global capital and liquidity rules with the goal of promoting a more resilient banking sector (BIS, 2011).

Chapter 7, by Maino and Tintchev, follows on the capital adequacy theme of the previous chapter by investigating the issue of stress testing when a banking system is interconnected or comprises a network of claims. Their framework models the capital asset ratios of banks by considering future losses and credit growth. They are also able to consider the critical issue of tail risk – the risk of extreme non-normal price movements. Overall, their approach has the advantage of providing a simple framework to integrate various systemic risk scenarios.

Durand, Gündüz and Thomazeau consider the important effect of liquidity on asset prices, specifically by developing a simplified model that estimates the endogenous liquidity parameter of a portfolio. Liquidity is exogenous due to the variability of bid-ask spreads for usual-sized transactions, while endogenous liquidity is due to the impact of liquidity on market prices when liquidating larger positions. They focus on endogenous liquidity, which measures the risk that the realized price of a transaction may be different from the pre-transaction price in both normal and stress periods. This price will then depend on (i) the size of the position relative to the overall market, (ii) the direction (long or short) of the position with respect to those of the other actors, and (iii) the market depth. The authors argue that, given its effects on prices, asset liquidity should be part of the regulatory framework, which is currently being developed by the Trading Book Group of the Basel Committee of Banking Supervision.

The impact of the UK banking crash on the implied volatility of option prices is then considered by So, Driouchi and Tan. They examine the information content of UK banking equity options of the four major UK banks: Barclays, RBS, Lloyds TSB and HSBC, using the Black–Scholes and Merton frameworks for the period leading to the fall 2008 global markets crash. Their findings suggest that the 2008 banking downturn could be foreseen, thereby confirming the relative superiority of options markets in predicting stock volatility and in signaling market sentiment ahead of other economic systems.

The chapter by Niklewski and Rodgers then investigates whether the Global Financial Crisis had a permanent impact on the benefits of international equity portfolio diversification. This is done by examining the conditional correlation between US equity markets and a number of developed and emerging/frontier markets. They conclude that the crisis has resulted in a permanent long-term increase in the correlation between the US and developed markets and also between the US and emerging/frontier markets. This conclusion is especially important for financial institutions that rely on the benefits of diversification to mitigate credit, and other types of risk, across their international asset portfolios.

The final offering in this section is a chapter by Maciel that develops a model which combines the properties of a hybrid GARCH model with fuzzy system theory. Maciel's model, termed a Fuzzy GJR–GARCH model, is better able to capture the behavior of volatility, which is known to both cluster and be asymmetric. When this model is applied to forecasting volatility on the S&P 500 and the Ibovespa Index it is able to provide more accurate results than either a standard GARCH or Fuzzy–GARCH estimation. Despite its complexity, this technology is able to make a significant contribution to the task of forecasting the risk present in asset prices.

III. Financial risk management in portfolios

Part III develops the theme of financial risk management but does so in the context of portfolios. There are six chapters (Chapters 12–17) in this section, with the first chapter by Lioui investigating the implication of predictability in asset returns for consumption and portfolio rules. The context of this chapter is the literature on dynamic asset pricing and asset allocation, which the author argues has the potential to solve some long-standing financial puzzles (for example, the equity premium puzzle). The objective of this theoretical work is to provide a closed form solution to a consumption/investment problem in incomplete markets, when an agent trades a riskless and a risky asset. The market price of risk (the state variable) is allowed to follow a mean reverting process that is imperfectly correlated with the risky asset. In addition to being risk averse, the agent has some preference for robustness and this is taken into account in the optimization problem. In this setting the author is able to obtain an explicit solution to the consumption/investment problem in *incomplete* markets.

In the next chapter, Frahm and Wiechers address the interesting question of how to measure the diversification effect in portfolios of risky assets. They do so by relating the degree of systematic risk to the total portfolio return variance. To illustrate their method they investigate monthly return data for S&P 500 constituents over the past fifty years. They discover that the average degree of diversification of naive portfolios barely exceeds 60 percent. In other words, at least 40 percent of the total risk of a naive portfolio could be diversified away, which highlights the benefits to investors from analysis of the covariance–variance structure of asset returns.

The chapter by Hitaj and Mercuri shifts discussion from investigation of the first two moments of portfolio and asset returns to the higher moments of a portfolio returns, namely skewness and kurtosis (return asymmetry and fat tails). The authors undertake an empirical analysis of hedge fund portfolio allocation assuming a Multivariate Variance Gamma distribution for returns. They begin by conducting a rolling window strategy for portfolio allocation and, after the estimation procedure, obtain optimal portfolio weights. They then analyze the impact of the level of risk aversion on these weights and compare the different portfolios obtained in out-of-sample periods.

Chapter 15, by Casati and Tabachnik, investigates the statistical properties of the maximum drawdown (termed the MDD) in financial time series. The MDD is an alternate measure of risk to measures such as Value-at-Risk, and measures the potential loss from the peak to the bottom of a price series. When price follows Brownian motion with drift, the authors' analytical predictions for the expected value of the MDD are well recovered by the Monte Carlo code they present in this chapter. Importantly, the numerical simulations allow for the recovery of the MDD distribution function in terms of a generalized extreme value distribution.

Hasan and Choudhry, in Chapter 16, investigate the effectiveness of dynamic stock index portfolio hedging, that is, the use of time-varying hedge ratios. Their analysis is undertaken on stock index futures trading in three emerging markets: Brazil, Hungary and South Africa. The authors apply five variations of a GARCH model to estimate the hedge ratios along with the conventional covariance method, and then compare the hedging effectiveness using both within-sample and out-of-sample forecasting performance. One key novelty of their approach is that they evaluate hedging effectiveness by calculating the Value-at-Risk and Minimum Capital Risk Requirement for portfolio returns obtained under alternative hedging models. Their results show that forecasting superiority varies with the market under investigation and the length of the forecast horizon.

The final chapter in the volume, by Leung and Liu, investigates the optimal timing approach to option portfolio risk management. The authors point out that while it is common for investors to use options for risk management, it is not clear exactly when an investor should optimally liquidate the option position in the market. They state that the optimal timing of liquidation will be a function of both the investor's subjective probability and the market risk-neutral pricing measure. The main contribution of their work is that they are able to identify situations where holding the option through expiration is optimal, under both a complete diffusion market and an incomplete stochastic volatility market.

In conclusion, this volume presents the latest research in the areas of financial risk management in three critical areas: corporate, financial and portfolio risk management. The chapters present both empirical and theoretical perspectives on issues that remain paramount despite the abating of the financial market volatility experienced in recent years. The prospects going forward are for more regulatory oversight and attention being paid to the modeling and measuring of financial risk. It is the editors' and authors' hope that this offering will contribute to this ongoing debate and provide valuable insights into the issues and appropriate practice of financial risk management.

References

Bank for International Settlements (BIS) (2011). Basel III: A Global Regulatory Framework for More Resilient Banks and Banking Systems. Basel, CH-4002. Switzerland.
http://www.bis.org/publ/bcbs189.pdf
Bens, D. A., Nagar, V., Skinner, D. J. and Wong, M. H. F. (2003). 'Employee Stock Options, EPS Dilution, and Stock Repurchases', *Journal of Accounting and Economics*, XXXVI, 51–90.
Smith, C. W. and Stulz, R. M. (1985). 'The Determinants of Firms' Hedging Policies', *Journal of Financial and Quantitative Analysis*, 20, 391–405.
Mackay, P. and Moeller, S. B. (2007) 'The Value of Corporate Risk Management', *Journal of Finance*, 62, 1379–419.

Notes on Contributors

Tim R. Adam is the Rudolf von Bennigsen Professor of Finance at Humboldt University, Berlin, Germany. He received a PhD in Economics from the University of Virginia in 1997, and has taught at internationally leading universities, such as the Massachusetts Institute of Technology, the University of Michigan, the Hong Kong University of Science & Technology, and the National University of Singapore. Professor Adam's primary research interests lie in the areas of corporate risk management, syndicated loans and mutual funds. His work has been published in leading journals, including the *Journal of Finance*, the *Journal of Financial Economics*, and the *Journal of Banking & Finance*.

Francesca Battaglia is Assistant Professor of Financial Markets and Institutions at the University of Naples 'Parthenope', Department of Accounting and Finance. Her main research interests focus on cooperative banks, securitization, governance of financial intermediaries and systemic risk. She is author of several publications on financial institutions, including several chapters in Palgrave Macmillan book editions ('Asset Pricing, Real estate and Public Finance over the Crisis', 'New issues in Financial and Credit Markets', 'Bank Performance, Risk and Securitization', in press) and articles in journals including *Applied Financial Economics* and *International Review of Financial Analysis*.

Jonathan A. Batten is Professor of Finance at Monash University, Melbourne, Australia. Previously he worked at the Hong Kong University of Science & Technology and Seoul National University. He is also the editor of *Emerging Markets Review* and associate editor of the *Journal of Banking & Finance* and has undertaken consulting work for the World Bank and the Asian Development Bank. His research interests include credit spread modeling, market integration, financial market development and non-linear dynamics. His work has been published in leading journals including *Applied Economics, Chaos, Journal of Financial and Quantitative Analysis, Journal of International Business Studies,* and the *World Bank Research Observer* amongst others.

Craig O. Brown is Assistant Professor of Finance at NUS Business School. His fields are financial economics, applied microeconometrics, international finance, and political economy. Professor Brown's current research interests include financial analysis, behavioral finance, investments in marketable securities by non-financial corporations, business groups, the intersection of politics and finance, government financial management, and the economics of government leadership. His research has appeared in the *Quarterly Journal of Economics* and the *Review of Financial Studies*. Professor Brown holds a BA in Economics from Rutgers University, in addition to a PhD in Finance from the University of Michigan.

Alessandro Casati is a quantitative researcher at Antares Technologies, Paris. He has a background in engineering and a PhD in Physics. His academic research has been related to turbulence modeling, non-linear dynamics and high performance computing; his work has been published in leading scientific journals including *Physical Review Letters*. His current experience and interests in quantitative finance are focused on algorithmic trading at medium and high frequencies.

Taufiq Choudhry is Professor of Finance at the University of Southampton, School of Management. Before that he was Professor of Finance at the University of Bradford. His research interests are in the areas of financial markets, international finance, forecasting and econometrics. He has published in *Review of Economics and Statistics, Economic Letters, Journal of International Money and Finance, Journal of Banking & Finance,* and *Journal of Forecasting*. He is also an associate editor of the *European Journal of Finance*.

Tarik Driouchi is Associate Professor of Financial and Management Studies at KCL, University of London. Prior to joining King's, he held academic appointments at Cranfield Postgraduate School of Management, the University of Cambridge and Aston University. Dr Driouchi's research is in the area of investment and decision-making under uncertainty, examining real options and options markets. His work has been published in *OMEGA – The International Journal of Management Science, International Journal of Services Sciences, European Journal of Operational Research, Journal of World Business*, and *Transportation Research B* amongst others.

Philippe Durand is Inspector at Banque de France and Head of Mission in the on-site banking supervision department of the Autorité de Contrôle Prudentiel et de Résolution. Philippe started his career as a front-office quant. He worked as head of quantitative research in a market risk management department, credit structurer and trader in several commercial banks before joining Banque de France in 2008. Philippe graduated from École Polytechnique (Paris), École Nationale de la Statistique et de d'Administration Économique (ENSAE, Paris), and has a master's in Probability (University of Paris VI). He has published several articles on quantitative finance.

Chitru S. Fernando is the John and Donnie Brock Chair and Professor of Finance at the University of Oklahoma Price College of Business, Research Fellow at the Wharton Financial Institutions Center, and Research Director of the OU Price College Energy Institute. He is published in major refereed journals including the *Journal of Finance, Journal of Financial Economics* and

Review of Financial Studies. He has served as a consultant to major institutions and corporations worldwide. He received a PhD (Finance) from Wharton; MA (Applied Economics) from the University of Pennsylvania; MS (Management) from the MIT Sloan School; MS (Technology and Policy) from MIT; and BSc (Mechanical Engineering) with First Class Honors from the University of Sri Lanka.

Gabriel Frahm studied Business Administration at the University of Cologne with a focus on Financial Markets and Statistics. In 2004 he finished his doctoral thesis in statistics and in 2009 he completed his habilitation in statistics and econometrics. He holds the chair for Applied Stochastics and Risk Management at the Helmut Schmidt University. His research interests include copulas, elliptical distributions, robust estimation of covariance matrices, and random matrix theory. Another field of interest is the statistical investigation of portfolio optimization. His contributions have been published in several journals such as the *Journal of Econometrics* and the *Journal of Multivariate Analysis*.

Janya Golubeva's teaching interests include investments, risk management, and energy. Her research focuses on various aspects of behavioral finance and analyzes the effects of psychological biases on managerial and investment choices. Her work has been published in the *Review of Financial Studies* and the *Journal of Financial Markets*. Her research interests also include energy markets, especially energy hedging. Prior to pursuing her PhD in Finance at the University of Utah, she worked in the Russian oil and gas industry for three years. Professor Golubeva is a member of the American Finance Association and the Financial Management Association.

Yalin Gündüz is a financial economist at the Research Center of Deutsche Bundesbank, Germany. Yalin completed his PhD at Karlsruhe Institute of Technology, and BSc and MSc studies at Middle East Technical University, Turkey. He was a Fulbright Scholar in 2000 and afterwards worked as a financial risk consultant for Citibank, Siemens and PwC. Recently, he visited New York University as a research scholar. His research interests include credit risk modeling, credit default swap markets and pricing, central counterparty platforms, market microstructure, banking regulation and sovereign risk. His work has been published in leading journals including *Review of Derivatives Research, Quantitative Finance, Physica A*, and the *Journal of Financial Services Research* amongst others.

Mohammad S. Hasan is Senior Lecturer in Finance at the University of Kent, Canterbury, UK. He previously held Associate Professor post at the King Fahd University of Petroleum and Minerals, Saudi Arabia and Senior Lecturer at the Sheffield Hallam University, UK. His research interests cover broad fields of financial economics, international finance, macro and monetary economics. He has authored 33 academically referred journal articles with selected publications appearing in *Applied Financial Economics, Economics Letters, Empirical Economics, European Journal of Finance, International Journal of Theoretical and Applied Finance, The Manchester School, Journal of Comparative Economics,* and *Journal of Policy Modelling.*

Asmerilda Hitaj is a junior researcher at the University of Milano, Bicocca, Italy, where she graduated in Economics and Finance. She has a master's in Risk and Asset Management from EDHEC Business School and a PhD in Mathematics applied to Financial Markets from the University of Milano. Her research focuses on portfolio allocation models in discrete and continuous time, risk, performance measures, and option pricing.

Tim Leung is Assistant Professor in the Industrial Engineering and Operations Research (IEOR) Department at Columbia University, New York. He holds a PhD in Operations Research and Financial Engineering from Princeton University. His research interests include portfolio optimization, derivatives trading strategies, leveraged ETFs, and employee stock options. Professor Leung's research has been funded by the National Science Foundation (NSF) and published in journals, such as *Mathematical Finance, Quantitative Finance,* and *SIAM Journal on Financial Mathematics.*

Abraham Lioui is Professor of Finance at EDHEC Business School. He also serves as Vice Academic Director of the PhD Program in Finance. His research interests in finance revolve around the valuation of financial assets, portfolio management, and risk management. His economics research looks at the relationship between monetary policy and the stock market. He has published in leading journals, including *Journal of Financial and Quantitative Analysis, Journal of Banking and Finance, Journal of Economic Dynamics and Control, Journal of International Money and Finance,* and *Management Science.* He is regularly invited to the program committee of the European Finance Association and Financial Management Association annual meetings and acts as track chair for Asset Pricing for the EuroFidai conference.

Peng Liu is currently a researcher at Campbell & Co., a hedge fund specializing in systematic managed futures and equity market-neutral strategies. His most recent research focuses on quantitative solutions for alpha extraction from global financial and commodities futures markets. Other research interests include credit risk, market timing, portfolio optimization, and option-implied information. Dr. Liu holds a PhD in Applied Mathematics and Statistics from Johns Hopkins University, and a BSc in Mathematics from Zhejiang University.

Leandro Maciel is a PhD student of Electrical Engineering at the University of Campinas, from where he also received his BSc in Economics and his MSc in Electrical Engineering. His research interests center on computational intelligence: fuzzy set theory and fuzzy logic, neural networks, and evolutionary computation with focus on problems in economics and finance.

Peter MacKay is Associate Professor at the Hong Kong University of Science and Technology. He previously served at Southern Methodist University (Dallas) and Laval University (Quebec). He is an associate editor for the *Multinational Finance Journal* and the *International Review of Financial Analysis*. His work appears in the *Journal of Finance, Review of Financial Studies, Journal of Financial and Quantitative Analysis,* and the *Journal of Banking & Finance*. His research spans several areas of corporate finance, namely, capital structure, corporate risk management, corporate investment, working capital management, and corporate governance. He has undertaken consulting work for the Venture-Capital and Alternative Investment Associations of Hong Kong.

Shane Magee is Senior Lecturer at Macquarie University's Applied Finance Centre, Sydney, Australia. Previously he was Senior Vice President in the corporate treasury division of Citigroup. His research interests include corporate risk management and risk governance in financial institutions.

Rodolfo Maino is a senior economist at the International Monetary Fund. In that capacity, he has worked on financial stability and central banking issues and contributed to the surveillance agenda for the Asia and Pacific and Africa regions at the IMF. Before joining the IMF in 2001, he served as a manager of international reserves, as a researcher at the Central Bank of Argentina, and he has worked as a financial analyst for Philip Morris and as an economist at the World Bank. He has also held positions in academia, teaching econometrics, finance, and statistics. He holds a PhD in economics, specialized in finance, and master's degrees in Economics and in Mathematical Statistics.

Maria Mazzuca is Assistant Professor of Banking and Finance at the University of Calabria, Italy, from where she holds a PhD in Banking and Finance. She was employed as a research fellow at University of Calabria (2004–6). She worked on several research projects with research grants (such as Prin 2007, co-financed by Italian Government, and Newfin-Bocconi University) and is also the author of several articles on securitization and disclosure in banks. Her main fields of research interest include Italian and European banks, securitization, credit risk transfer activity and banks disclosure.

Lorenzo Mercuri holds a postdoc position at the University of Bergamo, Italy. He graduated in Economics from the University of 'Politecnica delle Marche'. He has a PhD in Mathematics related to financial markets from the University of Milano, Bicocca. His research focuses on option pricing in continuous and discrete time models, EM algorithm and portfolio allocation.

Amrita Nain is Assistant Professor of Finance at Tippie College of Business at the University of Iowa. Previously she worked at the Desautels Faculty of Management at McGill University. Her research interests lie in the area of empirical corporate finance including mergers and acquisitions, private equity and IPOs. Her work has been published in leading journals including *Journal of Financial Economics, Review of Financial Studies,* and *Journal of Financial and Quantitative Analysis.*

Jacek Niklewski is Lecturer in Finance at Coventry University, Coventry, UK. He is currently working on a PhD in Financial Econometrics. Jacek holds two master's degrees with distinction. He currently teaches econometrics and fixed-income securities and has ongoing research interests focusing on: financial econometrics, portfolio management and also corporate social responsibility. He has publications in the finance area relating to option theory and has presented a number of conference papers in relation to portfolio management and corporate social responsibility.

Timothy Rodgers is Principle Lecturer in Economics and Finance at Coventry University, Coventry, UK. He holds a PhD and is Programme Manager for the MSc Investment Management at Coventry. He also supervises a number of PhD students. He has personal research interests in two main areas: financial markets and quality management in higher education. He has a number of publications in the finance area including a number of papers relating to market efficiency in Islamic markets and corporate capital structures. He is currently also researching portfolio management.

Daniel A. Rogers is Associate Professor of Finance at Portland State University. He teaches courses in corporate finance, valuation and derivatives, and has previously taught at Northeastern University, Massey University, and University of Utah. He has published research in the areas of corporate risk management and derivatives usage, managerial incentives arising from compensation and stock option repricing. His published work includes articles in the *Journal of Finance, Journal of Banking & Finance, Financial Management,* and *Journal of Applied Corporate Finance.* Prior to his life as an academic, Dr. Rogers held management positions with a national airline and a petroleum products distributor.

Ha Yan Raymond So is Investment Analyst at MacroValue Investors Ltd in Hong Kong and an affiliated researcher with the Department of Management of King's College London. He earned his master's degree in Finance from the Cranfield School of Management. His research interests include volatility forecasting, financial options and investments.

Serge Tabachnik is CEO and Founder of Antares Technologies. Previously, he was head of Yield Arbitrage at Capital Fund Management and was employed by Amaranth as Senior Risk Manager. Prior to his career in finance, Dr. Tabachnik was a Postdoctoral Fellow at Princeton University's Department of Astrophysics and lectured at both Oxford University and

EPFL. His work has been published in leading journals including *Nature, The Astrophysical Journal* and *Astronomy and Astrophysics*. He holds a PhD in Theoretical Physics from Oxford University and attended both EPFL and École Polytechnique in France, where he received a master's degree in Physics.

Zhiyuan Simon Tan is Assistant Professor of Accounting and Financial Management at King's College London. He obtained his PhD from the London School of Economics in 2010. His research interests include the role of financial intermediaries in corporate governance, and corporate information disclosure, communication, and utilization, particularly through the lens of financial analysts.

Kalin Tintchev is a senior research analyst at the International Monetary Fund's Monetary and Capital Markets Department. Since joining the IMF in 2001, he has worked on financial surveillance and stress testing in a number of countries that have participated in the IMF/World Bank Financial Sector Assessment Program (FSAP) and has published on financial stability issues. He is a PhD candidate in economics specializing in international finance and holds an MBA in Finance and master's degrees in Economics and International relations. His research interests include credit and liquidity risk modeling, cross-border contagion and systemic risk analysis.

Isabelle Thomazeau has 24 years of experience in the financial industry. She joined the Banque de France in 1999 as a member of the on-site banking supervision department of the Autorité de Contrôle Prudentiel et de Résolution. Previously she spent 10 years in Credit Lyonnais where she particularly contributed to the validation of pricing models and to the setup of 'scores' within the Groupe de Recherche Opérationnelle and to the elaboration of Risk Adjusted Return On Capital (RAROC) models within the Group Risks Department. She holds a physics doctorate from Paris-Orsay University and started her career in non-linear optics research.

Niklas Wagner is Professor of Finance at Passau University, Germany. After receiving his PhD in Finance, he held postdoctoral appointments at the Haas School of Business and at Stanford GSB. More recently, he was an academic guest to research universities in Asia, Australia and Europe as well as the US, and taught courses in risk and investment management for EDHEC business school. Professor Wagner is *International Review of Financial Analysis* subject editor and regularly serves as a referee for leading finance journals. His publications cover the areas of empirical asset pricing and applied financial econometrics as well as derivatives and risk management.

Christof Wiechers studied Mathematics and Economics at the University of Bielefeld and at Purdue University with a focus on Decision Theory and

Statistics. After finishing his studies in 2007, he joined the Graduate School of Risk Management at the University of Cologne. His doctoral studies at the chair for Statistics and Econometrics resulted in several publications on portfolio optimization and diversification. After his doctorate in 2011, he started to work in the insurance industry with a focus on risk management and Solvency II.

Part I
Corporate

1
Strategic Risk Management and Product Market Competition

Tim R. Adam and Amrita Nain

1.1 Introduction

How does competition affect corporate risk management strategies? The theoretical literature has derived conflicting predictions. Allayannis and Ihrig (2001) predict that firms operating in more competitive industries are more likely to hedge, while Mello and Ruckes (2008) predict that firms hedge less if competition is more intense. Adam, Dasgupta, and Titman (2007) show that competition can have a positive or negative impact on the number of firms that hedge in equilibrium. While the theoretical literature has produced conflicting answers, anecdotal evidence suggests that the competitive environment does affect firms' hedging strategies. For example, Brown (2001) reports that competitive pricing concerns in the product market, rather than the traditional models of hedging, determine how a major durable goods producer in the US hedges its FX exposures.

A related question is whether corporate hedging strategies are interdependent across firms; in other words, is the incentive of a firm to hedge affected by the hedging decisions of its competitors? Most theories of corporate risk management model firms in isolation, and therefore do not consider the possible interaction of hedging strategies between firms.[1] In contrast, Froot, Scharfstein and Stein (1993) argue that the nature of competition can affect a firm's optimal risk management strategy and may lead to hedging decisions that are different from the firm's rivals. Adam, Dasgupta, and Titman (2007) formally study the hedging decisions of firms in an industry equilibrium, and show that the incentive to hedge declines as more firms hedge.

The objective of this chapter is twofold. First, we empirically examine how competition affects corporate derivatives strategies, and second, we test whether firms' derivatives strategies are interdependent, as prior research has suggested. Examining such interdependence is also interesting from a modeling perspective, as it would indicate whether we need equilibrium models to better understand corporate risk management. We investigate these questions using hand-collected data on foreign currency derivatives usage in 1999 for a large sample of US firms.

We find that in more competitive industries, fewer firms hedge. While this finding does not prove causality, it is consistent with the notion that firms strategically decide not to hedge if they face more intense competition, as in Adam, Dasgupta and Titman (2007). The finding that in more competitive industries fewer firms hedge is due to smaller firms, which are less likely to use derivatives in more competitive industries. In contrast, larger firms are more likely to use derivatives in more competitive industries. These results imply that it is the smaller firms that behave in the strategic sense of Adam, Dasgupta and Titman (2007) by opting to not hedge when competition is high. Larger firms behave in the manner predicted by Allayannis and Ihrig (2001), that is, hedge when competition is high, profit margins are tight and shocks can't be passed through to prices. These results are robust to controlling for other determinants of derivatives usage, such as size of exposure, growth options, and financial policies, and support the prediction that competition has a negative impact on hedging of foreign exchange risk.

Next, we examine whether derivatives strategies are interdependent across firms. Derivatives strategies will be interdependent if a firm's exposure to exchange rate risk is affected by the hedging decisions of its competitors. Therefore, we examine firms' (ex-post) net FX exposures.[2] We find that firms' net FX exposures depend not only on a firm's own hedging decision, but also on the hedging decisions of its competitors. Consistent with Guay (1999) and Allayannis, Ihrig and Weston (2001), derivatives users have lower net FX exposures than derivatives non-users.[3] More importantly, however, as more firms in an industry use derivatives, the exposure of derivatives non-users increases, while the exposure of derivatives users declines. In other words, firms' net exposures are lowest if their hedging decisions conform to the hedging decisions of the majority, and are highest if they deviate from the hedging decisions of the majority. This result is robust to alternative estimation methods and alternative definitions of hedging in an industry.

In Adam, Dasgupta and Titman (2007) and Mello and Ruckes (2008), the interdependence between firms' hedging choices relies on the existence of imperfect competition. Therefore, we further support our empirical evidence by examining FX exposures in sub-samples of more competitive and less competitive industries. We find that, as expected, the relation between an individual firm's FX exposure and the derivatives choices of its competitors is stronger in less competitive industries.

Our results are significant for two reasons. First they show that the nature of competition can affect corporate derivatives strategies, and thus support theoretical predictions by Adam, Dasgupta and Titman (2007) and Mello and Ruckes (2008). Second, the results highlight that derivatives strategies are likely to be interdependent, which implies a need for equilibrium models to better understand corporate risk management behaviors.

Our results also contribute to several other strands of the literature. Most of the empirical literature on corporate risk management has examined how firm-specific factors, such as firm size, tax considerations, financial constraints, growth options, and managerial incentives affect firms' hedging strategies. We add to this literature by focusing on the relations between industry characteristics and hedging strategies.[4] In a related study, Allayannis and Weston (1999) find that firms that operate in lower mark-up (more competitive) industries are more likely to use FX derivatives, which seems to contradict our industry-level result. We show, however, that the relation between a firm's decision to hedge and measures of industry competitiveness is a function of firm size. Smaller firms are less likely to hedge if competition is more intense, while for larger firms it is the opposite. Thus, it is especially smaller firms that strategically choose not to hedge in the presence of competition as suggested by Adam, Dasgupta and Titman (2007).

Several researchers have observed the impact of competition on firms' risk exposures, and by deduction risk management strategies. Lewent and Kearney (1990) write on p. 19 '...the impact of exchange rate volatility on a company depends mainly on the companies' business structure, its industry profile, and the nature of its competitive environment.' Indeed, He and Ng (1998) and Williamson (2001) find that the degree of competition affects exposures: more competition implies larger exposures. We add to this literature by showing that aggregate derivatives decisions in an industry appear to affect the exposures of derivatives users and non-users differently.

Although our chapter is the first to show that adopting hedging strategies similar to the rest of the industry lowers a firm's exposure, the prediction that firms find safety in conforming to the majority's decision is not new. De Meza (1986) demonstrates that as the number of firms adopting a given production technology increases, output prices correlate more closely with production costs, providing firms with a better hedge against changes in the cost of production. Maksimovic and Zechner (1991) use the same theoretical argument to show that agency problems associated with debt need to be studied in a multi-firm framework because the risk of a project's cash flows is endogenously determined by the investment decisions of all firms in an industry.

The remaining chapter is structured as follows. Section 1.2 reviews the existing theories and derives testable predictions. The data sample and variables used in the econometric analysis are described in Section 1.3. Section 1.4 contains the econometric analysis, which focuses on the impact of competition on aggregate hedging strategies in an industry. Section 1.5 contains the econometric analysis, which examines whether derivatives strategies are interdependent across firms, and Section 1.6 concludes.

1.2 Theory and testable predictions

The theoretical literature demonstrates that the impact of competition on firms' hedging strategies is ambiguous. Allayannis and Ihrig (2001) show that exchange rate exposures rise as industry mark-ups, a proxy for the degree of competition, fall. This is because in less competitive industries, firms have a greater ability to adjust prices in response to cost shocks. In more competitive industries, output prices are set near marginal costs, so that the impact of cost shocks on a firm's profitability is larger. An implication is that firms that operate in more competitive industries face higher exposures and therefore are more likely to hedge.

In contrast, Adam, Dasgupta and Titman (2007) show that competition can have a positive or negative impact on firms' incentives to hedge, depending on whether hedging or not hedging is optimal in the absence of any competitive interaction between firms. In their model, volatility in input prices inflicts costs, due to a convex cost function, but also provides benefits, due to the presence of real options.[5] In the absence of any competitive interaction, firms will either hedge or remain unhedged, depending on whether the cost effect or the real option effect dominates. For example, if the market is sufficiently large then the cost effect dominates so that all firms hedge, while if the market is small the real option effect dominates so that all firms remain unhedged. In the presence of competitive interaction, however, firms also benefit from generating cash flows in states in which other firms are cash constrained, as in Shleifer and Vishny (1992). Since the value of hedging declines as more firms hedge, in equilibrium, some firms hedge, while others do not, even though all firms are ex-ante identical. The resulting heterogeneity in hedging strategies is determined by the degree of competition, and the slopes of the demand and marginal cost curves. An increase in competition, an increase in the slope of the demand curve, and a decrease in the slope of the marginal cost curve all cause more heterogeneity in firms' hedging decisions.

Mello and Ruckes (2008) also study firms' hedging decisions in an imperfectly competitive market, and predict that competition reduces the extent of hedging. Although hedging can reduce a firm's financial constraints, remaining unhedged carries the potential benefit of a large cash inflow relative to the firm's hedged peers. In such a case, the firm may gain a significant financial advantage, that is, lower marginal costs and hence increase market share, over its competitors that hedge. Due to this competitive factor, firms will not fully hedge their exposures. Controlled risk-taking may make it possible to gain a financial advantage. This discussion leads to testable predictions about the fraction of firms in an industry that choose to use derivatives. The arguments of Allayannis and Ihrig (2001) imply that the fraction of hedgers is higher in more competitive industries. In contrast, Adam, Dasgupta and Titman (2007) show that under some conditions, the fraction of hedgers can be lower in more competitive industries. These conflicting predictions lead us to test the following hypothesis.

> *H1: The degree of competition is positively or negatively correlated with the fraction of firms that use derivatives within an industry.*

We also test the Mello and Ruckes (2008) prediction that firms will not hedge their exposures fully when competition is more intense.

> *H2: The degree of competition is negatively correlated with the extent of derivatives usage.*

We control our analysis, as suggested by theory, for other determinants of corporate risk management, such as exposure levels, firm size, growth options, financial constraints, financial heterogeneity, and operating leverage.

In the traditional risk management literature, which studies a firm in isolation, a firm's net exposure is a function of only the firm's own characteristics and its own decision to hedge. In imperfectly competitive industries, however, a firm's risk exposure can also depend on the hedging decisions of its competitors. To see why, consider an imperfectly competitive industry, in which all firms are subject to a common shock to their marginal costs of production. When the shock occurs, firms adjust their profit maximizing output and the output price will change accordingly. As a result, output prices co-vary with the cost shock, as in Adam, Dasgupta and Titman (2007). Now suppose that, prior to the realization of the cost shock, firms are able to enter into derivative contracts that enable them to lock in their costs of production. Ceteris paribus, firms that have completely protected themselves from the shock make no changes to their outputs when the shock occurs.[6] As more firms choose to hedge the shock, output prices become less sensitive to the cost shock because fewer firms adjust output.

This dampening effect of hedging on the correlation between output prices and costs implies that the volatility of an individual unhedged (hedged) firm increases (decreases) with the fraction of hedged firms in the industry. In an industry where all firms hedge the cost shock, prices do not fluctuate with the cost shock. If a firm in this industry remains unhedged, it faces volatility in costs, which is not offset by volatility in output prices. Hedged firms, on the other hand, face constant costs as well as constant prices. In such an industry, profit variability of unhedged (hedged) firms is high (low). In contrast, when most firms in an industry are unhedged, output prices co-vary with costs, causing the profit variability of unhedged firms to be low relative to hedged firms. If a firm in this industry chooses to hedge, it has fixed costs but faces volatility in output prices. Thus, in largely unhedged industries, unhedged (hedged) firms should exhibit relatively low (high) net exposures.

Based on this discussion we test the following hypothesis.

H3: As more firms hedge in an industry, the exposure of derivatives non-users increases, while the exposure of derivatives users declines.

In Adam, Dasgupta and Titman (2007) and Mello and Ruckes (2008), the interdependence between firms' hedging choices relies on the existence of imperfect competition. We, therefore, further examine Hypothesis H3 in sub-samples of more competitive and less competitive industries. Since FX exposures are the most significant financial exposures for non-financial corporations, we conduct our tests using a comprehensive, hand-collected data set on the use of FX derivatives by publicly listed firms in the US.

1.3 Data sample and variables

To define the sample, we first selected all firms from the Compustat database for the year 1999, excluding financial firms (SIC 600–699) and utilities (SIC 491–494). Financial firms hold derivatives for purposes other than hedging, and utilities are regulated entities, and thus may not pursue shareholder-maximizing strategies. Furthermore, we exclude industries with less than three firms as reported by Compustat. We also exclude firms with negative or missing values for net sales, total assets and market values of equity. This yielded a total of 8442 observations. Then we collected information on firms' FX derivative holdings, by searching firms' 1999 10-K filings for text strings such as 'hedg', 'swap', 'cap', 'forward' and so on.[7] If a reference to any of the search terms was found, we read the surrounding text to confirm that it referred to FX derivatives holdings and classified the firm as an FX derivatives user accordingly. We also recorded the gross notional amounts of foreign exchange forwards, swaps and options outstanding if available. In cases where there were no contracts outstanding, but the firm did engage in FX risk management during the year, we took the notional amounts of derivatives that expired during 1999. If there were no references to the keywords, we classified the firm as a derivatives non-user for 1999.

Using this method, we identified 556 FX derivatives users. This number is comparable to the sample size of 497 FX derivatives users in Purnanandam (2008). The small difference in the number of FX derivatives users is to be expected since Purnanandam (2008) collects data as of calendar year 1997 and we collect data as of fiscal year 1999. Overall, FX derivatives usage is comparable to previous studies. For example, Graham and Rogers (2002) report a mean notional amount for FX derivatives of $558 million for the years 1994–5, or 8.06 percent of total assets, while in our sample it is $725 million, or 10.55 percent of total assets.

Next, we summarize the prevalence of derivatives usage by industry. We define an industry by its four digit SIC. There are a total of 827 industries in our sample, with an average (median) of 24.8 (13) firms per industry. To measure the prevalence of derivatives usage we use the market-value-weighted fraction of derivatives usage, which is defined as the sum of market values of FX derivatives users in a four digit SIC industry, divided by the sum of market values of all firms in that industry. We use a market value-weighted measure to account for the fact that larger firms represent a bigger share of industry output, and thus their hedging choices are more important to competitors than the hedging choices of smaller firms. There is significant variation in the prevalence of derivatives usage across industries, ranging from 0 to 1. In half the industries no firm uses derivatives. The average proportion of derivatives users is 22.4 percent, while in the top percentile of industries, the proportion of derivatives users is 87 percentor higher.

1.3.1 Variables

Since our analysis contains both firm-level and industry-level regressions, we construct both firm-level and industry-level variables. Prior research has revealed significant correlations between hedging strategies and several firm-specific variables, such as firm size, Tobin's q, leverage, liquidity, and dividend policy. See Geczy, Minton and Schrand (1997) for further justifications for these variables. We follow this literature and control our analysis for these standard variables. Variable definitions can be found in the Appendix.

Our main attention centers on measures of the degree of competition in an industry. We define several variables. The standard variables are the price-cost margin, used by Domowitz, Hubbard and Petersen (1986), Allayannis and Weston (1999), and Allayannis and Ihrig (2001), and measures of industry concentration, used by Lindenberg and Ross (1981). The rationale for these variables is that an increase in competition should depress firms' profit margins, ceteris paribus, and industries that are more concentrated are often viewed as less competitive.

We use two data sources to calculate price-cost margins. Following Allayannis and Weston (1999), we use data from the 1999 Annual Survey of Manufacturers published by the Bureau of Census to calculate the price-cost margin as follows.

$$PCM_{Census} = \frac{Value\,of\,Sales + \Delta\,Inventories - Payroll - Cost\,of\,Materials}{Value\,of\,Sales + \Delta\,Inventories}.$$

The change in inventories is included because the cost of materials measures the cost of all output produced. Allayannis and Weston's (1999) estimate of the price-cost margin ranges from 0.170 to 0.696 with an average at 0.35. We obtain price-cost margins for a total of 215 industries, ranging from 0.094 to 0.818 and averaging at 0.332 (see Table 1.1).

A limitation of the census data is that it is available only for the manufacturing sector. We therefore calculate a second measure, the sales-weighted

Table 1.1 Descriptive statistics

	Mean	Median	Std. dev.	Min.	Max.	Obs.
Notional value of foreign currency derivatives (in $ millions)	725.30	39.13	3407	0.05	54974	556
Scaled by book value of total assets	10.55%	4.39%	26.58%	0.00%	345.67%	556
Fraction of derivatives users (market-value-weighted)	0.224	0	0.337	0	1	827
Industry average hedge ratio	0.017	0	0.044	0	0.418	772
Fraction of exposed firms (market-value-weighted)	0.725	0.935	0.370	0	1	827
PCM	0.335	0.317	0.161	0	0.974	555
PCM_{Census}	0.332	0.333	0.096	0.094	0.818	215
Herfindahl $index_{Census}$	0.764	0.592	0.637	0.009	2.984	263
Concentration ratio (top four firms)	0.422	0.403	0.202	0.036	1	268
Concentration ratio (top eight firms)	0.556	0.564	0.214	0.066	1	265
PCM_HHI	0.520	0.50	0.226	0.10	1	210
PCM_4CON	0.521	0.50	0.224	0.10	1	214
Number of firms per four digit SIC industry	24.8	13	56.7	3	587	772
Median market value of assets (in millions of US$)	568.1	151.0	1641	7.236	19097	320
Median market-to-book ratio of assets	1.415	1.292	0.428	0.771	4.498	772
Median debt-equity ratio	0.366	0.247	0.391	0	4.305	768
Median quick ratio	1.213	1.139	0.437	0.139	4.101	772
Median dividend payout	0.028	0	0.104	0	1.356	772
Median foreign sales/total sales (exposed firms only)	0.317	0.248	0.235	0.009	1	754
FX exposure coefficients (all firms)	0.0015	0.0006	0.0224	−0.161	0.209	5837
FX exposure coefficients (derivatives users)	−0.0002	−0.0017	0.0138	−0.055	0.100	510
FX exposure coefficients (derivatives non-users)	0.0018	0.0009	0.023	−0.161	0.209	5327

Notes: This table presents summary statistics of all variables used in the analysis. Median variables are unweighted medians based on all firm observations within a four digit SIC industry. Variable definitions can be found in the Appendix.

average price-cost margin, using Compustat data, using the following formula,

$$PCM = \sum_{i=1}^{N} \frac{s_i}{s} \times \frac{s_i - c_i}{s_i},$$

where s_i is the net sales of firm i, c_i is the cost of goods sold of firm i, and s is the total sales of all single-segment firms in the same industry; N is the total number of single-segment firms per industry. If $PCM<0$, then we set it equal to zero for the calculation of the industry average. The change in inventories is excluded because the cost of goods sold does not contain the cost of inventories. We calculate the price-cost margin based on single-segment firms only, because multi-segment firms may engage in cross subsidization of their business segments, which would bias our measure of the competitiveness of the market.[8] Using Compustat data we obtain price-cost margins for 555 industries, which average at 0.335 and thus are similar to the price-cost margins derived from the Census data.

We use three measures of industry concentration provided by the US Census Bureau's 1997 Economic Census: the Herfindahl–Herschmann index, a four-firm concentration ratio, and an eight-firm concentration ratio, used by Lindenberg and Ross (1981). The Herfindahl–Herschmann index is calculated by summing the squares of the percentage value added by the 50 largest firms in the industry or the universe of firms in the industry, whichever is lower. The average index value is 0.764. The four-firm (eight-firm) concentration ratio captures the percent of value added accounted for by the four (eight) largest companies in the industry. The average values are 0.422 and 0.556 respectively.

In unreported analysis we find that all three concentration measures are significantly positively correlated ($\rho = 0.94$–0.97). Thus, it probably makes little difference whether industry concentration is measured by the Herfindahl index or by either one of the two concentration measures. The correlations between the price-cost margins and the three concentration measures are surprisingly low (0.176–0.250), however, which suggests that these variables measure different aspects of the degree of competition. Table 1.2 Panel A shows the breakdown of the manufacturing industries with below/above median price-cost margins and below/above median Herfindahl indices. If price-cost margins and concentration measures were singularly adequate measures of competition, then one would expect no/few industries in which margins are high and concentration is low and vice versa. Table 1.2 Panel A, however, indicates that there are significant numbers of industries with exactly these characteristics. It is unclear whether these industries are more or less competitive than average. This finding demonstrates the shortcomings of using only the price-cost margin or only a concentration measure to proxy for the degree of competition.

Table 1.2 Derivatives use and industry structure

Panel A: Number of industries in sample

	Herfindahl index$_{\text{Census}}$		
PCM$_{\text{Census}}$	Below median	Above median	Total
Below median	52	45	97
Above median	45	54	99
Total	97	99	196

Panel B: Fraction of derivatives users per industry (market-value-weighted)

	Herfindahl index$_{\text{Census}}$		
PCM$_{\text{Census}}$	Below median	Above median	Total
Below median	0.176	0.221	0.194
Above median	0.326	0.437	0.388
Total	0.241	0.345	0.292

Panel C: Industry average hedge ratio

	Herfindahl index$_{\text{Census}}$		
PCM$_{\text{Census}}$	Below median	Above median	Total
Below median	0.017	0.022	0.019
Above median	0.023	0.030	0.027
Total	0.020	0.026	0.023

Notes: This table shows the number of four digit SIC industries (Panel A), the market-value-weighted fraction of derivatives users (Panel B), and the industry average hedge ratio (Panel C) as functions of the price-cost margin (PCM) and the Herfindahl index. The industry average hedge ratio is defined as the sum of the notational values of FX derivatives of all firms divided by the sum of firms' market values of assets. All variable definitions can be found in the Appendix.

We address this issue in two ways. First, we construct two composite measures of industry competition based on the price-cost margin and either the Herfindahl index or the four-firm concentration ratio. The composite measure, *PCM_HHI*, is the average of the percentiles of the price-cost margin and the Herfindahl index. The composite measure, *PCM_4CON*, is the average of the percentiles of the price-cost margin and the four-firm concentration ratio. These composite measures have a high value if both the price-cost margin and the concentration measure are high, and a low value if both the price-cost margin and the concentration measure are low. We use these two variables as our primary measures of the degree of competition in an industry. Our second approach is to conduct sub-sample analyses on industries with above median price-cost margins and above median Herfindahl indices, which we interpret as less competitive industries, and on industries with below median price-cost margins and below median Herfindahl indices, which we interpret as more competitive industries.

We define several control variables to characterize the industries in our sample: firm size, industry financial constraints, and industry growth options. Since many studies have shown that large firms are more likely to use derivatives than small firms, we control our industry-level regressions for the *median firm size,* which we calculate as the unweighted median of the market value of firms' assets (market value of equity plus book values of debt and preferred stock) for each four digit SIC segment. Financial constraints and underinvestment problems have also been frequently linked to corporate derivatives usage. We measure *industry financial constraints* as the median values of the debt-equity ratio, the quick ratio and the dividend payout ratio in each four digit SIC segment. Similarly, we measure *industry growth options* as the median of the market-to-book ratio.[9] Finally, we create a measure of ex-ante exchange rate exposure. As in Graham and Rogers (2002), we define a firm as having ex-ante FX exposure if it disclosed foreign assets, foreign sales or foreign income in the Compustat geographic segment file, or disclosed non-zero values of foreign currency adjustments, exchange rate effect, or deferred foreign taxes in Compustat main files. Table 1.1 provides descriptive statistics of all variables.

1.4 The impact of competition on hedging strategies

In this section, we investigate whether competition is likely to have an impact on firms' derivatives strategies. To test Hypothesis H1, we conduct industry-level and firm-level tests. First, we estimate the relation between the degree of competition and the fraction of firms that use derivatives in an industry, controlling for other factors that might also affect the prevalence of derivatives usage in an industry. Next, we examine the relation between the degree of competition in an industry and a firm's probability of using derivatives. To test Hypothesis H2, we examine whether competition affects the extent of derivatives usage by a firm.

Table 1.2 shows the average fractions of derivatives users (Panel B) and the average hedge ratios (Panel C) in industries with above and below median Herfindahl indices and above and below median price-cost margins. The industry average hedge ratio is defined by the sum of the notational values of FX derivatives of all firms divided by the sum of market values of assets of all firms. Panel B shows that in more competitive industries (Herfindahl index and price-cost margin are both below median values) 17.6 percent of firms use derivatives, while in less competitive industries (Herfindahl

Table 1.3 Competition and the use of derivatives within industries

	I	*II*
Intercept	−1.431	−1.407
	(0.450)***	(0.431)***
PCM_HHI	0.708	
	(0.229)***	
PCM_4CON		0.753
		(0.228)***
Fraction of exposed firms	1.128	1.159
	(0.238)***	(0.233)***
ln Median market value of assets)	0.080	0.076
	(0.053)	(0.052)
Median market-to-book ratio of assets	−0.153	−0.190
	(0.150)	(0.126)
Median debt-equity ratio	−0.178	−0.184
	(0.242)	(0.239)
Median quick ratio	−0.005	0.000
	(0.125)	(0.120)
Median dividend payout	0.391	0.295
	(0.824)	(0.799)
Observations	180	184
Log likelihood	−131.6	−132.92
Pseudo R^2	0.15	0.16

Notes: This table reports industry-level tobit regressions of the (market-value-weighted) fraction of derivatives users in an four digit SIC industry on measures of the degree of competition and additional control variables. All variable definitions can be found in the Appendix. Medians refer to the industry median values of the firm-specific variables. Figures in parentheses represent heteroskedasticity-robust standard errors. Statistical significance is indicated by ***, **, and * for the 1%, 5% and 10% levels respectively.

index and price-cost margin are both above median values) 43.7 percent of firms use derivatives. Consistent with this result, the average hedge ratio is 1.7 percent in more competitive industries and 3 percent in less competitive industries. These univariate comparisons show that the degree of competition is negatively correlated with the prevalence and the extent of hedging.

In Table 1.3, we examine the relation between competition and the prevalence of derivatives usage in a multivariate setting in order to control for other factors that may also impact firms' decisions to use derivatives. Since there are a significant number of industries in which no firm uses derivatives, we estimate industry-level tobit regressions. We regress the market-value-weighted fraction of derivatives users on measures of the degree of competition and control variables. The results show that the two composite competition measures are significantly positively correlated with the fraction of derivatives users, which implies that in more competitive industries fewer firms hedge. This finding supports Adam, Dasgupta and Titman (2007) and Mello and Ruckes (2008) who argued that in competitive environments some firms may strategically reduce their hedge positions, or not hedge at all, in order to benefit from cash inflows when their competitors experience a cash outflow due to their hedging activities. These results are significant because they support the notion that there is a strategic component to corporate derivatives strategies, which most theories of corporate hedging have hitherto ignored. We note that, consistent with previous studies, the fraction of derivatives users in an industry is also a function of the fraction of exposed firms.

In Table 1.4, we examine a firm's probability of using FX derivatives by estimating a probit model. The dependent variable takes on a value of one if a firm uses FX derivatives in 1999 and zero otherwise. On the right hand side, we include our two composite measures of industry competition. In Table 1.4, Columns I and II show that our two composite measures, *PCM_HHI* and *PCM_4CON*, have negative but marginally significant relations with the fraction of hedgers. These results appear to contradict the positive relation between the fraction of hedgers and industry competitiveness shown in Table 1.3. The results in Columns III and IV of Table 1.4 show that this negative relation is due to large firms. We interact the measures of industry competition with firm size and include the interaction term as a control variable. The coefficient on the interaction of firm size and the two composite measures of industry competition is negative and statistically significant in both columns. This means that large firms are more likely to hedge when competition is high. However, consistent with Table 1.3, the coefficients on *PCM_4CON* and *PCM_HHI* are now positive and economically large, with the former also statistically significant. Thus, among small firms, the likelihood of using derivatives is smaller in more competitive industries.

For comparison with Allayannis and Weston (1999), we present a similar analysis using the price-cost margin based on Census data as a measure of competition. Column V of Table 1.4 shows that, as in Allayannis and Weston (1999), the price-cost margin is significantly negatively correlated with the probability of hedging. However, when the interaction of firm size and price-cost margin is included (Column VI), we see that the price-cost margin itself is positively related to the probability to hedge, while the interaction between size and price-cost margin has a significant negative relation with the probability of hedging. This analysis suggests that larger firms behave in the manner predicted by Allayannis and Ihrig (2001) – hedge when profit margins are tight and shocks can't be passed through to prices. In contrast, smaller firms behave in the strategic sense of Adam, Dasgupta and Titman (2007) and Mello and Ruckes (2008) by opting to not hedge when competition is greater.

Table 1.4 Competition and the probability of derivatives usage

	I	II	III	IV	V	VI
Intercept	−3.918	−3.904	−5.693	−6.040	−3.768	−6.149
	(0.337)***	(0.337)***	(0.973)***	(0.992)***	(0.340)***	(0.954)***
PCM_HHI	−0.588		1.972			
	(0.384)		(1.374)			
PCM_4CON		−0.637		2.452		
		(0.379)*		(1.404)*		
PCM_HHI × ln(firmsize)			−0.409			
			(0.213)*			
PCM_4CON × ln(firmsize)				−0.489		
				(0.214)**		
PCM_{Census}					−1.248	3.606
					(0.533)**	(1.823)**
PCM_{Census} × ln(firm size)						−0.707
						(0.259)***
Fraction of derivatives users	0.712	0.743	0.745	0.770	0.688	0.690
	(0.272)***	(0.269)***	(0.279)***	(0.278)***	(0.256)***	(0.282)**
FX exposure dummy	0.924	0.927	0.914	0.913	0.896	0.881
	(0.215)***	(0.216)***	(0.215)***	(0.216)***	(0.212)***	(0.210)***
ln(firm size)	0.377	0.376	0.661	0.716	0.384	0.738
	(0.043)***	(0.043)***	(0.152)***	(0.154)***	(0.043)***	(0.143)***
Market-to-book ratio of assets	−0.098	−0.099	−0.093	−0.094	−0.091	−0.084
	(0.039)**	(0.039)**	(0.038)**	(0.038)**	(0.037)**	(0.034)**
Debt-equity ratio	−0.054	−0.059	−0.051	−0.054	−0.063	−0.059
	(0.065)	(0.069)	(0.066)	(0.069)	(0.074)	(0.077)
Quick ratio	0.009	0.011	0.006	0.007	0.014	0.008
	(0.039)	(0.039)	(0.039)	(0.038)	(0.038)	(0.038)
Dividend payout ratio	0.213	0.209	0.190	0.183	0.189	0.216
	(0.132)	(0.133)	(0.133)	(0.134)	(0.131)	(0.130)*
Number of observations	859	863	859	863	863	863
Log likelihood	−197.86	−198.75	−196.49	−196.81	−197.05	−193.48
Pseudo R^2	0.38	0.37	0.38	.038	0.38	0.39

Notes: This table reports firm-level probit regressions of derivatives usage on measures of the degree of competition and additional control variables. The dependent variable takes a value of 1 if the firm reports using derivatives in 1999 and 0 otherwise. All variable definitions can be found in the Appendix. Figures in parentheses denote heteroskedasticity-robust standard errors. Statistical significance is indicated by ***, **, and * for the 1%, 5% and 10% levels respectively.

In unreported analysis we examine the impact of competition on a firm's extent of derivatives usage, because Mello and Ruckes (2008) predict that firms hedge less if competition is more intense. To test this hypothesis, we regress a firm's hedge ratio, calculated as notional amounts of outstanding FX derivatives over the book value of firm's total assets, on our composite measures of industry competition and several control variables using a tobit estimation. While the hedge ratio is correlated with exposure, firm size, Tobin's q, which is consistent with the existing literature, it appears to be unrelated to the degree of competition.[10] Mello and Ruckes (2008) further predict that when there is more heterogeneity in firms' financial strategies, then firms also hedge less. We find weak statistical support for this prediction. In industries in which debt levels are more heterogeneous, firms choose lower hedge ratios. These results show that the degree of industry competition has a significant impact on the decision to hedge, but not on the extent of hedging.[11]

A similar pattern exists in existing empirical literature on corporate risk management. While some of the rational theories of hedging do have some predictive power in explaining which firms hedge and which firms do not, the same theories largely fail to explain the extent of hedging.

1.5 The interdependence of hedging strategies

In this section, we examine whether corporate hedging strategies are interdependent, as equilibrium models such as the one developed by Adam, Dasgupta and Titman (2007) postulate. We are interested in examining whether a firm's hedging decision is related to the hedging decisions of the firm's competitors. Since the magnitude of a firm's FX exposure should capture an important incentive to hedge, we examine how the foreign exchange exposures of derivatives users and non-users are affected by the hedging decisions of other firms. Hypothesis H3 states that the exposure of derivatives non-users increases as more firms hedge in an industry, while the exposure of derivatives users declines.[12] To test this hypothesis, we first calculate each firms' FX exposure as described below.

1.5.1 Foreign exchange exposure of FX derivatives users and non-users

A large body of literature focuses on foreign currency exposure measurement. The standard approach is to regress stock returns on changes in exchange rates, controlling for the overall market return (see for example Jorion, 1990; He and Ng, 1998 and Dominguez and Tesar, 2001). Following this literature, we estimate the following time-series regression for each firm using monthly data from 1996 to 2000:

$$r_{it} = \beta_{i0} + \beta_{ix}\Delta EXCH_t + \beta_{im}r_{mt} + \varepsilon_{it}. \tag{1.1}$$

In equation (1.1), r_{it} is the monthly rate of return on firm i's stock; r_{mt} is the corresponding monthly rate of return (including distributions) on a value-weighted portfolio of NYSE/NASDAQ/AMEX stocks. The variable $\Delta EXCH_t$ is the monthly change in the value of the US dollar orthogonal to the market return.[13] The exchange rate is the trade-weighted value of the US dollar in terms of its major trading partners as calculated by the Federal Reserve Board. The coefficient β_{ix} measures a firm's (ex-post) net exposure to exchange rate movements of the US dollar.

As in previous studies, we find that the median foreign exchange exposure coefficients are generally small. Approximately 9 percent of the firms have significantly positive or significantly negative foreign exchange exposures. We are interested in comparing the foreign exchange exposures of FX derivatives users with that of non-users regardless of whether the exposure is positive or negative. Therefore, we take the absolute value of the estimated exposure coefficient and calculate the mean of the 'absolute' exposure for the two groups of firms. On average, firms using FX derivatives have significantly lower exposures to foreign exchange fluctuations than firms that do not use FX derivatives. The same conclusion prevails if we consider firms with positive and negativeβ_{ix} separately. In both sub-samples, the exposure of derivatives users is significantly smaller (closer to zero) than that of derivatives non-users. Thus, univariate tests show that, on average, FX derivatives users are less exposed to foreign currency fluctuations than FX derivatives non-users.[14]

1.5.2 The effect of industry hedging on individual firms' exposures

In this section, we examine how firms' exchange rate exposures are affected by their own hedging decisions and those of their competitors. In particular, we want to determine whether derivatives strategies are interdependent across firms.

We test the relation between β_{ix} and the fraction of hedgers in a multivariate framework. Since a more negative β_{ix} and a more positive β_{ix} both reflect higher exposures to exchange rates, we use the absolute value of the exposure coefficient as our dependent variable, and estimate the following regression using ordinary least squares:

$$|\hat{\beta}_{ix}| = \alpha_0 + \alpha_1 D_i + \alpha_2 D_i \times F_j + \alpha_3 F_j + \beta ControlVariables_i + u_i. \tag{1.2}$$

The dummy variable D_i takes on a value of one if a firm disclosed the use of FX derivatives and zero otherwise; F_j is our measure of the prevalence of hedging in firm *i*'s industry and is the same as the market-value-weighted fraction of derivatives users used previously with one minor change. When calculating the fraction of hedgers in firm i's industry, we exclude firm i's own hedging decision because it is already captured by the dummy variable *D*.

We focus on the coefficient of the interaction term. Since the exposure of an FX derivatives user (non-user) is expected to decrease (increase) with the fraction of hedged firms in the industry, we include an interaction term of D with F. We expect the coefficient on the interaction term, α_2, to be less than zero. A negative α_2 implies that in industries where hedging is widespread, unhedged firms are relatively more exposed to foreign exchange shocks than hedged firms. Likewise, it also implies that in industries where hedging is less common, unhedged firms are relatively less exposed to foreign exchange shocks than hedged firms.

Finally, we include the following control variables, which prior studies have found to be correlated with exposure coefficients and firms' decisions to use derivatives: firm size, debt-equity ratio, quick ratio, dividend payout ratio, and Tobin's Q. The construction of these variables is described in Section 1.3.1. Since a firm's involvement in foreign trade can affect its exposure, we include firm foreign sales divided by total sales as a control variable. Since there is no variation in F within an industry, we do not include industry dummies. However, we estimate regression (1.2) using industry-clustered standard errors to control for the possibility that observations on individual firms in a given industry may not be independent.[15]

The first column of Table 1.5 presents the regression estimates of equation (1.2). We focus on the coefficient of the interaction term, which is negative and significant as predicted, and larger in absolute value than the coefficient on the fraction of derivatives users. This implies that the net exposure of derivatives users declines relative to derivatives non-users as more firms use derivatives in the same industry. In contrast, the net exposure of derivatives non-users increases as more firms use derivatives in the same industry. An increase in the fraction of derivatives users by 0.1 increases the net exposure of non-users by 0.0002 or 10 percent relative to the mean, and decreases the exposure of users by 0.0001 or 50 percent relative to the mean. The coefficient on the derivatives user dummy shows that, in industries where the fraction of hedgers is zero, the FX exposures of derivatives users and non-users are not significantly different. In industries in which more than 10 percent of firms use derivatives, however, derivatives users have lower net FX exposures than derivatives non-users.

These results show that the net exposure of an individual firm is not only a function of a firm's own hedging decision, but also a function of the environment it operates in, for example, the hedging decisions of others. This implies that hedging decisions are likely to be interdependent as postulated by Adam, Dasgupta and Titman (2007). This result is robust to controlling for other factors that may also impact firms' exposure coefficients, such as firm size, the magnitude of firms' foreign sales, firm leverage, and firms' financial condition. In particular, we find that smaller and more levered firms, and firms that may be more financially constrained, as measured by the payout ratio, have larger FX exposures.

Table 1.5 Impact of derivatives usage on firms' FX exposures

		HI and PCM below median values	HI and PCM above median values
	All industries	More competitive industries	Less competitive industries
Intercept	0.024	0.021	0.022
	(0.001)***	(0.004)***	(0.006)**
Derivatives user dummy (D)	0.0003	0.004	0.025
	(0.001)	(0.002)**	(0.004)***
Fraction of derivatives users (F)	0.002	0.000	0.008
	(0.001)*	(0.003)*	(0.007)
D × F	−0.003	−0.006	−0.039
	(0.002)**	(0.003)	(0.008)***
Foreign sales/Total sales	−0.000	0.009	0.037
	(0.004)	(0.009)	(0.012)**
ln(Market value of assets)	−0.002	−0.002	−0.002
	(0.000)***	(0.001)***	(0.001)**
Debt-equity ratio	0.001	0.005	0.002
	(0.000)**	(0.003)	(0.005)
Quick ratio	0.000	0.000	0.000
	(0.000)	(0.000)	(0.000)
Dividend payout	−0.003	−0.002	−0.007
	(0.001)***	(0.003)	(0.002)**
R^2	0.08	0.16	0.08
N	4518	210	380

Notes: This table examines the impact of firms' individual and aggregate derivatives strategies on firms' foreign currency exposures. We estimate the following regression model using OLS:

$$\left|\hat{\beta}_{ix}\right| = \alpha_0 + \alpha_1 D_i + \alpha_2 F_j + \alpha_3 D_i \times F_j + \beta \text{ control variables}_i + u_i.$$

The dummy variable D_i takes a value of one if a firm disclosed the use of FX derivatives in 1999 and zero otherwise; F_j measures the fraction of derivatives users in firm *i*'s industry, calculated as the market value of firms in the industry that use FX derivatives divided by the market value of all firms in the industry. When calculating *F*, we exclude the firm's own hedging decision. All other variable definitions can be found in the Appendix. The second and third columns provide sub-sample analyses for more/less competitive industries (Herfindahl index and price-cost margin below/above median values). Standard errors, given in parentheses, are adjusted for heteroskedasticity and assume that observations are not necessarily independent within the same industry. Statistical significance is indicated by ***, **, and * for the 1%, 5% and 10% levels respectively.

The interdependence of derivatives strategies should be especially strong in industries in which firms possess pricing power, that is, less competitive industries, because in these industries aggregate hedging decisions have a stronger impact on the volatility of product prices. We therefore re-estimate equation (1.2) for two sub-samples: more competitive industries (price-cost margin and Herfindahl index are both below median) and less competitive

Table 1.6 Impact of derivatives usage on firms' positive and negative FX exposures

	Positive foreign currency exposure ($\hat{\beta}_{ix} > 0$)			Negative foreign currency exposure ($\hat{\beta}_{ix} < 0$)		
		HI and PCM below median values	HI and PCM above median values		HI and PCM below median values	HI and PCM above median values
	All industries	More competitive industries	Less competitive industries	All industries	More competitive industries	Less competitive industries
Intercept	0.027	0.028	0.026	−0.021	−0.014	−0.018
	(0.002)***	(0.007)***	(0.012)	(0.001)***	(0.004)***	(0.006)**
Derivatives user dummy (D)	−0.001	0.001	0.040	−0.001	−0.008	−0.017
	(0.001)	(0.003)	(0.008)***	(0.001)	(0.003)**	(0.005)**
Fraction of derivatives users(F)	0.002	−0.004	0.004	−0.003	−0.006	−0.011
	(0.002)	(0.004)	(0.011)	(0.002)*	(0.006)	(0.008)
D × F	−0.004	−0.002	−0.057	0.003	0.017	0.029
	(0.002)	(0.005)	(0.011)***	(0.002)	(0.006)***	(0.009)**
Foreign sales/Total sales	0.002	0.008	−0.014	0.004	−0.022	−0.096
	(0.005)	(0.008)	(0.058)	(0.005)	(0.015)	(0.028)**
ln(Market value of assets)	−0.002	−0.003	−0.002	0.001	0.001	0.001
	(0.000)***	(0.001)***	(0.001)	(0.000)***	(0.001)	(0.000)***

continued

Table 1.6 Continued

	Positive foreign currency exposure ($\hat{\beta}_{ix} > 0$)			Negative foreign currency exposure ($\hat{\beta}_{ix} < 0$)		
		HI and PCM below median values	HI and PCM above median values		HI and PCM below median values	HI and PCM above median values
	All industries	More competitive industries	Less competitive industries	All industries	More competitive industries	Less competitive industries
Debt-equity ratio	0.000	0.000	0.000	−0.001	−0.006	−0.003
	(0.000)	(0.003)	(0.004)	(0.000)**	(0.003)**	(0.006)
Quick ratio	0.000	0.000	0.000	−0.000	−0.000	−0.000
	(0.000)	(0.000)	(0.000)	(0.000)	(0.001)	(0.000)
Dividend payout	−0.002	−0.006	−0.009	0.004	0.003	0.013
	(0.001)	(0.004)	(0.002)***	(0.001)***	(0.003)	(0.003)***
R^2	0.09	0.22	0.09	0.07	0.24	0.09
N	2332	107	190	2186	103	190

Notes: In this table we analyze the impact of firms' individual and aggregate derivatives strategies on firms' foreign currency exposures, separating firms with positive foreign currency exposure ($\hat{\beta}_{ix} > 0$) from firms with negative foreign currency exposure ($\hat{\beta}_{ix} < 0$). Otherwise, the regression model is the same as in Table 1.5. Please see Table 1.5 for additional details. Standard errors, given in parentheses, are adjusted for heteroskedasticity and assume that observations are not necessarily independent within the same industry. Statistical significance is indicated by ***, **, and * for the 1%, 5% and 10% levels respectively.

industries (price-cost margin and Herfindahl index both above median). The regression estimates are also listed in Table 1.5. As expected, we find that the interaction effect is especially strong, both statistically and economically, in less competitive industries. While an increase in the fraction of derivatives users by 0.1 increases the net exposure of non-users by a statistically insignificant 0.0008, it decreases the exposure of users by 0.0039.[16] The coefficient on the interaction term is not statistically significant in more competitive industries.

So far we have treated positive and negative net FX exposures identically. However, a positive exposure coefficient implies that a general appreciation of the US dollar increases a firm's market value, for example because a firm is importing goods from abroad, or because domestic competition with foreign companies declines, while a negative exposure coefficient implies that a general depreciation of the US dollar increases a firm's market value, for example because a firm is exporting goods and the firm is becoming more competitive abroad. These are very different cases. It is therefore interesting to examine whether our prior results hold if we distinguish between positive and negative exposure coefficients.

In Table 1.6, we present regression estimates of equation (1.2) for positive β_{ix} and negative β_{ix} separately. Note that if β_{ix} is negative, lower values of the dependent variable imply larger exposures. Therefore, the expected signs of all coefficients flip. Our previous results prevail. In less competitive industries, the net exposure of derivatives users declines relative to non-users as the fraction of derivatives users increases. This relation is absent in more competitive industries. In the case of negative foreign exchange exposures, we find a positive coefficient on the interaction term; in other words, derivatives users have relatively lower (closer to zero) exposures if the fraction of derivatives users in the industry is high. Although the interaction term is statistically significant in both the more- and less-competitive sub-samples, the size of the coefficient is – again – larger in the less competitive industry sub-sample.

1.6 Conclusion

An extensive literature relates corporate derivatives strategies to firm-specific factors. Anecdotal evidence, however, suggests that industry-specific factors, such as the degree of competition, also affect risk management strategies. In fact, theoretical models by Adam, Dasgupta, and Titman (2007) and Mello and Ruckes (2008) imply that competition can be a first-order determinant of hedging decisions. In this chapter, we empirically examine how competition affects derivatives strategies, and whether risk management strategies are interdependent across firms, as the model by Adam, Dasgupta, and Titman (2007) suggests.

We find that the prevalence of derivatives usage in an industry is negatively correlated with competition; in other words, in more competitive industries fewer firms hedge. This effect is due to smaller firms, which are less likely to use derivatives in more competitive industries. In contrast, larger firms are more likely to use derivatives in more competitive industries. These results are consistent with some firms, that is, smaller firms, strategically choosing not to hedge an exposure in order to gain a competitive advantage when the market moves against hedged firms as proposed by Adam, Dasgupta, and Titman (2007) and Mello and Ruckes (2008).

We also find evidence suggesting an interdependence of risk management strategies across firms. We find that the (ex-post) net FX exposure of a firm is not only a function of its own hedging decision, but also of the hedging decisions of its competitors. In particular, as more firms hedge in an industry, the exposure of derivatives users declines, while the exposure of derivatives non-users increases. Thus, firms' net exposures are lowest if their hedging decisions conform to the hedging decisions of the majority, and are highest if they deviate from the hedging decisions of the majority.

These results have important implications for the theory of corporate risk management. The traditional literature has modeled a firm in isolation, and therefore disregarded the possibility of strategic interactions of risk management strategies. The empirical support for these models is weak, however. The results presented in this chapter demonstrate that such strategic interaction can be empirically relevant and not merely a theoretical possibility. Thus, to better understand corporate risk management strategies we need new equilibrium models that take the strategic interaction of hedging strategies into account.

Appendix

Definition of Variables

Variable name	Definition of variable
Notional value of foreign currency derivatives	Total notional value of foreign currency derivatives as disclosed on a firm's 1999 10-K form (in US$ millions)
Fraction of derivatives users (market-value-weighted)	Market value of firms in the industry that use FX derivatives divided by the market value of all firms in the industry
Industry average hedge ratio	Sum of the notational values of FX derivatives of all firms divided by the sum of firms' market values of assets

continued

Continued

Variable name	Definition of variable
Fraction of exposed firms (market-value-weighted)	Sum of market values of all firms that face ex-ante exchange rate exposure divided by the sum of market values of all firms in the industry
FX exposure dummy	Dummy variable that takes on a value of one if the firm faces ex-ante exchange rate exposure and zero otherwise. We define a firm as having ex-ante FX exposure if it disclosed foreign assets, foreign sales or foreign income in the Compustat geographic segment file, or disclosed non-zero values of foreign currency adjustments, exchange rate effect, or deferred foreign taxes in Compustat main files.
Foreign sales/Total sales	Foreign sales of a firm obtained from Compustat Geographic segment files divided by total sales of the firm
PCM	Price-cost margin calculated using Compustat data
PCM_{Census}	Price-cost margin calculated using Census data (industries that are covered by the 1999 Annual Survey of Manufacturers).
Herfindahl $index_{Census}$	Herfindahl–Herschmann index calculated by summing the squares of the percentage value added by the 50 largest firms in the industry or the universe of firms in the industry, whichever is lower, using Census data
Concentration ratio (top four firms)	The percent of value added accounted for by the four largest companies in the industry, using Census data
Concentration ratio (top eight firms)	The percent of value added accounted for by the eight largest companies in the industry, using Census data
PCM_HHI	Average of the percentiles of the price-cost margin and the percentiles of the Herfindahl index
PCM_4CON	Average of the percentile of the price-cost margin and the four-firm concentration ratio
Market value of assets (firm size)	Market value of equity plus book value of debt and preferred stock (in US$ millions)
Market-to-book ratio of assets	Ratio of the market value of assets over the book value of assets
Debt-equity ratio	Total debt divided by market value of equity

continued

Continued

Variable name	Definition of variable
Quick ratio	Current assets minus inventories all divided by current liabilities
Dividend payout	Total dividends paid over net income
FX exposure coefficient ($\hat{\beta}_{ix}$)	The FX exposure coefficient is estimated for 5837 firms using the following regression: $r_{it} = \beta_{i0} + \beta_{ix}\Delta EXCH_t + \beta_{im}r_{mt} + \varepsilon_{it}$, where r_t is the monthly rate of return on a firm's stock for the years 1996 till 2000, r_{mt} is the corresponding monthly rate of return on the value-weighted market index, and $\Delta EXCH_t$ is the monthly change in value of the US dollar orthogonal to the market return

Notes

The authors thank Yiorgos Allayannis, Sugato Bhattacharyya, Greg Brown, Sudipto Dasgutpa, Serdar Dinc, Martin Dierker, Amy Dittmar, Art Durnev, Philippe Jorion, Lutz Kilian, E. Han Kim, Francine Lafontaine, Adair Morse, Vikram Nanda, Linda Tesar, Anjan Thakor; participants of the 2004 European Finance Association Meetings, 2005 American Finance Association Meetings, 15th Annual Derivatives and Risk Management Conference (2005), 16th Annual Conference on Financial Economics and Accounting (2005); and participants of finance seminar series at – Bank of Canada, College of William and Mary, H.E.C. Montreal, McGill University, University of California (Irvine), University of Georgia, University of Miami, University of Michigan, University of Oklahoma, University of Toronto and University of Virginia (Darden) for helpful comments. The second author thanks Institut de Finance Mathématique de Montreal for research support. Any errors are our own.

1. See, for example, Stulz (1984), Smith and Stulz (1985), DeMarzo and Duffie (1991, 1995), Breeden and Viswanathan (1998), Leland (1998) and Morellec and Smith (2003).
2. We define a firm's (ex-post) net FX exposure as the sensitivity of the firm's stock returns to changes in the trade-weighted value of the US dollar in terms of its major trading partners.
3. Hentschel and Kothari (2001) find no differences in the overall risk measures of derivatives users and non-users.
4. Geczy, Minton and Schrand (1997) find significant variation in hedging practices across industries. Most of this variation cannot be explained by firm-specific factors alone, highlighting the potential importance of industry effects, such as competition, in explaining corporate hedging strategies.
5. Firms have the option to adjust their production capacities due to changes in their internal cash flows, which are a function of input prices. The value of this option increases with the volatility of input prices.

6. This argument relies on the presence of financial constraints.
7. FAS 105 requires all firms to report information about their off balance sheet financial instruments (including the notional amounts outstanding) for fiscal years ending after June 15, 1990. FAS 133, which came into effect in year 2000, increased the onus on companies to recognize derivatives gains and losses into the income statement. However, FAS 133 also removed the requirement that firms disclose the notional amounts of outstanding contracts. Consequently, from year 2000 onwards, many firms have stopped disclosing contract amounts of their derivatives positions. For this reason we collect derivatives data as of 1999.
8. Out of our initial sample, 6670 firms can be identified in the segment files as operating in only one business segment. We treat these as single-segment firms. If the net sales of single-segment firms differ from the sales reported in the segment file by more than 10 percent, then we delete the observation. We lose 333 observations. If the firm's primary two digit SIC code differs from the two digit SIC code in the segment file, we delete the observation. We lose 395 observations. If the firm's primary four digit SIC code differs from the four digit SIC code in the segment file, we use the four digit SIC code in the segment file.
9. We also used industry median credit rating and the highest credit rating in an industry as alternative measures of industry financial constraints. Since the credit rating variables were never found to be significantly related to derivatives strategies we excluded them from the reported analysis.
10. Results are unchanged if we limit the sample only to firms that use FX derivatives.
11. These results are available from the authors upon request.
12. Probit regressions with the derivatives usage dummy on the left hand side and fraction of hedgers on the right hand side may seem like an alternative method of investigating whether hedging choices are interdependent. Such regression is problematic, however. A positive relation is likely since a derivatives user is more likely to be drawn from an industry that has a greater fraction of derivatives users. Thus, a probit model will not reveal whether hedging strategies are interdependent.
13. Jorion (1990) points out that using changes in the exchange rate that are orthogonal to the market return may lead to econometric difficulties. We repeat our analysis using changes in the exchange rate instead of the residuals from a regression of exchange rates on the stock market return. Our exposure results do not change if we use this different set of exposure coefficients.
14. This finding is consistent with the results of Allayannis and Ofek (2001) who also find that FX derivatives users have lower foreign exchange exposures.
15. It is well recognized that in regression models where the dependent variable is an estimate, variation in the sampling variance causes heteroskedasticity. A common approach to this problem is to use a weighted least squares technique. However, Lewis and Linzer (2005) show that weighted least squares usually leads to inefficient estimates and underestimated standard errors. They find that in many cases, OLS with heteroskedasticity consistent standard errors yields better results. The clustered standard errors used here are heteroskedasticity consistent.
16. Results are similar if we create the sub-samples using a cross between the price-cost margin and the four-firm concentration ratio instead of the cross between price-cost margin and Herfindahl index.

References

Adam, T. R., Dasgupta, S. and Titman, S. (2007). Financial Constraints, Competition, and Hedging in Industry Equilibrium. *Journal of Finance*, 62, 2445–73.

Allayannis, G. and Ihrig, J. (2001). Exposure and Markups. *Review of Financial Studies*, 14, 805–35.

Allayannis, G., Ihrig, J. and Weston, J. (2001). Exchange-rate Hedging: Financial versus Operational Strategies. *American Economic Review*, 91, 391–5.

Allayannis, G. and Ofek, E. (2001). Exchange Rate Exposure, Hedging, and the Use of Foreign Currency Derivatives. *Journal of International Money and Finance*, 20, 273–96.

Allayannis, G. and Weston, J. P. (1999). The Use of Currency Derivatives and Industry Structure, in Brown, G. and Chew, D. (eds) *Corporate Risk: Strategies and Management*. Riskbooks.

Breeden, D. and Viswanathan, S. (1998). Why Do Firms Hedge? An Asymmetric Information Model. Unpublished manuscript.

Brown, G. (2001). Managing Foreign Exchange Risk with Derivatives. *Journal of Financial Economics*, 60, 401–48.

DeMarzo, P. and Duffie, D. (1991). Corporate Financial Hedging with Proprietary Information. *Journal of Economics Theory*, 53, 261–86.

DeMarzo, P. and Duffie, D. (1995). Corporate Incentives for Hedging and Hedge Accounting. *Review of Financial Studies*, 8, 743–71.

De Meza, D. (1986). Safety in Conformity but Profits in Deviance. *Canadian Journal of Economics*, 19, 261–9.

Dominguez, K. and Tesar, L. (2001). A Reexamination of Exchange Rate Exposure. *American Economic Review*, 91, Papers and Proceedings, 396–9.

Domowitz, I., Hubbard, R. G. and Petersen, B. C. (1986). The Intertemporal Stability of the Concentration-margins Relationship. *Journal of Industrial Economics*, 35, 13–34.

Froot, K., Scharfstein, D. and Stein, J. (1993). Risk Management: Coordinating Corporate Investment and Financing Policies. *Journal of Finance*, 48, 1629–57.

Geczy, C., Minton, B. and Schrand, C. (1997). Why Firms Use Currency Derivatives. *Journal of Finance*, 52, 1323–54.

Graham, J. and Rogers, D. (2002) Do Firms Hedge in Response to Tax Incentives. *Journal of Finance*, 57, 815–38.

Guay, W. (1999). The Impact of Derivatives on Firm Risk: An Empirical Examination of New Derivatives Users. *Journal of Accounting and Economics*, 26, 319–51.

He, J. and Ng, L. K. (1998). The Foreign Exchange Exposure of Japanese Multinational Corporations. *Journal of Finance*, 53, 733–53.

Hentschel, L. and Kothari, S. P. (2001). Are Corporations Reducing or Taking Risks with Derivatives? *Journal of Financial and Quantitative Analysis*, 36, 93–118.

Jorion, P. (1990). The Exchange-rate Exposure of U.S. Multinationals. *Journal of Business*, 63, 331–45.

Leland, H. E. (1998). Agency Costs, Risk Management, and Capital Structure. *Journal of Finance*, 53, 1213–43.

Lewent, J. and Kearney, A. J. (1990). Identifying, Measuring and Hedging Currency Risk at Merck. *Journal of Applied Corporate Finance*, 4, 19–28.

Lewis, J. B. and Linzer, D. A. (2005). Estimating Regression Models in Which the Dependent Variable Is Based on Estimates. *Political Analysis*, 13, 345–64.

Lindenberg, E. B. and Ross, S. A. (1981). Tobin's Q Ratio and Industrial Organization. *Journal of Business*, 54, 1–32.

Maksimovic, V. and Zechner, J. (1991). Debt, Agency Costs and Industry Equilibrium. *Journal of Finance*, 46, 1619–45.

Mello, A. and Ruckes, M. (2008). Financial Hedging and Product Market Rivalry. Unpublished manuscript.

Morellec, E. and Smith, C. W. (2003). Investment Policy, Financial Policies, and the Control of Agency Conflicts. Unpublished manuscript.

Purnanandam, A. (2008). Financial Distress and Corporate Risk Management: Theory and Evidence. *Journal of Financial Economics*, 87, 706–39.

Shleifer, A. and Vishny, R. W. (1992). Liquidation Values and Debt Capacity: A Market Equilibrium Approach. *Journal of Finance*, 47, 1343–66.

Smith, C. W. and Stulz, R. (1985). The Determinants of Firm's Hedging Policies. *Journal of Financial and Quantitative Analysis*, 48, 391–405.

Stulz, R. (1984). Optimal Hedging Policies. *Journal of Financial and Quantitative Analysis*, 19, 127–40.

Williamson, R. (2001). Exchange Rate Exposure and Competition: Evidence from the Automotive Industry. *Journal of Financial Economics*, 59, 441–75.

2
The Cash-Flow Risk of Corporate Market Investments

Craig O. Brown

2.1 Introduction

Over a long span of time, US aggregate risk has decreased while the risk for US nonfinancial corporations (or firms) has increased substantially.[1] This general finding has been observed using sales (Comin and Mulani, 2006), stock returns (Campbell et al., 2001) and cash flows (Irvine and Pontiff, 2009) in addition to earnings,[2] employment and capital investment (Comin and Philippon, 2005).

Like firm-level risk, corporate liquidity has increased substantially and is shown to be positively correlated with firm-level cash-flow risk.[3] The prevailing explanation is that corporate managers increase liquidity in response to a risky and uncertain environment. However, aggregate risk shrinks over time and cash growth should reduce subsequent firm-level risk. Therefore it is somewhat puzzling that, despite a downward trend in aggregate risk, there exists an upward trend in firm-level risk and corporate liquidity.

The solution to this problem might lie in the heterogeneity of corporate liquidity. The standard measure of corporate liquidity consists of three components: physical currency (or cash), credit lines, and short-term investments in marketable securities. Unlike cash, the other components of corporate liquidity might increase cash-flow risk. Do investments in marketable securities (or corporate market investments) have a significant effect on cash-flow risk? This chapter studies the total cash-flow risk associated with marketable securities and the causal relation between the growth in investments in marketable securities and cash-flow risk.

Corporate market investment (current and noncurrent), consisting of equity and debt securities, is substantial by itself, and has increased over time. Present-day corporate market investment can constitute well over 30 percent of total assets for many firms. When including noncurrent corporate market investment in the measure of liquid assets, it is not cash (42 percent) that constitutes the majority of liquid assets for firms that make market investments; it is corporate market investment (58 percent). This 58 percent consists of 28 percent noncurrent market investment and 30 percent current market investment.

The money-demand literature (and by extension the cash-management literature) presents a cash storage view of market investment risk which suggests that corporate market investment is a simple substitute for cash (Selden, 1961; Maddala and Vogel, 1967; Jeffers and Kwon, 1969) or a low-risk store of excess cash[4] (Miller and Orr, 1966, 1968). Alternatively, market investment might have substantial risk properties; it might decrease or increase total cash-flow risk significantly. The former outcome is consistent with risk management; the latter outcome is consistent with speculation. Risk management (or hedging behavior) can increase value (Smith and Stulz, 1985); speculation through market investments is not likely to increase value (Berk and Green, 2004). Hence, positive market investment risk might be associated agency costs (Jensen and Meckling, 1976), risk-taking incentives, and corporate governance (John, Litov and Yeung, 2008). This chapter evaluates the merits of the cash storage view of market investment risk (Jeffers and Kwon, 1969).

The cash storage view of market investment risk has roots in pre-1960 studies of corporate market investment (Chudson, 1945; Frazer, 1958), and should be qualified for modern firms given the change in investment behavior over time. Prior to 1960, investments held by firms were mostly 'safe' (Krishnamurthy and Vissing-Jorgensen, 2010; Gorton, Lewellen and Metrick, 2012); firms held roughly 75 percent of their market investments in US Treasuries with approximately 67 percent of their market investments maturing in one year or less (Jacobs, 1960). Over time, however, managers of firms have been investing less in short-term US Treasuries, and more in other types of securities (Jacobs, 1960; Heston, 1962). For some firms, traders manage market investments on a day-to-day basis.[5]

This chapter finds that market investments have a positive and significant impact on business cash-flow risk. The risk associated with market investments (or portfolio cash-flow risk) is roughly 90 percent of the risk associated with a firm's core business activities (or operating cash-flow risk).A standard-deviation increase in market investment growth has a risk effect that is 50 percent of the risk effect of a standard-deviation increase in capital expenditure. The effect of market investment growth on the subsequent cash-flow risk spread between total cash-flow risk (inclusive of portfolio cash flow) and operating cash-flow risk (excluding portfolio cash flow) is robust to firm and year fixed effects.

Brown (2013) argues that if managers invest in marketable securities as they would invest in capital stock, then market investments should be positively associated with capital investments. Scott (1979) argues that managers could invest in marketable securities to maximize value directly, but are likely to invest less as the tax rate increases. This chapter shows that market investment portfolio cash-flow risk increases with capital expenditure and decreases with the tax rate. Hence this chapter's evidence suggests that managers could be investing in marketable securities with an objective similar to that for general investment.

Brown (2013) argues that managers could invest in marketable securities in an effort to manage dividend and interest payments. This chapter shows that market investment portfolio cash-flow risk increases with promised commitments (dividend and interest payments). Hence this chapter's evidence suggests that managers could be using market investments to practice asset-liability management (ALM).

This chapter is primarily related to the literature on corporate risk-taking (Comin and Philippon, 2005; John, Litov and Yeung, 2008) and corporate liquidity (Eppen and Fama, 1968); it is also related to the literature on money demand (Barro and Fischer, 1976), and financial flexibility.

In the next section I define corporate market investment and study the investment profile of a modern nonfinancial firm. I then show how aggregate market investment size and the aggregate portfolio composition have changed in recent years. I continue with a rigorous analysis of the effect of market investment growth on cash-flow risk.

2.2 Corporate market investments: definition and example

What are corporate market investments? What types of market investments does a modern firm make?

Corporate market investments are recognized by the Financial Accounting Standards Board (FASB) in the Statement of Financial Accounting Standards (SFAS) No. 115[6] as 'investments in equity securities that have readily determinable fair values' and 'all investments in debt securities'. Market investments do not include unsecuritized loans, futures, forwards, options, or other derivatives recognized by SFAS No. 133. Moreover, market investments do not include treasury stock from repurchases or consolidated subsidiaries, but can include mortgage-backed securities and other securitized loans.

Google is a large public corporation in the internet and technology sector. Google's investments provide not only a good example of the diversity in the types of market investments, but also of diversity in the maturity of market investments. Figure 2.1 shows the liquid-asset amounts for the annual period ending 31 December 2011; the firm has total assets of approximately \$72.6 billion. The firm's cash holding excluding cash-equivalent marketable securities is equal to approximately \$4.7 billion. The firm's total market investment (excluding cash-equivalent marketable securities) is equal to approximately \$34.6 billion. Its market investment as a percentage of net assets (total assets minus cash minus cash-equivalent marketable securities minus market investments) is equal to approximately 124 percent. The

	As of December 31,	
	2010	2011
Cash and cash equivalents:		
Cash	$ 4,652	$ 4,712
Cash equivalents:		
Time deposits	973	534
Money market and other funds	7,547	4,462
U.S. government agencies	0	275
U.S. government notes	300	0
Foreign government bonds	150	0
Corporate debt securities	8	0
Total cash and cash equivalents	13,630	9,983
Marketable securities:		
Time deposits	307	495
U.S. government agencies	1,857	6,226
U.S. government notes	3,930	11,579
Foreign government bonds	1,172	1,629
Municipal securities	2,503	1,794
Corporate debt securities	5,742	6,112
Agency residential mortgage-backed securities	5,673	6,501
Market able equity securities	161	307
Total market able securities	21,345	34,643
Total cash, cash equivalents, and market able securities	$ 34,975	$ 44,626

Figure 2.1 An Example: Google
Notes: The figure presents Note 3 from the 10-K filing for Google Inc. for the annual period ended December 31, 2011. It presents amounts for the firm's various liquid assets. These amounts are from the December 2010 and December 2011 fiscal years (in millions of US dollars). Cash consists of demand deposits, physical currency and coin. US government agencies are securities issued by various federal agencies, other than the Treasury. Time deposits are deposits that depositors may withdraw after giving prior notice. Money market mutual funds are open-end investment companies that invest in short-term, liquid assets, including short-term municipal securities. US government notes are marketable securities issued by the Department of the Treasury. Foreign government bonds are obligations issued by foreign governments. Municipal securities are obligations issued primarily by state and local governments. Corporate debt securities are obligations issued by corporations. Agency residential mortgage-backed securities are claims on cash flows from residential mortgages. Marketable equity securities consist of equity or stock investments.

largest component of Google's market investment consists of US government notes ($11.6 billion), which make up approximately 41 percent of net assets. Google's market investments also include municipal securities ($1.8 billion), corporate debt securities ($6.1 billion), equity securities ($307 million), and agency residential mortgage-backed securities ($6.5 billion). Of the $34.3 billion of non-cash-equivalent debt marketable securities, $13.2 billion worth is due within 1 year (38.6 percent), $7.5 billion worth is due between 1 year and 10 years (21.8 percent), and $8.1 billion worth is due after 10 years (23.6 percent). Google obviously has a flexible investment policy: Google is not limited to investing a moderate amount of funds in short-term US Treasuries.

2.3 Aggregate market investments: size and composition

To understand the change in corporate market investment practices over time, this section presents evidence of the change in the aggregate portfolio composition over time.

Taking data from the Flow of Funds Accounts, Table 2.1 shows the time-series means of various types of market investment for three separate periods: Period 1 (1945 to 1964), Period 2 (1965 to 1984), and Period 3 (1985 to 2005). Period 1 firms place approximately 84 percent of their investible funds in US Treasury securities,[7] and on average, market investments are equal to approximately 8 percent of tangible assets. The Period 2 aggregate investment portfolio is more diverse than the Period 1 portfolio; investments in US Treasury securities comprise only 16.2 percent of all Period 2 market investments. On average, approximately 57 percent of all Period 2 market investments are classified as unidentified miscellaneous financial assets, with total market investments being equal to approximately 12 percent of tangible assets. Finally, Period 3 market investments are equal to approximately 53 percent of tangible assets, with over 90 percent of investments being classified as unidentified miscellaneous financial assets.

2.4 Hypothesis

This section presents and discusses the hypothesis that I use to study market investment risk-taking. This chapter's hypotheses are informed by three classes of models of liquid-asset demand: buffer-stock models, inventory models, and investment models.

Buffer-stock models explain the demand for all liquid assets (Patinkin, 1956). In a buffer-stock model, *the manager determines the optimal amount of liquid assets* to maintain, given various motives: the precautionary motive,[8] the transactions motive, the tax motive, the agency cost motive, and so on. Inventory models explain the demand for physical currency (or cash) by firms (Baumol, 1952; Miller and Orr, 1966, 1968; Eppen and Fama, 1968), given that managers can maintain liquid assets in two forms: cash and money assets. In an inventory model, *the manager recognizes the two forms, but is concerned only with determining the optimal amount of cash* to maintain over the course of the operating period. Inventory models are silent on the optimal amount of money assets.[9] Buffer-stock models and inventory models do not acknowledge the investment in marketable securities as an independent managerial decision. In an investment model, market investments are made

Table 2.1 Aggregate cash and corporate market investments by asset class: period means

	Period 1: 1945–64 Time-Series means			*Period 2: 1965–84* Time-Series means			*Period 3: 1985–2005* Time-Series means		
	Amount (in $BN, 2005)	% of TANA	% of MINV	Amount (in $BN, 2005)	% of TANA	% of MINV	Amount (in $BN, 2005)	% of TANA	% of MINV
Cash and cash equivalents	215.439	11.388	150.347	313.734	7.351	101.794	622.362	9.044	17.555
Foreign deposits	1.463	0.062	0.996	15.034	0.335	3.365	30.481	0.454	0.934
Checkable deposits and currency	199.971	10.681	139.678	198.228	4.744	73.831	238.026	3.646	7.796
Time and savings deposits	13.908	0.642	9.612	83.067	1.887	20.577	211.936	3.028	5.684
Money market funds	0.000	0.000	0.000	7.863	0.163	0.755	136.151	1.830	2.961
Security repurchase agreement	0.097	0.003	0.061	9.542	0.223	3.267	5.769	0.086	0.180
Market investments (MINV)	145.712	7.804	100.000	563.529	12.324	100.000	3689.712	53.040	100.000
Commercial paper	3.138	0.136	2.174	33.279	0.789	12.498	44.203	0.622	1.129
US Treasury securities	122.241	6.790	83.972	45.351	1.093	16.207	51.072	0.811	1.849
US Govt. agency securities	3.152	0.125	2.143	7.935	0.187	2.571	15.165	0.225	0.450
Municipal securities and loans	9.941	0.452	6.822	20.377	0.480	6.734	42.946	0.668	1.463
Mortgages	0.270	0.013	0.190	30.887	0.653	3.579	75.553	1.179	2.618
Mutual funds	0.199	0.007	0.132	4.154	0.095	1.258	73.707	1.021	1.774
Equity in GSE	0.183	0.007	0.125	0.210	0.006	0.156	0.000	0.000	0.000
Unidentified misc. investments	6.587	0.274	4.440	421.335	9.021	56.997	3387.067	48.514	90.717
Other identified financial assets	628.988	30.657	435.359	1823.302	42.312	563.670	3167.489	46.776	93.551
Consumer credit	57.595	2.902	39.944	77.486	1.857	28.662	89.702	1.383	2.981

continued

Table 2.1 Continued

	Period 1: 1945–64 Time-Series means			*Period 2: 1965–84* Time-Series means			*Period 3: 1985–2005* Time-Series means		
	Amount (in $BN, 2005)	% of TANA	% of MINV	Amount (in $BN, 2005)	% of TANA	% of MINV	Amount (in $BN, 2005)	% of TANA	% of MINV
Trade credit	406.469	19.887	281.456	1061.831	24.772	342.180	1637.159	24.434	49.815
Foreign direct investment	145.623	6.975	100.587	599.828	13.771	170.714	1193.288	17.257	33.156
Insurance receivables	193.019	0.893	13.373	75.988	1.739	21.204	218.306	3.273	6.724
Investment in FC subsidiaries	0.000	0.000	0.000	8.169	0.172	0.910	29.034	0.429	0.875
Tangible assets (TANA)	1996.542	100.000	1386.685	4271.995	100.000	1394.026	6687.987	100.000	204.772
Total assets	2986.682	149.850	2072.392	6972.560	161.986	2159.489	14200.000	208.860	415.878

Notes: The table provides time-series means of aggregate balance-sheet items (cash, financial assets, and tangible assets) for nonfarm nonfinancial corporations in the US economy. The full period is 1945 to 2005 (Federal Reserve Board of Governors) and is divided into three sub-periods: Period 1 (1945 to 1964), Period 2 (1965 to 1984), and Period 3 (1985 to 2005). All nominal balance-sheet items are converted to 2005 dollars using the Consumer Price Index. Foreign deposits are deposits, including negotiable certificates of deposit, held in foreign financial institutions. Checkable deposits consist of demand deposits, negotiable order of withdrawal (NOW) accounts and automatic transfer service (ATS) accounts. Currency is US currency and coin. Time and savings deposits are deposits that depositors may withdraw after giving prior notice. Money market mutual funds are open-end investment companies that invest in short-term, liquid assets, including short-term municipal securities. A security repurchase agreement is an agreement to sell an asset, in many cases a federal government security, accompanied simultaneously by an agreement that the seller will repurchase the asset at a later date at a higher price. Commercial paper consists of short-term unsecured promissory notes issued by financial and nonfinancial borrowers. US Treasury securities are marketable and securities issued by the Department of the Treasury. US Govt. agency securities are issued by various federal agencies, other than the Treasury. Municipal securities and loans are obligations issued primarily by state and local governments. Mortgages are loans that are secured in whole or in part by real property. Mutual fund shares are obligations issued by mutual funds; the category excludes money market mutual fund shares. Equity in government-sponsored enterprises (GSE) is equity ownership in Fannie Mae, the Farm Credit System, and the Federal Home Loan Banks. Unidentified miscellaneous claims are obtained directly as the total amount reported by original sources as 'other' financial assets. Consumer credit consists of short-term and intermediate-term loans to individuals. Trade credits are accounts receivable arising from the sale of business-related goods and services. Foreign direct investment is the acquisition of equity in, and the provision of loans to, US affiliates of foreign firms by the purchase of tangible or financial assets of US firms or the direct ownership of their equity shares; the 10 percent threshold that distinguishes direct investment from portfolio investment. Insurance receivables are deferred and unpaid life insurance premiums. Investment in finance company (FC) subsidiaries is the acquisition of equity ownership in the subsidiary companies. Among these subsidiaries, companies are the subsidiaries of motor vehicle manufacturers and the credit subsidiaries of major retailers.

with an objective similar to that for general investment through speculation (Keynes, 1936), portfolio choice (Tobin, 1955), or tax arbitrage (Scott, 1979).

Each type of model is associated with a different view of market investments. For a manager who is unconcerned about the form of liquid asset, buffer-stock models view market investments as being substitutes for cash. For a manager who would like to determine the optimal demand for cash given that deterministic and stochastic factors can influence the transfer between cash and money assets, inventory models view market investments as money assets: the residual after the manager takes the primary action (cash allocation). Investment models view market investment as the primary action; one that is made with an objective similar to that for general investment.

All three types of models have implications for cash-flow risk. Investment models appeal to a manager who makes market investments with the expectation that investments are risk-sensitive assets, which increase cash-flow risk. Buffer-stock models and inventory models appeal to a manager who is motivated to accumulate liquidity. For a manager who is motivated to invest in risk-sensitive assets, market investment has an increasing cash-flow risk effect. For a manager who would like to accumulate liquidity (for any reason) by investing in assets that are not risk sensitive, market investment has a decreasing cash-flow risk effect or no cash-flow risk effect.

For managers who would like to accumulate liquidity, market investments should consist of low-risk short-term securities (or cash-like securities) only (Tobin, 1955). Jeffers and Kwon (1969) study the demand for government securities by firms and find support for the cash storage view. The authors argue that traditional investment (in government securities) is, by and large, low risk and a simple store of cash.

This chapter examines market investment risk for the modern firm given the recent changes in market investment composition over time,[10] and the finding that corporate market investment is used for reasons other than cash storage (Brown, 2013). By itself, the fact that modern firms make noncurrent equity investments (without the intention to acquire other firms) is inconsistent with the view that managers limit their investments to low-risk short-term securities.

Although the Google example in Figure 2.1 provides some level of detail with respect to Google's holdings of cash, cash equivalents, and marketable securities, very few companies provide detailed accounting information of liquid-asset holdings. Given the general lack of accounting transparency with respect to corporate market investments, it is unclear the extent to which market investments are associated with business cash-flow risk.

The first hypothesis addresses whether market investment is indeed associated with business cash-flow risk.

Hypothesis 1 (Cash-Flow Risk) Market investment is *not* associated with business cash-flow risk.

In studying market investment risk for a manager who would like to accumulate liquidity, market investment growth could cause some cash-flow risk not because of speculation, but because managers are capturing a liquidity premium. Hence the cash-flow risk effect might not be economically meaningful when compared to the cash-flow risk effect of capital expenditure. Alternatively, if the market investment risk effect is economically significant when compared to the risk effect of capital expenditure, then managers could be investing with the intention of increasing risk significantly.

Corollary 1.1 (Economic Significance). Market investment risk is *not* comparable to capital investment risk.

2.5 Data

Aggregate data for private nonfarm nonfinancial corporations are taken from the Flow of Funds Accounts maintained by the Federal Reserve Board of Governors. Firm-level data are initially extracted from the Compustat Fundamentals database (annual update) for the years 1950 to 2011 (431,474 observations). I exclude foreign firms (60,386 observations deleted), then non-US currency observations (4219 observations deleted). I then exclude firms from minor US territories (1896 observations deleted), then firms that are not located in the US (3025 observations deleted). I then exclude financial firms (Standard Industrial Classification (SIC) codes between 6000 and 6999), utilities (SIC codes between 4900 and 4999). After the exclusions, the extraction sample contains 268,013 observations.

Starting with the extraction sample, I then exclude firm-year observations (73,892 observations) where data are missing (or negative) for market value of equity (CSHPRI * PRCC_F).[11] Next, I exclude firm-year observations where data are missing for all of the following items: investments and advances using the equity method (IVAEQ), investments and advances using the market method (IVAO), and short-term investments (IVST), and finally I exclude observations from fiscal years 1950 to 1969. The initial sample for years 1970 to 2011 contains 179,090 observations.

The noncurrent market investments variable is equal to noncurrent investments using the equity and market methods. The market investments variable is equal to short-term investments plus noncurrent market investments. Cash is cash plus short-term investments (CHE) minus IVST. Market investment growth is equal to the yearly change in the market investments variable. Cash growth is equal to the yearly change in the cash variable. Both growth variables are normalized by lagged net assets (net assets in year $t-1$).

All balance-sheet data used for cash-flow risk analysis are converted to 2011 dollars using a seasonally adjusted consumer price index (CPI). CPI data are extracted from the Federal Reserve Economic Data maintained by the Federal Reserve Bank of St. Louis. Informed by John, Litov, and Yeung (2008), all cash-flow risk variables are calculated as the rolling year-ahead eight-year standard deviation of cash flows. Operating cash-flow risk is calculated as the rolling year-ahead eight-year standard deviation of operating cash flow (OIBDP −TXT). Risk from market investment cash flows (or portfolio cash-flow risk) is calculated as the rolling year-ahead eight-year standard deviation of portfolio cash flow(Δ Market Investments + SIV − IVCH − IVSTCH). Total cash-flow risk (including cash flows from market investments) is calculated as the rolling year-ahead eight-year standard deviation of operating cash flow plus portfolio cash flow. Operating cash-flow risk, portfolio cash-flow risk, and total cash-flow risk are all normalized by total assets. Cash-flow risk spread is total cash-flow risk minus operating cash-flow risk. Given the requirement to use lagged net assets (as normalization for the growth variables) and eight-year rolling cash-flow risk variables, the effective sample period for cash-flow risk analysis is 1971 to 2002.

Capital expenditure is equal to the capital investments of the firm (CAPX). The size variable is equal to the market value of equity. The cash flow variable is equal to earnings before interest, taxes, depreciation and amortization (EBITDA) minus interest, minus taxes, minus common dividends (OIBDP −XINT −TXT −DVC). Leverage is equal to the market debt ratio, calculated as total debt (DLTT + DLC) divided by the sum of total debt and the market value of equity (CSHPRI * PRCC_F). Interest expense is equal to the interest payments of the firm (XINT). The dividend payout is equal to common dividends paid (DVC). The repurchase variable is equal to the purchase of the firm's own common stock and preferred stock minus the redemption of preferred stock (PRSTKC −PSTKRV), and R&D expense is equal to research and development expenditures (XRD) divided by sales (SALE). The market-to-book ratio is equal to net assets (AT −CHE −IVAEQ −IVAO) minus book equity (CEQ) plus the market value of equity, all divided by net assets. Sales growth is equal to the change in the logarithm of one plus sales. The strategic equity stake dummy variable is equal to one if noncurrent market investment using the equity method is greater than zero, thus representing a stake with significant control. Strategic equity change is equal to the yearly change in the strategic equity stake dummy variable.

The marginal tax rate is a trichotomous variable (Graham, 1996). The firm-year marginal tax rate variable is constructed based on taxable income, the top statutory tax rate, and the net operating loss (NOL) carry forward (TLCF). Following Graham and Kim (2009), taxable income is defined as operating income after depreciation plus non-operating income minus interest expense minus deferred taxes from the income statement (divided by the top statutory tax rate) plus extraordinary items and discontinued operations (divided by one minus the top statutory tax rate) plus special items (OIADP + NOPI −XINT −(TXDI/top tax rate) + (XIDO/(1 −top tax rate)) + SPI). The marginal tax rate is equal to the top statutory tax rate if taxable income is positive and there is no NOL carry forward (TLCF is zero or missing). The marginal tax rate is equal to half of the top statutory tax rate if either the taxable income is positive or there exists an NOL carry forward (without both conditions being satisfied). The marginal tax rate is equal to zero in all other cases.

All variables other than the cash-flow risk variables, strategic equity, market investment growth, cash growth, size, R&D expense, leverage, the market-to-book ratio, sales growth, strategic equity change, and the marginal tax rate are normalized by net assets. All variables are winsorized at the 1 percent tails to lessen the effect of extreme values. The sample used for total cash-flow risk analysis consists of 51,105 observations. The sample summary statistics are presented in Table 2.2.

2.6 Statistics and empirical analysis

Table 2.2 presents the variable definitions (in the legend) and lists the summary statistics for the variables used in this study. The mean for operating cash-flow risk (the year-ahead eight-year volatility of operating cash flow) is 11.8 percent. The mean for portfolio cash-flow risk (the year-ahead eight-year volatility of portfolio cash flow) is 10.4 percent. The mean for total cash-flow risk (the year-ahead eight-year volatility of operating cash flow plus portfolio cash flow) is 19.6 percent. The mean for the spread between total cash-flow risk and operating cash-flow risk is 7.8 percent. While there are negative values for the risk spread (the 10th percentile is equal to −0.055 percent), in most cases, portfolio cash-flow risk adds to operating cash-flow risk. The finding suggests that corporate market investments increase business cash-flow risk. When conducting a *t*-test for the cash-flow risk-spread mean of 7.8 percent, the resulting *p*-value is 0.000, thus rejecting Hypothesis 1.

Capital expenditure, cash flow, repurchases, interest expense, and dividend payout are all normalized by net assets (total assets minus cash minus market investments). Market investment growth and cash growth are normalized by lagged net assets (net assets in year $t-1$). Average market investment growth is 4.8 percent for the sample period used for total cash-flow risk analysis. However, with a standard deviation of 60.4 percent, there is substantial dispersion relative to the mean. Average cash growth is 6.8 percent with a standard deviation of 77.3 percent. The mean for capital expenditures (or the growth in capital stock) is 9.5 percent with a standard deviation of 10 percent. The mean for firm size is roughly $980 million (in 2011 US dollars). The mean values for leverage, the market-to-book ratio, cash flow, R&D expense, repurchases, sales growth, the marginal tax rate,

Table 2.2 Risk and corporate market investments: definitions and summary statistics

Variable name	Mean	sd.	N	Q50
Operating cash-flow risk	0.118	0.300	51105	0.040
Portfolio cash-flow risk	0.104	0.166	44707	0.047
Total cash-flow risk	0.196	0.475	51105	0.075
Risk spread	0.078	0.237	51105	0.015
Market investment growth	0.048	0.604	50021	0.000
Cash growth	0.068	0.773	50021	0.001
Capital expenditure	0.095	0.100	51105	0.064
Size	976.316	3379.021	51105	86.298
Leverage	0.247	0.244	51105	0.177
MTB ratio	3.376	8.870	51105	1.385
Cash flow	−0.111	1.079	51105	0.075
R&D expense	0.166	0.868	51105	0.000
Repurchases	−0.023	0.195	51105	0.000
Sales growth	0.084	0.316	51105	0.061
Marginal tax rate	0.346	0.112	51105	0.350
Interest expense	0.033	0.079	51105	0.020
Dividend payout	0.012	0.026	51105	0.000

Notes: The table provides summary statistics (for unstandardized variables) for observations in the sample. Data are from years 1970 to 2011 where *Log (Total cash-flow risk)* and lagged net assets have non-missing values. All nominal balance-sheet items are converted to 2011 dollars using a seasonally-adjusted consumer price index. *Market investments* are short-term investments plus noncurrent investments using the equity and market methods. *Noncurrent market investments* are noncurrent investments using the equity and market methods. *Capital expenditure* is capital investments. *Repurchases* is the net repurchase of common shares and preferred stock. *Cash flow* is EBITDA minus interest minus taxes minus common dividends. *Interest expense* is the interest expense of the firm. *Dividend payout* is equal to common dividend paid. *MTB Ratio* is total assets minus cash minus short-term investments minus noncurrent investments using the equity and market methods minus book value of equity plus the market value of equity, all normalized. All aforementioned variables are normalized by net assets (total assets minus cash minus short-term investments minus noncurrent investments using the equity and market methods). *Operating cash-flow risk is* the year-ahead eight-year volatility of operating cash flow. *Portfolio cash-flow risk is* the year-ahead eight-year volatility of investment cash flows from *Market investments*. *Total cash-flow risk is* the year-ahead eight-year volatility of total cash flow (operating cash flow plus portfolio cash flow). *Cash-flow risk spread* is *Total cash-flow risk* minus *Operating cash-flow risk*. *Market investment growth* is the change in market investment (current and noncurrent) normalized by lagged net assets. *Cash growth is* the change in cash holdings, normalized by lagged net assets. *Size* is the market value of equity. *Leverage* is market leverage. *R&D expense* is the research and development expenditures of the firm divided by sales. *Marginal tax rate* is the trichotomous variable for corporate tax rate (Graham, 1996). *Sales growth* is the change in the logarithm of sales. *Strategic equity* is a dummy variable equal to one if noncurrent investment using the equity method is positive, and zero otherwise. *Strategic equity change* is the yearly change in *Strategic equity*.

interest expense, and dividend payout are 24.7 percent, 3.376, −11.1 percent, 16.6 percent, −2.3 percent, 8.4 percent, 34.6 percent, 3.3 percent and 1.2 percent. Given the mean values for the sample, the evidence suggests that firms that report market investments have negative cash flow on average, but positive median cash flow.

2.6.1 Cash-flow risk analysis

The risk-spread evidence presented in Table 2.2 suggests that portfolio cash flows have a significant impact on overall business cash flow (Hypothesis 1). However, it is unclear whether the cash-flow risk from a standard investment in marketable securities has a significant impact on overall business cash flow (Hypothesis 1) and whether the cash-flow risk from a standard investment in marketable securities is comparable to the cash-flow risk from a standard investment in capital stock (Corollary 1.1).

The commonly held view is that capital expenditure (or the growth in capital stock) is the single most important manager-controlled determinant of business cash-flow risk. To understand the standard effect of market investments on business cash-flow risk, in Table 2.3 I investigate the differences in the means of various cash-flow risk measures by the growth in the amount of market investments on a firm's balance sheet (or market investment growth).

For operating cash flow, greater market investment growth is associated with lower operating cash-flow risk. The difference in means is approximately −3.5 percent and statistically significant at the 1 percent level. The finding is most likely representative of the idea that liquid-asset growth is associated with less business cash-flow risk. In support of the idea, Table 2.3 also shows evidence that, like market investment growth, cash growth is associated with less operating cash-flow risk.

However, for portfolio cash flow, greater market investment growth is associated with greater portfolio cash-flow risk, while cash growth has no significant effect on portfolio cash-flow risk. The difference in means for market investment growth is approximately 1.5 percent and statistically significant at the 1 percent level. The finding suggests that when firms increase market investments, there is a subsequent increase in portfolio cash-flow risk. The finding also suggests that the difference is not being driven by an omitted variable that is correlated with the motive for managers to accumulate liquidity in response to expected business cash-flow risk (if portfolio cash-flow risk were spuriously correlated with operating cash-flow risk).

For total cash flow (operating cash flow plus portfolio cash flow), greater market investment growth is associated with lower total cash-flow risk. The difference in means is approximately −1.6 percent and statistically significant at the 1 percent level. The finding again is most likely representative of the idea that liquid-asset growth is associated with less business cash-flow risk. In support of the idea, Table 2.3 also shows evidence that, like market investment growth, cash growth is associated with less total cash-flow risk.

Table 2.3 Risk and corporate market investments: differences in means

Variable Name (*t* – 1)		All	X > Median	X <= Median	Difference
		Operating cash-flow risk (*t*)			
Market investment growth	Mean	0.118	0.094	0.130	−0.035**
	se.	0.001	0.002	0.002	0.003
	N	50021	16572	33449	50021
Cash growth	Mean	0.118	0.113	0.123	−0.011**
	se.	0.001	0.002	0.002	0.003
	N	50021	25010	25011	50021
		Portfolio cash-flow risk (*t*)			
Market investment growth	Mean	0.105	0.114	0.099	0.015**
	se.	0.001	0.001	0.001	0.002
	N	43726	16570	27156	43726
Cash growth	Mean	0.105	0.106	0.103	0.002
	se.	0.001	0.001	0.001	0.002
	N	43726	21966	21760	43726
		Total cash-flow risk (*t*)			
Market investment growth	Mean	0.196	0.186	0.202	−0.016**
	se.	0.002	0.003	0.003	0.005
	N	50021	16572	33449	50021
Cash growth	Mean	0.196	0.191	0.202	−0.012**
	se.	0.002	0.003	0.003	0.004
	N	50021	25010	25011	50021
		Cash-flow risk spread (*t*)			
Market investment growth	Mean	0.078	0.091	0.072	0.019**
	se.	0.001	0.002	0.001	0.002
	N	50021	16572	33449	50021
Cash growth	Mean	0.078	0.078	0.079	−0.001
	se.	0.001	0.001	0.002	0.002
	N	50021	25010	25011	50021

Notes: This table presents differences in means of the cash-flow risk variables for the observations in the sample where *Log (Total cash-flow risk)* and lagged net assets have non-missing values. The cash-flow risk variables are *Operating cash-flow risk*, *Portfolio cash-flow risk*, *Total cash-flow risk*, and *Cash-flow risk spread*. Data are from years 1970 to 2011. The variable definitions are presented in Table 2; and +, *, ** denote statistical significance at the 10%, 5% and 1% levels in a two-sided test of the mean equal to zero.

To control for the relation between liquid-asset growth and business cash-flow risk, in Table 2.3 I investigate the risk spread: total cash-flow risk minus operating cash-flow risk. For the risk spread, greater market investment growth is associated with a greater cash-flow risk spread. The difference in means is approximately 1.9 percent and statistically significant at the 1 percent level. Cash growth has no significant effect on the cash-flow risk spread.

To understand the standard effect of market investments on business cash-flow risk, controlling for variables that might be correlated with cash-flow risk, I estimate, for various cash-flow risk measures, the effect of market investment growth on the subsequent logarithm of cash-flow risk.

2.6.2 Operating cash-flow risk

Table 2.4 column (1) presents the results of a regression for the base specification with year and industry effects, where the dependent variable is the logarithm of operating cash-flow risk. For ease of exposition, the independent variables are standardized in all regressions. Heteroskedasticity-robust standards errors are estimated and corrected for clustering at the firm level (White, 1982). For fixed T and large N, clustered standard errors are also robust to serial correlation of arbitrary forms (Arellano, 1987).

Consistent with John, Litov and Yeung (2008), operating cash-flow risk decreases with firm size. The coefficient in column (1) is approximately −45.6 percent; a standard-deviation increase in the firm size variable is associated with 45.6 percent less operating cash-flow risk. This finding supports the idea that larger companies are less risky. Controlling for firm size, operating cash-flow risk might increase with leverage because of managerial risk-shifting behavior (Jensen and Meckling, 1976). Alternatively, operating cash-flow risk might decrease with leverage because of the influence of debt holders (Morck and Nakamura, 1999; Acharya, Amihud and Litov, 2011). The findings in Table 2.4 support the idea that debt holders exert influence on firms. The market-leverage coefficient in column (1) is approximately −16.5 percent and is statistically significant at the 1 percent level; a standard-deviation increase in leverage is associated with 16.5 percent less cash-flow risk.

Consistent with a firm's tendency to capitalize on growth opportunities, operating cash-flow risk increases with the market-to-book ratio. The coefficient for the market-to-book ratio is approximately 16.2 percent and is statistically significant at the 1 percent level; a standard-deviation increase in the market-to-book ratio is associated with 16.2 percent greater cash-flow risk. Operating cash-flow risk decreases with cash flow. The cash-flow coefficient is approximately −20.3 percent and is statistically significant at the 1 percent level; a standard-deviation increase in the cash-flow variable is associated with 20.3 percent less cash-flow risk. Operating cash-flow risk decreases with the marginal tax rate. The coefficient for the marginal tax rate

Table 2.4 Risk and corporate market investments: comparing operating cash-flow risk to portfolio cash-flow risk

	Log (Operating cash-flow risk)		***Log (Portfolio cash-flow risk)***	
Log (Size)	−0.456	−0.456	−0.150	−0.150
	(45.199)**	(44.798)**	(7.440)**	(7.371)**
Leverage	−0.165	−0.164	−0.344	−0.344
	(18.054)**	(17.817)**	(17.657)**	(17.456)**
MTB Ratio	0.162	0.165	0.190	0.157
	(10.122)**	(10.186)**	(9.372)**	(7.561)**
Cash flow	−0.203	−0.200	−0.045	−0.065
	(9.049)**	(8.738)**	(1.484)	(2.096)*
R&D expense	0.139	0.139	0.182	0.176
	(15.434)**	(15.287)**	(13.082)**	(12.600)**
Repurchases	−0.077	−0.078	−0.026	−0.026
	(7.889)**	(7.807)**	(1.529)	(1.564)
Sales growth	0.035	0.037	−0.012	−0.019
	(7.108)**	(7.379)**	(1.263)	(2.037)*
Strategic equity change	0.003	0.005	−0.002	−0.006
	(1.103)	(1.732)+	(0.256)	(0.911)
Marginal tax rate	−0.185	−0.186	−0.134	−0.134
	(18.375)**	(18.199)**	(6.531)**	(6.467)**
Capital expenditure	0.075	0.076	0.079	0.075
	(10.520)**	(10.506)**	(5.419)**	(5.151)**
Interest expense	0.105	0.105	0.144	0.138
	(5.684)**	(5.659)**	(6.421)**	(6.050)**
Dividend payout	−0.053	−0.053	0.047	0.049
	(6.862)**	(6.755)**	(3.175)**	(3.238)**
Market investment growth		−0.012		0.099
		(2.296)*		(12.435)**
Year dummies	Yes	Yes	Yes	Yes
Industry dummies	Yes	Yes	Yes	Yes
Number of obs.	65890	64211	45561	44569
Model *p*-value	0.000	0.000	0.000	0.000

Notes: This table presents regression results for the sample where the dependent variables are presented in the row of headings. The variable definitions are presented in Table 2.

Data are from years 1970 to 2011. Heteroskedasticity-robust standards errors are estimated and corrected for clustering at the firm level. Absolute *t*-statistics are reported in parentheses. Model *p*-value shows the result for a test that all of the listed coefficients are jointly zero, and +, *, ** denote statistical significance at the 10%, 5% and 1% levels.

is approximately −18.5 percent and is statistically significant at the 1 percent level; a standard-deviation increase in the corporate tax rate is associated with 18.5 percent less cash-flow risk.

As expected, operating cash-flow risk increases with capital investment, R&D expenses, and interest expenses. The coefficient for capital investment is approximately 7.5 percent and is statistically significant at the 1 percent level; a standard-deviation increase in capital investment is associated with 7.5 percent greater cash-flow risk. The coefficient for R&D expenses is approximately 13.9 percent and is statistically significant at the 1 percent level; a standard-deviation increase in R&D expense is associated with 13.9 percent greater cash-flow risk. The coefficient for interest expenses is approximately 10.5 percent and is statistically significant at the 1 percent level; a standard-deviation increase in interest expense is associated with 10.5 percent greater cash-flow risk.

Consistent with the idea that firms that pay dividends should be able to maintain an ongoing commitment to shareholders, operating cash-flow risk decreases with dividend payout. The coefficient for dividend payout is approximately −5.3 percent and is statistically significant at the 1 percent level; a standard-deviation increase in the dividend payout is associated with 5.3 percent less cash-flow risk.

Firms might generate excess cash during risky periods of high sales growth. These firms might store this excess cash as market investments. Therefore I include sales growth as an independent variable. Operating cash-flow risk increases with sales growth. The coefficient for sales growth is approximately 3.5 percent and is statistically significant at the 1 percent level; a standard-deviation increase in sales growth is associated with 3.5 percent greater cash-flow risk.

Consistent with the findings in Table 2.3, column (2) of Table 2.4 shows evidence of a negative relation between market investment growth and subsequent operating cash-flow risk. The coefficient for market investment growth is approximately −1.2 percent and is statistically significant at the 1 percent level; a standard-deviation increase in market investment growth is associated with 1.2 percent less cash-flow risk. This finding suggests that reverse causality (due to the precautionary motive) for the relation between operating cash-flow risk and market investment growth is unlikely. Under reverse causality, the manager would accumulate liquid assets in the expectation of greater cash-flow risk.

2.6.3 Portfolio cash-flow risk

While the determinants of operating cash-flow risk are reasonably well understood, the determinants of portfolio cash-flow risk are not well understood. Brown (2013) argues that managers in their preference for market investments (relative to cash and excess cash) might be influenced by the speculative motive, tax arbitrage, and ALM. Brown also argues that managers who are influenced by the speculative motive and tax arbitrage tend not to be influenced to manage risk through ALM.

In Table 2.4 columns (3) and (4), I investigate the relation between portfolio cash-flow risk and the independent variables in the specification. As with the case of operating cash-flow risk, portfolio cash-flow risk is negatively related to firm size. The market-leverage coefficient in column (4) is approximately −34.4 percent and is statistically significant at the 1 percent level; a standard-deviation increase in leverage is associated with 34.4 percent less cash-flow risk. The finding supports the idea that debt holders exert influence on firms to take less market investment risk.

The effects of taxes, capital expenditure, interest expenses and dividends are all consistent with the findings in Brown (2013). The tax-rate coefficient in column (4) is approximately −13.4 percent and is statistically significant at the 1 percent level; a standard-deviation increase in the corporate tax rate is associated with 13.4 percent less cash-flow risk. The capital-expenditure coefficient is approximately 7.5 percent and is statistically significant at the 1 percent level; a standard-deviation increase in capital expenditure is associated with 7.5 percent greater cash-flow risk. Consistent with managers using riskier investments to manage promised commitments, the coefficients for interest expense and dividend payout are positive and statistically significant at the 1 percent level.

In Table 2.4, I control for changes in strategic investments when estimating the effect of market investment growth on portfolio cash-flow risk. Column (4) shows that portfolio cash-flow risk is unaffected by changes in strategic investments. The coefficient for strategic equity change is approximately −0.6 percent and not statistically significant.

Consistent with the findings in Table 2.3, column (4) of Table 2.4 shows evidence of a positive relation between market investment growth and subsequent portfolio cash-flow risk. The coefficient for market investment grows this approximately 9.9 percent and is statistically significant at the 1 percent level; a standard-deviation increase in leverage is associated with 9.9 percent greater cash-flow risk.

One important relation is that of cash flow with portfolio cash-flow risk. In column (3) of Table 2.4, the relation with cash flow is negative, but not statistically significant. However, cash flow is negatively related to market investment growth; that is, as a firm increases its operating cash flows, the firm tends not to increase its market investments. Controlling for market investment growth in column (4), the coefficient for cash flow is −6.5 percent and is statistically significant at the 5 percent level. The finding suggests that firms with negative cash flows have positive subsequent portfolio cash-flow risk.

2.6.4 Total cash-flow risk

In Table 2.5, I investigate the extent to which standard market investment growth is associated with subsequent total cash-flow risk. Table 2.5 also

Table 2.5 Risk and corporate market investments: total cash-flow risk and the cash-flow risk spread

	Log (Total cash-flow risk)			***Log (Cash-flow risk spread)***		
Log (Size)	−0.372	−0.371	−0.344	−0.202	−0.202	−0.183
	(29.417)**	(29.000)**	(24.125)**	(7.952)**	(7.852)**	(9.058)**
Leverage	−0.265	−0.264	−0.247	−0.451	−0.450	−0.442
	(23.398)**	(23.079)**	(15.809)**	(17.980)**	(17.676)**	(16.663)**
MTB Ratio	0.199	0.187	0.315	0.237	0.208	0.317
	(13.128)**	(12.195)**	(9.594)**	(10.436)**	(9.009)**	(7.048)**
Cash flow	−0.139	−0.149	−0.185	−0.085	−0.108	0.101
	(6.536)**	(6.836)**	(2.897)**	(2.426)*	(3.008)**	(0.756)
R&D expense	0.157	0.154	0.457	0.181	0.174	0.461
	(16.848)**	(16.414)**	(3.604)**	(10.590)**	(10.122)**	(4.192)**
Repurchases	−0.077	−0.076	−0.038	−0.045	−0.043	−0.039
	(7.363)**	(7.236)**	(3.132)**	(1.887)+	(1.797)+	(2.632)*
Sales growth	0.019	0.017	0.014	−0.017	−0.026	−0.024
	(3.198)**	(2.821)**	(1.941)+	(1.300)	(2.011)*	(1.672)
Strategic equity change	0.001	0.001	−0.001	−0.003	−0.014	−0.013
	(0.256)	(0.148)	(0.134)	(0.319)	(1.408)	(1.017)
Marginal tax rate	−0.186	−0.187	−0.184	−0.137	−0.138	−0.140
	(15.035)**	(14.933)**	(24.322)**	(5.290)**	(5.266)**	(9.720)**
Capital expenditure	0.082	0.080	0.072	0.087	0.081	0.059
	(9.116)**	(8.771)**	(11.682)**	(4.702)**	(4.336)**	(3.993)**

Interest expense	0.156	0.153	0.195	0.235	0.226	0.271
	(8.351)**	(8.193)**	(8.611)**	(7.913)**	(7.662)**	(12.499)**
Dividend payout	−0.007	−0.006	−0.004	0.047	0.049	0.060
	(0.667)	(0.556)	(0.630)	(2.580)**	(2.648)**	(5.273)**
Market investment growth		0.039	0.060		0.099	0.138
		(6.810)**	(4.947)**		(10.701)**	(5.664)**
Year dummies	Yes	Yes	No	Yes	Yes	No
Industry dummies	Yes	Yes	Yes	Yes	Yes	Yes
Number of obs.	51105	50021	50021	38131	37301	37301
Model *p*-value	0.000	0.000	0.000	0.000	0.000	0.000

Notes: This table presents regression results for the sample where the dependent variables are presented in the row of headings. Columns (3) and (6) use Fama–Macbeth regressions to estimate the coefficients. The variable definitions are presented in Table 2.

Data are from years 1970 to 2011. Heteroskedasticity-robust standards errors are estimated and corrected for clustering at the firm level. Absolute *t*-statistics are reported in parentheses. Model *p*-value shows the result for a test that all of the listed coefficients are jointly zero, and +, *, ** denote statistical significance at the 10%, 5% and 1% levels.

allows for a comparison of the effect of a standard increase in market investments on business cash-flow risk to the effect of a standard increase in capital stock on business cash-flow risk (Corollary 1.1).

Comparing column (2) of Table 2.5 to Table 2.3, the importance of multivariate analysis for total cash-flow risk is clear. While the difference in means between high market investment growth observations and low market investment growth observations is −1.6 percent, the coefficient for market investment growth in column (2) is approximately 3.9 percent and is statistically significant at the 1 percent level. The finding rejects the idea that market investment growth does not affect cash-flow risk. The coefficient for capital expenditure is 8 percent and is statistically significant at the 1 percent level. Using the specification in column (2), market investment growth has a risk effect that is roughly 50 percent of the risk effect of a corresponding increase in capital expenditure (Corollary 1.1).

2.6.5 Cash-flow risk spread

In Table 2.5, I also investigate the extent to which market investment growth is associated with the subsequent cash-flow risk spread. Column (5) of Table 2.5 shows that the coefficient for market investment growth is approximately 9.9 percent and is statistically significant at the 1 percent level. Moreover, the effects of taxes, capital expenditure, interest expenses and dividends are all consistent with the findings in Brown (2013). The tax-rate coefficient in column (4) is approximately −14 percent and is statistically significant at the 1 percent level; a standard-deviation increase in the tax rate is associated with 14 percent less cash-flow risk. The capital-expenditure coefficient is approximately 5.9 percent and is statistically significant at the 1 percent level; a standard-deviation increase in capital expenditure is associated with 5.9 percent greater cash-flow risk. Consistent with managers using riskier investments to manage promised commitments, the coefficients for interest expense and dividend payout are positive and statistically significant at the 1 percent level.

2.7 Robustness

This chapter finds that, controlling for size, leverage, the market-to-book ratio, cash flow, the marginal tax rate, capital expenditure, R&D expenses, repurchases, interest expense, dividend payout, sales growth and the change in strategic equity, a standard increase in market investment growth causes a significant increase in a firm's cash-flow risk spread (Hypothesis 1).

This section explores the robustness of the finding. In particular, are the results robust when controlling for unobserved heterogeneity at the firm level?

2.7.1 Firm fixed effects

Various time-invariant firm-level policies might affect the cash-flow risk spread. For instance, some firms might experience more security trading volatility when compared with other firms (allocation volatility). Some firms might exhibit lumpy investment over the sample period, which might require large market investment balances. To control for unobserved heterogeneity at the firm level, in Table 2.6 column (4) I estimate the effect of market investment growth on the cash-flow risk spread in a specification with firm fixed effects. The coefficient for market investment growth is 4.9 percent and is statistically significant at the 1 percent level. Hence the main result is robust when addressing unobserved heterogeneity at the firm level.

2.8 Conclusion

Today's market investments are quite different from the market investments of 1960. Market investment – on average – continues to grow, and previously moderate investment in US Treasuries has given way to larger and riskier market investment portfolios.

This chapter finds that market investments have a positive and significant impact on business cash-flow risk. The risk associated with market investments (or portfolio cash-flow risk) is roughly 90 percent of the risk associated with a firm's core business activities (or operating cash-flow risk).A standard-deviation increase in market investment growth has a risk effect that is 50 percent of the risk effect of a standard-deviation increase in capital expenditure. The effect of market investment growth on the subsequent cash-flow risk spread between total cash-flow risk (inclusive of portfolio cash flow) and operating cash-flow risk (excluding portfolio cash flow) is robust to firm and year fixed effects.

Market investment portfolio cash-flow risk increases with capital expenditure and decreases with the tax rate. Hence this chapter's evidence suggests that managers could be investing in marketable securities with an objective similar to that for general investment. In addition, market investment portfolio cash-flow risk increases with promised commitments (dividend and interest payments). Hence this chapter's evidence suggests that managers could be using market investments to practice ALM.

Rather than view market investment as a store of cash, we can use theories of investment, agency and risk management to understand the effect of market investments on risk. Regulators, for example, might want to take an economic approach to the classification of investment companies and the regulation of market investments. Currently, if a firm holds more than 40 percent of its total assets in market investments (excluding US Treasuries and cash equivalents) it can attract the attention of the US Securities and Exchange Commission (SEC) and might have to register as an investment

Table 2.6 Risk and corporate market investments: firm fixed effects

	Log (Portfolio Cash-Flow Risk)		*Log (Cash-Flow Risk Spread)*	
Log (Size)	−0.150	−0.098	−0.202	−0.160
	(7.371)**	(2.573)*	(7.852)**	(2.902)**
Leverage	−0.344	−0.120	−0.450	−0.137
	(17.456)**	(5.552)**	(17.676)**	(4.712)**
MTB Ratio	0.157	0.027	0.208	0.053
	(7.561)**	(1.637)	(9.009)**	(2.332)*
Cash flow	−0.065	0.011	−0.108	0.032
	(2.096)*	(0.429)	(3.008)**	(0.995)
R&D expense	0.176	0.020	0.174	0.004
	(12.600)**	(1.511)	(10.122)**	(0.253)
Repurchases	−0.026	0.011	−0.043	0.002
	(1.564)	(0.897)	(1.797)+	(0.130)
Sales growth	−0.019	−0.024	−0.026	−0.028
	(2.037)*	(3.395)**	(2.011)*	(2.682)**
Strategic equity change	−0.006	0.001	−0.014	−0.003
	(0.911)	(0.178)	(1.408)	(0.381)
Marginal tax rate	−0.134	−0.005	−0.138	0.008
	(6.467)**	(0.298)	(5.266)**	(0.367)
Capital expenditure	0.075	0.007	0.081	−0.003
	(5.151)**	(0.695)	(4.336)**	(0.211)
Interest expense	0.138	0.074	0.226	0.081
	(6.050)**	(3.186)**	(7.662)**	(2.685)**
Dividend payout	0.049	0.052	0.049	0.066
	(3.238)**	(3.348)**	(2.648)**	(3.439)**
Market investment growth	0.099	0.049	0.099	0.049
	(12.435)**	(8.798)**	(10.701)**	(7.539)**
Year dummies	Yes	Yes	Yes	Yes
Industry dummies	Yes	No	Yes	No
Number of obs.	44569	44569	37301	37301
Model *p*-value	0.000	0.000	0.000	0.000

Notes: This table presents regression results for the sample where the dependent variables are presented in the row of headings. The variable definitions are presented in Table 2.

Data are from years 1970 to 2011. Regressions in columns (2), (3), (5), and (6) use firm fixed effects. Heteroskedasticity-robust standards errors are estimated and corrected for clustering at the firm level. Absolute *t*-statistics are reported in parentheses. Model *p*-value shows the result for a test that all of the listed coefficients are jointly zero, and +, *, ** denote statistical significance at the 10%, 5% and 1% levels.

company. Instead of focusing on an arbitrary asset-based cutoff – which might no longer be relevant – regulators might want to focus on a general benefit-cost analysis of market investments. In general, efforts to determine the composition of a firm's market investments from publicly available information bear little fruit; greater transparency might improve financial market efficiency and financial system health.

This chapter's evidence suggests that corporate managers speculate using market investments; this behavior might be a cause for concern for investors. Concerned investors should therefore focus on the mechanisms that might reduce the speculation costs. In general, the costs of managerial entrenchment might be reduced by improved corporate governance voting practices (Bebchuk and Cohen, 2005) large activist shareholders (Shleifer and Vishny, 1986; Brav et al., 2008; Klein and Zur, 2009) the alignment of cash-flow rights and voting rights (Masulis, Wang and Xie, 2009; Gompers, Ishii and Metrick, 2010) and the quality of directors (Knyazeva, Knyazeva and Masulis, 2009; Chhaochharia and Grinstein, 2007).

Increased information and transparency might also reduce the costs of managerial entrenchment. On the other hand, managerial compensation might increase to offset the manager's costs of improved disclosure (Hermalin and Weisbach, 2011), which, given this chapter's results, might be counterproductive if the manager's compensation is too sensitive to volatility. Political considerations might also be important for the costs of managerial entrenchment (Roe, 2003; Morck, Wolfenzon and Yeung, 2005; Pagano and Volpin, 2005; Perotti and von Thadden, 2005; Bebchuk and Neeman, 2010). Future research should investigate how these factors affect market investment risk.

Notes

1. Research argues that sector diversification, financial development (Morck, Yeung, Yu, 2000; Li et al., 2004), expected stock returns (French, Schwert and Stambaugh, 1987), innovation (Chun et al., 2004; Comin and Mulani, 2009) and the firm's life cycle (Fink et al., 2010) can explain the increase in firm-level risk.
2. Wei and Zhang (2006) find that earnings quality is related to firm-level risk.
3. See Opler et al. (1997) for evidence of a positive correlation between firm-level cash-flow risk and corporate liquidity; see Bates, Kahle and Stulz (2009) for evidence of an increase in corporate liquidity over time.
4. In fact, Miller and Orr (1968) 'followed their (Baumol (1952) and his followers) precedents in assuming that earning assets are homogenous' and admittedly ignore 'the importance that runoffs from the portfolio can have in cash balance management.'
5. Douglas MacMillan, 'Google's Latest Launch: Its Own Trading Floor', *Bloomberg Businessweek*, 27 May, 2010.
6. SFAS No. 115 supersedes SFAS No. 12. SFAS No. 12 presents a standard for equity security accounting and the conditions under which equity investments should be recorded at cost or at market value.
7. Jacobs (1960) uses a survey method to show the various market investment components of a pre-1960 sample of corporations. He states that pre-1960 firms place

most of their investible funds in government debt. In addition, he alludes to the progression towards a higher non-Treasury component.

8. Liquid asset holdings can be used as a precaution against low future cash flow or uncertainty in the economy.
9. Tobin argues that money assets are those that are 'marketable, fixed in money value, and free of default risk.' Other assets such as corporate equity are not applicable in the cash-demand framework. These assets would fall in the category of general investment (Tobin, 1955; Scott, 1979). See Sprenkle (1969) for his assumption that even current market investments are made with the speculative motive in mind.
10. See Table 2.1 of this chapter.
11. I also eliminate firm-year observations for which net assets or dividend payout values are negative.

References

Acharya, V., Amihud, Y. and Litov, L. (2011). Creditor Rights and Corporate Risk-Taking. *Journal of Financial Economics*, 102, 150–66.

Arellano, M. (1987). Computing Robust Standard Errors for Within-Group Estimators. *Oxford Bulletin of Economics and Statistics*, 49, 431–4.

Bates, T.W., Kahle, K. M. and Stulz, R. M. (2009). Why Do U.S. Firms Hold So Much More Cash Than They Used To? *The Journal of Finance*, 64, 1985–2021.

Barro, R. J. and Fischer, S. (1976). Recent Developments in Monetary Theory. *Journal of Monetary Economics*, 2, 133–67.

Baumol, W. J. (1952). The Transactions Demand for Cash: An Inventory Theoretic Approach. *Quarterly Journal of Economics*, 66, 545–56.

Bebchuk, L. A. and Cohen, A. (2005). The Costs of Entrenched Boards. *Journal of Financial Economics*, 78, 409–33.

Bebchuk, L. A. and Neeman, Z. (2010). Investor Protection and Interest Group Politics. *Review of Financial Studies*, 23, 1089–119.

Berk, J. B. and Green, R. C. (2004). Mutual Fund Flows and Performance in Rational Markets. *Journal of Political Economy*, 112, 1269–95.

Brav, A., Jiang, W., Partnoy, F. and Thomas, R. (2008). Hedge Fund Activism, Corporate Governance, and Firm Performance. *The Journal of Finance*, 63, 1729–75.

Brown, C. O. (2013). Marketable Securities: Storage or Investment? Unpublished Working Paper.

Campbell, J. Y., Lettau, M., Malkiel, B. G. and Xu, Y. (2001). Have Individual Stocks Become More Volatile? An Empirical Exploration of Idiosyncratic Risk. *The Journal of Finance*, 56, 1–43.

Chhaochharia, V. and Grinstein, Y. (2007). Corporate Governance and Firm Value: The Impact of the 2002 Governance Rules. *The Journal of Finance*, 62, 1789–825.

Chudson, W. (1945). *The Pattern of Corporate Financial Structure*. National Bureau of Economic Research: New York, NY.

Chun, H., Kim, J., and Morck, R. (2004). Patterns of Comovement: The Role of Information Technology in the U.S. Economy. NBER Working Paper No. 10937.

Comin, D. and Mulani, S. (2006). Diverging Trends in Aggregate and Firm-level Volatility. *The Review of Economics and Statistics*, 88, 374–83.

Comin, D. and Philippon, T. (2005). The Rise in Firm-level Volatility: Causes and Consequences. *NBER Macroeconomics Annual*, 20, 167–228.

Eppen, G. D. and Fama, E. F. (1968). Solutions for Cash-Balance and Simple Dynamic Portfolio Problems. *The Journal of Business*, 41, 94–112.

Fink, J., Fink, K., Grullon, G. and Weston, J. (2010). What Drove the Increase in Idiosyncratic Volatility during the Internet Boom? *Journal of Financial and Quantitative Analysis*, 45, 1253–78.

Frazer, W. J., Jr. (1958). Large Manufacturing Corporations as Suppliers of Funds to the United States Government Securities Market. *The Journal of Finance*, 13, 499–509.

French, K. R., Schwert, G. W. and Stambaugh, R. (1987). Expected Stock Returns and Volatility. *Journal of Financial Economics*, 19, 3–29.

Gompers, P. A., Ishii, J. and Metrick, A. (2010). Extreme Governance: An Analysis of Dual-Class Firms in the United States. *Review of Financial Studies*, 23, 1051–88.

Gorton, G. B., Lewellen, S. and Metrick, A. (2012). The Safe Asset Share. Unpublished Working Paper.

Graham, J. R. (1996). Proxies for the Corporate Marginal Tax Rate. *Journal of Financial Economics*, 42, 187–221.

Graham, J. R. and Kim, H. (2009). The Effects of the Length of the Tax-Loss Carryback Period on Tax Receipts and Corporate Marginal Tax Rates. Unpublished Working Paper.

Hermalin, B. E. and Weisbach, M. S. (2011). Information Disclosure and Corporate Governance. *The Journal of Finance*, forthcoming.

Heston, A. W. (1962). An Empirical Study of Cash, Securities and Other Current Accounts of Large Corporations. *Yale Economic Essays*, II, 117–59.

Irvine, P. J. and Pontiff, J. (2009). Idiosyncratic Return Volatility, Cash Flows, and Product Market Competition. *Review of Financial Studies*, 22, 1149–77.

Jacobs, D. P. (1960). The Marketable Security Portfolios of Non-Financial Corporations, Investment Practices and Trends. *The Journal of Finance*, 15, 341–52.

Jeffers, J. R. and Kwon, J. (1969). A Portfolio Approach to Corporate Demands for Government Securities. *The Journal of Finance*, 24, 905–19.

Jensen, M. C. and Meckling, W. H. (1976). Managerial Behavior, Agency Costs and Ownership Structure. *Journal of Financial Economics*, 3, 305–60.

John, K., Litov, L. and Yeung, B. (2008). Corporate Governance and Risk-Taking. *The Journal of Finance*, 63, 1679–728.

Keynes, J. M. (1936). *The General Theory of Employment, Interest and Money*. Macmillan, New York, NY.

Klein, A. and Zur, E. (2009). Entrepreneurial Activism: Hedge Funds and Other Private Investors. *The Journal of Finance*, 64, 187–229.

Knyazeva, A., Knyazeva, D. and Masulis, R. W. (2009). Local Director Talent and Board Composition. Unpublished Working Paper.

Krishnamurthy, A. and Vissing-Jorgensen, A. (2010). The Aggregate Demand for Treasury Debt. Unpublished Working Paper.

Li, K., Morck, R., Yang, F. and Yeung, B. (2004). Firm Specific Variation and Openness in Emerging Markets. *The Review of Economics and Statistics*, 86, 658–69.

Maddala, G. S. and Vogel, R. C. (1967). Cross-Section Estimates of Liquid asset Demand by Manufacturing Corporations. *The Journal of Finance*, 22, 557–75.

Mark, R. (2003). *Political Determinants of Corporate Governance*. Oxford University Press, Oxford.

Masulis, R. W., Wang, C. and Xie, F. (2009). Agency Problems at Dual-Class Companies. *The Journal of Finance*, 64, 1697–727.

Miller, M. H., and Orr, D. (1966). A Model of the Demand for Money by Firms. *Quarterly Journal of Economics*, 80, 413–35.

Miller, M. H., and Orr, D. (1968). The Demand for Money by Firms: Extensions of Analytic Results. *The Journal of Finance*, 23, 735–59.
Morck, R. and Nakamura, M. (1999). Banks and Corporate Control in Japan. *The Journal of Finance*, 54, 319–39.
Morck, R., Wolfenzon, D. and Yeung, B. (2005). Corporate Governance, Economic Entrenchment and Growth. *Journal of Economic Literature*, 43, 657–722.
Morck, R., Yeung, B. and Yu, W. (2000). The Information Content of Stock Markets: Why Do Emerging Markets Have Synchronous Stock Price Movements? *Journal of Financial Economics*, 59, 215–60.
Opler, T., Pinkowitz, L., Stulz, R. and Williamson, R. (1999). The Determinants and Implications of Corporate Cash Holdings. *Journal of Financial Economics*, 52, 3–46.
Pagano, M. and Volpin, P. (2005). The Political Economy of Corporate Governance. *American Economic Review*, 95, 1005–30.
Patinkin, D. (1956). *Money, Interest, and Prices*. Row Peterson, Evanston.
Perotti, E. and von Thadden, E.-L. (2005). The Political Economy of Corporate Control and Labor Rents. *Journal of Political Economy*, 114, 145–74.
Scott, J. H., Jr. (1979). The Tax Effects of Investment in Marketable Securities on Firm Valuation. *The Journal of Finance*, 34, 307–24.
Selden, R. T. (1961). The Postwar Rise in the Velocity of Money a Sectoral Analysis. *The Journal of Finance*, 16, 483–545.
Shleifer, A. and Vishny, R. (1986). Large Shareholders and Corporate Control. *Journal of Political Economy*, 94, 461–88.
Smith, C. W. and Stulz, R. M. (1985). The Determinants of Firms' Hedging Policies. *The Journal of Financial and Quantitative Analysis*, 20, 391–405.
Sprenkle, C. M. (1969). The Uselessness of Transactions Demand Models. *The Journal of Finance*, 24, 835–47.
Tobin, J. (1955). A Dynamic Aggregative Model. *Journal of Political Economy*, 63, 103–15.
Wei, S. X. and Zhang, C. (2004). Why Did Individual Stocks Become More Volatile? *The Journal of Business*, 79, 259–92.
White, H. (1982). Maximum-Likelihood Estimation of Misspecified Models. *Econometrica*, 50, 1–25.

3
Foreign Currency Hedging and Firm Value: A Dynamic Panel Approach

Shane Magee

3.1 Introduction

The Modigliani and Miller (1958) irrelevance proposition suggests that in perfect capital markets a firm's hedging policy does not affect its value, since shareholders can undo any hedging activities implemented by the firm. Recent theories, however, argue that when capital markets are imperfect, hedging can increase a firm's value by influencing its expected taxes, expected financial distress costs and investment decisions.[1] More recently, researchers have examined the effect of hedging with derivatives on firm value. For example, Allayannis and Weston (2001) find that in a broad sample of firms, the value of firms that hedge foreign currency risk is, on average, 4.87 percent higher than non-hedgers, and Carter, Rogers and Simkins (2006) find that fuel hedging increases firm value by 5 to 10 percent for a sample of US airlines.

Guay and Kothari (2003), however, challenge the hypothesis that hedging with derivatives is associated with an increase in firm value. They find that potential gains on hedging portfolios are economically small and are unlikely to generate large changes in firm value. Guay and Kothari (2003) suggest that the increase in firm value documented in Allayannis and Weston (2001) is either driven by other risk management activities, such as operational hedges, that are correlated with derivatives use, or that the results are spurious. Consistent with this, Jin and Jorion (2006) find no relation between hedging and firm value for a sample of oil and gas producers.

Jin and Jorion (2006) argue that the positive relation between hedging and firm value documented in previous studies could be due to endogeneity. One possible source of endogeneity is reverse causality. That is, the positive relation between hedging and firm value documented in previous studies may be because higher firm value creates an incentive to hedge rather than hedging causing higher firm value. Another possible source of endogeneity is unobserved heterogeneity, which arises when time invariant unobservable firm specific factors affect both hedging and firm value. Allayannis and Weston (2001) and Carter, Rogers and Simkins (2006) use firm fixed effects to control for unobserved heterogeneity. However, the use of firm fixed effects requires that hedging is strictly exogenous, which ignores the possibility of feedback from past amounts of firm value to the current amount of hedging. If firms adjust the amount of their hedging in reaction to past amounts of firm value, then hedging is not strictly exogenous, and the estimated effect of hedging on firm value can be biased and inconsistent.

To control for these endogeneity problems, I estimate the effect of hedging on firm value in a dynamic panel framework, using the system generalized method of moments (GMM) estimator developed by Arellano and Bover (1995) and Blundell and Bond (1998). The dynamic panel framework captures persistence in firm value by including lagged firm value as an explanatory variable, while the system GMM estimator uses a first-difference transformation to control for unobserved firm heterogeneity, and uses lagged values of firm value and foreign currency hedging as instrumental variables to control for failure of the strict exogeneity assumption.

I estimate the effect of foreign currency hedging with derivatives on firm value, as measured by Tobin's Q, for a sample of 408 large US nonfinancial firms with foreign sales from operations abroad over the period 1996 to 2000. During this period the US dollar appreciated against the currencies of major US trading partners. Assuming firms with foreign sales have net long positions in foreign currency, hedging foreign currency risk is expected to increase firm value during this period. To facilitate comparison to previous studies, I initially assume that foreign currency hedging is strictly exogenous. I find a strong positive relation between foreign currency hedging and firm value when using lagged firm value as the only control variable, consistent with the univariate results of Allayannis and Weston (2001). This relation, however, is much weaker when I control for other factors that affect firm value. My results suggest that foreign currency hedging is associated with an increase in firm value of 6.33 percent when foreign currency hedging is assumed to be strictly exogenous. However, I find foreign currency hedging is positively related to past amounts of firm value and is therefore not strictly exogenous. After controlling for the dependence of foreign currency hedging on past amounts of firm value, I no longer find that foreign currency hedging affects firm value. This result also holds for firms with greater foreign currency risk. I find weak evidence, however, that foreign currency hedging is associated with a higher firm value for firms with a greater probability of financial distress.

The main contribution of this study is to show that foreign currency hedging is not strictly exogenous, and that, after controlling for the failure of the strict exogeneity assumption, foreign currency hedging has no effect on firm value. This study is also the first to examine the effect of hedging on firm value in a dynamic panel framework, which is appropriate when firm value is serially correlated.

The remainder of this chapter is organized as follows. Section 3.2 reviews prior research on hedging and firm value. Section 3.3 describes the empirical method. Section 3.4 describes the data and the variables used in the empirical analysis. Section 3.5 presents the results on the relation between foreign currency hedging and firm value. Section 3.6 concludes.

3.2 Prior research

Theories of hedging based on capital market imperfections suggest that hedging can increase firm value. For example, Stulz (1984) argues that risk averse managers may engage in hedging if their human capital and wealth are poorly diversified and if they believe the cost of hedging at the firm level is less than hedging on their own account. Smith and Stulz (1985) argue that if a firm's tax function is convex, hedging can reduce its expected tax liability by reducing the volatility of its taxable income. Smith and Stulz (1985) also argue that if financial distress is costly, hedging increases firm value by reducing the probability of financial distress, and hence the expected costs of financial distress. Froot, Scharfstein and Stein (1993) argue that with volatile cash flows and costly external finance, hedging can mitigate underinvestment by ensuring a firm has sufficient internal funds to finance valuable investment opportunities. DeMarzo and Duffie (1995) argue that hedging reduces noise related to exogenous factors from a firm's earnings, thereby making earnings a more informative signal of managerial ability. Leland (1998) argues that hedging can increase a firm's debt capacity, and therefore increases firm value due to the tax deductibility of interest payments.

A large body of empirical studies on this topic investigate which theory explains firms' actual hedging activities. For example, Knopf, Nam and Thornton (2002) find a positive relation between hedging and managerial share ownership, which is consistent with the managerial risk aversion argument. Graham and Rogers (2002) find that tax function convexity does not influence a firm's hedging activities, but hedging leads to greater debt capacity. Haushalter (2000) and Graham and Rogers (2002) find a positive relation between hedging and leverage, consistent with the view that greater expected financial distress costs cause greater hedging. Nance, Smith and Smithson (1993) and Geczy, Minton and Schrand (1997) find a positive relation between hedging and investment opportunities, consistent with the view that hedging mitigates the underinvestment problem. Finally, DaDalt, Gay and Nam (2002) find that hedging is associated with a reduction in information asymmetry.

The empirical evidence on the effect of hedging on firm value is mixed. Allayannis and Weston (2001) conclude that in a sample of large US multinationals, the value of firms that hedge foreign currency risk is, on average,

4.87 percent higher than non-hedgers. Carter, Rogers and Simkins (2006) find that fuel hedging increases firm value by 5 to 10 percent for a sample of US airlines. Mackay and Moeller (2007) control for the potential endogeneity of hedging with respect to firm value and find that hedging concave revenues and leaving concave costs exposed increases firm value by 2 to 3 percent for a sample of US oil refiners. Guay and Kothari (2003), on the other hand, find that the potential gains on hedging portfolios are small when compared to cash flows and firm size and are unlikely to generate large changes in firm value. Jin and Jorion (2006) also find that hedging does not affect firm value for a sample of US oil and gas producers.

To estimate the effect of hedging on firm value, researchers typically use pooled ordinary least squares or firm fixed effects. However, a consistent estimate of the effect of hedging on firm value using either pooled ordinary least squares or firm fixed effects requires that hedging is strictly exogenous. Strict exogeneity rules out the possibility of feedback from past amounts of firm value to the current amount of hedging. That is, under the strict exogeneity assumption, hedging affects firm value but firm value does not affect hedging. A weaker exogeneity assumption is that hedging is sequentially exogenous (or predetermined) in the sense that past amounts of firm value affect the current amount of hedging. The sequential exogeneity assumption appears reasonable given that both theoretical models and prior empirical studies suggest that firm value affects hedging. For example, if firms with higher valuations have many valuable investment opportunities and external financing is costly, then these firms may have greater incentives to hedge (Froot, Scharfstein and Stein, 1993). Consistent with this prediction, Nance, Smith and Smithson (1993), Geczy, Minton and Schrand (1997), and Gay and Nam (1998) find that investment opportunities are a determinant of hedging. Another explanation as to why hedging might not be strictly exogenous is that risk averse managers of firms with high valuations might hedge at the firm level to protect their incentive payments (Stulz, 1984). Given that the estimated increase in firm value documented in previous studies could be biased and inconsistent if hedging is not strictly exogenous, it is important to re-examine the question of whether hedging affects firm value after controlling for the possibility of feedback from past amounts of firm value to the current amount of hedging. This study addresses this issue.

3.3 Empirical method

I estimate the causal effect of foreign currency hedging on firm value using a dynamic GMM panel estimator. This estimator was introduced by Holtz-Eakin, Newey and Rosen (1988) and Arellano and Bond (1991) and further developed by Arellano and Bover (1995) and Blundell and Bond (1998). The econometric model to be estimated is

$$y_{it} = \alpha y_{i,t-1} + \gamma w_{it} + \mathbf{x}'_{it}\beta + c_i + u_{it} \text{ for } i = 1,\ldots,N \text{ and } t = 2,\ldots,T, \quad (3.1)$$

where y_{it} is firm value, as measured by Tobin's *Q*, for firm *i* in period *t*. The lagged value of this variable is included as an explanatory variable to capture persistence in firm value. This results in the entire history of the explanatory variables w_{it} and $\mathbf{x}_{it}$ being included in equation (3.1) so that the causal effect of the explanatory variables is conditioned on this history. The main variable of interest is w_{it}, the extent of foreign currency hedging for firm *i* in period *t*. The coefficient γ therefore measures the short-run effect of foreign currency hedging on firm value given $y_{i,t-1}$, with the long-run effect given by $\gamma/(1-\alpha)$. The vector $\mathbf{x}_{it}$ includes control variables, which are discussed in Section 3.4.3.2 below, and year dummies that capture common shocks to firm value of all firms. The unobserved effect c_i contains firm specific time invariant unobserved factors, such as managerial quality and managerial risk preferences, that may affect both foreign currency hedging and firm value. Finally, u_{it} is an error term, capturing all other omitted factors.

The GMM estimation procedure includes two important steps. The first step eliminates the unobserved firm specific time invariant effect c_i by first-differencing equation (3.1), resulting in

$$\Delta y_{it} = \alpha \Delta y_{i,t-1} + \gamma \Delta w_{it} + \Delta \mathbf{x}'_{it}\beta + \Delta u_{it} \quad \text{for } i = 1,\ldots,N \text{ and } t = 3,\ldots,T, \quad (3.2)$$

where $\Delta y_{it} = y_{it} - y_{i,t-1}, \Delta y_{i,t-1} = y_{i,t-1} - y_{i,t-2}, \Delta \mathbf{x}'_{it} = \mathbf{x}'_{it} - \mathbf{x}'_{i,t-1}$, and $\Delta u_{it} = u_{it} - u_{i,t-1}$. Estimation of equation (3.2) by ordinary least squares, however, results in inconsistent estimates because $y_{i,t-1}$ is correlated with $u_{i,t-1}$, and hence the explanatory variable $\Delta y_{i,t-1}$ is correlated with the error term Δu_{it}. The second step addresses this endogeneity problem by using lags of y_{it} dated $T-2$ and longer as instrumental variables for $\Delta y_{i,t-1}$, resulting in the following moment conditions:

$$E\left(y_{i,t-s}\Delta u_{it}\right) = 0 \quad \text{for } t = 3,\ldots,T \text{ and } s \geq 2. \quad (3.3)$$

For example, y_{i1} can be used as an instrument in the first-differenced equation at period $t = 3$, both y_{i1} and y_{i2} can be used as instruments in the first-differenced equation at period $t = 4$, and the vector $\left(y_{i1}, y_{i2}, \ldots, y_{i,T-2}\right)$ can be used as instruments in the first-differenced equation for period $t = T$.

Additional moment conditions can also be used, depending on the exogeneity assumptions of the explanatory variables w_{it} and $\mathbf{x}_{it}$. For example, if $\mathbf{z}_{it} \equiv \left(w_{it}, \mathbf{x}_{it}\right)$ is strictly exogenous in the sense that the explanatory variables are uncorrelated with all past, present and future realizations of the error term u_{it}, then the complete time series $\left(\mathbf{z}_{i1}, \mathbf{z}_{i2}, \ldots, \mathbf{z}_{iT}\right)$ can be used as instruments in each of the first-differenced equations. Assuming $\mathbf{z}_{it}$ is strictly exogenous results in the following additional moment conditions for the first-differenced equations:

$$E\left(z_{is}\Delta u_{it}\right) = 0 \quad \text{for } t = 3, \ldots, T \text{ and } s = 1, \ldots, T. \tag{3.4}$$

There are several econometric weaknesses with the first-differenced GMM estimator. First, Arellano and Bover (1995) argue that variables in levels may be poor instruments for first-differenced variables. In particular, if the time series y_{it} is highly persistent, Blundell and Bond (1998) find that lagged levels of the series are only weakly correlated with subsequent first-differences, so that the instruments for the first-differenced equations are weak. Using Monte Carlo experiments, Blundell and Bond (1998) show that the first-differenced GMM estimator has large finite sample bias and poor precision when the instruments are weak. Second, the coefficients on time invariant explanatory variables are not identified, because the first-differencing transformation eliminates these variables from the model. Furthermore, it may also be difficult to identify a causal effect if the explanatory variable of interest varies little over time for a given firm.

To address these problems I use the system GMM estimator developed by Arellano and Bover (1995) and Blundell and Bond (1998). The system GMM estimator combines the first-differenced equation in (3.2) with the levels equation in (3.1) and uses lagged levels as instruments for the first-differenced equations and lagged first-differences as instruments for the levels equations. Blundell and Bond (1998) show that the system GMM estimator has smaller finite sample bias and greater precision than the first-differenced GMM estimator when the explanatory variables are persistence. An additional advantage of the system GMM estimator is that it is now possible to identify the coefficients on time invariant explanatory variables or explanatory variables that vary little over time for a given firm. This is important because the main variable of interest in this study, the extent of foreign currency hedging, has a within firm standard deviation of only 3 percent and hence varies little over time for a given firm. Consequently, estimating equation (3.1) with only the first-differenced equations is unlikely to identify an association between foreign currency hedging and firm value, because the cross sectional variation is not exploited.

The equations in levels, however, still contain the unobserved firm specific time invariant effect c_i. Appropriate instruments must now be used to control for the unobserved firm specific time invariant effect. The system GMM estimator uses first-differences of the explanatory variables as instruments for the levels equations. These instruments are valid under the assumption that the correlation between the levels of the explanatory variables and the unobserved firm specific time invariant effect is constant over time. Under this assumption, the first-differences of the explanatory variables are uncorrelated with the unobserved firm specific time invariant effect. Assuming z_{it} is strictly exogenous results in the following moment conditions for the levels equations:

$$E\left(\Delta y_{i,t-1}\left(c_i + u_{it}\right)\right) = 0 \quad \text{for } t = 3, \ldots, T, \tag{3.5}$$

and

$$E\left(\Delta \mathbf{z}_{it}\left(c_i + u_{it}\right)\right) = 0 \quad \text{for } t = 2, \ldots, T. \tag{3.6}$$

The consistency of the system GMM estimator depends on the validity of the instruments and the absence of serial correlation in the error terms u_{it}. To address these concerns I use two specification tests suggested by Arellano and Bond (1991). The validity of the instruments can be tested using Hansen's (1982) test of overidentifying restrictions. This test produces a J statistic which has an asymptotic χ^2 distribution under the null hypothesis that the instruments are valid. The assumption that there is no serial correlation in the error terms u_{it} can be tested by testing for serial correlation in the first-differenced residuals. If the error terms, u_{it}, are not serially correlated, the first-differenced residuals should exhibit negative first-order serial correlation but no second-order serial correlation. Failure to reject the null hypothesis of both specification tests supports the use of the dynamic panel model.

Thus far, I have assumed that w_{it}, the extent of foreign currency hedging, is strictly exogenous in the sense that w_{it} is uncorrelated with all past, present and future realizations of the error term u_{is}. Strict exogeneity rules out the possibility of feedback from past amounts of firm value to the current amount of foreign currency hedging. Failure of the strict exogeneity assumption can result in a biased and inconsistent estimate of the effect of foreign currency hedging on firm value. Wooldridge (2002) presents the following regression based test for strict exogeneity using first-differences:

$$\Delta y_{it} = \delta w_{it} + \gamma \Delta w_{it} + \Delta \mathbf{x}'_{it}\beta + \Delta u_{it} \quad \text{for } i = 1, \ldots, N \text{ and } t = 2, \ldots, T. \tag{3.7}$$

Under the null hypothesis of strict exogeneity, $\delta = 0$. If $\delta \neq 0$, then past amounts of firm value affect the current amount of foreign currency hedging and a weaker sequential exogeneity assumption can be used to generate a consistent estimate of the effect of foreign currency hedging on firm value. Under sequential exogeneity, w_{it} is uncorrelated with current and future realizations of the error term but may be correlated with past realizations of the error term. If w_{it} is sequentially exogenous, moment condition (3.6) is still valid for the levels equations, and lags of w_{it} dated $T-1$ and longer can be used as instruments for Δw_{it} in the first-differenced equations. This results in the following additional moment conditions for the first-differenced equations:

$$E\left(w_{i,t-s}\Delta u_{it}\right) = 0 \text{ for } t = 3, \ldots, T \quad \text{and } s \geq 1. \tag{3.8}$$

3.4 Data

3.4.1 Sample

I construct a sample of 408 large US nonfinancial firms over the period 1996 to 2000, based on the screening criteria in Allayannis and Weston (2001). The sample consists of nonfinancial firms listed in Compustat's Industrial Annual Files with total assets of more than $500 million in each fiscal year between 1996 and 2000. I retain observations that meet the following criteria: the firm has no missing data on sales and market value; the firm is not financial (SIC codes 6000–6900); the firm is not a regulated utility (SIC codes 4900–4999); the firm's 10-K reports are available from EDGAR; and the firm discloses the notional value of its foreign currency derivative holdings, if any. I further restrict the sample to those firms that face ex-ante foreign currency risk. This is important because it allows me to interpret the absence of foreign currency derivatives as a decision not to hedge rather than a lack of foreign currency risk. I follow Allayannis and Ofek (2001) and Allayannis and Weston (2001), and define firms to have ex-ante foreign currency risk if they disclose foreign sales from operations abroad in the Compustat Geographic Segment files in the fiscal year of derivative usage. One concern with selecting firms based on their foreign sales from operations abroad is that a firm might not face ex-ante foreign currency risk due to its foreign sales being denominated in US dollars. I therefore exclude from the sample firms that state in their 10-K report that they do not have any foreign currency risk because the majority of their foreign sales are denominated in US dollars. The final sample consists of 408 firms from 1996 to 2000, or 1893 firm year observations, with 347 firms present in all 5 years.

During the sample period, Statement of Financial Accounting Standard (SFAS) 119 required firms to disclose the notional value, nature and terms of their derivative contracts. SFAS 119 also required firms to disclose whether they use derivatives for trading or nontrading purposes. I only examine foreign currency derivatives held for nontrading purposes. The Financial Accounting Standards Board issued SFAS 133 in June 1998 to supersede SFAS 119. SFAS 133, which is effective for fiscal years beginning July 15, 2000, requires firms to disclose the fair market value of their derivative contracts, but does not require the disclosure of notional values. Consequently, the last year of my sample is 2000 because the data are not sufficiently detailed after that time.

3.4.2 Dependent variable

Following earlier studies on the effect of hedging on firm value, I use Tobin's *Q* as the proxy for firm value. I use the market-to-book ratio as an approximation of Tobin's *Q*, which is calculated as the book value of assets minus the book value of common equity plus the market value of common equity, all divided by the book value of assets.[2] While it is possible to calculate more

Table 3.1 Serial correlation of Tobin's *Q*

	1996	1997	1998	1999	2000
1996	1.000				
1997	0.881	1.000			
1998	0.718	0.850	1.000		
1999	0.710	0.703	0.792	1.000	
2000	0.645	0.693	0.740	0.876	1.000

Notes: This table presents autocorrelation coefficients of Tobin's *Q*. The sample includes nonfinancial Compustat firms with assets greater than $500 million and foreign sales for 1996 to 2000. All coefficients are statistically significant at the 1% level.

complicated measures of Tobin's *Q*, the market-to-book ratio is commonly used as a proxy for Tobin's *Q* in the empirical corporate finance literature.[3] Furthermore, Allayannis and Weston (2001) find a high degree of correlation between the market-to-book ratio and more complicated measures of Tobin's *Q*. Table 3.1 presents autocorrelation coefficients of Tobin's *Q* for each of the years 1996 to 2000. The time series of Tobin's *Q* is highly persistent with the first-order autocorrelation coefficients ranging from a minimum of 0.792 to a maximum of 0.881. This suggests that a dynamic panel estimator should be used to capture the persistence in Tobin's *Q*.

3.4.3 Explanatory variables

3.4.3.1 Foreign currency hedging

Following previous research, I assume that firms conduct their hedging through the use of derivatives. Consequently, this study investigates the effect of hedging with foreign currency derivatives on firm value beyond any hedging firms can achieve with operating and financing decisions. I obtain data on each firm's foreign currency derivative holdings from 10-K filings available from EDGAR. I search each 10-K filing for text strings such as 'derivative', 'financial instrument', 'forward', 'hedg', and 'market risk'. If a reference is made to any of these key words, I read the surrounding text to obtain data on the year end total notional value of foreign currency forward, and option contracts. Following Allayannis and Ofek (2001), these values do not include currency swaps because these financial instruments are mainly used by firms to either convert foreign debt into domestic debt or to convert domestic debt into foreign debt.

I use a continuous variable to measure foreign currency hedging. The continuous variable is measured by the fiscal year end total notional value of foreign currency forward and option contracts divided by the book value of total assets for foreign currency derivative users, or zero for nonusers.[4] Several studies employ a dummy variable, indicating the decision to hedge with derivatives.[5] I prefer to use the continuous variable as a proxy for foreign currency hedging in all regression specifications because, unlike the continuous variable, the dummy variable does not capture the extent of foreign currency hedging with derivatives and hence cannot distinguish between those firms that significantly hedge and those that partly hedge. In addition, when the dummy variable is used as a proxy for foreign currency hedging, unreported multivariate regression results suggest the decision to hedge foreign currency risk does not affect firm value, regardless of whether foreign currency hedging is assumed to be strictly or sequentially exogenous. The continuous variable, on the other hand, illustrates that the extent of foreign currency hedging affects firm value when it is assumed to be strictly exogenous but no longer affects firm value when it is assumed to be sequentially exogenous.

3.4.3.2 Control variables

I include the following control variables, as used in Allayannis and Weston (2001).

1) *Firm Size*: The literature has found that firm size is positively related to both the decision to hedge and the extent of hedging.[6] Allayannis and Weston (2001) also find that firm size is negatively related to Tobin's Q. I use the natural logarithm of total assets to control for the possibility that Tobin's Q and foreign currency hedging are related through the size of the firm.

2) *Profitability*: Profitable firms are likely to have higher Tobin's Q ratios than less profitable firms. Consequently, if hedgers are more profitable, they are likely to have higher Tobin's Q ratios. I control for profitability with the ratio of net income to total assets. I expect a positive coefficient on this variable.

3) *Access to financial markets*: If hedgers have limited access to financial markets, their Tobin's Q ratios may be high because they invest only in those projects with the highest net present value. To proxy for the ability to access financial markets, I use a dummy variable which equals one if the firm paid dividends on common equity during the fiscal year, and zero otherwise. The rationale is that if a firm paid a dividend, it is less likely to be financially constrained because it could reduce its dividend to increase its level of investment (see Fazzari, Hubbard and Petersen, 1988). I expect a negative coefficient on this variable.

4) *Leverage*: A firm's capital structure may also be related to its value. For example, the trade off theory predicts that leverage increases firm value owing to the tax benefits of debt. Greater leverage can also act as a positive signal of managerial quality (Ross, 1977), suggesting a positive relation between leverage and firm value. On the other hand, several studies find a negative relation between leverage and investment opportunities owing

to the agency costs of debt (for example, Rajan and Zingales, 1995 and Faulkender and Petersen, 2006). Since Tobin's *Q* can also act as a proxy for investment opportunities, the findings in these studies suggest a negative relation between leverage and firm value. I control for differences in capital structure by using the ratio of total debt to total assets as a proxy for leverage, where total debt is defined as the sum of short-term debt and long-term debt.

5) *Investment opportunities*: Myers (1977) suggests that firm value also depends on future investment opportunities. Since Geczy, Minton and Schrand (1997) and Allayannis and Ofek (2001) find that hedgers are more likely to have larger investment opportunities, it is important to control for investment opportunities. I measure investment opportunities with the ratio of capital expenditures to total sales, the ratio of research and development expenditures to total sales and the ratio of advertising expenditures to total sales. I expect a positive coefficient on these variables.

6) *Industrial diversification*: Empirical evidence suggests that industrial diversification is negatively related to firm value (for example, Lang and Stulz (1994), Berger and Ofek (1995) and Servaes (1996)). I control for the effect of industrial diversification on firm value by using a dummy variable equal to one if the firm operates in more than one business segment, and zero otherwise. I expect a negative coefficient on this variable.

7) *Geographic diversification*: Following Christophe (1997) and Denis, Denis and Yost (2002), I use the ratio of foreign sales to total sales to measure geographic diversification. Previous empirical evidence on the effect of geographic diversification on firm value is ambiguous. For example Morck and Yeung (1991) and Bodnar, Tang and Weintrop (1999) find a positive relation between geographic diversification and firm value, while Christophe (1997) and Denis, Denis and Yost (2002) find a negative relation between geographic diversification and firm value. However, it is important to control for geographic diversification because firms with a higher percentage of foreign sales are more likely to hedge (see Geczy, Minton and Schrand (1997) and Allayannis and Ofek (2001)).

8) *Credit rating*: The credit quality of a firm, as reflected in its credit rating, may also affect firm value. I control for credit quality by constructing seven dummy variables that specify the credit rating of the firm.[7]

3.4.4 Summary statistics

Table 3.2 presents summary statistics on firm characteristics and the variables used in the analysis. The sample includes 1893 firm year observations with a mean (median) value of assets of $8583 ($2468) million and a mean (median) value of sales of $7455 ($2403) million. The mean (median) foreign sales to total sales ratio is 33.4 percent (32.1 percent). The mean (median) total notional value of foreign currency derivatives, as a percentage of total

Table 3.2 Summary statistics

Variable	*N*	Mean	Median	Std. dev.	Min.	Max.
Firm characteristics						
Total assets (millions)	1893	8583	2468	28390	503	437006
Total sales (millions)	1893	7455	2403	17906	224	206083
Dependent variable						
Tobin's Q	1893	2.296	1.707	1.833	0.453	19.152
Hedging variable						
Total FX derivatives to assets	1893	0.049	0.017	0.081	0.000	0.656
Control variables						
Firm size	1893	8.035	7.811	1.196	6.221	12.988
Net income to assets	1893	0.058	0.059	0.088	−1.149	0.578
Dividend dummy	1893	0.698	1.000	0.459	0.000	1.000
Debt to assets	1893	0.263	0.251	0.176	0.000	1.447
Capex to sales	1876	0.080	0.052	0.102	0.000	1.637
R&D to sales	1893	0.036	0.013	0.056	0.000	0.513
Advertising to sales	1893	0.012	0.000	0.036	0.000	0.352
Diversification dummy	1893	0.702	1.000	0.457	0.000	1.000
Foreign sales to total sales	1893	0.334	0.321	0.195	0.000	1.000

Notes: This table presents summary statistics for the variables used in the analysis. The sample includes nonfinancial Compustat firms with assets greater than $500 million and foreign sales for 1996 to 2000. *Tobin's Q* is the book value of assets minus the book value of common equity plus the market value of common equity, all divided by the book value of assets. *Total FX derivatives to assets* is the total notional value of foreign currency forward and option contracts divided by total assets. *Firm size* is the natural logarithm of total assets. *Net income to assets* is the ratio of net income to total assets. *Dividend dummy* is a dummy variable set equal to one if the firm paid dividends on common equity during the fiscal year, and zero otherwise. *Debt to assets* is the ratio of total debt to total assets. *Capex to sales* is the ratio of capital expenditure to total sales. *R&D to sales* is the ratio of research and development expenditure to total sales. *Advertising to sales* is the ratio of advertising expenditure to total sales. *Diversification dummy* is a dummy variable equal to one if the firm operates in more than one business segment, and zero otherwise. *Foreign sales to total sales* is the ratio of foreign sales to total sales.

assets, is 4.9 percent (1.7 percent). The mean (median) Tobin's Q is 2.296 (1.833), suggesting that the average firm is profitable with valuable investment opportunities. For the average (median) firm, the net income to assets ratio is 5.8 percent (5.9 percent), the debt to assets ratio is 26.3 percent (25.1 percent), the capex to sales ratio is 8.0 percent (5.2 percent), the R&D to sales ratio is 3.6 percent (1.3 percent), and the advertising to sales ratio is 1.2 percent (0.0 percent). Finally, 69.8 percent of the sample firms pay a dividend on common equity during the sample period and 70.2 percent of the sample firms operate in more than one business segment.

3.5 Results

In this section, I test the hypothesis that the extent of foreign currency hedging with derivatives increases Tobin's *Q*, a proxy for firm value. I begin the analysis by estimating the effect of foreign currency hedging on Tobin's *Q*, assuming that foreign currency hedging is strictly exogenous. Next, I test whether foreign currency hedging is strictly exogenous and then re-estimate the effect of foreign currency hedging on Tobin's *Q* after controlling for the dependence of foreign currency hedging on past amounts of Tobin's *Q*. Finally, I discuss the robustness of the results.

3.5.1 The effect of foreign currency hedging on Tobin's Q assuming foreign currency hedging is strictly exogenous

To facilitate comparison to previous studies, I estimate the regression model in equation (3.1) assuming that foreign currency hedging is strictly exogenous. Table 3.3 reports results for a one-step system GMM estimator, with asymptotic standard errors that are adjusted for heteroskedasticity (White, 1980) and firm clustering, which accounts for correlation across observations of a given firm.[8] Regression 1 in Table 3.3 reports the results of the effect of foreign currency hedging on Tobin's *Q* with lagged Tobin's *Q* as the only control variable. The coefficient on foreign currency hedging is positive and significant at the 1 percent level, which is consistent with the univariate results of Allayannis and Weston (2001). In regression 2 of Table 3.3, I include the control variables discussed in Section 3.4.3.2. The coefficient on foreign currency hedging is still positive, but it is only weakly related to Tobin's *Q*, with a *p*-value of 0.080. The estimated long-run effect of foreign currency hedging on Tobin's *Q* is 1.939,[9] suggesting that a change from no foreign currency hedging to the average amount of foreign currency hedging (for hedging firms) of 7.5 percent is associated with an in increase in firm value of 6.33 percent.[10]

Several control variables are statistically significant. For example, consistent with previous studies,[11] I find that Tobin's *Q* is positively related to profitability, research and development expenditure, and advertising expenditure. I also find a negative relation between Tobin's *Q* and leverage, which is consistent with the findings in Demsetz and Villalonga (2001) and Anderson and Reeb (2003).

Table 3.3 also reports tests for the absence of first-order and second-order serial correlation in the first-differenced residuals, in addition to Hansen's (1982) test of overidentifying restrictions (*J* statistic), which tests the validity of the instruments. As expected, I reject the null hypothesis of no first-order serial correlation in the first-differenced residuals. However, I cannot reject the null hypothesis of no second-order serial correlation in the first-differenced residuals at the 10 percent level for regression 1 and at the 5 percent level for regression 2 (the *p*-values are 0.103 and 0.074, respectively).

Table 3.3 The effect of foreign currency hedging on firm value: foreign currency hedging is strictly exogenous

Dependent variable: Tobin's Q_t	(1)	(2)
Tobin's $Q_{,t-1}$	**0.789**	**0.673**
	(0.000)	**(0.000)**
Total FX derivatives to assets$_t$	**1.310**	0.634
	(0.002)	(0.080)
Firm size$_t$		0.024
		(0.494)
Net income to assets$_t$		**2.368**
		(0.036)
Dividend dummy$_t$		−0.137
		(0.165)
Debt to assets$_t$		**−0.643**
		(0.003)
Capex to sales$_t$		−0.516
		(0.105)
R&D to sales$_t$		**3.998**
		(0.000)
Advertising to sales$_t$		**1.958**
		(0.036)
Diversification dummy$_t$		0.107
		(0.090)
Foreign sales to total sales$_t$		0.028
		(0.835)
Number of observations	1483	1469
AR(1) test (p-value)	0.001	0.001
AR(2) test (p-value)	0.103	0.074
Hansen's J statistic (p-value)	0.179	0.110

Notes: This table presents the results for one-step system GMM regressions of the effect of foreign currency hedging on firm value assuming that foreign currency hedging is strictly exogenous. The sample includes nonfinancial Compustat firms with assets greater than $500 million and foreign sales for 1996 to 2000. *Tobin's Q* is the book value of assets minus the book value of common equity plus the market value of common equity, all divided by the book value of assets. *Total FX derivatives to assets* is the total notional value of foreign currency forward and option contracts divided by total assets. *Firm size* is the natural logarithm of total assets. *Net income to assets* is the ratio of net income to total assets. *Dividend dummy* is a dummy variable set equal to one if the firm paid dividends on common equity during the fiscal year, and zero otherwise. *Debt to assets* is the ratio of total debt to total assets. *Capex to sales* is the ratio of capital expenditure to total sales. *R&D to sales* is the ratio of research and development expenditure to total sales. *Advertising to sales* is the ratio of advertising expenditure to total sales. *Diversification dummy* is a dummy variable equal to one if the firm operates in more than one business segment, and zero otherwise. *Foreign sales to total sales* is the ratio of foreign sales to total sales. The regressions include year dummies and credit quality controls (regressions 2 and 4 only), whose coefficient estimates are suppressed. The coefficient of the intercept is also suppressed. In parentheses are p-values based on standard errors adjusted for heteroskedasticity (White, 1980) and firm clustering. Variables significant at the 5% level or less are in bold.

Furthermore, the Hansen (1982) test for overidentifying restrictions shows that the null hypothesis of valid instruments is not rejected (the *p*-values for the *J* statistics of regressions 1 and 2 are 0.179 and 0.110 respectively).[12] Overall, the results from these tests support the dynamic panel specification.

3.5.2 Testing strict exogeneity

Table 3.4 reports the results of the regression based test of strict exogeneity in equation (3.7). Under the null hypothesis that foreign currency hedging is strictly exogenous, the coefficient on the level of foreign currency hedging in the first-differenced regression should be zero. Regression 1 reports the results with no control variables, while regression 2 includes control variables. The coefficients on the level of foreign currency hedging in regressions 1 and 2 are both positive with *p*-values of 0.024 and 0.016 respectively. I therefore reject the null hypothesis that foreign currency hedging is strictly exogenous and conclude that foreign currency hedging is related to past amounts of Tobin's *Q*.

3.5.3 The effect of foreign currency hedging on Tobin's Q assuming foreign currency hedging is sequentially exogenous

Since I reject the hypothesis that foreign currency hedging is strictly exogenous, I now investigate the effect of foreign currency hedging on Tobin's *Q* under the sequentially exogenous assumption. Table 3.5 reports results for a one-step system GMM estimator, with asymptotic standard errors that are adjusted for heteroskedasticity (White, 1980) and firm clustering. Regression 1 in Table 3.5 reports the results of the effect of foreign currency hedging on Tobin's *Q* with lagged Tobin's *Q* as the only control variable, while regression 2 in Table 3.5 includes the full set of control variables. Although the coefficients on the foreign currency hedging variables in the regressions are positive, they are statistically insignificant. These results highlight the importance of controlling for the failure of the assumption that foreign currency hedging is strictly exogenous. The most striking example is in the regression with lagged Tobin's *Q* as the only control variable. When foreign currency hedging is assumed to be strictly exogenous, its coefficient is positive and significant at the 1 percent level. When foreign currency hedging is assumed to be sequentially exogenous, however, the coefficient is positive but is no longer statistically significant.

Table 3.5 also reports several specification tests. First, the test for no second-order serial correlation in the first-differenced residual is not rejected at the 10 percent level for regression 1 and at the 5 percent level for regression 2 (the *p*-values are 0.103 and 0.074, respectively). Second, the *p*-values for the Hansen (1982) test for overidentifying restrictions show that the null hypothesis of valid instruments is not rejected (the *p*-values for regressions 1 and 2 are 0.366 and 0.255 respectively). Finally, I also report the

Table 3.4 Testing whether foreign currency hedging is strictly exogenous

Dependent variable: ΔTobin's Q_t	(1)	(2)
Total FX derivatives to assets$_t$	**0.941**	**0.997**
	(0.024)	**(0.016)**
ΔTotal FX derivatives to assets$_t$	−1.926	−2.039
	(0.178)	(0.153)
ΔFirm size$_t$		−0.018
		(0.923)
ΔNet income to assets$_t$		**1.427**
		(0.018)
ΔDividend dummy$_t$		0.250
		(0.127)
ΔDebt to assets$_t$		**−0.882**
		(0.027)
ΔCapex to sales$_t$		−0.575
		(0.161)
ΔR&D to sales$_t$		−1.818
		(0.207)
ΔAdvertising to sales$_t$		−2.076
		(0.547)
ΔDiversification dummy$_t$		**0.181**
		(0.027)
ΔForeign sales to total sales$_t$		0.309
		(0.207)
Number of observations	1483	1467

Notes: This table presents the results of testing whether foreign currency hedging is strictly exogenous using first-differenced regressions. The sample includes nonfinancial Compustat firms with assets greater than $500 million and foreign sales for 1996 to 2000. The symbol Δ is the first-difference operator. *Tobin's Q* is the book value of assets minus the book value of common equity plus the market value of common equity, all divided by the book value of assets. *Total FX derivatives to assets* is the total notional value of foreign currency forward and option contracts divided by total assets. *Firm size* is the natural logarithm of total assets. *Net income to assets* is the ratio of net income to total assets. *Dividend dummy* is a dummy variable set equal to one if the firm paid dividends on common equity during the fiscal year, and zero otherwise. *Debt to assets* is the ratio of total debt to total assets. *Capex to sales* is the ratio of capital expenditure to total sales. *R&D to sales* is the ratio of research and development expenditure to total sales. *Advertising to sales* is the ratio of advertising expenditure to total sales. *Diversification dummy* is a dummy variable equal to one if the firm operates in more than one business segment, and zero otherwise. *Foreign sales to total sales* is the ratio of foreign sales to total sales. The regressions include year dummies and credit quality controls (regression 2 only), whose coefficient estimates are suppressed. The coefficient of the intercept is also suppressed. In parentheses are *p*-values based on standard errors adjusted for heteroskedasticity (White, 1980) and firm clustering. Variables significant at the 5% level or less are in bold. The coefficient on Total FX derivatives to assets$_t$ equals zero under the null hypothesis of strict exogeneity.

Table 3.5 The effect of foreign currency hedging on firm value: foreign currency hedging is sequentially exogenous

Dependent variable: Tobin's Q_t	(1)	(2)	(3)
Tobin's $Q_{,t-1}$	**0.791**	**0.675**	**0.678**
	(0.000)	**(0.000)**	**(0.000)**
Total FX derivatives to assets$_t$	1.398	0.599	0.871
	(0.227)	(0.603)	(0.327)
Firm size$_t$		0.023	
		(0.516)	
Net income to assets$_t$		**2.378**	**2.351**
		(0.032)	**(0.031)**
Dividend dummy$_t$		−0.133	−0.137
		(0.170)	(0.168)
Debt to assets$_t$		**−0.674**	**−0.662**
		(0.003)	**(0.002)**
Capex to sales$_t$		−0.551	−0.511
		(0.103)	(0.103)
R&D to sales$_t$		**3.970**	**3.922**
		(0.000)	**(0.000)**
Advertising to sales$_t$		1.985	1.861
		(0.089)	(0.090)
Diversification dummy$_t$		0.110	0.064
		(0.087)	(0.083)
Foreign sales to total sales$_t$		0.011	
		(0.952)	
Number of observations	1483	1469	1469
AR(1) test (*p*-value)	0.001	0.001	0.001
AR(2) test (*p*-value)	0.103	0.074	0.074
Hansen's *J* statistic (*p*-value)	0.366	0.255	0.322
Difference in Hansen (*p*-value)	0.605	0.559	

Notes: This table presents the results for one-step system GMM regressions of the effect of foreign currency hedging on firm value when foreign currency is sequentially exogenous. All regressions use lagged levels and first-differences of Total FX derivatives to assets as internal instruments. In regression 3, firm size and the ratio of foreign sales to total sales are used as additional instruments. The sample includes nonfinancial Compustat firms with assets greater than $500 million and foreign sales for 1996 to 2000. *Tobin's Q* is the book value of assets minus the book value of common equity plus the market value of common equity, all divided by the book value of assets. *Total FX derivatives to assets* is the total notional value of foreign currency forward and option contracts divided by total assets. *Firm size* is the natural logarithm of total assets. *Net income to assets* is the ratio of net income to total assets. *Dividend dummy* is a dummy variable set equal to one if the firm paid dividends on common equity during the fiscal year, and zero otherwise. *Debt to assets* is the ratio of total debt to total assets. *Capex to sales* is the ratio of capital expenditure to total sales. *R&D to sales* is the ratio of research and development expenditure to total sales. *Advertising to sales* is the ratio of advertising expenditure to total sales. *Diversification dummy* is a dummy variable equal to one if the firm operates in more than one business segment, and zero otherwise. *Foreign sales to total sales* is the ratio of foreign sales to total sales. The regressions include year dummies and credit quality controls (regressions 2 and 4 only), whose coefficient estimates are suppressed. The coefficient of the intercept is also suppressed. In parentheses are *p*-values based on standard errors adjusted for heteroskedasticity (White, 1980) and firm clustering. Variables significant at the 5% level or less are in bold.

results for difference in Hansen tests. The difference in Hansen test examines the validity of the assumption that foreign currency hedging is sequentially exogenous. It compares the *J* statistic under the weaker assumption of sequential exogeneity to the *J* statistic under the stronger strict exogeneity assumption. Under the null hypothesis, foreign currency hedging is sequentially exogenous, while it is strictly exogenous under the alternative. The *p*-values for the difference in Hansen test show that I cannot reject the null hypothesis that foreign currency hedging is sequentially exogenous. Consequently, the difference in Hansen test provides additional evidence against the assumption that foreign currency hedging is strictly exogenous.

I also examine the strength of the instruments used for foreign currency hedging in the first-differenced and levels equations by running reduced form regressions.[13] For the first-differenced equation, the first and second lags of the level of foreign currency hedging are strong instruments, while the third and fourth lags are potentially weak. For the levels equations, the first-difference of foreign currency hedging is strongly related to the level of foreign currency hedging. To gauge the impact of the potentially weak instruments on the previous results, I re-estimate the system GMM model with only the first and second lags of foreign currency hedging as instruments and find that the overall outcome is consistent with my previous results. I also strengthen the instrument set with external instruments. The system GMM estimates in regression 2 of Table 3.5 suggest that firm size and foreign sales can be omitted from the model specification. This suggests that I may be able to strengthen the instrument set by including firm size and foreign sales as external instruments, and test their validity. Prior empirical research suggests that firm size and foreign sales should be positively related to foreign currency hedging (for example, Geczy, Minton and Schrand, 1997 and Allayannis and Ofek, 2001). Regression 3 in Table 3.5 reports the system GMM results using firm size and foreign sales as external instruments. Although the coefficient on foreign currency hedging has increased, it is still statistically insignificant with a *p*-value of 0.327. Additionally, the increase in the *p*-value for the Hansen (1982) test for overidentifying restrictions indicates that firm size and foreign sales are valid instruments.

3.5.4 Robustness

After finding that foreign currency hedging no longer affects firm value under the sequential exogeneity assumption, I now explore the effect of foreign currency hedging on firm value for those firms that are most likely to benefit from foreign currency hedging. For example, firms with greater foreign currency risk are more likely to benefit from foreign currency hedging than firms with low foreign currency risk. In addition, Smith and Stulz (1985) suggest that firms with a greater probability of financial distress are also likely to benefit from foreign currency hedging. I maintain the assumption that foreign currency hedging is sequentially exogenous, and include the full set of control variables discussed in Section 3.4.3.2 throughout the subsequent analysis.[14]

I examine the effect of foreign currency hedging on firm value for firms with low foreign currency risk and high foreign currency risk, as measured by the ratio of foreign sales to total sales. I define firms with a ratio of foreign sales to total sales less than or equal to the 50th percentile as low foreign sales firms. Otherwise, firms are considered to be high foreign sales firms. The results are presented in Panel A of Table 3.6. I find that the effect of foreign currency hedging on firm value for firms with greater foreign sales is positive but insignificant (the *p*-value is 0.157).

I also examine the effect of foreign currency hedging on firm value for firms with a low probability of financial distress and firms with a high probability of financial distress. My proxy for a firm's probability of financial distress is its one year distance to default, which is estimated using Merton's (1974) structural default model. The distance to default measures the difference between the asset value of a firm and the face value of its debt, scaled by the standard deviation of the firm's asset value. A lower distance to default is associated with a greater probability of financial distress. I define firms with a distance to default less than or equal to the 50th percentile as low distance to default firms. Otherwise, firms are considered to be high distance to default firms. The results are presented in Panel B of Table 3.6. The coefficient on foreign currency hedging is positive. but it is only weakly related to Tobin's Q for low distance to default firms (the *p*-value is 0.099), indicating that foreign currency hedging is associated with an increase in firm value for firms with a greater probability of financial distress.

3.6 Conclusion

Much of the empirical literature that has examined the effect of hedging with derivatives on firm value implicitly assumes that hedging is strictly exogenous, which rules out the possibility of feedback from past amounts of firm value to the current amount of hedging. However, both theoretical and empirical studies suggest that firm value affects hedging. In this study, I estimate the effect of the extent of foreign currency hedging with derivatives on firm value using a dynamic panel estimator, which allows me to control for unobservable firm specific factors and feedback from past amounts of firm value to the current amount of firm value and foreign currency hedging. My results suggest that foreign currency hedging is associated with an increase in firm value when foreign currency hedging is assumed to be strictly exogenous. However, I find foreign currency hedging depends on past amounts of firm value and is therefore not strictly exogenous. After controlling for the dependence of foreign currency hedging on past amounts of firm value, I find foreign currency hedging no longer affects firm value. This is contrary to the findings reported in Allayannis and Weston (2001). This result holds

Table 3.6 Robustness tests

	Panel A: Foreign sales	
Dependent variable: Tobin's Q_t	Low foreign sales	High foreign sales
Tobin's Q_{t-1}	**0.718**	**0.637**
	(0.000)	**(0.000)**
Total FX derivatives to assets$_t$	2.151	2.309
	(0.331)	(0.157)
AR(2) test (p-value)	0.385	0.275
Hansen's J statistic (p-value)	0.171	0.324
	Panel B: Distance to default	
Dependent variable: Tobin's Q_t	Low distance to default	High distance to default
Tobin's Q_{t-1}	**0.539**	**0.414**
	(0.001)	**(0.001)**
Total FX derivatives to assets$_t$	1.271	−2.060
	(0.099)	(0.308)
AR(2) test (p-value)	0.072	0.109
Hansen's J statistic (p-value)	0.248	0.218

Notes: This table presents several robustness tests for one-step system GMM regressions of the effect of foreign currency hedging on firm value when foreign currency is sequentially exogenous. Lagged levels and first-differences of Total FX derivatives to assets are used as internal instruments. The sample includes nonfinancial Compustat firms with assets greater than $500 million and foreign sales for 1996 to 2000. Panel A compares firms with low foreign sales (defined as the ratio of foreign sales to total sales ≤ 50th percentile) to firms with high foreign sales (defined as the ratio of foreign sales to total sales >50th percentile). Panel B compares firms with a low distance to default (defined as distance to default ≤ 50th percentile) to firms with a high distance to default (defined as distance to default >50th percentile). *Tobin's* Q is the book value of assets minus the book value of common equity plus the market value of common equity, all divided by the book value of assets. *Total FX derivatives to assets* is the total notional value of foreign currency forward and option contracts divided by total assets. The regressions include the following control variables, whose coefficient estimates are suppressed: the natural logarithm of the book value of total assets; the ratio of net income to the book value of total assets; a dummy variable set equal to one if the firm paid dividends on common equity during the fiscal year, and zero otherwise; the ratio of total debt to the book value of total assets; the ratio of capital expenditure to total sales; the ratio of research and development expenditure to total sales; the ratio of advertising expenditure to total sales; a dummy variable equal to one if the firm operates in more than one business segment, and zero otherwise; the ratio of foreign sales to total sales; year dummies; and credit quality controls. The coefficient of the intercept is also suppressed. In parentheses are p-values based on standard errors adjusted for heteroskedasticity (White, 1980) and firm clustering. Variables significant at the 5% level or less are in bold.

for firms with greater foreign currency risk. However, I do find weak evidence that foreign currency hedging is associated with an increase in firm value for firms with a greater probability of financial distress.

This study has two implications for future research on the effect of hedging on firm value. First, researchers should consider a dynamic panel framework when the current amount of firm value depends on past amounts of firm value. Second, researchers should test the assumption that hedging is strictly exogenous and control for the failure of this assumption.

Notes

I thank Don Adams, Phil Dolan, Doug Foster, Alexander Ljungqvist, Anna D. Martin, Elizabeth Sheedy, Tom Smith, Bruno Solnik and seminar participants at the 2008 FIRN Doctoral Tutorial, the 2008 Australasian Finance and Banking Conference, and the 2009 Eastern Finance Association Annual Meeting for helpful comments and suggestions. Financial support from the Macquarie University Applied Finance Centre is gratefully acknowledged. All remaining errors are mine.

1. For example, in Smith and Stulz (1985), hedging can increase firm value by reducing expected taxes or expected financial distress costs. In Froot, Scharfstein and Stein (1993), hedging can reduce underinvestment costs when cash flow is volatile and external finance is costly.
2. I also use industry adjusted Tobin's Q as a proxy for firm value and obtain similar results.
3. See for example Allayannis and Weston (2001), Coles, Daniel and Naveen (2008), Jin and Jorion (2006), Mackay and Moeller (2007), Palia (2001), Porta, Lopez-de-Silanes, Shleifer and Vishny (2002), Shin and Stulz (1998), and Villalonga and Amit (2006).
4. Total notional values have been used in Berkman and Bradbury (1996), Gay and Nam (1998), Howton and Perfect (1998), Allayannis and Ofek (2001), and Knopf, Nam and Thornton (2002).
5. See for example, Nance, Smith and Smithson (1993), Mian (1996), Geczy, Minton and Schrand (1997), Haushalter (2000), Allayannis and Ofek (2001), and Allayannis and Weston (2001).
6. See Geczy, Minton and Schrand (1997), Haushalter (2000), Allayannis and Ofek (2001), and Graham and Rogers (2002) for empirical evidence regarding the relationship between firm size and derivatives use.
7. I follow Allayannis and Weston (2001) and use one dummy for AAA firms, one for AA+ to AA-, one for A+ to A-, one for BBB+ to BBB-, one for BB+ to BB-, one for B+ to B-, and one for CCC+ and below.
8. Although a more efficient two-step system GMM estimator is available, Blundell and Bond (1998) find that inference based on the one-step estimator can be more reliable than the two-step estimator, even in moderately large samples. The one-step system GMM estimator has recently been used in Cheung and Wei (2006).
9. The long-run effect is calculated as: foreign currency hedging coefficient/(1 - lagged Tobin's Q coefficient) $= 0.634/(1-0.673) = 1.939$.
10. This is calculated as: long-run effect/average Tobin's $Q \times$ average amount of hedging for hedging firms $=$ $1.939/2.296 \times 7.5\% = 6.33\%$.
11. See for example Lang and Stulz (1994), Palia (2001), Denis, Denis and Yost (2002), and Anderson and Reeb (2003).
12. Although there is weak evidence of second-order serial correlation in the first-differenced residuals of regression 2, the Hansen (1982) test for overidentifying restrictions shows that the null hypothesis of valid instruments is not rejected.
13. Examining the strength of the instruments with reduced form regressions is difficult when using system GMM because of the way in which the instruments are

created and also because the first-differenced and levels equations are estimated in a system.

14. My qualitative results are similar when assuming foreign currency hedging is strictly exogenous.

References

Allayannis, G. and Ofek, E. (2001). Exchange Rate Exposure, Hedging, and the Use of Foreign Currency Derivatives. *Journal of International Money and Finance*, 20, 273–296.

Allayannis, G. and Weston, J. P. (2001). The Use of Foreign Currency Derivatives and Firm Market Value. *Review of Financial Studies*, 14, 243–76.

Anderson, R. C. and Reeb, D. M. (2003). Founding-family Ownership and Firm Performance: Evidence from the S&P 500. *Journal of Finance*, 58, 1301–28.

Arellano, M. and Bond, S. (1991). Some Tests of Specification for Panel Data: Monte carlo Evidence and an Application to Employment Equations. *Review of Economic Studies*, 58, 277–97.

Arellano, M. and Bover, O. (1995). Another Look at the Instrumental Variable Estimation of Error-components Models. *Journal of Econometrics*, 68, 29–51.

Berger, P. G. and Ofek, E. (1995). Diversification's Effect on Firm Value. *Journal of Financial Economics*, 37, 39–65.

Berkman, H. and Bradbury, M. E. (1996). Empirical Evidence on the Corporate Use of Derivatives. *Financial Management*, 25, 5–13.

Blundell, R. and Bond, S. (1998). Initial Conditions and Moment Restrictions in Dynamic Panel Data Models. *Journal of Econometrics*, 87, 115–43.

Bodnar, G. M., Tang, C. and Weintrop, J. (1999). Both Sides of Corporate Diversification: The Value Impacts of Geographic and Industrial Diversification. Working Paper, John Hopkins University.

Carter, D. A., Rogers, D. A. and Simkins, B. J. (2006). Does Hedging Affect Firm Value? Evidence from the US Airline Industry. *Financial Management*, 35, 53–86.

Cheung, W. K. A. and Wei, K. C. J. (2006). Insider Ownership and Corporate Performance: Evidence from the Adjustment Cost Approach. *Journal of Corporate Finance*, 12, 906–25.

Christophe, S. E. (1997). Hysteresis and the Value of the U.S. Multinational Corporation. *The Journal of Business*, 70, 435–62.

Coles, J. L., Daniel, N. D. and Naveen, L. (2008). Boards: Does One Size Fit All. *Journal of Financial Economics*, 87, 329–56.

DeMarzo, P. M. and Duffie, D. (1995). Corporate Incentives for Hedging and Hedge Accounting. *Review of Financial Studies*, 8, 743–71.

Demsetz, H. and Villalonga, B. (2001). Ownership Structure and Corporate Performance. *Journal of Corporate Finance*, 7, 209–33.

Denis, D. J., Denis, D. K. and Yost, K. (2002). Global Diversification, Industrial Diversification, and Firm Value. *Journal of Finance*, 57, 1951–79.

Faulkender, M. and Petersen, M. A. (2006). Does the Source of Capital Affect Capital Structure? *Review of Financial Studies*, 19, 45–79.

Fazzari, S. M., Hubbard, R. G. and Petersen, B. C. (1988). Financing Constraints and Corporate Investment. Brookings Papers on Economic Activity 1988, 141–95.

Froot, K. A., Scharfstein, D. S. and Stein, J. C. (1993). Risk Management: Coordinating Corporate Investment and Financing Policies. *Journal of Finance*, 48, 1629–58.

Gay, G. D. and Nam, J. (1998). The Underinvestment Problem and Corporate Derivatives Use. *Financial Management*, 27, 53–69.

Geczy, C., Minton, B. A. and Schrand, C. (1997). Why Firms Use Currency Derivatives. *Journal of Finance*, 52, 1323–54.

Graham, J. R. and Rogers, D. A. (2002). Do Firms Hedge in Response to Tax Incentives? *Journal of Finance*, 57, 815–39.

Guay, W. and Kothari, S. P. (2003). How Much Do Firms Hedge with Derivatives? *Journal of Financial Economics*, 70, 423–61.

Hansen, L. P. (1982). Large Sample Properties of Generalized Method of Moments Estimators. *Econometrica*, 50, 1029–54.

Haushalter, G. D. (2000). Financing Policy, Basis Risk, and Corporate Hedging: Evidence from Oil and Gas Producers. *Journal of Finance*, 55, 107–52.

Holtz-Eakin, D., Newey, W. and Rosen, H. S. (1988). Estimating Vector Autoregressions with Panel Data. *Econometrica*, 56, 1371–95.

Howton, S. D. and Perfect, S. B. (1998). Currency and Interest-Rate Derivatives Use in US Firms. *Financial Management*, 27, 111–21.

Jin, Y. and Jorion, P. (2006). Firm Value and Hedging: Evidence from U.S. Oil and Gas Producers. *Journal of Finance*, 61, 893–919.

Knopf, J. D., Nam, J. and Thornton, J. H. (2002). The Volatility and Price Sensitivities of Managerial Stock Option Portfolios and Corporate Hedging. *Journal of Finance*, 57, 801–13.

Lang, L. H. P. and Stulz, R. M. (1994). Tobin's Q, Corporate Diversification, and Firm Performance. *The Journal of Political Economy*, 102, 1248–80.

Leland, H. E. (1998). Agency Costs, Risk Management, and Capital Structure. *Journal of Finance*, 53, 1213–43.

Mackay, P. and Moeller, S. B. (2007). The Value of Corporate Risk Management. *Journal of Finance*, 62, 1379–419.

Merton, R. C. (1974). On the Pricing of Corporate Debt: The Risk Structure of Interest Rates. *Journal of Finance*, 29, 449–70.

Mian, S. L. (1996). Evidence on Corporate Hedging Policy. *Journal of Financial and Quantitative Analysis*, 31, 419–39.

Modigliani, F. and Miller, M. H. (1958). The Cost of Capital, Corporation Finance and the Theory of Investment. *American Economic Review*, 48, 261–97.

Morck, R. and Yeung, B. (1991). Why Investors Value Multinationality. *The Journal of Business*, 64, 165–87.

Myers, S. C. (1977). Determinants of Corporate Borrowing. *Journal of Financial Economics*, 5, 147–75.

Nance, D. R., Smith, C. W., Jr. and Smithson, C. W. (1993). On the Determinants of Corporate Hedging. *Journal of Finance*, 48, 267–84.

Palia, D. (2001). The Endogeneity of Managerial Compensation in Firm Valuation: A Solution. *Review of Financial Studies*, 14, 735–64.

Porta, R. L., Lopez-de-Silanes, F., Shleifer, A. and Vishny, R. (2002). Investor Protection and Corporate Valuation. *Journal of Finance*, 57, 1147–70.

Rajan, R. G. and Zingales, L. (1995). What Do We Know About Capital Structure? Some Evidence from International Data. *Journal of Finance*, 50, 1421–60.

Ross, S. A. (1977). The Determination of Financial Structure: The Incentive-signalling Approach. *Bell Journal of Economics*, 8, 23–40.

Servaes, H. (1996). The Value of Diversification during the Conglomerate Merger Wave. *Journal of Finance*, 51, 1201–25.
Shin, H.-H. and Stulz, R. M. (1998). Are Internal Capital Markets Efficient? *Quarterly Journal of Economics*, 113, 531–52.
Smith, C. W. and Stulz, R. M. (1985). The Determinants of Firms' Hedging Policies. *Journal of Financial and Quantitative Analysis*, 20, 391–405.
Stulz, R. M. (1984). Optimal Hedging Policies. *Journal of Financial and Quantitative Analysis*, 19, 127–40.
Villalonga, B. and Amit, R. (2006). How Do Family Ownership, Control and Management Affect Firm Value? *Journal of Financial Economics*, 80, 385–417.
White, H. (1980). A Heteroskedasticity-consistent Covariance Matrix Estimator and a Direct Test for Heteroskedasticity. *Econometrica*, 48, 817–38.
Wooldridge, J. M. (2002) *Econometric Analysis of Cross Section and Panel Data*. Cambridge, Massachusetts: The MIT Press.

4

Repurchases, Employee Stock Option Grants, and Hedging

Daniel A. Rogers

4.1 Introduction

A large literature exists regarding stock repurchases by corporations. Recently, attention has focused on the link between employee stock options and repurchases. Business press and corporate disclosures often tie these two activities together. For example, in Microsoft's 2003 10-K filing, footnote 14 to the financial statements states,[1]

> *We repurchase our common shares primarily to manage the dilutive effects of our stock option and stock purchase plans, and other issuances of common shares.*

Recent research (Bens et al., 2003; Fenn and Liang, 2001; Kahle, 2002 and Weisbenner, 2000) documents that employee and executive stock option programs affect equity repurchase decisions. The principal arguments underlying the relation between options and repurchases are (1) that repurchases alleviate dilution of earnings per share, (2) that repurchases are used to 'fund' stock option programs, and (3) that executive options increase incentives to substitute repurchases for dividends as a form of payout.

In this chapter, I explore a fourth possible argument that might explain the observed relation between repurchases and employee options. When shares are repurchased then reissued to employees to satisfy option exercises, the firm has effectively locked in a cost of shares in advance. This strategy would be quite similar to the forward purchase of commodities or currencies, as practiced by many firms. In other words, repurchasing shares to provide a pool of shares for option exercises is a hedging strategy.

A natural implication of this hedging argument for stock repurchases is that the number of options granted should be positively related to the number of shares repurchased. Prior studies largely analyze the relations between the total number of options (or total number of vested options) and repurchases. Unfortunately, an association between a 'stock' amount of options and the 'flow' of repurchases cannot be cleanly interpreted in a panel data set. By looking at the flow of option grants over a number of years, I am able to examine whether there is a statistical pattern between repurchases and new employee options. The first contribution of this study is to analyze the relation between employee option grants and repurchases during 1993–2003 by a randomly selected sample of 151 S&P 500 firms.

The analysis shows that employee option grants are positively related to contemporaneous stock repurchases. With the exception of employee option exercises, other possible option variables do not exhibit statistical power in explaining repurchase activity. The existence of a positive relation between option grants and stock repurchases implies that firms are able to lock in a cost for future shares expected to be issued to satisfy employee option exercises for some portion of their current option grants.[2]

Given that a positive relation is documented between option grants and stock repurchases, the analysis further explores possible rationales to explain cross-sectional variation in the relation between repurchases and option grants. The most robust results show that the extent of R&D expenditures is positively related to the measure of stability of repurchases relative to option grants, and that firms with lower long-term debt ratios exhibit less variability between repurchases and option grants. This set of results can be explained from at least two perspectives. First, from risk management theory, Froot, Scharfstein, and Stein (1993) argue that firms with more growth options in their investment opportunity sets have more to gain from hedging. If the R&D variable is a proxy for greater growth options, then the results presented here are consistent with this theory. Additionally, Froot et al. (1993) argue that firms facing greater financial constraints are more prone to the underinvestment problem. If lower debt ratios are indicative of firms that face greater costs associated with debt financing, then the relation shown between debt and repurchase-to-grant stability is consistent with the theory that firms hedge to avoid expected underinvestment costs.

Alternatively, greater R&D could be indicative of more intangible assets. If firms with more intangible assets are harder to value, then firms with more R&D should face greater uncertainty about future exercise prices and would find more value from locking in a price for future share obligations to employees if this practice reduces the information asymmetry between firm insiders and outside investors.

The chapter proceeds as follows. Section 4.2 provides background on prior research examining the relation between stock repurchases and options. The discussion in Section 4.3 provides a review of the price uncertainty introduced by option grants, and how theories of optimal hedging may be related to this uncertainty. In Section 4.4, the option and repurchase data are introduced. Section 4.5 provides analyses to address whether corporate stock repurchases are related to option grants. Section 4.6 explores whether the relation between repurchases and option grants may be explained by theories of optimal risk management, and Section 4.7 provides concluding comments.

4.2 Literature on repurchases and stock options

Recent research illustrates that stock options provide significant explanatory power for repurchase activity. Weisbenner (2000) provides initial evidence on the link between options and repurchases. In a cross-sectional regression using 1995 data on repurchases, he illustrates that employee options outstanding are positively related to repurchases. He also uses data for 144 firms from 1990–8, and finds that changes in shares outstanding are negatively related to option grants made during each of the last three years. He interprets his findings as consistent with the idea that firms repurchase stock to reduce the earnings dilution of employee option programs.

Using Execucomp data during 1993–7, Fenn and Liang (2001) find that executive options outstanding are positively related to repurchases. While their results are seemingly consistent with the hypothesis that option-holding managers prefer to substitute repurchases for dividends, it is not possible to rule out other option-related explanations given that they do not use broad-based employee options in their analysis.

Kahle (2002) uses a cross-sectional sample of firms announcing open-market repurchases. She contrasts this sample against a set of firms announcing dividend increases, and finds that employee options outstanding exhibit a statistically strong positive relation with the decision to announce a repurchase. Employee options outstanding are also positively related to repurchase activity. She further finds that both relations are principally associated with exercisable employee options. She interprets this evidence as supportive that repurchases are used to fund employee option programs. Kahle's study also incorporates executive options. She finds that executive options outstanding are positively related to the decision to repurchase, but do not affect repurchase activity. Thus, she concludes that managers use repurchases as a substitute form of payout to maximize the value of their options.

Bens et al. (2003) focus their examination on the hypothesis that firms repurchase shares in amounts that allow for maintenance of EPS growth. Their sample consists of a panel of large firms during 1996–9. They find that the change in diluted shares occurring because of stock price effects on existing unexercised options has a positive effect on the number of shares repurchased. They also control for the dilutive nature of newly granted options, but find no relation between dilution from newly granted options and repurchases. They also document a positive relation between executive options outstanding and repurchases.

This chapter adds to prior literature on three dimensions. First, I directly analyze whether option grants and repurchases are related. Weisbenner

(2000) finds that option grants are negatively related to changes in shares outstanding. However, Jagannathan, Stephens, and Weisbach (2000) argue that change in shares outstanding is a problematic measure of repurchases. Others among the aforementioned papers focus only on the relation between repurchases and options outstanding to test their hypotheses.[3]

The second innovation from this study is that it incorporates not only the cross-section of firms' repurchases and option activity, but also incorporates a significant time series of these data. Repurchases represent a flow of shares while outstanding options represent a stock of shares. While it may be reasonable to expect that repurchases are related to outstanding options in the cross-section, the hypothesized relation becomes less clear as time series data are added to the cross-sectional data, because total options outstanding are a function of the cumulative effect of each firm's grant and exercise activity. If there is a relation between actual repurchase activity and employee options over time, then it might better be represented by a flow variable such as option grants or exercises.

Finally, this research provides preliminary analyses as to whether commonly cited hedging rationales can explain the cross-sectional differences in firms' relations between option grants and repurchases. The results offer guidance for future research on optimal hedging of option grant liabilities.

4.3 Option grants and hedging as a possible motivation for repurchases

4.3.1 Price risk of employee option grants

Granting stock options creates an uncertain future obligation for the shareholders of the firm. The market price of the stock at the time of exercise is unknown at the grant date. Additionally, the issuer does not know if the option will be exercised during the option's life.

Suppose the option is exercised at an unspecified time prior to or at the expiration date. At this date, the firm's stock price must be greater than the exercise price of the employee's option. The firm is obligated to supply the employee with a share of the company's stock in exchange for the employee's payment of the exercise price. The difference between the firm's stock price and the option's exercise price at this future date represents a source of uncertainty for the company's shareholders. If the firm must issue a new share of stock, shareholders bear an opportunity cost equal to the difference of the two prices.

Recent research of repurchases and employee options suggest that firms are concerned with dilution of EPS (Bens et al., 2003 and Kahle, 2002). If this is the case, a firm might monetize the opportunity cost mentioned above by repurchasing a share of its stock prior to or on the exercise date. Suppose that the repurchase takes place on the exercise date; then the full amount of the opportunity cost is monetized.

Rather than issue a new share or repurchase a share for subsequent issue at the time of option exercise, the firm can repurchase a share before the exercise date. The company can issue this share from its inventory to satisfy an option exercise transaction, and therefore remove some of the uncertainty regarding the size of the opportunity cost. By purchasing a share in advance, the firm locks in an economic cost of the share subsequently used to satisfy the employee option obligation.

If taken to the limit, the firm can eliminate all uncertainty associated with the opportunity cost of a future employee option exercise by repurchasing a share of stock when the option is granted. Given that most employee options are granted at-the-money (Murphy, 2002), this practice would be akin to a forward purchase type of operational hedging strategy, such as an airline buying jet fuel and storing it for later consumption.

The ex-post economic outcome of using shares repurchased at the grant date to hedge option grant liabilities depends upon the firm's stock price performance between the option grant and exercise dates, as well as its dividend-adjusted cost of equity capital. For example, suppose a firm grants an at-the-money option when its stock price is $20. Suppose the firm's continuously compounded dividend yield is 3 percent, and its continuously compounded cost of equity capital is 8 percent. After five years, its stock price is expected to be $25.68. If the price is exactly $25.68 five years after the grant date and the option is exercised, the ex-post economic cost of the option grant to shareholders ($5.68 at year 5) is identical if (1) the firm repurchased the share for $20 at the option grant date, or (2) the firm repurchases the share at the exercise date for $25.68 (or simply issues a new share of stock to satisfy the exercised option).[4]

Ex-post, shareholders prefer the firm to repurchase the share at the grant date if the actual stock price on the exercise date is greater than $25.68, or repurchase at the exercise date (or not repurchase at all) if the price is below $25.68. Thus, the future value of the stock calculated with the dividend-adjusted cost of equity represents the break-even level of the strategy of hedging the option grant liability by repurchasing a share at the grant date. The firm can choose to lock in the ex-post economic cost of the option grant by repurchasing a share at the grant date, or can allow the ex-post cost to vary depending upon the exercise date stock price.

The discussion of the previous paragraph implies that hedging an option grant liability by repurchasing stock yields a positive net payoff to shareholders if the stock price appreciation is greater than should be rationally expected ex-ante. This is not to say that shareholders view greater stock price appreciation as a bad thing if employees hold options. If the firm's employees have truly created value in excess of investor expectations, the repurchase is still a good strategy. However, suppose the firm's share price appreciation is high because of a deviation from its fundamental value. Because employees are able to choose when to exercise, an unsustainably high price allows for employees to buy shares that are not only cheap because of expected price appreciation, but also because of the market's mispricing of the firm's stock. For example, Jensen (2005) discusses Enron as an extreme example of the types of problems that can occur when a firm's stock becomes overpriced.

The discussion so far presumes that an employee option granted is ultimately exercised. This will not always be the case. First, it is not a certainty that the stock price will be greater than the exercise price during time periods when the employee is eligible to exercise the option. Additionally, the employee might not continue to be employed with the company past the option's vesting period, thus the option is canceled. The higher the likelihood that the option will not be exercised, the less likely the firm will choose to repurchase a share to satisfy the employee option obligation. Thus, if firms repurchase shares at the time of option grant as a forward purchase hedge, the ratio of shares repurchased to options granted is likely to be well below one.

4.3.2 Hedging option grant price risk and risk management theory

The price risk associated with option grants obviously is very different from the sorts of price risk normally considered when analyzing rationales for hedging. For example, airlines might choose to enter into contracts to hedge their cost of future jet fuel purchases. If unhedged, sharply higher fuel prices could cause significantly lower cash flow with detrimental consequences for the airline's investment plans and/or financing options (Carter, Rogers and Simkins, 2006). In the case of option grant uncertainty, the 'bad' outcome occurs when the firm's stock price increases at a rate in excess of its dividend-adjusted cost of equity. The larger the disparity, the greater the opportunity cost borne by the firm's shareholders. While some might argue that a higher stock price is never a bad outcome, Jensen (2005) provides a compelling argument that an unsustainably high stock price can cause management to engage in wealth destruction. In this section of the chapter, I discuss how the price risk associated with option grants relates to traditional theories of corporate risk management.

Theoretic rationales for hedging include the following motives: (1) hedging to reduce expected underinvestment/distress costs, (2) hedging to increase borrowing capacity, (3) hedging to reduce the effects of information asymmetry, (4) hedging because of managers' risk aversion, and (5) hedging because of tax function convexity.[5]

Reduction of expected underinvestment/distress costs is a commonly cited motive for hedging.[6] Smith and Stulz (1985) argue that hedging reduces expected financial distress costs by reducing the probability of bankruptcy. However, protection against bankruptcy is clearly inconsistent with repurchasing stock to hedge the price uncertainty of future option exercises.

Froot et al. (1993) extend the Smith and Stulz argument by endogeneizing bankruptcy costs. Their theory proposes hedging as a mechanism to reduce expected underinvestment costs by providing cash flow during periods in which the firm would otherwise be forced to access external capital markets to finance valuable investment opportunities.

The framework cited in the prior paragraph might hold some promise to potentially explain a hedging strategy of repurchasing stock to protect against the stock price risk associated with future option exercises. As mentioned previously, there exists significant evidence that firms repurchase shares prior to option exercise. Suppose a firm repurchases stock just prior to option exercise. A 'bad' outcome occurs when the firm's stock price has appreciated at a rate in excess of the dividend-adjusted cost of equity since the date of the option grant. In such a situation, the firm must use more cash to repurchase the stock. This extra expenditure leaves less for investment. If firms hedge option grant uncertainty by repurchasing stock, then subsequent cash flows will be less influenced by the need to repurchase stock at prevailing market prices. Firms could choose to avoid cash flow consequences altogether by issuing new shares to satisfy option exercises, but this explanation presumes that firms do not care about the potential for dilution effects associated with issuing new shares.

One prediction from the above discussion is that firms with greater investment opportunities might be more likely to repurchase shares in conjunction with granting options. Option-intensive firms are typically considered to be firms with more growth opportunities, and Core and Guay (2001) find that variables proxying for growth options (that is, R&D) are positively related to employee option usage and new grants.

Theoretical evidence suggests that potential for an increase in borrowing capacity may provide a legitimate motive for hedging stock option grants. Mozes and Raymar (2001) discuss stock repurchases in the context of offering a hedge against the possibility of issuing new shares in the future. To finance a portion of the stock repurchase, debt is issued. The value of hedging comes from the value of the increased tax shield to the hedger.[7] This type of value effect is consistent with the theoretic arguments of Leland (1998) and the empirical findings of Graham and Rogers (2002). The underinvestment hypothesis might also predict a positive relation between debt levels and hedging if debt level is a proxy for financial constraints. On the other hand, Froot et al. (1993) argue that firms hedge to avoid issuance of additional debt capital, thus their framework implies that hedging firms likely exhibit lower debt ratios.

Hedging might serve as a mechanism to reduce costs associated with information asymmetry. DeMarzo and Duffie (1991) argue that a firm's management should hedge based on private information that cannot be conveyed costlessly to shareholders. Breeden and Viswanathan (1998) suggest that high-quality managers have incentives to hedge away uncertainty about performance so that the market can more precisely infer ability.

The information asymmetry hypothesis also seems to provide a plausible reason for firms to reduce the price risk associated with option grants. If firms with greater information asymmetry face more uncertainty about future stock price, then repurchasing stock to lock in the economic cost of options might make sense, because the information asymmetry creates greater risk exposure.

While risk aversion of managers is an unobservable characteristic, the common practice in hedging literature is to examine incentives supplied by the manager's holdings of company stock and options (Tufano, 1996; Knopf, Nam and Thornton, 2002 and Rogers, 2002). Smith and Stulz (1985) suggest that portfolio holdings with linear payoffs provide more incentive for managers to engage in hedging. Additionally, from a non-hedging perspective, repurchases increase management's proportionate ownership stake.

On the other hand, if managers are option holders, they may be opposed to hedging by repurchasing stock. Managers may want to utilize capital for the purposes of risky positive NPV investment, rather than repurchasing stock. Alternatively, they may view repurchase of company stock as a positive NPV project, suggesting a positive link between executive options and hedging via repurchases.

The tax convexity motive does not offer a convincing rationale for hedging stock option grants.[8] Hedging stock option grants by repurchasing stock does not alter a firm's current taxable income; rather the exercise of stock options may reduce taxable income during a future time period (when exercise occurs). As such, I do not explore a tax convexity argument in this chapter.

4.4 Data – repurchases and stock options

The sample is gathered from the population of S&P 500 firms listed in the Compustat database as of July 2004. Because much of the data are hand-collected, I limit the sample to approximately 30 percent of the composition of the index, and the final sample consists of 151 randomly selected firms. Data are gathered from the SEC EDGAR database as far into the past as data availability allows through 2003. EDGAR filings are first available in late 1993, so the first year of data for many of the sample firms is 1993.

The number of common shares repurchased during each year is collected for each of the sample firms.[9] The number of shares repurchased is found in either the Statement of Shareholders' Equity or the footnote regarding shareholder equity. This methodology, while time-consuming, overcomes the difficulties associated with other proxies of measuring stock repurchase activity (Jagannathan et al., 2000).

I also hand-collect the following employee option data from all 10-K filings available on EDGAR: option grants, options exercised, total options outstanding, and total exercisable options outstanding. In addition, I collect the weighted average exercise prices of grants, exercised options, and total options, although these data items are often not available until filings for the 1996 calendar year.

Finally, I gather executive option data from the Execucomp database and proxy statement filings on EDGAR. I gather data on the total number of executive options granted to the five highest-paid executives, the total number of options exercised by these executives, the total number of options that are exercisable (that is, vested), and the total number of options (exercisable and unexercisable).

The repurchase and option data are scaled by the number of shares outstanding at the end of the prior fiscal year. Table 4.1 shows summary statistics. Across 1496 firm-years, the mean percentage of shares repurchased is 1.83 percent. The average percentage of options granted is 2.23 percent. The magnitude of repurchases as a percentage of option grants displays considerable variation. For example, repurchases as a percentage of option grants exhibit a median of 35.67 percent, with 25th and 75th percentiles of 0 and 158 percent, respectively. Nevertheless, it is difficult to interpret the magnitude of the repurchases relative to option grants without considering the effect of other motives for repurchasing shares.

Table 4.1 also illustrates summary statistics for the primary control variables used in subsequent multivariate analyses of repurchase activity. The average sample firm has market value of equity of approximately $6,063 million (that is, natural logarithm equals 8.71).

The level of free cash flow is defined as operating cash flow from the Statement of Cash Flow minus capital expenditures minus dividends. This amount is scaled by book value of total assets. Free cash flow measures the degree to which the firm has additional cash to distribute as repurchases, and we should observe a positive relation between repurchases and free cash flow.

The ratio of market value of assets relative to book value provides an estimate of investment opportunities. Firms with greater investment opportunities would be expected to distribute less cash to shareholders. Capital expenditures scaled by total assets serve as an additional control variable to proxy for investment opportunities.

The use of debt capital provides an alternative mechanism to distribute cash to investors. As financial leverage grows, smaller amounts of cash are available to pay to shareholders. Thus, we expect a negative relation between debt ratio and repurchases. Because repurchases may serve as a substitute for dividend payments, I also include the dividend yield as a control variable.

Table 4.1 Data summary statistics

	Obs.	Mean	Std dev.	Median	25th %ile	75th %ile
Repurchase and option variables:						
Shares repurchased	1496	1.83%	2.83%	0.69%	0.00%	2.65%
Options granted	1496	2.23%	2.91%	1.56%	0.83%	2.66%
Options granted – executives	1491	0.38%	0.75%	0.22%	0.08%	0.43%
Options exercised	1488	1.08%	1.37%	0.70%	0.30%	1.41%
Options exercised – executives	1489	0.15%	0.40%	0.04%	0.00%	0.15%
Options outstanding	1496	8.10%	6.84%	6.93%	4.12%	10.28%
Options outstanding – executives	1489	1.65%	1.79%	1.24%	0.53%	2.13%
Exercisable options	1474	4.06%	3.34%	3.39%	1.97%	5.41%
Exercisable options – executives	1489	0.90%	1.08%	0.60%	0.23%	1.18%
Repurchases/grants	1460	241.75%	1886.59%	35.67%	0.00%	158.38%
Financial control variables						
Natural log of market capitalization	1493	8.71	1.22	8.61	7.87	9.42
Free cash flow-to-total assets	1501	3.77%	9.15%	2.48%	−0.56%	7.37%
Market-to-book of assets	1493	1.96	2.19	1.29	0.84	2.18
Capital expenditures-to-total assets	1501	6.73%	6.51%	5.30%	2.50%	8.65%
Long-term debt-to-total assets	1501	17.93%	14.70%	15.31%	6.14%	28.05%
Dividend yield	1500	1.77%	1.85%	1.26%	0.26%	2.72%
Percentage stock price change (current year)	1499	19.66%	52.81%	11.34%	−9.35%	38.10%
Percentage stock price change (prior year)	1487	18.57%	52.33%	10.01%	−10.48%	37.54%
Volatility of stock – daily (current year)	1500	2.41%	1.16%	2.13%	1.59%	2.88%
Volatility of stock – daily (prior year)	1489	2.39%	1.15%	2.12%	1.58%	2.87%

Notes: This table shows distributional statistics for the repurchase and option variables. Variables (with the exception of repurchases/grants) are divided by the lagged number of common shares outstanding. This table also shows the variables used in subsequent regression analysis of repurchases to control for relevant corporate financial characteristics.

Characteristics of firm return and risk might be important in explaining stock repurchases. For example, there is significant evidence that price declines are associated with higher levels of repurchase announcements and activity (Stephens and Weisbach, 1998 and Kahle, 2002). I control for price change effects by including one-year percentage stock price changes for both the year of and the year prior to the repurchase date. I also include the standard deviation of daily stock returns during each of the two years.

4.5 Are option grants a determinant of repurchase activity?

A direct implication of discussion from earlier in the chapter is that granting employee options creates a risk exposure that firms might find optimal to hedge. If firms repurchase stock contemporaneously with granting of options, then a positive relation between option grants and repurchases is predicted. In this section, I explore this hypothesis.

I initially examine the hypothesis by performing a Tobit random effects regression of the following form:[10]

$$\begin{aligned}\text{REP\_NUM}_{i,t} = {} & \alpha_0 + \alpha_1 \text{LN\_MKCAP}_{i,t-1} + \alpha_2 \text{FCF}_{i,t} + \alpha_3 \text{MB}_{i,t-1} + \alpha_4 \text{CAPX}_{i,t} \\ & + \alpha_5 \text{LTD}_{i,t-1} + \alpha_6 \text{DIV\_YLD}_{i,t} + \alpha_7 \text{PRC\_CHG}_{i,t} \\ & + \alpha_8 \text{PRC\_CHG}_{i,t-1} + \alpha_9 \text{VOL}_{i,t} + \alpha_{10} \text{VOL}_{i,t-1} \\ & + \alpha_{11} \text{GRT\_OPT}_{i,t} + \alpha_{12} \text{EXD\_OPT}_{i,t} \\ & + \alpha_{13-22} \text{YEAR INDICATORS} + \mu_i + \varepsilon_{i,t} \qquad (4.1)\end{aligned}$$

where,

REP_NUM = number of shares repurchased divided by shares outstanding at the prior fiscal year end,

LN_MKCAP = natural logarithm of the market value of equity,

FCF = free cash flow, defined as net cash flow from operating activities minus cash dividends and capital expenditures, divided by book value of assets at the prior fiscal year end,

MB = the sum of market value of equity, book value of total interest-bearing debt, and book value of preferred stock divided by the book value of assets,

CAPX = capital expenditures divided by book value of assets at the prior fiscal year end,

LTD = long-term debt divided by the book value of assets,

DIV_YLD = dividend yield,

PRC_CHG = percentage stock price change during the fiscal year,

VOL = standard deviation of daily returns during the fiscal year,

GRT_OPT = number of options granted divided by the number of shares outstanding at the prior fiscal year end,

EXD_OPT = number of options exercised divided by the number of shares outstanding at the prior fiscal year end,
YEAR INDICATORS = dummy variables indicating years 1994–2003,
μ_i = firm-specific error term.

The first ten explanatory variables are financial controls discussed in Section 4.4. An option exercise variable is included to control for the possibility that firms use repurchases as a way of making shares available when options are exercised. Alternatively, firms might use cash proceeds from option exercises to fund stock repurchases.

Table 4.2 Effect of option grants on common share repurchases

Panel A Models with option grant and exercise variables

	Model 1	Model 2	Model 3
Log of market capitalization	0.0032	0.0031	0.0029
	(0.026)	(0.039)	(0.046)
Free cash flow to assets	0.0752	0.0771	0.0758
	(0.000)	(0.000)	(0.000)
Market-to-book of assets	–0.0038	–0.0037	–0.0037
	(0.000)	(0.000)	(0.000)
Capital expenditures	–0.0272	–0.0212	–0.0235
	(0.232)	(0.349)	(0.299)
Long-term debt to assets	–0.0619	–0.0619	–0.0634
	(0.000)	(0.000)	(0.000)
Dividend yield	–0.0005	–0.0006	–0.0005
	(0.626)	(0.513)	(0.598)
Percentage stock price change (current yr)	–0.0086	–0.0067	–0.0090
	(0.000)	(0.003)	(0.000)
Percentage stock price change (prior yr)	–0.0003	0.0007	–0.0004
	(0.890)	(0.752)	(0.859)
Volatility of daily returns (current yr)	–0.5014	–0.4992	–0.4561
	(0.001)	(0.001)	(0.003)
Volatility of daily returns (prior yr)	–0.3916	–0.4094	–0.3763
	(0.035)	(0.027)	(0.043)
Option grants/shares outstanding	0.1057	0.1355	
	(0.049)	(0.010)	
Exercised options/shares outstanding	0.2609		0.3107
	(0.018)		(0.004)
Year dummies	Yes	Yes	Yes
Number of observations	1478	1486	1478
Number of censored observations	495	496	495
Wald chi-squared	189.08	180.49	184.19
P-value	0.000	0.000	0.000
Log likelihood	1670.2	1683.3	1668.3

continued

Table 4.2 Continued

Panel B Coefficient estimates on other option variables

	Only option variable	Alternative variable and exercised options	Alternative variable and grants and exercises
Option grants/shares outstanding	0.1355 (0.010)		
Exercised options/shares outstanding	0.3107 (0.004)		
Total options/shares outstanding	0.0251 (0.229)	0.0139 (0.518)	−0.0050 (0.840)
Vested options/shares outstanding	0.0376 (0.376)	0.0264 (0.532)	0.0157 (0.711)
Exec grants/shares outstanding	0.1770 (0.396)	0.0957 (0.651)	−0.2095 (0.415)
Exec exercises/shares outstanding	0.5599 (0.125)	0.0203 (0.962)	−0.0078 (0.986)
Exec total options/shares outstanding	0.0605 (0.513)	0.0259 (0.781)	−0.0429 (0.667)
Exec vested options/shares outstanding	0.2039 (0.112)	0.1863 (0.141)	0.1479 (0.247)

Notes: This table shows coefficients from Tobit random effects regressions of the number of common shares repurchased during the fiscal year divided by common shares outstanding at the end of the prior fiscal year on the listed independent variables; P-values are shown in parentheses below the Tobit coefficient estimates. Panel A illustrates the results for all variables included in the models. Panel B shows only results for option variables. Model 1 of Panel B illustrates estimates for each variable when it is used as the only option variable. Model 2 shows results for option variables from a model that includes option exercises, and Model 3 includes option grants and exercises in addition to each of the listed option variables individually.

Model 1 of Panel A in Table 4.2 illustrates positive relations between repurchase activity and both employee option grants and exercises. The relation between option exercises and repurchases is consistent with either an option funding hypothesis as suggested by Kahle (2002) or with an argument that employee payments to exercise options are used to fund stock repurchases (Bens et al., 2003). Nevertheless, the positive relation between option grants and repurchases implies that firms' option granting activity drives more concurrent stock repurchases.

Not surprisingly, there is a high correlation between option grants and exercises. The sample data exhibit a positive correlation of approximately

53 percent between these two variables. Models 2 and 3 of Panel A in Table 4.2 show results of the models if I include each option variable separately. In both cases, the results are similar to those of Model 1, and the option variables exhibit stronger statistical significance if included individually.

The high correlation between option grants and exercises typically is true among many of the potential option variables. For example, the correlation between option grants and total options outstanding is 65 percent. Given this fact, the relation between option grants and repurchases might reflect a broader relation between options and repurchases that cannot be attributed solely to option grants. To assess this possibility, I repeat the regressions discussed earlier but replace the option grant and exercise variables with each of the alternative option variables: total options, exercisable options, executive grants, executive exercises, total executive options, and executive exercisable options.

Panel B of Table 4.2 shows Tobit coefficients and p-values on the other option variables. The first column of Panel B shows results from models in which each variable is included individually. For example, the coefficients on option grants and exercised options shown in Panel B correspond to Models 2 and 3 of Panel A. While all of the coefficients are positive, none are statistically significant at conventional levels. The next column of Panel B shows results of models that include each option variable individually and exercised options. The final column of Panel B also includes option grants as an explanatory variable. The alternative option variables illustrate even less statistical power to explain repurchases. Meanwhile, the coefficients on the option grant and exercise variables retain similar in magnitude and statistical significance in models in which other option variables are included.[11]

4.6 Does 'optimal' risk management explain the relation between repurchases and option grants?

Having documented a positive relation, on average, between repurchases and option grants within the sample firms, the analysis now moves to examining whether firms that repurchase stock in conjunction with option grants are practicing optimal risk management. In other words, do firms with low variation between repurchases and option grants exhibit characteristics that would be expected of hedgers according to risk management theories?

This question is answered through the following general process. First, I identify a variable to proxy for the likelihood that firms are using repurchases to hedge option grants. Then, a model is tested to determine whether these firms exhibit financial characteristics consistent with hedging theory.

4.6.1 Identification of option grant hedging proxy variable

As opposed to much of the empirical hedging literature in which 'hedging' firms are selected based on some directly observable variable, this study cannot rely on such direct observation. Below, I describe a possible proxy variable to measure hedging of the price risk exposure occurring from employee stock option grants.

The hedging proxy variable utilizes the volatility of the ratio of shares repurchased to options granted. Specifically, for each firm in the sample, I measure the coefficient of variation for the ratio. For firms with larger coefficients of variation, there is a lower likelihood that option grants are a determining factor of repurchases. Therefore, this coefficient of variation serves as an inverse measure of each firm's possible hedging of option grant price risk.

Table 4.3 provides summary statistics of the coefficient of variation of the repurchases-to-grant ratio and the ratio's mean across the 140 sample firms with at least one year of stock repurchases. The first column of Table 4.3 shows the average coefficient of variation is 1.58 with a median value of 1.40. The second column highlights that there is significant variation in the ratio of repurchases-to-grants, but the interquartile range of 0.50–2.38 implies that, on average, firms tend to repurchase stock and grant options of similar magnitudes. The following columns of Table 4.3 segregate the distributions into coefficient of variation quartiles from lowest to highest. The most notable observation from the quartile breakdowns is that the median repurchase-to-grant ratio declines considerably over the two highest coefficient of variation quartiles. Thus, the relation between repurchases and option grants is more tenuous for firms that repurchase less stock, grant more employee options, or both. In subsequent regressions, I include both repurchase and option grant variables as additional control variables.

To verify the effectiveness of the hedging proxy variable described above, I re-estimate the random effects Tobit regression model shown in Model 1 of Table 4.2, including the interaction of the option grant variable and the inverse of the coefficient of variation of the repurchase-to-grant ratio as an additional variable. This interaction term exhibits a statistically much stronger relation with repurchases than does the option grant variable (p-value of the coefficient is less than 0.005 in all specifications). This result confirms that firms displaying less variation in the univariate relation between option grants and repurchases also exhibit stronger positive relations in a multivariate setting.

4.6.2 Regression analyses

In this section of the chapter, I present the results from regressions of the option grant hedging proxy variable on firm characteristics to assess whether

Table 4.3 Summary statistics: firm repurchases-to-grant ratio averages and variabilities

	Full sample (140 obs)		**Lowest quartile**		**2nd quartile**		**3rd quartile**		**Highest quartile**	
	Repurchase-to-grants		*Repurchase-to-grants*		*Repurchase-to-grants*		*Repurchase-to-grants*		*Repurchase-to-grants*	
	Coef of var	*Mean*	*Coef of var*	*Mean*	*Coef of var*	*Mean*	*Coef of var*	*Mean*	*Coef of var*	*Mean*
Average	1.58	2.64	0.74	2.15	1.21	1.74	1.79	1.95	2.57	4.72
Median	1.40	1.13	0.75	1.36	1.20	1.53	1.78	0.95	2.48	0.62
Std dev.	0.73	6.17	0.19	3.26	0.12	1.37	0.17	2.64	0.39	11.41
25th percentile	1.02	0.50	0.61	0.98	1.14	0.74	1.69	0.41	2.23	0.23
75th percentile	2.05	2.38	0.89	1.83	1.28	2.43	1.91	2.58	2.82	2.22
Minimum	0.24	0.01	0.24	0.21	1.02	0.04	1.40	0.02	2.10	0.01
Maximum	3.32	57.67	1.01	19.63	1.40	5.06	2.04	12.07	3.32	57.67

Notes: This table shows summary statistics for the coefficient of variation and mean of the repurchases-to-grants ratio across 140 randomly selected S&P 500 firms with at least one year of repurchase activity during 1993–2003. The first two columns display statistics for the full sample, and the following four sets of columns show distributions within each coefficient of variation quartile.

relations between repurchases and option grants conform to predictions from hedging theory.[12] First, I briefly review the explanatory variables used in the option grant hedging model.

Firm size is measured by the natural logarithm of each firm-year observation's market capitalization. Firm size is commonly employed to measure the extent to which a firm might be able to utilize scale economies in their risk management activities. Alternatively, firm size is sometimes used as a proxy for expected costs of financial distress or the degree of information asymmetry.

The amount of free cash flow might be related to option grant hedging for at least two different reasons. First, firms with greater free cash flow show more ability to repurchase stock, thus might exhibit more stability in their repurchase behavior relative to option grants. Second, firms that generate less free cash flow may face more binding financial constraints, and as such, be more susceptible to underinvestment problems.

Market-to-book ratio is often used to reflect a firm's growth opportunities, and thus, if option grant hedging follows the investment opportunities hypothesis, then a positive relation is expected.

Capital structure and payout variables might be useful in explaining option grant hedging. Long-term debt is a common variable used to test financial distress and underinvestment arguments for hedging. I also explore the relation between debt issuance and option grant hedging to test whether hedging firms differ in their external financing behavior. Finally, dividend yield might provide a measure of financing constraints.

Stock price volatility and change variables are included to assess whether the variability and behavior of a firm's stock price plays a meaningful role in the relation between repurchases and option grants. If firms with more historically volatile stock prices face more uncertainty about future stock price, then volatility can be viewed as a measure of risk exposure. Past price changes might provide market timing arguments for hedging, or could illustrate that firms base option grant hedging decisions on prior stock price performance.

Research and development (R&D) expenditures are often used as a proxy variable for growth opportunities. Alternatively, R&D might provide a measure of information asymmetry, and could be viewed as an intangible asset with more uncertain future value. Regardless of the explanation employed, the prediction that R&D should be positively related to option grant hedging is unambiguous.

Executive holdings of options and shares can affect hedging decisions based on risk aversion arguments. Option holdings are often associated with more risk-seeking behavior and less hedging. Meanwhile, executive stock holdings create more risk averse tendencies and are related to greater hedging activity.

Models 1 and 2 of Table 4.4 display the means of coefficient results from regressions performed annually for each year from 1993–2003. The hedging proxy variables are computed for each firm, so these are not allowed to vary over time. The first column of Table 4.4 presents OLS estimates from the regression of the repurchase-to-grant coefficient of variation without industry control indicators included, while the second column shows results if I include dummy variables indicating 2-digit SIC codes. As in Minton and Schrand (1999), I assess the statistical significance of the mean coefficients with a z-statistic calculated using the t-statistics from the annual regressions.[13]

From the results of the first two models of Table 4.4, I make several observations. First, addition of industry control variables improves the explanatory power of the regressions significantly. Model 1 shows that the annual regressions explain from 19 to 34 percent of the variability in the coefficient of variation of repurchase-to-grant ratios. In Model 2, the R-squared range increases to 47–84 percent for the annual regressions.

Second, while the regression without industry controls shows a number of significant relations between independent variables and the option grant hedging proxy variable, many of the results disappear after adding the industry control variable. In particular, Model 1 shows the following relations with option grant hedging that become insignificant or change signs after inclusion of industry controls (note that I reverse the signs when discussing results of these regressions because the coefficient of variation is an inverse measure of hedging): positive size effect, positive free cash flow effect, negative capital expenditures effect, negative dividend yield effect, negative volatility effect, and negative executive stock holding effect.

Third, only a few relations are robust to the inclusion of industry effects. Long-term debt shows a negative relation with option grant hedging, and R&D expenditures exhibit a positive relation. Taken together, these two relations can be viewed as evidence supporting the investment opportunities framework of optimal hedging. Firms that optimally choose low debt ratios because of high financial distress costs and that also spend greater amounts on R&D are more likely to exhibit stable repurchase activity relative to new option grants. On the other hand, contrary to the predictions of managerial risk aversion hedging arguments, executive option holdings show a positive relation with the option grant hedging variable.

Finally, after controlling for industry effects, market-to-book ratio shows a negative relation with option grant hedging and executive share holdings exhibit a positive association. The market-to-book result is inconsistent with an investment opportunities argument for hedging, but rather suggests that firms with undervalued stock relative to firms in the same industry classification are more likely to repurchase in conjunction with option grants. The executive share holding result could be viewed as consistent with a risk aversion framework; however, it could be argued that managers with more stock

Table 4.4 Determinants of the extent of option grant hedging

Independent variables	***Model 1***	***Model 2***	***Model 3***	***Model 4***
Log of market capitalization	−0.0479	−0.0240	0.0284	0.0570
	−3.71	−1.80	2.95	5.05
Free cash flow to assets	−0.6286	0.7412	−0.3403	0.6646
	−2.61	1.58	−2.08	1.91
Market-to-book of assets	−0.0034	0.0537	−0.0033	0.0459
	−0.25	2.78	−0.60	2.37
Capital expenditures	0.9913	0.4928	−0.3694	−0.2975
	2.70	1.08	−1.82	−1.01
Long-term debt to assets	1.0021	1.5035	0.3267	1.0136
	6.44	4.20	2.76	2.64
Net debt issuance to assets	0.1163	0.9428	0.0588	0.6115
	0.14	0.69	0.24	0.32
Dividend yield	0.0580	0.0126	0.0313	−0.0034
	6.45	0.97	5.36	−0.27
Volatility of stock during current year	10.9545	7.8701	5.4183	0.9072
	2.60	1.62	1.42	0.49
Volatility of stock during prior year	10.0358	4.0641	9.3120	5.9102
	2.09	1.46	2.57	1.56
Percentage stock price change (current yr)	−0.0673	−0.0852	−0.0192	−0.0408
	−0.39	−1.57	0.35	−0.45
Percentage stock price change (prior yr)	−0.0549	−0.0056	−0.0501	−0.0420
	−0.02	−0.61	−0.16	−0.89
R&D expenditures	−2.8848	−3.8470	−1.3310	−1.4180
	−7.56	−7.44	−4.63	−4.86

continued

Table 4.4 Continued

Independent variables	***Model 1***	***Model 2***	***Model 3***	***Model 4***
Vested executive options/shares	−6.8616	−11.2171	−3.2296	−3.0836
outstanding	−2.91	−2.91	−0.88	−1.14
Shares held by executives/shares	0.5190	−1.4084	0.5526	−0.6968
outstanding	2.88	−4.93	6.49	−4.14
Option grants/shares outstanding	−2.7323	−2.0914	−2.1623	−1.9136
	−0.59	0.00	−1.08	−0.41
Shares repurchased/shares	−5.1428	−6.9157	−2.1485	−4.4786
outstanding	−3.43	−5.36	−1.96	−4.02
Coefficient of variation of			0.5897	0.5771
repurchases to exercises			21.05	9.25
Constant	1.4568	0.9347	0.0750	1.0943
	9.98	3.04	0.61	3.12
2-digit SIC industry dummies included	No	Yes	No	Yes
Number of observations	1,374	1,374	1,374	1,374
Range of annual R-squared	0.1929–0.3394	0.4665–0.8410	0.5165–0.5681	0.6731–0.8518

Notes: This table presents the means of coefficient results from annual regressions of an option grant hedging proxy variable. The dependent variable is the coefficient of variation of the repurchase-to-grant ratio (an inverse measure of hedging), and OLS regressions are utilized with t-statistics calculated using robust standard errors. Independent variables are defined as in earlier tables. Average coefficients from annual regressions using 1993–2003 data are listed first (with four decimal places) with z-statistics of the hypotheses that mean coefficients are equal to zero shown beneath each average coefficient. The z-statistics are calculated as $z = \bar{t}/\sigma(t)/(N-1)^{0.5}$, where $\bar{t}$ and $\sigma(t)$ are the mean and standard deviation of the annual t-statistics and N is equal to 11.

will be more inclined to repurchase, because of perceived undervaluation of the stock. This interpretation could also clarify the positive relation between executive option holdings and option grant hedging.

One concern about the dependent variable in the regression models is that it may be proxying for the variability of repurchases with a different option variable. In Table 4.2, I demonstrate that option exercises exhibit an even stronger relation with repurchases than is evident between grants and repurchases. Thus, there might be a concern that the coefficient of variation of repurchases-to-grants could conceivably be reflecting the variability of the relation between repurchases and option exercises. To address this issue, I include the coefficient of variation of the repurchases-to-exercises ratio as an explanatory variable in the regressions. Models 3 and 4 of Table 4.4 show the results of the regressions with this variable included.

Inclusion of the variability of repurchases-to-exercises provides considerable improvements in the explanatory power of most of the annual regressions. Repurchase-to-exercise variability shows a very strong positive relation with repurchase-to-grant variability. However, its inclusion affects almost none of the results shown in Models 1 and 2 of Table 4.4. The one notable exception is that firm size shows a negative relation with option grant hedging in Models 3 and 4. This result is consistent with the idea that firms facing greater information asymmetry are more likely to hedge the uncertainty associated with option grants. Alternatively, if smaller firms face greater financial constraints, these firms may be more likely to underinvest.

4.7 Conclusion

Repurchases of common stock are often linked to employee stock option programs, both in the business press and in corporate disclosures regarding repurchase programs. This relation has been confirmed by empirical studies of corporate repurchase behavior relative to direct measures of options outstanding.

In this chapter, I extend research of the association between repurchases and employee stock options by studying repurchase activity relative to option grants. Using a randomly selected sample of 151 S&P 500 firms, I document a significant association between repurchases and employee options granted, after controlling for other motives for stock repurchases. The analysis conducted in this chapter highlights an important extension to prior analyses of stock repurchases and employee options. Specifically, variables reflecting the flow of corporate option programs will better reflect incentives to repurchase stock if examining corporate behavior over time.

The finding of a positive relation between repurchases and option grants within firms suggests that some firms may be hedging price risk associated with option grants. I explore this possibility by constructing a proxy variable to measure the stability of each sample firm's repurchases relative to its stock option grants, and conduct multivariate regressions of this variable on financial characteristics that proxy for rationales of optimal risk management.

The most robust finding from the hedging regressions is that firms with lower leverage and higher R&D expenditures are more likely to be hedging option grant uncertainty. This set of results is consistent with the idea that investment opportunities and financing constraints are important determinants in corporate hedging decisions. This is a notable result that is consistent with much of the empirical research in corporate risk management, despite the differing type of price risk exposure associated with granting stock options as compared to more traditional risk exposures examined in other hedging research.

Notes

I appreciate comments from Peter Brous, Keith Jakob, Kathy Kahle, Frank Kerins, Ruben Trevino, participants of the Financial Management Association and Southern Finance Association annual meetings, and seminar participants at Massey University, Portland State University, Seattle University, and University of Montana. I also am grateful for the efforts of Sowmya Devarajan, Gang Liu, and Jie Shen in gathering data for this project.

1. Microsoft discontinued granting stock options to employees during its 2004 fiscal year, and now grants restricted stock as its standard form of equity-based pay.
2. The evidence presented in this analysis does not contradict the well-known result that repurchases serve as a mechanism to offset the EPS dilution occurring as options become in-the-money. In unreported analysis, I find that corporate repurchases are positively associated with option grants occurring in the concurrent year, as well as with those granted during the prior two years. Interested readers may request the omitted analysis by contacting me at drogers@pdx.edu.
3. While Bens et al. (2003) possess data on option grants, they do not include this variable as a possible explanatory factor of repurchases. Instead, they construct a variable measuring the dilutive impact of option grants, and find that this variable offers no power in explaining repurchases. They disclose that the correlation between this 'grant dilution' variable and option grants is 36 percent.
4. The ex-post economic cost is merely the future value of the ex-ante cost (Black–Scholes value) calculated for the option assuming a risk-free rate equal to the expected price appreciation and assuming no volatility.
5. These commonly cited rationales for hedging are put forth in articles by Bessembinder (1991), DeMarzo and Duffie (1991), Froot et al. (1993), Leland (1998), Mello and Parsons (2000), Smith and Stulz (1985), and Stulz (1984).
6. Empirical work by Allayannis and Weston (2001), Gay and Nam (1998), Géczy, Minton and Schrand (1997), Graham and Rogers (2002), and Haushalter (2000) mention such costs as an important force in determining corporate hedging.
7. This borrowing is not risk-free. If options are not exercised, then the 'collateral' for the borrowing is never monetized.

8. In tests using a cross-section of firms, Graham and Rogers (2002) show that tax function convexity is not related to hedging with derivatives.
9. All share-related data collected (shares repurchased, options granted, grant price, and so on) are adjusted for stock splits.
10. As illustrated in Table 4.1, over 25 percent of the firm-year observations exhibit zero repurchases (in other words, the dependent variable in equation (1) is censored), so the Tobit specification corrects for the censoring bias. A random effects model is utilized to control for the panel data aspect of the dataset.
11. To conserve space, this chapter omits discussion of various analyses conducted to explore the robustness of the relation between option grants and repurchases. Interested readers may contact me at drogers@pdx.edu to request this omitted portion of the chapter.
12. To conserve space, this chapter omits an additional set of multivariate analyses that incorporates the set of firms that never repurchase stock. Interested readers may contact me at drogers@pdx.edu to request this portion of the analysis.
13. The calculation is $z = \bar{t}/\sigma(t)/(N\text{-}1)^{0.5}$, where $\bar{t}$ and $\sigma(t)$ are the mean and standard deviation of the annual t-statistics and N is equal to 11.

References

Allayannis, G. and Weston, J. P. (2001). The Use of Foreign Currency Derivatives and Firm Market Value. *Review of Financial Studies*, XIV, 243–76.

Bens, D. A., Nagar, V., Skinner, D. J. and Wong, M. H. F. (2003). Employee Stock Options, EPS Dilution, and Stock Repurchases. *Journal of Accounting and Economics*, XXXVI, 51–90.

Bessembinder, H. (1991). Forward Contracts and Firm Value: Investment Incentive and Contracting Effects. *Journal of Financial and Quantitative Analysis*, XXVI, 519–32.

Breeden, D. and Viswanathan, S. (1998). Why Do Firms Hedge? An Asymmetric Information Model. Unpublished Working Paper, Fuqua School of Business, Duke University.

Carter, D. A., Rogers, D. A. and Simkins, B. J. (2006). Does Hedging Affect Firm Value? Evidence from the US Airline Industry. *Financial Management*, XXXV (1), 53–86.

Core, J. E. and Guay, W. R. (2001). Stock Option Plans for Non-executive Employees. *Journal of Financial Economics*, LXI, 253–87.

DeMarzo, P. and Duffie, D. (1991). Corporate Financial Hedging with Proprietary Information. *Journal of Economic Theory*, LIII, 261–86.

Fenn, G. W. and Liang, N. (2001). Corporate Payout Policy and Managerial Stock Incentives. *Journal of Financial Economics*, LX, 45–72.

Froot, K., Scharfstein, D. and Stein, J. (1993). Risk Management: Coordinating Investment and Financing Policies. *Journal of Finance*, XLVIII, 1629–58.

Gay, G. D. and Nam, J. (1998). The Underinvestment Problem and Corporate Derivatives Use. *Financial Management*, XXVII (4), 53–69.

Géczy, C., Minton, B. A. and Schrand, C. (1997). Why Firms Use Currency Derivatives. *Journal of Finance*, LII, 1323–54.

Graham, J. R. and Rogers, D. A. (2002). Do Firms Hedge in Response to Tax Incentives? *Journal of Finance*, LVII, 815–39.

Haushalter, G. D. (2000). Financing Policy, Basis Risk, and Corporate Hedging: Evidence from Oil and Gas Producers. *Journal of Finance*, LV, 107–52.

Jagannathan, M., Stephens, C. P. and Weisbach, M. S. (2000). Financial Flexibility and the Choice between Dividends and Stock Repurchases. *Journal of Financial Economics*, LVII, 355–84.

Jensen, M. C. (2005). Agency Costs of Overvalued Equity. *Financial Management*, XXXIV (1), 5–19.

Kahle, K. M. (2002). When a Buyback Isn't a Buyback: Open Market Repurchases and Employee Options. *Journal of Financial Economics*, LXIII, 235–61.

Knopf, J. D., Nam, J. and Thornton, J. H., Jr. (2002). The Volatility and Price Sensitivities of Managerial Stock Option Portfolios and Corporate Hedging. *Journal of Finance*, LVII, 801–13.

Leland, H. E. (1998). Agency Costs, Risk Management, and Capital Structure. *Journal of Finance*, LIII, 1213–43.

Mello, A. S. and Parsons, J. E. (2000). Hedging and Liquidity. *Review of Financial Studies*, XIII, 127–53.

Minton, B. A. and Schrand, C. (1999). The Impact of Cash Flow Volatility on Discretionary Investment and the Costs of Debt and Equity Financing. *Journal of Financial Economics*, LIV, 423–60.

Mozes, H. A. and Raymar, S. B. (2001). Granting and Hedging Employee Stock Options: Tax Motivation and Empirical Tests. Unpublished Working Paper, Fordham University Graduate School of Business Administration.

Murphy, K. J. (2002). Explaining Executive Compensation: Managerial Power vs. the Perceived Cost of Stock Options. *University of Chicago Law Review*, LXIX, 847–69.

Rogers, D. A. (2002). Does Executive Portfolio Structure Affect Risk Management? CEO Risk-taking Incentives and Corporate Derivatives Usage. *Journal of Banking and Finance*, XXVI, 271–95.

Smith, C. W., Jr. and Stulz, R. M. (1985). The Determinants of Firms' Hedging Policies. *Journal of Financial and Quantitative Analysis*, XX, 391–405.

Stephens, C. P. and Weisbach, M. S. (1998). Actual Share Reacquisitions in Open-market Repurchase Programs. *Journal of Finance*, LIII, 313–33.

Stulz, R. M. (1984). Optimal Hedging Policies. *Journal of Financial and Quantitative Analysis*, XIX, 127–40.

Tufano, P. (1996). Who Manages Risk? An Empirical Examination of Risk Management Practices in the Gold Mining Industry. *Journal of Finance*, LI, 1097–137.

Weisbenner, S. J. (2000). Corporate Share Repurchases in the 1990s: What Role Do Stock Options Play? Unpublished Working Paper, Federal Reserve Board of Governors.

5

Do Managers Exhibit Loss Aversion in Their Risk Management Practices? Evidence from the Gold Mining Industry

Tim R. Adam, Chitru S. Fernando, and Evgenia Golubeva

For years, hedging made Southwest Airlines Co. the most consistently profitable airline in the US. But included in its third-quarter earnings, released Thursday, was a $247 million accounting charge, which reflected the decline in the value of its hedges as the price of oil dropped during the quarter. The charge caused Southwest, which had a healthy operating profit, to post a quarterly net loss for the first time in 17 years. 'Southwest is looking for opportunities to "de-hedge" some of its fuel,' Gary Kelly, the airline's chief executive, said Thursday. 'Low fuel prices are a good thing ... and an opportunity that we'll want to take the best advantage of that we can.' *Wall Street Journal*, 'Fuel Hedges Cloud Airline Results,' 17 October 2008.

5.1 Introduction

Despite a considerable body of theoretical literature that advances rationales for why and how managers can create value for shareholders by hedging corporate risk exposures,[1] empirical studies of corporate hedging underscore the significant gap that continues to persist between theory and practice.[2] Indeed, the recent empirical evidence that a majority of managers engage in selective hedging by using derivatives strategies to time the market,[3] despite the lack of any evidence that such hedging strategies create value for shareholders,[4] provides support for the notion that managerial behavior can deviate from the pure rationality assumed by the neoclassical theories of hedging.

In this chapter, we study the risk management activities of a sample of North American gold mining firms and present new evidence that lends strong support for behavioral explanations of some practices associated with corporate hedging. A growing body of literature, both theoretical and empirical, studies the impact of managerial behavioral biases on corporate decisions.[5] Several managerial biases, including loss aversion, mental accounting, and overconfidence, have been found to affect corporate investment policies, capital structure decisions, mergers and acquisitions, security offerings, and investment bank relationships.[6] To the best of our knowledge, ours is the first study to examine whether managerial loss aversion and mental accounting also affects corporate risk management decisions.[7]

Recent anecdotal evidence shows that, like in the aforementioned case of Southwest Airlines, gold mining firms move swiftly to cut or eliminate their hedges after losing money on contracts due to rising gold prices. According to the Wall Street Journal (17 March 2008), 'last year, in the largest cut since 2002, gold mining companies reduced their committed hedged positions by 35%.' One prominent example is the de-hedging of Barrick Gold (Wall Street Journal, 28 July 2004) when, facing rising gold prices, 'Barrick reduced its hedge position to 13.9 million ounces, down 850,000 ounces in the quarter,' which contributed to its 42 percent drop in quarterly net income. We have uncovered no public announcements or other anecdotal evidence to suggest a similarly swift response when gold prices are moving downwards.

Consistent with the anecdotal evidence, our study of quarterly hedging changes in our sample of gold mining firms reveals that managers systematically reduce their hedge positions in response to market movements against the hedge (that is, gold price increases) in the previous quarter. While the correlation between hedging changes and gold price changes is negative, we do not observe a similarly prompt reaction to gold price decreases, suggesting that any increases in hedging that accompany gold price declines occur more gradually. This asymmetric reaction is puzzling from the standpoint of rational value-maximizing behavior on the part of managers. For firms that already have open derivatives positions, losses and gains on derivatives positions are offset by gains and losses on the underlying exposures being hedged, resulting in a minimal net change in value, if any. Additionally, since some firms may commence hedging only after gold price declines that elevate their likelihood of financial distress, we would expect a sharper hedging response to gold price declines than to increases.

While the observed asymmetry is inconsistent with the existing theories of hedging, it is consistent with the presence of loss aversion in the managers of our sample firms (Kahneman and Tversky, 1979; Kahneman and Tversky, 1984; Tversky and Kahneman, 1991) which implies a higher sensitivity to losses than to gains of equal magnitude. For example, while oil prices were rising, Southwest Airlines' fuel hedging activities were regarded as state-of-the-art, but when oil prices fell and the fuel hedges began to generate losses, Southwest Airlines moved swiftly to unwind its hedge positions despite realizing offsetting gains from lower fuel prices. Similar to the case of Southwest Airlines, hedging losses in our sample of gold mining firms are offset by gains in their underlying gold holdings. Yet, gold mining firms seem to treat these hedging losses as 'real' losses and react accordingly. A possible explanation for treating hedging losses as 'real' losses without regard to the gain in the underlying position arises from mental accounting. The concept of mental accounting was first proposed by Thaler (1980, 1985) and summarized by Grinblatt and Han (2005) as follows: 'The main idea is that decision makers tend to segregate different types of gambles into separate accounts ... by ignoring possible interactions.' Thus, mental accounting implies that managers regard losses on derivatives positions separately from simultaneous gains on the underlying position. A risk management policy influenced by loss aversion and mental accounting implies that managers will implement hedging strategies that minimize derivatives losses.

In summary, the new evidence we document about the time-series properties of corporate derivatives practices is consistent with the possibility that managerial loss aversion and mental accounting affect derivatives strategies. Our findings are robust to numerous controls for alternative rational explanations, and contribute to the growing literature on behavioral biases by showing that managerial behavioral biases can also impact corporate risk management. Recognizing that managers sometimes deviate from strict rationality is likely to improve our understanding of corporate risk management decisions and help close the gap between the observed practice of risk management and the extant neoclassical theory that seeks to explain it.

The remainder of the chapter is organized as follows. Section 5.2 discusses the relevant behavioral theories and derives testable hypotheses. Section 5.3 describes our sample, the construction of our variables and the empirical methodology. Section 5.4 presents the empirical evidence on how hedging responds to gold price changes. Section 5.5 summarizes the results and presents our conclusions.

5.2 Empirical hypotheses

The objective of this chapter is to investigate the potential effects on corporate risk management decisions of two managerial behavioral biases: mental accounting and loss aversion. *Mental accounting* (Thaler, 1980, 1985) implies that managers maintain separate mental accounts for different decision variables. Mental accounting may lead to sub-optimal decisions if managers ignore the possible interdependencies of the decision variables when making decisions, that is, managers make decisions for each mental account separately. For example, Sautner and Weber (2009) report that managers are more likely to sell shares acquired from exercising options than shares acquired through required stock investments. This behavior is consistent with mental accounting. Loughran and Ritter (2002) provide an explanation for IPO underpricing based on mental accounting: managers do not mind underpricing as long as it is not larger than the 'gain' between the midpoint of the filing-price range and the first-day closing price. Ljungqvist and Wilhelm (2005) show that behavioral factors can explain the likelihood that firms will switch IPO underwriters for subsequent offerings and the fees that underwriters charge for such offerings. Coleman (2007) uses an experimental survey setting to study managerial choices over risky alternatives and finds evidence that the surveyed managers maintain separate mental accounts for the consequences of decision outcomes and for the probabilities of those outcomes. In the context of risk management, mental accounting implies that managers maintain one account for derivatives-related gains and losses, and a separate account for the gains and losses on the underlying asset. Thus, managers exhibiting mental accounting may make decisions related to their derivatives portfolio while disregarding the gains/losses on the underlying asset.

The literature on cognitive biases ties mental accounting to another behavioral bias known as *loss aversion* (Kahneman and Tversky, 1979; Kahneman and Tversky, 1984; Tversky and Kahneman, 1991). Loss aversion implies that individuals are more sensitive to losses than they are to gains of equal magnitude, and strongly prefer the avoidance of future losses to the prospect of future gains. That is, they exhibit non-standard utility functions. In the context of corporate risk management decisions, loss aversion implies that managers would be significantly more averse to potential losses of upside gains when firms are hedged and the market moves against the hedge, than they would value the benefit of gains that help the firm offset downside losses when the market moves in favor of the hedge. Experimental evidence by Tversky and Kahneman (1991) suggests that when comparing gains and losses of equal economic magnitude, loss-averse individuals outweigh losses over gains by a factor of two.

Mental accounting coupled with loss aversion implies that individuals tend to be loss averse over specific accounts rather than their overall position. For example, Barberis and Huang (2001) argue that investors exhibit loss aversion over individual stocks in their portfolios rather than over their overall portfolios. In the corporate risk management context, mental accounting coupled with loss aversion implies that managers are more sensitive to derivatives losses than to derivatives gains, and at least partially ignore any offsetting effects in the hedged positions. Moreover, Tversky and Kahneman (1991) review considerable prior evidence which suggests that managers who are loss averse will also react more intensely to losses than to gains by moving to reverse actions that led to the loss (see also Thaler and Johnson, 1990). Therefore, managers who exhibit mental accounting and loss aversion will reduce their hedge positions when they result in hedging losses, but will not systematically increase their hedge positions when they result in hedging gains.[8]

It could be argued that shareholders, rather than managers, are potentially affected by some of the above behavioral biases and exert pressure on rational managers to react asymmetrically. However, while shareholders observe gold price changes, they do not fully observe dynamic hedging strategies or the resulting variation in derivatives cash flows. Therefore, it is unlikely that shareholder pressure can fully underlie all our empirical hypotheses. We discuss other alternative explanations in Section 5.3 below.

5.3 Data and methodology

5.3.1 Data and variables

Our sample consists of 92 gold mining firms in North America, which are included in the *Gold and Silver Hedge Outlook*, a quarterly survey of derivatives activities conducted by Ted Reeve, an analyst at Scotia McLeod, from 1989 through 1999, when he discontinued the survey.[9] These 92 firms represent the majority of firms in the gold mining industry (see Tufano, 1996) and Adam and Fernando, 2006). Firms not included in the survey tend to be small or privately held corporations.

The survey contains information on all outstanding gold derivatives positions, their size and direction, maturities, and the respective delivery prices for each instrument (forwards, spot-deferred contracts, gold loans and options). This derivatives data is described in detail in Adam (2002). We hand-collect operational data: gold production (in ounces), production costs per ounce of gold, and gold reserves, from firms' annual reports. The data on firm characteristics such as size, market-to-book, leverage, liquidity, existence of a credit rating, and payment of quarterly dividends comes from Compustat. All variable notations and definitions are provided in Appendix.

We measure the extent of derivatives usage at a given point in time t with time to maturity i by a hedge ratio $HR(i)_t$, defined as follows:

$$HR(i)_t = \frac{N(i)_t}{E_t[\text{Prod}_{t+i}]}, \tag{5.1}$$

Where $N(i)_t$ is the sum of the firm's derivatives positions in place at time t(in ounces of gold) that mature in i years, weighted by their respective deltas, as in Tufano (1996); $E_t[\text{Prod}_{t+i}]$ is the firm's expectation of its gold production (in ounces of gold) at time $t+i$ as of time t. The maturity i of a derivatives position can be 1, 2, 3, 4, or 5 years, although most derivatives activity takes place with contracts that mature within three years. To check robustness of our results we aggregate (a) contracts with one to three years maturity and (b) contracts with one to five years maturity.

The derivatives survey reports the expected production for each hedge horizon i whenever a firm has derivatives positions outstanding that mature in i years. If a firm does not hedge a particular maturity, then the expected production figures are missing. In this case we use the actual gold production in year $t+i$. Since most firms do not hedge their gold production beyond three years, the problem of missing expected production figures increases with the hedge horizon. Therefore, we also define an alternate hedge ratio, $HR_{Res}(i)_t$, that does not rely on expected production but scales a firm's total derivatives position by its total gold reserve (see Jin and Jorion, 2006):

$$HR_{\mathrm{Res}}(i)_t = \frac{N(i)_t}{\mathrm{Gold\ Reserve}_t}. \tag{5.2}$$

In addition to helping overcome potential issues associated with missing production data, scaling by reserves is also a useful robustness check of our analysis using production-based hedge ratios, due to the possibility that some time-series variation in the production-based hedge ratio may be due to unplanned variations in expected production rather than a change in the firm's derivatives positions. We observe these hedge ratios every quarter from December 1989 to December 1999. Table 5.1 provides descriptive statistics of our variables.

5.3.2 Methodology

Our basic methodology is to run panel regressions with firm fixed effects in order to focus on the time-series variation in hedge ratios. We estimate the loss aversion hypothesis on the whole sample and, for robustness, on the subsample of firms that hedge in the sample period (that is, have at least one non-zero hedge ratio). We test our hypothesis on both groups of firms to avoid the possibility that sample selection bias could affect the results for the subsample of hedgers, and because we do not know ex ante that non-hedgers will persist in not hedging throughout our sample period. Keeping non-hedgers in the sample will make a finding in support of the loss aversion hypothesis less likely, ex post. A firm that has a zero hedge ratio will not reduce the hedge ratio in response to a gold price increase. At the same time, a firm that has a zero hedge ratio may increase the hedge ratio in response to a gold price decrease. Therefore, by keeping non-hedgers in the sample we decrease (increase) the unconditional probability of observing a significant reaction to increases (decreases) in the price of gold, which would work against the loss aversion hypothesis. We then check the robustness of our results by taking non-hedgers out of the sample.

In our initial tests, we estimate the sensitivity of the hedge ratio to past changes in the price of gold while controlling for firm characteristics that may affect the fundamental hedging needs of the firm, as well as seasonal dummies and a time trend. Subsequently, we consider the possibility that the initial level of the hedge ratio may affect the firm's reaction to the gold price change.

For robustness we repeat our tests using the two-step Heckman (1979) procedure with selection to control for any potential selection in bias in our sample of firms that hedge. In the first stage, we model the existence of hedging activity as a function of variables that are predicted by

Table 5.1 Descriptive statistics of hedge ratios and firm characteristics

Variable	Mean	Standard deviation	Minimum	Maximum	Number of observations
One-year hedge ratio	0.2874	0.3179	0.0000	1.0000	1875
Two-year hedge ratio	0.1552	0.2418	0.0000	1.0000	1879
Three-year hedge ratio	0.0779	0.1722	0.0000	1.0000	1901
Four-year hedge ratio	0.0363	0.1135	0.0000	1.0000	1935
Five-year hedge ratio	0.0271	0.1092	0.0000	0.9990	1952
Aggregate 3-yr. ratio, (production)	0.1716	0.2402	0.0000	1.0000	1460
Aggregate 3-yr. ratio, (reserves)	0.0465	0.0738	0.0000	0.6620	1460
Aggregate 5-yr. ratio, (reserves)	0.0575	0.0961	0.0000	0.9857	1460
Quarterly gold price change	−3.0569	17.7753	−48.9000	52.0000	1781
Size	5.5771	1.7608	1.0460	9.3604	1858
Market-to-Book ratio	1.9381	1.1137	0.2985	9.0819	1647
Debt-to-Equity ratio	0.4619	1.0772	0.0000	21.2707	1205
Quick ratio	4.2476	9.7254	0.0065	141.5172	1161
Dividend dummy	0.4701	0.4993	0.0000	1.0000	1289
Rating dummy	0.2454	0.4305	0.0000	1.0000	1312
Altman's Z-score	4.9900	13.5111	−22.8560	126.8310	1618

Notes: Descriptive statistics are estimated on the pooled dataset. The sample consists of quarterly observations from 1989 to 1999 for a sample of 92 North American gold mining firms as reported in Gold and Silver Hedge Outlook. The table reports summary statistics for the following variables: hedge ratios of various maturities as well as aggregate hedge ratios estimated as the sum of the firm's derivatives positions in place in quarter t (in ounces of gold), weighted by their respective deltas, scaled either by expected production or by reserves; quarterly price changes per ounce of gold; firm size measured as the logarithm of the market value of assets; market-to-book ratio of assets; ratio of book debt to book equity; quick ratio; dividend dummy variable equal to one if the firm paid quarterly dividend; credit rating dummy variable equal to one if a firm reports a credit rating; and Altman's (1968) Z-score. Firm characteristics are from Compustat.

extant hedging theory to be determinants of hedging –firm size, market-to-book ratio, liquidity, leverage, dividend payment, credit rating, and the likelihood of financial distress (Tufano, 1996; Haushalter, 2000). We say that a firm has hedging activity if two conditions hold: (1) the beginning or the end-of-quarter hedge ratio is non-zero; and (2) cash flows from derivatives positions in the previous quarter are non-zero. In the second stage of the Heckman two-step procedure, we test whether the hedge ratio is sensitive to past changes in the price of gold for the firms that exhibit hedging activity as described above. Further methodological details are provided in Section 5.4.

Previous studies of managerial behavioral biases take a cross-sectional approach by examining a variety of characteristics that are likely to affect the degree to which individual managers exhibit behavioral biases, including personal and professional characteristics (age, gender, tenure, education, and so on) and personal wealth management practices (the tendency to hold disproportionate amounts of one's own firm's stock, and the failure to exercise vested options).[10] Our unique data, which contains quarterly observations on all outstanding gold derivatives positions of a sample of 92 North American gold mining firms from 1989 to 1999, and therefore allows us to infer actual derivatives transactions on a quarterly basis, permits us to focus on time-series patterns that may characterize behavioral biases by examining how managers as a group respond to market movements.

We control for alternative rational explanations that could explain an asymmetric response to changes in gold prices. One such explanation for closing out losing derivatives positions may be liquidity pressure or financial distress (Mello and Parsons, 2000). In particular, if a firm has insufficient liquidity or is otherwise financially constrained, it is possible that managers may be forced to close out losing positions due to margin calls, whereas they would not face such margin pressure from profitable positions. Therefore, we control for a firm's liquidity and likelihood of financial distress to allow for this possibility by including a dividend dummy, rating dummy, quick ratio, leverage and Altman's (1968) Z-score as control variables.[11]

5.4 Empirical results

In this section, we test the loss aversion hypothesis, which predicts that managers systematically reduce their hedge positions when they produce hedging losses but do not systematically increase their hedge positions when they produce hedging gains. Initially, we test this hypothesis by examining how the change in the hedge ratio is related to the previous quarter's change in the gold price, while allowing for asymmetry effects and controlling for relevant firm characteristics. Thereafter, we repeat our tests while allowing for the possibility that the relation between hedge ratio changes and gold price changes may be affected by the initial level of the hedge ratio. We conclude by carrying out robustness checks.

We begin by examining the relationship between hedge ratio changes and gold price changes without allowing for asymmetry. We normalize past changes in the price of gold by the initial gold price level, thereby making gold *returns* our main independent variable of interest:

$$RTNGOLD_{t-1} = \Delta GOLD_{t-2,t-1}/GOLD_{t-2}, \tag{5.3}$$

since a given dollar change in the price of gold is likely to be perceived differently depending on the prevailing gold price level.[12]

Table 5.2 reports the results of the regression:

$$\Delta HR_t = a + b \cdot RTNGOLD_{t-1} + CONTROLS_{t-1} + \varepsilon_t. \tag{5.4}$$

We control for past changes in firm characteristics which may also explain a hedge ratio adjustment following a change in the gold price. As our control variables, we choose the change in size, liquidity (quick ratio), leverage, market-to-book, Altman's Z-score, dividend dummy, and credit rating dummy, to accommodate the possibility that a change in the price of gold may change the fundamental hedging needs of the firm, or cause liquidity pressure and financial distress. In addition, we control for seasonal variation using seasonal dummies, clustering of some observations across quarters, and a time trend. The time trend is a variable equal to zero for the first sample observation (December of 1989) and increasing by 0.25 each quarter. Finally, in Models (3), (6), (9), and (12), we report the results obtained on a reduced sample with non-hedgers (firms reporting a zero hedge ratio for the entire sample period) excluded from the sample.

The evidence in Table 5.2 suggests that firms adjust hedge ratios in response to changes in the price of gold, and that this adjustment occurs primarily for short hedge horizons. The coefficient is highly significant, both statistically and economically, for the one-year hedge ratio. A one standard deviation (5.27 percent) increase in the price of gold makes the average firm reduce its one-year hedge ratio by about 10 percent relative to the sample mean. For the aggregate three-year and five-year hedge ratios, the gold return coefficient is smaller in magnitude and sometimes insignificant, although the sign is still negative.[13] We also notice that hedge ratios respond to changes in liquidity and that this effect too occurs at short horizons. A reduction in the quick ratio, which indicates a decrease in liquidity, makes the firm reduce its one-year hedge positions, and vice versa. However, the long-term hedge positions appear to be unaffected by liquidity changes.

Forcing an equal response to gold price increases and decreases in our regression specification (4) does not allow a test of our main hypothesis that the hedge ratio response to gold price changes is asymmetrically stronger

Table 5.2 Relationship between hedging and past gold returns

	One-year hedge ratio			Aggregate 3-year ratio scaled by production			Aggregate 3-year ratio scaled by reserves			Aggregate 5-year ratio scaled by reserves		
	(1)	(2)	(3)	(4)	(5)	(6)	(7)	(8)	(9)	(10)	(11)	(12)
Intercept	0.0264**	−0.0012	−0.001	0.0212***	0.0251*	0.0266*	−0.0043*	−0.0051	−0.0054	−0.0056	−0.0043	−0.0044
	−2.19	(−0.06)	(−0.05)	−2.53	−1.65	−1.69	(−1.79)	(−1.07)	(−1.07)	(−1.50)	(−0.61)	(−0.60)
RTNGOLD	−0.3926***	−0.5979**	−0.6013**	−0.1935***	−0.3174**	−0.3230**	−0.0183	−0.0495	−0.0513	−0.0501	−0.1205*	−0.1223*
	(−3.05)	(−2.47)	(−2.42)	(−3.09)	(−2.09)	(−2.06)	(−0.75)	(−1.55)	(−1.56)	(−1.39)	(−1.68)	(−1.66)
ΔSIZ		0.0521	0.0543		0.0329	0.0342		0.0063	0.0063		0.0014	0.0001
		−1.11	−1.11		−1.16	−1.15		−0.84	−0.82		−0.15	−0.13
ΔZ		−0.0011	−0.0012		0	0		0	0		−0.0002	−0.0002
		(−1.45)	(−1.61)		−0.01	(−0.09)		(−0.16)	(−0.14)		(−0.50)	(−0.52)
ΔQCK		0.0017***	0.0017***		0.0006**	0.0007**		0	0		0.0002	0.0002
		−4.35	−4.34		−2	−2.02		−0.29	−0.24		−1.45	−1.44
ΔMB		0.0166	0.0168		0.0115	0.012		−0.0014	−0.0015		0.0055	0.0056
		−1.04	−1.01		−0.89	−0.89		(−0.51)	(−0.53)		−1.18	−1.16
ΔDE		−0.0307	−0.029		0.0622	0.0641		0.0064	0.0065		−0.004	−0.0039
		(−1.56)	(−1.42)		−1.41	−1.42		−1.1	−1.09		(−0.38)	(−0.36)
ΔDIV		−0.0399	−0.0393		−0.0231	−0.0227		−0.0025	−0.0025		−0.0045	−0.0044
		(−0.48)	(−0.47)		(−0.61)	(−0.59)		(−0.39)	(−0.39)		(−0.40)	(−0.39)
ΔRAT		0.0857	0.0978		−0.007	0.0018		−0.0032	−0.0034		0.0064	0.007
		−1.48	−1.55		(−0.29)	−0.08		(−0.53)	(−0.52)		−1.32	−1.39
R^2	0.0582	0.0785	0.0804	0.0474	0.0808	0.0832	0.0045	0.0234	0.0243	0.0046	0.0167	0.0169
F−statistic	7.3	3.25	3.25	7.66	3.06	3.48	1.11	1.78	1.81	1.34	1.42	1.42
Observations	1,501	618	596	1,266	523	501	1,344	581	559	1,510	661	639
Clusters	93	37	36	88	36	35	81	38	37	82	38	37

Notes: The table presents the results of the panel regressions with firm fixed effects of hedge ratio changes in the current quarter, ΔHR_t, on past relative changes in the price of gold, $RTNGOLD_{t-1} = \Delta GOLD_{t-2,t-1}/GOLD_{t-2}$. We control for changes in the following firm characteristics: *SIZ*, firm size measured as the logarithm of the market value of assets; *Z*, Altman's Z-score; *QCK*, quick ratio; *MB*, market-to-book ratio of assets; *DE*, ratio of book debt to book equity; *DIV*, dummy variable equal to one if the firm paid quarterly dividend; and *RAT*, dummy variable equal to one if a firm reports a credit rating. Models (3), (6), (9), and (12) are estimated on a reduced sample with non-hedgers excluded. All of the models include seasonal dummy variables and a time trend, and ***, **, * indicate significance at the 1%, 5% and 10% levels, respectively. Robust t-statistics accounting for cluster effects are given in parentheses.

for gold price increases. Therefore, we next run the following regression to capture any asymmetric response:

$$\Delta HR_t = a + b_1 \cdot RTNGOLD_{t-1} \cdot I_1 + b_2 \cdot RTNGOLD_{t-1} \cdot I_2 + CONTROLS_{t-1} + \varepsilon_t. \tag{5.5}$$

In this regression, I_1 is a dummy variable that equals one if the change in the gold price during the last quarter was positive, and equals zero otherwise; and I_2 is a dummy variable that equals one if the change in the price of gold was negative, and equals zero otherwise. The sensitivity of hedge ratios to gold price increases is determined by b_1, while the sensitivity to gold price decreases is determined by b_2.

The results, presented in Table 5.3, are striking. In every model, regardless of the hedge ratio specification and presence of control variables, the coefficient b_1 is strongly negative and statistically significant. At the same time, the coefficient b_2 is always statistically insignificant. That is, increases in the price of gold are followed by significant de-hedging in the next quarter, while decreases in the price of gold do not elicit a correspondingly rapid increase in hedging. This result is robust to the inclusion of changes in firm characteristics that may affect the firm's hedging needs. The result is also economically significant. A one standard deviation (5.27 percent) increase in the price of gold leads to a reduction of around 17 percent in the one-year hedge ratio relative to its sample mean, with the magnitude of the reaction diminishing with the hedging horizon. Finally, we continue to observe that at short horizons, hedge ratio adjustments are sensitive to variations in liquidity. Once again, Models (3), (6), (9), and (12) present the results obtained on a reduced sample with non-hedgers excluded.

We next allow for the changes in hedge ratio to be affected by the initial hedge ratio. If a firm has a low hedge ratio or does not hedge, the subsequent change in the hedge ratio is likely to be positive, all else equal. A non-hedger may either remain a non-hedger or decide to start hedging, thus making the hedge ratio adjustment positive, on average, for such firms. In addition, firms with very low levels of hedge ratios are more likely to under-hedge, thereby increasing the likelihood of a subsequent increase in hedging. Following the same logic, a firm with a very high level of hedging is more likely to reduce its hedge ratio, all else equal. Hence, we expect to observe a negative relationship, all else equal, between the initial level of hedge ratio and the subsequent change. In other words, we can posit a systematic negative impact of the initial hedge ratio on the subsequent change, which exists irrespective of changes in the price of gold or other factors. In this section, we test whether our earlier results are robust to the inclusion of this permanent impact into the regression. We re-run regression (5) with one more

Table 5.3 Relationship between hedging and past gold returns with asymmetry

	One-year hedge ratio			Aggregate 3-year ratio scaled by production			Aggregate 3-year ratio scaled by reserves			Aggregate 5-year ratio scaled by reserves		
	(1)	(2)	(3)	(4)	(5)	(6)	(7)	(8)	(9)	(10)	(11)	(12)
Intercept	0.0424***	0.0131	0.0132	0.0311***	0.0336*	0.0353*	−0.0022	−0.0034	−0.0036	−0.0034	−0.0015	−0.0016
	−3.29	−0.64	−0.63	−2.95	−1.88	−1.91	(−0.69)	(−0.65)	(−0.66)	(−0.86)	(−0.22)	(−0.23)
RTNGOLD I_1	−0.6905***	−0.9432***	−0.9624	−0.3622***	−0.5091**	−0.526	−0.0615**	−0.0877**	−0.0919**	−0.0954**	−0.1813*	−0.1849*
	(−3.60)	(−3.24)	(−3.21)	(−3.28)	(−2.13)	(−2.13)	(−2.00)	(−2.56)	(−2.62)	(−2.06)	(−1.97)	(−1.96)
RTNGOLD I_2	0.0182	−0.0636	−0.04	0.0547	−0.0089	0.0054	0.0429	0.0168	0.0195	0.0147	−0.019	−0.0174
	−0.1	(−0.22)	(−0.13)	−0.48	(−0.05)	−0.03	−0.73	−0.26	−0.28	−0.18	(−0.14)	(−0.12)
ΔSIZ		0.0461	0.0487		0.0266	0.0279		0.0052	0.0053		0	−0.0001
		−0.99	−1		−0.97	−0.97		−0.7	−0.68		(−0.01)	(−0.01)
ΔZ		−0.001	−0.0011		0	0		0	0		−0.0001	−0.0001
		(−1.29)	(−1.43)		−0.1	0		(−0.11)	(−0.08)		(−0.45)	(−0.47)
ΔQCK		0.0017***	0.0017***		0.0006*	0.0006*		0	0		0.0002	0.0002
		−4.13	−4.1		−1.92	−1.93		−0.24	−0.19		−1.38	−1.37
ΔMB		0.0127	0.0124		0.01	0.0102		−0.0018	−0.002		0.0047	0.0048
		−0.89	−0.84		−0.82	−0.8		(−0.66)	(−0.70)		−1.06	−1.03
ΔDE		−0.0317	−0.0295		0.0605	0.0628		0.0062	0.0063		−0.0044	−0.0042
		(−1.69)*	(−1.53)		−1.38	−1.39		−1.07	−1.07		(−0.42)	(−0.39)
ΔDIV		−0.0408	−0.0403		−0.0235	−0.023		−0.0026	−0.0027		−0.0048	−0.0047
		(−0.49)	(−0.48)		(−0.62)	(−0.60)		(−0.44)	(−0.44)		(−0.43)	(−0.42)
ΔRAT		0.0929*	0.1080*		−0.0019	0.0089		−0.0022	−0.002		0.0078	0.0088
		−1.67	−1.82		(−0.08)	−0.39		(−0.35)	(−0.29)		−1.39	−1.43
R^2	0.062	0.0851	0.0873	0.0504	0.0849	0.0878	0.0064	0.0259	0.027	0.0053	0.0182	0.0185
F-statistic	7.1	3.67	3.87	7.33	2.85	3.38	1.56	2.12	2.25	1.38	1.54	1.54
Observations	1,501	618	596	1,266	523	501	1,344	581	559	1,510	661	639
Clusters	93	37	36	88	36	35	81	38	37	82	38	37

Notes: The table presents the results of the panel regressions with firm fixed effects of hedge ratio changes in the current quarter, ΔHR_t, on past relative changes in the price of gold in the previous quarter, $RTNGOLD_{t-1} = \Delta GOLD_{t-2,t-1}/GOLD_{t-2}$, while allowing for an asymmetric response in the hedge ratio to gold price increases and decreases. Indicator variables I_1 (I_2) are equal to 1 if gold return was positive (negative). We control for changes in the following firm characteristics: *SIZ*, firm size measured as the logarithm of the market value of assets; *Z*, Altman's Z-score; *QCK*, quick ratio; *MB*, market-to-book ratio of assets; *DE*, ratio of book debt to book equity; *DIV*, dummy variable equal to one if the firm paid quarterly dividend; *RAT*, dummy variable equal to one if a firm reports a credit rating. Models (3), (6), (9), and (12) are estimated on a reduced sample with non-hedgers excluded. All of the models include seasonal dummy variables and a time trend, and ***, **, * indicate significance at the 1%, 5% and 10% levels, respectively. Robust t-statistics accounting for cluster effects are given in parentheses.

term added to the specification:

$$\Delta HR_t = a + b_1 \cdot RTNGOLD_{t-1} \cdot I_1 + b_2 \cdot RTNGOLD_{t-1} \cdot I_2 + CONTROLS_{t-1} + c \cdot HR_{t-1} + \varepsilon_t. \tag{5.6}$$

In (6), HR_{t-1} is the beginning-of-quarter level of the hedge ratio. We expect the coefficient c to be negative. We also expect the coefficient b_1 to be negative and b_2 to be zero, consistent with the results reported in Table 5.3.

Table 5.4 presents the results of our regression (6) with firm characteristics, seasonal dummies, and a time trend used as controls, as in Table 5.3. We can see that our hypothesis regarding the systematic effect of the initial level of hedge ratio is confirmed: the coefficient for HR_{t-1} is universally negative and strongly significant. We observe a marked improvement in the model fit as evidenced by the increase in R^2 compared to those reported in Table 5.3. Therefore, including the initial level of hedge ratio in the regression is important for modeling hedging adjustments of firms. At the same time, our inference regarding the effect of changes in the price of gold remains virtually unaffected. The coefficient b_1 is still negative and significant: a one standard deviation (5.27 percent) increase in the price of gold leads to a 10 percent reduction in the one-year hedge ratio relative to the sample mean, with economic significance diminishing with hedging horizon as before. This result indicates that firms robustly reduce their hedge ratios in response to increases in the price of gold. At the same time, we observe no significant response to decreases in the price of gold over the quarterly time intervals of our study.

As an additional robustness check, we control for the possibility of selection bias in our sample by allowing for the two sequential decisions of the firm, (1) whether or not to be a hedger and (2) conditional on being a hedger, the choice of the level of hedging. We estimate the two-step Heckman procedure with selection. In the first stage, we estimate a PROBIT model, where the dependent variable is the 'hedging activity' dummy, equal to zero if either (1) the firm has zero hedge ratios in both the beginning and the end of quarter t; or (2) the firm had zero cash flows from hedging operations in quarter t-1.[14] We estimate the likelihood of hedging activity as a function of several firm characteristics: size, market-to-book ratio, the ratio of book debt to book equity, quick ratio, dividend-payer status, existence of a credit rating, and Altman's Z-score. In the second stage, we estimate the relationship between the changes in hedge ratio and past changes in the price of gold conditional on the firm being an active hedger.

The results from the second stage of the Heckman procedure are presented in Table 5.5.[15] These results are consistent with our previous findings reported in Table 5.4. We continue to observe a significant negative relationship between changes in hedge ratio and past changes in the price of gold only when these changes are positive, and the relationship is the strongest

Table 5.4 Relationship between hedging and past gold returns: effect of initial hedge ratio

	One-year hedge ratio			Aggregate 3-year ratio scaled by production			Aggregate 3-year ratio scaled by reserves			Aggregate 5-year ratio scaled by reserves		
	(1)	(2)	(3)	(4)	(5)	(6)	(7)	(8)	(9)	(10)	(11)	(12)
Intercept	0.1291***	0.1077***	0.1119***	0.0552***	0.0528***	0.0559***	0.009	0.0039	0.004	0.0028	0.0022	0.0025
	−5.93	−3.2	−3.25	−4.28	−2.95	−3.01	−1.63	−0.44	−0.45	−0.38	−0.17	−0.19
RTNGOLD I_1	−0.3968**	−0.7120***	−0.7303	−0.2135**	−0.3963*	−0.4138	−0.0233	−0.0573*	−0.0611*	−0.028	−0.1022	−0.105
	(−2.42)	(−3.74)	(−3.71)	(−2.41)	(−1.92)	(−1.93)	(−0.74)	(−1.74)	(−1.82)	(−0.70)	(−1.55)	(−1.55)
RTNGOLD I_2	−0.1364	−0.2125	−0.1889	−0.0043	−0.0846	−0.0624	0.0164	−0.014	−0.0107	−0.0362	−0.0962	−0.0936
	(−0.86)	(−0.81)	(−0.71)	(−0.04)	(−0.54)	(−0.38)	−0.37	(−0.27)	(−0.20)	(−0.57)	(−0.87)	(−0.83)
HR_{t-1}	−0.4672***	−0.5360***	−0.5358***	−0.3298***	−0.3009***	−0.3009***	−0.3486***	−0.2531***	−0.2536***	−0.3499***	−0.3280***	−0.3285***
	(−13.13)	(−10.39)	(−10.38)	(−8.32)	(−7.00)	(−6.95)	(−9.67)	(−8.94)	(−9.00)	(−11.51)	(−9.63)	(−9.65)
CONTROLS		YES	YES		YES	YES		YES	YES		YES	YES
R^2	0.1509	0.1452	0.1504	0.0603	0.0721	0.0756	0.1265	0.0746	0.0766	0.1055	0.0956	0.0972
F-statistic	33.59	28	29.21	15.42	12	12.09	20.12	12.58	12.46	25.15	64.56	64.16
Observations	1,501	618	596	1,266	523	501	1,344	581	559	1,510	661	639
Clusters	93	37	36	88	36	35	81	38	37	82	38	37

Notes: The table presents the results of the panel regressions with firm fixed effects of hedge ratio changes in the current quarter, ΔHR_t, on past relative changes in the price of gold in the previous quarter, $RTNGOLD_{t-1} = \Delta GOLD_{t-2,t-1}/GOLD_{t-2}$, while allowing for the effect of the initial hedge ratio and asymmetry effects. Indicator variables I_1 (I_2) are equal to one if gold return was positive (negative), and HR_{t-1} is the level of the hedge ratio at the beginning of quarter. We control for changes in the following firm characteristics: *SIZ*, firm size measured as the logarithm of the market value of assets; *MB*, market-to-book ratio of assets; *DE*, ratio of book debt to book equity; *QCK*, quick ratio; *DIV*, dummy variable equal to one if the firm paid quarterly dividend; *RAT*, dummy variable equal to one if a firm reports a credit rating; and *Z*, Altman's Z-score. Models (3), (6), (9), and (12) are estimated on a reduced sample with non-hedgers excluded. Non-hedgers are firms that report no hedging over the entire sample period. All of the models include seasonal dummy variables and a time trend, and ***, **, * indicate significance at the 1%, 5% and 10% levels, respectively. Robust t-statistics accounting for cluster effects are given in parentheses.

Table 5.5 Relationship between hedging and past gold returns conditional on hedging activity: second stage of the two-step Heckman regression with selection

	One-year hedge ratio	Aggregate 3-year ratio scaled by production	Aggregate 3-year ratio scaled by reserves	Aggregate 5-year ratio scaled by reserves
	(1)	(2)	(3)	(4)
Intercept	0.1623***	0.0337	−0.0040	0.0053
	(3.71)	(1.36)	(−0.42)	(0.49)
RTNGOLD I_1	−1.1368***	−0.4991*	−0.0665	−0.1389
	(−4.13)	(−1.80)	(−1.20)	(−1.50)
RTNGOLD I_2	0.0805	−0.3583	−0.0584	−0.1552
	(0.25)	(−1.59)	(−0.80)	(−1.04)
HR_{t-1}	−0.2344***	−0.0705**	−0.1019***	−0.1907***
	(−3.27)	(−2.06)	(−2.95)	(−5.24)
Inverse Mills	−0.1254***	−0.0275**	−0.0072	−0.0259**
Ratio	(−3.08)	(−2.17)	(−1.47)	(−2.63)
CONTROLS	YES	YES	YES	YES
R^2	0.2161	0.1478	0.0646	0.1061
F-statistic	5.22	9.39	6.36	11.62
Observations	432	366	430	495
Clusters	31	27	33	34

Notes: The table reports the results of the second stage of the two-step Heckman procedure. In the first stage. We estimate the likelihood of hedging activity in a given quarter. In the second stage, we regress hedge ratio changes in the current quarter, ΔHR_t, on past relative changes in the price of gold in the previous quarter, $RTNGOLD_{t-1} = \Delta GOLD_{t-2,t-1}/GOLD_{t-2}$, while allowing for the effect of the initial hedge ratio and asymmetry effects. Indicator variables I_1 (I_2) are equal to one if gold return was positive (negative). We control for the level of the hedge ratio at the beginning of quarter as well as for changes in the following firm characteristics: firm size measured as the logarithm of the market value of assets; market-to-book ratio of assets; ratio of book debt to book equity; quick ratio; dummy variable equal to one if the firm paid quarterly dividend; dummy variable equal to one if a firm reports a credit rating; and Altman's Z-score. The regressions include the Inverse Mills ratio estimated on the first stage of the Heckman procedure. All of the models include seasonal dummy variables and a time trend, and ***, **, * indicate significance at the 1%, 5% and 10% levels, respectively. Robust t-statistics accounting for cluster effects are given in parentheses.

for the short-horizon hedge ratio. We observe no significant relationship between changes in hedge ratio and past decreases in the price of gold. As before, the initial level of the hedge ratio is negative and significant across all hedging horizons.

In all our specifications, we control for alternative explanations based on extant hedging theories that may help explain firms' hedge ratio adjustments following gold price changes. In particular, we control for firm characteristics such as liquidity and financial distress using a firm's quick ratio, leverage, Altman's Z-score, dividend dummy, and credit rating dummy.

These additional controls do not affect our principal results in any of the specifications that we employ. We also include these variables in a non-linear fashion, for example, by including the interaction of the change in liquidity with the change in gold price. These additional tests do not affect our findings either and are available upon request. We repeat all our tests using the dollar change in the price of gold in place of gold return, with robust results. Finally, our results are robust to including the gold dummy as a separate independent variable, to allow for the intercept term to vary with the direction of gold price change.

5.5 Conclusions

We add to the growing body of literature that documents the presence of managerial behavioral biases in a variety of corporate finance settings, including investment and capital structure policy, mergers and acquisitions, security offerings and investment bank relationships, by showing that the effect of these behavioral biases also extends to corporate hedging decisions. We study how firms change their hedge positions in response to past changes in the gold price, using a ten-year sample of North American gold mining firms that has been widely studied in the literature. Consistent with anecdotal evidence, we find that managers promptly and systematically decrease their hedge positions following past increases in the gold price, while we do not find a similar prompt increase in their hedges following past gold price declines. We interpret this evidence as consistent with managerial loss aversion and mental accounting; in other words, managers act to minimize losses from derivatives positions, while paying less regard to the performance of the underlying position. Our findings provide some of the first evidence that corporate hedging strategies are affected by managerial behavioral biases, and suggest that recognizing the presence of these biases will help bridge the gap between the theory and practice of corporate risk management.

Appendix

Variable Notations and Definitions

ΔGOLD is the change in the price of gold over the quarter.

Hedge Ratios

HR1 – HR5 are the hedge ratios from one- to five-year maturities, respectively;

A3 is the aggregate hedge ratio that aggregates the hedge positions over one-, two-, and three-year horizons, scaled by the expected production;

A3R is the aggregate hedge ratio that aggregates the hedge positions over one-, two-, and three-year horizons, scaled by gold reserves;
A5R is the aggregate hedge ratio that aggregates the hedge positions over one-, two-, three-, four- and five-year horizons, scaled by gold reserves.

Firm Characteristics

SIZ is the logarithm of the market value of assets ($ million);
MB is the market-to-book ratio of assets;
DE is the ratio of book debt to book equity;
QCK is the quick ratio;
DIV is a dummy variable equal to one if the firm paid quarterly dividend;
RAT is a dummy variable equal to one if a firm reports a credit rating;
Z is the Altman's (1968) Z-score (higher value of Z corresponds to lower probability of bankruptcy).

Notes

We thank the editor, Peter MacKay for inviting this chapter and Seth Hoelscher for research assistance.

1. See, for example, Stulz (1984), Smith and Stulz (1985), Froot, Scharfstein and Stein (1993), DeMarzo and Duffie (1995), Leland (1998), Mello and Parsons (2000), Chidambaran, Fernando and Spindt (2001), and Mackay and Moeller (2007).
2. See, for example, Tufano (1996), Mian (1996), Geczy, Minton and Schrand (1997), Graham and Smith (1999), Haushalter (2000), and Graham and Rogers (2002).
3. See, for example, Dolde (1993), Stulz (1996), Bodnar, Hayt and Marston (1998), and Glaum (2002).
4. See Adam and Fernando (2006) and Brown, Crabb and Haushalter (2006).
5. Baker, Ruback, and Wurgler (2007) provide a comprehensive review of the literature on behavioral corporate finance.
6. Studies include Roll (1986), Loughran and Ritter (2002), Heaton (2002), Ljungqvist and Wilhelm (2005), Malmendier and Tate (2005, 2008), Ben-David, Graham and Harvey (2007), Billett and Qian (2008), Goel and Thakor (2008), Sautner and Weber (2009), and Gervais, Heaton and Odean (2009).
7. Adam, Fernando and Golubeva (2012) provide evidence of managerial overconfidence in the context of corporate risk management.
8. Loss aversion has been commonly associated in the investments literature with a reluctance to sell losing investments, that is, the disposition effect (Shefrin and Statman, 1985), which arises when the heightened sensitivity to losses generates an attempt to gamble out of a sure loss (unless the sensitivity to losses is itself dynamically affected by the loss, in which case the disposition effect may not obtain (Thaler and Johnson, 1990)). However, drawing a parallel to the disposition effect is not straightforward in the context of corporate hedging since one cannot clearly say that keeping a hedge open is more of a gamble than closing it out. Nonetheless, the basic premise of loss aversion – the higher sensitivity to losses than to gains of equal magnitude – implies that managers will more likely notice and act upon a derivatives loss associated with corporate hedging.

9. While some post-2000 hedging data is available from accounting disclosures and other sources, this data lacks the level of detail and consistency across firms that has made the Scotia McLeod survey data invaluable for many empirical studies of corporate hedging, including Tufano (1996, 1998), Fehle and Tsyplakov (2005), Adam and Fernando (2006), and Brown, Crabb and Haushalter (2006).
10. See, for example, Ben-David, Graham and Harvey (2007) and Malmendier and Tate (2005).
11. The FAS 133 accounting standard, which made a significant departure from past accounting practice by requiring derivatives contracts to be marked to market, could also potentially affect the way managers react to market movements. However, our findings are unlikely to be affected by this change since our sample ends around the same time FAS 133 went into effect (in mid-1999).
12. While we report regression results that employ gold return as the independent variable, we also repeated our tests using dollar changes in the price of gold. The results of those tests are available upon request and are similar to the results obtained using gold returns.
13. Our finding of especially strong results when we use the short-term hedge ratio (up to one-year maturity) is consistent with prior studies showing that hedgers are more active in the shorter-term maturities (see, for example, Bodnar, Hayt and Marston, 1998).
14. We also run the first stage estimation using only the first condition (non-zero hedge ratios) to define hedging activity and obtain similar results. They are not reported due to space constraints but are available on request.
15. The results from the first stage are not presented here for brevity but are available from the authors. The first-stage results show that firms that exhibit hedging activity are large firms with low growth opportunities (as indicated by low market-to-book ratios), conservative leverage policies, and higher financial constraints/low liquidity. These results are consistent with the previously reported findings by Geczy, Minton and Schrand (1997), Bodnar, Hayt and Marston (1998) and Haushalter (2000).

References

Adam, T. R. (2002). Do Firms Use Derivatives to Reduce their Dependence on External Capital Markets? *European Finance Review,* 6, 163–87.

Adam, T. R. and Fernando, C. S. (2006). Hedging, Speculation, and Shareholder Value. *Journal of Financial Economics,* 81, 283–309.

Adam, T. R., Fernando, C. S., and Golubeva, E. (2012). Managerial Overconfidence and Corporate Risk Management. Working Paper.

Altman, E. I. (1968). Financial Ratios, Discriminant Analysis and the Prediction of Corporate Bankruptcy, *Journal of Finance,* 23, 589–609.

Baker, M., Ruback, R. S. and Wurgler, J. (2007). Behavioral Corporate Finance: A Survey, in Eckbo, E. (ed.) *The Handbook of Corporate Finance: Empirical Corporate Finance.* Elsevier/North Holland: New York.

Barberis, N. and Huang, M. (2001). Mental Accounting, Loss Aversion, and Individual Stock Returns. *Journal of Finance,* 56, 1247–92.

Ben-David, I., Graham, J. R., and Harvey, C. R. (2007). Managerial Overconfidence and Corporate Policies. Working Paper.

Billett, M. T. and Qian, Y. (2008). Are Overconfident CEOs Born or Made? Evidence of Self-Attribution Bias from Frequent Acquirers. *Management Science,* 54, 1037–51.
Bodnar, G. N., Hayt, G. S., and Marston, R. C. (1998). Wharton Survey of Derivatives Usage by US Non-Financial Firms. *Financial Management,* 27, 70–91.
Brown, G. W., Crabb, P. R. and Haushalter, D. (2006). Are Firms Successful at Selective Hedging? *Journal of Business,* 79, 2925–49.
Chidambaran, N. K., Fernando, C. S. and Spindt, P. A. (2001). Credit Enhancement through Financial Engineering: Freeport McMoRan's Gold-denominated Depositary Shares. *Journal of Financial Economics,* 60, 487–528.
Coleman, L. (2007). Risk and Decision Making by Finance Executives: A Survey Study. *International Journal of Managerial Finance,* 1, 108–24.
DeMarzo, P. M., and Duffie, D. (1995). Corporate Incentives for Hedging and Hedge Accounting. *Review of Financial Studies,* 8, 743–72.
Dolde, W. (1993). The Trajectory of Corporate Financial Risk Management. *Journal of Applied Corporate Finance,* 6, 33–41.
Fehle, F. and Tsyplakov, S. (2005). Dynamic Risk Management: Theory and Evidence. *Journal of Financial Economics,* 78, 3–47.
Froot, K. A., Scharfstein, D. S. and Stein, J. C. (1993). Risk Management: Coordinating Corporate Investment and Financing Policies. *Journal of Finance,* 48, 1629–58.
Géczy, C. C., Minton, B. A. and Schrand, C. (1997). Why Firms Use Currency Derivatives. *Journal of Finance,* 52, 1323–54.
Gervais, S., Heaton, J. B. and Odean, T. (2009). Overconfidence, Compensation Contracts and Labor Markets. Working Paper.
Glaum, M. (2002). The Determinants of Selective Exchange-Risk Management – Evidence from German Non-Financial Corporations. *Journal of Applied Corporate Finance,* 14, 108–21.
Goel, A. and Thakor, A. (2008). Overconfidence, CEO Selection and Corporate Governance. *Journal of Finance,* 63, 2737–84.
Graham, J. and Rogers, D. (2002). Do Firms Hedge in Response to Tax Incentives. *Journal of Finance,* 57, 815–38.
Graham, J. R. and Smith, C. W. (1999). Tax Incentives to Hedge. *Journal of Finance,* 54, 2241–62.
Grinblatt, M. and Han, B. (2005). Prospect Theory, Mental Accounting, and Momentum. *Journal of Financial Economics,* 78, 311–39.
Haushalter, G. D. (2000). Financing Policy, Basis Risk, and Corporate Hedging: Evidence from Oil and Gas Producers. *Journal of Finance,* 55, 107–52.
Heaton, J. B. (2002). Managerial Optimism and Corporate Finance. *Financial Management,* Summer, 33–45.
Heckman, J. J. (1979). Sample Selection as a Specification Error. *Econometrica,* 47, 153–61.
Jin, Y. and Jorion, P. (2006). Firm Value and Hedging: Evidence from US Oil and Gas Producers. *Journal of Finance,* 61, 893–919.
Kahneman, D. and Tversky, A. (1979). Prospect Theory: An Analysis of Decisions under Risk. *Econometrica,* 47, 313–27.
Kahneman, D. and Tversky, A. (1984). Choices, Values and Frames. *American Psychologist,* 39, 341–50.
Leland, H. E. (1998). Agency Costs, Risk Management, and Capital Structure. *Journal of Finance,* 53, 1213–43.
Ljungqvist, A. and Wilhelm, W. J., Jr. (2005). Does Prospect Theory Explain IPO Market Behavior? *Journal of Finance,* 60, 1759–90.

Loughran, T. and Ritter, J. R. (2002). Why Don't Issuers Get Upset About Leaving Money on the Table in IPOs? *Review of Financial Studies,* 15, 413–43.

MacKay, P. and Moeller, S. B. (2007). The Value of Corporate Risk Management. *Journal of Finance,* 62, 1379–419.

Malmendier, U. and Tate, G. (2005). CEO Overconfidence and Corporate Investment. *Journal of Finance,* 60, 2661–700.

Malmendier, U. and Tate, G. (2008). Who Makes Acquisitions? CEO Overconfidence and the Market's Reaction. *Journal of Financial Economics,* 89, 20–43.

Mello, A. and Parsons, J. (2000). Hedging and Liquidity. *Review of Financial Studies,* 13, 127–53.

Mian, S. (1996). Evidence on Corporate Hedging Policy. *Journal of Financial and Quantitative Analysis,* 31, 419–39.

Roll, R. (1986). The Hubris Hypothesis of Corporate Takeovers. *Journal of Business,* 59, 197–216.

Sautner, Z. and Weber, M. (2009). How Do Managers Behave in Stock Option Plans? Clinical Evidence from Exercise and Survey Data. *Journal of Financial Research,* 32, 123–55.

Shefrin, H. and Statman, M. (1985). The Disposition to Sell Winners Too Early and Ride Losers Too Long: Theory and Evidence. *Journal of Finance,* 40, 777–90.

Smith, C. W. and Stulz, R. M. (1985). The Determinants of Firms' Hedging Policies. *Journal of Financial and Quantitative Analysis,* 20, 391–405.

Stulz, R. M. (1984). Optimal Hedging Policies. *Journal of Financial and Quantitative Analysis,* 19, 127–40.

Stulz, R. M. (1996). Rethinking Risk Management. *Journal of Applied Corporate Finance,* 9, 8–24.

Thaler, R. H. (1980). Towards a Positive Theory of Consumer Choice. *Journal of Economic Behavior and Organization,* 1, 39–60.

Thaler, R. H. (1985). Mental Accounting and Consumer Choice. *Marketing Science,* 4, 199–214.

Thaler, R. H. and Johnson, E. J. (1990). Gambling with the House Money and Trying to Break Even: The Effects of Prior Outcomes on Risky Choice. *Management Science,* 36, 643–60.

Tufano, P. (1996). Who Manages Risk? An Empirical Examination of Risk Management Practices in the Gold Mining Industry. *Journal of Finance,* 51, 1097–137.

Tufano, P. (1998). The Determinants of Stock Price Exposure: Financial Engineering and the Gold Mining Industry. *Journal of Finance,* 53, 1051–52.

Tversky, A. and Kahneman, D. (1991). Loss Aversion in Riskless Choice: A Reference-Dependent Model. *Quarterly Journal of Economics,* 106, 1039–61.

Part II

Intermediaries

6
Does Securitization Affect Banks' Liquidity Risk? The Case of Italy

Francesca Battaglia and Maria Mazzuca

6.1 Introduction

During the decade 2003–13, credit securitization has greatly developed in Italy. Theory and empirical literature have investigated many issues related to this topic, such as its capacity to contribute to achieving capital arbitrage (Calomiris and Mason, 2004) or its efficacy as a risk management technique (Cantor and Rouyer, 2000). Nonetheless, many questions remain open, especially in reference to the Italian market, which has not yet been sufficiently studied. Furthermore, in recent months, the interest of academics, managers and regulators towards this financial technique has increased due to the financial crisis (which started in the subprime mortgages sector in the US).

The considerations above explain the potential interest in this topic. The present study aims to more deeply investigate the real value and consequences of credit securitization. We believe that the contribution/consequences – both in macroeconomic and microeconomic terms (more closely observed in this study) – that this financial technique has for the originator banks is not yet well understood.

We intend to explore the relationship between securitization and liquidity position in banks by answering the following research questions: does securitization affect the originator banks? Does securitization produce effects on a bank's liquidity? We investigate the effects of securitizations on liquidity by focusing on a sample composed of all the Italian banks that placed at least one securitization during the period 2000–9. The choice of time-frame is based on the fact that in 1999 the Italian law on loan securitization was introduced. Our dataset is hand-collected and original; moreover, it contains updated information on all securitizations placed by the Italian banks during the period considered.

If we turn to analyzing the effects of securitization on banks' risk, we find that the relationship is not obvious. Via securitization, banks should transfer part of the risk embedded in their portfolios of assets to other subjects. In this sense, the ex post risk of the originator banks should be reduced. On the other hand, the ex post risk of the bank depends on the use of the liquidity originated via securitization. In fact, the ex post risk of the bank does not decrease if the originator bank invests this liquidity in risky (or riskier than before) assets. The same applies if banks use the proceeds to expand their loans business, thus incurring more systemic risk (Franke and Krahnen, 2005). Furthermore, we have to consider the technical and economic goals that drive banks' securitization activities. For instance, under the old Basel Capital Accord, banks had incentives to transfer the less risky assets, maintaining in their portfolio the riskier ones, in order to achieve regulatory capital arbitrage (Passmore and Sparks, 2004; Calem and LaCour-Little, 2004; Ambrose et al., 2005; Calomiris and Mason, 2004).

To summarize, although the immediate effect of each (cash) securitization is represented by an increase in liquidity for originators, it is not evident that this liquidity improves the overall liquidity position of the securitizing banks. Our research questions come from the previous considerations and from the knowledge that, so far, there are no other studies dealing with this topic.

To test our research hypotheses, using different specifications and estimation methods, we adopt an ordered probit model, in which the changes of the originator banks' liquidity are linked to a set of regressors, including two securitization dummy variables (securitization and previous securitization), plus a vector of control variables. All variables are lagged by one year. To test the robustness of our results, we perform several sensitivity analyses. First, following Berger et al. (2010) we use different cutoffs to define what constitutes a substantial change in liquidity position. Then, we run regressions using an ordered logit. In all cases, referring to the key independent variables (securitization dummy and previous securitization dummy), we obtain results that are similar to the main findings and that confirm the positive relationship between securitization and liquidity. Finally, we perform additional analyses in which we run regressions separately for the pre-crisis period (2000–6) and the crisis period (2007–9). Although the small number of observations means that it has not been possible to develop reliable estimates for the period after 2006, the results referring to the pre-crisis period (2000–6) generally confirm the relevance of the securitization variables for the liquidity of the originator banks.

Our study contributes to the empirical literature on the effects of securitization for banks in several ways. First, we analyze the relationship between securitization and the liquidity risk of the originator banks. To our knowledge there are no previous studies focusing on this item. Second, despite the importance of the Italian securitization market, there is a research void on it. To date, Agostino and Mazzuca (2011) are the only authors to have analyzed the securitization determinants in the Italian market. The other empirical studies, which focus on the drivers and/or motivations for securitization, concern the US market or, more recently, Europe. There are still very few studies that refer to specific European countries (Martínez-Solano et al., 2009; Cardone-Riportella et al., 2010) both consider the Spanish market). In the light of these considerations, we believe that it is interesting to consider other geographical contexts with differently developed capital markets, different banking sector structures and, in some cases, different legislation and regulation systems. Third, to develop our analysis, we use an original and updated dataset. Furthermore, unlike previous studies, our analysis covers the period 2000–9, including the financial crisis years. We believe that this represents an important research opportunity. Finally, we apply an ordered probit model to test the effects of securitization. To our knowledge, this methodology has not been employed in the past in this context.

The remainder of the chapter is organized as follows. In Section 6.2, we analyze the relevant literature. In Section 6.3, we describe our estimation framework, sample and data, and variables. In Section 6.4, we present and discuss the empirical analysis and its results. In Section 6.5, we report the results of the additional analysis and the robustness tests. Finally, in Section 6.6, we summarize and conclude.

6.2 Literature review

The studies on securitization can be grouped into two main streams of literature: those dealing with the theory of securitization (why banks securitize) and those dealing with the effects of securitization. The first group of studies has shown that banks can use securitization to transfer/reduce the risk to free up equity or to reduce capital requirements (also for possible arbitrages), to increase the diversification of their portfolio, to increase liquidity/restructure assets and liabilities, and to enhance their loan portfolios (Greenbaum and Thakor, 1987; Pavel and Phillis, 1987; Donahoo and Shaffer, 1988; Wolfe, 2000; DeMarzo, 2005; Agostino and Mazzuca, 2011).

For the purposes of the present work, studies focusing on the effects of securitization are more relevant. They consider the phenomenon according to different perspectives. In detail, a first stream of this literature deals with the effects of securitization on the banks' lending activity and on the monetary policy (Loutskina and Strahan, 2009; Estrella, 2002; Altunbas et al., 2010).

Other studies concern the potential effects of securitization on financial stability. Hansel and Krahnen (2007) analyze the European Collateralized Debt Obligation (CDO) and show that the credit risk transfer activity enhances the systemic risk (equity beta) of the issuing bank, and that overall credit securitization increases the bank's risk appetite. Uhde and Michalak (2010) study securitization and systemic risk in the European banking sector by analyzing a sample of European listed banks from the period 1997–2007.

They find that securitization has a negative impact on the banks' financial soundness, a positive impact on leverage and return volatility and a negative effect on profitability. Nijiskens and Wagner (2011) build up two separate datasets, one for Collateralized Loan Obligation (CLO) and another for Credit Default Swap (CDS) banks, and analyze the two sub-samples during the period 1997–2006. They estimate the relationship between credit risk transfer activities (CLO issues and CDS trading) by banks and the systemic risk measured by the issuer/trading banks' beta (using an augmented Capital Asset Pricing Model (CAPM)). Their results show that, after their first use of CLOs and CDSs, the betas of the issuer/trading banks increase significantly.

From a microeconomic point of view – the one adopted in this chapter – several other studies investigate: (1) the effects of securitization on the pricing of loans with reference to the primary mortgage market, (2) the positive effects of securitization on the performance (profitability) of the originator banks, and (3) the relationship between securitization and risk for the originator banks. Studies concerning the third point are more relevant for the purposes of the present work. Dionne and Harchaoui (2003) examine the Canadian financial sector and conclude that securitization has a negative effect on capital ratios and that there exists a positive link between a bank's risk and securitization. Also, Uzun and Webb's (2007) findings go in the same direction. The results of the previous studies provide evidence for the so-called capital arbitrage theory.

6.3 Estimation framework, data and variables

In this section, we first describe our regression framework, then examine the sample and the data, and finally focus on the explanation of the key independent variables (securitization and previous securitization), the dependent variable (changes in banks' liquidity position) and the control variables.

6.3.1 Estimation framework

To address whether and how securitization affects banks' liquidity, by adopting an ordered probit model, we regress changes in banks' liquidity on a securitization dummy, a previous securitization dummy and a set of control variables. The employment of an ordinal-dependent variable allows us to analyze the behavior of the bank *i*, in terms of probability, distinguishing between changes in bank behavior and relatively constant behavior. In particular, focusing on changes of 2 percent,[1] our dependent variable takes on the following values:

a. one if the bank experienced a drop in risk-taking or liquidity creation (relative to the previous year) of more than 2 percent (DECR);
b. two if the banks' risk-taking and their liquidity creation moved within a range of +/−2 percent (CONST);

c. three if the banks' risk-taking and their liquidity creation increased by more than 2 percent (INCR).

We estimate the following model specification:

$$\Pr(y_{it} = j) = \Phi(X'_{i,t-1}\beta), \quad j = 1,2,3 \tag{6.1}$$

in which the ordered outcomes are modeled to arise sequentially as the latent variable, y*, crosses progressively higher thresholds.[2] In detail, $y_{it} = 1$, 2 or 3 depending on whether the change in risk-taking and liquidity of bank *i* at time *t* respectively decreases, remains within a definite range or increases; Pr is the probability, Φ is the standard cumulative normal probability distribution, $X_{i,t-1}$ is the vector of securitization (dummy) variables and control variables (described in Section 6.3.3), all lagged by one year; as usual, β parameters are estimated by maximum likelihood.

In the ordered probit model the sign of the regression parameters, β, can be immediately interpreted as determining whether the latent variable, y*, increases with the regressor. If β_j is positive, then an increase in $X_{i,j}$ necessarily decreases the probability of being in the lowest category ($y_i = 1$) and increases the probability of being in the highest category ($y_i = 3$). So, referring to the risk-taking, a positive β for the securitization dummy (or the previous securitization dummy) indicates that an increase of these variables corresponds to an increased probability that the bank will belong to the upper risk-taking category (that is, greater than 2 percent). Conversely, a negative β indicates that an increase in securitization variables determines a decrease in the probability that bank *i* will belong to the higher risk-taking group. All regressors are lagged by one year for two main reasons. First, we assume that the analyzed independent variables fully affect the risk indicator (that is, the dependent variable) only in the year following the considered event (please note that our dependent variable is represented by a risk-based accounting ratio); second, recognizing that this may not be sufficient, we intend to address a potential endogeneity concern in our analysis.

6.3.2 Sample and data

To test the relationship between securitization and banks' liquidity (liquidity position), we first need to separate all the banks that placed at least one cash securitization[3] during the period considered (2000–9), from banks that did not. To this end, we employ the Securitisation.it[4] database, providing information on all the cash securitizations carried out from 1999 onwards. From this database we draw a list of deals that solely originated from banks.

We mostly employ microdata from the banks' financial statements (balance sheets and income statements) and, additionally, some non-accounting information, such as the status of the bank on the official listing and the measure of capital for regulatory purposes. All these data are drawn from the Bankscope-Bureau van Djik database. With reference to the M&As operations made up by the originator banks, we draw information both from the Bankscope-Bureau van Djik database and from the banks' financial statements.

Our sample includes all commercial banks with headquarters (including the registered office) in Italy, for which the data needed to estimate the econometric model were available. More precisely, our sample banks are all the intermediaries present in the supervisory register of the Bank of Italy (according to article No. 106 of TUB, the Italian Banking Law) and classified as commercial banks (and incorporated as limited liability companies) or savings banks (*banche popolari/casse di risparmio*). Cooperative credit banks (BCCs) are not included in the sample because of their special nature. In fact, the behavior of cooperative banks is special in terms of both activity and size, and a comparative analysis between them and other banks would incur the risk of providing biased results. Furthermore, in Italy these banks do not engage in securitization as a single originator; rather, they participate in multi-originator transactions. Presumably, this choice depends on the fact that smaller institutions tend to benefit from jointly pooling assets; for example, they may obtain a better rating because of the added diversification (Martin-Oliver and Saurina, 2007). Because the model we estimate is applicable only to separate, individual banks, it would be difficult to apply our research methodology to Italian cooperative banks. For the same reason, we do not consider other multi-lender transactions.

It should be noted that, due to the lack of many values in different years for the different variables, the final sample is composed of 276 observations relating to 49 banks in the period 2000–9.

6.3.3 Variables

6.3.3.1 Key independent variables: securitization dummy and previous securitization dummy

To capture the securitization activity placed by the Italian banks during the analyzed period, in model (1) we consider two different securitization dummy variables. First, we include a securitization dummy (SEC), which is coded one if the specific bank securitizes in the considered year, and zero otherwise. Since we suppose that securitization begins to produce its effects in a reasonably short period of time, we lag this variable by one year (as mentioned above, the same applies to all other independent variables).

The other securitization regressor (PREV_SEC) accounts for the previous securitizations developed by the considered bank. This variable is coded one if the bank placed at least one securitization in the years before the year considered, and zero otherwise. This dummy variable is also lagged by one year. We decide to add this variable because a consolidated expertise may represent an incentive to use the securitization channel once again (Agostino and Mazzuca, 2011).

According to Santomero and Trester (1998), we expect that securitization (and previous securitization) produces positive effects on banks' liquidity position (negative on banks' liquidity risk).

6.3.3.2 Dependent variable: the liquidity ratio

To capture the effects of securitization on banks' liquidity risk we use an accounting-based indicator: the liquidity ratio (liquid assets/customer and short-term funding, LIQUID, that here has to be considered as an inverse measure of liquidity risk). Since previous studies dealing with the effects of securitization have not specifically analyzed this feature, it is not possible to refer to papers that have already employed this indicator.

6.3.3.3 Control variables

Since the liquidity position of a bank could be affected by factors other than securitization, we include a set of control variables in model (1). All of the control variables (except for dummy variables) are measured in terms of changes. For ease of exposition, we discuss these variables below according to their levels.

To control for specific bank characteristics, we include variables that might explain differences in banks' risks. In detail, we consider the following accounting-based variables: the loans ratio (total loans/total assets, LOANS), the equity ratio (equity/total assets percent, EQUITY_RATIO), the total assets (natural log of total assets, SIZE), the impaired loan ratio (impaired loans/gross loans, IMP_LOANS), and the return on equity (net income/total assets, ROA).[5]

The direction of the expected relation between the previous variables and the dependent one varies from one regressor to another. The expected direction of the relation with the LOANS variable is negative for the liquidity position (and positive for liquidity risk).

The relation between risk and capital is not obvious. Stolz (2002, p. 17) states that 'theories related to banks' choice of risk and capital levels suggest that risk and capital decisions are simultaneously determined and interrelated... Besides, banks may have an incentive to increase portfolio risk and/or leverage due to moral hazard resulting from incomplete contracting and/or hidden action together with limited liability and deposit insurance. Countervailing effects may come from managerial risk aversion, and dynamic considerations such as the loss of the bank's charter value in case of bankruptcy. Competition also plays a role via its impact on bank rents.' It follows that we are not sure about the expected direction of the relation between EQUITY_RATIO and bank's risk.

The SIZE variable is expected to be positively correlated with the liquidity risk because a larger bank may have a greater capacity to absorb risk, or because some banks are 'too big to fail' (Berger et al., 2010). On the other hand, due to the size-related diversification benefits and economies of scale, the larger banks should be less risky. Furthermore, the managers of larger banks could take advantage of the benefits of risk diversification to further push the risk profile of the bank (Hughes et al., 2001). Also, the results of the empirical literature produced mixed results, and it seems there is no general support for a specific relationship between the size of the bank and its risk level (for example, De Nicolò, 2000; Stever, 2007). It follows that we have no specific expectations about the direction of this relation.

The IMP_LOANS variable is employed to control for portfolio quality. This regressor should be negatively related to liquidity (and positively to liquidity risk). In fact, since it represents a proxy of the deterioration of quality loans, the greater its impact, the lower the banks' liquidity.

Finally, we include ROA to control for profitability, and expect a negative sign because it is assumed that the most profitable banks are also those who are employed in more profitable activities, which are typically characterized by a lower degree of liquidity (Kwan and Eisenbeis, 1996; Laeven and Levine, 2009).

Furthermore, we add other control variables that do not have an accounting nature: the Tier 1 ratio (TIER1); the M&As – a dummy variable, accounting for the banks' involvement in M&As; and the crisis dummy variable (CRISIS), accounting for the presence of the financial crisis.

We can apply to TIER1 the same considerations used for the bank's capitalization. Nonetheless, the literature has studied this relation deeply, with a focus on the different incentives deriving from (tighter) capital requirements for banks to increase/decrease their risk. Higher capital requirements should mitigate the moral hazard problem. Some authors focus on the strengthened bank monitoring incentives that accompany higher bank capital (for example, Allen et al., 2011; Mehran and Thakor, 2011). On the other hand, the relation between capital and risk could be positive. For example, Koehn and Santomero (1980), in examining (in the pre-Basel scenario) individual bank behavior with reference to capital requirement (without an imposed asset composition), state that banks could react to an increase in capital requirement by shifting into riskier portfolios. Furthermore, Calomiris and Kahn (1991) also show that a capital structure with sufficiently high demand deposits (and by implication lower equity) leads to more effective monitoring of bank managers by informed depositors, and hence a smaller likelihood of bad investment decisions. Thus, banks with higher capital, and consequently a lower proportion of the portfolio financed by demandable deposits, may operate with higher credit risk and insolvency risk. Morrison and White (2005) argue that if banks do not have enough equity at stake, they may be tempted to make excessively risky investments. For a survey of the theoretical and empirical literature, see, for example, Stolz (2002). As a conclusion, we are not sure about the expected direction of the relation between TIER1 and bank's risk.

The M&As variable is a dummy coded one if bank *i* is involved in an M&A in the analyzed year, and zero otherwise. In general, the relationship between the M&A variable and risk is expected to be negative, due to the decrease in bad loans as a result of more efficient screening and monitoring activities (Focarelli et al., 1999). As a consequence, the specific relation between M&As and liquidity risk is expected to be negative, while for the dependent variable of model (1) the expected relation should be positive, due to the increased chances for the merged banks to finance their liquidity needs (Carletti et al., 2003).

The CRISIS variable is a dummy coded one during the year 2007–9 and zero in the previous years (2000–6). The expected relationship between crisis and the bank's liquidity risk (liquidity position) is positive (negative). There could be several reasons for this. For example, we could expect a positive (negative) relationship due to the fact that, during the crisis, banks have come to rely more on short-term funding (Gertler et al., 2011), or because banks no longer have access to the interbank market.

6.4 Empirical analysis and results

Table 6.1 summarizes some relevant statistical information for the key independent variables, for the dependent variable, and for the control variables. While the regressions are run based on changes, we report means of levels and changes for all the variables.

Because many of our variables have large positive and negative outliers, we winsorize them at 5 percent. Winsorizing at 5 percent involves assigning to outliers beyond the 5th and 95th percentiles a value equal to the value of the 5th or 95th percentile in order to limit the influence of outliers on the regression. In all cases, the observations are clustered at the bank level. In fact, because in our sample the same bank may be present in different years, it seems appropriate to allow the errors to be correlated for the same intermediary over time. Moreover, by doing so, we obtain standard errors that are robust with respect to heteroskedasticity.[6]

As in the probit models, the direction of the coefficient relationships only provides information on the direction of the impact of each determinant (independent variables) on the probability that the bank will become riskier; to obtain the direct impact of each explanatory variable on the probability that the event of interest will occur (which depends on the value taken by all other regressors included in the equation), one has to compute the

Table 6.1 Summary statistics for the dependent variable, the key independent variables and the control variables

	Variable	Obs.	Mean of level	Mean of change
Dependent variable	Liquidity	428	32.24435	0.6665274
Key independent variables	Sec	500	0.274	n.a.
	Prev_sec	500	0.632	n.a.
Control variables	Loans	450	0.6844478	0.0963422
	Equity_ratio	454	0.1483919	0.0621452
	Size	455	15.86279	0.0094635
	Imp_loans	417	3.504574	0.8864065
	Tier1	435	9.869195	0.0306219
	Roa	450	0.5700048	0.7556208
	Crisis	500	0.3	n.a.
	M&A	500	0.158	n.a.

Notes: Sec is a dummy coded one if a bank places at least one securitization in a year, zero otherwise; Prev_sec is a dummy coded one if a bank places at least one securitization in the period before the analyzed year, zero otherwise; Crisis is a dummy coded one during the year 2007–9 and zero in the previous years (2000–6); M&A is a dummy coded one if the bank *i* is involved in a M&A in the analyzed year and zero otherwise; Size is measured as ln of total assets; the other variables are described in Section 3.3. Continuous variables are winsorized at 5 percent.

Source: Authors' elaborations.

marginal effect of each explanatory variable by assuming a given (representative) value for all other variables. In the present work, for the computation of each partial effect, we consider all other variables at their sample mean. We do not need to standardize the regressors, because they are all expressed in the same measurement units.[7] In Panel A of Table 6.2, we show only the marginal effect referring to class three, which corresponds to the upper liquidity class where changes are greater than 2 percent.

Table 6.2 reports the results obtained by estimating model (1). The dependent variable is represented by changes in the liquidity ratio of 2 percent. Panel A summarizes the main results of the regression, which refers to the overall time period (2000–9), while Panel B shows the estimates referring to the sub-period 2000–6.

The main regression coefficients (Panel A) demonstrate that securitization is positive and significant at 5 percent, while the variable that considers the previous securitizations is positive and significant at 10 percent. In general, the results provide evidence that securitization produces positive effects on the bank's liquidity position, and thus negative effects on the bank's liquidity risk. Estimates suggest that the immediate effect of securitizations, consisting of an increase in liquidity, tends to persist at least for the year

Table 6.2 Ordered probit models focusing on liquidity changes of 2 percent for the overall period (2000–9) and for the pre-crisis years (2000–6)

	Panel A: Liquidity Δ 2% Period: 2000–9			Panel B: Liquidity Δ 2% Period: 2000–6	
	Coefficients (1)	Robust standard errors (2)	Marg. effects. (3)	Coefficients (1)	Robust standard errors (2)
Key variables					
Sec	0.5844828**	0.2629084	0.0010334	0.7119733**	0.3312663
Prev_sec	0.6590299*	0.3908019	0.00055	0.9212524**	0.4446664
Control variables					
Loans	0.1192852*	0.0718632	0.0001151	1.69793*	0.8693669
Equity_ratio	0.7621858**	0.3679568	0.0007351	0.2399359	0.4379972
Size	1.724459	6.868621	0.0016632	15.54873**	7.387916
Imp_loans	0.0231053	0.017698	0.0000223	0.1632805***	0.0574797
Tier1	0.1643187	0.2900978	0.0001585	−0.2264371	0.5215158
Roa	0.0006236	0.0113097	6.01*E* − 07	0.0040653	0.0087573
M&A	−9.561826***	1.787112	−0.0380539	−7.133093***	0.257551
Crisis	0.4204033	0.5987503	0.0005681		
Number di obs	276			188	
Log pseudolikelihood	−42.392634			−16.718591	
Number of banks (clusters)	46			41	
Prob > chi^2	0			0	
Pseudo R^2	0.1911			0.4409	

Notes: Dependent variable – Panels A and B: changes in liquidity (Δ liquidity) of 2 percent.
(a) We estimate ordered probit models for changes in liquidity of 2 percent. The dependent variable takes on the value one if there was a drop in liquidity of at least 2 percent relative to the previous year, it takes on the value two if liquidity remained within the interval +/−2 percent, and it takes on the value three if there was an increase in liquidity of more than 2 percent; (b) all explanatory variables are lagged one year, except the crisis dummy; (c) all the explanatory variables (except the dummy variables) are measured in changes; (d) columns 2 of Panel A and Panel B report robust standard errors; (e) column 3 of Panel A presents the marginal effects referring to the outcome three, that is the upper liquidity category (changes > 2 percent); (f) time effects are included in all estimation. * Significant at 10 percent. ** Significant at 5 percent. *** Significant at 1 percent.

Source: Authors' elaboration.

following the operation: the securitization for the banks' originator determines a reduction of the illiquidity of the portfolio (Santomero and Trester, 1998). These findings are consistent with Agostino and Mazzuca (2011) and with Martin-Oliver and Saurina (2007), who focused on the Italian and Spanish markets, respectively. Both studies, in terms of analyzing the securitization drivers, demonstrate that the main determinant of securitization is represented by the opportunity of increasing liquidity, and hence also the possibility of diversifying the originators' sources of funding. A further explanation could be related to the use of the liquidity coming from securitizations. Banks may employ this additional liquidity for other purposes that are not consistent with the increase of bank's profitability, such as the reduction of leverage or the restructuring of the assets portfolio in order to make it more liquid.

The results of the main regression show the strongly negative influence of the M&As variable (positive relationship with liquidity risk). The relationship of this regressor is unexpected. Unlike the previous literature (Carletti et al., 2003), it seems that the Italian banks involved in M&As do not achieve advantages in terms of liquidity, but experience a relevant liquidity problem. Furthermore, the EQUITY_RATIO is positively significant at 5 percent, and the better-capitalized banks seem to be more liquid. Finally, the LOANS regressor is marginally significant with an unexpected positive relationship.

We then perform an additional analysis in which we run regressions separately for crisis years (2007–9) and non-crisis years (2000–6). However, Panel B of Table 6.2, which shows the results of this further analysis, do not present the estimates referring to the years 2007–9, because the lack of information relating to that time horizon does not allow model (1) to achieve the convergence. So, Table 6.2 shows only the results relating to the sub-period 2000–6.

We decide to perform this additional analysis for two main reasons. First, during the crisis years the Italian banks employ securitization to create assets that are eligible as collateral for refinancing operations with the Central Bank. Second, because during crisis periods banks generally operate under more difficult conditions, it could be possible that our regressors (that is, key variables and control variables) could affect the banks' risks in a different way, thereby producing biased results. In general, we expect that in non-crisis years securitization produces more significant effects in terms of liquidity.

The results shown in Panel B are similar to those of Panel A. In detail, with reference to the securitization variables (SEC and PREV_SEC), the coefficients are positive and significant at 5 percent. These findings confirm those referring to the overall period (2000–9). Furthermore, these estimates confirm our expectations: in the pre-crisis years securitization produces the most important effects on the liquidity of the originator banks. Also in Panel B, the M&A dummy is highly significant and negative.

6.5 Further analyses

In this section, to further verify our results, we implement a set of robustness checks concerning the model specification and the estimation method.

First, we use alternative cut-offs for the dependent variables to check whether our results are sensitive to our choice of 2 percent cut-offs. Panels A and B of Table 6.3 show the results of these further analyses, which employ changes of 1 percent and 3 percent, respectively. The results obtained generally confirm the findings obtained in the main regression (Panel A of Table 6.2).

The results of these tests show that when we consider changes in liquidity of 3 percent (Panel B), the securitization dummy (SEC) is significant at 5 percent. The positive direction of the relationship results in an increase of the banks' liquidity. The previous securitization variable loses significance, while the M&A dummy is still negative and significant at 1 percent. Also, the estimates relating to the 1 percent cut-off (Panel A) are consistent with our expectations and confirm the main regression results. In particular, we underline that the coefficient of the securitization dummy is once again positive and significant at 10 percent, instead of 5 percent (Panel B).

We also employ alternative cut-offs (1 percent and 3 percent) with reference to the sub-period 2000–6, as shown in Table 6.4.

When we consider the 3 percent changes (Panel B), the securitization variable is highly significant and positive, according to what we expect for the pre-crisis years in which securitization should more greatly affect the banks' liquidity. Moreover, this result confirms the findings obtained by implementing the main regression (2 percent cut-off). The previous securitization variable loses significance, although its significance is still positive. Finally, the estimates for the sub-period confirm the strong and negative significance of the M&A. When we consider the 1 percent cut-off (Panel B), the key independent variables lose significance, as is the case for the estimates related to the overall period (2000–9).

As a second sensitivity check referring to the model specification, we change some control variables. In detail, recognizing that banks of different size classes have different balance sheet compositions (Berger et al., 2005), we rerun all calculations including a size dummy variable, which is coded one if the size of bank *i* in year *t* is below the yearly median bank size and zero otherwise,[8] with no change in the main results.[9] Then, assuming that the different capitalization of a securitizing bank can affect its risk-taking in a different way, we split our sample into poorly- and better-capitalized banks and create a new dummy variable (equity_ratio dummy) by using as a cut-off

Table 6.3 Ordered probit models focusing on alternative cut-offs (1 percent and 3 percent) for the overall period (2000–9)

	Panel A: Liquidity Δ 1%			Panel B: Liquidity Δ 3%		
	Coefficients (1)	Robust standard errors (2)	Marg. effects (3)	Coefficients (1)	Robust standard errors (2)	Marg. effects (3)
Key variables						
Sec	0.4294527*	0.245597	0.046416	0.4990432**	0.2197654	0.0023732
Prev_sec	0.1896156	0.3455659	0.0163219	0.4201647	0.2963706	0.001128
Control variables						
Loans	0.1192821	0.07742	0.0107498	0.1350012*	0.0782537	0.0004132
Equity_ratio	0.2768941*	0.172492	0.0249539	0.3092115	0.2578399	0.0009463
Size	0.73721	7.270747	0.0664378	1.257892	7.753399	0.0038498
Imp_loans	0.0228779	0.0167189	0.0020618	0.0223398	0.0148617	0.0000684
Tier1	−0.0049129	0.2901373	−0.0004428	0.167513	0.2933531	0.0005127
Roa	0.0003496	0.0101827	0.0000315	0.0049554	0.0095691	0.0000152
M&A	−0.4449225	0.4883136	−0.0316187	−7.105924***	0.8483329	−0.0314841
Crisis	0.3214926	0.4101381	0.0322245	0.2343045	0.6218242	0.0008338
Number of obs.	276			276		
Log pseudolikelihood	−52.424466			−35.916729		
Number of banks (clusters)	46			46		
Prob > chi^2	0			0		
Pseudo R^2	0.1003			0.1646		

Notes: Dependent variables – Panel A: changes in liquidity of 1%; Panel B: changes in liquidity of 3 percent.
(a) We estimate ordered probit models for changes in liquidity of 1 percent and 3 percent. The dependent variable takes on the value one if there was a drop in liquidity of at least 1 or 3 percent relative to the previous year, it takes on the value two if liquidity remained within the interval +/−1 percent or +/−3 percent and it takes on the value three if there was an increase in liquidity of more than 1 or 3 percent; (b) all explanatory variables are lagged one year, except the crisis dummy; (c) all the explanatory variables (except the dummy variables) are measured in changes; (d) columns 2 of Panel A and Panel B report robust standard errors; (e) columns 3 of Panel A and Panel B present the marginal effects referring to the outcome three, that is the upper liquidity category (changes > 1 percent and > 3 percent); (f) time effects are included in all estimation. * Significant at 10 percent. ** Significant at 5 percent. *** Significant at 1 percent.

Source: Authors' elaborations.

Table 6.4 Ordered probit models focusing on alternative cut-offs (1 percent and 3 percent) for the sub-period (2000–6)

	Panel A: Liquidity Δ 1% Period 2000–6		Panel B: Liquidity Δ 3% Period 2000–6	
	Coefficients (1)	Robust standard errors (2)	Coefficients (1)	Robust standard errors (2)
Key variables				
Sec	0.4778189	0.345837	0.7108679***	0.2910275
Prev-sec	0.182162	0.52876	0.0885543	0.3587145
Control variables				
Loans	0.947793	0.792317	0.6922983	0.5637696
Equity_ratio	0.0319632	0.376321	0.0603242	0.2939447
Size	11.00047*	6.783074	10.54976*	6.367361
Imp_loans	0.1319029**	0.054562	0.105842***	0.0363367
Tier1	−0.2500876	0.439697	−0.4404055	0.7545275
Roa	0.0022826	0.011092	0.0083199	0.0104929
M&A	−7.580473***	0.30093	−6.62465***	0.3670842
Number of obs.	188		188	
Log pseudolikelihood	−22.5301		−13.518122	
Number of banks (clusters)	42		41	
Prob>chi^2	0		0	
Pseudo R^2	0.319		0.414	

Notes: Dependent variables - Panel A: changes in liquidity of 1 percent; Panel B: changes in liquidity of 3 percent.
(a) We show the probit models estimates only for the sub-period 2000-06 (see Part 4). The dependent variable takes on the value one if there was a drop in liquidity of at least 1 or 3 percent relative to the previous year, it takes on the value two if liquidity remained within the interval +/−1 percent or +/−3 percent and it takes on the value three if there was an increase in liquidity of more than 1 or 3 percent; (b) all explanatory variables are lagged one year, except the crisis dummy; (c) all the explanatory variables (except the dummy variables) are measured in changes; (d) columns 2 of Panel A and Panel B report robust standard errors; (e) columns 3 of Panel A and Panel B present the marginal effects referring to the outcome three, that is the upper liquidity category (changes >1 percent and > 3 percent); (f) time effects are included in all estimation. * Significant at 10 percent. ** Significant at 5 percent. *** Significant at 1 percent.

Source: Authors' elaboration.

the bank's yearly median equity ratio.[10] We then reestimate our regressions, but our findings remain qualitatively unchanged.[11]

With reference to the robustness test concerning the estimation method, we reestimate all our liquidity regressions by using an ordered logit model in order to verify that our results are insensitive to the choice of modeling technique.

The general formula for an ordered logit model with three categories expresses the probability of observation *i* of variable Y falling into category *j* in year *t* as:

$$P(Y_{i,t>j}) = \frac{\exp(\alpha_j + \beta X_{i,t-1})}{1 + \exp(\alpha_j + \beta X_{i,t-1})}, \quad j = 1,2 \tag{6.2}$$

and

$$P(Y_{i,t}) = 1 - P(Y_{i,t} > 1), \tag{6.3}$$

where $X_{i,t-1}$ is the vector of the independent variables for observation i in year $t-1$, while the αs are the intercepts and the βs are the slope coefficients.[12]

Table 6.5 reports all regression results obtained using the ordered logit model: these findings are qualitatively similar to those obtained by employing model (1). This suggests that our results are not driven by the modeling technique we chose. By analogy with the results reported in Tables 6.2, 6.3 and 6.4, in Table 6.5 we present the logit estimated coefficients instead of the odds ratios.

6.6 Conclusions

In the present study we analyze the effects of securitization on Italian banks' liquidity during the period 2000–9. To test our research hypotheses, we adopt an ordered probit model, in which the changes in the originator banks' liquidity are linked to a set of regressors including two securitization dummy variables (securitization and previous securitization), plus a vector of control variables. All the independent variables are lagged by one year. The empirical findings generally confirm that securitization produces positive effects on the originator bank's liquidity. The PREV_SEC variable, which takes into account the 'know-how effect', is less relevant. Unexpectedly, the M&A dummy is highly negatively significant. The bank's size is less important, and becomes significant at 5 percent with a positive sign only in the pre-crisis period (the larger banks appear to be more liquid).

To account for the crisis effects, we implement separate estimates with reference to the time periods 2000–6 and 2007–9. When the pre-crisis year is considered, both of the securitization variables (SEC and PREV_SEC) are significant and positive. These results are consistent with our expectations.

Table 6.5 Ordered logit models for different cut-offs (1 percent, 2 percent and 3 percent) referring to the overall period (2000–9)

	Panel A: Liquidity Δ 2%		Panel B: Liquidity Δ 1%		Panel C: Liquidity Δ 3%	
	Coefficients (1)	Robust standard errors (2)	Coefficients (1)	Robust standard errors (2)	Coefficients (1)	Robust standard errors (2)
Key variables						
Sec	1.223037**	0.582043	0.9530232*	0.5237064	1.091063**	0.4994228
Prev_sec	1.252714	0.892457	0.4285291	0.7971932	8.43E-01	6.45E-01
Control variables						
Loans	0.1965855*	0.119367	0.1965855*	0.119367	0.2293703*	0.1217144
Equity_ratio	0.5741374**	0.33941	0.5741374*	0.3394102	0.6087393	0.5652574
Size	−2.109763	15.56191	−2.109763	15.56191	−2.675435	17.46754
Imp_loans	0.0365073	0.031939	0.0365073	0.0319387	0.0372556	0.0282837
Tier1	−0.0209456	0.709966	−0.0209456	0.7099657	0.348657	0.6691333
Roa	−0.0006505	0.020888	−0.0006505	0.0208876	0.0088118	0.0188071
M&A	−40.10625***	2.676296	−1.108248	1.260799	−36.78658***	0.4983549
Crisis	0.9083668	1.389232	0.6398321	0.9368613	0.474086	1.492426
Number of obs.	276		276		276	
Log pseudolikelihood	−42.89939		−52.717979		−36.301346	
Number of banks (clusters)	46		46		46	
Prob > chi^2	0		0		0	
Pseudo R^2	0.1815		0.0953		0.1557	

Notes: Dependent variable – Panels A, B and C: changes in liquidity of 2 percent, 1 percent and 3 percent respectively.
(a) The table presents results based on ordered logit models for different cut-offs: 2 percent, 1 percent and 3 percent. The dependent variable takes on the value one if there was a drop in liquidity of at least 2 percent, 1 percent or 3 percent relative to the previous year, it takes on the value two if liquidity remained within the interval +/−2 percent, 1 percent or 3 percent, and it takes on the value three if there was an increase in liquidity of more than 2 percent, 1 percent or 3 percent; (b) all explanatory variables are lagged 1 year, except the crisis dummy; (c) all the explanatory variables (except the dummy variables) are measured in changes; (d) columns 1 present the coefficients, odds ratios are available upon request; (e) columns 2 report robust standard errors; (f) time effects are included in all estimation. * Significant at 10 percent. ** Significant at 5 percent. *** Significant at 1 percent.

Source: Authors' elaboration.

We do not present the estimates referring to the years 2007–9, because the lack of information relating to that time horizon prevents model (1) from achieving convergence.

To verify the results of the empirical analysis, we implement different robustness tests. First, we use alternative cut-offs in the ordered probit models. These findings substantially confirm our main regression results. Second, we change the model specification by modifying some control variables and obtaining qualitative, unchanged results. Finally, we run further regressions using the ordered logit model: the results are similar to those obtained when we employ the ordered probit model.

The main implication of the chapter for the banks' risk management is that in some contexts, such as the Italian one, securitization does not necessarily produce negative effects in terms of a bank's risk. In fact, the increase in credit risk is accompanied by a reduction of liquidity needs/liquidity increase/drop of liquidity risk. From the perspective of regulators, our results support the initiatives undertaken by the Basel Committee in order to define an international framework for liquidity risk and to strengthen global capital and liquidity rules with the goal of promoting a more resilient banking sector (Basel Committee on Banking Supervision, 2009, 2011).

To summarize, the findings of this research show that securitization does not produce, for banks, the negative effects associated with it, thus confirming its effectiveness as a financial tool for asset management activity (as well as for funding) of the financial intermediaries.

The main limitation of our study is related to the geographic area analyzed, although we do not exclude the possibility that future research focusing on the effects of securitization could study a larger sample, including other European banks, to identify possible differences to Italian ones. Another potential stream of research could investigate whether different types of securitization (distinguished according to the type of underlying asset classes, such as non-performing loans, residential mortgages, leasing receivables, and so on) differently affect banks' risk-taking. Finally, we could split our original sample into two subgroups, listed and non-listed banks, in order to consider the effect of securitization on other types of banks' risks (for example beta and idiosyncratic risk).

Notes

1. We specify that in a robustness test, we use alternative cut-offs.
2. We decide to adopt an ordered probit model because our dependent variables are not really, but can be considered as, a synthesis of a latent continuous variable.
3. We do not study synthetic securitization because during the period under consideration the number of synthetic deals was rather limited among Italian banks. However, we do not exclude the possibility that future research could adapt our analysis framework to study synthetic securitization, focusing on the effects on banks' risks. Furthermore, we do not consider on-balance-sheet securitizations,

for example covered bonds, because they were not employed in Italy during the period analyzed.

4. Securitisation.it is the website of *130 Finance*, an independent advisor for the analysis and structuring of securitizations. This company is the editor of the cited website, containing the data used for the present research.
5. Barth et al. (2006) adopt the same method.
6. For other contributions that adopt the same method, see Barth et al. (2006), Muiño Vázquez and Trombetta (2009).
7. In fact, with the exception of the dummy variables, ratios are expressed as a percentage.
8. We split our sample into small and large banks using the yearly median bank size as the cut-off.
9. All estimates are available upon request.
10. The dummy EQUITY_RATIO variable is coded one if the equity ratio of bank i in the year t is above the yearly median equity ratio, and zero otherwise.
11. All estimations are available upon request.
12. In our models, the equations are:

$$P(Y_{i,t} = DECR) = 1 - \frac{\exp(\alpha_1 + \beta X_{i,t-1})}{1 + \exp(\alpha_1 + \beta X_{i,t-1})} \tag{6.4}$$

$$P(Y_{i,t} = CONST) = \frac{\exp(\alpha_1 + \beta X_{i,t-1})}{1 + \exp(\alpha_1 + \beta X_{i,t-1})} - \frac{\exp(\alpha_2 + \beta X_{i,t-1})}{1 + \exp(\alpha_2 + \beta X_{i,t-1})} \tag{6.5}$$

$$P(Y_{i,t} = INCR) = \frac{\exp(\alpha_2 + \beta X_{i,t-1})}{1 + \exp(\alpha_2 + \beta X_{i,t-1})}. \tag{6.6}$$

References

Agostino, M. and Mazzuca, M. (2011). Empirical Investigation of Securitization Drivers: The Case of Italian Banks. *The European Journal of Finance*, 17 (8), 623–48.

Allen, F., Carletti, E. and Marquez, R. (2011). Credit Market Competition and Capital Regulation. *Review of Financial Studies*, 24 (4), 983–1018.

Altunbas, Y., Gambacorta, G. and Marques-Ibanez, D. (2010). Does Monetary Policy Affect Bank Risk-Taking? Working Paper No. 298, March, BIS.

Ambrose, B. W., LaCour-Little, M. and Sanders, A. B. (2005). Does Regulatory Capital Arbitrage or Asymmetric Information Drive Securitization. *Journal of Financial Services Research*, 28 (1–3), 113–33.

Barth, M. E., Landsman, W., Lang, M. and Williams, C. D. (2006). Accounting Quality: International Accounting Standards and US GAAP. http://ssrn.com/abstract=897241, date accessed December 2009.

Basel Committee on Banking Supervision (2011). Basel III: A global Regulatory Framework for More Resilient Banks and Banking Systems. http://www.birs.org (home page), June.

Basel Committee on Banking Supervision, Bank for International Settlement (2009). International Framework for Liquidity Risk Measurement, Standards and Monitoring – Consultative Document. http://www.birs.org (home page).

Berger, A., Bouwman, C. H. S., Kick, T. and Schaeck, K. (2010). Bank Risk Taking and Liquidity Creation Following Regulatory Interventions and Capital Support. Discussion Paper Series 2, Deutsche Bundesbank, No. 05/2010.

Berger, A. N., Clarke, G. R. G., Cull, R., Klapper, L. and Udell, G., (2005). Corporate Governance and Bank Performance: A Joint Analysis of the Static, Selection, and Dynamic Effects of Domestic, Foreign, and State Ownership. Working Paper No. 3632, June, World Bank Policy Research.

Calem, P. S. and LaCour-Little, M. (2004). Risk-based Capital Requirements for Mortgage Loans. *Journal of Banking and Finance*, 28(2), 647–72.

Calomiris, C. and Kahn, C. M. (1991). The Role of Demandable Debt in Structuring Optimal Banking Arrangements. *American Economic Review*, 81, 497–513.

Calomiris, C. W. and Mason, J. (2004). Credit Card Securitization and Regulatory Arbitrage. *Journal of Financial Services Research*, 26(1), 5–27.

Cantor, R. and Rouyer, S. (2000). Another Perspective on Credit Risk Transfer and Securitization. *Journal of Risk Finance*, 1 (6.2), 1–11.

Cardone-Riportella, C., Samaniego-Medina, R. and Trujillo-Ponce, A. (2010). What Drives Bank Securitization? The Spanish Experience. *Journal of Banking and Finance*, 34 (11), 2639–51.

Carletti, E., Hartmann, P. and Spagnolo, G. (2003). Bank Mergers, Competition and Liquidity. Working Paper Series No. 292, European Central Bank, 1–44.

De Nicolò, G. (2000). Size, Charter Value and Risk in Banking: An International Perspective. Board of Governors of the Federal reserve System, International Finance Discussion Paper No. 689.

DeMarzo, P. M. (2005). The Pooling and Tranching of Securities: A Model of Informed Intermediation. *Review of Financial Studies*, 18 (1), 1–35.

Dionne, G. and Harchaoui, T. M. (2003). Bank's Capital, Securitization and Credit Risk: An Empirical Evidence for Canada. Working Paper, January.

Donahoo, K. K. and Shaffer, S. (1988). The Impact of Capital Requirements on the Securitization Decision. Research Paper No. 8820, Federal Reserve Bank of New York.

Estrella, A. (2002). Securitization and the Efficacy of Monetary Policy. *Economic Policy Review*, 8 (1), 1–13.

Focarelli, D., Panetta, F. and Salleo, C. (1999). Why Do Banks Merge? Working Paper, Bank of Italy, No. 361, 1–54.

Franke, G. and Krahnen, J. P. (2005). Default Risk Sharing between Banks and Markets: The Contribution of Collateralized Debt Obligations. NBER Working Papers 11741, National Bureau of Economic Research, Inc.

Gertler, M., Kiyotaki, N. and Queralto, A. (2011). Financial Crises, Bank Risk Exposure and Government Financial Policy. N.Y.U. and Princeton, September, 1–38.

Greenbaum, S. I. and Thakor, A. V. (1987). Bank Funding Modes. Securitization versus Deposits? *Journal of Banking and Finance*, 11, 379–401.

Hansel, D. N. and Krahnen, J.-P. (2007). Does Securitization Reduce Bank Risk? Evidence from the European CDO Market. Finance Department, Goethe University Frankfurt, March 20.

Hughes, J. P., Mester, L. J. and Moon, C. (2001). Are Scale Economies in Banking Elusive or Illusive? Evidence Obtained by Incorporating Capital Structure and Risk-taking into Models of Bank Production Checking Accounts and Bank Monitoring. *Journal of Banking and Finance*, 25, 2169–208.

Iazzolino, G., Migliano G. and Gregorace, E. (2013). Evaluating Intellectual Capital for Supporting Credit Risk Assessment: An Empirical Study. *Investment Management and Financial Innovations*, 10(2), 44–54.

Koehn, M., and Santomero, A. M. (1980). Regulation of Bank Capital and Portfolio Risk. *Journal of Finance*, 35, 1235–50.

Kwan, S. and Eisenbeis, R. A. (1996). Bank Risk, Capitalization and Inefficiency. Working Paper Series No. 96-35, The Wharton Financial Institutions Center, University of Pennsylvania, Wharton, PA.

Laeven, L. and Levine, R. (2009). Bank Governance, Regulation and Risk Taking. *Journal of Financial Economics,* 93, 259–75.

Loutskina, E. and Strahan, P. E. (2009) Securitization and the Declining Impact of Bank Finance on Loan Supply: Evidence from Mortgage Originations. *Journal of Finance,* LXIV, 2, 861–89.

Martínez-Solano, P., Yagüe-Guirao, J. and López-Martínez, F. (2009). Asset Securitization: Effects on Value of Banking Institutions. *European Journal of Finance,* 15 (6.2), 119–36.

Martin-Oliver, A. and Saurina, J. (2007). *Why Do Banks Securitize Assets.* Banco de Espana.

Mehran, H. and Thakor, A. V. (2011). Bank Capital and Value in the Cross-section. *Review of Financial Studies,* 24 (4), 1019–67.

Morrison, A. D. and White, L. (2005). Crises and Capital Requirements in Banking. *American Economic* Review, 95, 1548–72.

Nijiskens, R. and Wagner, W. (2011). Credit Risk Transfer Activities and Systemic Risk: How Banks Became Less Risky Individually but Posed Greater Risks to the Financial System at the Same Time. *Journal of Banking and Finance,* 35 (6), 1391–8.

Passmore, S. W. and Sparks, R. (2004). Putting the Squeeze on the Market for lemons: Government-sponsored Mortgage Securitization. *Journal of Real Estate Finance and Economic,* 13 (1), 27–44.

Pavel, C. and Phillis, D. (1987). Why Commercial Banks Sell Loans: An Empirical Analysis. Economic Perspectives, Federal Reserve Bank of Chicago, May, 3–14.

Santomero, A. M. and Trester, J. J. (1998). Financial Innovation and Bank Risk Taking. *Journal of Economic Behaviour & Organization,* 35, 25–37.

Stever, R. (2007). Bank Size, Credit and the Sources of Bank Market Risk. BIS Working Papers No. 238, 1–31.

Stolz, S. (2002). The Relationship between Bank Capital, Risk-Taking, and Capital Regulation: A Review of the Literature. Kiel Working Paper No. 1105, Kiel Institute for World Economics.

Uhde, A. and Michalak, T. C. (2010). Securitization and Systemic Risk in European Banking: Empirical Evidence. *Journal of Banking and Finance,* 34 (12), 3061–77.

Uzun, H. and Webb, E. (2007). Securitization and Risk: Empirical Evidence on US Banks. *Journal of Risk Finance,* 8 (1), 11–23.

Vázquez, F. M. and Trombetta, M. (2009). Does graph Disclosure Bias Reduce the Cost of Equity Capital? *Accounting and Business Research,* 39 (6.2), 83–102.

Wolfe, S. (2000). Structural Effects of Asset-backed Securitization. *European Journal of Finance,* 6, 353–69.

7
Stress Testing Interconnected Banking Systems

Rodolfo Maino and Kalin Tintchev

7.1 Introduction

The recent financial crisis turned the spotlight on the issue of stress testing financial institutions. Until the crisis, risk monitoring and stress testing were built around the safety and soundness of individual institutions. In the aftermath of the crisis, stress tests adopted a new role by incorporating elements of the increased interconnectedness among banks, brokers, insurance companies, and hedge funds. Indeed, for many years after the crisis, stress test models failed to incorporate this interconnectedness and the amplification of distress triggered by financial sector institutions.

As recently highlighted by Schmieder et al. (2011), stress tests need to fulfill three key conditions as management tools. First, the assumptions about the level of adverse shocks (scenarios) and their duration should be plausible but severe enough to appropriately assess the resilience of individual institutions and the system. Second, the framework used to assess the impact of adverse shocks on solvency (resilience) has to be sufficiently risk sensitive, which requires changes of risk parameters to be based on economic measures of solvency, in addition to statutory ones, which are usually not sufficiently risk sensitive. Third, the results of the tests should be easy to communicate to decision makers (for example, policy makers and senior bank managers) and market participants.

This chapter presents an integrated framework to examine risks from the macro environment and banks' interconnectedness, and assesses the resilience of the banking system to aggregate and idiosyncratic shocks. In particular,

- a general setup is advanced to design the scope and methodology of stress tests based on hypothetical data;
- the stress test exercise assesses the resilience of the banks in the system both individually and in peer groups by size;

- in addition to various scenarios, a range of single-factor shocks are simulated, including deterioration of the quality of the entire portfolio and individual sectors, defaults of the largest obligors, interbank contagion, exchange rate and interest rate shocks, and a systemic deposit run;
- the framework discusses a macro-risk model based on banks' capital asset ratios as a function of expected losses and credit growth, using a generalized method of moments to calibrate shocks to credit quality and credit growth; and
- a series of statistical simulations are used to find the distributions of banks' credit losses and economic capital.

This analysis is complemented by an assessment of individual banks' contributions to systemic risk. Using quantile regressions, we estimate a simple measure of systemic risk, which captures tail risk comovement among banks in the system. The main contribution of this chapter is to advance a simple framework to integrate systemic risk scenarios that assess the impact of aggregate and idiosyncratic factors. The analysis is based on CreditRisk+ to estimate banks' credit portfolio loss distributions, making no assumptions about the cause of default.

The chapter is structured as follows. Section 7.2 advances a macro-risk stress testing model with simulations for credit portfolio loss distributions. Section 7.3 presents systemic macro- and micro-risk stress tests using quantile regressions, while Section 7.4 discusses how to design sensitivity tests depending on the shocks at hand. Concluding thoughts are advanced in Section 7.5.

7.2 Credit risk stress testing

7.2.1 Related literature

The purpose of system-focused stress testing is to identify common vulnerabilities across institutions that can lead to a systemic failure (Jones et al., 2004). As common vulnerabilities are often driven by banks' exposure to macroeconomic risks, such stress tests typically aim to understand how changes in macroeconomic variables impact the stability of the financial system.

Early applied stress testing frameworks, such as Čihák (2007), provide an Excel-based format to quantify the impact of credit, market and liquidity shocks on the banking system. Excel-based tests are easy to implement, but are based on ad hoc shocks since the link between bank losses and the macro environment is not modeled explicitly and bank assets typically do not change over the stress test horizon. Ong, Maino and Duma (2010) caution against the use of extreme ad hoc shocks in stress tests, as there is always a shock that is sufficiently large to break the banking system. Second-generation frameworks such as Schmieder et al. (2011) extend the approach to allow banks' risk-weighted assets (RWA) to change under stress.

The link between credit quality and macroeconomic fundamentals has been investigated empirically. Sorge (2004), Chan-Lau (2006), Foglia (2009), Quagliariello (2009), and Borio et al. (2012), among others, provide overviews of existing models, which for the most part use a reduced-form 'satellite' approach to map exogenous macro shocks into credit quality indicators. In particular, Foglia (2009) distinguishes between approaches that model banks' nonperforming loans (NPL) or loan-loss provisions (LLP), and models that focus on household and corporate default rates. Espinoza and Prasad (2010) and Nkusu (2011), among others, incorporate feedback effects from banks' credit quality to the real economy.

Other stress testing models focus on interdependencies among financial institutions. Segoviano and Goodhart (2009) view banking systems as portfolios of banks and model the system's portfolio multivariate density to derive banking stability measures that embed the distress dependencies among financial institutions. Gray and Jobst (2010), on the other hand, model the financial sector as a portfolio of individual contingent claims, which allows them to define their joint put option value as the multivariate density of each institution's individual marginal distribution of contingent liability. Other systemic risk indicators, such as CoVar (Adrian and Brunnermeier, 2009) and CoRisk (Chan-Lau, 2010), are derived using econometric methods and measure individual institutions' contributions to systemic risk.

The global crisis demonstrated that financial risks need to be assessed in a systemic perspective that considers potential spillovers across institutions and the interaction of multiple risk factors. The integrated approach to systemic risk stress testing is still developing. One early integrated framework developed by the Oesterreichische National bank (Boss et al., 2006) combines 'satellite' credit and market risk models with an interbank network model. The RAMSI model of the Bank of England (Aikman et al., 2009), which is one of the most comprehensive frameworks, includes a vector autoregression that simulates macro scenarios, 'satellite' models for credit risk, market risk, and net interest income, as well as embedded market liquidity shocks. In a recent paper, Barnhill Jr. and Schumacher (2011) model correlated systemic liquidity and solvency risks.

This chapter aims to contribute to existing research along two dimensions. First, it advances a simple method to construct integrated systemic risk scenarios, which assess the marginal contributions to systemic risk of both macroeconomic and idiosyncratic factors.[1] Second, the chapter derives a stylized theoretical model, which measures the impact of future credit losses, credit growth and net interest income on banks' capital to risk-weighted asset ratio (CAR). The model incorporates credit growth's direct effects on

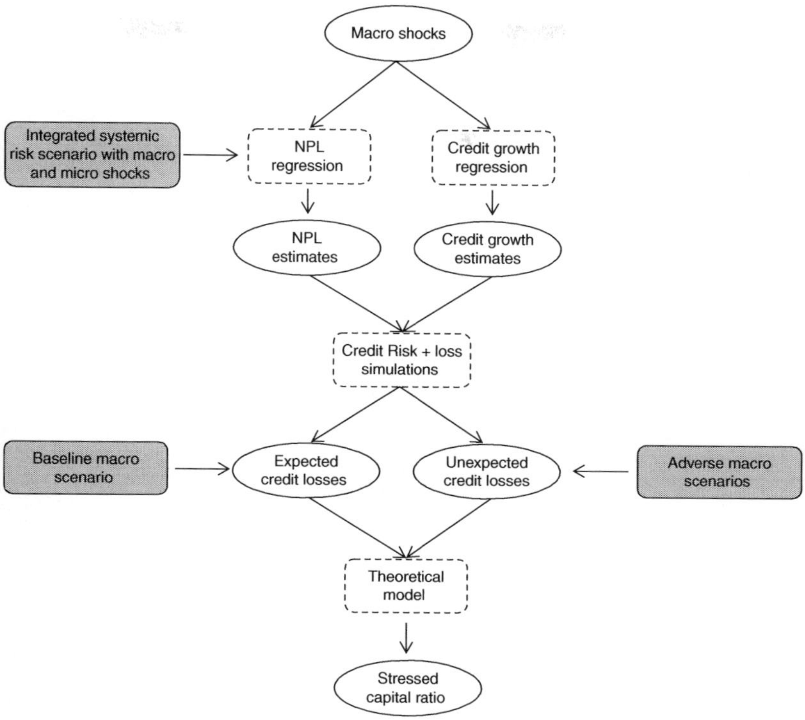

Figure 7.1 Macrofinancial stress testing framework

Note: Dashed rectangles – tools; solid ovals – inputs/outputs; striped rectangles – scenarios.

Source: Authors' estimates.

RWA and indirect effects on future credit losses, which, to our knowledge, have not been examined in prior research.

Moreover, we study the linkages between credit risk and the real economy in a simple macrofinancial framework, using econometric and statistical methods.[2] We use the framework to measure the impact of various scenarios on banks' solvency. In this section, we investigate the linkages between the macroeconomic environment, banks' credit quality and credit growth. In the next section, we design integrated scenarios that simulate simultaneous macro and micro shocks to credit quality.[3] The macrofinancial stress testing framework involves the following modeling steps (Figure 7.1).

- First, we model econometrically banks' credit quality and credit growth as a function of a set of risk factors and use the regression estimates to project banks' NPL ratios and credit growth under various scenarios.

- Second, we use the regression projections to model banks' credit portfolio loss distributions in CreditRisk+ and gauge expected losses and economic capital.
- Third, we derive a simple theoretical model, where banks' CARs are functions of future credit losses, credit growth and the net interest spread. Incorporating the credit loss and credit growth projections into the theoretical model allows us to estimate the impact of the scenarios on banks' CARs.

7.2.2 Theoretical credit risk model

One common approach to credit risk stress testing assumes that banks' assets do not change over the stress test horizon. Thus, loss projections are deducted directly from banks' present CARs.[4] Although convenient for short modeling horizons, such an approach involves a high degree of simplification. Also, abstracting from credit growth effects, this approach may underestimate the buildup of risks during a credit boom. RWA may increase significantly over longer stress test horizons, and banks would need additional capital to maintain stable CARs. Higher credit growth also implies higher exposures at default and thus higher credit losses when the boom goes bust. In this section, we develop a stylized model that attempts to incorporate such effects.

We model bank capital adequacy as a function of future credit quality, credit growth and profitability. Negative shocks to capital adequacy arise in the model from banks' mispricing of credit risk. The approach is highly simplified and assumes a banking system that is engaged in traditional intermediation. Thus, banks rely solely on net interest income to cover their operating expenses and credit losses, accumulating the residual as capital.[5] Credit is fully weighted in RWA, and operating expenses represent a fixed fraction of credit. Net interest income depends on credit growth, credit quality, and the spread between bank loan and deposit rates. Spreads are reset by the banks at the beginning of each period and remain unchanged until the end of the period. Banks do not raise new capital and distribute dividends only if this will not reduce their CARs. Under these assumptions, bank *i's* capital and RWA at time $t+1$ would evolve as follows:

$$\Delta Capital_{i,t,+1} = Credit_{i,t+1} \times Spread_{i,t+1} - Expenses_{i,t+1} - Credit\ Loss_{i,t+1} \tag{7.1}$$

$$\Delta RWA_{i,t+1} = Credit_{i,t+1} - Credit_{i,t} - Credit\ Loss_{i,t+1} \tag{7.2}$$

$$Expenses_{i,t+1} = \theta Credit_{i,t+1} \tag{7.3}$$

$$Spread_{i,t+1} = Net\ Interest\ Income_{i,t+1} / Credit_{i,t+1} \tag{7.4}$$

Capital accumulation in (7.1) depends on future credit losses, future credit (net of NPL) and the net interest spread.[6] Accumulation of RWA in (7.2), on the other hand, is driven by future credit growth and credit losses. Thus, changes in banks' CARs depend on the tradeoff between the accumulation of new capital and new RWA. If banks trade new capital for new RWA at a rate that is equal to their present CAR, their capital adequacy will remain unchanged. However, if they accumulate capital at a lower rate, their CARs will decline.

Baseline: We define the baseline as the most likely outcome. In this scenario, banks are able to correctly forecast shocks to credit quality and credit growth using the prevailing outlook. Therefore, they choose a spread that would fully absorb the shocks and keep CAR constant. Thus, in the baseline, condition (7.5) holds and banks' CARs do not change:

$$CAR_{i,t+l}^{Baseline} \equiv \frac{\Delta_{i,t+l}}{\Delta RWA_{i,t+l}} \equiv \frac{Capital_{i,t}}{RWA_{i,t}} \equiv CAR_{i,t}^{Baseline} \tag{7.5}$$

Equations (7.1), (7.2), and (7.5) define a system with three unknowns – credit losses, credit growth and the net interest spread. We substitute (7.1) and (7.2) into (7.5) and solve for the 'baseline' spread as a function of 'baseline' credit losses and credit growth:

$$Spread_{i,t+1}^{*} = \theta + \frac{Credit\,Loss_{i,t+1}^{Baseline}}{Credit_{i,t}(1 + Credit\,Growth_{i,t+1}^{Baseline})} \times (1 - CAR_{i,t}) + \frac{Credit\,Growth_{i,t+1}^{Baseline}}{1 + Credit\,Growth_{i,t+1}^{Baseline}} \times CAR_{i,t}. \tag{7.6}$$

Expression (7.6) defines the condition under which the spread would fully absorb the shocks, keeping CAR constant. The weights *(1-$CAR_{i,t}$)*and $CAR_{i,t}$ sum to unity and depend on banks' initial condition. The more a bank is initially in distress, the bigger the weight placed on credit losses and the smaller the weight placed on credit growth. A macrofinancial regression model forecasts banks' NPL ratios and credit growth, which are used in CreditRisk+ to find the credit portfolio loss distributions. 'Baseline' credit losses are assumed to equal the mean of the distribution. Finally, the projections are substituted in (7.6) to find the 'baseline' spread:

$$NPL_{i,t+1}^{Baseline} = f(Macro_{i,t+1}^{Outlook}) \tag{7.7}$$

$$Credit\,Growth_{i,t+1}^{Baseline} = f(Macro_{i,t+1}^{Outlook}) \tag{7.8}$$

$$Credit\,Loss_{i,t+1}^{Baseline} = Expected\,Credit\,Loss_{CreditRisk+}^{Outlook}. \tag{7.9}$$

Adverse scenarios: We simulate adverse macro scenarios, in which shocks diverge significantly from the baseline. At the beginning of the period the banks set the spreads in line with the baseline projections, which are the most likely outcome. Since the spreads can be reset only at the end of the period, after the shocks to credit quality and credit growth have been realized, deviations from the baseline have impact on CARs. Also, in adverse scenarios, credit losses are assumed to correspond to the 99th percentile of the distribution:

$$NPL_{i,t+1}^{ScenarioA} = f(Macro_{i,t+1}^{ScenarioA}) \tag{7.10}$$

$$Credit\,Growth_{i,t+1}^{ScenarioA} = f(Macro_{i,t+1}^{ScenarioA}) \tag{7.11}$$

$$Credit\,Loss_{i,t+1}^{ScenarioA} = Credit\,Loss99\%_{CreditRisk+}^{ScenarioA}. \tag{7.12}$$

To estimate the impact on banks' capital and RWA, in (7.13) and (7.14) we use the scenario credit losses and credit growth projections, while retaining the 'baseline' spread:

$$\Delta Capital_{i,t+1}^{ScenarioA} = Credit_{i,t+1}^{ScenarioA} \times Spread_{i,t+1}^{*} - Expenses_{i,t+1}^{ScenarioA} - Credit\,Loss_{i,t+1}^{ScenarioA} \tag{7.13}$$

$$\Delta RWA_{i,t+1}^{ScenarioA} = Credit_{i,t+1}^{ScenarioA} - Credit_{i,t}^{ScenarioA} - Credit\,Loss_{i,t+1}^{ScenarioA}. \tag{7.14}$$

Thus, banks' CARs become functions of the magnitude of the credit quality and credit growth surprises under each scenario. The larger the deviations of credit losses and credit growth from the baseline projections the bigger the impact of the scenario on banks' CARs. The model can be estimated for multiple periods, depending on the assumed horizon.

7.2.3 Empirical credit risk model

This theoretical model is linked to a regression model, which investigates the linkages between credit risk, credit growth, and the macro environment. Exploiting quarterly data, we estimate two dynamic-panel equations that model credit quality and credit growth as functions of exogenous macro-risk factors. The empirical model has the following specification:

$$NPL_{i,t} = Y_{i,t}'\beta + \alpha_i + \varepsilon_{i,t} \tag{7.15}$$

$$Credit\,Growth_{i,t} = X_{i,t}'\gamma + \delta_i + \eta_{i,t}. \tag{7.16}$$

where $NPL_{i,t}$ denotes the NPL ratio of bank *i* at time *t*; *Credit* $Growth_{i,t}$ stands for a year-on-year percentage change in total private sector credit of bank *i* at time *t*; $Y_{i,t}'$ and $X_{i,t}'$ denote vectors of endogenous and predetermined variables, including lag(s) of the dependent variables and the macro-risk factors, $i = 1,\ldots,N$, is the cross-sectional dimension, $t = 1,\ldots,T$, is the time dimension, α_i and δ_i are time-invariant individual fixed effects; and $\varepsilon_{i,t}$ and $\eta_{i,t}$ are disturbances. We allow the explanatory variables to vary between the two equations and consider up to four lags to provide sufficient response time to the dependent variables.

It is well known that dynamic specifications lead to inference problems in panel data models. The Ordinary Least Squares (OLS) levels estimator would produce inconsistent, upward-biased estimates since by construction there is a positive correlation between the lagged dependent variable and unobserved individual fixed effects (Bond, 2002). Fixed effects can be removed with the Within Groups (WG) estimator, which is based on deviations of the observations from their means. However, WG estimation would induce endogeneity in the transformed lagged dependent variable, which is negatively correlated by construction with the transformed error term. Thus, the WG estimator would be biased downwards.

Generalized Method of Moments (GMM) estimators have been proposed for panels with endogenous regressors. GMM estimation offers inference that is asymptotically efficient, while relying on relatively weak statistical assumptions. The Arellano and Bond (1991) one-step 'difference' GMM estimator transforms the panel data model in first differences to remove the individual effects, and uses lagged levels of the variables as instruments for the endogenous differences. The estimator is based on all available orthogonality conditions that exist between the lagged endogenous variables and the disturbances, and is the most efficient in the class of linear instrumental variables estimators. Arellano and Bover (1995) and Blundell and Bond (1998) develop an augmented version of the estimator, known as 'system' GMM, which is based on extra moment conditions and has better finite sample properties. The conditions are derived from the model in levels and combined with moment conditions for the model in first differences. The 'system' GMM estimator tends to outperform the 'difference' estimator when series are highly autoregressive.

We exploit the 'xtabond2' estimation procedure discussed in Roodman (2006), which has been implemented in STATA (see Drukker, 2008). Since we have a small unbalanced panel, the forward orthogonal deviations transform, proposed by Arellano and Bover (1995), was used instead of first differencing. The orthogonal-deviations transform does not subtract the previous observation, but the average of all available future observations. Thus, the transform preserves the sample size in panels with gaps, where differencing would reduce the number of available observations. The robustness of GMM inference depends on the number of available data points. Since we have a small panel, we also exploit an alternative estimator, due to Hausman and Taylor (1981), which fits a random-effects model with lagged instruments. We also utilize the WG and Pooled OLS estimators, which are biased downward and upward respectively, but still provide useful lower and upper bounds for the estimation.

The model was simulated with each of the estimators discussed above. The estimates suggest that credit quality and credit growth are largely driven by real GDP growth and inflation (Table 7.1). The coefficients have the expected signs and appear robust to alternative specifications. NPL ratios are correlated negatively with GDP growth and positively with inflation. Lending to the private sector, on the other hand, is associated positively with GDP growth and negatively with inflation. It takes approximately three quarters for GDP growth to affect NPLs and credit growth, while inflation affects credit quality and credit growth in two quarters and one quarter, respectively. The large coefficients on the autoregressive terms indicate presence of strong inertia in the dependent variables.

7.2.4 Modeling banks' credit portfolio losses in CreditRisk+

Next, we project NPL ratios and credit growth under each scenario. The baseline assumes robust GDP growth and credit growth, and moderate inflation. The high-inflation scenario envisages a spike in inflation, while the slowdown scenario envisages a sharp economic slowdown. The regression estimates suggest that the system's NPL ratio would increase by around 27 percent, and growth of credit to the private sector would decelerate to around 14 percent in the inflation scenario. By contrast, the system's NPL ratio would increase by nearly 60 percent and credit growth would decelerate to roughly 7 percent in the slowdown scenario.

We use the projections to model banks' credit portfolio loss distributions in CreditRisk+, which allows us to assess the economic capital that a bank has at risk by holding the credit portfolio. We focus on the large loans in each bank's portfolio. Required inputs for the simulation include borrowers' probabilities of default, banks' exposures at default and recovery rates. Since default probabilities are not readily available, we proxy them with the provisioning rates required for each loan classification.[7] CreditRisk+ estimates the portfolio value-at-risk (VaR) based on distributional assumptions detailed in Box 7.1 and Appendix I.

In order to simulate macro scenarios in CreditRisk+ we proceed as follows:

- initial loan default probabilities are increased by the projected rise in NPL ratios;
- exposure at default is found by multiplying the loan balances by the credit growth projections;
- a 25 percent recovery rate is assumed on all loans;
- under the previous assumptions, banks' credit portfolio loss distributions are generated before and after the shocks; and
- unexpected losses from the simulations and the credit growth projections from the regression analysis are fed into the theoretical model to gauge the impact on CARs.

Table 7.1 Macro determinants of credit risk (2002–10)[a] (in percent, unless indicated otherwise)

	Difference GMM[b]	System GMM[c]	Hausman-Taylor[d]	Within Group[e]	Pooled OLS
Credit quality equation: NPL to total loans					
NPL ratio (t–1)	0.49***	0.57***	0.57***	0.52***	0.60***
	0.00	*0.00*	*0.00*	*0.00*	*0.00*
NPL ratio (t–1)	0.47***	0.52***	0.34***	0.33***	0.37***
	0.00	*0.00*	*0.00*	*0.00*	*0.00*
Real GDP growth	−0.16***	−0.13***	−0.16**	−0.16***	−0.15**
(t–3)[f]	*0.00*	*0.01*	*0.03*	*0.01*	*0.04*
Inflation (t–2)[g]	0.14***	0.14***	0.13***	0.13**	0.13**
	0.01	*0.01*	*0.01*	*0.02*	*0.01*
Constant		−0.54***	1.36	1.18*	0.52
	...	*0.45*	*0.15*	*0.09*	*0.54*
Number of	296	306	306	306	306
observations R2	...	...	...	*0.61*	*0.61*
Credit growth equation: Private sector credit growth					
Private sector credit	0.67***	0.72***	0.68***	0.68***	0.73***
growth (t–1)[h]	*0.00*	*0.00*	*0.00*	*0.00*	*0.00*
Real GDP	0.61**	0.61**	0.60**	0.61*	0.59**
growth (t–3)	*0.03*	*0.03*	*0.04*	*0.08*	*0.04*
Inflation (t–1)	−0.48***	−0.49***	−0.49***	−0.48***	−0.50***
	0.01	*0.01*	*0.01*	*0.00*	*0.01*
Fiscal balance	0.27*	0.24*	0.26*	0.27*	0.23
to GDP (t–2)	*0.07*	*0.10*	*0.08*	*0.10*	*0.12*
Constant		7.25**	7.14**	8.24***	7.01***
	...	*0.02*	*0.02*	*0.00*	*0.02*
Number of	254	264	264	264	264
observations R2	...	...	...	...	...

Notes: [a] P-values are in italic; * denotes significance at the 10 percent level; ** at the 5 percent level;*** at the 1 percent level.

[b] Arellano-Bond (1991) one-step 'difference' GMM estimator with forward orthogonal deviations transform; robust variance-convariance matrix.

[c] Bludell and Bond (1998) one-step 'system' GMM estimator with forward orthogonal deviations transform; robust variance-convariance matrix.

[d] Hausman-Taylor panel data random-effects model with endogenous covariates.

[e] Fixed effects (within group) panel data estimator.

[f] Year-on-year real GDP growth.

[g] Year-on-year percent change in the CPI index (2005=100).

[h] Year-on-year percent change in total loans.

Source: Authors' estimates.

Box 7.1 CreditRisk+

CreditRisk+ is a portfolio credit risk model, which can be used to generate estimates of the expected (average) and unexpected (extreme) losses in a bank's portfolio. The model was developed by Credit Suisse First Boston in 1997 and can be applied to any credit instrument, including loans, bonds and derivatives. We utilize a modified version of the model implemented at the IMF (see Avesani et al., 2006).

CreditRisk+ takes a portfolio approach to credit risk. The model is tractable and obtains, under some statistical assumptions, a closed-form solution for the distribution of portfolio losses, using analytical techniques similar to those applied in the insurance industry. The model treats credit risk as a sudden event rather than a continuous change. Since credit risk is a binary outcome - default or no default - CreditRisk+ has been characterized in the literature as a 'default mode' model as opposed to other models (for example, Credit Metrics) that are based on non-default credit quality migrations (see Saunders and Allen, 2010).

Since the exact timing of default events and total number of defaults cannot be predicted, default is modeled as a continuous random variable with a probability distribution. In contrast to structural models (for example, Merton, 1974) CreditRisk+ makes no assumptions about the cause of default. Its theoretical underpinnings are similar to intensity-based models. CreditRisk+ models the default process in a portfolio with a large number of loans with relatively small default probabilities, which are independent of one another. Under these assumptions, the frequency of default events can be closely approximated by the Poisson distribution, which is more appropriate than the normal distribution for estimating the probability that a given number of defaults will occur within a specific time period (see Appendix I).

7.2.5 Main findings

The stress test outcomes reported in Table 7.2 reveal banks' vulnerability to macroeconomic shocks. The system's CAR declines from 9.4 percent to 5.2 percent in the inflation scenario and to 4.5 percent in the slowdown scenario. The two scenarios have a broadly similar impact on capital adequacy. Although the slowdown scenario has higher NPLs, its impact is somewhat mitigated by lower credit growth. By contrast, the bigger increase in RWA in the inflation scenario partly offsets the smaller credit losses. Higher credit growth implies higher exposures at default and higher potential losses, everything else being equal. Thus, not considering credit growth effects may underestimate the risks from the inflation scenario.

Table 7.2 Summary stress test results (in percent, unless indicated otherwise)

	Banking system		Large banks		Medium banks		Small banks	
	CAR	Tier 1 ratio	CAR	Tier 1 ratio	CAR	Tier 1 ratio	CAR	Tier 1 ratio
Reported CAR	16.3	12.9	15.2	11.3	16.6	13.8	65.9	65.9
Adj. CAR[a]	9.4	4.9	11.8	6.2	2.9	0.5	53.2	53.1
A. Sensitivity analysis								
Credit risk								
40 percent increase in NPLs[b]	7.8	3.3	10.7	5.1	0.5	−1.9	47.2	47.2
Downgrade of 30 percent of standard loans to substandard[c]	3.7	−1.0	6.1	0.1	−2.9	−5.4	51.7	51.7
Credit concentration risk								
Default of single largest borrower	5.8	1.2	9.4	3.7	−2.9	−5.4	47.0	47.0
Default of two largest borrowers	3.4	−1.2	8.0	2.2	−6.8	−9.2	36.6	36.6
Sectoral credit downgrades[d]								
Agriculture	8.7	4.2	11.	5.3	2.5	0.2	52.4	52.4
Construction	6.7	2.2	9.1	3.5	0.2	−2.2	52.7	52.7
Manufacturing	6.5	2.1	9.3	3.6	−0.5	−2.9	50.1	50.0
Mining	7.1	2.6	9.4	3.8	0.8	−1.5	50.4	50.4
Trade	6.1	1.6	8.5	2.9	−0.4	−2.7	49.5	49.5
Exchange rate risk								
20 percent currency appreciation	9.2	4.8	11.7	6.1	2.7	0.4	51.4	51.4

continued

Table 7.2 Continued

	Banking system		Large banks		Medium banks		Small banks	
	CAR	Tier 1 ratio	CAR	Tier 1 ratio	CAR	Tier 1 ratio	CAR	Tier 1 ratio
25 percent currency depreciation	9.6	5.2	12.0	6.4	3.1	0.7	55.3	55.3
Interest rate risk								
250 basis points upward shift	9.8	5.3	12.2	6.6	3.3	0.9	55.1	55.1
300 basis points downward shift	8.9	4.4	11.4	5.7	2.4	0.1	50.8	50.8
B. Scenario analysis								
Interbank contagion risk								
First-round effects[e]	8.2	4.4	8.1	4.5	−0.2	−1.4	33.2	33.2
Second-round effects[f]	7.5	3.8	7.3	3.7	−0.4	−1.7	32.2	32.2
Macroeconomic scenarios								
High-inflation scenario	5.2	1.0	8.9	3.7	−3.1	−5.5	27.5	27.5
Slowdown scenario	4.5	−0.1	8.7	3.1	−4.8	−7.4	24.4	24.4

Notes: [a] Adjusted for underprovisioning.
[b] Past-due, substandard, doubtful, and loss loans increase uniformly by 40 percent.
[c] 30 percent of standard (performing) loans are downgraded to substandard.
[d] 20 percent of sectoral loans are downgraded to loss.
[e] Measures direct effects from a simultaneous default of five undercapitalized small banks in the interbank market, assuming a loss given default of 50 percent.
[f] Measures second-round effects from defaults of two other banks.

Source: Authors' estimates.

Figure 7.2 shows the loss distribution of the average bank credit portfolio before and after the shock in the slowdown scenario. The distribution was generated by averaging over the banks' portfolios and using the average loan balances and default probabilities in CreditRisk+. The shock shifts the distribution to the right, with banks' expected and 99th percentile losses increasing by 70 percent and 50 percent, respectively. Unexpected losses, defined as the difference between the 99th percentile loss and the mean of the distribution, exceed capital, suggesting that the system's capital buffers will be insufficient to absorb the shock.

7.3 Systemic risk stress tests

7.3.1 Systemic risk drivers

Similarly to Kaufman and Scott (2003), we define systemic risk as the risk of a systemic failure, as opposed to risks associated with an individual institution that is evidenced by an increase in the comovement among institutions. As such, systemic risk can be viewed as a function of aggregate (macro) and idiosyncratic (micro) risk factors. Aggregate shocks are common to all institutions and arise from the broader economy, whereas idiosyncratic shocks are institution-specific.

In the previous section we modeled banking system distress from a macro perspective as a reduced-form function of aggregate risk factors. Our approach implicitly assumes that idiosyncratic factors are independent of one another and would not have systemic implications. This assumption allowed us to quantify the default risk of an individual bank in isolation from the default risk of the remaining banks in the system. However, in interconnected banking systems the system's VaR is not a simple sum of individual banks' VaRs, since distress at one institution may spread to other institutions. We define the risk of systemic spillovers in this framework as the risk that an idiosyncratic shock could have implications for the stability of the whole system.

The risk of systemic spillovers is assessed with a simple indicator measuring tail risk comovement among the banks in the system. The indicator, which we dub 'CoStress', builds upon the insights in Adrian and Brunnermeier (2009) and Chan-Lau (2010). The CoStress measure for bank i is defined as the level of systemic stress conditional on bank i being in distress. Thus, the marginal contribution of bank i to systemic risk will be the difference between the level of systemic stress conditional on bank i being in distress and conditional on its 'normal' (median) state. In order to capture tail risk effects, we model the 90th percentile of the conditional quantile function of the banks' NPL ratios using quantile regression.

Quantile regression is a modeling technique introduced by Koenker and Bassett (1978) that is especially useful for systemic risk analysis, where

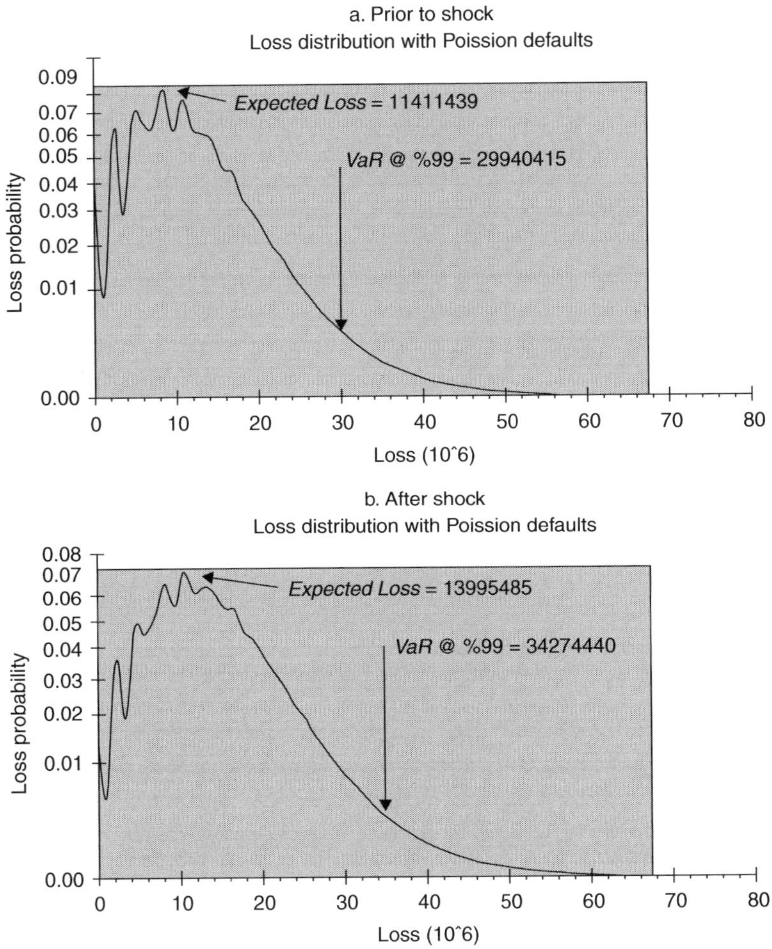

Figure 7.2 Slowdown scenario: average bank's portfolio loss distribution

Source: Authors' estimates.

extreme values are important. In contrast to OLS, which models the conditional mean function of a response variable Y given X=x, quantile regression models the conditional quantile function of Y given X=x. Since in systemic risk analysis the coefficients are likely to depend on the quantile, or the level of stress, quantile regression allows us to focus on the conditional distribution at the quantile of interest (for example, the 90th percentile). Thus, quantile regression appears better suited to capturing nonlinear effects, which are likely to be present at higher levels of stress (see Box 7.2).

Box 7.2 Quantile Regression

The quantile regression method estimates the conditional quantile function by solving an optimization problem. While OLS regression minimizes the sum of squared residuals to obtain an estimate of the conditional mean function, quantile regression minimizes the sum of weighted absolute residuals to obtain an estimate of the conditional quantile function (further details on the minimization problem are presented in Appendix II).

The use of quantile regression is justified by the properties of the data (Figure 7.3). We fit the NPL ratio of one bank against the NPL ratios of all other banks using two alternative methods: quantile regression and OLS. Superimposed on the scatter plot are the fitted values of seven quantile regressions corresponding to the 0.05, 0.10, 0.25, 0.50, 0.75, 0.90, and 0.95 percentiles. The quantile regression estimate of the conditional median function is the dashed line, whereas the OLS estimate of the conditional mean function is the dotted line. The two lines diverge significantly due to asymmetry of the conditional density and sensitivity of OLS to outliers.

Quantile regressions are better suited to modeling heterogeneous conditional distributions than OLS (Koenker and Hallock, 2001). First, there

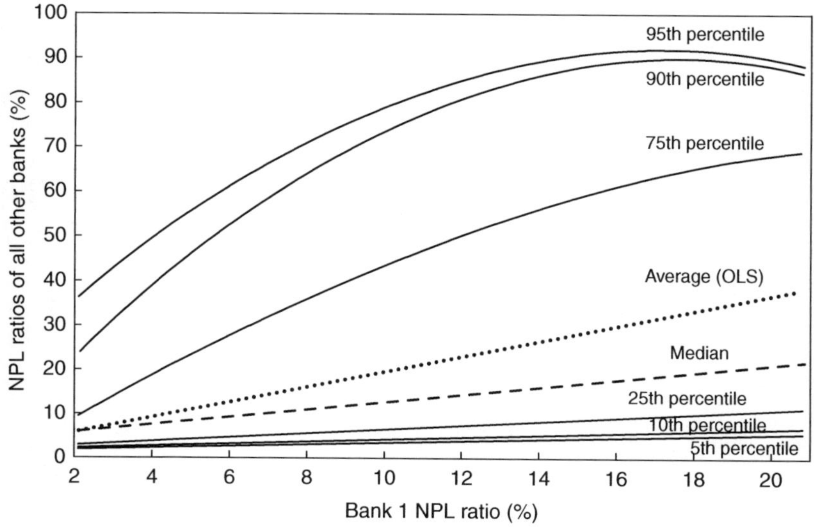

Figure 7.3 Quantile regression lines

Source: Author' estimates

Box 7.2 Continued

is a tendency for the dispersion of banks' NPL ratios to increase with the distress level of the 'explanatory' bank. Second, the narrow spacing in the lower quantiles reveals higher density and shorter lower tail, while the wide spacing in the upper quantiles indicates lower density and longer upper tail. Finally, the spacing decreases sharply between the 90th and 95th percentiles as the upper tail fattens at the end of the distribution.

7.3.2 Empirical model

We model tail risk comovement among the banks in the system as a function of common and idiosyncratic risk factors. We assume that the lenders in our sample are vulnerable to commodity price shocks and include a commodity price index as a common risk factor. To model idiosyncratic risk we add an individual bank's NPL ratio as an explanatory variable.[8] The regression model utilizes a logistic functional form put forward by Wilson (1997a, 1997b), which takes into account that NPL ratios are bounded between zero and one. The model has the following general specification:

$$NPL_{\tau,t} = a_\tau + \beta_\tau NPL_{t-1} + \sum_{n}^{N} \beta_{\tau,n} CRF_{n,t} + \beta_{\tau,j} NPL_{j,t} + \varepsilon_{\tau,t} \tag{7.17}$$

where $NPL_{\tau,t}$ is the 90th percentile of the conditional quantile distribution ($\tau = 0.90$) of the logit transformation of banks' pooled NPL ratios, excluding bank *j*; NPL_{t-1} is a one-quarter lag of the dependent variable; CRF_n denotes the n-th common risk factor; *NPLj* is the NPL ratio of 'explanatory bank' j, a_τ is the intercept and $\varepsilon_{\tau,t}$ is the disturbance.

We estimate the model separately for each 'explanatory' bank and refer to the prediction as the CoStress measure of bank *j* – the level of systemic stress conditional on distress at bank *j*. Following Adrian and Brunnermeier (2009), we define bank *j*'s marginal contribution to systemic risk (MCSR) as the percentage point difference between the systemic risk indicator (CoStress) conditional on an extreme shock to the bank and conditional on its median state:

$$MCSR_j = \beta_{\tau=0.9,j} (\hat{N}PL_{\tau=0.9,macro}^{\text{system} \mid \text{NPL}_{j,\tau=0.9}} - \hat{N}PL_{\tau=0.5,macro}^{\text{system} \mid \text{NPL}_{j,\tau=0.5}}) \tag{7.18}$$

where MCSR is defined as the difference between the average fitted NPL ratio conditional on bank *j* being in distress ($NPLj, \tau = 0.90$) and in its median state ($NPLj, \tau = 0.50$). The shocks are calibrated with historical data. Since

		Idiosyncratic risk factor	
		Median state	Extreme state
Aggregate risk factor	Median state	Scenario A	Scenario B
	Extreme state	Scenario C	Scenario D

Figure 7.4 Systemic risk scenarios

Source: Authors' estimates.

CoStress depends not only on idiosyncratic factors but also on the aggregate macroeconomic and banking environment, in order to find the marginal contribution of bank j to systemic risk we need to keep other factors constant. This estimation procedure enables us to rank individual banks by their systemic importance.

7.3.3 Systemic risk scenarios

We expand the methodology to accommodate scenarios that assess the marginal contributions to systemic risk of both aggregate and idiosyncratic factors. Since we have two types of risk factors – aggregate and idiosyncratic – and shocks of two magnitudes – a median shock and an extreme shock – we have four possible outcomes (see Figure 7.4): (i) *Scenario A*: median aggregate and idiosyncratic shocks; (ii) *Scenario B*: median aggregate shock and extreme idiosyncratic shock; (iii) *Scenario C*: extreme aggregate shock and median idiosyncratic shock; and (iv) *Scenario D*: extreme aggregate and idiosyncratic shocks. Using the quantile regression line, we project banks' NPL ratios under each scenario. 'Shocked' variables assume their median historical value, if the shock is 'normal', and the 90th percentile of the distribution, if the shock is extreme. Scenario A, where the common risk factor and the 'explanatory' bank are in their 'normal' states, is the baseline.

To calculate the marginal contributions of aggregate and idiosyncratic risk factors we take the difference between the fitted CoStress indicators in two scenarios. For example, the MCSR of an extreme idiosyncratic shock, when the aggregate risk factor is in 'normal' state, is equal to $\hat{NPL}_B - \hat{NPL}_A$, whereas the contribution of an extreme aggregate shock, when the idiosyncratic factor is in its 'normal' state, is defined as $\hat{N}PL_C - \hat{N}PL_A$. Analogously, the marginal contribution of an extreme idiosyncratic shock, when the aggregate factor is in extreme state, is calculated as $\hat{N}PL_D - \hat{N}PL_C$. Finally, the marginal contribution to systemic risk of an extreme aggregate shock when the idiosyncratic factor is in an extreme state is measured as $\hat{N}PL_D - \hat{N}PL_B$.[9]

7.3.4 Main findings

We fit the CoStress measure under each scenario. CoStress and MCSRs of aggregate and idiosyncratic factors are shown in Table 7.3. The estimates suggest that aggregate risk factors have a greater contribution to systemic risk. CoStress increases by around 75 percent following an extreme shock to commodity prices and the system's lagged NPL ratio. By contrast, individual banks contribute to systemic risk to a lesser degree, with CoStress increasing on average by around 10 percent. Naturally, scenario D, in which both aggregate and idiosyncratic factors are in extreme states, has the biggest impact on systemic risk.

Nevertheless, a simultaneous shock to several banks would be significant from a systemic perspective. For example, the impact of a simultaneous shock to five banks with the largest MCSR is broadly similar to that of an extreme aggregate shock. Noticeably, we find that due to nonlinearities in the prediction, the marginal impact of an extreme shock to one of the factors is bigger when there is an extreme shock to the other factor. For example, the impact of an extreme idiosyncratic shock is bigger in the presence of an extreme aggregate shock.

Although the small sample complicates the formal analysis of the determinants of banks' systemic importance, we plot banks' MCSR against bank-specific indicators such as NPL ratios, share of the system's NPLs, share of the system's total assets, and extent of interbank borrowing. The estimates, albeit heavily influenced by outliers, suggest that MCSRs depend on banks' interconnectedness, proxied by dependence on interbank borrowing. This finding is broadly similar to that in Adrian and Brunnermeier (2009) who find a weak relationship between banks' unconditional VaRs and their MCSRs.

Finally, the quantile regression estimates were used to model banks' conditional VaRs in CreditRisk+. Figure 7.5 illustrates this concept using a network structure, where banks' VaRs are conditional on a tail event at another bank. To estimate the conditional VaR we use the quantile regression line to project the bank's NPL ratio conditional on an extreme (90th percentile) shock to the 'explanatory' bank and simulate that bank's conditional credit portfolio loss distribution in CreditRisk+. Table 7.4 shows the conditional VaR of five banks with the largest MCSRs. Bank 2 emerges as systemically important

Table 7.3 Systemic risk scenarios (in percent, unless indicated otherwise)

	Predicted CoStress indicator conditional on shock to bank j (j=1,2,...,12)[a]												
	System average	Bank 1	Bank 2	Bank 3	Bank 4	Bank 5	Bank 6	Bank 7	Bank 8	Bank 9	Bank 10	Bank 11	Bank 12
A. Systemic risk scenarios													
Scenario A: median idiosyncratic shock/median aggregate shock	26.7	28.3	28.5	26.3	26.9	26.6	26.0	25.0	26.3	26.3	26.7	26.9	26.6
Scenario B: extreme idiosyncratic shock/median aggregate shock	29.2	29.6	31.3	27.6	30.3	28.6	29.1	31.3	26.7	28.2	28.9	27.6	31.7
Scenario C: median idiosyncratic shock/extreme aggregate shock	46.3	47.1	48.5	45.5	46.6	44.4	45.4	45.3	46.3	45.9	45.5	45.9	49.3
Scenario D: extreme idiosyncratic shock/extreme aggregate shock	49.4	48.7	51.9	47.1	50.7	46.9	49.2	53.1	46.8	48.4	48.3	46.7	55.4
B. MCSR of aggregate and idiosyncratic factors													
MCSR of extreme idiosyncratic shock when aggregate risk is in the median state (transition) from scenario A to B	2.5	1.3	2.8	1.3	3.3	2.0	3.1	6.3	0.4	2.0	2.2	0.7	5.1

Table 7.3 Continued

	Predicted CoStress indicator conditional on shock to bank j (j=1,2,. . . ,12)[a]												
	System average	Bank 1	Bank 2	Bank 3	Bank 4	Bank 5	Bank 6	Bank 7	Bank 8	Bank 9	Bank 10	Bank 11	Bank 12
MCSR of extreme idiosyncratic shock when aggregate risk is in the extreme state (transition) from scenario C to D	3.1	1.6	3.4	1.6	4.1	2.5	3.9	7.8	0.5	2.5	2.7	0.8	6.2
MCSR of extreme aggregate shock when idiosyncratic risk is in the median state (transition) from scenario A to C	19.6	18.8	20.0	19.2	19.7	17.8	19.4	20.3	19.9	19.7	18.8	18.9	22.7
MCSR of extreme aggregate shock when idiosyncratic risk is in the extreme state (transition) from scenario B to D	20.2	19.1	20.5	19.5	20.4	18.3	20.1	21.8	20.1	20.2	19.4	19.1	23.7

Notes: [a] The CoStress measure is defined as the 90th percentile of the NPL ratios of the banks in the system. Extreme shocks are defined as the 90th percentile of the historical distribution of the variables, whereas median shocks – as the 50th percentile of the distribution.

Source: Authors' estimates.

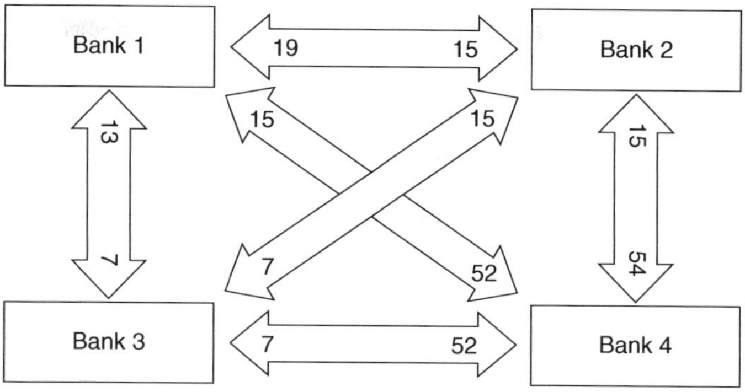

Figure 7.5 CoVaR network structure[a]

Notes: [a]After Adrian and Brunnermeier (2009). The figure shows VaRs of banks at the end of the arrow conditional on distress at the banks at the origin.

Source: Authors' estimates.

within the group. CreditRisk+ could be also used to derive banks' VaRs conditional on integrated systemic risk scenarios that include shocks not only to individual banks, but also to the macro-risk factors.

7.4 Sensitivity analysis

The scenario analysis was complemented by single-factor sensitivity tests, which assessed banks' resilience to credit and market risks, liquidity shocks and interbank contagion. The sensitivity tests gauged the impact of the shocks on banks' CARs using a relatively standard set of techniques (see Čihák, 2007). This section discusses key assumptions and findings.

7.4.1 Shocks

A number of sensitivity tests focused on credit and concentration risks, given their importance for the banking system. The following shocks were used in the exercise: (i) a 40 percent uniform increase in adversely classified loans across all loan categories (past due, substandard, doubtful, and loss); (ii) a 30 percent downgrade of performing loans to substandard; (iii) a simultaneous default of the single largest and two largest obligors; and (iv) a 20 percent default rate on banks' lending to agriculture, mining, construction, trade and manufacturing sectors. The tests for market and liquidity risks and interbank contagion applied the following shocks: (i) a 25 percent (20 percent) simultaneous depreciation (appreciation) against all major currencies; (ii) a parallel upward (downward) shift in the yield curve of 250 basis points (300 basis points); (iii) a five-day systemic deposit run resulting in a cumulative outflow of 20 percent of total deposits in domestic currency; and

Table 7.4 Conditional value-at-risk (VaR)[a] (in percent of bank capital)

	Bank 1	Bank 2	Bank 3	Bank 4	Bank 5	Unconditional VaR (1)	Cumulative conditional VaR[b] (2)	Difference (2)-(1)
Bank 1	12	18	12	14	12	112	21	9
Bank 2	135	129	135	136	134	129	154	25
Bank 3	28	31	27	29	28	27	33	6
Bank 4	269	283	268	254	266	254	325	71
Bank 5	27	28	27	28	26	26	32	6

Notes: [a] 90 percent VaR of the bank in the row, conditional on a shock to the bank in the column.
[b] Conditional on shocks to the five banks, which are assumed to be independent.

Source: Authors' estimates.

(iv) a simultaneous default of five undercapitalized banks on their interbank exposures.

7.4.2 Methodology and assumptions

7.4.2.1 Credit risk

Credit risk stress tests simulated downgrades of various magnitudes to the loan rating transition matrix. The impact on banks' CARs was gauged by deducting the increase in required provisions from capital. In addition, banks' default risk was assessed using Z scores derived from accounting data. Z scores measure distance to default in standard deviations of the asset return (ROA), with lower scores corresponding to higher default risk. The Z score was estimated over a three-year rolling window using the following formula:

$$Zscore = \frac{(ROA + capital/assets)}{\sigma_{ROA}} \tag{7.19}$$

where *ROA* is return on assets, capital/assets is capital to asset ratio, and σ_{ROA} denotes the standard deviation of *ROA* over the estimation window.

7.4.2.2 Market risk

Banks' sensitivity to interest rate risk was assessed in a repricing gap model. The model measures the impact of interest rate shocks on the cumulative gap between interest-earning assets and liabilities. In addition, FX risk was gauged by conducting sensitivity analysis on the banks' net open FX position in all currencies.

7.4.2.3 Liquidity risk and interbank contagion

The liquidity stress tests simulated a five-day systemic deposit run leading to a cumulative outflow of around 23 percent of deposits in domestic currency. It was further assumed that banks have at their disposal 70 percent of their liquid assets in domestic currency readily available to meet daily withdrawals. Interbank contagion risk was assessed by sensitivity analysis on the matrix of net interbank exposures. The test assumed that five banks with low capital buffers would default simultaneously on their interbank obligations and simulated the systemic impact, including second-round effects from defaults of other banks.

7.4.3 Main findings

Credit risk emerged as a major vulnerability in the banking system. A number of banks with weak capital buffers and high NPL ratios are vulnerable even to moderate credit quality shocks. Vulnerability to credit risk is exacerbated by large single obligor and sectoral concentrations. In particular, the following observations were noted.

Table 7.5 Distribution of stress test results (in percent, unless indicated otherwise)

	Distribution of banks by CAR (number of banks)			Distribution of banks by CAR (in percent of total assets)			Recapitalization[a] % of GDP
	<4%	4%–14%	>14%	<4%	4%–14%	>14%	
Reported CAR	0	4	10	0.0	34.4	65.6	0.1
Adj. CAR[b]	3	5	6	5.2	58.0	36.9	2.3
A. Sensitivity analysis							
Credit risk							
40 percent increase in NPLs[c]	5	4	5	15.2	76.8	8.0	2.7
Downgrade of 30 percent of standard loans to substandard[d]	6	4	4	39.4	56.4	4.2	4.1
Credit concentration risk							
Default of single largest borrower	5	5	4	15.2	80.6	4.2	3.4
Default of two largest borrowers	6	4	4	39.4	56.4	4.2	4.1
Sectoral credit downgrades[e]							
Agriculture	3	6	5	5.2	86.9	8.0	2.5
Construction	5	5	4	15.2	80.6	4.2	3.0
Manufacturing	5	5	4	15.2	80.6	4.2	3.1
Mining	4	6	4	13.5	82.4	4.2	3.3
Trade	5	4	5	15.2	76.8	8.0	3.2
Exchange rate risk							
20 percent currency appreciation	4	5	5	6.9	85.1	8.0	2.3

25 percent currency depreciation	3	5	6	5.2	58.0	36.9	2.3
Interest rate risk							
250 basis points upward shift	2	6	6	4.6	58.5	36.9	2.2
300 basis points downward shift	4	5	5	6.9	85.1	8.0	2.4
B. Scenario analysis							
Interbank contagion risk							
First-round effects[f]	7	3	4	35.5	60.3	4.2	1.8
Second-round effects[g]	8	2	4	42.7	53.1	4.2	2.0
Macroeconomic scenarios							
High-inflation scenario	5	5	4	15.2	80.6	4.2	3.8
Slowdown scenario	5	5	4	15.2	80.6	4.2	3.9

Notes: [a] Capital injection needed to restore banks' CARs to 14 percent.
[b] Adjusted for underprovisioning.
[c] Past-due, substandard, doubtful, and loss increase uniformly by 40 percent.
[d] 30 percent of standard (performing) loans are downgraded to substandard.
[e] 20 percent of sectoral loans are downgraded to loss.
[f] Measures direct effects from a simultaneous default of five undercapitalized small banks in the interbank market, assuming a loss given default of 50 percent.
[g] Measures second-round effects from defaults of two other banks.

Source: Authors' estimates.

- A 40 percent increase in problem loans would erode the capital buffers of banks, accounting for around 15 percent of the system's assets (Table 7.5). Severe shocks to loan quality, such as a downgrade of 30 percent of performing loans to substandard or a simultaneous default of the two largest obligors would deplete Tier 1 capital.
- A simultaneous default of five undercapitalized banks on their interbank loans would undermine the solvency of two other banks, including a systemically important one.
- Exposure to direct FX and interest rate risks is small. More banks would suffer moderate losses if the domestic currency appreciated due to the banks' prevailing long net open FX positions. A 20 percent simultaneous appreciation against all currencies would have negligible impact on capital adequacy.
- Asset-liability mismatches are small, thus net interest income's sensitivity to interest rate shocks is generally low. However, FX and interest rate risks indirectly exacerbate credit risk by weakening borrowers' repayment capacity.
- Recent trends show improvements in bank liquidity. Although the system as a whole is in a position to withstand a hypothetical five-day deposit run, liquid assets would fall to around 7 percent of total assets. Medium-sized banks appear particularly vulnerable to the shock, and two banks would require liquidity assistance (Table 7.6).

Table 7.6 Liquidity and z-score stress test results (in percent, unless indicated otherwise)

	Banking system[a]	Large banks	Medium banks	Small banks
Initial Position				
Liquid assets to total assets[a]	18.6	20.8	13.0	21.4
Liquid assets to total deposits[a]	42.5	45.0	33.8	111.2
Liquidity Shock Scenario[b]				
Liquid assets to total assets	7.2	8.2	4.4	15.4
Liquid assets to total deposits	19.2	20.7	13.1	86.0
Z Score[c]				
December 2007	37.1	20.8	71.8	48.6
December 2009	7.7	15.2	3.4	2.9
June 2010	10.1	19.1	5.0	4.5

Notes: [a] Liquid assets in domestic currency.
[b] 5-day deposit run leading to an outflow of 22.5 percent of deposits in domestic currency.
[c] Default risk index defined as the sum of ROA and the capital to asset ratio divided by the standard deviation of ROA. Lower Z score indicates higher default risk.

Source: Authors' estimates.

- Default risk remains high for medium and small banks, which have z scores that are well below pre-crisis levels.

7.5 Conclusion

An integrated framework for systemic risk analysis needs to consider risks from both the macroeconomic environment and banks' interconnectedness. This research uses a general setup to present a simple framework to assess the resilience of a banking system to aggregate and idiosyncratic shocks, advancing a toolbox that can be used in financial sector risk assessments. In this framework:

- banks' CARs are modeled in a format that considers the simultaneous impact of future credit losses, credit growth, and the net interest spread;
- the analysis focuses on economic measures of solvency and uses a generalized method of moments to calibrate the shocks to NPLs and credit growth;
- uncertainty about banks' future losses is modeled in CreditRisk+, which relies on analytical techniques to find the banks' credit portfolio loss distributions;
- a simple systemic risk indicator is proposed to measure tail risk comovement among the banks in the system; and
- quantile regressions and CreditRisk+ are used to model banks' conditional VaRs.

Appendix I

Default Risk Modeling in CreditRisk+[10]

CreditRisk+ derives banks' portfolio loss distributions in a two-stage process. The first stage estimates the frequency of defaults and the severity of losses, while the second stage derives the loss distribution. While the frequency of defaults in a time period, within a loan portfolio of obligors with different probabilities, can be approximated by a Poisson distribution, the loss distribution depends both on the frequency of default occurrence and on the severity of the loss, and would not be Poisson in general. The amount lost in a given default would be equal to the exposure to the obligor less a recovery amount.

Since it is difficult to estimate the severity of the loss on an individual loan-by-loan basis, the exposures, net of recoveries, are grouped into discrete loan bands, and the exposure for each band is approximated by a common average. Loss distributions are derived for each exposure band, which are accumulated across bands to generate an overall distribution. Given its simplicity, the model has parsimonious data requirements. The inputs required for the estimation of the basic model are the loans in a bank's portfolio, their default probabilities and recovery rates. Default probabilities can be approximated by obligors' credit ratings or other proxies such as NPLs, required provisioning rates, and so on.

The basic statistical theory behind the default event process in CreditRisk+ is as follows. The model assumes that in a portfolio with N obligors each exposure has a known probability of default over a one-year time horizon. Let p_A denote the annual probability of default for obligor A. To examine the portfolio loss distribution, the model introduces a probability generating function, which is defined using an auxiliary variable z:

$$F(z) = \sum_{n=0}^{\infty} p(n\,defaults)z^n. \tag{7.20}$$

Since for an individual obligor there are two states of the world – default or no default – the probability generating function for a single obligor can be defined as:

$$F_A(z) = 1 - p_A + p_A Z = 1 + p_A(Z - 1) \tag{7.21}$$

Since the individual default events are assumed to be independent, the probability generating function for the whole portfolio represents the product of the individual probability generating functions:

$$F(z) = \prod_A F_A(z) = \prod_A (1 + p_A(z-1)) \tag{7.22}$$

$$\log F(z) = \sum_A \log(1 + p_A(z-1)). \tag{7.23}$$

Since the individual default probabilities are assumed to be small, the logarithms can be replaced using the expression:

$$\log(1 + p_A(z-1)) = p_A(z-1). \tag{7.24}$$

In the limit, equation (23) simplifies to:

$$F(z) = e^{\sum_A p_A(z-1)} = e^{\mu(z-1)} \tag{7.25}$$

where the expected number of defaults in the portfolio is given by:

$$\mu = \sum_A p_A. \tag{7.26}$$

The distribution corresponding to the probability generating function is found by a Taylor expansion:

$$F(z) = e^{\mu(z-1)} = e^{-\mu(z-1)}e^{\mu z} = \sum_{n=0}^{\infty} \frac{e^{-\mu}\mu^n}{n!} z^n. \tag{7.27}$$

If the individual default probabilities are small, the probability of having n default events in the portfolio in one year would be equal to:

$$\Pr(n\,defaults)\frac{e^{-\mu}\mu^{n}}{n!}. \tag{7.28}$$

Equation (28) is the Poisson distribution for the probability of n defaults, which does not depend on the number of exposures or individual default probabilities. The distribution's only parameter is the expected number of defaults μ. The default probabilities have to be uniformly small, albeit not the same. The Poisson process assumed by the basic model implies that the mean of the distribution equals its variance. Since the variance of the default rate was found to be significantly higher in historical data, especially for lower quality exposures, it follows that the Poisson assumption would underestimate actual default probabilities. To capture the fatter tails of observed loss distributions, Credit Suisse First Boston extended the basic model to allow for pairwise default correlations among obligors.

Appendix II

Quantile Regression

The minimization problem reduces to solving the following expression:

$$\min_{\beta}\sum\rho_{\tau}(y_i-\xi(x_i,\beta)) \tag{7.29}$$

where y is the dependent variable, $\xi(x_i,\beta)$ is a linear parametric function of the explanatory variable x_i, and $\rho_{\tau}(.)$ is a weighting function for each observation, such as:

$$\rho_{\tau}(k) \;=\; k(\tau - I(k<0)), \quad 0<\tau<1 \tag{7.30}$$

where $I(.)$ denotes the indicator function. The weights depend on the quantile of interest.

To fit the median quantile, the minimization equates the number of positive and negative residuals, while the residuals are weighted asymmetrically to yield other quantiles. The minimization leads to a linear program, which can be solved by applying the simplex method.

Quantile regression has certain advantages over other methods such as OLS and extreme value theory (EVT) for modeling systemic risk.

- First, the technique captures the differential impact of the covariates at various distributional quantiles and is thus better suited to modeling heterogeneous distributions (Chen, 2005). Quantile regressions fit the data better in the upper quantiles, where the estimated regression lines exhibit a steeper slope and a nonlinear relationship.

- Second, although conditional quantiles could be modeled by fitting OLS regressions on various quantiles of the data, the slopes of the fitted quantile curve and mean curve in this case will remain the same since the change represents simply a locational shift in the conditional NPL distribution, which does not affect its scale and shape. This approach could create small-sample problems in the upper and lower tails of the distribution that are often encountered by EVT modeling techniques. Given their focus on the extreme tail of the distribution, standard EVT techniques have been found less suitable for credit risk analysis (see Lucas et al., 2002).
- Third, quantile regression is based on less rigid distributional assumptions than OLS and is thus more robust to outliers. While OLS assume that errors are normally distributed, quantile regression makes no distributional assumptions regarding the error term since the covariance matrices are estimated using bootstrap methods, which do not require residuals and explanatory variables to be independent.

7.6 Acknowledgments

The authors would like to thank Li Lian Ong and Laura Kodres for their useful comments. All remaining mistakes are the responsibility of the authors.

Notes

The views expressed in this chapter are those of the authors and do not necessarily represent those of the IMF or IMF policy.

1. The approach does not require data on bilateral interbank exposures.
2. The exercise that follows is based on fictional data generated with the sole purpose of presenting the scope and advantages of using the framework.
3. Stein (2011) describes some limitations of scenario-based approaches as a sole mechanism for assessing portfolio risk.
4. See for example Čihák (2007).
5. Given our focus on credit risk, we consider only the banking book and do not consider other assets and income sources, which are, however, easy to incorporate and would not affect the basic results. Thus, we do not model shocks to the trading book, which would have an impact on CARs, as well as noninterest sources of income (for example fees and commissions).
6. $Credit_{i,t+1}$ denotes net performing (interest-earning) credit, excluding NPL. The difference between net interest income, operating expenses and credit losses should be adjusted for taxes, dividends and other relevant deductions.
7. The provisioning rates that we use are as follows: 3 percent for loans that are performing; 5 percent for past due; 25 percent for substandard; 50 percent for doubtful; and 100 percent for loss. Alternatively, one could use default probabilities derived from banks' own internal risk management data systems, if available, or borrowers' credit risk ratings.

8. A drawback of this approach is that the common factor and the 'explanatory' NPL ratio may be interrelated, inducing multicollinearity in the estimation. One could extract common factors from the data and use the factors and their orthogonal components (see Chan-Lau, 2010). A caveat of this approach is that the shocks cannot be linked directly to the macro environment.
9. $\hat{NPL}$ denotes the CoStress values, and the subscripts denote the scenario.
10. The discussion to follow is based on the methodology outlined in Credit Suisse First Boston (1997).

References

Adrian, T. and Brunnermeier, M. (2009). CoVaR. *Mimeo,* Princeton University.

Aikman, D., Alessandri, P., Eklund, B., Gai, P., Kapadia, S., Martin, E., Mora, N., Sterne, G. and Willison, M. (2009). Funding Liquidity Risk in a Quantitative Model of Systemic Stability. *Bank of England Working Paper* 372.

Arellano, M. and Bond, S. (1991). Some Tests of Specification for Panel Data: Monte Carlo Evidence and an Application to Employment Equations. *The Review of Econometric Studies,* 58, 277–97.

Arellano, M. and Bover, O. (1995). Another Look at the Instrumental Variables Estimation of Error-Components Models. *Journal of Econometrics,* 68, 29–51.

Arvai, Z., Driessen, K. and Otker-Robe, I. (2009). Regional Financial Interlinkages and Financial Contagion within Europe. *IMF Working Paper* 6.

Avesani, R. G., Liu, K., Mirestean, A. and Salvati, J. (2006). Review and Implementation of Credit Risk Models of the Financial Sector Assessment Program. *IMF Working Paper* 134.

Barnhill, T., Jr. and Schumacher, L. (2011). Modeling Correlated Systemic Liquidity and Solvency Risks in a Financial Environment with Incomplete Information. *IMF Working Paper* 263.

Blundell, R. and Bond, S. (1998). Initial Conditions and Moment Restrictions in Dynamic Panel Data Models. *Journal of Econometrics* 87.

Bond, S. (2002). Dynamic Panel Data Models: A Guide to Micro Data Methods and Practice. *CEMMAP Working Paper* 09.

Borio, C., Drehmann, M. and Tsatsaronis, K. (2012). Stress-Testing Macro Stress Testing: Does it Live Up to Expectations? *BIS Working Paper* 369.

Boss, M., Krenn, G., Puhr, C. and Summer, M. (2006). Systemic Risk Monitor: A Model for Systemic Risk Analysis and Stress Testing of Banking Systems. *Oesterreichische National Bank Financial Stability Report* 11.

Chan-Lau, J. (2006). Fundamentals-Based Estimation of Default Probabilities: A Survey. *IMF Working Paper* 149.

Chan-Lau, J. (2010). The Global Financial Crisis and Its Impact on the Chilean Banking System. *IMF Working Paper* 108.

Chen, C. (2005). An Introduction to Quantile Regression and the QUANTREG Procedure. *SAS Institute Paper,* 213–30.

Čihák, M. (2007). Introduction to Applied Stress Testing. *IMF Working Paper* 59.

Credit Suisse First Boston (1997). CreditRisk+: A Credit Risk Management Framework.

Drukker, D. M. (2008). Econometric Analysis of Dynamic Panel-Data Models Using STATA. *Summer North American STATA Users Group Meeting,* July 2008.

Espinoza, R. and Prasad, A. (2010). Nonperforming Loans in the GCC Banking System and Their Macroeconomic Effects. *IMF Working Paper* 224.

Foglia, A. (2009). Stress Testing Credit Risk: A Survey of Authorities' Approaches. *International Journal of Central Banking*, September, 9–44.
Gray, D. and Jobst, A. A. (2010). New Directions in Financial Sector and Sovereign Risk Management. *Journal of Investment Management*, 8 (1), 23–8.
Hausman, J. and Taylor, W. (1981). Panel Data and Unobservable Individual Effects. *Econometrica*, 49, 1377–98.
Jones, M. T., Hilbers, P. and Slack, G. (2004). Stress Testing Financial Systems: What to Do When the Governor Calls. *IMF Working Paper* 127.
Kaufman, G. G. and Scott, K. E. (2003). What is Systemic Risk, and Do Bank Regulators Retard or Contribute to It? The Independent Review, VII (3, 371–91. Koenker, R. and Bassett, G. (1978). Regression Quantiles. *Econometrica*, 46 (1), 33–50.
Koenker, R. and Hallock, K. F. (2001). Quantile Regression. *Journal of Economic Perspectives*, 15 (4), 143–56.
Lucas, A., Klaassen, P., Spreij, P. J. C. and Straetmans, S. (2002). Extreme Tails for Linear Portfolio Credit Risk Models. *Proceedings of the Third Joint Central Bank Research Conference*, Basle, 271–83.
Merton, R. C. (1974). On the Pricing of Corporate Debt: The Risk Structure of Interest Rates. *Journal of Finance*, 29(2), 449–70.
Nkusu, M. (2011). Nonperforming Loans and Macrofinancial Vulnerabilities in Advanced Economies. *IMF Working Paper* 161.
Ong, L. L., Maino, R. and Duma, N. (2010). Into the Great Unknown: Stress Testing with Weak Data. *IMF Working Paper* 282.
Quagliariello, M. (ed.) (2009). *Stress Testing the Banking System: Methodologies and Applications*, 1st edn. Cambridge University Press.
Roodman, D. (2006). How to Do Xtabond2: An Introduction to 'Difference' and 'System' GMM in STATA. *Center for Global Development Working Paper* 103.
Saunders, A. and Allen, L. (2010). *Credit Risk Management In and Out of the Financial Crisis: New Approaches to Value at Risk and Other Paradigms*, 1st edn. John Wiley & Sons.
Schmieder, C., Puhr, C. and Hasan, M. (2011). Next Generation Balance Sheet Stress Testing. *IMF Working Paper* 83.
Segoviano, M. A. and Goodhart, C. (2009). Banking Stability Measures. *IMF Working Paper* 4.
Sorge, M. (2004). Stress Testing Financial Systems: An Overview of Current Methodologies. *BIS Working Paper* 165.
Stein, R. (2011). The Role of Stress Testing in Credit Risk Management. *Moody's Research Labs Working Paper* 2011/05/01.
Wilson, T. (1997a). Portfolio Credit Risk (I). *Risk Magazine*, September, 111–17.
Wilson, T. (1997b). Portfolio Credit Risk (II). *Risk Magazine*, October, 56–61.

8

Estimating Endogenous Liquidity Using Transaction and Order Book Information

Philippe Durand, Yalin Gündüz and Isabelle Thomazeau

8.1 Introduction

The liquidity of instruments has been a key area of financial research on its own within the past decades, where theoretical and empirical studies have shown statistically significant effects of liquidity on asset prices. Recent research has treated the impacts of liquidity as fundamental and incorporated liquidity-adjusted modifications into the original Capital Asset Pricing Model (CAPM) framework (Acharya and Pedersen, 2005). There is also a vast literature on the implications of liquidation risk (Huang, 2003; Duffie, Garleanu and Pedersen, 2007; Longstaff, 2009). An important review of the literature on liquidity and asset prices can be found in Amihud, Mendelson and Pedersen (2005).

Although intense interest in the field of liquidity has given rise to theoretical and empirical research, the analyses were usually undertaken under the assumption that asset liquidity is exogenously given. Studies looking at endogenous asset liquidation costs with abnormal transaction sizes have not received adequate attention in the literature. A major contribution has been proposed by Cetin, Jarrow, Protter, and Warachka (2006). In their paper, the authors first model the liquidity using stochastic supply curves: consecutive purchases are executed at higher prices while consecutive sales are transacted at lower prices. The authors describe the impact of liquidity costs on the price of a European call option and calibrate the liquidity parameters they introduced on intraday equity price observations. A more recent study that incorporates constrained asset prices due to illiquidity is Wagner (2011). Our intuition overlaps with the results of the portfolio choice model presented in the paper, such that asset prices fall below the fundamentals when the supply of assets runs out in the short run.

In this study, we distinguish *exogenous* liquidity, which corresponds to the variability of bid-ask spreads for usual-sized transactions, from *endogenous* liquidity, which corresponds to the impact of liquidity on market prices when liquidating larger positions. We leave aside exogenous liquidity, which has been intensively studied in the literature through various analyzes, and focus on endogenous liquidity, which measures the risk that the realized price of a transaction may be different from the pre-transaction price in both normal and stress periods. This price will then depend on (i) the size of the position relative to the overall market, (ii) the direction (long or short) of the position with respect to those of the other actors, and (iii) the market depth. The concept is also shown to generalize to the case of collective liquidation or to the case where all market participants react in the same way, and therefore cause the overall one-way transaction size in the market to be large and illiquid.

The Basel Committee on Banking Supervision (BCBS) has already stated the necessity of taking endogenous liquidity into account for the valuation of portfolios in Articles 700 and 701 of the Basel II framework (BCBS, 2006) and in the Technical Document 'Supervisory guidance for assessing banks' financial instrument fair value practices' (BCBS, 2009), but probably it could be better specified, deepened, and expanded. On the other hand, current accounting rules do not allow endogenous liquidity to be recognized in the accounting results. For example, the November 2006 issue of the International Accounting Standards Board Discussion Paper (IASB, 2006) specifies that 'the quoted price shall not be adjusted because of the size of the positions relative to trading volume.'

We apply an endogenous liquidity concept-based model to two sources in order to understand two different phenomena. An order book of equity prices has been used so as to reveal any *not-yet-realized* endogenous liquidity effects – effects that become real if a new order is executed. We show that there is a significant parameter for liquidity, derived from the *not-yet-realized* transactions in the order book, which indicates the importance of endogenous liquidity and signals a high liquidity cost for large transaction sizes.

Second, we apply our model to a set of credit default swap transactions in order to find a *realized* endogenous liquidity component. Our results indicate that a *realized* component is not present in CDS prices, since a large transaction would not actually have happened in first place due to the high costs of transacting, leaving us only with the realized transactions without endogenous liquidity. We conclude that it is highly probable that traders are placing 'iceberg' orders in the CDS market, simply by slicing the large transactions into several small pieces to avoid liquidity constraints. A further explanation is that traders know exactly where endogenous liquidity starts when they execute their transactions.

We aim to fill the gap in the liquidity literature by presenting a simplified model to estimate the endogenous liquidity parameter of a portfolio. The intuitive model calculates a liquidity-adjusted price by making use of data made available from repositories and order books. Our results with *realized* and *not-yet-realized* endogenous liquidity have an important impact on the incorporation of liquidity in the market risk framework. Given its effects on prices, asset liquidity should definitely be a part of the regulatory framework, amendments to which are currently being developed by the Trading Book Group of the BCBS.

The rest of the chapter is organized as follows: Section 8.2 introduces the concept of endogenous liquidity in detail. Section 8.3 presents the theoretical modeling of the endogenous liquidity parameter. While Section 8.4 brings the results with *not-yet-realized* liquidity in order books into discussion, Section 8.5 looks at whether *realized* endogenous liquidity is priced in CDS transactions. The conclusion summarizes our findings and lays out issues for further research and for supervisory authorities.

8.2 Defining endogenous liquidity

Bangia, Diebold, Schuermann and Stroughair (2002) and Bervas (2006) are among the studies which recognized the importance of distinguishing between exogenous and endogenous liquidity in the sense that we define.[1] Below a certain size, transactions may be traded at the bid-ask price quoted in the market (exogenous liquidity), and above this size the transaction will be conducted at a price below the initial bid or above the initial ask, depending on the sign of the trade (endogenous liquidity). There could be a threshold for the size of the transaction above which endogenous (il)liquidity will happen, whereas trades below this threshold occur in accordance with the liquidity measured by the bid-ask spreads.

Exogenous liquidity risk, which corresponds to a normal variation of bid-ask spreads under normal market conditions, can be easily integrated into a VaR framework. However, incorporating endogenous liquidity risk into a VaR computation is not straightforward from a theoretical point of view. The impact of the liquidation of a position on market prices may be highly significant, especially in financial institutions' trading books. Although the academic literature on portfolio valuation and VaR computation is quite rich, a small number of endogenous liquidity applications are present, since liquidity reserves are not held to be compliant with accounting standards. Among studies that looked at the implications of endogenous liquidity risk on portfolios and VaR frameworks, Jarrow and Protter (2005) and Rogers and Singh (2005), describe an optimal liquidation strategy and deduce a market value for the expected liquidation price.

While the usual bid-ask cost is a linear function of the size of the transaction, this is no longer the case for endogenous liquidity costs. As a consequence, when we include endogenous liquidity, the price of a portfolio that is made of several sub-portfolios is no longer the sum of the price of each individual sub-portfolio. This result, though intuitive, contradicts current accounting practices.

8.3 The model

In this section we introduce a simplified model which incorporates the estimation of the endogenous liquidity component, and mention some possible extensions to the model.

8.3.1 General presentation

Let us consider an investor holding a portfolio of quantity N (N>0) of a single asset having a price S_0 at time T_0. In the spirit of exponential demand and supply curves introduced by Cetin, Jarrow, Protter and Warachka (2006), we model the endogenous liquidity to be represented by an exponential function $e^{-\lambda}$, λ being a positive or a null parameter. This parameter would represent the impact on the market of selling one unit of the asset, so its estimation depends particularly on the liquidation horizon chosen. The exponential decay assumption should cause the following observation. The first asset is sold at a price of S_0. Because of the impact on the market of selling the first stock, the second stock may be sold at a price $e^{-\lambda}S_0$, and the nth stock at $e^{-(n-1)\lambda}S_0$. In this model, we compute a sequential liquidation price of a portfolio, supposing that no other investor will liquidate his portfolio at the same moment; this price does not incorporate the impact of a systemic crisis, where all the investors would try to sell their portfolios at the very same second.

The valuation with the liquidity adjustment (V) of the portfolio is the sum of the prices of the assets. We then have:

$$V_{liquidity\ adjustments}(T_0) = \sum_{n=1}^{n=N} e^{-(n-1)\lambda} \times S_0 = \frac{1-exp(-\lambda N)}{1-exp(-\lambda)} S_0 \tag{8.1}$$

When λ tends to 0, $V_{liquidity\ adjustments}(T_0)$ coincides with the valuation without liquidity adjustments: $V_{liquidity\ adjustments}(T_0) = N \times S_0$. The price is then a linear function of the size of the position, and no second-order volume effects or liquidation costs are considered.

Let us now show how we can derive a simplified relationship from this equation. Using Taylor's expansion,

$$e^x = 1 + \frac{x}{1!} + \frac{x^2}{2!} + \cdots, \quad -\infty < x < \infty \tag{8.2}$$

in equation (1) and assuming both $x = -\lambda N$ and $x = -\lambda$ to be small, we obtain:

$$\frac{V}{S_0}\left(1 - \frac{\lambda}{2}\right) = N\left(1 - \frac{\lambda}{2}N\right) \tag{8.3}$$

The same logic can be applied when buying a stock repetitively. This last equation provides a basic relationship between volumes and prices, and will be further developed in Section 8.5.1 for the special case of CDS transactions.

8.3.2 Extensions

This simple approach has been used by Cetin, Jarrow, Protter and Warachka (2006) to better take into account the liquidity costs when pricing derivatives: for a cash product market maker, the endogenous liquidity cost is not necessarily the cost of unwinding his position, but the cost of hedging his positions. Using the same model, Possamai, Soner and Touzi (2010) obtain a Taylor expansion of these liquidity costs, which would allow an option price to be written incorporating liquidity as a correction of its price, ignoring the impact of liquidity.

In the same way, for highly correlated instruments (for example a portfolio of interest rate swaps in the same currency and on the same underlying), endogenous liquidity costs could be estimated on a portfolio basis, but not at a transaction level.

8.4 Results with 'not-yet-realized' endogenous liquidity

While Cetin, Jarrow, Protter and Warachka (2006) use intraday transaction information to estimate the λ parameters introduced in Section 8.3, this section presents how they can be estimated using order book information. In our approach of modeling endogenous liquidity, we presume that order books and transactions contain different market information about the liquidity parameter. Order books, being a list of buy and sell orders, contain all the intentions of traders, although they are *not yet realized*. The order book does not provide real transaction prices, but prices on which traders and market makers agree to deal. So the endogenous liquidity coefficient measured on these data may correspond to the liquidity costs they would agree to include in their prices. This 'raw' form of information should actually be a correct source to observe the (intended) effects of the transaction size on prices.

8.4.1 Order book datasets

Since full order book information is not readily available, we used the data from order books available on the Boursorama website, which gives real-time quotations of Euronext for the ten best buy and sell orders. Ten entities from various business sectors and sizes were selected: Accor (hotel industry), Axa (insurance company), BNP Paribas (banking), Boiron (pharmaceutical laboratories), Bouygues (telecommunications, construction), Carrefour (supermarkets), Fleury Michon (food manufacturing), LVMH (wines and spirits, fashion and leather goods, perfume and cosmetics, watches and jewelry), Peugeot (automobiles), Total (energy producer and provider). All these firms are from the CAC 40 except for the two smallest, Boiron and Fleury

Table 8.1 Boursorama order book close-of-business data for Accor on 5 July 2011

Bid orders	Bid quantity	Bid price	Ask orders	Ask quantity	Ask price
2	3507	31.150	1	20	31.200
1	1278	31.145	1	1142	31.215
1	2845	31.135	1	800	31.220
2	10,011	31.130	3	11,529	31.245
1	7350	31.125	1	20	31.250
1	575	31.120	1	9012	31.285
3	7062	31.100	3	7363	31.290
1	8392	31.095	2	9945	31.295
2	9509	31.090	2	645	31.300
1	3964	31.080	1	746	31.310
15	**54,493**	**Total**	**16**	**41,222**	**Total**

Michon. We retrieved close of business data from 5 July to 29 July 2011, which corresponds to a dataset of 19 trading days.

8.4.2 Estimation methodology and numerical results for a single entity

The methodology below is used to estimate the value of the parameter λ for each entity and each day similarly. We present here the basic steps of the methodology, illustrating it with the particular case for only a single entity, Accor.

8.4.2.1 Extraction of data

The daily closing price data were extracted from the available order books. The content of this extraction is illustrated in Table 8.1 as of 5 July 2011.

The first three columns correspond to selling orders (bids), whereas the final three columns show intention for buying orders (asks). The columns *Orders* indicate how many orders have been placed for trading at a given price (respectively for sell and buy), and *Quantity* is the quantity of stocks corresponding to these orders (respectively for sell and buy). For a party adding a new order, these prices can be considered as marginal prices, in other words if a party wants to sell 5000 stocks, the price will be 31.150 for the first 3507 stocks, 31.145 for the following 1278, and 31.135 for the remaining part.

8.4.2.2 Estimation of the liquidity parameter

After the order book data were extracted, the order book marginal prices were plotted as a function of the cumulated quantity of stocks in the order book, with the following convention: the quantities of stocks N are positive for long positions (which have to be sold to be taken out of the order book),

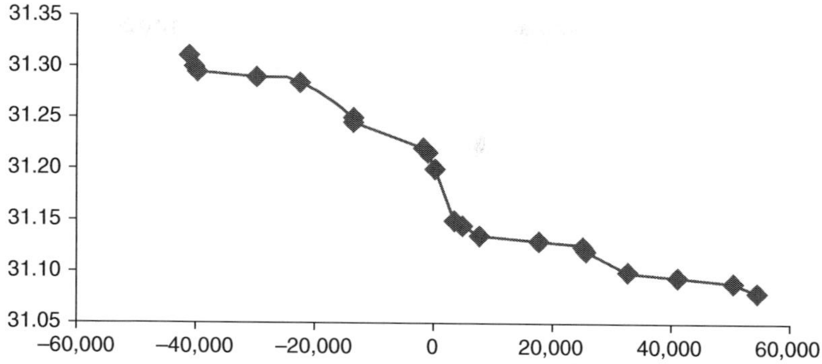

Figure 8.1 Stock prices versus cumulated quantity for Accor stocks as on 5 July 2011

and negative for short positions (which have to be bought to be taken out). Figure 8.1 presents this function as of 5 July 2011.

As explained in Section 8.3, the model supposes that the marginal price S of a stock is linked to the quantity N by the following relationship, where S_0 is the first stock price:

$$S = e^{-(N-1)\lambda} S_0 \tag{8.4}$$

So, assuming that N is approximately equal to $N-1$, this relationship can be rewritten as:

$$lnS = aN + b \tag{8.5}$$

where $a = -\lambda$ and $b = \ln S_0$. By fitting this function to the data from the order book, we obtained a value for λ. Table 8.2 presents the results of this process for each of the 19 days of our sample.

We observe that the R^2 coefficients, which measure the goodness-of-fit (the correlation between the theoretical and the empirical marginal prices), are quite high. On the other hand, the estimated λ parameters are quite small, mostly at the 10^{-8} level.

8.4.2.3 Descriptive statistics for lambda

We obtained a time series of λ in Section 8.4.2.2. We can plot the total quantity of stocks from the 10 best bids and asks in the order book and the lambda for the period of 19 days, as illustrated for Accor stocks in Figure 8.2.

In Figure 8.2, $-\lambda$ has been depicted instead of λ, since its correlation with the quantity of stocks is clearer. From this time series, we were able to compute several descriptive statistics, including:

- average value of $-\lambda$: -8.03E-08;
- standard deviation σ of the λ time series: $\sigma = 1.86$E-08;

Table 8.2 Results of the regression between the marginal price and the cumulative quantity of Accor stocks for the 5–29 July 2011 period

July	05	06	07	08	11	12	13	14	15	18
$a = -\lambda$ (in 10^{-8})	−8.45	−7.65	−11.40	−7.01	−5.59	−6.75	−6.13	−8.57	−7.51	−6.35
σ (in 10^{-8})	0.56	0.53	0.79	0.30	0.48	0.46	0.48	0.65	0.23	0.66
$-\lambda / \sigma$	−15.20	−14.40	−14.40	−23.70	−11.50	−14.70	−12.70	−13.20	−32.90	−9.62
R^2	93%	92%	92%	97%	88%	92%	90%	91%	98%	84%
July		19	20	21	22	25	26	27	28	29
$a = -\lambda$ (in 10^{-8})		−7.40	−7.74	−8.28	−8.13	−7.13	−7.36	−7.48	−9.14	−14.00
σ (in 10^{-8})		0.43	0.29	0.44	0.84	0.85	0.66	0.38	0.62	1.25
$-\lambda / \sigma$		−17.40	−27.00	−18.80	−9.67	−8.39	−11.20	−19.90	−14.90	−11.20
R^2		94%	98%	95%	84%	80%	87%	96%	92%	87%

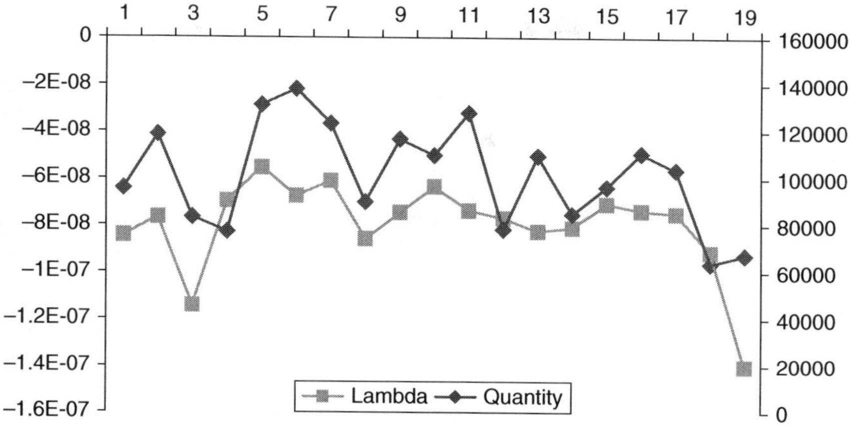

Figure 8.2 Time evolution of $-\lambda$ and of the total quantity of assets between 5–29 July 2011

- average stock price: 30.56;
- correlation between $-\lambda$ and total quantity of stocks: ρ ($-\lambda$, Quantity) = 0.65;
- weighted λ (average of the daily λ estimation weighted by the size of the corresponding order book): 7.75E-08;
- weighted σ (standard deviation of the weighted λ time series): 118.34;
- weighted λ/price (weighted λ normalized by the average price of the stock): 2.37E-06.

8.4.2.4 *Impact of endogenous liquidity*

It is also possible to estimate the liquidity-adjusted price portfolios of different sizes, and the impact (in percent) of the endogenous liquidity on their valuation, by making use of equation (1). The results are shown in Table 8.3. Since the estimation of the λ parameter is based on the 10 best bids and 10 best asks, the calculation of the impact for large portfolios is only indicative.

8.4.3 Results for the full dataset

The same computations were performed for the nine other entities. Table 8.4 shows the results of the estimation process.

The λ/σ ratio is reasonable and the weighted λ/weighted σ ratio is quite high, which indicates a very good quality of the weighted λ estimation. Being independent from a split of equity, the weighted λ/price ratio can be compared across entities. The results in Table 8.4 show that it is a good indicator of the liquidity: the smallest values of this ratio correspond to the most liquid entities, whereas the highest values are obtained for the two least liquid (and also the smallest) entities of the sample, Fleury Michon and

Table 8.3 Example of estimations of the impacts of the endogenous liquidity adjustments on the valuation of the portfolio for Accor

Size of the position[a] (EUR)	Adjusted price (EUR)	Difference (EUR)	Impact (%)
1,000,000	998,687	1313	0.1
10,000,000	9,869,748	130,252	1.3
50,000,000	46,854,370	3,145,630	6.3
100,000,000	87,939,581	12,060,419	12.1

Notes: [a]The total market capitalization of Accor is around EUR 5 billion, the daily volume of transactions is generally between EUR 1 million and 50 million.

Boiron. Additionally, the correlations between – λ and the size of the order book (in term of quantity of assets) are quite high, as shown in Table 8.5.

These high values indicate that the λ parameter was able to capture volume effects inside the order book. The λ parameter, normalized by the price, is shown to be a good indicator of liquidity.

8.4.4 Conclusion for 'not-yet-realized' endogenous liquidity

This section concludes by summarizing the findings with not-yet-realized endogenous liquidity. Although the estimation of the liquidity parameter was undertaken on a very small set of data during a volatile period (5–29 July 2011), it yielded some interesting conclusions.

- For each asset and for each end of day, a strong relationship has been found between quantities and prices, measured by a high R^2 coefficient from the regressions with these data.
- For each asset, the estimation of the λ parameter remains relatively stable and robust over the whole observation period, which even includes highly volatile days. When weighted by the size of the order book, the robustness of this estimation is even higher.
- The temporal evolutions show that the correlation between –λ and the size of the order book is generally very high: the issues of estimating the λ parameter and the daily volume are extremely similar.
- When normalized by the price of the relevant stock, λ/price is a good indicator of its liquidity.
- The impact of the endogenous liquidity on the valuation of the portfolio using the estimated λ parameter seems quite realistic.

Extensions to our analysis should incorporate a larger sample of order books in order to generalize these results. Further studies should also control for variance similar to this analysis so as to avoid the effects of volatile periods.

Table 8.4 Descriptive statistics for the 10 entities in the sample: λ, weighted λ values, and their corresponding standard deviations

	λ(Average)	σ	$\frac{\lambda}{\sigma}$	weighted λ	weighted σ	$\frac{\text{weighted } \lambda}{\text{weighted } \sigma}$	$\frac{\text{weighted } \lambda}{\text{price}}$
Accor	8.03E-08	1.87E-08	4.30	7.75E-08	6.55E-10	118.34	2.37E-06
Axa	9.78E-09	2.24E-09	4.37	9.08E-09	1.00E-10	90.43	1.32E-07
BNP Paribas	5.99E-08	4.04E-08	1.48	2.96E-08	7.16E-10	41.32	1.40E-06
Boiron	1.35E-05	3.53E-06	3.84	1.30E-05	1.47E-07	88.29	4.00E-04
Bouygues	4.94E-08	1.11E-08	4.47	4.76E-08	4.08E-10	116.66	1.31E-06
Carrefour	1.56E-08	6.31E-09	2.47	1.44E-08	1.99E-10	72.33	3.18E-07
Fleury Michon	1.57E-05	2.68E-06	5.86	1.52E-05	7.36E-08	206.86	5.33E-04
LVMH	8.61E-08	2.23E-08	3.87	7.96E-08	4.61E-10	172.80	1.01E-05
Peugeot	7.00E-08	1.37E-08	5.11	6.76E-08	6.71E-10	100.78	2.01E-06
Total	**1.95E-08**	**7.70E-09**	**2.53**	**1.74E-08**	**2.36E-10**	**73.94**	**6.79E-07**

Table 8.5 Correlations between $-\lambda$ and the total quantity of assets

	$\rho(-\lambda, \text{Quantity})$
Accor	65.0%
Axa	82.5%
BNP Paribas	84.3%
Boiron	51.8%
Bouygues	73.1%
Carrefour	65.8%
Fleury Michon	82.1%
LVMH	82.1%
Peugeot	69.3%
Total	77.3%

8.5 Results with realized endogenous liquidity

The question of whether our results with *not-yet-realized* order books can be extended to actually *realized* transactions is both theoretical and empirical. Does endogenous liquidity appear as an observable parameter in repetitive transactions? Does a dry-up in the market show up as a significant liquidity parameter in prices? Theoretically, a *realized* transaction is free of any liquidity constraints. It may have happened during a dry-up, yet nevertheless it happened because a counterparty could be found and a transaction size agreed. In a *realized* transaction, the counterparty facing illiquidity (sell side when there is a shortage of buyers) was able to find a buy-side counterparty.

Cetin, Jarrow, Protter and Warachka (2006) estimated the endogenous liquidity from the price of *realized* intraday transactions in listed instruments. We extend this analysis by using the information created by the new trade repositories and estimate the endogenous liquidity component of OTC market CDSs. We base our analysis on a set of CDS transactions with the following extension of the model presented in Section 8.3. We test empirically whether transaction size has an effect on the market portfolio of CDS transaction prices.

8.5.1 Application to CDS transactions

If we now consider a CDS portfolio at time T_0, with S_0 being the price of one unit of CDS, we can write:

$$S_0 = Premium_0. \tag{8.6}$$

The valuation of the portfolio at T_0 is:

$$V(T_0) = Premium \times N \tag{8.7}$$

where N is the total notional of the portfolio. The *Premium*, (the price for a notional N) is expressed in basis points. Therefore, equation (3) becomes:

$$\frac{Premium}{Premium_0}\left(1-\frac{\lambda}{2}\right)=1-\frac{\lambda}{2}N \tag{8.8}$$

or:

$$Premium \approx Premium_0 - \frac{\lambda}{2} \times Premium_0 \times N \tag{8.9}$$

This equation suggests that a linear regression of the premium on the volume N (which is the notional amount of CDS) would reveal the parameter λ.

8.5.2 CDS transaction datasets

Our unique dataset comes from the Depository Trust & Clearing Corporation (DTCC), which claims to capture data on 99 percent of CDS transactions worldwide. In our analysis, we used information only from new trades, whereas DTCC provides assignment, amendment and termination data as well. The transactions in our set are spread out over the June 2009–December 2010 period.

We have used two distinct datasets in order to understand the effects of realized endogenous liquidity. The first dataset consists of single-name CDS transactions of the top 10 most liquid sovereigns in 2009 and 2010. These are Turkey, Greece, Spain, Italy, Portugal, Germany, France, UK, Brazil, Mexico, Russia and Argentina, in descending order of the number of transactions. Russia and Argentina enter the top 10 only in 2009, whereas France and the UK only show up in 2010. When the transactions of both years are merged, we find that 2159 transactions have taken place where we observe a trade price.[2] 2059 of these trades are denominated in USD. Besides undertaking robustness checks with the EUR-denominated sample, we concentrate on USD-denominated trades due to their high dominance in the data. The total volume covered by this sample is USD 24.2 billion, and these 2059 transactions have an average notional of USD 11.7 million.

The second dataset is constructed by choosing single names for which CDS trades exist. It has been decided to alternatively look at single names from a real investment bank portfolio,[3] instead of top 10 liquid sovereign names. This larger dataset consists of 40732 confirmed trades with a conventional spread from 126 distinct entities. Among other currencies of notional volumes in the sample, USD-denominated trades cover a volume of around USD 175 billion, whereas EUR-denominated trades have a total volume of around EUR 113 billion.

8.5.3 Empirical results

We calibrated the λ parameter on DTCC data by making use of both datasets described in Section 8.5.2 and applying equation (7) to them. With this simplifying relationship, λ should ideally be a significant positive parameter.

Table 8.6 tabulates the results arising from regressing the CDS premiums on their volumes. On a given day, a total of 15 observations that have the same maturity, currency, and underlying entity were taken as a required minimum to be able to undertake the regression of the market portfolio.

In Table 8.6, it can be observed that all the observations have a minimum of 15 trades on a given day and a five-year initial maturity. The λ parameter is negative in six cases out of nine, and significant in only two cases, both of which are negative. This result can be interpreted to be due to either (i) selection of the ten most liquid sovereign entities, so that no endogenous λ parameter indicating a liquidity premium is significant; (ii) selection of a highly liquid time period for CDS in general, which would exacerbate the effects in (i); (iii) selection of the market portfolio instead of individual counterparty portfolios, which mixes up the buy and sell (positive and negative) effects on the λ parameter, ending up in an 'average', but insignificant, λ parameter; (iv) notional amounts in the regressions being smaller than a size leading to a price change: traders tending to split a large trade into several small orders to optimize liquidity costs; and (v) making use of *realized* transactions as a dataset, where actually no endogenous liquidity parameter is present, since the transactions have already been realized, possibly in smaller sizes.

In order to find out which of these conclusions can make sense, a second dataset, in which not only the liquid entities are present, is used. Despite this, a similar time period has been utilized due to data restrictions, and so the conclusion arising from (ii) cannot be ruled out yet. Table 8.7 presents the results with the second dataset arising from a benchmarking of a portfolio constructed by choosing single names for which CDS trades exist, as described in Section 8.5.2.

It is observed that the λ parameter is significant in 21 cases out of 54; however, in 9 out of 21 significances, the lambda has a negative sign. Besides that, the remaining positive significances are quite small: as a case in point, in the case of regression (10), a volume of USD 100 million changes the prices by only 0.296 bp. It could be concluded that any endogenous effect cannot be isolated.

These results strengthen the conclusion that CDS traders tend to split a large trade into several small orders to avoid liquidity costs (iv), which means that they have a clear idea of where the endogenous liquidity starts. Moreover, it can be more firmly stated that endogenous liquidity is not observed in a 'realized' OTC transactions dataset (v). Using liquid CDS entities (i) or a liquid time horizon (ii) does not affect in any way the robustness of these results. Unfortunately, the number of individual counterparty transactions is still not enough to test conclusion (iii), which remains unsolved. Since we are unable to distinguish buyer-initiated and seller-initiated trades, a mostly insignificant λ parameter may not be surprising. However, at the portfolio level of analysis, it can be stated that endogenous liquidity is not priced

Table 8.6 Parameter estimation results with the regressions using the first dataset

No.	Entity	n	Trade date	Term. date	Currency	Lambda	t-stat	p-value	Sig.
1	FRANCE	20	05-May-10	20-Jun-15	USD	−3.55E-10	−0.05	0.9593	
2	FRANCE	20	20-Dec-10	20-Mar-16	USD	3.20E-14	1.60	0.1262	
3	FRANCE	15	10-Dec-10	20-Dec-15	USD	−2.63E-14	−3.50	0.0032	**
4	GERMANY	60	28-Apr-10	20-Jun-15	USD	−2.77E-09	−2.08	0.0417	*
5	GERMANY	18	23-Apr-10	20-Jun-15	USD	−1.92E-09	−0.64	0.5312	
6	GREECE	152	19-Feb-10	20-Mar-15	USD	−8.01E-11	−0.10	0.9166	
7	GREECE	16	26-Feb-10	20-Mar-15	USD	−5.05E-10	−1.32	0.2064	
8	ITALY	16	10-May-10	20-Jun-15	USD	3.30E-09	0.60	0.5576	
9	SPAIN	18	10-Feb-10	20-Mar-15	USD	8.34E-10	1.22	0.2370	

Notes: ** Indicates significance at 99% level; * Indicates significance at 95% level.

Table 8.7 Parameter estimation results with the regressions using the second dataset

No.	Entity	n	Trade date	Term. date	Currency	Lambda	t-stat	p-value	Sig.
1	AXA	18	14-Dec-10	20-Dec-15	EUR	1.51E-12	0.83	0.4188	
2	AXA	18	20-Dec-10	20-Mar-16	EUR	−2.64E-12	−1.12	0.2793	
3	CLARIANT AG	18	29-Nov-10	20-Dec-15	EUR	−3.14E-10	−0.81	0.4290	
4	CONTINENTAL AG	40	02-Feb-10	20-Mar-15	EUR	−7.10E-09	−2.37	0.0225	*
5	CONTINENTAL AG	16	29-Oct-09	20-Dec-14	EUR	1.31E-08	2.85	0.0117	*
6	CONTINENTAL AG	28	31-Jul-09	20-Sep-14	EUR	−9.91E-10	−0.75	0.4622	
7	ENEL S.P.A.	16	20-Oct-09	20-Dec-14	EUR	2.47E-09	1.60	0.1282	
8	ENEL S.P.A.	24	29-Jan-10	20-Mar-15	EUR	−6.22E-09	−1.11	0.2759	
9	ENEL S.P.A.	34	04-Feb-10	20-Mar-15	EUR	5.19E-10	0.34	0.7392	
10	FORD MOTOR COMPANY	16	05-Oct-09	20-Jun-12	USD	2.82E-15	2.75	0.0141	*
11	FORD MOTOR COMPANY	16	09-Feb-10	20-Mar-15	USD	7.26E-09	1.49	0.1549	
12	FORD MOTOR COMPANY	16	12-Jan-10	20-Mar-15	USD	2.44E-09	3.94	0.0012	**
13	FORD MOTOR COMPANY	26	14-Sep-09	20-Sep-14	USD	−4.06E-14	−1.59	0.1241	
14	FORD MOTOR COMPANY	38	15-Sep-09	20-Sep-14	USD	5.92E-09	4.40	0.0001	**
15	FORD MOTOR COMPANY	22	07-May-10	20-Jun-15	USD	1.08E-09	0.14	0.8908	
16	FORD MOTOR CREDIT CO.	24	07-Apr-10	20-Jun-12	USD	−4.11E-09	−21.33	0.0000	**
17	GANNETT CO., INC.	22	30-Nov-09	20-Mar-12	USD	3.93E-10	12.18	0.0000	**
18	HSBC BANK PLC	20	17-Dec-10	20-Dec-14	EUR	4.67E-08	3.58	0.0019	**
19	HSBC BANK PLC	18	17-Dec-10	20-Mar-13	EUR	1.53E-08	0.62	0.5450	
20	INTESA SANPAOLO SPA	16	29-Jan-10	20-Mar-15	EUR	−6.36E-09	−0.54	0.5983	
21	INTESA SANPAOLO SPA	20	03-Dec-10	20-Dec-15	EUR	1.14E-07	3.27	0.0039	**
22	INTESA SANPAOLO SPA	16	29-Nov-10	20-Dec-15	EUR	7.12E-08	1.15	0.2665	
23	JAPAN	16	09-Mar-10	20-Mar-15	USD	−4.42E-10	−0.14	0.8926	
24	JAPAN	28	15-Apr-10	20-Jun-15	USD	−1.78E-09	−13.49	0.0000	**
25	JAPAN	24	22-Apr-10	20-Jun-15	USD	−5.52E-09	−7.83	0.0000	**
26	JAPAN	120	25-Feb-10	20-Mar-15	USD	9.81E-10	17.05	0.0000	**
27	JAPAN	18	26-Jan-10	20-Mar-15	USD	9.97E-09	15.15	0.0000	**
28	JAPAN	30	27-Jan-10	20-Mar-15	USD	−1.73E-10	−0.60	0.5512	

continued

Table 8.7 Continued

No.	Entity	n	Trade date	Term. date	Currency	Lambda	t-stat	p-value	Sig.
29	JAPAN	16	28-Jan-10	20-Mar-15	USD	−3.78E-09	−1.37	0.1909	
30	JAPAN	20	05-Oct-10	20-Dec-15	USD	−1.62E-09	−10.17	0.0000	**
31	JAPAN	16	22-Sep-10	20-Dec-15	USD	2.56E-09	0.35	0.7274	
32	JAPAN	26	29-Oct-10	20-Dec-15	USD	−7.71E-10	−29.18	0.0000	**
33	JAPAN	24	06-May-10	20-Jun-15	USD	1.47E-09	2.16	0.0406	*
34	JPMORGAN CHASE	16	28-Apr-10	20-Jun-15	USD	3.39E-09	0.58	0.5722	
35	JPMORGAN CHASE	16	30-Apr-10	20-Jun-15	USD	1.89E-09	0.72	0.4845	
36	JPMORGAN CHASE & CO.	26	19-Oct-10	20-Dec-15	USD	1.99E-09	0.69	0.4942	
37	KINGDOM OF THAILAND	22	14-May-10	20-Jun-15	USD	−1.27E-09	−1.44	0.1633	
38	LLOYDS TSB BANK	32	14-May-10	20-Jun-20	EUR	3.62E-22	3.81	0.0006	**
39	LLOYDS TSB BANK PLC	16	18-Oct-10	20-Dec-15	EUR	−2.30E-08	−0.60	0.5557	
40	LLOYDS TSB BANK PLC	18	14-Dec-10	20-Dec-15	EUR	1.35E-12	1.10	0.2872	
41	LLOYDS TSB BANK PLC	18	20-Dec-10	20-Mar-16	EUR	−3.55E-15	−0.36	0.7258	
42	LLOYDS TSB BANK PLC	54	24-Nov-10	20-Dec-15	EUR	9.34E-10	0.66	0.5138	
43	MORGAN STANLEY	30	03-Dec-09	20-Jun-16	EUR	3.24E-14	1.60	0.1203	
44	MORGAN STANLEY	16	12-May-10	20-Jun-15	USD	−2.27E-09	−1.51	0.1504	
45	PORTUGAL TELECOM INT.	34	04-Feb-10	20-Mar-15	EUR	2.82E-10	0.18	0.8545	
46	REP.OF PHILIPPINES	16	05-Mar-10	20-Mar-15	USD	1.51E-09	1.69	0.1100	
47	REP.OF PHILIPPINES	24	06-Aug-10	20-Sep-15	USD	−5.74E-10	−2.50	0.0196	*
48	SUPERVALU	18	22-Jul-10	20-Sep-15	USD	1.29E-09	4.85	0.0001	**
49	TELECOM ITALIA SPA	20	13-Apr-10	20-Jun-15	EUR	5.24E-09	0.87	0.3944	
50	THYSSENKRUPP AG	18	11-Feb-10	20-Mar-15	EUR	1.02E-08	1.28	0.2158	
51	UNITED BUSINESS MEDIA	24	21-Sep-10	20-Dec-15	EUR	−1.60E-22	−3.31	0.0029	**
52	UNITED BUSINESS MEDIA	26	16-Sep-10	20-Sep-15	EUR	3.00E-13	6.37	0.0000	**
53	VERIZON COMMS	16	01-Jul-09	20-Dec-11	USD	1.36E-14	1.21	0.2431	
54	WESTFIELD MANAGEMENT	32	11-Feb-10	20-Dec-10	USD	−5.13E-14	−1.39	0.1740	

Notes: ** Indicates significance at 99% level; * Indicates significance at 95% level.

into credit default swap prices. This observation supports the findings of Longstaff, Mithal and Neis (2005), who state that CDSs are contracts and not securities. Therefore, they can be arbitrarily created at any time, which makes them invulnerable to liquidity effects.

8.6 Conclusion and implications on supervision

Endogenous liquidity is a reality, but currently it is not considered for the accounting valuation of portfolios. Approaches to integrate it into this valuation, in particular using intraday prices on equities and for pricing derivatives products, exist. One of the difficulties lies in estimating the introduced endogenous liquidity parameter. In this chapter, we tried to build a composite picture for estimation techniques by using either trade repositories for CDS or the order book for listed equities. No endogenous liquidity component could be identified on CDS transactions, showing probably that market participants know full well where endogenous liquidity costs start, and prefer to split large transactions into several small ones. On the other hand, the use of order book information made it possible to estimate not-yet-realized endogenous liquidity parameters. Our study on the equity order book could probably be extended to other types of listed transactions, such as bonds or futures.

The evidence provided in our study shows that incorporating endogenous liquidity into the mark-to-market valuation of portfolios is feasible and realistic. Even if not recognized in the accounting results, it should be used to estimate prudential valuation, as requested by the BCBS, such that difference between prudent valuations and accounting valuations is taken from the capital, and the different risk measures (standardized or internal model) are estimated on these prudent valuations. Varying the value of the introduced endogenous liquidity parameters would give information on an institution's exposure to liquidity risk.

Introducing endogenous liquidity into the valuation of the portfolios would be extremely useful for several reasons.

- **Systemic risk** would be abated in two ways. First, it would help to address some issues associated with too-big-to-fail institutions. Indeed, the endogenous liquidity cost increases with the size of a position; as a result, the marginal profit of a new transaction will be negatively correlated to the size of the positions. Second, it would mitigate herding behavior as endogenous prudential liquidity reserves should prevent institutions from accumulating similar exposure to the same risks.
- The endogenous liquidity reserve would also help mitigate the **cyclicality** of the BCBS market risk framework. It would address, in particular, the case of market stress affecting the realized price of transactions. Moreover, as introducing endogenous liquidity reserves would decrease the

volatility of profit and loss (P&L), this would also contribute to reducing procyclicality.

- Taking valuation risk better into account should decrease the **volatility** of P&L, and thus dampen the incentives for short-term risk-taking.
- Recognizing endogenous liquidity risk should **penalize short positions:** since these are more exposed to endogenous liquidity via squeeze risk, introducing endogenous liquidity into the valuation should particularly penalize them.
- Endogenous liquidity should improve the computation of reserves. Although excluded from the current International Financial Reporting Standards (IFRS) rules, these reserves could be accumulated for future administrative costs as well. This will diminish upfront profits by some trading desks, and therefore will **impact traders' compensations** without necessarily decreasing the long-term profit of institutions.
- Finally, as adjusting the endogenous liquidity reserve would reduce the not-yet-realized part of the P&L but would not impact the realized part, it could represent a first step toward the **unification of prudential valuations/risk measures between the trading book and the banking book** (marked-to-market P&L converging towards accrued P&L).

Notes

This chapter has been developed during the Trading Book Group (TBG)/Research Task Force (RTF) Joint Work Stream of the Basel Committee for Banking Supervision. We thank the participants of the TBG/RTF Joint Work Stream, the RTF Frankfurt Workshop in February 2011, the TBG Ottawa Meetings in August 2011, and the RTF Istanbul Workshop in December 2011 for their constructive comments. This study presents ideas of the authors, which are not necessarily those of Deutsche Bundesbank, of the Autorité de Controle Prudentiel, or of Banque de France.

1. Our definition can be traced as an interpretation of the terminology of Nikolau (2009), where the author describes endogeneity to be the link of liquidity risk to the market conditions.
2. One should note that these are transactions in which at least one counterparty is supervised in Germany.
3. The restriction that at least one counterparty is of German origin still holds. The name of the investment bank could not be published due to confidentiality restrictions.

References

Acharya, V. and Pedersen, L. H. (2005). Asset Pricing with Liquidity Risk. *Journal of Financial Economics*, 77 (2), 375–410.

Amihud, Y., Mendelson, H. and Pedersen, L. H. (2005). Liquidity and Asset Prices. *Foundations and Trends in Finance*, 1 (4), 269–364.

Bangia, A., Diebold, F. X., Schuermann, T. and Stroughair, J. D. (2002). Modeling Liquidity, in Figlewski, S. and Levich, R. M. (eds) *Risk Management: The State of the*

Art. The New York University Salomon Center Series on Financial Markets and Institutions, Vol. 8, pp. 3–14. Springer, New York.

Basel Committee on Banking Supervision (2006). International Convergence of Capital Measurement and Capital Standards, Bank for International Settlements, Technical Report.

Basel Committee on Banking Supervision (2009). Supervisory Guidance for Assessing Banks' Financial Instrument Fair Value Practices, Bank for International Settlements, Technical Report.

Bervas, A. (2006). Market Liquidity and Its Incorporation into Risk Management. *Banque de France, Financial Stability Review*, 8, 63–79.

Cetin, U., Jarrow, R., Protter, P. and Warachka, M. (2006). Pricing Options in an Extended Black Scholes Economy with Illiquidity: Theory and Empirical Evidence. *Review of Financial Studies*, 19 (2), 493–529.

Duffie, D., Garleanu, N., and Pedersen, L. (2007). Valuation in Over-the-Counter Markets. *Review of Financial Studies*, 20 (5), 1865–900.

Huang, M. (2003). Liquidity Shocks and Equilibrium Liquidity Premia. *Journal of Economic Theory*, 109 (1), 104–29.

International Accounting Standards Board (2006). Fair Value Measurements, Technical Report, November, pp. 23–24.

Jarrow, R. A. and Protter, P. E. (2005). Liquidity Risk and Risk Measure Computation. *Review of Futures Markets,* 11 (1), 27–39.

Longstaff, F. (2009). Portfolio Claustrophobia: Asset Pricing in Markets with Illiquid Assets. *American Economic Review*, 99 (4), 1119–44.

Longstaff, F. A., Mithal, S., and Neis, E. (2005). Corporate Yield Spreads: Default Risk or Liquidity? New Evidence from the Default Swap Market. *Journal of Finance,* 60 (5), 2213–53.

Nikolaou, K. (2009). Liquidity (Risk) Concepts, Definitions and Interactions. European Central Bank Working Paper Series, No. 1008.

Possamai, D., Soner, H. M. and Touzi, N. (2010). Large Liquidity Expansion of Super-Hedging Costs, Les Cahiers de la Chaire, Technical Report, No. 35.

Rogers, L. C. G. and Singh, S. (2005). Option Pricing in an Illiquid Market. University of Cambridge, Technical Report.

Wagner, W. (2011). Systemic Liquidation Risk and the Diversity-Diversification Trade-Off, *Journal of Finance,* 66 (4), 1141–75.

9
The 2008 UK Banking Crash: Evidence from Option Implied Volatility

Ha Yan Raymond So, Tarik Driouchi, and Zhiyuan Simon Tan

9.1 Introduction

The 2007–9 Great Recession reached its culmination point in 15 September 2008 with the demise of Lehman Brothers and the near collapse of the global financial system. A major banking crash would follow as a result of impending stock markets mayhem and abnormal credit risk contagion (Bartram and Bodnar, 2009; Longstaff, 2010). UK banking institutions in particular were severely affected by this turn of events. The oligopolistic structure of the industry and the weight of financial services in the UK economy did not facilitate recovery ex-post. Although losses incurred were somewhat unpredictable, the crisis itself did not come as a surprise. Early signs for a global downturn looming could be spotted in standard economic indicators as early as summer/fall 2006 (Mihm, 2008; Reinhart and Rogoff, 2008). Financial markets' indicators would follow suit soon after with mild and sporadic warnings from index options.[1] In this contribution we examine whether similar warning signals could be patterned in equity options markets (for options on individual stocks) in the UK. Specifically, we analyze the information efficiency of option IV as a predictor of (future) realized stocks downside volatility –a proxy for bank soundness and downside risk –of the four major UK banks around the 2008 global markets crash.[2] Given that the event was mainly banking-driven, it is interesting to shed light on the interaction between banks' stock prices and the volatilities implied by transactions prices for their exchange-listed options during the time leading to the crash. Prior research has already established that variances induced from banking equity options prices are better (but biased) forecasts of bank stock volatility, and hence bank failure probability, than traditional frameworks used in the financial services sector to monitor banking turbulence (for example, Swidler and Wilcox, 2002). However, this evidence is specific to US banks and, though comprehensive time wise, did not cover banking-specific crises at the time.

In this study we examine related IV dynamics for UK high street banks in the particular context of the fall 2008 banking crash. We follow the behavior of banking options IVs from 2006 to 2008 and analyze predictive power and information content vis-à-vis the subsequent behavior of the underlying banks' stock prices. We emphasize the case of UK banks because of their heavy weight in the global financial system, their significant role in the recent subprime financial crisis, the relative liquidity of equity options written on UK banking stocks, and the need for further (derivatives) markets-based research on banking risk and soundness (see for example Ioannidis et al., 2010; Liadaki and Gaganis, 2010; Trutwein and Schiereck, 2011).

Several studies have attempted to examine the information content of option implied volatility around crisis phenomena or highly uncertain events (for example, Bates, 1991; Gemmill, 1992; Poteshman, 2006). Such works would mainly revolve around the trading dynamics of index and foreign exchange options (for example, Bhabra et al., 2001; Cao et al., 2005; Dupoyet, 2006). Research on equity options and their implied volatility, however, is relatively scarce (Taylor et al., 2010; Elkamhi and Ornthanalai, 2010; Xing et al., 2010). Regarding the 2007–9 Great Recession, contributions on the forecasting ability of options markets are probably still emerging, but are usually not on banking downside risk (Figlewski, 2009; Birru and Figlewski, 2009; Cao et al., 2011; Trutwein and Schiereck, 2011). Here, we are concerned with the predictive power of IV as a forecast for bank stock downside volatility realized during the peak of the 2007–9 financial crisis. If we can obtain information from options markets regarding expected/future downturns, proactive –rather than reactive –and coordinated measures can be adopted by senior bankers and regulators to prevent systemic banking failure, and protect the real economy against severe economic shocks. IV inputs from options markets can be employed in conjunction with, and as inputs to, other warning and risk management systems (for example, ratings, yield spreads, value-at-risk, credit default swap (CDS) spreads and so on) to gauge banking distress in advance and signal markets downturn well ahead of backward looking financial and economic metrics (see for example Hamalainen et al., 2012 and the case of Northern Rock).

Options prices data over 2006–8 for four of the five largest UK banks at the time, Barclays, RBS, HSBC and Lloyds TSB, are analyzed to examine possible evidence of aggregate market opinion prior to September/October 2008 of an imminent banking downfall. The relationship between banks' stock downside volatility and IV from a set of OTM put options written on individual banking stocks is investigated under the elementary Black–Scholes (1973) and Merton (1976) jump diffusion, hereafter BS and MJD respectively, IV frameworks. OLS and 2SLS regressions are conducted using several prediction windows to test, with daily but Newey–West adjusted overlapping data, if and to what extent implied volatility could be a (un)biased predictor of banking (future) volatility and downside risk realized during the fall of 2008. Together with information on incidents happening during the two years prior to the crisis peak we are able validate the hypothesis of investors' bearish opinion about UK banks, confirming that despite intermittent evidence of bullish behavior and indecisiveness in the market the fall 2008 banking crash could to a relevant degree be predicted before its occurrence.[3] We also corroborate the previously established (lead-lag) association between IV and realized volatility (RV) with the former acting as a superior predictor of the latter. Additional results from variance decomposition and instrumented IV regressions did highlight the interdependencies across banks and the effects of US markets on UK banking downside risk. These results call for a better incorporation of options-based market information in existing risk management and stress-testing techniques used by bankers and regulators to assess financial services performance/distress and diagnose the likelihood of banking failure.

The remainder of the chapter proceeds as follows. Section 9.2 discusses related research and implied volatility frameworks. Section 9.3, on data and methods, describes our analytical setup. Section 9.4 summarizes our findings and covers implications while Section 9.5 concludes.

9.2 Background

The use of option IV as a forecast for asset volatility is well documented (Poon and Granger, 2005; Mayhew, 1995).Whether examining call or put options contracts, the basic intuition is that volatility implied in options prices is reflective of the general market view or expectations about future movements in the underlying up to the options' exercise or expiry dates. Fears of downside occurrences can be revealed broadly in put options prices' deviations (see for example Cao et al., 2010). Bullish sentiment on the other hand can be foreseen in call options prices' movements. The forecasting efficiency of option IV generally depends on several factors besides the analytical model used for price and value synchronization (the IV model). Such factors would be related to option maturity and moneyness, liquidity and market microstructure issues, and firm specific characteristics (Cheng et al., 2000; Taylor et al., 2010). Examples of IV models encountered in the literature are based on Brownian motion (Beckers, 1981), jump diffusion (Bates, 1996), model-free (Jiang and Tian, 2005), and stochastic volatility characteristics (Hull and White, 1987; Heston, 1993). The choice of model is subject to the nature of risk and uncertainty in financial markets, the type of underlying asset traded, and the distributions of options and underlying returns.

Research on the information content of implied option volatility can be categorized generally into studies comparing the efficiency of a number of proxies for volatility and performance prediction (Cao et al., 2005; Mixon, 2009), and studies examining the dynamics of options markets around uncertain events (for example, financial crises, elections, or market crashes) (Gemmill and Saflekos, 2000; Low, 2004). This includes the investigation of rational bubbles and analysis of trading patterns and market sentiment (for example, via trading volumes, liquidity and risk neutral distributions) (Bates, 1991, 1996; McIntyre and Jackson, 2009). The general consensus is that option IV is an efficient but biased predictor of future stock/index returns and future volatility.[4] In this research we are concerned with the forecasting ability of equity options markets for the 2008 global banking downturn. We investigate and compare the predictive power and information efficiency of options IV around the fall 2008 banking crash, in particular emphasizing the debacle of UK 'high street' banks.

Examples of papers related to this area include Rappoport and White (1994) on the 1929 crash, Bates (1991) on the 1987 crash, and Fung (2007) on the 1997 Hong Kong stock market collapse. For instance, Rappoport and White use BS volatility implied from the optionality of US collateralized brokers' loans to analyze and confirm investors' expectations of a stock market crash during the late 1920s. In a similar context, Bates (1991) studies the (mis)pricing of OTM call and put options on S&P 500 futures during the 1985–7 period, to reveal that the 1987 stock market crash was expected and signaled by options prices ex-ante. Other studies comprise Bhabra et al. (2001) on the 1997 Korean economic crisis and Cheng et al. (2000) on the pricing behavior of index options in Hong Kong prior to and throughout the Asian financial crisis. Research related to more recent events and the 2007–8 credit crunch include Birru and Figlewski (2009), Longstaff (2010) and Trutwein and Schiereck (2011).

However, not many of the above options markets' focused works are devoted specifically to banks and banking crises (see for instance Dwyer and Tkac, 2009; Demyanyk and Hasan, 2012; Barros et al., 2012; Eichler et al., 2011 and Dietrich and Wanzenried, 2011 as relevant examples of studies on banking risk analysis and prediction but not from the perspective of options markets).[5] Swidler and Wilcox (2002), Crouhy (2002), Hamalainen et al. (2012) and to a lesser extent –due to their emphasis of firms' CDS spreads – Cao et al. (2010) and Trutwein and Schiereck (2011) are among the few contributions related to options markets' predictive efficiency.[6] Swidler and Wilcox (2002) present US evidence that bank risks in the form of stock prices dumps can be predicted by the implied volatility calculated from corresponding equity options prices. In their research, the authors emphasize the case of three US banks, Bank of America, Citicorp and Great Western Financial, which had options traded for their study period, specifically investigating the relationship between bank equity volatility and BS option implied volatility. The results attained suggest that implied volatility had predictive power to future volatility realized during their study period but was a biased forecast. Swidler and Wilcox (2002) add further that IV contains not only important information about common movements across bank equity, but also bank-specific movements in bank risks with leverage and size as meaningful determinants. The authors conclude that adding a measure of implied volatility to existing banking risk monitoring measures would be useful in evaluating the failure probability of banks and is very likely to provide relevant information about banking risk, especially that this information is cheap, objective and timely (Swidler and Wilcox, ibid). Fung (2007) and Cao et al. (2011) share a similar view on this matter with respect to risk and market turbulence in general.

We argue that IV measures from banking equity options should be used responsibly and more extensively to understand and signal risk in financial services. Given the relative efficiency of options markets, different ranges of implied volatilities can be integrated in existing risk warning systems to regularly monitor banking downside risk and possibly alleviate crash and recession eventualities/expectations. There are not many empirical studies testing whether options prices could provide forward information regarding the financial crisis that started in 2007 and resulted in the fall of Lehman Brothers and the distress of many other banks globally.[7] Here we investigate whether the peak of the crisis could have been anticipated ex-ante and how far equity options markets can inform us about the downturn of UK individual banking stocks. We study the relationship between implied volatility during 2006–8 and future downside volatility realized by UK high street banking stocks prior to and during the fall 2008 banking crash, specifically (1) verifying the forecasting power of IV as a superior predictor of stock volatility and (2) examining whether the UK banking downturn could be signaled ex-ante. By assessing thoroughly the lead-lag relationship between options implied volatility and equity volatility and the downside risk of the main UK financial institutions, we extend the very recent US-based banking risk findings of Trutwein and Schiereck (2011) on the (reverse) association between CDS spreads and options volatility during the 2007–8 period.[8]

With the implied volatility being computed from the examples of IV models discussed above, least square regressions are usually implemented in the extant literature to analyze the relationship between implied volatility and future realized volatility (Taylor et al., 2010). In line with prior studies in this area (Christensen and Prabhala, 1998; Ederington and Guan, 2005; Swidler and Wilcox, 2002), the following model is implemented:

$$\ln \sigma_{r,t,T} = \beta_0 + \beta_1 \ln \sigma_{I,t,T} + \varepsilon \tag{9.1}$$

where $\sigma_{r,t,T}$ denotes the future (downside) realized volatility[9] of the specific banking stock analyzed based on daily returns from time t to T; $\sigma_{I,t,T}$ denotes the volatilities implied by daily settlement prices of (banking) equity options (with maturity T) written on their corresponding underlying assets;β_0 is the

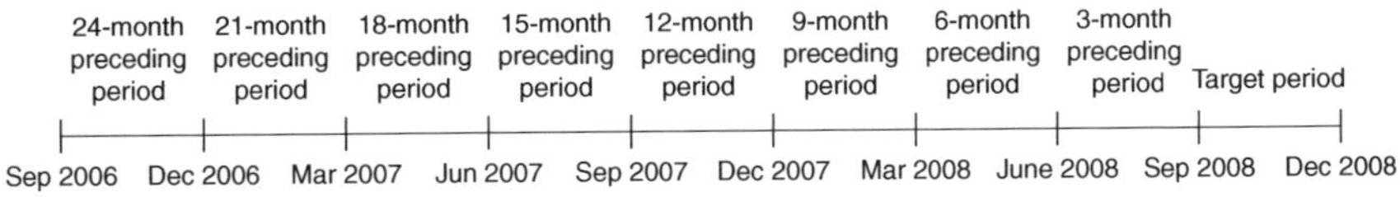

Figure 9.1 Target and preceding periods timeline for signaling tests

intercept, β_1 is the coefficient of implied volatility. If implied volatility contains information about future volatility, β_1 should be a non-zero figure. If implied volatility is an un-biased forecast of realized volatility, β_0 should be 0 and β_1 should be 1. If implied volatility is efficient, the residual ε should be uncorrelated with any variable in the market's information set. The above model is used to (1) verify the forecasting power of IV as a superior predictor of stock volatility during the 2006–8 period and (2) to examine whether the fall 2008 UK banking downturn could have been signaled in advance. For robustness purposes and to account for endogeneity effects in IV from prior IVs, equation (1) was also tested using an instrumented procedure where, depending on the overall number of preceding periods available,

$$\ln \sigma_{r,t} = \beta_0 + \beta_1 \ln \sigma_{I,t-1} + \varepsilon \tag{9.2}$$

where:

$$\sigma_{I,t-1} = f(\sigma_{I,t-2}, \sigma_{I,t-3}, \ldots \sigma_{I,t-n}); \tag{9.3}$$

$\sigma_{r,t}$, represents the ex-post realized downside volatility estimated based on the last 22 daily returns of the specific banking stock analyzed for a given target period (see Section 9.3 for further details on data procedures and timelines), $\sigma_{I,t-1,}$ denotes the volatilities implied by daily settlement prices of options written on the corresponding underlying asset for the preceding periods schedule outlined in Figure 9.1. A similar robustness procedure was also followed to capture general volatility effects of S&P implied volatility index VIX and FTSE implied volatility index VFTSE on bank IV. The predicted IV from VIX and subsequently (backdated) VFTSE was then used as an independent variable in equation (2).

In order to assess the predictive power of IV and verify whether a banking downturn could be anticipated at the aggregate level, the analysis is conducted on daily settlement prices of equity put options traded in the UK. We focus on OTM and near the money put options because these are fairly liquid prior and during crisis events and are indicative of downside risk expectations in the market (Latane and Rendleman, 1976; Gemmill, 1986; Bates, 1991). Implied volatilities are computed through reverse computation of the Black and Scholes (1973) and the Merton (1976) jump diffusion option pricing models.[10] Details of methodology and data used are discussed in Section 9.3.

9.3 Data and methods

9.3.1 Models and variables specifications

9.3.1.1 *Black and Scholes implied volatility*

The Black and Scholes (1973) model is employed as the basis for calculating BS implied volatility in our study. The pricing formula for a put option under this framework is expressed as follows:

$$P_t = K_t e^{-r_t T_t} N(-d_2) - S_t e^{-q_t T_t} N(-d_1) \tag{9.4}$$

where:

$$d_1 = \frac{(\ln(S_t/K_t) + (r_t - q_t)T_t + \sigma_t^2 T_t/2)}{\sigma_t \sqrt{T_t}} \quad \text{and} \quad d_2 = d_1 - \sigma_t \sqrt{T_t}$$

with K, S, T, r, σ and q the usual inputs of the Black–Scholes equation. By solving (9.4) numerically, with σ_t as the unknown, implied volatility for each option price observed in the market can be obtained.

9.3.1.2 *Jump diffusion implied volatility*

The Merton (1976) model is used for our comparative jump diffusion MJD IV estimates. This approach, being suitable in the context of crises events, aims to capture discontinuous stock returns and incorporates jump effects to the pricing apparatus. The price P'_t of a put option under this framework can be written as:

$$P'_t = \sum_{n=0}^{\infty} \frac{e^{-\lambda' T}(\lambda' T)^n}{n!} f_n \tag{9.5}$$

where λ is the average number of jumps occurring per year or period, $\lambda' = \lambda(1+k)$, k is the average jump size as a percentage of the stock price and f_n is the standard Black–Scholes put option price. The variance rate v is $v = \sigma_t^2 + \frac{ns^2}{T}$. The risk free rate is given by $r - \lambda k + \frac{n\gamma}{T}$, where $\gamma = \ln(1+k)$. By solving (9.6) numerically, with σ_t as the required output, implied volatility can be determined. Parameters estimations can be obtained using standard RMSE minimization.

9.3.1.3 *Time to maturity*

Time to maturity is measured by the number of calendar days between the trade day and the maturity day divided by the number of calendar days in a whole year. A standardized 365 days was used for this purpose. The effect of this standardization should not affect the calculation of implied volatilities except for options with very short lives.

9.3.1.4 *Realized (downside) volatility*

Realized volatility is measured by computing the sample standard deviation of the daily stock returns in the sample period and then adjusting it to an annualized quantity. The number of trade days in a year was taken as 252. The annualized realized volatility is expressed as

$$\sigma_{r,t,T} = \sqrt{\frac{\sum_{i=t}^{T}(R_i - \bar{R})^2}{n-1}} \times \sqrt{252} \tag{9.6}$$

where $\sigma_{r,t,T}$ is the realized volatility in period t, R_i is the daily return and $\bar{R}$ is the mean daily return for the sample period. RV was mainly employed in the general predictive performance regressions (that is, IV predicting RV throughout the entire 2006–8 period).

For crisis signaling purposes, ex-post realized downside volatility was estimated according to the following procedure (see for example Low, 2004)

$$\sigma_{r,t,T} = \sqrt{\frac{\sum_{i=t-21}^{t}(R_{d,i} - MAR)^2}{n-1}} \times \sqrt{252} \tag{9.7}$$

Where $\sigma_{r,t}$ is the downside realized volatility estimated based on the latest 22 daily return of the banking stock, $R_{d,t}$ is the downside daily return of the banking stock on day t and MAR is the minimum acceptable return (zero in this case) on day t.

9.3.2 Data

Realized (downside) volatilities are calculated from daily settlement prices of the underlying equities, while implied volatilities (IV) are computed from daily settlement prices of the corresponding European equity put options. Stocks and options prices were obtained from Thomson Datastream. At the early stages of the research, put option prices for the five main UK high street banks at the time, HBOS, Barclays, Lloyds TSB, HSBC and Royal Bank of Scotland, were collected for the period of 1 January 2005 to 31 December 2008. However, HBOS was dropped from the study due to severe data unavailability. Data obtained from Thomson Datastream was available as shown in Table 9.1.

Other than the daily settlement prices of options, data collected included strike prices (K) and maturity date for each individual put option. Implied volatilities were computed under BS and MJD both described above using daily options prices observed in the market. Option prices and stock prices were adjusted for dividend payments. UK gilts rates were used as the risk-free rate (R_f) in computing the implied volatilities. As explained above, this data was collected for two related purposes. First, we verified that option IV was a superior predictor of stock volatility during 2006–8. The regression

Table 9.1 Data availability for option prices

Stock	Number of options	Available period
HSBC	466	1 Jan 2005–31 Dec 2008
RBS	818	
Lloyds	454	
Barclays	626	

design for this particular task is in line with prior research on the information content of options prices and uses the ex-ante stock realized volatility as a dependent variable. Subsequent findings are reported in Table 9.3. Second, we examined whether the unusual volatility surrounding the 2008 banking crash could be signaled in options prices ex-ante using a number of preceding periods of implied volatility. For this purpose, we adopted a modified regression design and employed the ex-post downside realized volatility as a dependent variable for our target period of downside volatility, plus made the Newey and West (NW) (1987) adjustment for standard errors and serial correlation controls (see also Cao et al., 2010; Yu et al., 2010). This allowed us to calculate the realized volatility with a short period of returns instead of using the length of the preceding period. Moreover, in the proposed signaling design the target period was not immediately following the preceding period. Instead, a gap of different lengths was left to test the predictive power of implied volatility with different time windows prior to the crisis peak or high volatility period. This signaling design is illustrated in Figure 9.1.[11] Table 9.4 reports related findings.

Similar to Yu et al. (2010) and others (for example Mixon, 2009; Cao et al., 2010), we implemented the NW adjustment/correction to minimize overlapping problems faced with the use of daily observations in realized volatility regressions. We also accounted for endogenous/exogenous IV effects by running 2SLS regressions where (1) IV was a function of prior periods' IVs and (2) IV was also a function of VIX or (backdated) VFTSE respectively.[12] IV for each preceding period is computed from (OTM) put option prices for that period. As previously stated, realized downside volatility (RDV) (see Low, 2004) is included as a dependent variable in this research to verify the information content of OTM put prices regarding exclusive downside risk signals.[13] The detailed schedule of preceding periods employed for our crash prediction tests is shown in Figure 9.1. The use of multiple preceding periods for these tests is aimed at gauging and monitoring investors' future expectations – at various time intervals (quarterly and bi-monthly) prior to the crash –of what would happen to banks' stock prices in fall 2008. This also explains the existence of gaps between the preceding and target periods adopted for these tests as observed in Figure 9.1. With respect to the general

Table 9.2 Descriptive statistics and correlation matrix

Variable	Mean	Std dev.	Max.	Min.	Barclays IV	Lloyds IV	RBS IV	HSBC IV	VFTSE
Barclays IV	0.3915	0.1078	0.6730	0.2681					
Lloyds IV	0.4866	0.1623	0.9498	0.2999	0.8543				
RBS IV	0.5081	0.1177	0.7657	0.2740	0.8263	0.5619			
HSBC IV	0.2373	0.0651	0.4072	0.1047	0.9064	0.8345	0.6691		
VFTSE	0.1974	0.0583	0.3486	0.1074	0.5356	0.3535	0.7141	0.4625	
VIX	0.1833	0.0588	0.3224	0.0989	0.5687	0.3908	0.6954	0.5079	0.9292

Table 9.3 RV and IV association for 2006–8

	Independent variables		
Stock	Cst.	IV	R^2
HSBC	0.055 (0.999)	0.920 (18.478)	84.59%
RBS	0.300 (8.567)	0.715 (10.672)	51.08%
Lloyds	0.063 (4.083)	0.943 (27.012)	88.92%
Barclays	0.242 (7.818)	0.916 (20.123)	83.90%

Note: * t-statistics in parentheses.

forecasting power of IV as a predictor of realized stock volatility, we employ the full range of daily IV data available for 2006–8 with no gap between target and preceding periods. This was also done to assess the extent to which option implied volatility could be built up in stock volatility on a day-to-day basis, specifically reflecting how investors can immediately incorporate option implied volatility information in their equity valuation estimates.

Our main period of interest (our target) is fall 2008. Signaling regressions are, hence, set up with realized downside volatilities starting in September 2008 as the dependent variable, with implied volatilities from the preceding periods as the independent constructs. We focus our analysis on OTM put options as implied volatility computed from OTM put option prices can have better predictive power than both at-the-money (ATM) puts and in-the-money (ITM) puts for crisis periods and downside volatility events. This is also in accordance with the market expectations of a possible downturn. A target period of three months, September 2008 to November 2008, is used in our signaling tests for the calculation of realized downside volatilities for each of the four stocks. This is to keep the crash prediction objective more in line with the high volatility period resulting from Lehman Brothers collapse and the distress of other banks globally. That also justifies the use of daily options prices. Regarding the calculation of downside realized volatilities, a one-month period was employed. The use of short periods in calculating the RDV instead of using a longer period (for example, 3 months, 1 year) as in other research could provide a better sensitivity of the volatility realized during the crisis peak because 'memory' effects are somewhat reduced. The use of a shorter period to calculate the realized volatility can also offer the benefit of less overlapping in data. To further reduce the effect of overlapping in data, our attention is mainly on regressions with the implied volatility as the main variable explaining realized (downside) deviations in stock returns. The telescoping problem does not exist in the signaling design as ex-post realized volatilities instead of ex-ante realized volatilities are calculated. Our statistical output is NW adjusted for all regressions (general and signaling).

Table 9.4 Realized downside volatility results 2006–8: crash signaling

	Barclays					HSBC				
	Cst	IV	F	R^2	MJD	Cst	IV	F	R^2	MJD
3 months	0.7745 (1.715)	0.4093 (2.8246)	12.6782	0.1675	+9% R2 +5% Beta	4.9580 (13.3711)	0.9148 (16.3175)	323.2188	0.8369	Idem
6 months	−3.3855 (−6.5072)	−0.6189 (−5.8332)	39.1062	0.3830	+11% R2 +5% Beta	−5.4397 (−15.617)	−0.8732 (−12.494)	202.1833	0.7624	+10% R2 +5% Beta
9 months	1.8135 (8.1549)	0.8655 (11.059)	188.1130	0.7491	+2% R2 +1% Beta	3.1773 (6.9843)	0.8714 (9..2253)	198.6961	0.7593	+0.6% R2 +0.3% Beta
12 months	0.3291 (1.3957)	0.5013 (3.3629)	21.1477	0.2513	Idem	4.4762 (6.9864)	0.8033 (8.4317)	114.6014	0.6453	Idem
15 months	1.0737 (2.2879)	0.4720 (3.267)	18.0571	0.2228	+3% R2 +1% Beta	3.6967 (7.3197)	0.8499 (9.1962)	163.9411	0.7224	+0.3% R2 +0.15% Beta
18 months	−4.3424 (−2.1245)	−0.2613 (−1.882)	4.6173	0.0683	+316% R2 +104% Beta	−16.6837 (−9.6426)	−0.7564 (−8.9778)	84.2378	0.5721	+28% R2 +13% Beta
21 months	−9.8954 (−2.6927)	−0.4986 (−2.5294)	20.8458	0.2486	+85% R2 +36% Beta	4.5728 (4.1615)	0.7449 (5.1592)	78.5456	0.5549	Idem
24 months	−15.3149 (−12.5724)	−0.9221 (−12.0645)	357.7080	0.8503	+2% R2 +1% Beta	14.1083 (9.0207)	0.8427 (9.4571)	154.4017	0.7102	Idem

continued

Table 9.4 Continued

	Lloyds					RBS				
	Cst	IV	*F*	R^2	MJD	Cst	IV	*F*	R^2	MJD
3 months	−1.2369	0.8833	223.7452	0.7803	Idem	2.8077 (4.0941)	0.5489 (4.3085)	27.1670	0.3013	Idem
6 months	−4.2302 (−6.4781)	−0.4557 (−3.5078)	16.5096	0.2076	+16% R2 +8% Beta	−1.8820 (−2.6955)	−0.6015 (−2.5095)	24.7550	0.3225	Idem
9 months	−1.4313 (−4.8008)	0.3789 (2.0135)	10.5638	0.1436	+2% R2 +1% Beta	1.8180 (2.9877)	0.5694 (3.6287)	30.2298	0.3243	+2%R2 +1% Beta
12 months	−2.0734 (−10.8015)	−0.0085 (−0.0553)	0.0045	0.0001	+3166% R2 +470% Beta	0.3873 (0.5348)	0.1620 (0.7747)	1.6976	0.0262	Idem
15 months	−1.1432 (−1.5688)	0.2391 (1.183)	3.8193	0.0572	Idem	1.4299 (1.299)	0.3133 (1.4858)	6.8578	0.0982	Idem
18 months	−9.3051 (−13.3792)	−0.8381 (−10.4263)	148.6755	0.7024	Idem					
21 months										
24 months										

Note: * t-statistics in parentheses.

Further details on data constructs and the components of equations (1–2) are provided below.

9.3.2.1 Regressions data characteristics

To perform the regression analyses and investigate the relationship between realized (downside) volatility and IV of the period(s) preceding our targets – specifically the information content of options implied volatility around and surrounding the fall 2008 banking crash – data collected for each individual UK banking stock was handled according to the following procedures. (1) Realized downside volatility was computed for the target (crisis) period September 2008 to November 2008. This was done for our crash prediction tests. (2) Realized volatility was computed for the 2006–8 period to verify the lead-lag association between IV and RV and assess the predictive power of the former. (3) For a pool of options available for the various preceding periods, OTM puts were selected for every period. Options with long and short maturities were both sampled. Near the money (OTM) put options were chosen as instruments of analysis.[14] (4) For each sample, after maturity matching, implied volatilities were computed using the Black and Scholes and Merton jump diffusion models. (5) Regressions analyses were implemented according to the specifications outlined in Section 9.2 and findings were aggregated using the average of results obtained for the appropriately selected contracts. Overall findings are reported in Section 9.4.

9.4 Findings

9.4.1 Descriptive statistics

Table 9.2 presents descriptive statistics and shows correlations among banks, and associations between each bank BS IV and the VIX and VFTSE indices. Significant variation can be observed in IV values, highlighting investors' fear and lack of certainty about the future. Despite exhibiting some idiosyncratic movements, correlation coefficients are far above those reported in previous studies (Swidler and Wilcox, 2002), suggesting that herding might have been in operation during the period or simply reflecting the oligopolistic nature of the sector in the UK. This also indicates that industry effects were relatively dominant. This specific phenomenon can be accentuated in the context of credit crunches. Each bank IV correlates significantly with VFTSE and VIX, underlining also market and systemic effects. Figure 9.2 highlights these dynamics comparatively among the four banks. IVs for RBS, Barclays and Lloyds were considerably above VIX and VFTSE, reaching unusual levels at times. On the other hand, HSBC shows less evidence of downside risk fears than the other three banks. This might be explained by HSBC's well diversified market operations worldwide and other idiosyncratic considerations.

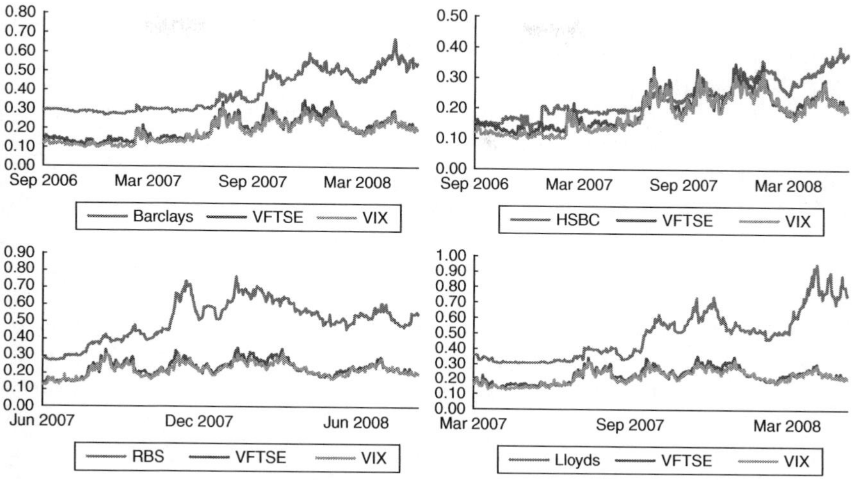

Figure 9.2 Bank IV versus VIX and VFTSE

Section 9.4.2 reports our main regression findings (general and signaling). First, we verify the forecasting power of IV as a superior predictor of RV during 2006–8. Second, we examine whether the UK banking downturn could be signaled ex-ante. Specific NW adjusted regression outcomes are presented in Tables 9.3 and 9.4 for RV and RDV predictions respectively.

9.4.2 Regression results

Table 9.3, on the general predictive performance of IV, shows realized volatility findings for the four banks throughout the entire 2006–8 period. Results confirm the lead-lag association between options markets information and equity markets information. Regression outputs validate the hypothesis that option implied volatility is an efficient but biased predictor of realized stock volatility. This is line with outcomes from prior research (for example, Swidler and Wilcox, 2002; Fung, 2007; Yu et al., 2010). Note that despite the relatively good accuracy of findings, the predictive power of RBS IVs tends to be weaker than that of Barclays, HSBC and Lloyds IVs. Given that these results confirm the superior information content of implied volatility, we can now turn to our (crash) signaling regressions.

Table 9.4 summarizes our crash predictions tests. The various regressions for the preceding periods used follow –subject to data availability –the timelines described in Figure 9.1. To verify prediction power and IV model accuracy, comparative MJD results are also added to the analysis. In terms of forecasting efficiency, Barclays and HSBC have the best predictive power overall because of significant option trading volume on their options (proxied by the number of different strikes available for trade relative to RBS and

Lloyds) and better quality maturity matching. A number of consistent patterns emerge for the four banks. Downside risk fears could be observed 3, 9, 12 and 15 months prior to the period of interest, with positive but biased predictive associations between IVs and the dependent variables.[15] Pessimistic sentiment was not necessarily present 6, 18, 21 and 24 months before the crash, with possibly bullish or indecisive expectations among Barclays, RBS and Lloyds options' investors. This signifies that in the 15 months leading to the crash, downside risk fears were present four times out of five (seven out of ten times if we consider the two-months preceding periods findings) for these three banks and also HSBC. No sign of bearishness was observed prior to that and as far as 2005, implying that there were no downside risk fears or expectations for 2008 more than two years before the crash for the four banks.[16] However, HSBC IV analysis underlined negative aggregate expectations 21 and 24 months prior to the target period. This can be explained by HSBC's significant exposure to the US subprime market at the time, the global status of the business and their strong US presence relative to the other three banks, and perhaps their early appreciation of the consequences of the subprime bubble burst. These conclusions usually hold when using two months preceding periods' IVs. For instance, downside expectations were detected 8, 11 and 14, but not 5 and 17 months before the crash for the four banks. Bearish sentiment was again present among HSBC's options investors 20 and 23 months prior to the target period. This did not happen in the case of the other three banks. An interesting finding thought was that crash fears were possibly alleviated during the two months immediately preceding the fall 2008 events (that is, non-positive betas were observed for Barclays, Lloyds and RBS but positive betas were found for HSBC).[17] This is consistent with the economics and nature of stock market crashes.

In general, findings suggest that the fall 2008 UK banking stocks' debacle was in a way expected. It was explained by options markets more than once at various time intervals (prior and during the so called credit crunch period) and as early as June 2007. It was not necessarily foreseen between March and June 2007 or before (that is, a lack of crash was signaled). However, results hint at the possibility of earlier detection in the US market as evidenced by HSBC IV results for the last quarter of 2006 and the first quarter of 2007. These findings were validated after controlling for endogeneity and using preceding IVs as instrumented variables in the 2SLS procedures (see for example Christensen and Prabhala, 1998). The statistical analyses using VIX and (backdated) VFTSE as instruments were also consistent with these findings as directions of associations and qualitative conclusions were generally unchanged.

For the four UK banks analyzed, significant drops in share prices were expected for fall 2008 by options' investors, especially during the 15 months leading to the crash. This is depicted clearly in Figure 9.3, with strong evidence/symmetry for Barclays, Lloyds and HSBC. Although observable, such

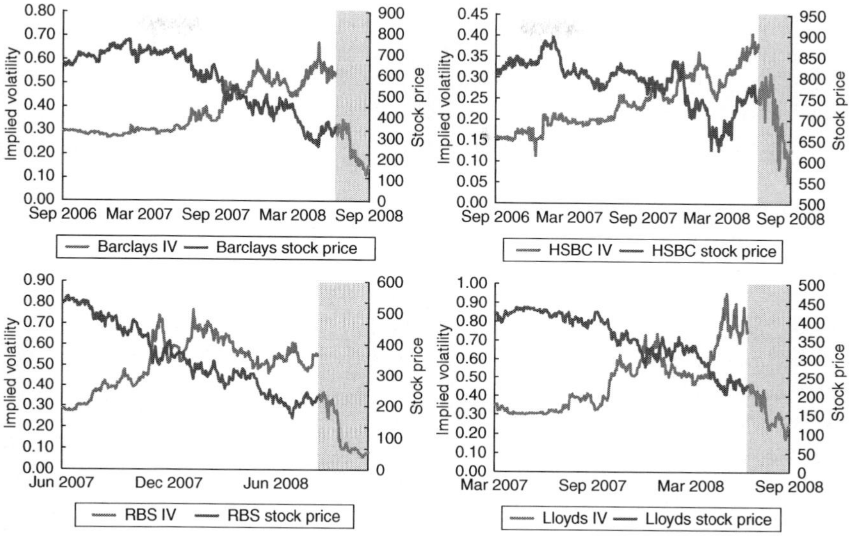

Figure 9.3 Bank IV versus share price

an IV-share price pattern is less evident in the RBS case because of the impact of the ABN AMRO acquisition of early 2008 on the distribution of options returns. Nevertheless, overall results imply that the crash was likely to be anticipated ex-ante and that it possibly happened because it was due to happen! Additional regression outcomes also reveal that VIX and VFTSE were important determinants of banking IV signifying important markets effects and international contagion/interaction from/with the US market. With respect to information efficiency comparisons, MJD results generally showed as expected that jump diffusion IVs tend to provide additional explanatory power to BS IVs, particularly in the second half of the credit crunch, although only marginally at times (see Table 9.4 for percentage changes in R^2 and betas). This finding confirms that with the right calibration, option IV models based on discontinuous returns assumptions can be superior in signaling abnormal events occurrences. This also hints at the need to consider models and frameworks that go beyond 'normal' uncertainty principles to signal and warn about extreme volatility events in financial markets (for example, infinite variance, behavioral finance, and so on).

Based on the above, it can be said that despite a number of similarities with prior crash events, the fall 2008 banking collapse was more analogous to a major volcanic eruption than to a violent earthquake. The credit crunch period served as a build-up to such an eruption. The scrutiny around banks at the time, and well publicized turbulence during the second half of 2007 and first part of 2008 (credit squeeze and illiquidity contagion) all pointed to the possibility of a major downturn, confirming that a crash was on the cards by then. Our options IV results confirm this and corroborate the timing of such a crash at least 15 months before the events. Nonetheless, the unusual level of uncertainty surrounding markets still managed to create indecisiveness among investors at times. This was specifically observed between March and June 2008.[18] Indeed, this period coincides with rumors/news of possible bailouts, and announcements of shares repurchases among banks to stimulate and enhance credit and asset liquidity in the market resulting into a temporary alleviation of fears in the short run. It appears also that during this specific period (the second half of the credit crunch period), and as a consequence of mood swinging markets and volatile IVs, investors ended up trading on news and announcements rather than on fundamentals and sound investment judgment, confirming the level of confusion surrounding markets at the time.[19]

These findings reveal that although IV is an efficient predictor of future volatility it is not an unbiased forecast, implying that other factors (such as implied correlation and options Greeks) need to be considered to account for the unexplained components of the statistical regressions. This concerns IV type measures from other markets (OTC, CDS and so on), firm specific characteristics and fundamentals, and interactions and implied correlations among these markets. Nevertheless, the advantages of IV based indicators compared to more traditional measures of risk and default are that they are forward looking and can be useful in signaling rational bubbles, investors' fears/expectations and aggregate market sentiment. On the whole, the predictive power of the statistically significant regressions is in accord with the equity options IV findings of Cao et al. (2010) for 2001–6.

Analysis of contagion and interactions among the four banks during the credit crunch period divulged via IVs variance decomposition[20] that RBS and HSBC were the main sources of uncertainty because of their non-negligible exposure to the US subprime market. At the same time, there was no one dominant source of uncertainty among banks throughout the period. Another interesting finding, however, was that RBS and HSBC did significantly impact on Barclays and Lloyds and viceversa. This confirmed that risk contagion did emanate from the US subprime market and was diffused throughout national banking systems to feed back into the larger integrated system and so on. This happened incrementally – with a number of distress episodes nationally and internationally (for example, Bear Stearns) –until the collapse of Lehman Brothers, and the rest is history.

9.5 Conclusions

In this chapter, we assessed the predictive power and efficiency of options prices with respect to the fall 2008 global banking crash prior to and during the 2007 credit crunch, emphasizing the information content of UK banking equity options implied volatility surrounding this exceptional period in financial markets history. Despite a number of issues related to information availability and data overlapping/mismatching problems, results show that IV is an efficient but biased predictor of future realized (downside) volatility and that a stock price collapse was predicted (more than once) for each bank prior to our target periods, therefore explaining the possibility of a market crash. Evidence of indecisiveness was also occasionally present because of investors' lack of certainty about the future and noise trading tendencies in the market. Equity options markets sent warning signals in advance of what would happen in autumn 2008 to the UK banking sector, high street banks in particular. Therefore, there was scope for senior bankers and regulators to intervene proactively rather than reactively in minimizing banking failure and reducing the impact of second moment shocks in the economy. The interaction among markets (for example, CDS markets) is quite important and might provide additional evidence on the information content of derivatives markets around the 2007–9 Great Recession. From a risk management standpoint, the large concentration of banks in the financial services sector in the UK (a total of 73 percent market share for the four banks analyzed) might have worsened the situation relative to other countries. A more competitive structure would have alleviated contagion and illiquidity risks in the sector.

As option implied volatility can inform investors and investment professionals about abnormal events beforehand, forward looking risk-monitoring mechanisms from markets with options characteristics, real and financial, should be incorporated more extensively but responsibly (for example, to avoid economic signaling problems where cause and effects relationships are reversed or are no longer stable) in warning systems for an early detection of financial crises turbulence. Besides the usual metrics used for risk screening in banking, implied volatility (and other option-related financials) with a number of preceding periods' ranges should be employed effectively and efficiently, in parallel to other banking soundness indicators, as part of a robustly integrated risk management framework to gauge market fears or downside risk in financial services. Similar to the use of VIX and VFTSE[21] as indicators of negative expectations in the US and UK stock markets, global and local IV banking indexes could also be employed to monitor banking risks and contagion in the economy. Meanwhile, IV should be analyzed with its determinants to see what other factors (for example, fundamental data inputs), besides markets interactions, also affect the relationship between RV and IV in order to track banking performance, at the firm and industry level, appropriately and responsibly. Such measures or information proxies could be used on a regular basis as additional indicators for distress, default and downside risk occurrence in the context of banking supervision and regulation.

Limitations of this study concern sample size and the relatively short study period. We have emphasized banking cases with appropriate and significant data that were also meaningful to our period of analysis: the fall 2008 banking crash for UK high street banks. In spite of using daily observations, our results are overall acceptable, robust and meaningful. Possible extensions to this work could consider volume (for example, Spyrou, 2011) and liquidity factors, as well as investigating whether abnormal trading activity was also occurring prior to the crash to confirm whether the latter was expected/signaled ex-ante. The major change observed in the number of different strikes available for trade between 2006 and 2007 for each of the four sets of equity options analyzed would seem to suggest so. Other research avenues could compare our findings with outputs from stochastic volatility models and expand results to US, Asia-Pacific and EU financial services firms, as this would relate also to the global banking contagion during this special period in markets history. Models to capture abnormal uncertainty and discontinuities in the underlying assets movements may also be useful in providing better forecasts. An additional research opportunity is to examine the risk neutral distributions of options prices for the various banks investigated using both daily and intra-day data. This would require the use of a continuous range of exercise prices for both call and puts options contracts. Finally, considering behavioral factors as inputs to options IV frameworks might inform us about investors' trading tendencies more clearly, and should enlighten us about components and characteristics of uncertainty that might not necessarily be captured by existing option pricing models.

Notes

Part of this research is based on the first author's MSc Dissertation at Cranfield University (2009).

1. Signs of episodic but incremental turbulence in the VIX index can be traced back to 2007.
2. The largest banks in the country in terms of assets value in December 2007 were RBS, Barclays, HSBC, HBOS and Lloyds. Subsequent to the exceptional events of fall 2008, HBOS and Lloyds were merged into one entity.
3. Comparative findings also confirm that with appropriate parameters estimation and calibration, IV outcomes provided by jump diffusion options pricing models can be more adequate for financial crises signaling.
4. Indeed, option IV can provide additional forecasting information relative to historical volatility for index options and liquid equity options (see Taylor et al., 2010).
5. Among these studies, Eichler et al. (2011) analyze the short term and long term default probabilities of a number of US banks under a compound real options lens for 2007, revealing that defaulting and overtaken institutions in 2008–9 were showing higher long term crisis risk prior to the fall 2008 crash.

6. Focusing on the 2007–9 events and studying mainly the interaction between equity and credit markets for that period, Trutwein and Schiereck (2011) analyze the association(s) between CDS spreads and equity returns (option implied volatility to a lower degree) of the major US financial institutions to reveal the amplified lead-lag relationship between equity and credit markets, and the positive but somewhat simultaneous interaction between option IV and CDS spreads when markets are very unstable. Although such a study is not focused on the information content of equity options and the interaction between implied volatility and stock volatility, its findings complement ours by shedding light on the information content of derivatives markets in the context of US financial services. However, the relationship between option IV and CDS spreads is out of the scope of this chapter.
7. It is now generally accepted that the 2007–9 Great Recession was composed of (1) the 2007–8 credit crunch and (2) the 2008–9 economic downturn.
8. It is interesting to note that in their robustness checks of US financial services, Cao et al. (2010) find strong evidence for the lead–lag relationship between option IV and CDS spreads for the 2001–6 data period, confirming the superiority of IV as a predictor of future realized volatility.
9. Because we emphasize the downside risk dynamics of the major UK banks during our study period, realized volatility findings for our crash prediction tests – though leading to similar conclusions – are not shown here.
10. As discussed before, theory suggests that this model can be more suitable for discontinuous price changes and crisis events. We use it here for comparison vis-à-vis the Black–Scholes model IV.
11. Preceding periods of two months duration were also considered in the analysis with comparable results.
12. Findings under these procedures were generally consistent with the statistical outcomes presented in Section 9.4.
13. This was done specifically to reduce noise effects and use a cleaner measure of bank downside risk.
14. See Gemmill (1986) on near the money options' vega properties and forecasting efficiency.
15. Based on the scarce data available, a similar finding was observed for HBOS 9 months prior to the crash period. The 12 months IV findings for Lloyds and RBS were mainly due to maturity mismatch induced from lack of data for that specific preceding period for the two banks.
16. Evidence of bullishness could actually be observed in call and put options prices of Barclays and HSBC 27 and 30 months before the crash. Such behavior is consistent with the bubble hypothesis and the theory of business cycles.
17. This also suggests that HSBC options traders and investors were possibly better informed than other UK banks' investors.
18. It is also worth mentioning that bearish sentiment was not necessarily reflected in option prices between March and June 2007, even for HSBC.
19. Specifically, five, six and two months prior to the target period.
20. We thank Yaxin Sun for her useful inputs on this part of the analysis.
21. VFTSE was only introduced to the UK market in the summer (June) of 2008.

References

Barros, C. P., Managi, S. and Matousek, R. (2012). The Technical Efficiency of the Japanese Banks: Non-radial Directional Performance Measurement with Undesirable Output. *Omega*, 40 (1), 1–8.

Bartram, S. and Bodnar, G. M. (2009). No Place to Hide: The Global Crisis in Equity Markets in 2008/2009. *Journal of International Money and Finance*, 28 (8), 1246–92.

Bates, D. S. (1991). The Crash of '87: Was It Expected? The Evidence from Options Markets. *Journal of Finance*, 46 (3), 1009–44.

Bates, D. S. (1996). Jumps and Stochastic Volatility: Exchange Rate Processes Implicit in Deutsche Mark Options. *The Review of Financial Studies*, 9 (1), 69–107.

Beckers, S. (1981). Standard Deviations Implied in Option Prices as Predictors of Future Stock Price Variability. *Journal of Banking & Finance*, 5 (3), 363–81.

Bhabra, G. S., Gonzalez, L., Kim, M. S. and Powell, J. G. (2001). Volatility Prediction during Prolonged Crises: Evidence from Korean Index Options. *Pacific Basin Finance Journal*, 9 (2), 147–64.

Birru, J. and Figlewski, S. (2012). Anatomy of a Meltdown: The Risk Neutral Density for the S&P 500 in the Fall of 2008. *Journal of Financial Markets*, 15 (2),151–80.

Black, F. and Scholes, M. (1973). The Pricing of Options and Corporate Liabilities. *Journal of Political Economy*, 81 (3), 637.

Cao, C., Li, H. and Yu, F. (2005). Is Investor Misreaction Economically Significant? Evidence from Short- and Long-term S&P 500 Index Options. *Journal of Futures Markets*, 25 (8), 717–52.

Cao, C., Yu, F. and Zhong, Z. (2010). The Information Content of Option-implied Volatility for Credit Default Swap Valuation. *Journal of Financial Markets*, 13 (3), 321–43.

Cao, C., Yu, F. and Zhong, Z. (2011). Pricing Credit Default Swaps with Option-Implied Volatility. *Financial Analysts Journal*, 67 (4), 67–76.

Cheng, L. T. W., Fung, J. K. W. and Chan, K. C. (2000). Pricing Dynamics of Index Options and Index Futures in Hong Kong Before and During the Asian Financial Crisis. *Journal of Futures Markets*, 20 (2), 145–66.

Christensen, B. J. and Prabhala, N. R. (1998). The Relation between Implied and Realized Volatility. *Journal of Financial Economics*, 50 (2), 125–50.

Crouhy, M. (2002). Comments on 'Information about Bank Risk in Options Prices'. *Journal of Banking & Finance*, 26 (5), 1059–64.

Demyanyk, Y. and Hasan, I. (2010). Financial Crises and Bank Failures: A Review of Prediction Methods. *Omega*, 38 (5), 315–24.

Dietrich, A. and Wanzenried, G. (2011). Determinants of Bank Profitability before and during the Crisis: Evidence from Switzerland. *Journal of International Financial Markets, Institutions and Money*, 21 (3), 307–27.

Dupoyet, B. (2006). Information Content of Cross-Sectional Option Prices: A Comparison of Alternative Currency Option Pricing Models on the Japanese Yen. *Journal of Futures Markets*, 26 (1), 33–59.

Dwyer, G. P. and Tkac, P. (2009). The Financial Crisis of 2008 in Fixed-Income Markets. *Journal of International Money and Finance*, 28 (8), 1293–316.

Ederington, L. and Guan, W. (2005). The Information Frown in Option Prices. *Journal of Banking & Finance*, 29 (6), 1429–57.

Eichler, S., Karmann, A. and Maltritz, D. (2011). The Term Structure of Banking Crisis Risk in the United States: A Market Data Based Compound Option Approach. *Journal of Banking & Finance*, 35 (4), 876–85.

Elkamhi, R. and Ornthanalai, C. (2010). Market Jump Risk and the Price Structure of Individual Equity Options. *Working Paper*.

Figlewski, S. (2009). Viewing the Financial Crisis from 20,000 Feet Up. *Journal of Derivatives*, 16 (3), 53–61.

Fung, J. K. W. (2007). The Information Content of Option Implied Volatility Surrounding the 1997 Hong Kong Stock Market Crash. *Journal of Futures Markets*, 27 (6), 555–74.

Gemmill, G. (1986). The Forecasting Performance of Stock Options on the London Traded Options Market. *Journal of Business Finance & Accounting*, 13 (4), 535–46.

Gemmill, G. (1992). Political Risk and Market Efficiency: Tests Based in British Stock and Options Markets in the 1987 Election. *Journal of Banking & Finance*, 16 (1), 211–31.

Gemmill, G. and Saflekos, A. (2000). How Useful are Implied Distributions? Evidence from Stock Index Options. *The Journal of Derivatives*, 7 (3), 83–91.

Hamalainen, P., Pop, A., Hall, M. and Howcroft, B. (2012). Did the Market Signal Impending Problems at Northern Rock? An Analysis of Four Financial Instruments. *European Financial Management*, 18 (1), 68–87.

Heston, S. L. (1993). A Closed-Form Solution for Options with Stochastic Volatility with Applications to Bond and Currency Options. *Review of Financial Studies*, 6 (2), 327.

Hull, J. and White, A. (1987). The Pricing of Options on Assets with Stochastic Volatilities. *Journal of Finance*, 42 (2), 281–300.

Ioannidis, C., Pasiouras, F. and Zopounidis, C. (2010). Assessing Bank Soundness with Classification Techniques. *Omega*, 38 (5), 345–57.

Jiang, G. J. and Tian, Y. S. (2005). The Model-Free Implied Volatility and Its Information Content. *Review of Financial Studies*, 18 (4), 1305–42.

Latane, H. A. and Rendleman Jr, R. J. (1976). Standard Deviations of Stock Price Ratios Implied in Option Prices. *Journal of Finance*, 31 (2), 369–81.

Liadaki, A. and Gaganis, C. (2010). Efficiency and Stock Performance of EU Banks: Is There a Relationship? *Omega*, 38 (5), 254–9.

Longstaff, F. A. (2010). The Subprime Credit Crisis and Contagion in Financial Markets. *Journal of Financial Economics*, 97 (3), 436–50.

Low, C. (2004). The Fear and Exuberance from Implied Volatility of S&P 100 Index Options. *Journal of Business*, 77 (3), 527–46.

Mayhew, S. (1995). Implied Volatility. *Financial Analysts Journal*, 51 (4), 8–20.

McIntyre, M. L. and Jackson, D. (2009). Market Moves and the Information Content of Option Prices. *International Review of Economics & Finance*, 18 (2), 327–40.

Merton, R. C. (1976). Option Pricing When Underlying Stock Returns Are Discontinuous. *Journal of Financial Economics*, 3(1–2), 125–44.

Mihm, S. (2008). Dr. Doom. *The New York Times*. New York.

Mixon, S. (2009). Option Markets and Implied Volatility: Past versus Present. *Journal of Financial Economics*, 94 (2), 171–91.

Newey, W. and West, K. (1987). A Simple, Positive Semi-Definite, Heteroskedasticity and Autocorrelation Consistent Covariance Matrix. *Econometrica*, 55 (3), 703–8.

Poon, S.-H. and Granger, C. (2005). Practical Issues in Forecasting Volatility. *Financial Analysts Journal*, 61 (1), 45–56.

Poteshman, A. M. (2006). Unusual Option Market Activity and the Terrorist Attacks of September 11, (2001). *Journal of Business*, 79 (4), 1703–26.

Rappoport, P. and White, E. N. (1994). Was the Crash of 1929 Expected? *American Economic Review*, 84 (1), 271–81.

Reinhart, C. M. and Rogoff, K. S. (2008). Is the 2007 US Sub-prime Financial Crisis So Different? An International Historical Comparison. *American Economic Review*, 98 (2), 339–44.

Spyrou, S. (2011). Are Broad Market Shocks Anticipated by Investors? Evidence from Major Equity and Index Options Markets. *International Review of Financial Analysis*, 20 (3), 127–33.

Swidler, S. and Wilcox, J. A. (2002). Information about Bank Risk in Options Prices. *Journal of Banking and Finance*, 26 (5), 1033–57.

Taylor, S. J., Yadav, P. K. and Zhang, Y. (2010). The Information Content of Implied Volatilities and Model-free Volatility Expectations: Evidence from Options Written on Individual Stocks. *Journal of Banking & Finance*, 34 (4), 871–81.

Trutwein, P. and Schiereck, D. (2011). The Fast and the Furious-Stock Returns and CDS of Financial Institutions under Stress. *Journal of International Financial Markets, Institutions and Money*, 21 (2), 157–75.

Xing, Y., Zhang, X. and Zhao, R. (2010). What Does the Individual Option Volatility Smirk Tell Us About Future Equity Returns? *Journal of Financial and Quantitative Analysis*, 45 (3), 641–62.

Yu, W. W., Lui, E. C. K. and Wang, J. W. (2010). The Predictive Power of the Implied Volatility of Options Traded OTC and on Exchanges. *Journal of Banking & Finance*, 34 (1), 1–11.

10
International Portfolio Diversification and the 2007 Financial Crisis

Jacek Niklewski and Timothy Rodgers*

10.1 Introduction and aims

By diversifying stock selection on an international basis, portfolio managers hope to improve the trade-off between risk and reward through a reduction in within-portfolio correlation levels. Although the benefits of this procedure can be considerable, the process of stock selection is not always clear cut. It was argued more than twenty years ago by French and Poterba (1991) that behavioral factors, such as biases in investor expectations, can lead to under-diversification in the international dimension. Portfolio managers wanting to optimize their stock selection can now be seen to face another important issue; namely, whether or not financial crisis results in significant long-term permanent changes in between-market correlation levels.

The benefits of diversification depend on the extent to which markets are correlated. Although the general trend in both economic integration and market correlation has been for them to increase over time (Goetzmann et al., 2005), the long-term impact that the 2007 financial crisis had is questionable. Contagion theory (Forbes and Rigobon, 2002) would suggest that the impact of a crisis on correlation will often be short term and result in short-lived spikes in correlation. However, recent evidence from Markwat et al. (2009) showed that global contagion events can be long and drawn out processes.

The argument can be made that the impact of financial crisis may be permanent rather than short-term contagion. Minsky (1992), amongst others, suggested that crisis can have a major impact on the 'architecture' of financial markets. Whalen (2008) described the 2007 crisis as a 'Minsky moment' and argued that the crisis has resulted in wide ranging structural changes across global financial markets.

We recognize that it is difficult to draw a clear distinction between the 2007 crisis and the subsequent euro crisis. However, in this chapter we argue there is a *prima facie* case that the 2007 financial crisis in itself resulted in long-term structural changes in the correlations between US and international regional markets. If permanent change did occur in response to a financial crisis, it will have important implications for the management of international equity portfolios.

The remainder of this chapter is structured as follows: Section **10.2** examines lessons from the literature in respect to what determines the degree of between-market correlation. Section **10.3** discusses and presents the hypotheses tested. Section **10.4** describes data and methodology used. Section **10.5** presents and discusses the results and finally, Section **10.6** draws some preliminary conclusions.

10.2 Lessons from the literature

A large number of studies examined the benefits of portfolio internationalization (for example: Laopodis, 2005; Lucey and Muckley, 2011; Meric et al., 2008). Solnik (1995) showed that these benefits can be large. Using data from 1966–71, he identified that a well-diversified international portfolio reduced risk by about half for a US investor. The size of such benefits will, however, be determined by how these between-market correlations change over time.

A series of further studies showed there to be a clear upward trend in correlations over time (Barari, 2004; Kearney and Lucey, 2004; Swanson, 2003). Bekaert et al. (2002) argued that this trend reflects the impact of globalization and increasing market integration. This is supported by a number of related studies in the literature; for example, Jagannathan and Wang (1996) found that as economic production becomes less segmented and more integrated (as measured by business-cycle convergence) financial integration increases. This type of effect has been found to be particularly apparent in Europe, where equity market integration increased significantly after 1996 in response to the rapid economic and financial integration associated with convergence within the European Union (Fratzschler, 2002). More recent studies, for example, Goetzmann et al. (2005) also argued that there is robust historical evidence that market correlation is in fact strongly influenced by market globalization on a world-wide basis. This argument is supported in a developing-Asia context by Yu et al. (2010) who found that rates of market integration increased significantly from around 2007–8.

Elsewhere in the literature researchers have argued that there are short-term fluctuations in correlation related to changes in market volatility. Both Longin and Solnik (1995) and also Solnik et al. (1996) argued that short-term correlation increases can be seen in terms of the greater volatility found in the bear phase of market cycles. The assertion that correlation increases during times of high market volatility is a theme that runs throughout a lot of the literature. For example, Karolyi and Stulz (1996) and also Ramchand and Susmel (1998), found correlation to be higher between US and other markets during high-volatility periods. Other researchers argue that findings such as these possibly related to the impact of stock market trends rather than to volatility *per se*. Later work by Longin and Solnik (2001) found that correlation increased during bear markets phases and You and Daigler (2010) argued that a consequence of this is that the benefits of international diversification can be asymmetric. The latter found a reduction in portfolio diversification benefits during bear market phases. It was argued by Bekaert and Wu (2000) that the asymmetric impact on correlation of different market phases is possibly due to negative shocks producing two interacting effects. Namely, an effect related to changes in investor's expectations of the conditional variance and a second effect related to changes in leverage as markets fall.

Further evidence from the 1997 Asian financial crisis appeared to support the argument that market volatility and the phase of the stock market cycle are important factors in determining the short-term impact of a crisis on cross-country market correlation. Schwebach et al. (2002) found the Asian crisis to have had a similar effect to that found during business-downturns and bear markets. Using world equity benchmark shares they identified that cross-country correlations increased. These correlations ranged from 0.180–0.274 during the first phase of the crisis, before rising to 0.451–0.531 during the second phase.

It can be noted that the Schwebach et al. (2002) study used a relatively short time series. This means that it is not possible to tell from their work whether or not the changes found were limited to being short-term contagion effects or represented long-term structural change. Long-term structural change as the result of crisis would not be unexpected. Garnaut (1998) argued that the Asian crisis in fact had a major structural impact on the region.

We argue in this chapter that in the context of the 2007 financial crisis, any changes in correlations are likely to be long-term and in response to structural changes in financial markets. We discuss this in more detail in the next section. We also acknowledge the importance of the volatility-correlation relationship identified in the literature and note that historically volatility levels have been higher in emerging/frontier markets than in developed markets. We therefore ask whether or not the fact that the 2007 crisis was mainly a developed market phenomena will have an impact on the relative volatilities of developed and emerging/frontier markets, and as a consequence, whether or not this may have a further possible impact on correlations.

10.3 Hypotheses tested

An examination of the literature reveals that financial crisis can potentially have both short-term and long-term impacts on equity market correlations. Long-term structural change effects are found to be associated not only with the trend of increasing globalization but also with the impact of crisis-induced changes in the 'architecture' of the financial system.

Crotty (2009) traced the origins of the 2007 financial crisis in the US to the New Financial Architecture (NFA) of the previous two decades, having effectively eliminated the regulatory regime developed in response to the 1930s Great Depression. He argued that the NFA resulted in excessive risk taking, stimulated excessive leverage and also led to the development of financial market complexity and opaqueness. He saw the main consequence of this as being the dramatic increases in the size of the financial sector relative to the rest of the economy.

Crotty argued that the economic and social impact of the NFA has been viewed in most countries as being detrimental and that as a consequence the NFA needed reform. The 2007 crisis can be seen as presenting the opportunity to implement this reform. Moshirian (2011) showed that crisis often leads to the emergence of new national and international financial institutions. One of the responses to the 2007 crisis has been, for example, the Basel III accord (BIS, 2012). This is designed to strengthen bank capital requirements and introduces new regulatory requirements on liquidity and leverage. The crisis also stimulated a worldwide debate on the merits of separating investment banking from commercial banking (which in a US context would be a reintroduction of the Glass-Steagall Act). Other research has suggested that corporate governance structures have undergone re-examination as these have been found to have a significant impact on managerial risk taking behavior (King and Wen, 2011). As well as new regulatory responses, the 'financial architecture' has seen massive adjustment through changes in market attitudes to risk. For example, New York Federal reserve chairman Timothy Geithner commented on the huge impact that de-leveraging had on financial markets during 2007 (Geithner, 2008).

We believe that Whalen (2008) is right in describing the 2007 crisis as a 'Minsky moment'. Furthermore, we argue that the resulting changes to the world's 'financial architecture', and the consequent changes in levels of integration between its respective financial systems, will impact on the long-term correlation between equity markets. We also argue that a further consequence of the crisis may have been that long-term changes have occurred in the relative volatilities of markets; this given that the crisis affected developed and emerging/frontier markets in widely differing ways. Such changes, as Gupta and Mollik (2008) identified, can influence correlations. We argue that because of the greater impact of the financial crisis on developed markets, there will possibly be greater similarities in the changes experienced by the US and other developed markets than there will be between the changes experienced by the US and emerging/frontier markets.

On the basis of the above arguments we test the following hypotheses.

Hypothesis 1: there has been a long-term post-crisis structural change in the conditional correlations between the US equity market and other developed regional markets.

Hypothesis 2: there has been a long-term post-crisis structural change *of a different magnitude* in the conditional correlations between the US equity market and emerging/frontier regional markets.

Hypothesis 3: conditional correlations between US and regional markets have been affected by long-term post-crisis structural changes in the relative conditional volatilities of these US and regional markets.

10.4 Data, descriptive statistics and methodology

An important issue that we face in this study is identifying the starting and ending points of the financial crisis. This is a potentially problematical issue as their dates are open to interpretation. For the purposes of this chapter we use 11 May 2007 and 1 January 2010 as these respective dates. In order to identify any long-term structural changes in the conditional correlation, conditional volatility and ratio of conditional volatility relationships the chapter undertakes a series of Welch comparison-of-mean tests and Wilcoxon rank-sum tests. We enhance the robustness of the results, and also ensure that we can account for any 'contamination' of the data from the subsequent euro crisis,[1] by using a number of different test observation periods. We undertake a series of tests using 62,124 and 176 weekly pre-crisis observation periods and 62 and 124 weekly post-crisis observation periods. The 124 week sample was chosen on the basis that this represents the maximum post-crisis period of data available for analysis. The 62 week period represents half of this maximum period and the 176 week period prior to the crisis was chosen as it represents a long period of relatively stable correlation.

Although problems in the US sub-prime market began to become apparent in 2006, it was not until the middle of May 2007 that stock prices across the US financial sector as a whole began to fall (based on weekly closing values of Dow Jones US Financials index) and volatility across the market began to increase significantly. Market perceptions in respect to the development of the crisis can be approximated by using the VIX index (Chicago Board Options Exchange Market Volatility Index). This index is often described as a 'fear gauge', given that it reflects market volatility expectations over the following 30 days. From around the middle of 2007 the VIX can be observed as rising above its historical mean levels and remaining high throughout the crisis period. As the crisis began to wane the VIX began to mean-revert back towards its historical average. For the purposes of this study we have identified the point of approximate reversion to the mean as being the end point of the crisis.[2] It can be argued that the crisis ended earlier than this date, in June 2009, which is the point that the National Bureau of Economic Research (NBER) identified as being the end of the contraction phase of the business cycle (NBER, 2012). However, up to the end of 2009 the VIX showed market volatility to be still significantly above its historical average. It was not until January 2010 that President Obama declared that the markets had been stabilized, and that in effect the crisis was over (US Treasury, 2010). We believe that although our choice of end date may possibly be a little conservative, this adds to the overall robustness of the analysis.

The source of the data used in this study is MSCI (2012). Weekly data is used that runs from 12 July 2002 to 11 May 2012; this gives 514 observations. We use MSCI 'standard' indices (based on large- and mid-capitalization stocks); these are derived from closing-price-based weekly total returns (adjusted for dividend payments) and are based in US dollars. The weekly logarithmic returns of the respective indices used in the study are presented in Figure 10.1.

The conditional correlation is estimated between the US and a series of (i) developed market regional indices and (ii) emerging/frontier market regional indices. The constituent countries of the regional indices used are shown below in brackets.

Developed regions:

- EMU (Austria, Belgium, Finland, France, Germany, Greece, Ireland, Italy, Netherland, Portugal, Spain);
- EUROPE ex EMU (Denmark, Norway, Sweden, Switzerland, UK);
- PACIFIC (Australia, Hong Kong, Japan, New Zealand, Singapore).

Emerging/frontier regions:

- BRIC (Brazil, Russia, India, China);
- EM EUROPE (Czech Republic, Hungary, Poland, Russia, Turkey);
- EM LATIN AMERICA (Brazil, Chile, Colombia, Mexico, Peru);
- EM ASIA (China, India, Indonesia, Korea, Malaysia, Philippines, Taiwan, Thailand);
- EFM AFRICA (Egypt, Kenya, Mauritius, Morocco, Nigeria, South Africa, Tunisia).

The 2007 crisis resulted in equity markets across the world starting to fall significantly towards the end of 2008, with most markets reaching their trough in early 2009. The returns data in Figure 10.1 show that most markets experienced increases in volatility towards the end of 2008 and also during 2009 as the financial crisis reached its peak.

Table 10.1 identifies that returns made in emerging/frontier markets over the full sample period covered by the dataset were generally higher than those made in their developed market counterparts. The respective

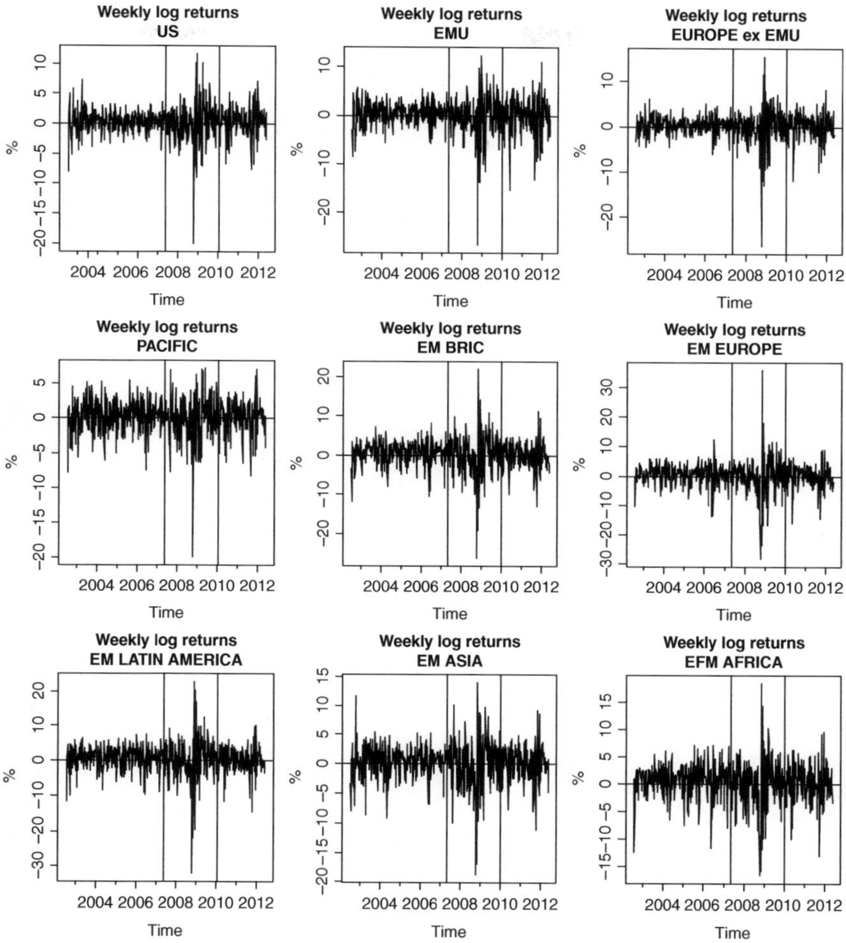

Figure 10.1 Weekly logarithmic returns shown in percentages over the period 12 July 2002 to 11 May 2012

Note: The two vertical lines represent 11 May 2007 and 1 January 2010.

mean, median and standard deviation of returns were also on the whole higher in the emerging/frontier regions. This is as would be expected given that higher returns are normally associated with higher risk (volatility). During this period the unconditional correlations between the US and developed-world regional indices can be seen as having been generally higher than the correlations between the US and emerging/frontier market indices.

Table 10.1 Summary statistics of weekly percentage returns 12 July 2002 to 11 May 2012

	US	EMU	EUROPE ex EMU	PACIFIC	BRIC	EM EUROPE	EM LATIN AMERICA	EM ASIA	EFM AFRICA
Median	0.21	0.51	0.50	0.21	0.82	0.70	0.84	0.54	0.68
Mean	0.12	0.10	0.15	0.10	0.32	0.25	0.38	0.22	0.30
Min.	−20.05	−26.64	−26.45	−20.01	−26.47	−28.46	−32.25	−18.77	−16.74
Max.	11.58	12.37	15.51	7.29	21.92	36.01	22.78	13.95	18.45
Std dev.	2.67	3.65	3.14	2.74	4.06	4.89	4.59	3.44	3.71
Uncond. correlation with US	1.00	0.83	0.83	0.62	0.72	0.62	0.78	0.64	0.63

This chapter measures correlations by applying the dynamic conditional correlation multivariate GARCH model (DCC-MGARCH) proposed by Engle (2002) and Engle and Sheppard (2001).

Different ARMA specifications of the mean equation were tested through the examination of: the significance of the coefficients, information criteria and the Ljung-Box test for autocorrelation in the standardized residuals. The simplest form of the mean equation (that includes only a constant) was found to be the most appropriate and ARMA(0,0) is used on the basis that it was the most parsimonious of the models found as acceptable in the tests undertaken.

As well as testing the specification of the mean equation, specifications of different forms of the variance equation were also examined. Different orders and specifications of the GARCH model were explored using significance tests of the coefficients and also using the Ljung-Box and ARCH LM tests of the squared standardized residuals.

Alternative asymmetric GARCH specifications were tested: GJR GARCH (Glosten, Jagannathan and Runkle, 1993), EGARCH (Nelson, 1991) and TGARCH (Zakoian, 1994). A specification of TGARCH(1,1) was found to be the most appropriate way of dealing with asymmetries in the data.

The multivariate specification of the DCC element of the model was identified as being (1,1) through an examination of the significance of the coefficients and also through the use of information criteria.

The univariate specifications reject the null hypothesis of normality in the series of standardized residuals using the Jarque-Bera and Shapiro-Wilk tests.

The full model used in the chapter is expressed as follows.

Mean equation:

$$\mathrm{r}_{\mathrm{i,t}} = \mu_{\mathrm{i}} + \varepsilon_{\mathrm{i,t}} \tag{10.1}$$

where the residuals are assumed to be conditionally multivariate-normal.

Variance equation:

$$\sqrt{h_{i,t}} = \omega_i + \alpha|\varepsilon_{i,t-1}| + \gamma_i|\varepsilon_{i,\mathrm{t}-1}|I(\varepsilon_{i,\mathrm{t}-0} < 0) + \beta_i\sqrt{h_{i,t-1}} \tag{10.2}$$

DCC equation:

$$\mathrm{Q_t} = (1 - \alpha - \beta)\bar{\mathrm{Q}} + \alpha v_{\mathrm{t}-1}v'_{\mathrm{t}-1} + \beta\mathrm{Q}_{\mathrm{t}-1} \tag{10.3}$$

where v_{t} represents the residuals standardized by their conditional standard deviation.

The estimated model is presented in Appendix, Table 10.A.1. All the coefficients were found to be positive but not all were found to be statistically significant. The insignificant parameters were mainly found in relation to the developed markets; their insignificance could possibly reflect non-normality in the conditional distribution.

The impact of financial crisis on the conditional correlation is examined using two tests; this is done for comparative purposes and also in order

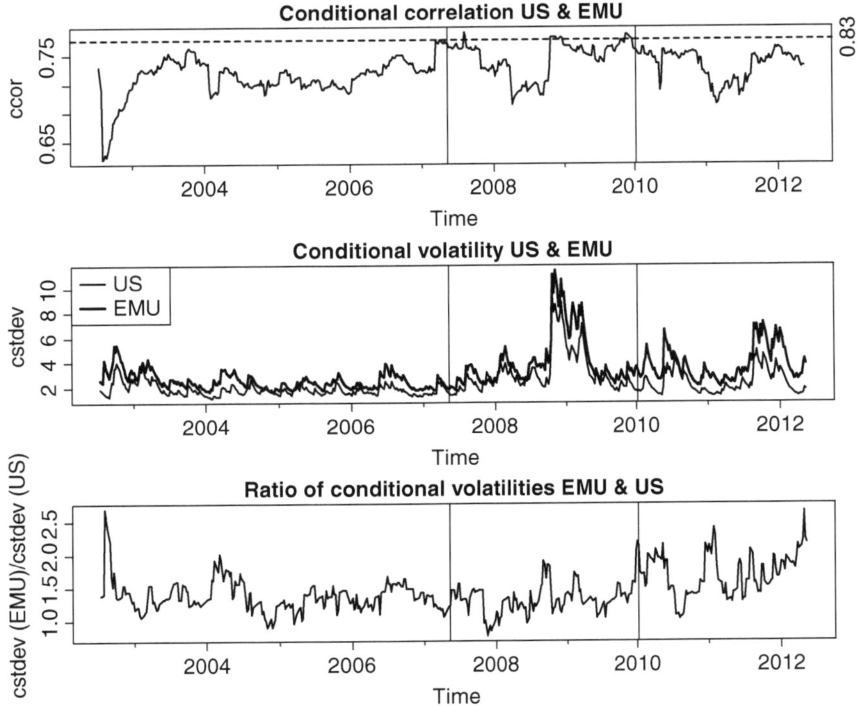

Figure 10.2 Relationship between weekly logarithmic returns of US and developed region stock indices

Notes: The graphs show the conditional correlation, conditional volatility and the ratio of conditional volatilities between the US and respective indices over the period 12 July 2002 to 11 May 2012. The two vertical lines represent the start (11 May 2007) and the end (1 January 2010) of the crisis. The dashed line represents unconditional correlation over the period from 12 July 2002 to 11 May 2012. The ratio of conditional volatilities is calculated as conditional volatility of the developed region divided by conditional volatility of the US.

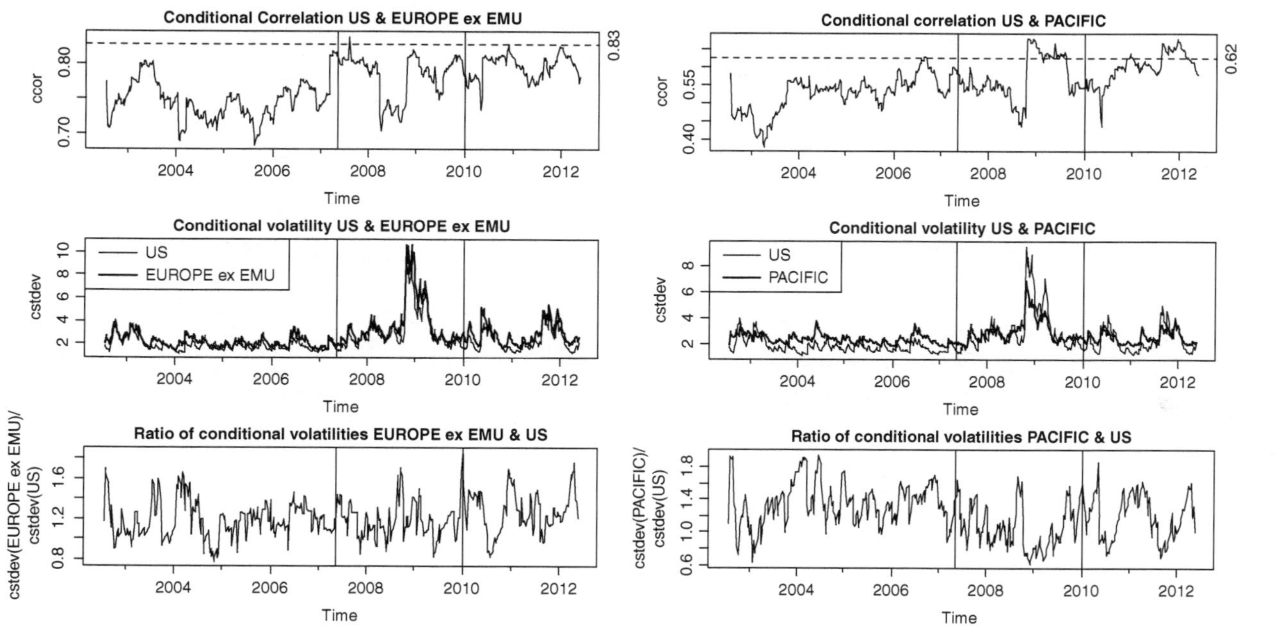

Figure 10.2 Continued

Table 10.2 Statistical significance of differences between pre-crisis and post-crisis mean: conditional correlations, conditional volatilities and ratio of conditional volatilities (US and developed region stock markets)

Index	Sample length before/ after	Mean correlation with US pre-crisis period[a]	Mean correlation with US post-crisis period[b]	Percentage change in mean correlation	Welch two sample t-test p-value	Wilcoxon rank sum test p-value	Mean volatility pre-crisis period[a]	Mean volatility post-crisis period[b]
US	62/62	–	–	–	–	–	1.720	2.140
	124/124	–	–	–	–	–	1.734	2.304
EMU	62/62	0.788	0.786	−0.254	0.790	0.099*	2.367	3.397
	124/124	0.771	0.782	1.427	0.000***	0.000***	2.318	3.787
EUROPE	62/62	0.766	0.797	4.047	0.000***	0.000***	2.091	2.634
ex EMU	124/124	0.749	0.796	6.275	0.000***	0.000***	2.068	2.837
PACIFIC	62/62	0.571	0.574	0.525	0.593	0.273	2.373	2.416
	124/124	0.553	0.599	8.318	0.000***	0.000***	2.303	2.545

Notes: [a]The 62 observation period runs from 10 March 2006 to 11 May 2007; the 124 observation period runs from 31 December 2004 to 11 May 2007. [b]The 62 observation period runs from 1 January 2010 to 4 March 2011; the 124 observation period runs from 1 January 2010 to 11 May 2012. The average percentage changes across all samples for the mean of conditional correlations, conditional volatilities and ratios of conditional volatilities are 3.390 percent, 29.957 percent and 6.131 percent respectively. The ratio of conditional volatilities is calculated as conditional volatility of a developed region divided by conditional volatility of US. Results for a 176 observation period pre-crisis running from 2 January 2004 to 11 May 2007 and a 124 observation post-crisis period running from 1 January 2010 to 11 May 2012 are available upon request from authors.
*Significant at 10%, ** Significant at 5%, *** Significant at 1%.

to add to the robustness of the results. The tests applied are the Welch (1938) t-test and the Wilcoxon (1945) rank sum test (also known as the Mann–Whitney–Wilcoxon (1947) test). The former compares the difference between sample means and the latter compares the difference between sample location parameters. The tests are used to compare the values of the conditional correlation and volatilities in the pre-crisis period of 10 March 2006–11 May 2007 (62 observations) against the values in the post-crisis period of 1 January 2010–4 March 2011 (62 observations). For robustness additional tests were undertaken for comparative purposes using longer pre-crisis and post-crisis periods: 31 December 2004–11 May 2007 (124 observations) against 1 January 2010–11 May 2012 (124 observations). A further series of tests producing similar results are not reported (using 176 observations from 2 January 2004–11 May 2007 against 124 observations from 1 January 2010–11 May 2012).

10.5 Results and discussion

10.5.1 Conditional correlation between US and developed region markets

The conditional correlations between US and developed-region weekly returns are shown in Figure 10.2. The reaction of these correlations to the financial crisis

Table 10.2 Continued

Percentage change in mean volatility	Welch two sample t-test p-value	Wilcoxon rank sum test p-value	Mean ratio of volatilities with US pre-crisis period[a]	Mean ratio of volatilities with US post-crisis period[b]	Percentage change in mean ratio of volatilities	Welch two sample t-test p-value	Wilcoxon rank sum test p-value
24.42	0.000***	0.020**	–	–	–	–	–
32.872	0.000***	0.000***	–	–	–	–	–
43.515	0.000***	0.000***	1.373	1.661	20.976	0.000***	0.000***
63.374	0.000***	0.000***	1.339	1.697	26.736	0.000***	0.000***
25.968	0.000***	0.000***	1.210	1.284	6.116	0.033**	0.020**
37.186	0.000***	0.000***	1.194	1.279	7.119	0.000***	0.000***
1.812	0.548	0.567	1.403	1.222	−12.901	0.000***	0.000***
10.508	0.000***	0.000***	1.350	1.198	−11.259	0.000***	0.000***

appears to be similar across all three developed regions, although there was some variation in timings. An initial fall in correlation with EMU countries was observed in the period immediately after May 2007. This can be interpreted as indicating that stock prices in this region responded relatively slowly to the initial declines in the US market. Non-EMU European countries however appeared to track the US market more closely. A large proportion of this index relates to the UK and Swiss markets and therefore the tendency for this index to track the US closely possibly reflects the relatively high importance of the financial services sectors in these countries.

The crisis appears to have had a positive impact on conditional correlations and volatilities across all three developed regions towards the end of 2008. From Figure 10.2, a spike in correlation can be identified as occurring in late 2010 between the US and EUROPE ex EMU and also between US and PACIFIC. At the same time there were pronounced increases in the conditional volatilities across all developed regions. Interestingly, however, the ratio of the conditional volatilities did not change substantially; in effect, market volatilities were moving very much in step as might be expected during a contagion event.

As the crisis subsided the conditional volatilities fell in all regions and in the post-crisis period (with the VIX index mean-reverting to approximately pre-crisis levels at the start of January 2010) and conditional correlation levels stabilized.

Table 10.2 identifies changes in mean correlation and volatility levels between the pre- and post-crisis periods. It can be noted that the estimates appear largely robust to changes in the sample length; however, the longer sample period mean correlation and mean ratio of volatilities values are generally a little lower for both pre- and post-crisis periods. A third set of results using a 176 pre-crisis period and a 124 post-crisis period are not reported given that they produced very similar results.

The mean comparison tests indicate that, with the possible exception of EMU, mean correlation levels were higher in the post-crisis period. This is indicative of a long-term increase in post-crisis conditional correlations. The average post-crisis increase in mean correlations across all samples is 3.39 percent. The 124-period sample test shows a statistically significant increase in correlations between the US and all three developed regions. There were however regional differences; for example, there is an increase of about 6.3 percent (from 0.749 to 0.796) in respect to Non-EMU Europe, which can be compared to an increase of about 1.43 percent in respect to EMU.

The effect of the crisis on the correlations can be contrasted with the impact that it had on the volatilities. Table 10.2 identifies that all the developed markets in the sample showed higher volatility than the US both pre-crisis and post-crisis. It is also interesting to note that in two out of the three cases the volatility of US markets fell relative to its developed country counterparts subsequent to the crisis ending. The possible implications that this had for correlation levels will be discussed in a later section.

We argue that the results from these tests give support for Hypothesis 1. We contend that the finding of statistically significant increases in the long-term conditional correlations between the US and other developed region markets means that the 2007 crisis has to be seen as being more than just a transitory contagion event. Our findings are consistent with the argument of Whalen (2008) that the financial crisis resulted in permanent changes in the world's 'financial architecture'. The increase in the conditional correlation can possibly be explained as being a result of the world-wide structural changes in the banking and regulatory framework that occurred in response to the crisis. As was identified by Moshirian (2011) responses to the financial crisis of governments in the developed world have been highly coordinated, and we have also seen significant levels of de-leveraging and a rolling back of the investment banking activities throughout the developed economies (Geithner, 2008). We would argue that the findings from our study lend support to the argument that the increase in the coordination of the world regulatory framework, and the constraints this has placed on trading activities, has had a positive long-term impact on the correlation of stock market price movements between developed regions.

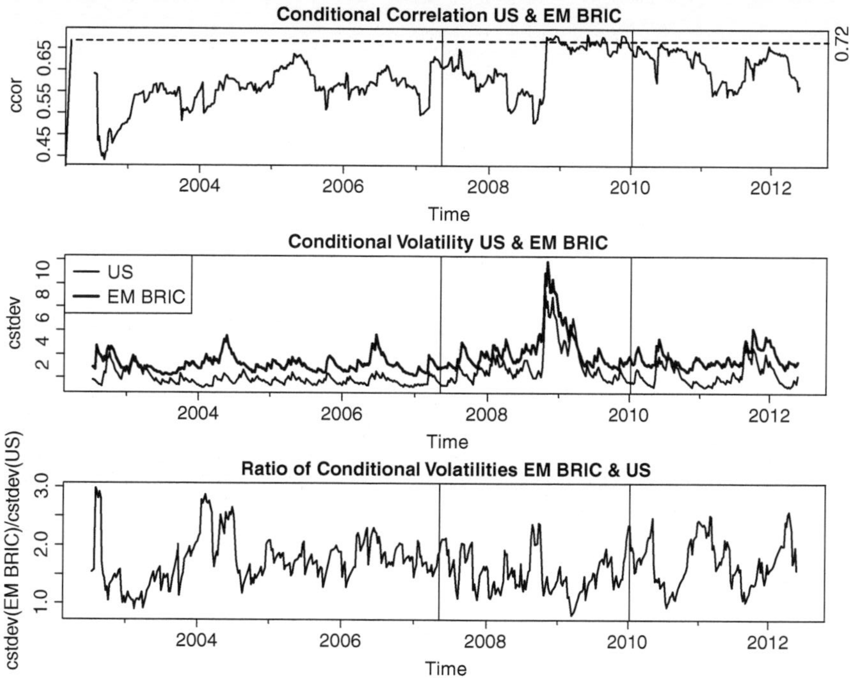

Figure 10.3 Relationship between weekly logarithmic returns of US and emerging/frontier country stock indices

Notes: The graphs show the conditional correlation, conditional volatility and the ratio of conditional volatilities between the US and respective indices over the period12 July 2002 to 11 May 2012. The two vertical lines represent the start (11 May 2007) and the end (1 January 2010) of the crisis. The dashed line represents unconditional correlation over the period from 12 July 2002 to 11 May 2012. The ratio of conditional volatilities is calculated as conditional volatility of the emerging/frontier region divided by conditional volatility of the US.

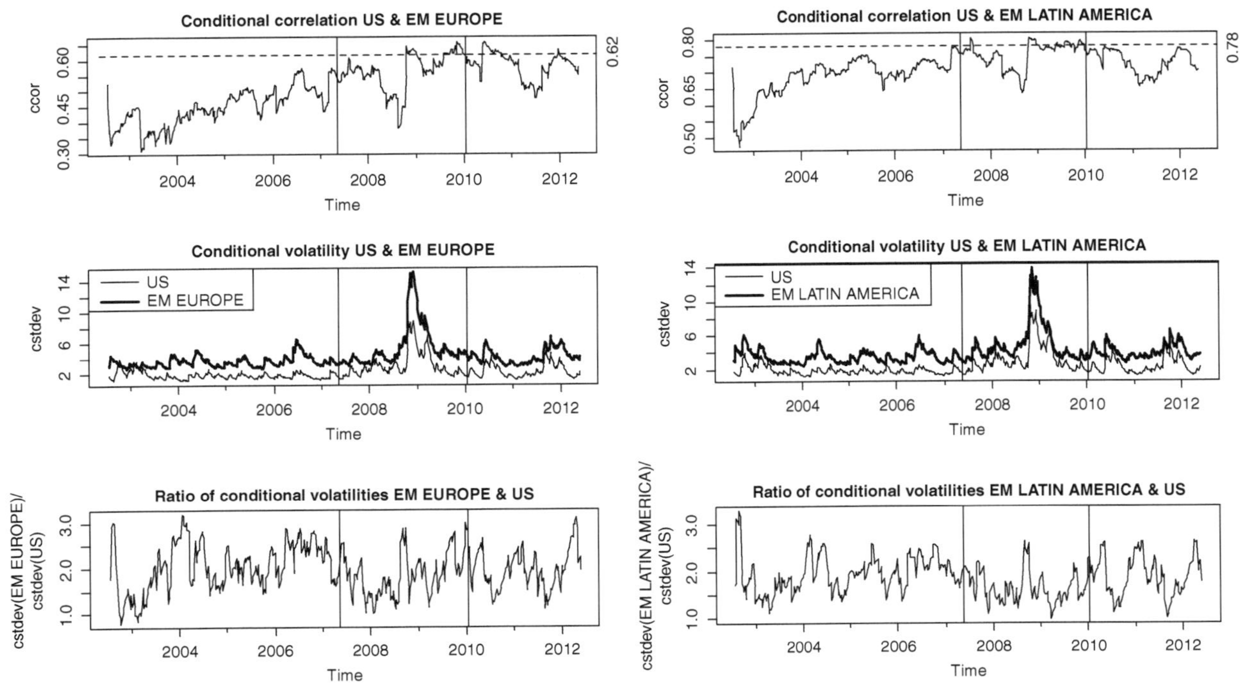

Figure 10.3 Continued

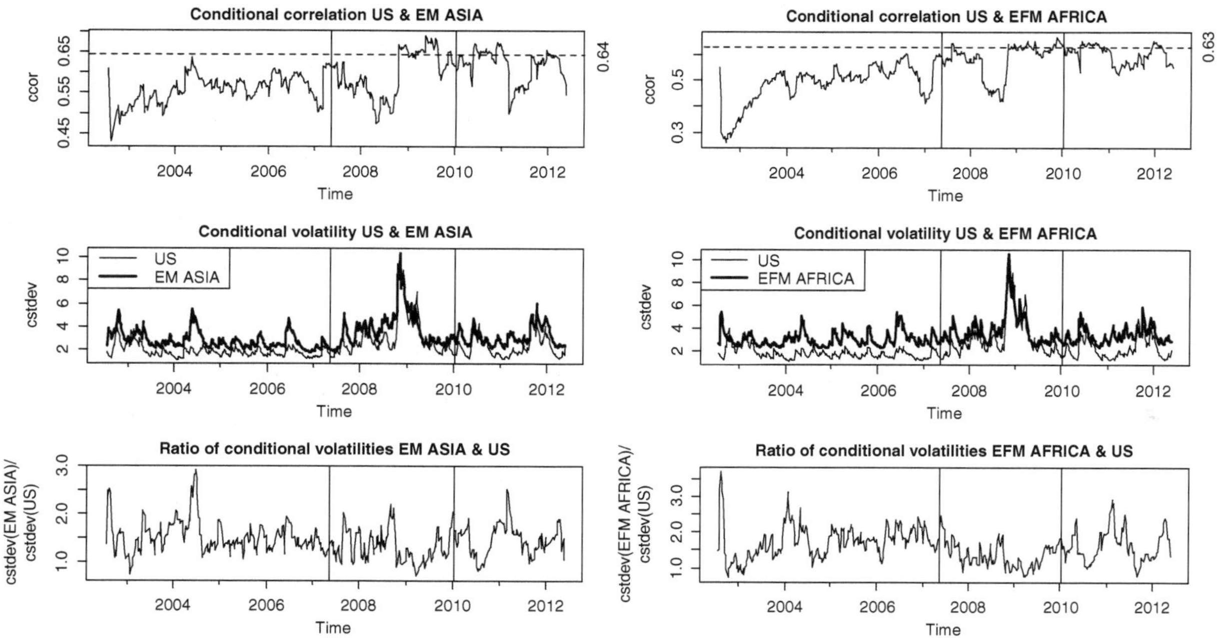

Figure 10.3 Continued

Table 10.3 Statistical significance of differences between pre-crisis and post-crisis mean: conditional correlations, conditional volatilities and ratio of conditional volatilities (US and emerging/frontier region stock markets)

Index	Sample length before/after	Mean correlation with US pre-crisis period[a]	Mean correlation with US post-crisis period[b]	Percentage change in mean correlation	Welch two sample t-test p-value	Wilcoxon rank sum test p-value	Mean volatility pre-crisis period[a]	Mean volatility post-crisis period[b]
US	62/62	–	–	–	–	–	1.720	2.140
	124/124	–	–	–	–	–	1.734	2.304
BRIC	62/62	0.624	0.683	9.455	0.000***	0.000***	3.206	3.473
	124/124	0.629	0.668	6.200	0.000***	0.000***	3.096	3.688
EM EUROPE	62/62	0.514	0.606	17.899	0.000***	0.000***	4.058	3.931
	124/124	0.496	0.582	17.339	0.000***	0.000***	3.748	4.197
EM LATIN	62/62	0.724	0.739	2.072	0.005***	0.004***	3.664	3.851
AMERICA	124/124	0.719	0.729	1.391	0.014**	0.008***	3.511	4.003
EM ASIA	62/62	0.575	0.634	10.261	0.000***	0.000***	2.533	2.933
	124/124	0.571	0.618	8.231	0.000***	0.000***	2.516	3.164
EFM AFRICA	62/62	0.532	0.613	15.226	0.000***	0.000***	3.326	3.300
	124/124	0.530	0.599	13.019	0.000***	0.000***	3.218	3.440

Notes: [a, b] Samples as described in Table 10.2. The average percentage changes across all samples for the mean of conditional correlations, conditional volatilities and ratios of conditional volatilities are 10.109 percent, 13.364 percent and −7.739 percent respectively. Ratio of conditional volatilities is calculated as conditional volatility of an emerging/frontier region divided by conditional volatility of the US. *Significant at 10%, ** Significant at 5%, *** Significant at 1%.

10.5.2 Conditional correlation between US and emerging/frontier region markets

The impact of the financial crisis appears to have been less severe on emerging/frontier regional financial markets; it can be argued that this was possibly a result of their lower-leveraged financial sectors and their smaller investment banking sectors. It might be expected that a possible consequence of this could be that changes in the conditional correlations between the emerging/frontier regional markets and the US may be found to be of a different size from the changes in correlations between the US and other developed markets.

From Figure 10.3 it can be identified that the reaction of the conditional correlation to the financial crisis appears to be similar in all the emerging/frontier regions in the sample. As was also found in respect to developed regional markets, there was an initial fall in correlation in May 2007, which indicated that these parts of the world responded relatively slowly to the initial falls in the US market. This was then followed by a spike in correlation that occurred towards the end of 2008.

In the BRIC countries, for example, correlation rose from a low of about 0.548 just prior to the crisis to a peak of about 0.730 during the crisis period. This spike in correlation was accompanied by a spike in the conditional volatility. Interestingly, the spikes found in the conditional volatilities across

Table 10.3 Continued

Percentage change in mean volatility	Welch two sample t-test p-value	Wilcoxon rank sum test p-value	Mean ratio of volatilities with US pre-crisis period[a]	Mean ratio of volatilities with US post-crisis period[b]	Percentage change in mean ratio of volatilities	Welch two sample t-test p-value	Wilcoxon rank sum test p-value
24.419	0.000***	0.020**	–	–	–	–	–
32.872	0.000***	0.000***	–	–	–	–	–
8.328	0.030**	0.003***	1.868	1.774	−5.032	0.157	0.334
19.121	0.000***	0.000***	1.796	1.735	−3.396	0.151	0.142
−3.130	0.416	0.349	2.381	1.963	−17.556	0.000***	0.000***
11.980	0.000***	0.000***	2.185	1.956	−10.481	0.000***	0.000***
5.104	0.162	0.112	2.141	1.949	−8.968	0.005***	0.026**
14.013	0.000***	0.000***	2.039	1.880	−7.798	0.001***	0.001***
15.792	0.001***	0.000***	1.471	1.490	1.292	0.739	0.581
25.755	0.000***	0.000***	1.456	1.467	0.755	0.765	0.632
−0.782	0.840	0.962	1.946	1.680	−13.669	0.000***	0.000***
6.899	0.010***	0.003***	1.867	1.633	−12.533	0.000***	0.000***

the emerging/frontier markets tended to be higher than the increase experienced in the US; this being despite the fact that the financial crisis was predominantly a developed market phenomena. It is possible that this was due to the world-wide nature of the crisis prompting developed country investors to withdraw money from emerging markets. It can be observed that since the 1990s, downturns in developed markets have triggered large underperformance in emerging markets. This may partially reflect the ways in which institutional investors operate. For example, Credit Suisse argues that pension fund investment in emerging markets is problematical given that it is restricted by strict liquidity rules. Funds are required to mark-to-market their assets daily, forcing rapid divestments if assets fall in relation to liability thresholds (Emerging Markets, 2010).

Table 10.3 identifies changes in mean conditional correlation and conditional volatility levels between the pre- and post-crisis periods. It can be noted that, as was the case with the developed market sample, the estimates appear largely robust to changes in the sample length and that the longer sample period mean values are generally a little lower for both the correlations and the ratios of volatilities.

From the 124-period sample test set it can be identified that subsequent to the end of the crisis in January 2010 mean correlation levels were higher than in the pre-crisis period. In addition, it can be noted that all of these increases were statistically significant. In, for example, the emerging/frontier

Africa region, correlation increased by about 13 percent to 0.599 (from 0.530) and for EM ASIA it increased by about 8.2 percent to 0.618.

These results appear to lend *prima facie* support to Hypothesis 2. They suggest the correlations between the US and emerging/frontier regional markets have risen by a different magnitude to the increases in correlation between US and developed markets. The mean increase across all samples was found to be 10.11 percent for emerging/frontier markets compared to the 3.39 percent mean increase found for the developed markets (from Table 10.2). In the next section we argue that a possible explanation for this difference in size can be found in the differences by which the relative conditional volatilities changed between the two sample groups. The influence of volatility on correlation is well recognized in the literature. For example, both Longin and Solnik (1995) and also Solnik et al. (1996) showed there to be a relationship between correlation levels and the changes in volatility.

10.5.3 Conditional correlations and the ratio of conditional volatilities

One possible explanation of the apparent long-term increases in market correlation is that they are the consequence of changes to the 'financial architecture' resulting in greater financial regulation and significant de-leveraging in developed markets. This would not however account for the differences found in the sizes of the increases in correlation in the emerging/frontier market and developed market sample datasets. A possible explanation of this difference lies in the different ways in which the conditional volatilities responded to the crisis.

We argue in this chapter that the differences in correlation found between developed and emerging/frontier markets may reflect the impact of two separate factors. Firstly, the effect of changes to the 'financial architecture' that have a positive impact on correlation. Secondly, the effect of changes in the ratio of volatilities between the second market and the US market. We find evidence to suggest that the effect on correlations of the second factor works in *opposite* directions in developed and emerging/frontier regional markets.

The importance of volatility on correlation was identified by Knif and Pynnonen (2007) and also Jithendranathan (2005); the latter found that an asymmetric decrease in volatility can alter the correlation between markets. Our study found that the volatilities of developed and emerging/frontier markets relative to the US market responded differently to the 2007 crisis. From Tables 10.2 and 10.3 it can be identified that in most instances the ratio of the conditional volatility with the US *increased* in respect to developed markets but *decreased* in respect to emerging/frontier markets.

We argue in this chapter that developed markets showed a relatively small increase in their correlation with the US because the positive impact on correlations associated with the change in the world's 'financial architectures' was partially offset by the *increase* in their conditional volatility relative to the US. This can be contrasted with emerging/frontier markets, where the larger increases in the conditional correlation can be explained in terms of the positive impact associated with 'financial architecture' effects being augmented by the impact of the *fall* in the volatility of emerging markets relative to the US (which has an additional positive impact on correlation levels).

We use the following regression model to examine this relationship in more detail:

$$\rho_{i,t} = \alpha_i + \beta_{1i} \frac{Volatility_{market,t}}{Volatility_{US,t}} + \beta_{2i} dummy\ variable_t + \varepsilon_t \tag{10.4}$$

where $\rho_{i,t}$ is the conditional correlation between the regional and the US indices, $\frac{Volatility_{market,t}}{Volatility_{US,t}}$ is the ratio of conditional volatility between the regional market and the US market, $dummy\ variables_t$ is an intercept dummy variable which equals 0 (10.1) for observation before (after) the crisis, *i* refers to the index and *t* to time.

The impact of the crisis on the 'financial architecture' is identified through the intercept dummy variable, which distinguishes between pre- and post-crisis periods. The parameter values presented in Table 10.4 are found to be mainly positive for both the developed and emerging markets. They are also largely significant, especially in respect to emerging markets (providing additional support for our Hypothesis 1).

The regression shown in equation (10.4) was run with the same three sample observation periods used in Tables 10.2 and 10.3; for consistency we report the results for the same 62 and 124 observation periods in Table 10.4. The sign on the ratio of volatilities variable is negative for both groups. This provides support to our Hypothesis 3, that market conditional correlations are partly determined by relative conditional volatilities. We only find statistical significance in respect to the emerging/frontier markets for this variable, which may possibly reflect the fact that the size of the change in the ratio of volatilities was generally smaller in respect to the developed countries.

We would argue that although these results are not unequivocal, they do provide significant support to the third hypothesis. They are also consistent with the literature; Gupta and Mollik (2008), for example, also found that changes in the relative volatilities of developed and emerging markets influenced their correlation.

10.6 Conclusion

This chapter asks whether or not the 2007 financial crisis resulted in a long-term structural change in the conditional correlation relationship between returns in the US equity market and the returns in international equity markets. This is important from the perspective of optimal portfolio selection, as increases in correlation reduce the benefits associated with international

Table 10.4 Regression results of factors affecting the conditional correlations (US and developed/emerging/frontier region stock markets)

Index	Sample length before[a]/after[b]	Constant	Ratio of conditional volatilities with US	Intercept dummy	Adj. R^2	F test p-value
EMU	62/62	0.822 (0.000***)	−0.025 (0.242)	0.006 (0.786)	0.062	0.008***
	124/124	0.773 (0.000***)	−0.001 (0.948)	0.012 (0.496)	0.044	0.001***
EUROPE ex EMU	62/62	0.800 (0.000***)	−0.028 (0.167)	0.033 (0.007***)	0.374	0.000***
	124/124	0.771 (0.000***)	−0.019 (0.165)	0.049 (0.000***)	0.519	0.000***
PACIFIC	62/62	0.563 (0.000***)	0.006 (0.774)	0.005 (0.869)	−0.013	0.793
	124/124	0.570 (0.000***)	−0.012 (0.581)	0.044 (0.039**)	0.264	0.000***
BRIC	62/62	0.692 (0.000***)	−0.037 (0.029**)	0.056 (0.003***)	0.570	0.000***
	124/124	0.668 (0.000***)	−0.022 (0.077*)	0.037 (0.037**)	0.268	0.000***
EM EUROPE	62/62	0.614 (0.000***)	−0.042 (0.000***)	0.074 (0.000***)	0.702	0.000***
	124/124	0.482 (0.000***)	0.006 (0.710)	0.088 (0.000***)	0.527	0.000***
EM LATIN AMERICA	62/62	0.830 (0.000***)	−0.050 (0.041**)	0.006 (0.766)	0.399	0.000***
	124/124	0.753 (0.000***)	−0.017 (0.292)	0.007 (0.696)	0.051	0.001***
EM ASIA	62/62	0.645 (0.000***)	−0.047 (0.364)	0.060 (0.003***)	0.522	0.000***
	124/124	0.632 (0.000***)	−0.042 (0.123)	0.048 (0.003***)	0.392	0.000***
EFMAFRICA	62/62	0.643 (0.000***)	−0.057 (0.000***)	0.066 (0.053*)	0.543	0.000***
	124/124	0.600 (0.000***)	−0.037 (0.014**)	0.060 (0.001***)	0.485	0.000***

Notes: [ab] Sample as described in Table 10.2. The ratio of conditional volatilities is calculated as conditional volatility of a developed/emerging/frontier region divided by conditional volatility of the US. P-values are presented in brackets below the coefficients. Standard errors have been corrected for autocorrelation and heteroskedasticity using Newey-West correction. Intercept dummy variable is equal to 0 (1) for observations before (after) the crisis.
* Significant at 10%, ** Significant at 5%, *** Significant at 1%.

$$\text{Regression equation}: \rho_{i,t} = \alpha_i + \beta_{1i}\frac{Volatility_{market,t}}{Volatility_{US,t}} + \beta_{2i} dummy\ variable_t + \varepsilon_t.$$

portfolio diversification. Previous researchers such as Longin and Solnik (2001) identified short-term correlation increases during bear market phases, and others, such as You and Daigler (2010), argued that there was a short-term reduction in portfolio diversification benefits during these periods. We believe however that this chapter produces evidence to suggest that the 2007 financial-crisis-related increases in conditional correlations are *permanent*. If this is the case it will have major implications for the ways in which US investors use international diversification in their portfolio selection.

We find *prima facie* evidence to support the hypothesis that economic structural adjustment has resulted in long-term increases in the correlation between the US and developed markets and also between the US and emerging/frontier markets.

The second key finding is that the *magnitude* of the increase in correlation appears to be greater in respect to emerging/frontier markets. For example, from pre-crisis to post-crisis the correlation between BRIC countries and the US rose by 6.2 percent to 0.668. It also increased between the US and EM ASIA by 8.2 percent to 0.618 and between the US and emerging frontier Africa by 13 percent to 0.599. We argue in this chapter that there is a *prima facie* case for the argument that the increases in correlation found are possibly a consequence of two interrelated factors. First, the global tightening of regulations and the de-leveraging effects seen across much of the world financial sector in response to the crisis. And second, the impact of the crisis on relative market conditional volatilities. It was found that in most instances post-crisis volatility *rose* in other developed markets relative to the US and that post-crisis volatility *fell* in emerging/frontier markets relative to the US. We would argue that this difference possibly explains why we found greater increases in the correlation with the US in respect to emerging/frontier markets than in respect to developed-economy markets.

Appendix

Table 10.A.1 DCC(1,1)-TGARCH(1,1) model for the logarithmic returns for the nine MSCI indices

Parameter	Estimate	Std. error	t value	Pr(>|t|)
US				
μ	0.112375	0.060353	1.861970	0.062608*
ω	0.176424	0.121118	1.456630	0.145218
α	0.125609	0.076503	1.641900	0.100612
γ	1.000000	0.391318	2.555460	0.010605**
β	0.826713	0.105525	7.834290	0.000000***
EMU				
μ	0.165232	0.081702	2.022370	0.043138**
ω	0.231389	0.120612	1.918460	0.055053*
α	0.113870	0.052256	2.179080	0.029326**

continued

Table 10.A.1 Continued

Parameter	Estimate	Std. error	t value	Pr(>|t|)
γ	1.000000	0.240486	4.158250	0.000032***
β	0.838841	0.070210	11.947600	0.000000***
EURORE ex EMU				
μ	0.201190	0.109583	1.835960	0.066363*
ω	0.219127	0.118019	1.856700	0.063353*
α	0.117188	0.060649	1.932220	0.053332*
γ	1.000000	0.285764	3.499390	0.000466***
β	0.827790	0.080246	10.315620	0.000000***
PACIFIC				
μ	0.109969	0.113864	0.965790	0.334149
ω	0.247988	0.170572	1.453860	0.145984
α	0.075309	0.039314	1.915590	0.055418*
γ	0.921783	0.405580	2.272750	0.023041**
β	0.847973	0.081597	10.392260	0.000000***
BRIC				
μ	0.466896	0.158356	2.948400	0.003194***
ω	0.331698	0.201699	1.644520	0.100069
α	0.101471	0.034261	2.961710	0.003059***
γ	0.685051	0.267757	2.558480	0.010513**
β	0.827542	0.073186	11.307330	0.000000***
EM EUROPE				
μ	0.307575	0.138342	2.223290	0.026197**
ω	0.253707	0.111582	2.273720	0.022983**
α	0.090235	0.027841	3.241050	0.001191***
γ	0.655310	0.274521	2.387100	0.016982**
β	0.871520	0.037822	23.042940	0.000000***
EM LATIN AMERICA				
μ	0.434562	0.167056	2.601300	0.009287***
ω	0.320633	0.160301	2.000190	0.045479**
α	0.084149	0.024202	3.476890	0.000507***
γ	1.000000	0.298997	3.344520	0.000824***
β	0.853897	0.052929	16.132740	0.000000***
EM ASIA				
μ	0.327047	0.084670	3.862620	0.000112***
ω	0.324017	0.127986	2.531660	0.011352**
α	0.112531	0.032175	3.497470	0.000470***
γ	0.810159	0.264753	3.060060	0.002213***
β	0.806754	0.054841	14.710700	0.000000***

continued

Table 10.A.1 Continued

Parameter	Estimate	Std. error	t value	Pr(>|t|)
EFM AFRICA				
μ	0.344854	0.155949	2.211330	0.027013**
ω	0.552053	0.283479	1.947420	0.051484*
α	0.100831	0.031708	3.179960	0.001473***
γ	1.000000	0.318689	3.137860	0.001702***
β	0.757527	0.099462	7.616230	0.000000***
DCC				
α	0.023365	0.003143	7.433910	0.000000***
β	0.937110	0.010067	93.085660	0.000000***

Notes: Mean equation:

$$r_{i,t} = \mu_i + \varepsilon_{i,t} \tag{A.1}$$

Variance equation:

$$\sqrt{h_{i,t}} = \omega_i + \alpha_i|\varepsilon_{i,t-1}| + \gamma_i|\varepsilon_{i,t-1}|I(\varepsilon_{i,t-1} < 0) + \beta_i\sqrt{h_{i,t-1}} \tag{A.2}$$

DCC equation:

$$Q_t = (1 - \alpha - \beta)\bar{Q} + \alpha v_{t-1}v'_{t-1} + \beta Q_{t-1} \tag{A.3}$$

where v_t represent standardized residuals by their conditional standard deviation.
* Significant at 10%, ** Significant at 5%, *** Significant at 1%.
Estimation based on 513 observations using R (2012) and rgarch package (Ghalanos, 2011).

Notes

* Corresponding author.

1. The first significant developments in the euro crisis were after the end-point of the 2007 financial crisis identified in this chapter. A Eurostat report dated 8 January 2010 first highlighted irregularities in the reporting of the Greek deficit, and it was not until April 2010 that the eurozone countries first agreed to set up a safety net of €30 billion for Greece. The subsequent €78 billion bailout of Ireland was agreed in November 2010 and a further bailout of Portugal was agreed in May 2011. The developing crisis appears to have had only a marginal impact on US markets during the period of our analysis. From 1 January 2010 to 4 March 2011 (week 62 in our analysis) the S&P 500 rose from 1133 to 1321 and by 11 May 2012 (week 124) it reached 1353. Within the eurozone itself the DAX 30 first fell by a substantial amount from 25 July 2011 (significantly after our week 62) and, after a period of recovery, started to resume its downward trend from 15 March 2012.
2. The mean daily closing value of the VIX over the period 3 January 2000–11 May 2012 was 21.72. The index began to show a significant increase above this level from the middle of 2007, peaking at 79.13 on 20 October 2008. It began to revert to the mean value during 2009 and by 28 December 2009 was at 21.58; approximately the long-term mean. Although there was a subsequent period of high volatility

during May and June 2010, the post-crisis mean of 21.15 covering the period 4 January 2010–11 May 2012 approximated to the long-term mean. Data source: Yahoo (2012).

References

Barari, M. (2004). Equity Market Integration in Latin America: A Time-Varying Integration Score Analysis. *International Review of Financial Analysis*, 13, 649–68.

Bekaert, G., Harvey, C. R. and Lumsdaine, R. L.(2002). Dating the Integration of World Equity Markets. *Journal of Financial Economics*, 65, 203–47.

Bekaert, G. and Wu, G. (2000). Asymmetric Volatility and Risk in Equity Markets. *Review of Financial Studies*, 13, 1–42.

BIS (2012) Basel III – Basel Committee on Banking Supervision, http://www.bis.org/bcbs/basel3.htm, date accessed 22 May 2012.

Crotty, J. (2009). Structural Causes of the Global Financial Crisis: A Critical Assessment of the 'New Financial Architecture'. *Cambridge Journal of Economics*, 33 (4), 563–80.

Emerging Markets (2010) Institutional Investment: Into the breach, http://www.emergingmarkets.org/Article/2690752/INSTITUTIONAL-INVESTMENT-Into-the-breach.html, date accessed 22 May 2012.

Engle, R. (2002). Dynamic Conditional Correlation – A Simple Class of Multivariate GARCH Models. *Journal of Business and Economic Statistics*, 20, 339–50.

Engle, R. F. and Sheppard, K. (2001). Theoretical and Empirical Properties of Dynamic Conditional Correlation Multivariate GARCH. *NBER Working Paper* 8554.

Forbes, K. J. and Rigobon, R. (2002). No Contagion, Only Interdependence: Measuring Stock Market Co-movements. *Journal of Finance*, 57 (5), 2223–61.

Fratzschler, M. (2002). Financial Market Integration in Europe: On the Effects of Euro area on Stock Markets. *International Journal of Finance and Economics*, 7, 165–93.

French, K. R. and Poterba, J. M. (1991). Investor Diversification and International Equity Markets. *American Economic Review*, 81 (2), 222–6.

Garnaut, R. (1998). The Financial Crisis: A Watershed in Economic Thought About East Asia. *Asian-Pacific Economic Literature*, 12 (1), 1–11.

Geithner, T. (2008). Comments by New York Fed President Timothy Geithner. *Wall Street Journal*, 30 May.

Ghalanos, A. (2011) rgarch: Flexible GARCH modelling in R, http://r-forge.r-project.org/projects/rgarch/, date accessed 18 May 2012.

Glosten, L. R., Jagannathan, R. and Runkle, D. E. (1993). On the Relation between the Expected Value and the Volatility of the Nominal Excess Return on Stocks. *Journal of Finance*, 48 (5), 1779–801.

Goetzmann, W. N., Li, L. and Rouwenhorst, K. G. (2005). Long-term Global Market Correlations. *Journal of Business*, 78 (1), 1–38.

Gupta, R. and Mollik, A. T. (2008). Volatility, Time Varying Correlation and International Portfolio Diversification: An Empirical Study of Australia and Emerging Markets. *International Research Journal of Finance and Economics*, 18, 18–37.

Jagannathan, R. and Wang, Z. (1996). The Conditional CAPM and the Cross-Section of Expected Returns. *Journal of Finance*, 51 (1), 3–53.

Jithendranathan, T. (2005). What Causes Correlations of Equity Returns to Change Over Time? A Study of the US and the Russian Equity Markets. *Investment Management and Financial Innovation*, 4, 69–79.

Karolyi, G. A. and Stulz, R. M.(1996). Why Do Markets Move Together? An Investigation of U.S.-Japan Stock Return Comovements. *Journal of Finance*, 51, 951–86.

Kearney, C. and Lucey, B. M.(2004). International Equity Market Integration: Theory, Evidence and Implications. *International Review of Financial Analysis*, 13, 571–83.

King, T.-H.D. and Wen, M.-M. (2011). Shareholder Governance, Bondholder Governance, and Managerial Risk-Taking. *Journal of Banking & Finance*, 35 (3), 512–31.

Knif, J. and Pynnonen, S.(2007). Volatility Driven Changes in Stock Return Correlation Dynamics. *Managerial Finance*, 33 (3), 220–35.

Laopodis, N. T.(2005). Portfolio Diversification Benefits within Europe: Implications for a US Investor. *International Review of Financial Analysis*, 14, 455–76.

Longin, F. and Solnik, B. (1995). Is the Correlation in International Equity Returns Constant: 1960-1990? *Journal of International Money and Finance*, 14, 3–26.

Longin, F. and Solnik, B. (2001). Extreme Correlation of International Equity Markets. *Journal of Finance*, 56, 649–76.

Lucey, B. M. and Muckley, C. (2011). Robust Global Stock Market Interdependencies. *International Review of Financial Analysis*, 20, 215–24.

Mann, H. B. and Whitney, D. R. (1947). On a Test of Whether One of Two Random Variables Is Stochastically Larger Than the Other. *Annals of Mathematical Statistics*, 18, 50–60.

Markwat, T., Kole, E. and van Dijk, D. (2009). Contagion as a Domino Effect in Global Stock Markets. *Journal of Banking & Finance*, 33 (11), 1996–2012.

Meric, I., Ratner, M. and Meric, G. (2008). Co-movements of Sector Index Returns in the World's Major Stock Markets in Bull and Bear Markets: Portfolio Diversification Implications. *International Review of Financial Analysis*, 17, 156–77.

Minsky, H. P. (1992). The Financial Instability Hypothesis. *The Jerome Levy Economics Institute, Working Paper 74*.

Moshirian, F. (2011). The Global Financial Crisis and the Evolution of Markets, Institutions and Regulation. *Journal of Banking & Finance*, 35 (3), 502–11.

MSCI (2012) MSCI Global Equity Indices, http://www.msci.com/products/indices/, date accessed 18 May 2012.

NBER (2012) US Business Cycle Expansions and Contractions, http://www.nber.org/cycles/cyclesmain.html,date accessed 18 May 2012.

Nelson, D. B.(1991). Conditional Heteroskedasticity in Asset Returns: A New Approach. *Econometrica*, 59 (2), 347–70.

R (2012) The R Project for Statistical Computing, http://www.r-project.org/index.html, date accessed 18 May 2012.

Ramchand, L. and Susmel, R. (1998). Volatility and Cross Correlation across Major Stock Markets. *Journal of Empirical Finance*, 5, 397–416.

Schwebach, R. G., Olienyk, J. P. and Zumwalt, J. K. (2002). The Impact of Financial Crises on International Diversification. *Global Financial Journal*, 13, 147–61.

Solnik, B. H. (1995). Why Not Diversify Internationally Rather Than Domestically? *Financial Analysts Journal*, 51 (1), 89–94.

Solnik, B., Bourcrelle, C. and Fur, Y. L. (1996). International Market Correlation and Volatility. *Financial Analysts Journal*, 52, 17–34.

Swanson, P. E. (2003). The Interrelatedness of Global Equity Markets, Money Markets, and Foreign Exchange Markets. *International Review of Financial Analysis*, 12, 135–55.

US Treasury (2010) Troubled Asset Relief Program: Two Year Retrospective, http://www.treasury.gov/initiatives/financial-stability/briefing-room/reports/agency_reports/Documents/TARP%20Two%20Year%20Retrospective_10%2005%2010_transmittal%20letter.pdf, date accessed 18 May 2012.

Welch, B. L.(1938). The Significance of the Difference between Two Means When the Population Variances Are Unequal. *Biometrika*, 29, 350–62.

Whalen, C. J. (2008). The Credit Crunch: A Minsky Moment. *Studi e Note di Economia,* XIII (1), 3–21.

Wilcoxon, F. (1945). Individual Comparisons by Ranking Methods. *Biometrics*, 1, 80–3.

Yahoo (2012) VIX Index, http://uk.finance.yahoo.com/q?s=%5EVIX, date accessed 22 May 2012.

You, L. and Daigler, R. (2010). The Strength and Source of Asymmetric International Diversification. *Journal of Economics and Finance*, 34 (3), 349–64.

Yu, I.-W., Fung, K.-P. And Tam, C.-S. (2010). Assessing Financial Market Integration in Asia – Equity Markets. *Journal of Banking & Finance*, 34 (12), 2874–85.

Zakoian, J. M. (1994). Threshold Heteroskedastic Models. *Journal of Economic Dynamics and Control*, 18 (5), 931–55.

11

A Hybrid Fuzzy GJR-GARCH Modeling Approach for Stock Market Volatility Forecasting

Leandro Maciel

11.1 Introduction

Accurately measuring and forecasting stock market volatility plays a crucial role for asset and derivative pricing, hedge strategies, portfolio allocation and risk management. Since the 1987 stock market crash, academics, practitioners and regulators have investigated the development of financial time series models with changing variance over time in order to avoid huge investment losses due to their exposure to unexpected market movements (Allen and Morzuch, 2006, Carvalho et al., 2005, Lin et al., 2012). Indeed, volatility, as a measure of financial security prices fluctuation around its expected value, is one of the primary inputs in decision making processes under uncertainty, justifying its growing interest in the financial and economic literature (Kapetanios et al., 2006, Lux and Kaizoji, 2007).

Stock returns volatility is often characterized by some stylized facts, such as volatility clusters, persistence, leptokurtic data behavior and time-varying volatility. A convenient framework for dealing with time-dependent volatility in financial markets concerns the autoregressive conditional heteroscedasticity (ARCH) model, proposed by Engle (1982), becoming a popular tool for volatility modeling. Providing a more flexible structure, Bollerslev (1986) introduced the Generalized ARCH (GARCH) model, which combines the ARCH and autoregressive moving average (ARMA) models. The GARCH model estimates jointly a conditional mean and conditional variance equation, and it is characterized by a fat tail and excess of kurtosis, regularly used in studying the daily returns of stock market data (Han and Park, 2008).[1]

Despite the success of GARCH model, it has been criticized for failing to capture the asymmetric volatility (Liu and Hung, 2010), since for stock prices, negative shocks to returns generally have large impacts on their volatility than positive shocks. To overcome these limitations, extensions of the GARCH model have been proposed, comprising a class of asymmetric GARCH models. The exponential GARCH (EGARCH), developed by Nelson

(1991), and the GJR-GARCH, proposed by Glosten et al. (1993), are the main representatives of GARCH-family models assuming persistence. These models include the asymmetric responses of volatility to positive and negative shocks, but they do not simulate stock fluctuations with volatility clustering well. Howsoever, these effects can be modeled by modifications of linear models, while others require nonlinear approaches, less commonly used in practice due to their complexity (Hung, 2011b).

Methods based on artificial intelligence have been extensively applied as a flexible way to describe complex dynamics of various economic and financial problems (Haofei et al., 2007; Racine, 2001). Hamid and Iqbal (2004) suggested the use of an artificial neural network (ANN) model to predict the volatility of S&P 500 index futures prices. Bildirici and Ersin (2009) enhanced GARCH-family models with ANN to forecast the volatility of daily returns in Istanbul Stock Exchange. On the other hand, Hajizadeh et al. (2012) proposed a scheme in which the estimates of volatility obtained by an EGARCH model are fed forward to an ANN model, considering the S&P 500 index prices.

A radial basis function neural network with Gaussian activation functions and robust clustering algorithms to model the conditional volatility of the Spanish electricity pool prices was suggested by Coelho and Santos (2011). The authors showed that their model performed better than traditional linear models to predict upward and downward movements in electricity future prices. Concerning the issue of derivative securities pricing, Wang (2009) integrated a GJR-GARCH model into an ANN option-pricing model and indicated that their approach provides higher predictability than other volatility methodologies. Providing similar results, Wang et al. (2012) and Tseng et al. (2008) also evaluated volatility forecasting performance in option pricing combining neural networks and GARCH-family models.

Tino et al. (2001) introduced a recurrent neural network model to simulate daily trading of straddles on financial indexes based on predictions of daily volatility. The authors showed that while GARCH models cannot generate any significantly positive profit, the use of recurrent networks can generate a statistically significant excess profit. Moreover, Tung and Quek (2011) jointed a self-organizing neural network and option straddle-based approach to financial volatility trading. Compared with several benchmarks, the proposed methodology demonstrated that its ability to forecast the future volatility enhances investments profits. Despite its high ability to deal with the problem of volatility forecasting, ANN drawbacks include its 'black box' nature, greater computational burden, proneness to overfitting, and the empirical nature of model development.

Due to these shortcomings, models based on fuzzy theory appear as an alternative methodology to evaluate high nonlinear systems (Zadeh, 2005; Savran, 2007). Popov and Bykhanov (2005) combined the concept of fuzzy rules and GARCH approach to model volatility of financial time series. The conditional volatility forecasting of foreign exchange rates returns was considered by Geng and Ma (2008), using a functional fuzzy inference system applied to the GARCH model. Hung (2009a) adopted the method of fuzzy logic systems to modify the threshold values for an asymmetric GARCH model. Based on simulations, the author showed that the forecasting performance is significantly improved if the leverage effect of clustering is considered along with the use of fuzzy systems and GARCH approaches.

Thavaneswaran et al. (2009) proposed a fuzzy weighted possibilistic model for option valuation based on the estimation and forecasting of financial volatility, considered as fuzzy numbers. They stated that fuzzy assumptions are more flexible and reveal promising results for option pricing as an intuitive way to look at the uncertainty in the model's parameters. To capture the volatility conditional distribution on higher-order moments such as skewness, a GARCH-Fuzzy-Density method for volatility density forecasting was proposed by Helin and Koivisto (2011). The model provided more accurate density forecasts for the higher-order moment varying processes than traditional GARCH models.

Combining the concepts of fuzzy systems and artificial neural networks, Chang et al. (2011) suggested the use of a hybrid adaptive network-based fuzzy inference system (ANFIS) to forecast the volatility of the Taiwan stock market. The authors indicated that the proposed model is superior to other methods with regard to error measures. Furthermore, Luna and Ballini (2012) introduced an adaptive fuzzy system to forecast financial time series volatility and compared their method with a GARCH model. The results indicate the higher performance of the adaptive fuzzy approach for volatility forecasting purposes.

A hybrid Fuzzy-GARCH model was suggested by Hung (2009b). The model comprises a functional fuzzy inference system with a GARCH model, optimized using a genetic algorithm framework. Similarly, Hung (2011a) and Hung (2011b) proposed a fuzzy system method to analyze clustering in GARCH models using genetic algorithms and particle swarm optimization, respectively, to estimate the parameters. The author indicates that the model offers significant improvements in forecasting stock market volatility, outperforming some GARCH-family models.

Hence, this work combines a GJR-GARCH model and fuzzy systems to develop a Fuzzy GJR-GARCH model. The proposed model is based on a collection of fuzzy rules in the form of IF-THEN statements, in which its structure comprises a GJR-GARCH model. The methodology also considers both volatility asymmetry and volatility clustering. Moreover, the Fuzzy GJR-GARCH includes clustering estimation using a subtractive clustering algorithm to provide a more autonomous model, based on data-knowledge, different from the approach proposed by Hung (2011a), which considers expert knowledge to determine the number of stock return clusters. Computational experiments illustrating the effectiveness of the Fuzzy GJR-GARCH model are provided by modeling and forecasting the volatility of S&P 500 (US) and Ibovespa (Brazil) indexes from 3 January 2000 through 30 September 2011, in comparison with some GARCH-family models and a current Fuzzy-GARCH method proposed by Hung (2011a).

The choice regarding a GJR-GARCH specification is justified by the evidence of volatility asymmetry in stock market data (Martens et al., 2009). Furthermore, other studies have found evidence in favor of the GJR-GARCH model (Brailsford and Faff, 1996; Taylor, 2004). For emerging stock market data, Ng and McAleer (2004) suggested that GARCH and GJR-GARCH models are superior to the RiskMetrics (Morgan, 1996) model in forecasting stock market volatility; however, neither GARCH nor GJR-GARCH dominates the other. Despite extensive literature on volatility model evaluation, no consensus exists suggesting the most appropriate method for assessing which model has the optimal performance in forecasting volatility (Liu and Hung, 2010).

The process of optimizing the Fuzzy GJR-GARCH model parameters is highly complex and nonlinear. A differential evolution (DE) based parameter estimation algorithm is suggested in this work in order to provide the optimal solution for the proposed model, since in this approach there is no requirement that the search space is differentiable or continuous, unlike some traditional optimization techniques. A nature-inspired metaheuristic, the DE algorithm, proposed by Storn and Price (1997), performs difference of the parameters vectors in order to search the optimal solution in a fitness function landscape. In a comparison to several other evolutionary computation algorithms, the main features that make the DE algorithm an attractive optimization tool are: simplicity of implementation;[2] high accuracy and robustness to deal with many problems including separable, non-separable, modal and multimodal objective functions (Zhang and Sanderson, 2003); very few control parameters (three in classical DE); and finally, for expensive and large scale optimization problems, the space complexity of DE is quite slow as compared to most other evolutionary algorithms.

The Fuzzy GJR-GARCH model has novel features in comparison to the existing approaches in the literature. First, the proposed method combines a fuzzy scheme with a GJR-GARCH model, providing a more realistic framework that captures both asymmetries and volatility clustering. Second, the Fuzzy GJR-GARCH model avoids the process of tuning the number of fuzzy rules by considering a subtractive clustering algorithm. Third, this work proposes a simple and efficient differential evolution algorithm to optimize the model parameters. Finally, empirical results consider comparisons with GARCH-type models and also with a recent Fuzzy-GARCH approach proposed by Hung (2011a), estimated with PSO as in its original version and with the differential evolution algorithm suggested.

After this introduction, the reminder of this chapter is organized as follows. The proposed Fuzzy GJR-GARCH model and the current Fuzzy-GARCH approach related in the literature are described in Section 11.2. Section 11.3 discusses the DE-based optimization algorithm of the Fuzzy GJR-GARCH parameters estimation. Computational experiments evaluating the potential of the proposed method for stock market data volatility modeling and forecasting are reported in Section 11.4. Finally, Section 11.5 concludes and suggests issues for further investigation.

11.2 The Fuzzy GJR-GARCH model

11.2.1 GARCH-type models

The Generalized Autoregressive Conditional Heteroskedasticity model, GARCH(p,q), considers the current conditional variance dependent on the p past conditional variances as well as the q past squared innovations. Let $y_t = 100 \times (\ln P_t - \ln P_{t-1})$ denote the continuously compounded rate of stock returns from time $t-1$ to t, where P_t is the daily closing stock price at time t. The GARCH(p,q) model can be written as:

$$y_t = \sigma_t \xi_t \tag{11.1}$$

$$\sigma_t^2 = \omega + \sum_{i=1}^{q} \alpha_i y_{t-i}^2 + \sum_{j=1}^{p} \beta_j \sigma_{t-j}^2 \tag{11.2}$$

where ξ_t is a sequence of independent and identically distributed (i.i.d.) random variables with zero-mean and unit variance, σ_t^2 is the conditional variance of ξ_t, and ω, α_i and β_j are unknown coefficients to be estimated, assuming (Bollerslev, 1986):

$$\omega > 0, \quad \alpha_i \geq 0, \quad i = 1,2,\ldots,q, \quad q > 0,$$

$$\beta_j \geq 0, \quad j = 1,2,\ldots,p, \quad p > 0,$$

$$\sum_{i=1}^{q} \alpha_i + \sum_{j=1}^{p} \beta_j < 1. \tag{11.3}$$

The GARCH model reduces the number of parameters required by considering the information in the lag(s) of the conditional variance in addition to the lagged y_{t-i}^2 term(s) as in ARCH-type models. GARCH models' simplicity and ability to capture persistence of volatility explain its empirical and theoretical appeal. However, it fails to capture the asymmetric influence of negative and positive shocks differently. On the other hand, the GJR-GARCH model provides a mechanism to account for leverage effects of price change on conditional variance. The GJR-GARCH(p,q) model is given by:

$$\sigma_t^2 = \omega + \sum_{i=1}^{q} \alpha_i y_{t-i}^2 + \sum_{j=1}^{p} \beta_j \sigma_{t-j}^2 + \sum_{i=1}^{q} \gamma_i S_{t-i}^- y_{t-i}^2 \tag{11.4}$$

where $S_{t-i}^{-}=1$ if $y_{t-i}<0$, and $S_{t-i}^{-}=0$ if $y_{t-i}\geq 0$, and γ_i are unknown parameters to be estimated. In this case, the following conditions must be satisfied (Glosten et al., 1993):

$$\omega>0,\ \ \alpha_i\geq 0,\ \ i=1,2,\ldots,q,\ \ q>0,$$

$$\beta_j\geq 0,\ \ j=1,2,\ldots,p,\ \ p>0,\ \ \alpha_i+\gamma_i\geq 0,$$

$$\sum_{i=1}^{q}\alpha_i+\sum_{j=1}^{p}\beta_j+\frac{1}{2}\sum_{i=1}^{q}\gamma_i<1. \tag{11.5}$$

Despite the GJR-GARCH model including the asymmetric responses of volatility to positive and negative shocks, it does not simulate stock fluctuations with volatility clustering well. This fact can lead to poor adequacy and forecast ability. Therefore, the proposal of a Fuzzy GJR-GARCH approach appears as a potential tool for volatility modeling and forecasting in the presence of volatility clustering and leverage effects.

11.2.2 The Hybrid Fuzzy GJR-GARCH model

Fuzzy inference systems are universal approximations that can estimate nonlinear continuous functions uniformly with arbitrary accuracy (Hung, 2011b; Savran, 2007; Ji et al., 2007). Besides the GJR-GARCH model considering the differential effects of the propagations of volatility caused by negative and positive shocks, a fuzzy approach provides the capability to simulate stock fluctuations with volatility clustering. The proposed Fuzzy GJR-GARCH model is describe by a collection of fuzzy rules in the form of IF-THEN statements in order to describe the stock market fluctuations via a GJR-GARCH model. Therefore, the kth rule of the Fuzzy GJR-GARCH(p,q) is written as:

$$\mathcal{R}^k: \text{IF}\ \ y_{t-1}\ \ \text{is}\ \ \Gamma^k\ \ \text{THEN}$$

$$y_{kt}=\sigma_{kt}\xi_{kt},\ \sigma_{kt}^2=\omega_k+\sum_{i=1}^{q}\alpha_{ki}y_{t-i}^2+\sum_{j=1}^{p}\beta_{kj}\sigma_{t-j}^2+\sum_{i=1}^{q}\gamma_{ki}S_{t-i}^{-}y_{t-i}^2 \tag{11.6}$$

where Γ^k is the kth fuzzy set (membership function) to describe the stock market return y (for $k=1,2,\ldots,R$), R is the number of fuzzy rules, and y_{t-1} is the previous value of the stock market's returns.

To describe the grade of membership of y_{t-1} in Γ^k, a Gaussian membership function[3] is assumed:

$$\Gamma^k(y_{t-1})=\exp\left(-\frac{1}{2}\left(\frac{y_{t-1}-c^k}{r^k}\right)^2\right) \tag{11.7}$$

where c^k is the center (focal point) of the kth local model, and r^k is a positive constant which defines the zone of influence of the respective cluster.

The collection of the R rules assembles a model as a combination of local models. The contribution of a local model to the overall output is proportional to the normalized degree of firing of each rule, expressed as:

$$\lambda^k(y_{t-1}) = \frac{\Gamma^k(y_{t-1})}{\sum_{l=1}^{R}\Gamma^l(y_{t-1})} \tag{11.8}$$

The Fuzzy GJR-GARCH model output is calculated by weighted averaging of individual rules' contributions:

$$y_t = \sigma_t \xi_t, \text{ and } \sigma_t^2$$

$$= \sum_{k=1}^{R} \lambda^k(y_{t-1}) \left[\omega_k + \sum_{i=1}^{q} \alpha_{ki} y_{t-i}^2 + \sum_{j=1}^{p} \beta_{kj} \sigma_{t-j}^2 + \sum_{i=1}^{q} \gamma_{ki} S_{t-i}^- y_{t-i}^2\right]$$

$$= \frac{\sum_{k=1}^{R} \Gamma^k(y_{t-1}) \left[\omega_k + \sum_{i=1}^{q} \alpha_{ki} y_{t-i}^2 + \sum_{j=1}^{p} \beta_{kj} \sigma_{t-j}^2 + \sum_{i=1}^{q} \gamma_{ki} S_{t-i}^- y_{t-i}^2\right]}{\sum_{k=1}^{R} \Gamma^k(y_{t-1})}$$

$$= \frac{\sum_{k=1}^{R} \exp\left(-\frac{1}{2}\left(\frac{y_{t-1}-c^k}{r^k}\right)^2\right) \left[\omega_k + \sum_{i=1}^{q} \alpha_{ki} y_{t-i}^2 + \sum_{j=1}^{p} \beta_{kj} \sigma_{t-j}^2 + \sum_{i=1}^{q} \gamma_{ki} S_{t-i}^- y_{t-i}^2\right]}{\sum_{k=1}^{R} \exp\left(-\frac{1}{2}\left(\frac{y_{t-1}-c^k}{r^k}\right)^2\right)}. \tag{11.9}$$

The Fuzzy GJR-GARCH model in (11.9) is a nonlinear time-varying equation to model the behavior of complex dynamic systems as stock market volatility processes, including mechanisms to ensure the description of volatility stylized facts, such as volatility dependence, leverage effects and volatility clustering.

The parameters of the Fuzzy-GARCH model can be estimated by minimizing a mean squared error criterion, which is reasonable to obtain success (Haykin, 2001). Therefore, the optimization objective function is defined as:

$$E(\mathbf{x}) = \sum_{l=1}^{N} (y_l - \hat{y}_l)^2 \tag{11.10}$$

where $\mathbf{x} = (\omega_1, \ldots, \omega_R, \alpha_{11}, \ldots, \alpha_{Rq}, \beta_{11}, \ldots, \beta_{Rp}, \gamma_{11}, \ldots, \gamma_{Rq})$ is the parameter set, y_l represents the stock market (actual) data sample for $l = 1, 2, \ldots, N$, N is the number of data points, and $\hat{y}_l$ is the stock market data estimated by the Fuzzy GJR-GARCH model in equation (11.9).

The objective function in (11.10) is a highly nonlinear function of $\mathbf{x}$. Simulations analysis showed that conventional gradient search methodologies produce poor estimates or even are not capable of finding the global minimum of $E(\mathbf{x})$ in equation (11.10). In this work, to estimate the Fuzzy GJR-GARCH parameters, a differential evolution algorithm was proposed.

The number of rules and its respective focal points (c^k) and spreads (r^k) were set using the Subtractive Clustering (SC) algorithm, proposed by Chiu (1994). SC uses the data points as candidate prototype cluster centers. The capability of a point to be a cluster center is evaluated through its potential, a measure of the spatial proximity between a particular point y_i and all other data points:

$$\rho_i = \frac{1}{N}\sum_{j=1}^{N} e^{-r||y_i - y_j||^2}, \quad i = 1, 2, \ldots, N \tag{11.11}$$

where ρ_i denote the potential of the ith data point, r is a positive constant which defines the zone of influence of the cluster, and N is the number of points.

The value of the potential is higher for a data point that is surrounded by a large number of close data points. Therefore, it is reasonable to establish such a point to be the center of a cluster. The potential of all other data points is reduced by an amount proportional to the potential of the chosen point and inversely proportional to the distance to this center. The next center is also found as the data point with the highest (after this subtraction) potential. The procedure is repeated until the potential of all data points is reduced below a certain threshold.[4]

11.2.3 Current Fuzzy-GARCH model approach

For comparison purposes, the suggested Fuzzy GJR-GARCH model was also compared with a current Fuzzy-GARCH approach related in the literature and proposed by Hung (2011a). Hence, the kth rule of the Fuzzy-GARCH(p,q) method is written as:

$$\mathcal{R}^k : \text{IF } y_{t-1} \text{ is } \Gamma^k \text{ THEN}$$

$$y_{kt} = \sigma_{kt}\xi_{kt}, \ \sigma_{kt}^2 = \omega_k + \sum_{i=1}^{q} \alpha_{ki} y_{t-i}^2 + \sum_{j=1}^{p} \beta_{kj}\sigma_{t-j}^2. \tag{11.12}$$

In this case, rules' consequents are comprised by a GARCH(p,q) model, instead of a GJR-GARCH(p,q) process. Similarly to equation (11.9), the Fuzzy-GARCH model output is calculated by weighted averaging of individual rules' contributions:

$$y_t = \frac{\sum_{k=1}^{R} \exp\left(-\frac{1}{2}\left(\frac{y_{t-1}-c^k}{r^k}\right)^2\right)\left[\omega_k + \sum_{i=1}^{q}\alpha_{ki}y_{t-i}^2 + \sum_{j=1}^{p}\beta_{kj}\sigma_{t-j}^2\right]}{\sum_{k=1}^{R} \exp\left(-\frac{1}{2}\left(\frac{y_{t-1}-c^k}{r^k}\right)^2\right)}. \tag{11.13}$$

Hung (2011a) applied a PSO algorithm to estimate the parameter set $\mathbf{x} = (\omega_1, \ldots, \omega_R, \alpha_{11}, \ldots, \alpha_{Rq}, \beta_{11}, \ldots, \beta_{Rp})$ of the Fuzzy-GARCH model. Nevertheless, this work adopts the same methodology as in Hung (2011a), that is using PSO, and also optimized Fuzzy-GARCH parameters with the differential evolution algorithm considered. Moreover, the number of rules and their focal points in Fuzzy-GARCH were performed with subtractive clustering.

11.3 Fuzzy GJR-GARCH parameters estimation with DE

The Fuzzy GJR-GARCH model estimation problem in equation (11.10) is summarized as follows:

$$\min_{\mathbf{x}\in\Theta} E(\mathbf{x}) \tag{11.14}$$

where Θ is the parameter space which defines viable solutions satisfying equation (11.5) by the coefficients $(\omega_1, \ldots, \omega_R, \alpha_{11}, \ldots, \alpha_{Rq}, \beta_{11}, \ldots, \beta_{Rp}, \gamma_{11}, \ldots, \gamma_{Rq})$. The fitness (objective) function is given as follows:

$$\min_{\mathbf{x}\in\Theta} \sum_{l=1}^{N} \left(y_{lt} - \sqrt{\sum_{k=1}^{R} \lambda^k(y_{t-1}) \left[\omega_k + \sum_{i=1}^{q}\alpha_{ki}y_{t-i}^2 + \sum_{j=1}^{p}\beta_{kj}\sigma_{t-j}^2 + \sum_{i=1}^{q}\gamma_{ki}S_{t-i}^{-}y_{t-i}^2\right] \xi_{lt}} \right)^2. \tag{11.15}$$

Alternatively, the objective function associated with the Fuzzy-GARCH model is expressed as:

$$\min_{\mathbf{x}\in\Theta'} \sum_{l=1}^{N} \left(y_{lt} - \sqrt{\sum_{k=1}^{R} \lambda^k(y_{t-1}) \left[\omega_k + \sum_{i=1}^{q}\alpha_{ki}y_{t-i}^2 + \sum_{j=1}^{p}\beta_{kj}\sigma_{t-j}^2\right] \xi_{lt}} \right)^2 \tag{11.16}$$

where Θ' is the parameter space of viable solutions satisfying equation (11.3) by the coefficients $(\omega_1, \ldots, \omega_R, \alpha_{11}, \ldots, \alpha_{Rq}, \beta_{11}, \ldots, \beta_{Rp})$.

The optimization problems in (11.15) and (11.16) were solved by using a differential evolution algorithm for the Fuzzy GJR-GARCH and Fuzzy-GARCH models, respectively. Additionally, the PSO algorithm proposed by

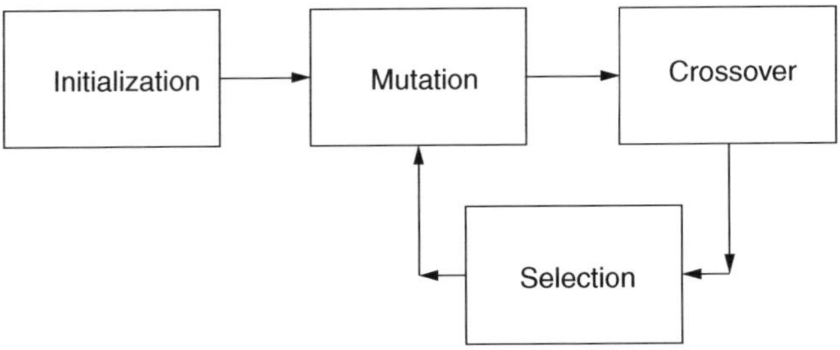

Figure 11.1 Main stages of the DE algorithm

Hung (2011a) was considered to optimize the Fuzzy-GARCH approach as in its original version.

Differential evolution is a vector population-based stochastic method for global optimization, introduced by Storn and Price (1997). The main idea behind the DE algorithm consists in a generation scheme of experimental parameters vectors that will disturb the population vector in order to evolve and find a desirable end. The main stages which comprise the DE algorithm are: initialization, mutation, crossover and selection. DE works through a simple cycle of these stages, illustrated in Figure 11.1. Each stage is described as follows for the case of Fuzzy GARCH-type parameters optimization. Finally, the PSO algorithm (Hung, 2011a) is also reported.

11.3.1 Initialization

Consider an optimization problem in a D-dimensional real parameter space $\Re^D$. The population Φ is comprised by $NP \times D$ dimensional real-valued parameter vectors, described as:

$$\Phi_{\mathbf{x},G} = \left[\mathbf{x}_{1,G}, \mathbf{x}_{2,G}, \ldots, \mathbf{x}_{NP,G}\right]^T, \quad G = 0, 1, \ldots, G_{max} \tag{11.17}$$

$$\mathbf{x}_{i,G} = \left[x_{1,i,G}, x_{2,i,G}, \ldots, x_{D,i,G}\right], \quad i = 1, 2, \ldots, NP \tag{11.18}$$

where $G = 0, 1, \ldots, G_{max}$ denotes the generation counter and NP the number of population vectors.

According to Storn and Price (1997), based on several benchmark optimization problems, a reasonable choice for NP is between $5 \cdot D$ and $10 \cdot D$, but NP must be at least 4 to ensure that DE will have enough mutually different vectors with which to work. Moreover, the literature has shown that DE control parameters setting is a specific empirical procedure (Das and Suganthan, 2011). In order to avoid non-convergence (low population size) and higher computational time complexity (high population size), $NP = 10 \cdot D$ was considered in this work.

Each population vector, also know as a *chromosome*, forms a candidate solution to the problem. In the case of the Fuzzy GJR-GARCH model estimation problem the real parameter space has dimension $D = (R + R \times q + R \times$

$p+R\times q)=R(1+2q+p)$. Otherwise, when the Fuzzy-GARCH model is taken into account, $D=(R+R\times q+R\times p)=R(1+q+p)$. The initial population (at $G=0$), as in the classical DE algorithm, is set as:

$$x_{i,j,1}=\varepsilon_{i,j},\ \ j=1,2,\ldots,D,\ \ i=1,2,\ldots,NP \tag{11.19}$$

where $\varepsilon_{i,j}$ is an uniformly distributed random number lying between 0 and 1 and is instantiated independently for each component of the ith vector.

Das and Suganthan (2011) pointed out that evolutionary computation algorithms such as DE have the advantage of not depending on the choice of initial values, since any point in the parameter space has a not null probability of being chosen. Moreover, the population is comprised only by viable solutions, that is satisfying equations (11.3) and (11.5) for the Fuzzy-GARCH and Fuzzy GJR-GARCH models, respectively.

11.3.2 Mutation

The mutation is a perturbation in the gene characteristic of a chromosome with a random element. In DE algorithms, a parent vector from the current generation is called a *target* vector, a mutant vector obtained through the differential mutation operation is the *donor* vector, and an offspring formed by recombining the donor with the target vector is known as *trial* vector.

In the classical DE-mutation operator, three distinct parameter vectors $\mathbf{x}_{r_1^i}$, $\mathbf{x}_{r_2^i}$ and $\mathbf{x}_{r_3^i}$ are sampled randomly from the current population, in order to create the donor vector for each ith target vector. The indices r_1^i, r_2^i and r_3^i, different from the base vector index i, are mutually exclusive integers randomly chosen from the range $[1,NP]$. The mutation operator can be described as:

$$\mathbf{v}_{i,G}=\mathbf{x}_{r_1^i,G}+F\cdot\left(\mathbf{x}_{r_2^i,G}-\mathbf{x}_{r_3^i,G}\right) \tag{11.20}$$

where $\mathbf{v}_{i,G}$ is the donor vector and F is the mutation scale factor, a scalar number usually in the interval $[0.4,1]$.

The mutation process is shown in Figure 11.2 on a two-dimensional parameter space, including constant cost contours of an arbitrary objective function.

In this case, the mutation uses a randomly selected vector $\mathbf{x}_{r_1^i}$ and only one weighted difference vector $F\cdot\left(\mathbf{x}_{r_2^i}-\mathbf{x}_{r_3^i}\right)$ to perturb it. However, there are several variants of mutation operator which are different to expression (11.20). The perturbations, for example, which set the base vector to the current best vector or a linear combination of various vectors are widely applied. In this work, the classical mutation operator described was considered, since it performs very well for a wide range of problems, and as stated by Price and Rönkkönen (2006), mutation operators' variants need further investigation to determine under which circumstances they perform well.

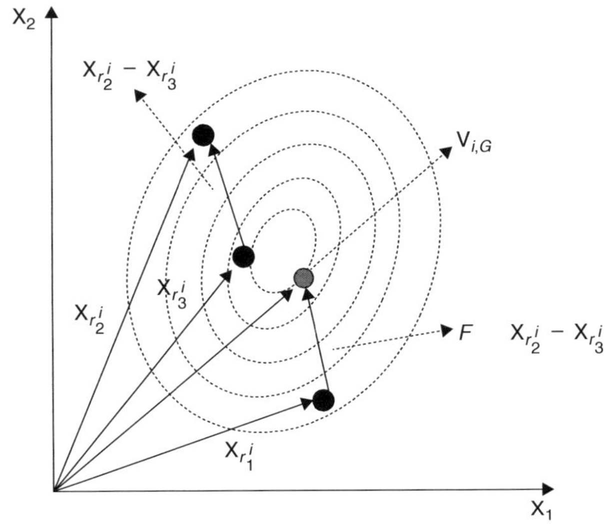

Figure 11.2 DE mutation scheme in two-dimensional parametric space

11.3.3 Crossover

After generating the donor vector through mutation, the next step in the DE algorithm is to apply the crossover operator. This stage provides the potential diversity enhancement of the population, which exchanges parameters of the mutation vector $\mathbf{v}_{i,G}$ and the target vector $\mathbf{x}_{i,G}$ to generate the so-called trial vector $\mathbf{u}_{i,G} = \left[u_{1,i,G}, u_{2,i,G}, \ldots, u_{D,i,G}\right]$. In this work, it the most common form of crossover operation, uniform (or binomial), was considered, defined as:

$$u_{j,i,G} = \begin{cases} v_{j,i,G} & \text{if } \left(\varepsilon_{i,j} \leq Cr \text{ or } j = j_{rand}\right) \\ x_{j,i,G} & \text{otherwise,} \qquad\qquad \forall\, j = 1, 2, \ldots, D \end{cases} \tag{11.21}$$

where $\varepsilon_{i,j}$ is a uniformly distributed random number lying between 0 and 1, which is called new for each jth component of the ith parameter vector, $j_{rand} \in [1, 2, \ldots, D]$ is an index chosen randomly, which guarantees that $\mathbf{u}_{i,G}$ gets at least one component from $\mathbf{v}_{i,G}$, and finally, Cr is called the *crossover rate*, a control parameter of the DE crossover operator, which lies in the interval $[0, 1]$ and defines the number of parameters expected to change in a population member.

Figure 11.3 illustrates an example of a crossover process in differential evolution, where it is clear that the population diversity is enhanced by exchanging some components of the target ($\mathbf{x}$) and donor ($\mathbf{v}$) vectors.

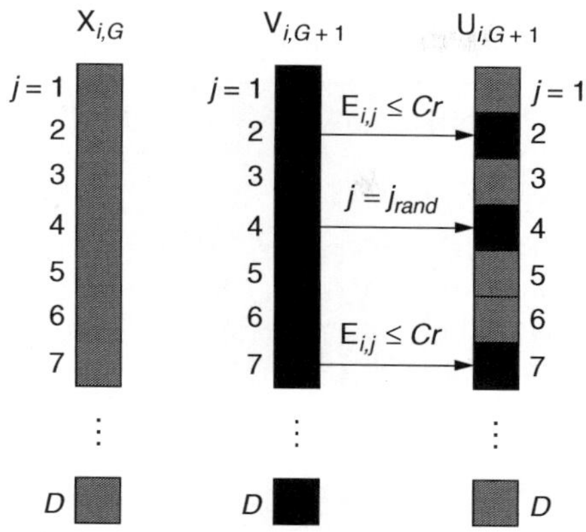

Figure 11.3 DE uniform crossover scheme example

11.3.4 Selection

Finally, the *selection* step determines whether the target or the trial vector survives to the next generation $G = G + 1$, as the following condition:

$$\mathbf{x}_{i,G+1} = \begin{cases} \mathbf{u}_{i,G} & \text{if } E(\mathbf{u}_{i,G}) \leq E(\mathbf{x}_{i,G}) \\ \mathbf{x}_{i,G} & \text{if } E(\mathbf{u}_{i,G}) > E(\mathbf{x}_{i,G}) \end{cases} \tag{11.22}$$

where $E(\mathbf{x})$ is the fitness function to be minimized.

The population size over generations is kept constant. Therefore, the new trial vector replaces the corresponding target vector in the next generation if it provides an equal or lower value of the objective (fitness) function.[5] Otherwise, the target vector is retained in the population. It must be noted that this selection criteria never deteriorates the fitness status, since the population either gets better or remains the same, in terms of objective function value. Nevertheless, this criteria enables DE-vectors to move over flat fitness landscapes with generations (Das and Suganthan, 2011).

11.3.5 Algorithm

Now that the classical DE algorithm steps, that is initialization, mutation, crossover and selection, have been described, the whole algorithm for the Fuzzy GJR-GARCH parameters identification is presented below in pseudo-code.

Algorithm. DE algorithm for the Fuzzy GJR-GARCH identification

Initialize randomly a initial population $\Phi_0 \in [0,1]$
Initiate $G = 1$
while $G < G_{max}$ **do**
  for $i = 1$ to NP **do** for each individual sequentially
    Generate a donor vector $\mathbf{v}_{i,G}$
    Generate a trial vector $\mathbf{u}_{i,G}$
    if $E(\mathbf{u}_{i,G}) \leq E(\mathbf{x}_{i,G})$ **then**
      $\mathbf{x}_{i,G+1} = \mathbf{u}_{i,G}$
    else
      $\mathbf{x}_{i,G+1} = \mathbf{x}_{i,G}$
    end if
  end for
  G=G+1
end while

In the algorithm suggested, the termination criteria is the number of iterations or generations, G_{max}. However, it can be defined as a termination condition when the best fitness of the population does not change according to a threshold over successive generations, or alternatively, when some pre-specified objective function value was reached. The control parameters are: F, Cr and G_{max}.

11.3.6 The Fuzzy-GARCH PSO-based algorithm

In order to optimize the Fuzzy-GARCH model proposed by Hung (2011a), this work considered the PSO-based algorithm, as reported in its original formulation by the author, and also the differential evolution methodology suggested, previously described. This subsection presents the PSO algorithm.

Particle swarm optimization is a population-based stochastic algorithm that attempts to generate better solutions to find a desirable end (Hung, 2011a). Each swarm consists of many particles, which represents a possible solution to an optimization problem. Each particle is characterized by its position and velocity. In PSO, particles evolve in the search space in three ways: (i) by moving in the previous direction; (ii) by moving toward the optimum (present location); or (iii) by moving toward the best solution for the entire swarm (population). Over iterations an improvement in the performance is achieved.

The first step is to randomly generate a swarm of S particles in the form of possible solution vectors for the Fuzzy-GARCH model. The position and velocity of the ith particle at the kth iteration are represented as $\mathbf{p}_i^k = (p_{i,1}^k, p_{i,2}^k, \ldots, p_{i,R(1+p+q)}^k)$ and $\mathbf{v}_i^k = (v_{i,1}^k, v_{i,2}^k, \ldots, v_{i,R(1+p+q)}^k)$, respectively. Thus, the second step updates the position and velocity of each particle according to:

$$v_{i,j}^{k+1} = \chi \cdot v_{i,j}^{k} + \mu_1 \cdot \varepsilon_1 \cdot (l_{i,j} - p_{i,j}^{k}) + \mu_2 \cdot \varepsilon_2 \cdot (g_j - p_{i,j}^{k}) \tag{11.23}$$

$$p_{i,j}^{k+1} = p_{i,j}^{k} + v_{i,j}^{k+1} \tag{11.24}$$

where χ is the linearly decreasing inertia weight, μ_1 and μ_2 are acceleration coefficients, ε_1 and ε_2 are uniformly distributed random variables lying between 0 and 1, $l_{i,j}$ is the value of the objective function along the jth dimension for the best position for the ith particle, and g_j is the value of the fitness function along the hth dimension for the global best position found by all particles in the swarm (Hung, 2011a).

Parameters μ_1, μ_2 and χ are related as follows (Clerc and Kennedy, 2002):

$$\chi = \frac{2}{|2 - (\mu_1 + \mu_2) - \sqrt{(\mu_1 + \mu_2)^2 - 4(\mu_1 + \mu_2)}|}. \tag{11.25}$$

In the third step, the fitness function value $E(\mathbf{x})$ of each particle, updated with equations (11.23) and (11.24), is calculated. If the objective function value for the new particle is higher than that of the local optimum ($l_{i,j}$) in its present location, then the local optimum is replaced by the new particle (Hung, 2011a). Moreover, if the previous condition holds and the fitness value for the new particle is higher than that of all the particles in the swarm, then this population's optimum value is also replaced by the new particle. This process repeats until the maximum number of iterations (G) is achieved, as the termination criteria.[6] The PSO control parameters are: μ_1, μ_2, χ, S and G. Nevertheless, the number of rules and their focal points were set using subtractive clustering algorithm.

11.4 Empirical results and analysis

To illustrate the performance of the proposed Fuzzy GJR-GARCH model for modeling and forecasting stock market volatility, this work focuses on daily prices of S&P 500 (US) and Ibovespa (Brazil) over the period from 3 January 2000 through 30 September 2011, in comparison with GARCH and GJR-GARCH models, and with the Fuzzy-GARCH model proposed by Hung (2011a). Moreover, the Fuzzy-GARCH approach was optimized using PSO as in its original version and using the DE algorithm suggested in this chapter. The daily stock return series were generated by taking the natural logarithm difference of the daily stock index and the previous day's stock index and multiplying by 100, as described previously. The data sample was partitioned into two parts. The in-sample period consists of data from 3 January 2000 through 29 December 2005, and the forecast out-of-sample period is from 2 January 2006 through 30 September 2011.

Table 11.1 shows the basic statistical characteristics of the return series. The average daily returns are negative for S&P 500 and positive for Ibovespa. The daily returns display evidence of skewness and kurtosis.

The returns series are skewed towards the left, characterized by a distribution with tails that are significantly thicker than for a normal distribution. J-B test statistics further confirm that the daily returns are non-normal distributed. As compared with Gaussian distribution, the kurtosis in S&P 500 and Ibovespa suggest that their daily returns have fat-tails (Table 11.1). Ibovespa index has a higher kurtosis than S&P 500, which explains the fact that emerging countries show in general a more leptokurtic behavior. Under the null hypothesis of no serial correlation in the squared returns, the Ljung-Box $Q^2(10)$ statistics infer a linear dependence for both series considered. Furthermore, the Engle's ARCH test for the squared returns reveals strong ARCH effects, which provides evidence in support of GARCH effects (that is, heteroskedasticity). Accordingly, these preliminary analyses of the data encourage the adoption of a sophisticated model, which embodies fat-tailed features, and of conditional models to allow for time-varying volatility.

Despite GARCH-type models being able to capture fat-tails and conditional volatility, they do not consider volatility clustering, as characterized by Fama (1965). The stock indexes are shown in Figure 11.4, and the correspondent returns are given in Figure 11.5. Particularly, in Figure 11.5 the context of volatility clustering became more clear.

Table 11.1 Descriptive statistics of daily returns of S&P 500 and Ibovespa

	S&P 500	Ibovespa
Mean	−0.0073	0.0378
Max	10.9572	13.6766
Min	−9.4695	−12.0961
Std. Dev.	1.3787	1.9493
Skewness	−0.1580	−0.1066
Excess Kurtosis	3.6701	7.4814
J-B[a]	234.9483*	277.1270*
$Q^2(10)$[b]	789.7362*	683.9531*
ARCH Test (10)[c]	1109.1934*	1082.7409*

Notes: [a] is the statistics of Jarque-Bera normal distribution test.
[b] is the Ljung-Box Q test for the 10th order serial correlation of the squared returns.
[c] Engle's ARCH test also examines for autocorrelation of the squared returns.
* Significant at 5 percent.

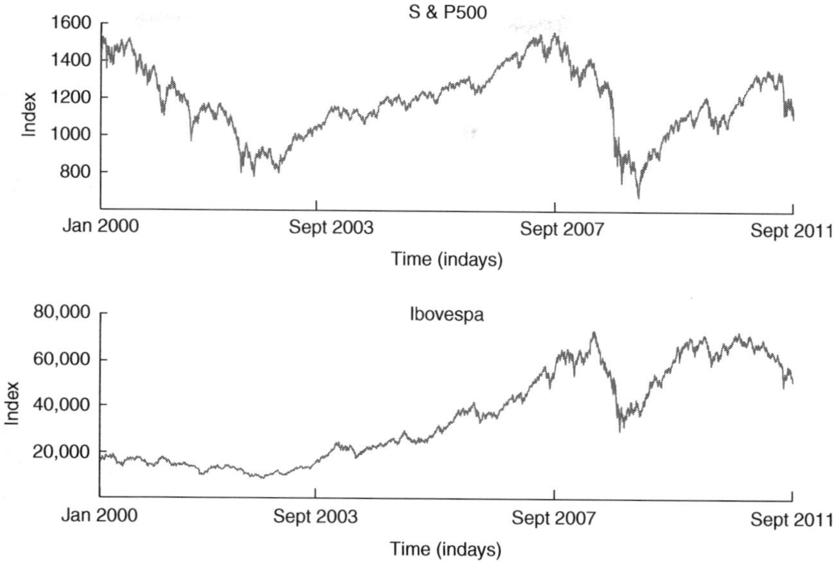

Figure 11.4 Daily closing stock price indexes for S&P 500 and Ibovespa

In order to select the best lag parameters for the Fuzzy GJR-GARCH and Fuzzy-GARCH models, and GARCH-type specifications, also considered in this work, the Bayesian information criterion (BIC) and Akaike's information criterion (AIC) were performed (Akaike, 1974; Schwarz, 1978). The models with various combinations of (p,q) parameters ranging from $(1,1)$ to $(15,15)$ were calibrated on return data. According to BIC and AIC criteria the best specification for all GARCH-type models was $(1,1)$, that is $p=1$ and $q=1$. The next step is to select the appropriate number of fuzzy rules for each data series, therefore, the subtractive clustering algorithm was applied. Figure 11.6 reports the membership functions for S&P 500 and Ibovespa indexes, which illustrates that these financial markets are asymmetric. In both economies evaluated, the clustering algorithm found three rules, that could be interpreted as *negative*, *medium* and *positive* returns.

Computational experiments were conducted to chose appropriate control parameters for the Fuzzy GARCH-type models, according to different values for these parameters and compared in terms of accuracy for a fixed number of generations. Simulations are comprised of 100 runs. Figures 11.7 and 11.8 display the boxplot analysis of the control parameters for S&P 500 and Ibovespa indexes, respectively, using the Fuzzy GJR-GARCH model. This approach is a convenient way of graphically depicting groups of numerical data through their five summaries: the sample minimum, sample maximum,

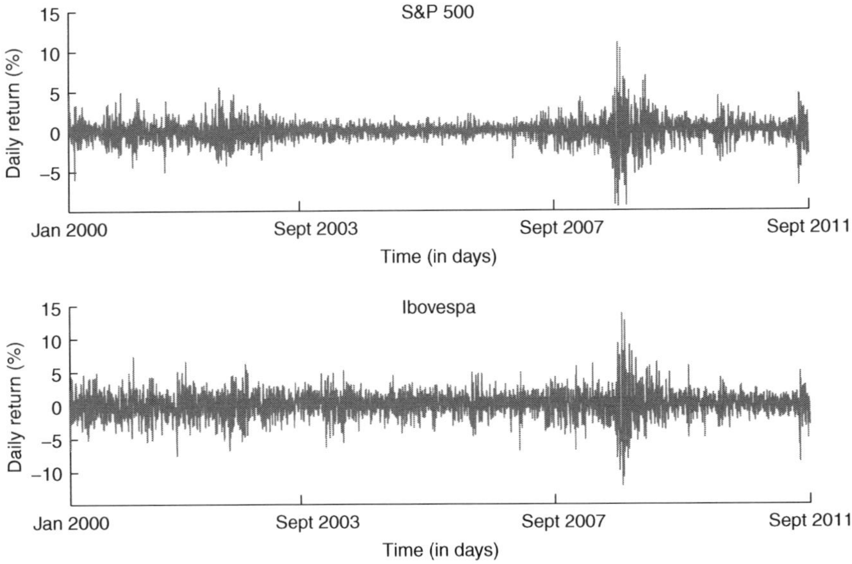

Figure 11.5 S&P 500 and Ibovespa daily returns

median, upper quartile, and largest observation. A boxplot may also indicate which observations, if any, might be considered outliers. The spacings between the different parts of the box help indicate the degree of dispersion (spread) and skewness in the data. Therefore, control parameters identified by a low mean, in terms of objective function value, and low dispersion are chosen as the ones which provide better results to the problem of volatility forecasting.

Considering the mutation scale factor (F), shown in Figure 11.7, one must note that more stable results, in terms of lower median and spread, are attained on the intervals [0.8,0.9] and [0.8,0.95] for S&P 500 and Ibovespa, respectively. Otherwise, higher spread and fitness value are observed, with high probability of providing suboptimal objective function values. On the other hand, the boxplot dispersions for the crossover rate (Cr) are more stable for both economies evaluated (Figure 11.8). A range of parameters which performs better accuracy for S&P 500 lies in the interval [0.86,0.89], whereas for Ibovespa it corresponds to the interval [0.89,0.96].

Moreover, the Fuzzy-GARCH control parameters setting adopts the same procedure, that is, by the boxplot analysis with 100 runs for both DE and PSO-based optimization techniques. Table 11.2 indicates the control parameters associated with each model, stock index and optimization procedure.

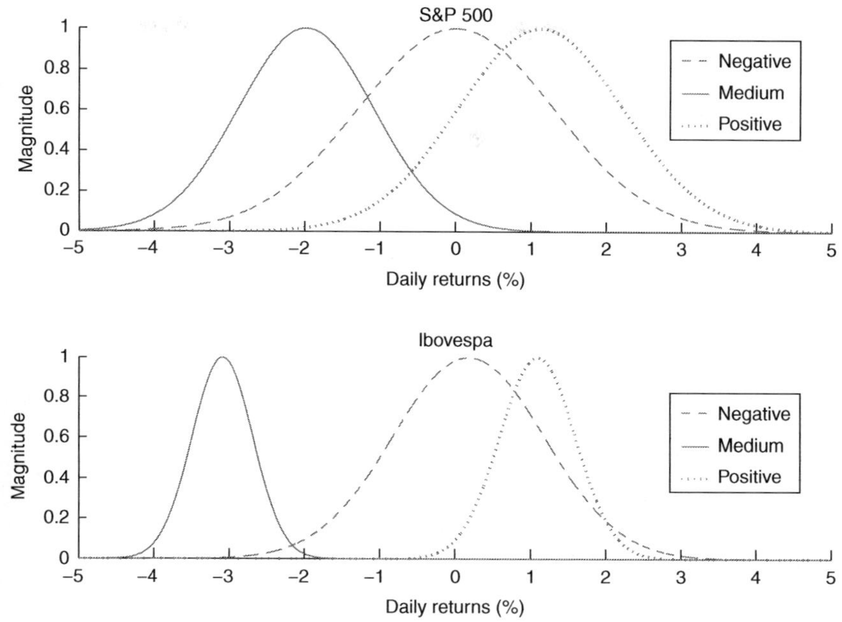

Figure 11.6 The membership functions for the S&P 500 and Ibovespa indexes

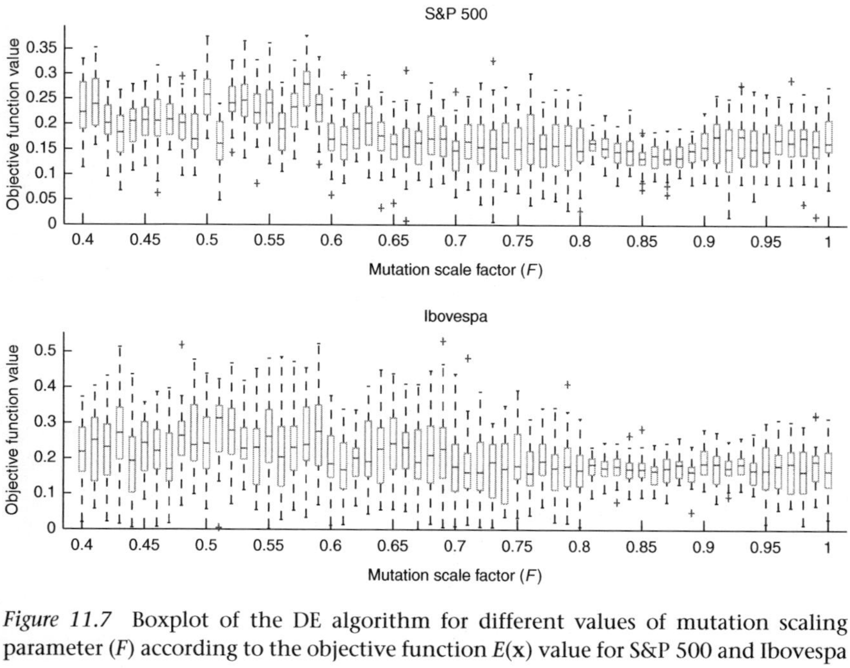

Figure 11.7 Boxplot of the DE algorithm for different values of mutation scaling parameter (F) according to the objective function $E(\mathbf{x})$ value for S&P 500 and Ibovespa

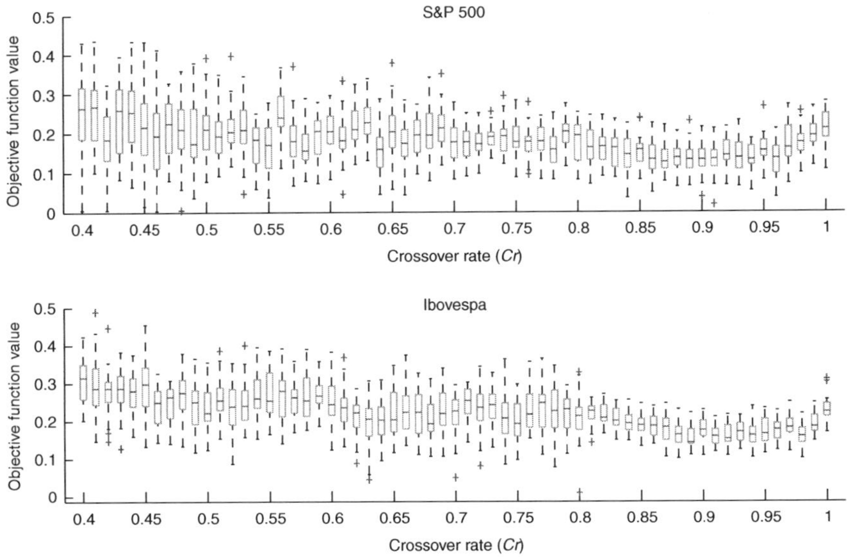

Figure 11.8 Boxplot of the DE algorithm for different values of crossover rate (*Cr*) according to the objective function $E(\mathbf{x})$ value for S&P 500 and Ibovespa

Table 11.2 Fuzzy GARCH-family models control parameters

	Fuzzy-GARCH (PSO)		Fuzzy-GARCH (DE)		Fuzzy GJR-GARCH (DE)	
	S&P 500	Ibovespa	S&P 500	Ibovespa	S&P 500	Ibovespa
F	–	–	0.80	0.79	0.85	0.84
Cr	–	–	0.89	0.98	0.91	0.94
μ_1	2.06	2.04	–	–	–	–
μ_2	2.03	2.11	–	–	–	–
χ	0.74	0.68	–	–	–	–
S	45	50	–	–	–	–

Figure 11.9 shows the objective function value ($E(\mathbf{x})$) behavior over the number of generations for S&P 500 and Ibovespa indexes to estimate the Fuzzy GJR-GARCH coefficients using the differential evolution algorithm proposed, and also the Fuzzy-GARCH model using particle swarm optimization and differential evolution. The fitness functions of the DE-based estimation method are exponential and rapidly converge at successful results in 25 generations, mainly when the S&P 500 index is considered (Figure 11.9). Despite its simplicity, lower number of control parameters and no

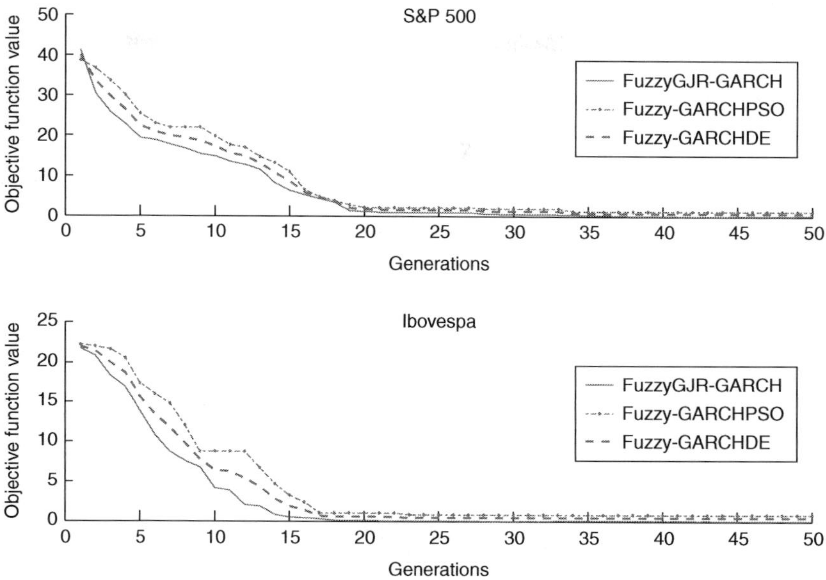

Figure 11.9 Objective function E(x) evaluated using DE algorithm for S&P 500 and Ibovespa

requirements about the parameter space stability, the DE also provides a fast convergence in a low number of iterations.[7] In terms of fit and convergence, the Fuzzy GJR-GARCH model provides better results in comparison with the Fuzzy-GARCH model optimized with PSO and DE algorithms. However, these differences became more clear when the adjustment, in terms of error measures, is considered.

The parameters estimates for in-sample data associated with the S&P 500 and Ibovespa indexes are shown in Table 11.3. Considering stable conditions, the parameters estimates all converge and, by taking the *t*-statistic into account, the proposed Fuzzy GJR-GARCH model effectively estimates the daily return data.[8] Moreover, it must be noted that US and Brazilian markets are asymmetric and exhibit the leverage effect as confirmed by the estimated coefficients.

Volatility forecasts comparison was conducted for one-step ahead horizon in terms of mean squared forecast error (MSFE), mean absolute forecast error (MAFE), and mean percentage forecast error (MPFE) defined as follows:

$$MSFE = \frac{1}{M}\sum_{i=1}^{M}\left(\sigma_i^2 - \hat{\sigma}_i^2\right)^2 \tag{11.26}$$

Table 11.3 Estimated parameters for the S&P 500 and Ibovespa stock indexes using the Fuzzy GJR-GARCH, Fuzzy-GARCH, optimized with PSO and DE, GARCH(1, 1) and GJR-GARCH(1, 1) models

		S&P 500	
Model	Parameter	Value	*t*-Statistic
Fuzzy GJR-GARCH	$(\omega_1,\alpha_{11},\beta_{11},\gamma_{11})$	(0.004, 0.030, 0.937, 0.033)	(1.483, 3.928, 44.827, 4.092)
	$(\omega_1,\alpha_{21},\beta_{21},\gamma_{21})$	(0.015, 0.028, 0.913, 0.029)	(2.546, 3.764, 41.039, 3.894)
	$(\omega_1,\alpha_{31},\beta_{31},\gamma_{31})$	(0.080, 0.055, 0.798, 0.036)	(2.306, 2.192, 16.443, 9.117)
Fuzzy-GARCH (PSO)	$(\omega_1,\alpha_{11},\beta_{11},\gamma_{11})$	(0.002, 0.027, 0.922, 0.028)	(1.446, 4.092, 42.112, 3.984)
	$(\omega_1,\alpha_{21},\beta_{21},\gamma_{21})$	(0.015, 0.028, 0.913, 0.029)	(2.462, 3.532, 39.110, 3.913)
	$(\omega_1,\alpha_{31},\beta_{31},\gamma_{31})$	(0.077, 0.061, 0.769, 0.033)	(2.376, 2.243, 17.283, 9.472)
Fuzzy-GARCH (DE)	$(\omega_1,\alpha_{11},\beta_{11},\gamma_{11})$	(0.004, 0.031, 0.940, 0.035)	(1.500, 3.872, 44.956, 4.192)
	$(\omega_1,\alpha_{21},\beta_{21},\gamma_{21})$	(0.011, 0.031, 0.942, 0.026)	(2.453, 3.664, 41.110, 3.980)
	$(\omega_1,\alpha_{31},\beta_{31},\gamma_{31})$	(0.076, 0.060, 0.803, 0.034)	(2.299, 2.219, 15.973, 9.215)
GARCH	(ω,α,β)	(0.059, 0.046, 0.865)	(6.532, 7.901, 40.103)
GJR-GARCH	$(\omega,\alpha,\beta,\gamma)$	(0.022, 0.079, 0.850, 0.084)	(5.973, 8.183, 32.225, 10.927)

Fuzzy GJR-GARCH	$(\omega_1, \alpha_{11}, \beta_{11}, \gamma_{11})$	(0.002, 0.025, 0.844, 0.028)	(1.309, 2.827, 34.857, 4.938)
	$(\omega_1, \alpha_{21}, \beta_{21}, \gamma_{21})$	(0.011, 0.021, 0.793, 0.034)	(3.029, 3.559, 36.294, 3.774)
	$(\omega_1, \alpha_{31}, \beta_{31}, \gamma_{31})$	(0.077, 0.049, 0.766, 0.033)	(1.993, 2.574, 19.903, 7.358)
Fuzzy-GARCH (PSO)	$(\omega_1, \alpha_{11}, \beta_{11}, \gamma_{11})$	(0.003, 0.029, 0.832, 0.021)	(1.422, 2.714, 32.991, 4.835)
	$(\omega_1, \alpha_{21}, \beta_{21}, \gamma_{21})$	(0.013, 0.020, 0.769, 0.033)	(3.201, 3.445, 35.100, 3.866)
	$(\omega_1, \alpha_{31}, \beta_{31}, \gamma_{31})$	(0.069, 0.047, 0.809, 0.030)	(2.082, 2.665, 21.022, 7.465)
Fuzzy-GARCH (DE)	$(\omega_1, \alpha_{11}, \beta_{11}, \gamma_{11})$	(0.005, 0.030, 0.904, 0.031)	(1.509, 2.911, 36.445, 5.029)
	$(\omega_1, \alpha_{21}, \beta_{21}, \gamma_{21})$	(0.010, 0.024, 0.765, 0.032)	(3.101, 3.448, 37.104, 3.833)
	$(\omega_1, \alpha_{31}, \beta_{31}, \gamma_{31})$	(0.080, 0.047, 0.813, 0.030)	(2.092, 2.633, 19.223, 7.431)
GARCH	(ω, α, β)	(0.036, 0.081, 0.794)	(4.726, 6.990, 36.772)
GJR-GARCH	$(\omega, \alpha, \beta, \gamma)$	(0.034, 0.056, 0.881, 0.031)	(3.778, 5.994, 29.736, 9.693)

Table 11.4 Models' performance to volatility forecasting for one-step Ahead

Index	Model	MSFE	MAFE	MPFE
S&P 500	Fuzzy GJR-GARCH	0.1983	0.3652	0.3795
	Fuzzy-GARCH (PSO)	0.2573	0.5001	0.4822
	Fuzzy-GARCH (DE)	0.2209	0.4653	0.4407
	GARCH	0.5704	0.7076	0.8366
	GJR-GARCH	0.5839	0.7298	0.8420
Ibovespa	Fuzzy GJR-GARCH	0.6099	0.7912	0.2852
	Fuzzy-GARCH (PSO)	0.9726	0.9019	0.4494
	Fuzzy-GARCH (DE)	0.8801	0.8603	0.3855
	GARCH	1.4487	1.2403	0.6723
	GJR-GARCH	1.4230	1.1955	0.6511

$$MAFE = \frac{1}{M}\sum_{i=1}^{M} |\sigma_i^2 - \hat{\sigma}_i^2| \tag{11.27}$$

$$MPFE = \frac{1}{M}\sum_{i=1}^{M} \frac{|\sigma_i^2 - \hat{\sigma}_i^2|}{\sigma_i^2} \tag{11.28}$$

where M is the number of out-of-sample observations, σ_i^2 is the actual volatility at forecasting period i, measured as the squared daily return, and $\hat{\sigma}_i^2$ is the forecast volatility at i.

Table 11.4 provides the performance of the evaluated models to predict the S&P 500 and Ibovespa stock indexes volatilities. The proposed Fuzzy GJR-GARCH model performs better than all remaining models since their structure provides a combination of rules for estimating forecast errors and also a mechanism to deal with leverage effects. The Fuzzy-GARCH model performs better than GARCH-family models, however, a better fit was attained when the model was optimized with the DE algorithm. The GJR-GARCH and GARCH models demonstrate similar results, but the GJR model presents slight lower errors than the GARCH model when the Ibovespa index is considered.

Although all performance measures of forecasting accuracy have been extensively employed in practice, they do not reveal whether the forecast of a model is statistically superior to another one. Therefore, it is imperative to use additional tests to help comparison among two or more competing models in terms of forecasting accuracy.

This work adopts the parametric Morgan-Granger-Newbold (MGN) test, proposed by Diebold and Mariano (1995). This test is often employed when the assumption of contemporaneous correlation of errors is relaxed. The statistic for this test can be computed using:

$$\text{MGN} = \frac{\hat{\rho}_{sd}}{\left(\frac{1-\hat{\rho}_{sd}^2}{M-1}\right)^{\frac{1}{2}}} \tag{11.29}$$

where $\hat{\rho}_{sd}$ is the estimated correlation coefficient between $s = e_1 + e_2$, and $d = e_1 - e_2$, with e_1 and e_2 the residuals of two models adjusted, for example Fuzzy GJR-GARCH model versus GARCH-type approaches. In this case, the statistic is distributed as Student distribution with $M - 1$ degrees of freedom, and M is the number of out-of-sample observations. For this test, if the estimates are equally accurate (null hypothesis), then the correlation between s and d will be zero.

The results from the MGN test, shown in Table 11.5, are in line with our results. MGN statistics reveal that the proposed Fuzzy GJR-GARCH model is a superior predictor for forecasting S&P 500 and Ibovespa indexes than traditional GARCH-type models and the Fuzzy-GARCH model, optimized both by PSO and DE algorithms. Considering the Fuzzy-GARCH model, one may infer that, for the different optimization algorithms, the results are competitive. Moreover, this model outperforms both GARCH-type specifications. The MGN test also suggests that GARCH and GJR-GARCH are equally accurate.

Finally, one must compare the volatility forecasting methodologies in terms of computational complexity. Table 11.6 reports the processing time for each algorithm to estimate its respective parameters. All algorithms were carried out using Matlab® on a laptop equipped with 4 GB and Intel®i3CPU.

According to Table 11.6, the GARCH and GJR-GARCH models are computationally more efficient than all the other models. However, the time required to estimate the Fuzzy GJR-GARCH model does not differ significantly from GARCH-type methods, which are also effective in dynamic environments. Comparing the optimizers, PSO and DE, for Fuzzy-GARCH estimation, it must be noted that DE provides a lower computational time than the PSO algorithm.

The proposed hybrid model exhibits high capability of forecasting volatility of the real market returns evaluated by considering both stock market asymmetry and volatility clustering; it also outperformed Fuzzy-GARCH, GARCH and GJR-GARCH methodologies in statistical terms. Moreover, a DE-based optimization algorithm improves the capability of the Fuzzy GJR-GARCH and Fuzzy-GARCH to obtain accurate parameters in a simple mechanism without restrictions about the parameter space and with a fast convergence.

Table 11.5 MGN statistics for volatility forecast for S&P 500 and Ibovespa

S&P 500				
	Fuzzy-GARCH (PSO)	Fuzzy-GARCH (DE)	GARCH	GJR-GARCH
Fuzzy GJR-GARCH	3.0928	2.7364	3.7645	3.6661
	(0.0020)	(0.0063)	(0.0001)	(0.0002)
Fuzzy-GARCH (PSO)	–	1.8040	2.9817	2.8911
	–	(0.0714)	(0.0029)	(0.0038)
Fuzzy-GARCH (DE)	–	–	2.7114	2.7991
	–	–	(0.0068)	(0.0052)
GARCH	–	–	–	0.3108
	–	–	–	(0.7559)

Ibovespa				
	Fuzzy-GARCH (PSO)	Fuzzy-GARCH (DE)	GARCH	GJR-GARCH
Fuzzy GJR-GARCH	2.8115	2.7365	3.3937	3.4928
	(0.0050)	(0.0063)	(0.0007)	(0.0004)
Fuzzy-GARCH (PSO)	–	1.7265	2.6998	2.5874
	–	(0.0845)	(0.0070)	(0.0098)
Fuzzy-GARCH (DE)	–	–	2.8009	2.7991
	–	–	(0.0052)	(0.0052)
GARCH	–	–	–	0.9530
	–	–	–	(0.3407)

Notes: The relevant *p*-values are shown beneath each test statistic in parentheses.

Table 11.6 Computational processing time (in seconds) for S&P 500/Ibovespa indexes

Models	Fuzzy GJR-GARCH	Fuzzy-GARCH (PSO)	Fuzzy GARCH (DE)	GARCH	GJR-GARCH
Time	23.11/22.87	28.55/27.62	22.35/21.19	12.87/11.82	14.17/13.09

11.5 Conclusion

Since the 1987 stock market crash, modeling and forecasting financial market volatility has received a great deal of attention from risk managers, regulators, academics and all markets participants in general. Volatility forecasting plays a central role in several financial applications such as asset allocation and hedging, option pricing and risk analysis. GARCH-family models are the approaches most commonly applied to model and forecast assets returns volatility, since they accommodate some volatility stylized facts such as persistence and time-varying volatility. However, despite the success of the GARCH model, it has been criticized for failing to capture asymmetric volatility. Therefore, a new class of asymmetric GARCH specifications, such as the GJR-GARCH model, for example, has recently been introduced in the literature. These models include the asymmetric responses of volatility to positive and negative shocks, but they do not simulate stock fluctuations with volatility clustering well.

Hence, this chapter proposed a new hybrid model named Fuzzy GJR-GARCH for stock market return volatility modeling and forecasting. The model combines both fuzzy inference systems and the conditional variance GJR-GARCH model to deal with time-varying volatility in the presence of leverage effects and also volatility clustering. The proposed model is based on a collection of fuzzy rules in the form of IF-THEN statements, in which its structure comprises a GJR-GARCH model. This chapter also suggested the use of a DE algorithm to estimate the parameters of the proposed methodology, since it comprises a high nonlinear and complex optimization problem. Computational experiments illustrating the effectiveness of the Fuzzy GJR-GARCH model were provided by modeling and forecasting the volatility of S&P 500 (United States) and Ibovespa (Brazil) indexes from 3 January 2000 through 30 September 2011, in comparison with some GARCH-family models and with a current Fuzzy-GARCH method proposed by Hung (2011a), optimized with PSO, as in its original version, and with the DE algorithm proposed.

The results revealed the potential of the Fuzzy GJR-GARCH approach to the problem of volatility forecasting, providing more accurate results than GARCH-type models and the Fuzzy-GARCH method, estimated with PSO and DE algorithms, in terms of fitness accuracy and statistical tests. Moreover, the DE-based algorithm converged with stable condition in a simple structure, with low computation complexity and few control parameters, not requiring stable conditions to the parameter space like traditional gradient search methods. Future research shall include applications of the Fuzzy GJR-GARCH approach in financial decision making problems related to volatility such as option pricing, portfolio selection and risk modeling (Value-at-Risk).

Acknowledgments

This work was supported by the Coordination for the Improvement of Higher Education Personnel (Capes). The author thanks the Brazilian Review of Finance for helpful comments that improved this work as in previous publication in vol. 10, no. 3, September 2012. The Editors are also gratefully acknowledged.

Notes

1. Several distinctive approaches have also been conducted for modeling and forecasting stock market volatility, including realized volatility models (Hansen and Lunde, 2006), intra-day volatility measure (Ceretta et al., 2011), and stochastic volatility (Fouque et al., 2000).
2. Methods based on particle swarm optimization (PSO) are also straightforward to implement, however, Das et al. (2009) and Rahnamayan et al. (2008) pointed out a largely better performance of DE against PSO in some varieties of problems.
3. Wang and Mendel (1992) stated that a fuzzy system with Gaussian membership function has been shown to be a universal approximation of any nonlinear function on a compact set.
4. For more details about the subtractive clustering algorithm see Chiu (1994).
5. Objective function value and fitness concepts are interchangeable, since a lower objective function value corresponds to higher fitness, for minimization problems.
6. For more details about the PSO-based Fuzzy-GARCH optimization algorithm see Hung (2011a).
7. The parameters of GARCH and GJR-GARCH models were estimated using the traditional maximum likelihood method, in which the log-likelihood function is computed from the product of all conditional densities of the prediction residuals.
8. A 95 percent confidence interval corresponds to a t-statistic greater than 2, which is a measure of the number of standard deviations where the estimate for the parameter is non-zero (Hung, 2011b).

References

Akaike, H. (1974). A new look at the statistical model identification. *IEEE Transactions on Automatic Control*, 19, 716–23.

Allen, P. G. and Morzuch, B. J. (2006). Twenty-five years of progress, problems, and conflicting evidence in econometric forecasting. What about the next 25 years? *International Journal of Forecasting*, 22, 475–92.

Bildirici, M. and Ersin, Ö. O. (2009). Improving forecasts of GARCH family models with the artificial neural networks: an application to the daily returns in Istanbul Stock Market Exchange. *Expert Systems with Applications*, 36, 7355–62.

Bollerslev, T. (1986). Generalized autoregressive conditional heteroscedasticity. *Journal of Econometrics*, 31, 307–27.

Brailsford, T. J. and Faff, R. W. (1996). An evaluation of volatility forecasting techniques. *Journal of Banking and Finance*, 20, 419–38.

Caretta, P. S., de Barba, F. G., Vieira, K. M. and Casarin, F. (2011). Previsï£¡o da volatilidade intradiï£¡ria: Anï£¡lise das distribuiï£¡ï£¡es alternativas. *Brazilian Review of Finance*, 9, 209–26.

Carvalho, M. C., Freire, M. A., Medeiros, M. C. and Souza, L. R. (2005). Modeling and forecasting the volatility of Brazilian asset returns: a realized variance approach. *Brazilian Review of Finance*, 4, 321–43.

Chang, J., Wei, L. and Cheng, C. (2011). A hybrid ANFIS model based on AR and volatility for TAIEX forecasting. *Applied Soft Computing*, 11, 1388–95.

Chiu, S. L. (1994). Fuzzy model identification based on cluster estimation. *Journal of Intelligent Fuzzy Systems*, 2, 267–78.

Clerc, M. and Kennedy, J. (2002). The particle swarm explosion, stability, and convergence in a multidimensional complex space. *IEEE Transactions on Evolutionary Computation*, 6, 58–73.

Coelho, L. S. and Santos, A. A. P. (2011). A RBF neural network model with GARCH errors: application to electricity price forecasting. *Electric Power Systems Research*, 81, 74–83.

Das, S., Abraham, A., Chakraborty, U. K. and Konar, A. (2009). Differential evolution using a neighborhood based mutation operator. *IEEE Transactions on Evolutionary Computation*, 13, 526–53

Das, S. and Suganthan, P. N. (2011). Differential evolution: a survey of the state-of-the-art. *IEEE Transactions on Evolutionary Computation*, 15, 4–31.

Diebold, F. X. and Mariano, R. S. (1995). Comparing predictive accuracy. *Journal of Business and Economic Statistics*, 13, 253–65.

Engle, R. F. (1982). Autoregressive conditional heteroscedasticity with estimates of the variance of United Kingdom inflation. *Econometrica*, 50, 987–1007.

Fama, E. F. (1965). The behavior of stock market price. *Journal of Business*, 38, 34–105.

Fouque, J., Papanicolaou, G. and Sircar, R. (2000). Mean reverting stochastic volatility. *International Journal of Theoretical and Applied Finance*, 3, 101–42.

Geng, L. and Ma, J. (2008). TSK fuzzy inference system based GARCH model for forecasting exchange rate volatility. *Annals of the Fifth International Conference on Fuzzy Systems and Knowledge Discovery*, 103–7, Shandong, China.

Glosten, L. R., Jagannathan, R. and Runkle, D. E. (1993). On the relation between the expected value and the volatility of the nominal excess return on stocks. *Journal of Finance*, 48, 1779–801.

Hajizadeh, E., Seifi, A., Fazel Zarandi, M. H. and Turksen, B. (2012). A hybrid modeling approach for forecasting the volatility of S&P 500 index return. *Expert Systems with Applications*, 39, 431–6.

Hamid, S. A. and Iqbal, Z. (2004). Using neural networks for forecasting volatility of S&P 500. *Journal of Business Research*, 57, 1116–25.

Han, H. and Park, J. Y. (2008). Time series properties of ARCH processes with persistent covariates. *Journal of Econometrics*, 146, 275–92.

Hansen, P. R. and Lunde, A. (2006). Realized variance and market microstructure noise (with discussion). *Journal of Business and Economic Statistics*, 24, 127–61.

Haofei, Z., Guoping, X., Fangting, Y. and Han, Y. (2007). A neural network model based on the multi-stage optimization approach for short-term food pricing forecasting in China. *Expert Systems with Applications*, 33, 347–56.

Haykin, S. (2001). *Adaptive Filter Theory*, 4th edn. Prentice Hall, Englewood Cliffs, New Jersey, 989.

Helin, T. and Koivisto, H. (2011). The GARCH-Fuzzy Density method for density forecasting. *Applied Soft Computing*, 11, 4212–25.

Hung, J. (2009a). A fuzzy asymmetric GARCH model applied to stock markets. *Information Sciences*, 179, 3930–43.

Hung, J. (2009b). A fuzzy GARCH model applied to stock market scenario using a genetic algorithm. *Expert Systems with Applications*, 36, 11710–17.

Hung, J. (2011a). Adaptive Fuzzy-GARCH model applied to forecasting the volatility of stock markets using particle swarm optimization. *Information Sciences*, 181, 4673–83.

Hung, J. (2011b). Applying a combined fuzzy systems and GARCH model to adaptively forecast stock market volatility. *Applied Soft Computing*, 11, 3938–45.

Ji, Y., Massanari, R. M., Ager, J., Yen, J., Miller, R. E. and Ying, H. (2007). A fuzzy logic-based computational recognition-primed decision model. *Information Sciences*, 177, 4338–53.

Kapetanios, G., Labhard, V. and Price, S. (2006). Forecasting using predictive likelihood model averaging. *Economic Letters*, 91, 373–9.

Lin, E. M. H., Chen,C. W. S. and Gerlach, R. (2012). Forecasting volatility with asymmetric smooth transition dynamic range models. *International Journal of Forecasting*, 28, 384–99.

Liu, H. and Hung, J. (2010). Forecasting S&P-100 stock index volatility: the role of volatility asymmetry and distributional assumption in GARCH models. *Expert Systems with Applications*, 37, 4928–34.

Luna, I. and Ballini, R. (2012). Adaptive fuzzy system to forecast financial time series volatility. *Journal of Intelligent & Fuzzy Systems*, 23, 27–38.

Lux, T. and Kaizoji, T. (2007). Forecasting volatility and volume in the Tokyo stock market: long memory, fractality and regime switching. *Journal of Economic Dynamics and Control*, 31, 1808–43.

Martens, M., van Dijk, D. and de Potter, M. (2009). Forecasting S&P 500 volatility: long memory, level shifts, leverage effects, day-of-the-week seasonality, and macroeconomic announcements. *International Journal of Forecasting*, 25, 282–303.

Morgan, J. P. (1996) *Risk Metrics: Technical Document*, 4th edn. Morgan Guaranty Trust Company, New York, 74.

Nelson, D. B. (1991). Conditional heteroscedasticity in asset returns: a new approach. *Econometrica*, 59, 347–70.

Ng, H. G. and McAleer, M. (2004). Recursive modeling of symmetric and asymmetric volatility in the presence of extreme observations. *International Journal of Forecasting*, 20, 115–29.

Popov, A. A. and Bykhanov, K. V. (2005). Modeling volatility of time series using fuzzy GARCH models. *Annals of the 9th Russian-Korean International Symposium on Science and Technology*, 687–92, Novosibirsk, Russia.

Price, K. V. and Rönkkönen, J. T. (2006). Comparing the uni-modal scaling performance of global and local selection in a mutation-only differential evolution algorithm. *Annals of the IEEE Congress of Evolutionary Computation*, 2034–41, Vancouver, Canada.

Racine, J. (2001). On the nonlinear predictability of stock returns using financial and economic variables. *Journal of Business and Economic Statistics*, 19, 380–2.

Rahnamayan, S., Tizhoosh, H. R. and Salama, M. A. (2008). Opposition-based differential evolution. *IEEE Transactions on Evolutionary Computation*, 12, 64–79.

Savran, S. (2007). An adaptive recurrent fuzzy system for nonlinear identification. *Applied Soft Computing*, 7, 593–600.

Schwarz, G. (1978). Estimating the dimension of model. *The Annuals of Statistics*, 6, 461–4.

Storn, R. and Price, K. V. (1997). Differential evolution – a simple and efficient heuristic for global optimization over continuous spaces. *Journal of Global Optimization*, 11, 341–59.

Taylor, J. W. (2004). Volatility forecasting with smooth transition exponential smoothing. *International Journal of Forecasting*, 20, 273–86.

Thavaneswaran, A., Appadoo, S. S. and Paseka, A. (2009). Weighted possibilistic moments of fuzzy numbers with applications to GARCH modeling and option pricing. *Mathematical and Computer Modeling*, 49, 352–68.

Tino, P., Schittenkopf, C. and Dorffner, G. (2001). Financial volatility trading using recurrent neural networks. *IEEE Transactions on Neural Networks*, 12, 865–74.

Tseng, C., Cheng, S., Wang, Y. and Peng, J. (2008). Artificial neural network model of the hybrid EGARCH volatility of the Taiwan stock index option prices. *Physica A: Statistical Mechanisms and Its Applications*, 387, 3192–200.

Tung, W. L. and Quek, C. (2011). Financial volatility trading using a self-organising neural-fuzzy semantic network and option straddle-based approach. *Expert Systems with Applications*, 38, 4668–88.

Wang, C., Lin, S., Huang, H. and Wu, P. (2012). Using neural network for forecasting TXO price under different volatility models. *Expert Systems with Applications*, 39, 5025–32.

Wang, L. and Mendel, J. M. (1992). Fuzzy basis functions, universal approximation, and orthogonal least-squares learning. *IEEE Transactions on Neural Networks*, 2, 807–14.

Wang, Y. (2009). Nonlinear neural network forecasting model for stock index option price: hybrid GJR-GARCH approach. *Expert Systems with Applications*, 36, 564–70.

Zadeh, L. (2005). Toward a generalized theory of uncertainty (GTU) – an outline. *Information Sciences*, 172, 1–40.

Zhang, J. and Sanderson, A. C. (2003). JADE: adaptive differential evolution with optional external archive. *IEEE Transactions on Evolutionary Computation*, 13, 945–58.

Part III
Portfolios

12
Robust Consumption and Portfolio Rules When Asset Returns Are Predictable

Abraham Lioui

12.1 Introduction

In his seminal contribution, Merton (1971) solved for the dynamic asset allocation of an expected utility maximizer in a continuous time setting and with an infinite horizon. He showed that when the agent derives utility from intermediate consumption, a closed form solution to the consumption/investment problem exists if the economy is affected by a state variable following a mean reverting process and perfectly positively correlated with the traded risky asset. Wachter (2002) showed that a closed form solution exists under finite horizon when the markets are still complete, that is when there is a perfect negative correlation between the traded risky asset and the state variable. In incomplete markets, a closed form solution is known to exist only when the agent derives utility solely from terminal wealth. Kim and Omberg (1996) consider a setting where a state variable following a mean reverting process is imperfectly correlated to the traded risky asset while the agent has utility only from terminal wealth. In this setting, they showed that a closed form solution exists. Recently, Liu (2007) extended the previous findings to the case where asset returns are quadratic in mean reverting state variables. He obtained explicit solutions in complete markets with intermediate consumption and in incomplete markets with only terminal wealth.

Thus, whether an explicit solution to the consumption/investment problem exists in incomplete markets is still an open issue. However, there are several techniques which provide an approximate solution to this problem. Amongst these techniques, the most popular one is that introduced by Campbell and Viceira (1999) which consists in log linearizing the agent budget constraint. The portfolio strategy is then shown to be linear in the state variable and the consumption to wealth ratio quadratic in the state variable. Recently, Brandt and Santa Clara (2006) simply suggested assuming that the conditional portfolio strategy is linear in the state variables.

In the absence of a closed form solution, it is hard to assess the relevance of the approximate solutions provided by these techniques. For example, in complete markets, we do have an explicit solution where the optimal portfolio choice is highly non linear in the state variables with intermediate consumption. However, as clearly exposed by Wachter (2002), when the state variable is around its long run mean, the risky asset demand is nearly linear. Having a similar finding for the incomplete markets case may provide a sound theoretical foundation for these approximations.

Our aim in this chapter is to provide for the first time a closed form solution to a consumption/investment problem in incomplete markets. Our setting is the by now standard one of an agent trading a riskless asset and a risky asset. The market price of risk (the state variable) follows a mean reverting process imperfectly correlated with the risky asset. In addition to being risk averse, our agent has some preference for robustness. Namely, the agent faces some model uncertainty, and therefore takes this into account in his optimization problem. Uppal and Wang (2003) and Maenhout (2004), building on the seminal contribution of Anderson et al. (2003) in continuous time, addressed the impact of preference for robustness on portfolio choice. They introduced a particular penalty function that preserved the homotheticity, relative to wealth, of the economic agent decisions and which revealed itself to be very useful to understanding the impact of homothetic preference for robustness on dynamic asset allocation. Maenhout (2004) considered the case of a constant opportunity set with identical parameter of preference for robustness for all the sources of risk in the economy and showed that the portfolio strategy of a risk averse agent with homothetic preference for robustness is equivalent to the portfolio strategy of an expected utility maximizer with increased effective risk aversion. In Maenhout (2006), the results have been extended to account for predictability. However, his framework allows markets to be incomplete so that only the terminal wealth case is solved in closed form. Uppal and Wang (2003) allowed for differential degrees of preference for robustness and provided an explicit solution when asset returns follow geometric Brownian motions. They showed that accounting for model misspecification could explain under-diversification. In a related paper, Cao et al. (2005) show that model uncertainty could explain the limited market participation so widely documented in the literature. Liu et al. (2005) introduce jumps into the Uppal and Wang (2003) and Maenhout (2004) setting and derive market equilibrium. Uncertainty aversion towards rare events was useful in explaining the empirical smirk encountered in option markets. Finally, Leippold et al. (2008) analyzed the implications of learning for the equilibrium in a financial market where agents have preference for robustness.

This chapter is the first work to consider the consumption/investment problem under preference for robustness. It is a direct extension of Maenhout (2006) who considers only utility from terminal wealth. Surprisingly, in this case and under a suitable parametrization of the penalty function, we are able to obtain an explicit solution to the consumption/investment problem in *incomplete* markets. We try hereafter to provide an intuition for this finding.

Consider a standard financial market where a riskless asset with constant interest rate and a risky asset with constant volatility are traded. The market price of risk (the state variable) follows a mean reverting process which is imperfectly correlated with the risky asset. The agent has a finite horizon and derives utility from intermediate consumption. When the agent is only risk averse, the value function of the agent is known to solve a PDE (Partial Differential Equation), which is usually highly non linear. However, the non linearity term cancels out when the correlation is perfect between the risky asset and the state variable. This is also the case when the agent has some preference for robustness. When the correlation is imperfect, the non linear term is multiplied by a complicated function made of the correlation coefficient, the parameter of risk aversion and the parameter of preference for robustness. We can thus find the value of the parameter of robustness such that this function cancels out, maintaining a correlation different from 1 or −1. Therefore, preference for robustness introduces an additional degree of freedom in making the solution to the PDE linear, thus allowing for a closed form solution.

Hence we obtain a closed form solution which resembles the closed form solution in complete markets and finite horizon obtained by Wachter (2002). The demand for the risky asset is highly non linear in the state variable; this is also the case for the consumption to wealth ratio, which is not quadratic in the state variable. Qualitatively, these findings question the linearity generally delivered by the approximating solutions suggested so far in the literature.

We then calibrate the model to assess the quantitative impact of these non linearities on the optimal demand for the risky asset. For a wide range of values of the state variable, it is very hard to distinguish the outcome of our closed form solution from a solution that would simply assume that the demand for the risky asset is linear. As a consequence, this chapter provides a sound support to these approximating solutions, at least for the quantitative analysis of the consumption/investment problem in incomplete markets.

Our calibration also contributes to the ongoing debate on the existence of asset return predictability and its implications for asset allocation. Model uncertainty was well known to be costly for the investor. For example, DeMiguel et al. (2009) found that, when accounting properly for estimation error, the simple '1/N' strategy is far from being inefficient relative to a battery of more or less sophisticated strategies, accounting in particular for the intertemporal nature of asset allocation. Nevertheless, Avramov (2002, 2004) and Wachter and Warusawitharana (2009) claim that even under model uncertainty, a long term investor should still follow dynamic asset allocation. These papers account for model misspecification using Bayesian analysis. Preference for robustness is a complementary way to account for unknown priors. Our calibrations show that intertemporal hedging demand represents up to 50 percent of total demand and therefore up to 100 percent of the myopic demand, and this weight is highly affected by preference for robustness.

The remainder of the chapter proceeds as follows. In the next section, we derive a general result related to the possibility of obtaining a closed form solution under incomplete markets and preference for robustness. We then apply these results in the setting à la Kim and Omberg (1996) and calibrate them using US data. The last section contains some concluding remarks. A technical point related to the solution of the main PDE in the text is dealt with in the Appendix.

12.2 A general result

In this section we derive the implications of homothetic preference for robustness for the existence of a closed form solution in a general setting where the agent derives utility from intermediate consumption.

Consider a standard economy where agents can trade a riskless asset, that is a money market account, and a risky asset. The dynamics of the asset prices are written as:

$$\frac{dB_t}{B_t} = r(X_t)\,dt \tag{12.1}$$

$$\frac{dS_t}{S_t} = \mu_S(X_t)\,dt + \sigma_S(X_t)\,dZ_t^S \tag{12.2}$$

where B stands for the riskless asset's price and S stands for the risky asset's price; Z_t^S is a standard Brownian motion under the reference model (probability) *P*; r is the short term interest rate; μ_S is the drift while σ_S is the diffusion coefficient (volatility) of the risky asset's price dynamics. In addition, $r(X_t)$, $\mu_S(X_t)$ and $\sigma_S(X_t)$ are assumed to be well-behaved functions of a state variable which follows a diffusion process:

$$dX_t = \mu_X(X_t)\,dt + \sigma_X(X_t)\left[\rho dZ_t^S + \sqrt{1-\rho^2}dZ_t^X\right] \tag{12.3}$$

where ρ stands for the correlation between the risky asset price dynamics and the state variable price dynamics; $\rho = -1$ is the case considered by Wachter (2002) while Merton (1971) considered the case $\rho = 1$. Kim and Omberg (1996), for example, consider the case $-1 \le \rho \le 1$.

Since all the processes in what follows depend upon this state variable, we will use the short-hand notation $r_t \equiv r(X_t)$, $\mu_{S_t} \equiv \mu_S(X_t)$, $\sigma_{S_t} \equiv \sigma_S(X_t)$, $\mu_{X_t} \equiv \mu_X(X_t)$ and $\sigma_{X_t} \equiv \sigma_X(X_t)$.

Together with the reference model P, the agent also considers in her decision-making process models that are related to this reference model in the following manner:

$$\left.\frac{d\hat{P}}{dP}\right|_t = \hat{\eta}_t \tag{12.4}$$

where

$$\hat{\eta}_t = \exp\left\{\int_0^t \kappa_s' dZ_s - \frac{1}{2}\int_0^t \left(\kappa_s'\kappa_s\right) ds\right\} \tag{12.5}$$

and $\hat{\eta}$ is the Radon–Nykodim derivative of the alternative model $\hat{P}$ relative to the reference model P; κ_s is a 2×1 dimensional vector to be found endogenously as part of the investor optimization problem as explained below.

Under the alternative model, the dynamics (1) and (2) become:

$$\frac{dS_t}{S_t} = \left[\mu_{S_t} + \Sigma_{S_t}'\kappa_t\right] dt + \Sigma_{S_t}' d\hat{Z}_t \tag{12.6}$$

$$dX_t = \left[\mu_{X_t} + \Sigma_{X_t}'\kappa_t\right] dt + \Sigma_{X_t}' d\hat{Z}_t \tag{12.7}$$

where $\Sigma_{S_t} = \begin{bmatrix} \sigma_{S_t} \\ 0 \end{bmatrix}$, $\Sigma_{X_t} = \sigma_{X_t}\begin{bmatrix} \rho \\ \sqrt{1-\rho^2} \end{bmatrix}$ and $\hat{Z}_t = \begin{bmatrix} \hat{Z}_t^S \\ \hat{Z}_t^X \end{bmatrix}$ is a standard two dimensional Brownian motion under the alternative model $\hat{P}$ (Girsanov Theorem).

Agents can trade these assets continuously, in a frictionless financial market. The investor's wealth dynamics is written as:

$$\frac{dW_t}{W_t} = \alpha_t \frac{dS_t}{S_t} + (1-\alpha_t)\frac{dB_t}{B_t} - C_t dt \tag{12.8}$$

where α is the fraction of wealth invested into the risky asset and C is the consumption rate. The agent chooses her optimal controls by maximizing the expected utility of her intertemporal consumption taking into account her preference for robustness. Namely, the agent solves:

$$\max_{\{\alpha\}_{t=0}^T,\{C\}_{t=0}^T} \ \min_{\{\kappa\}_{t=0}^T} E^{\hat{P}} \left\{\int_0^T \left[e^{-\beta s}\frac{C_s^{1-\gamma}}{1-\gamma} + \frac{1}{2\psi_s}\kappa_s'\kappa_s\right] ds\right\} \tag{12.9}$$

subject to the budget constraint (12.8); $\beta > 0$ stands for the subjective discount factor and γ is the parameter of relative risk aversion. The second term in the agent's objective function stands for the penalty due to deviations from the reference model. When ψ_S is equal to 0, the penalty is infinite and therefore the agent will not deviate from the reference model (no preference for robustness). We consider only the case of intermediate consumption, but adding a bequest does not present any particular complication.

To ensure that the optimal controls will be homothetic in wealth as is desirable from an economic standpoint, we follow the simplifying assumption in Maenhout (2004) and assume that the penalty function can be written[1] as:

$$\psi_t = \frac{\theta}{(1-\gamma)J_t} \tag{12.10}$$

where θ is a positive constant, and we use the specific form $V_t = e^{-\beta t}J_t$ for the agent's value function.

The Hamilton–Jacobi–Bellman equation (HJB hereafter) for the agent's optimization problem is written:

$$\max_{\{\alpha\}_{t=0}^{T},\{C\}_{t=0}^{T}} \min_{\{\kappa\}_{t=0}^{T}} \left\{ \begin{array}{l} \dfrac{C^{1-\gamma}}{1-\gamma} - \beta J + \dfrac{\partial J}{\partial t} + WJ_W\left[r+\alpha\left(\mu_S - r\right)\right] - CJ_W \\ +\dfrac{1}{2}J_{WW}W^2\alpha^2\sigma_S^2 + \mu_X J_X + \dfrac{1}{2}J_{XX}\sigma_X^2 \\ +W\alpha\rho\sigma_S\sigma_X J_{XW} + \dfrac{1}{2\psi}\kappa'\kappa + WJ_W\alpha\Sigma_S'\kappa + J_X\Sigma_X'\kappa \end{array} \right\} = 0 \tag{12.11}$$

where we use standard notation for the derivatives of the function J with respect to its arguments. The boundary condition for this problem is $J_T = 0$.

Starting with the minimization part of this HJB equation, we obtain:

$$\kappa^* = -\psi\left[W\, J_W\alpha\Sigma_S + J_X\Sigma_X\right] \tag{12.12}$$

which characterizes the worst case scenario or determines the model under which the agent is optimizing.[2] Substituting into (12.11) yields:

$$\max_{\{\alpha\}_{t=0}^{T},\{C\}_{t=0}^{T}} \left\{ \begin{array}{l} \dfrac{C^{1-\gamma}}{1-\gamma} - \beta J + \dfrac{\partial J}{\partial t} + WJ_W\left[r+\alpha\left(\mu_S - r\right)\right] - CJ_W \\ +\dfrac{1}{2}\left[J_{WW} - \psi J_W^2\right]W^2\alpha^2\sigma_S^2 + \mu_X J_X + \dfrac{1}{2}J_{XX}\sigma_X^2 \\ +W\alpha\rho\sigma_S\sigma_X\left[J_{XW} - \psi J_W J_X\right] - \dfrac{1}{2}\psi J_X^2\sigma_X^2 \end{array} \right\} = 0. \tag{12.13}$$

Under standard expected utility, J is conjectured to have the following form:

$$J_t = \frac{W^{1-\gamma}}{1-\gamma}\left(f(t,X_t)\right)^{\gamma} \tag{12.14}$$

for a suitable function f. Using this conjecture (12.14) for J and the specification (12.10) for the penalty function, we can rewrite (12.13) in the following simplified form:

$$\max_{\{\alpha\}_{t=0}^{T},\{C\}_{t=0}^{T}} \left\{ \begin{array}{l} \frac{C^{1-\gamma}}{1-\gamma} - \beta\frac{W^{1-\gamma}}{1-\gamma}f^{\gamma} + \frac{W^{1-\gamma}}{1-\gamma}\gamma\frac{\partial f}{\partial t}f^{\gamma-1} + W^{1-\gamma}f^{\gamma}\left[r+\alpha\left(\mu_S - r\right)\right] \\ -CW^{-\gamma}f^{\gamma} - \frac{1}{2}\left(\gamma+\theta\right)W^{1-\gamma}f^{\gamma}\alpha^2\sigma_S^2 + \frac{W^{1-\gamma}}{1-\gamma}\gamma f^{\gamma-1}\mu_X f_X \\ +W^{1-\gamma}\alpha\rho\sigma_S\sigma_X f_X\frac{1-\gamma-\theta}{1-\gamma}\gamma f^{\gamma-1} \\ +\frac{1}{2}\frac{W^{1-\gamma}}{1-\gamma}f^{\gamma-1}\gamma\sigma_X^2\left[f_{XX} + \left(\left(\gamma-1\right) - \frac{\theta}{1-\gamma}\gamma\right)f^{-1}f_X^2\right] \end{array} \right\}$$

$$= 0. \tag{12.15}$$

The optimal rules for consumption and portfolio holding are:

$$C^* = Wf^{-1}$$
$$\alpha^* = \frac{1}{\gamma+\theta}\frac{\mu_S - r}{\sigma_S^2} + \frac{1-\gamma-\theta}{\gamma+\theta}\frac{\gamma}{1-\gamma}\frac{\sigma_X\rho}{\sigma_S}f_Xf^{-1}. \tag{12.16}$$

Substituting into (12.15) and simplifying yields:

$$\begin{aligned} &1 + \frac{\partial f}{\partial t} + \frac{1}{2}\sigma_X^2 f_{XX} + \left(\mu_X + \frac{1-\gamma-\theta}{\gamma+\theta}\frac{\sigma_X\rho}{\sigma_S}\left(\mu_S - r\right)\right)f_X \\ &+\left(\frac{1-\gamma}{\gamma}r - \beta\frac{1}{\gamma} + \frac{1}{2}\frac{1-\gamma}{\gamma}\frac{1}{\gamma+\theta}\frac{\left(\mu_S-r\right)^2}{\sigma_S^2}\right)f \\ &+\frac{1}{2}\left(-\frac{1-\gamma}{\gamma} - \frac{\theta}{1-\gamma} + \frac{1-\gamma-\theta}{1-\gamma}\frac{1-\gamma-\theta}{\gamma+\theta}\rho^2\right)\gamma f^{-1}f_X^2\sigma_X^2 = 0. \end{aligned} \tag{12.17}$$

The last term of the left hand side of this HJB equation brings about strong non linearities that prevent any possible closed form solution in general. Cases with a closed form solution to (12.17) are those where such a term cancels out. Thus, for a closed form solution à la Kim and Omberg (1996) to be possible, the following condition should hold:

$$-\frac{1-\gamma}{\gamma} - \frac{\theta}{1-\gamma} + \frac{1-\gamma-\theta}{1-\gamma}\frac{1-\gamma-\theta}{\gamma+\theta}\rho^2 = 0. \tag{12.18}$$

Note first that we do recover the well-known result that when there is *no* preference for robustness($\theta = 0$), this condition becomes:

$$\rho^2 - 1 = 0$$

and therefore an explicit solution exists only when markets are complete ($\rho = \pm 1$). This is the feature at the origin of the closed form solutions in Brennan and Xia (2002) and Sangvinatsos and Wachter (2005). Although these authors consider incomplete markets, the expected inflation idiosyncratic risk is not priced, and this allowed an explicit solution under intermediate consumption.

When markets are *complete* and there *is* a strictly positive homothetic preference for robustness, this condition becomes:

$$\frac{1-\gamma-\theta}{1-\gamma}\frac{1-\gamma-\theta}{\gamma+\theta}-\frac{1-\gamma}{\gamma}-\frac{\theta}{1-\gamma}=0, \tag{12.19}$$

which simplifies to the unique solution:

$$\theta=0, \tag{12.19}$$

which is impossible! Therefore, the presence of preference for robustness prevents us from obtaining a standard closed form solution to the optimal consumption/investment problem in a complete market setting à la Wachter (2002).

Now consider the *incomplete* markets case. One may wonder whether there is a parameter θ solving (12.18) in this case. Note that (12.18) is a quadratic equation in θ, and we can write it as:

$$\left(\rho^2-1\right)\gamma\theta^2-\left[2\gamma(1-\gamma)\left(\rho^2-1\right)+1\right]\theta+\left(\rho^2-1\right)(1-\gamma)^2\gamma=0. \tag{12.20}$$

The discriminant of this quadratic equation is:

$$\Delta=1+4\gamma(1-\gamma)\left(\rho^2-1\right)>0 \tag{12.21}$$

for $\gamma>1$. We thus get two solutions:

$$\theta^*=1-\gamma+\frac{1-\sqrt{1+4(1-\gamma)\gamma\left(\rho^2-1\right)}}{2\gamma\left(\rho^2-1\right)} \tag{12.22}$$

and

$$\theta^{**}=1-\gamma+\frac{1+\sqrt{1+4(1-\gamma)\gamma\left(\rho^2-1\right)}}{2\gamma\left(\rho^2-1\right)}. \tag{12.23}$$

For solution (12.22) or (12.23) to be acceptable, they must be positive. Simple investigations show that, for any reasonable values of the parameter of relative risk aversion and of the coefficient of correlation, θ^* and θ^{**} are negative and are not thus admissible.

So far, we have a negative result: when the economic agent features preference for robustness, there is no explicit solution even when markets are complete. An exponential affine solution for the value function is obtained when the parameters of the model satisfy a condition (condition (12.18)) and markets are incomplete. We have however shown that this condition (12.18) is unlikely to be met with reasonable parameters values.

In what follows we suggest a simple twist to the traditional setting for an explicit solution to be possible.

12.3 Finding an explicit solution

A simple conceptual change to the classical robust decision making setting allows us to obtain an interesting and original result that an explicit solution is obtainable under incomplete markets. The developments below are heuristic and far from providing the axiomatic background necessary for the suggested preference's representation. They follow the approach of Maenhout (2004) whereby a particular form of the penalty function, although *ad hoc*, allows interesting insights into the optimal portfolio choice of an agent featuring preference for robustness.

One could write the investor's optimization problem as:

$$\max_{\{\alpha\}_{t=0}^{T},\{C\}_{t=0}^{T}} \max_{\{\kappa\}_{t=0}^{T}} E^{\hat{P}} \left\{ \int_0^T \left[e^{-\beta s} \frac{C_s^{1-\gamma}}{1-\gamma} + \frac{1}{2\psi_s} \kappa_s{}' \kappa_s \right] ds \right\} \tag{12.24}$$

where the penalty function is:

$$\psi_t = \frac{\theta}{(1-\gamma) J_t}.$$

Variable definitions are as before, and θ is now *negative*. All the previous findings are preserved. For example, under a mean reverting state variable, the solution to the consumption/investment problem will be the usual one even when markets are incomplete. While this conceptual change seems formally admissible, it is worth investigating its economic implications as to our understanding of the impact of preference for robustness on dynamic consumption/investment problems.

A preliminary issue to address is whether $\gamma + \theta$ is still positive when θ $(= \theta^*)$ is negative. This is necessary to ensure that the agent will hold a long position in the risky asset for speculative purposes when the market price of risk is positive. From (12.22), we have:

$$|\theta^*| = \gamma - 1 - \frac{1 - \sqrt{1 + 4(1-\gamma)\gamma\left(\rho^2 - 1\right)}}{2\gamma\left(\rho^2 - 1\right)} < \gamma$$

$$\Leftrightarrow \frac{2\gamma\left(\rho^2 - 1\right) + 1 - \sqrt{1 + 4(1-\gamma)\gamma\left(\rho^2 - 1\right)}}{2\gamma\left(\rho^2 - 1\right)} > 0 \tag{12.25}$$

$$\Leftrightarrow 2\gamma\left(\rho^2 - 1\right) + 1 - \sqrt{1 + 4(1-\gamma)\gamma\left(\rho^2 - 1\right)} < 0$$

$$\Leftrightarrow 2\gamma\left(1 - \rho^2\right) + \sqrt{1 + 4(1-\gamma)\gamma\left(\rho^2 - 1\right)} > 1.$$

This condition always holds for $\gamma > 1$. Therefore, assuming that the penalty function is negative does not contradict reasonable economic behavior.

This slight conceptual change into the now standard formulation of a robust consumption/portfolio choice problem changes the qualitative impact of preference for robustness on portfolio choice. To see this, consider the optimal portfolio rule (12.16) that one can write as:

$$\alpha^* = \frac{1}{\gamma+\theta}\frac{\mu_S - r}{\sigma_S^2} + \left(1 - \frac{1}{\gamma+\theta}\right)\frac{\gamma}{\gamma-1}\frac{\sigma_X\rho}{\sigma_S} f_X f^{-1}. \tag{12.26}$$

When the agent derives utility from terminal wealth only, Maenhout (2006) showed that the optimal portfolio strategy of the agent with homothetic preference for robustness is equivalent to an expected utility agent with an increased (effective) risk aversion. One implication of (12.26) is that this result will no longer hold under intermediate consumption. The reason for this is as follows. The equivalence shown in Maenhout (2006) does not extend to the welfare of the agent or function f defined in (12.14) but holds only for the portfolio strategy. Under terminal wealth, f cancels out in the intertemporal hedging component since f_X is a linear function of X times f (this is due to the exponential form of f). Under intermediate consumption, f will no longer cancel out since f_X is no longer a proportional function of f. Since f is related to the agent's welfare, and the latter is different for an agent with expected utility and tilted risk aversion and an agent with preference for robustness, the equivalence that holds under terminal wealth breaks down when there is intermediate consumption.

Another point worth noting is the relative impact of preference for robustness on the speculative demand and the intertemporal hedging demand. The portfolio rule (12.26) has the usual form of a weighted average between the speculative component and the intertemporal hedging component. Yet the impact of preference for robustness depends on the sign of θ. In the usual case, where θ is positive, preference for robustness tends to reduce the demand for speculative motives and to increase the demand for intertemporal hedging. This is a natural consequence of the increase in effective risk aversion of the agent when the agent derives utility only from terminal wealth. But this interpretation is only correct if we have equivalence between preference for robustness and increased effective risk aversion. This is not the case in the consumption/investment problem as explained above. Therefore, a better way to understand this behavior is to remember that the risky asset price's dynamics under the worst case model are written as:

$$\frac{dS_t}{S_t} = \left[\mu_{S_t} - \frac{\theta}{\gamma+\theta}\left[\mu_{S_t} - r - \frac{\gamma}{\gamma-1}\sigma_{S_t}\sigma_{X_t}\rho f_{X_t} f^{-1}\right]\right] dt + \Sigma_{S_t}' d\hat{Z}_t. \tag{12.27}$$

It is known from Maenhout (2006) that a stochastic investment opportunity set mitigates the impact of preference for robustness on the drift of the risky asset and thus the risk premium under the alternative model. Assume for the sake of simplicity that $\left[\mu_{S_t} - r - \frac{\gamma}{\gamma-1}\sigma_{S_t}\sigma_{X_t}\rho f_{X_t} f^{-1}\right] > 0$. In this case, when $\theta > 0$, preference for robustness implies a decrease in the risky asset's risk premium and therefore a reduction in the speculative demand for the risky asset. When $\theta < 0$, preference for robustness increases the drift of the risky asset and therefore will increase the demand for speculative purposes.

In the following section we solve explicitly for the optimal consumption/investment in a setting à la Kim and Omberg (1996).

12.4 Application

In this section we solve explicitly in a classical case first introduced by Merton (1971). In this case, the agent trades in a riskless asset with constant interest rate r and a risky asset with constant volatility. The market price of risk, the state variable in this setting, follows a mean reverting stochastic process. This setting has been used by, amongst others, Kim and Omberg (1996), Lioui and Poncet (2001), Wachter (2002) and Maenhout (2006).

The riskless asset's price dynamics is:

$$\frac{dB_t}{B_t} = r dt. \tag{12.28}$$

Under the reference model, the risky asset's price dynamics is:

$$\frac{dS_t}{S_t} = [r + \sigma_S X_t]\, dt + \sigma_S dZ_t^S \tag{12.29}$$

where σ_S is the asset's constant volatility and X_t is the Sharpe ratio of the asset, which is actually the state variable that makes the opportunity set stochastic.

Under the reference model, the state variable has the following dynamics:

$$dX_t = \phi_X [\mu_X - X_t]\, dt + \sigma_X \left[\rho dZ_t^S + \sqrt{1-\rho^2} dZ_t^X\right] \tag{12.30}$$

where ϕ_X, μ_X and σ_X are strictly positive constants.

We assume that condition (12.18) holds. We thus have to solve for:

$$\begin{aligned}
&1 + \frac{\partial f}{\partial t} + \frac{1}{2}\sigma_X^2 f_{XX} \\
&+ \left\{\sigma_X \rho X_t \left(\gamma - \frac{\gamma}{1-\gamma}\theta\right)\frac{1-\gamma}{\gamma}\frac{1}{\gamma+\theta} + \varphi_X [\mu_X - X_t]\right\} f_X \\
&+ \left\{\frac{1}{2}\frac{1}{\gamma+\theta}\frac{1-\gamma}{\gamma}X_t^2 - \beta\frac{1}{\gamma} + \frac{1-\gamma}{\gamma}r\right\} f = 0.
\end{aligned} \tag{12.31}$$

Following Liu (2007), we can show that the solution to (12.31) is (see the Appendix)

$$f(t,T,X_t) = \int_t^T \exp\left\{A(t,T) + B(t,T)X_t + C(t,T)X_t^2\right\}dt \tag{12.32}$$

where A(t,T) is given in the Appendix,

$$B(t,T) = \frac{4\varphi_X \mu_X}{\Delta}\frac{1-\gamma}{\gamma}\frac{1}{\gamma+\theta}\frac{\left(1-e^{-\frac{\Delta(T-t)}{2}}\right)^2}{2\Delta-(b_2+\Delta)\left(1-e^{-\Delta(T-t)}\right)}$$

$$C(t,T) = \frac{1-\gamma}{\gamma}\frac{1}{\gamma+\theta}\frac{1-e^{-\Delta(T-t)}}{2\Delta-(b_2+\Delta)\left(1-e^{-\Delta(T-t)}\right)}$$

and

$$b_1 = 2\sigma_X^2$$

$$b_2 = 2\left(\sigma_X \rho \frac{1-\gamma-\theta}{\gamma+\theta} - \varphi_X\right)$$

$$b_3 = \frac{1}{2}\frac{1-\gamma}{\gamma}\frac{1}{\gamma+\theta}$$

$$\Delta^2 = b_2^2 - 4b_1 b_3 = 4\left(\sigma_X \rho \frac{1-\gamma-\theta}{\gamma+\theta} - \varphi_X\right)^2 - 4\frac{1-\gamma}{\gamma}\frac{1}{\gamma+\theta}\sigma_X^2 > 0.$$

We can thus write the optimal portfolio rule explicitly as:

$$\alpha_t^* = \frac{1}{\gamma+\theta}\frac{X_t}{\sigma_S} + \frac{1-\gamma-\theta}{\gamma+\theta}\frac{\int_t^T\left(\frac{\gamma}{1-\gamma}B(s,T)+2C(s,T)X_t\right)\exp\left\{A(s,T)+B(s,T)X_t+C(s,T)X_t^2\right\}ds}{\int_0^T \exp\left\{A(s,T)+B(s,T)X_t+C(s,T)X_t^2\right\}ds}\frac{\sigma_X \rho}{\sigma_S}. \tag{12.33}$$

This portfolio strategy has several interesting features. First we note that it has the traditional components: a mean-variance component (the first term on the right hand side) and an intertemporal hedging component (the second term on the right hand side). The myopic component is similar to the one obtained by Kim and Omberg (1996), Campbell and Viceira (1999), Wachter (2002) and Maenhout (2006).

The intertemporal hedging component has a similar structure to the one we usually encounter in complete markets (Wachter, 2002) or incomplete markets where the state variables are still perfectly hedgeable (Brennan and Xia, 2002) and Sangvinatsos and Wachter, 2005). Yet, this component is highly non linear in the state variable and therefore very different from the linear portfolio strategy exhibited by Campbell and Viceira (1999), for example, when using some approximations and infinite horizon.

Another noticeable feature of the portfolio strategy above is that it is no longer equivalent to the strategy followed by an expected utility investor with tilted risk aversion. One main reason stems from the weighted average feature of the intertemporal hedging component as explained by Wachter (2002) in complete markets. Maenhout (2004, 2006) equivalence results hold for the optimal strategy and not the welfare. Namely, the value function of an agent with preference for robustness is not equal to the value function of an expected utility maximizer with a tilted parameter of risk aversion. Since the intertemporal hedging component involves the value function, this is why we no longer have the equivalence shown by Maenhout (2004).

One important variable, for the literature on portfolio choice and on asset return predictability literature, is the consumption to wealth ratio (see Lettau and Ludvigson, 2001). Using (12.16) and (12.32), we have:

$$\frac{C_t}{W_t} = \left[\int_t^T \exp\left\{A(t,T) + B(t,T)X_t + C(t,T)X_t^2\right\}dt\right]^{-1}. \tag{12.34}$$

Here again, we see an important difference with the approximate solution of Campbell and Viceira (1999). They obtained a ratio which is a quadratic function of the state variable, while it turns out to be highly non linear in our case.

Overall, the closed form solution obtained here shows that the optimal policies in incomplete markets, like in complete markets, are non linear in the state variables.

Table 12.1 Baseline parameter values

Rate of time preference (β)	0.0052
Interest rate (r)	0.0014
Volatility of X (σ_X)	0.0189
Speed of mean reversion of X (ϕ_X)	0.0226
Unconditional mean of X (μ_X)	0.0788
Volatility of the risky asset (σ_S)	0.0436
Correlation between X and the risky asset (ρ)	−0.93
Horizon (T)	60

Notes: This table provides the parameters used in the calibration. They are taken from Wachter (2002) who obtained these parameters from the discrete values obtained by Barberis (2000) and Campbell and Viceira (1999). All the parameters are in monthly units.

We now calibrate the results and, for this purpose and to make our findings comparable to others, we use the parameter values of Wachter (2002) which are based on the discrete time values of Barberis (2000). As it appears in the calibration exercise conducted by Maenhout (2006), the estimates are sensitive to the samples and the data frequency. We address this issue below.

In Table 12.1, we provide the parameter values used in the simulations. They correspond to Table 12.1 in Wachter (2002) except for the correlation coefficient which equals −1 in Wachter (2002) while we use as the baseline −0.93, as in Maenhout (2006). The baseline horizon has been set at 60 months whenever necessary.

Figure 12.1 shows the total demand for the risky asset, the hedging demand as a percentage of this total demand and the consumption to wealth ratio as a function of the horizon. Four values of the parameter of risk aversion are considered, $\gamma = 2$, 3, 5, and 10. The corresponding parameters of preference for robustness are (in absolute value) 0.18, 0.69, 2.20 and 6.76.

The total demand for the risky asset tends to decrease with risk aversion and preference for robustness and to increase with the horizon. However, this demand flattens at long horizons. For example, for a parameter of risk aversion of 10 and preference for robustness of 6.76, this demand is 71 percent at a horizon of 1 year and 104 percent at a horizon of 10 years, but it is 'only' 114 percent at a horizon of 20 years. Since the myopic component is independent from the horizon, this behavior of the total demand of the risky asset reflects the behavior of the intertemporal hedging component. As a fraction of total demand, the intertemporal hedging demand increases with both the horizon and the risk aversion/preference for robustness. For example, for a parameter of risk aversion of 10 and preference for robustness of 6.76, it represents 10.27 percent of total demand at a one-year horizon and 38.66 percent at a ten-year horizon, but it is only 43.91 percent at a 20-year horizon. Thus, for a given horizon, total demand decreases with risk aversion/preference for robustness while intertemporal hedging demand relative to total demand increases.

As to the consumption/wealth ratio, it decreases with the horizon in a convex way and tends to flatten for long horizons. For example, for a parameter of risk aversion of 10 and preference for robustness of 6.76, this ratio is 8.57 percent at a one-year horizon; it decreases to 1.13 percent at a ten-year horizon, but it is still 0.75 percent at a 20-year horizon. Of particular interest is the fact that risk aversion/preference for robustness have little impact on this ratio. For example, at a five-year horizon, the ratio is 1.98 percent when $\gamma = 2$ and $\theta = 0.18$, while it is 1.93 percent when $\gamma = 10$ and $\theta = 6.76$.

Figure 12.2 shows the total demand for the risky asset, the hedging demand as a percentage of this total demand and the consumption to wealth ratio as a function of the state variable. Total demand is increasing in the state variable while intertemporal hedging demand is decreasing. The behavior of the total demand is almost linear in the state variable; this is because

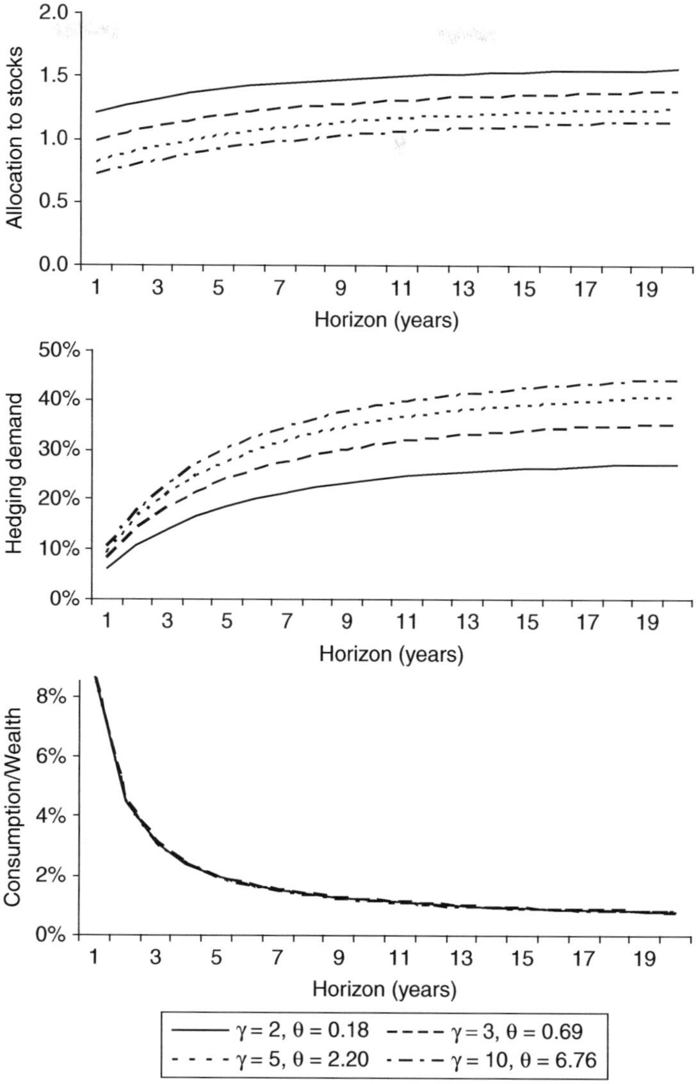

Figure 12.1 The total demand for the risky asset, the hedging demand and the consumption to wealth ratio as a function of the investor's horizon

Note: The baseline parameters are given in Table 12.1. The horizon is in years, the hedging demand is expressed in percentage of total demand and the consumption/wealth ratio is in percentage; θ stands for the absolute value of the parameter of preference for robustness.

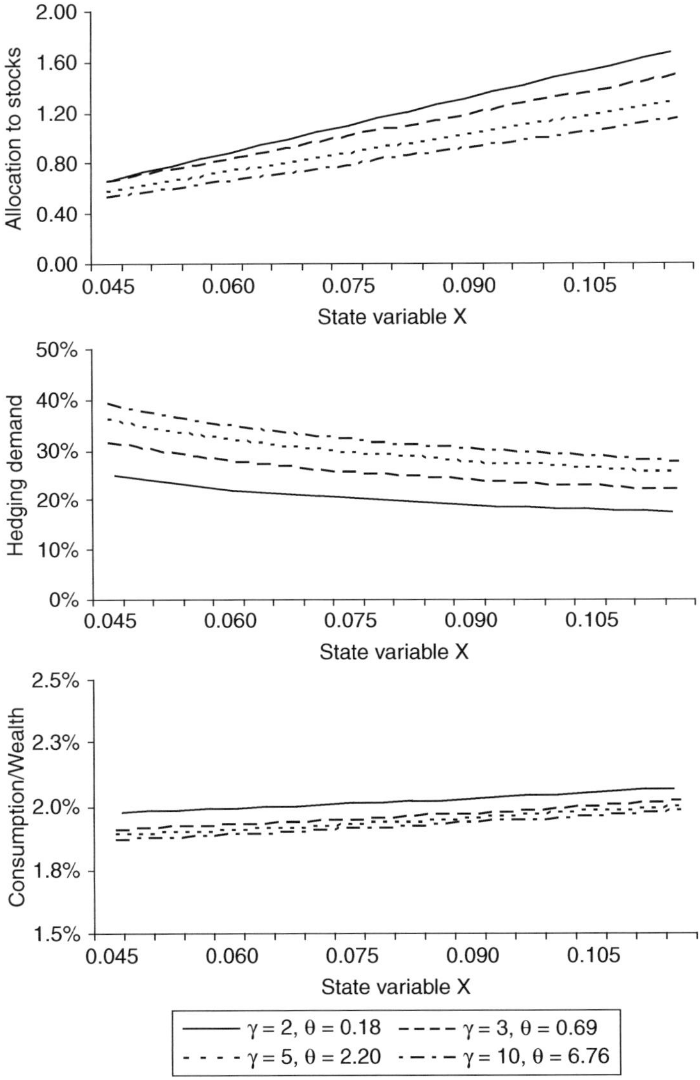

Figure 12.2 The total demand for the risky asset, the hedging demand and the consumption to wealth ratio as a function of the market risk premium

Notes: The baseline parameters are given in Table 12.1. The hedging demand is expressed in percentage of total demand and the consumption/wealth ratio is in percentage; θ stands for the absolute value of the parameter of preference for robustness.

the intertemporal hedging demand tends again to flatten while the myopic part of the total demand is still linear in the state variable. As a consequence, it does not seem unreasonable to assume that the total demand is linear in the state variable, as obtained by Campbell and Viceira (1999) using approximations. The relatively small impact of the state variable on the intertemporal hedging demand reappears in the behavior of the consumption to wealth ratio. This ratio is almost insensitive to changes in the state variable, although the structural form suggested some strong non linearities.

Figure 12.3 shows the changes in the different variables with respect to the coefficient of correlation. It must be remembered that this coefficient is in some sense a measure of the degree of market incompleteness: the closer to 0 it is, the more incomplete the markets are. Hence the risky asset does not allow any hedge of the state variable, and thus of the stochastic changes in the opportunity set, at all.

An a priori difficulty in interpreting the findings in Figure 12.3 is that the coefficient of correlation has a direct impact on the total demand for the risky asset and an indirect impact through the parameter of preference for robustness. However, it turns out that the impact of the changes in the coefficient of correlation on this parameter is marginal. Consider for example the case where the parameter of risk aversion is 10. When the correlation is 0, the parameter for robustness is (in absolute value) 8.10, while it is 8.02 when the coefficient of correlation is 0.4, thus a decrease of only 1 percent. When the coefficient of correlation is 0.8, the decrease in the coefficient of preference for robustness is 7 percent. Extreme changes of the parameter for robustness appear only at high levels of the correlations coefficient, and this is a direct consequence of the convergence of the coefficient to 0 when the correlation converges to ± 1.

As a consequence, we can reasonably see the changes in the different variables for a correlation between -0.8 and 0.8 as coming mainly from the direct impact of the coefficient of correlation. As such, the total demand for the risky asset is decreasing as a direct consequence of the decrease in the intertemporal hedging demand. It must be remembered that, to the extent that the parameter of preference for robustness is stable, the myopic demand is marginally affected by changes in the correlation. This behavior of the intertemporal hedging demand is a direct consequence of the behavior of the minimum variance hedge ratio that it contains and that involves the correlation coefficient. As can be seen from the impact on the consumption/wealth ratio, it seems that the correlation has a marginal impact on the state variable dependent part of the intertemporal hedging component.

Finally, we investigate the impact of the parameters of the dynamics of the state variable on the different policy functions. As can be seen from the calibration in Maenhout (2006), the estimated parameters of the state variable are sensitive to the sample period and data frequency.[3] This point has

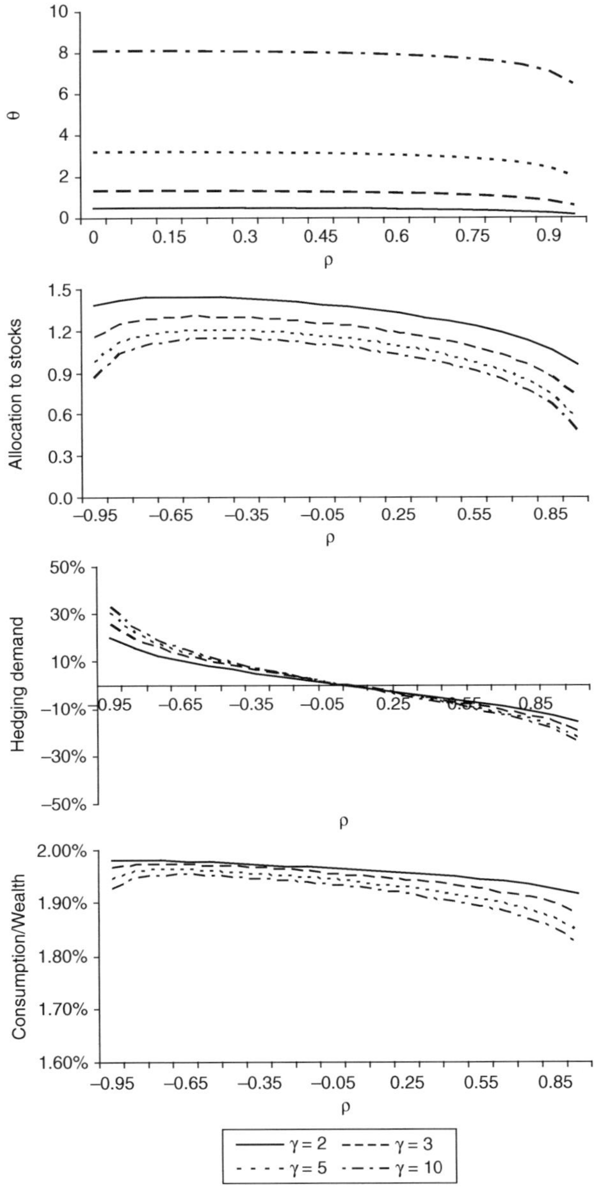

Figure 12.3 The total demand for the risky asset, the hedging demand, the consumption to wealth ratio and the parameter of preference for robustness as a function of the correlation between the risky asset and the state variable

Notes: The baseline parameters are given in Table 12.1. The hedging demand is expressed in percentage of total demand and the consumption/wealth ratio is in percentage; θ stands for the absolute value of the parameter of preference for robustness.

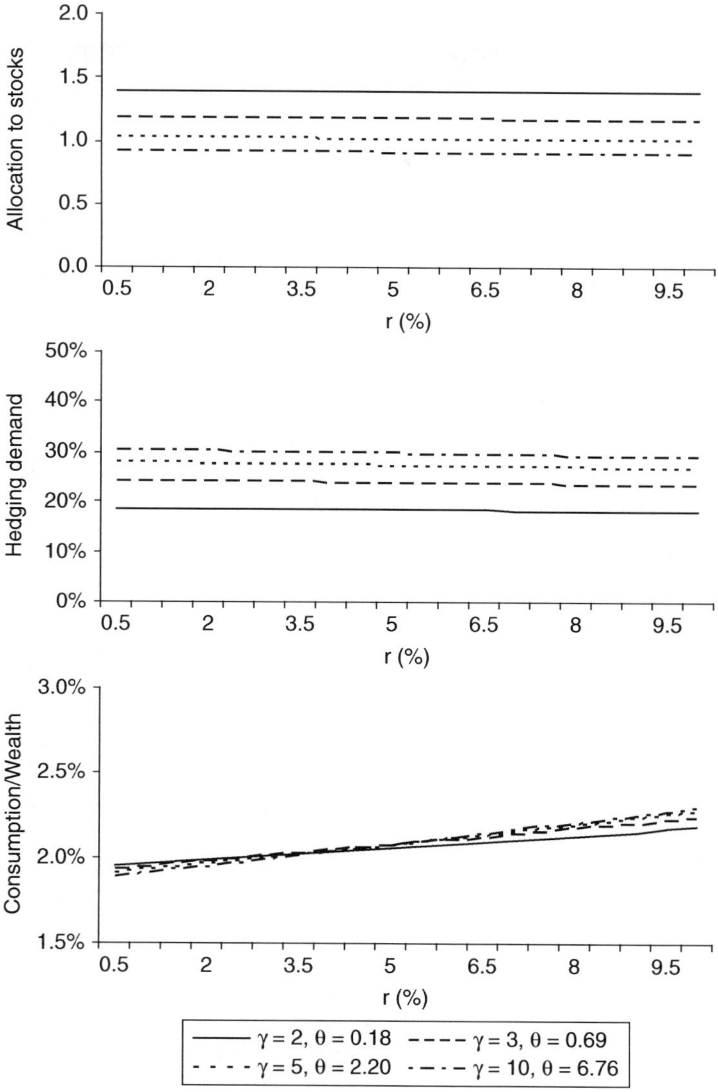

Figure 12.4 The total demand for the risky asset, the hedging demand and the consumption to wealth ratio as a function of the interest rate

Notes: The baseline parameters are given in Table 12.1. The hedging demand is expressed in percentage of total demand and the consumption/wealth ratio is in percentage; θ stands for the absolute value of the parameter of preference for robustness.

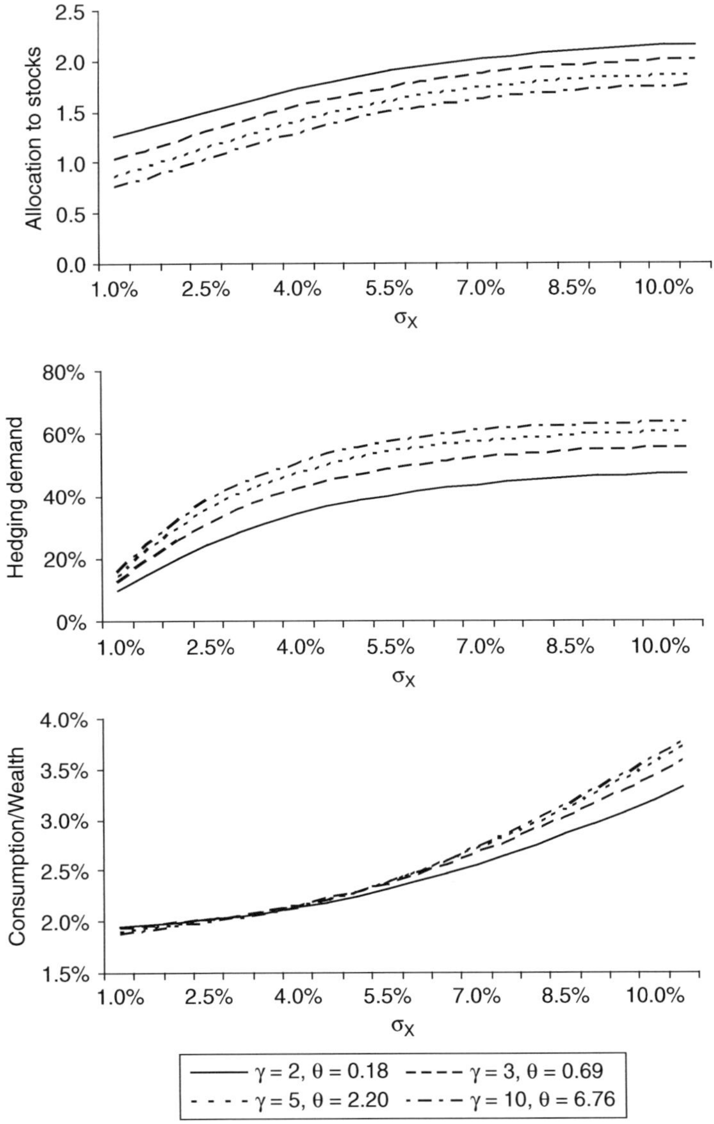

Figure 12.5 The total demand for the risky asset, the hedging demand and the consumption to wealth ratio as a function of the volatility of the state variable

Notes: The baseline parameters are given in Table 12.1. The hedging demand is expressed in percentage of total demand and the consumption/wealth ratio is in percentage; θ stands for the absolute value of the parameter of preference for robustness.

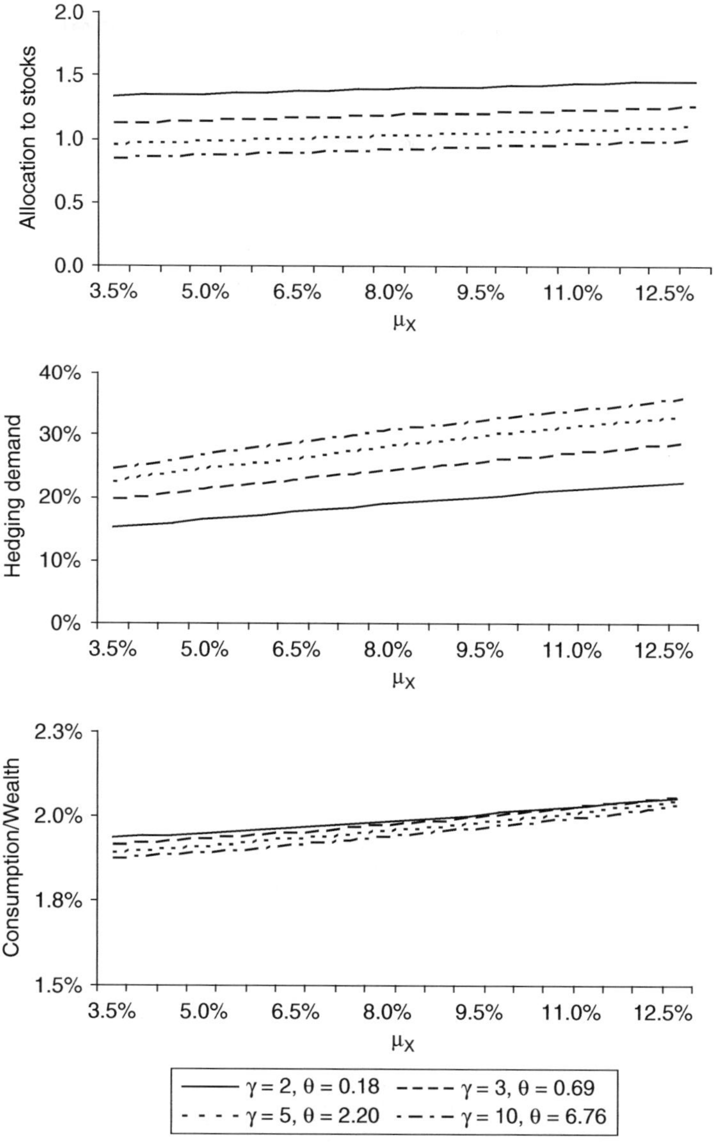

Figure 12.6 The total demand for the risky asset, the hedging demand and the consumption to wealth ratio as a function of the state variable's long run mean

Notes: The baseline parameters are given in Table 12.1. The hedging demand is expressed in percentage of total demand and the consumption/wealth ratio is in percentage; θ stands for the absolute value of the parameter of preference for robustness.

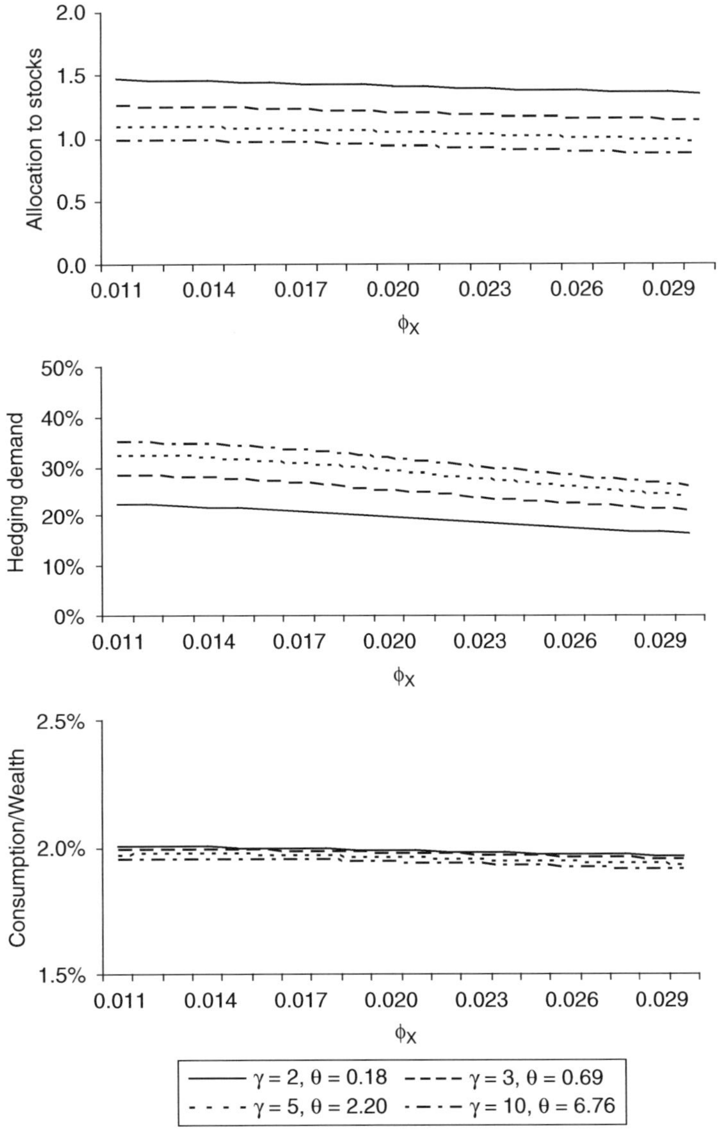

Figure 12.7 The total demand for the risky asset, the hedging demand and the consumption to wealth ratio as a function of the state variable's speed of mean reversion

Notes: The baseline parameters are given in Table 12.1. The hedging demand is expressed in percentage of total demand and the consumption/wealth ratio is in percentage; θ stands for the absolute value of the parameter of preference for robustness.

not been given enough attention so far, although it is important. A starting point of the robust portfolio analysis is that the agent knows a reference model and considers models close to this reference model. But like the priors in the Bayesian approach to portfolio choice, the agent may have some difficulties even choosing a reference model. As a consequence, it is legitimate to ask whether the lack of information on the reference model has great importance.

In Figures 12.4 to 12.7, we show the impact of the parameters of the dynamics of the state variable and of the interest rate on the policy functions. The most notable thing is that the set of parameters used to start with seems to have little importance except for the volatility of the state variable. The higher the volatility is, the higher the consumption to wealth ratio. This is quite intuitive since the riskier the state variable is, the less reliable it is for predictability. Therefore, the agent simply tends to consume more today.

12.5 Conclusion

The literature on dynamic asset pricing and dynamic asset allocation under preference for robustness or ambiguity aversion is by now voluminous. Worth citing are the comprehensive literature reviews by Epstein and Schneider (2010), Etner et al. (2009), Gilboa et al. (2008), Guidolin and Rinaldi (2010) and Wakker (2008). They all point to the potential of such a paradigm for solving long standing financial puzzles such as the equity premium puzzle, the interest rate puzzle, the excess volatility puzzle and even the local bias puzzle. An ultimate paper in this direction is the one by Ju and Miao (2012) whereby the authors apply the smooth ambiguity aversion paradigm to derive asset market equilibrium quantities.

The present chapter suggested some issues that have not been covered and a potential strength of this paradigm that had previously been overlooked. Dynamic asset allocation will certainly gain from systematically incorporating the lessons from the ambiguity aversion literature.

Appendix

For completeness, we provide here a derivation of (12.32). Let us first consider the PDE:

$$\begin{aligned} 0 &= \hat{f}_t + \frac{1}{2}\sigma_X^2 \hat{f}_{XX} \\ &+ \left\{ \sigma_X \rho X_t \left(\gamma - \frac{\gamma}{1-\gamma}\theta \right) \frac{1-\gamma}{\gamma} \frac{1}{\gamma+\theta} + \phi_X [\mu_X - X_t] \right\} \hat{f}_X \qquad \text{(a)} \\ &+ \left\{ \frac{1}{2} \frac{1}{\gamma+\theta} \frac{1-\gamma}{\gamma} X_t^2 - \beta \frac{1}{\gamma} + \frac{1-\gamma}{\gamma} r \right\} \hat{f} \end{aligned}$$

and let us guess the following solution:

$$\hat{f}(0, X_0) = \int_0^T \exp\left\{A(t,T) + B(t,T)X_t + C(t,T)X_t^2\right\}dt. \tag{b}$$

Substituting (b) into (a) yields the following system:

$$\frac{\partial A(t,T)}{\partial \tau} = \sigma_X^2 C(t,T) + B(t,T)\phi_X\mu_X + \frac{1}{2}\sigma_X^2 B(t,T)^2 - \beta\frac{1}{\gamma} + \frac{1-\gamma}{\gamma}r$$

$$\frac{\partial B(t,T)}{\partial \tau} = 2\sigma_X^2 C(t,T)B(t,T) + \left[\sigma_X\rho\frac{1-\gamma-\theta}{\gamma+\theta} - \phi_X\right]B(t,T) + 2\phi_X\mu_X C(t,T)$$

$$\frac{\partial C(t,T)}{\partial \tau} = 2\sigma_X^2 C(t,T)^2 + \left[2\rho\sigma_X\frac{1-\gamma-\theta}{\gamma+\theta} - 2\phi_X\right]C(t,T) + \frac{1}{2}\frac{1}{\gamma+\theta}\frac{1-\gamma}{\gamma} \tag{c}$$

where τ stands for $T - t$. Solving using standard integration tables yields B and C given at the outset of the Proposition, A could be obtained in closed form or solved using standard quadrature techniques (Kim and Omberg, 1996).

To see that $f = \hat{f}$, just apply Lemma 2 of Liu (2007).

Notes

1. While Maenhout (2004) considers an identical parameter of preference for robustness for all the sources of risk, Uppal and Wang (2003) allow for different levels of preference for robustness depending on the subset of assets. For a lucid discussion see Guidolin and Rinaldi (2010).
2. More on this vector in Uppal and Wang (2003) and Maenhout (2004).
3. See Maenhout (2006, table 1, p. 153).

References

Anderson, E., Hansen, L. P. and Sargent, T. (2003). A Quartet of Semigroups for Model Specification, Robustness, Prices of Risk and Model Detection. *Journal of the European Economic Association*, 1 (1), 68–123.

Avramov, D. (2002). Stock Return Predictability and Model Uncertainty. *Journal of Financial Economics*, 64, 423–58.

Avramov, D. (2004). Stock Return Predictability and Asset Pricing Models. *The Review of Financial Studies*, 17, 699–738.

Barberis, N. (2000). Investing for the Long Run When Returns are Predictable. *Journal of Finance*, 55, 225–64.

Brandt, M. and Clara, P. S. (2006). Dynamic Portfolio Selection by Augmenting the Asset Space. *Journal of Finance*, 61, 2187–217.

Brennan, M. and Xia, J. (2002). Dynamic Asset Allocation under Inflation. *Journal of Finance*, 57 (3), 1201–38.

Campbell, J. and Viceira, L. (1999). Consumption and Portfolio Decisions when Expected Returns Are Time Varying. *Quarterly Journal of Economics*, 114, 433–95.

Cao, H., Wang, T. and Zhang, H. (2005). Model Uncertainty, Limited Market Participation and Asset Prices. *Review of Financial Studies*, 18, 1219–51.

DeMiguel, A-V., Garlappi, L. and Uppal, R. (2009). Optimal Versus Naive Diversification: How Inefficient Is the 1/N Portfolio Strategy? *Review of Financial Studies*, 22 (5), 1915–53.

Epstein, L.G. and Schneider, M. (2010). Ambiguity and Asset Markets. NBER Working Paper No. 16181.

Etner, J., Jeleva, M. and Tallon, J.-M. (2009). Decision Theory under Uncertainty. Documents de Travail du Centre d'Economie de la Sorbonne No. 2009.64.

Gilboa, I., Postlewaite, A. W. and Schmeidler, D. (2008). Probability and Uncertainty in Economic Modeling. *Journal of Economic Perspectives*, 22, 173–88.

Guidolin, M. and Rinaldi, F. (2010). Ambiguity in Asset Pricing and Portfolio Choice. Working Paper Federal Reserve Bank of Saint Louis and Manchester Business School.

Ju, N. and Miao, J. (2012). Ambiguity, Learning and Asset Returns. *Econometrica*, 80, 559–91.

Kim, T. and Omberg, E. (1996). Dynamic Nonmyopic Portfolio Behavior. *Review of Financial Studies*, 9 (1), 141–61.

Leippold, M., Trojani, F. and Vanini, P. (2008). Learning and Asset Prices under Ambiguous Information. *Review of Financial Studies*, 21, 2565–97.

Lettau, M. and Ludvigson, S. (2001). Consumption, Aggregate Wealth, and Expected Stock Returns. *Journal of Finance*, LVI (3), 815–49.

Lioui, A., and Poncet, P. (2001). On Optimal Portfolio Choice under Stochastic Interest Rates. *Journal of Economic Dynamics and Control*, 25, 1141–865.

Liu, J. (2007). Portfolio Selection in Stochastic Environments. *Review of Financial Studies*, 20, 1–39.

Liu, J., Pan, J. and Wang, T. (2005). An Equilibrium Model of Rare Event Premia and Its Implication for Option Smirks. *Review of Financial Studies*, 18 (1), 131–64.

Maenhout, P. (2004). Robust Portfolio Rules and Asset Pricing. *Review of Financial Studies*, 17 (4), 951–83.

Maenhout, P. (2006). Robust Portfolio Rules and Detection-error Probabilities for a Mean-reverting Risk Premium. *Journal of Economic Theory*, 128 (1), 136–63.

Merton, R. (1971). Optimum Consumption and Portfolio Rules in a Continuous Time Model. *Journal of Economic Theory*, 3, 373–413.

Sangvinatsos, A. and Wachter, J. (2005). Does the Failure of the Expectations Hypothesis Matter for Long Term Investors? *Journal of Finance*, LX (1), 179–230.

Uppal, R. and Wang, T. (2003). Model Misspecification and Underdiversification. *Journal of Finance*, 58 (6), 2465–86.

Wachter, J. (2002). Portfolio and Consumption Decisions under Mean Reverting Returns: An Exact Solution for Complete Markets. *Journal of Financial and Quantitative Analysis*, 37, 63–91.

Wachter, J. and Warusawitharana, M. (2009). Predictable Returns and Asset Allocation: Should a Skeptical Investor Time the Market? *Journal of Econometrics*, 148, 162–78.

Wakker, P. P. (2008). Uncertainty, in Durlauf, S. and Blume, L. (eds) *The New Palgrave Dictionary of Economics*, 2nd edn. Palgrave Macmillan.

13

A Diversification Measure for Portfolios of Risky Assets

Gabriel Frahm and Christof Wiechers

13.1 Introduction

The benefits of diversification are well known and indeed diversification is frequently applied in real-life portfolio optimization. The first proof of portfolio diversification is given by Markowitz (1952). In his seminal paper, Markowitz provides a normative basis of portfolio choice which has led to modern portfolio theory. The mean-variance framework has become standard knowledge in finance theory.

Nevertheless, a direct application of the mean-variance approach is heavily deprecated by many practitioners and is still a matter of debate in the scientific community. The expected returns as well as the variances and covariances of asset returns are unknown. According to Markowitz (1952) the unknown parameters have to be approximated by 'observation and experience'. This leads to estimation errors which represent an additional and essential source of risk.

Klein and Bawa (1976) as well as Chopra and Ziemba (1993) test the out-of-sample performance of sample-based mean-variance portfolios and find that the results are far worse than suggested by theory. The latter authors emphasize that errors with respect to expected returns are about ten times as important as errors in variances and covariances. Accordingly, Best and Grauer (1991) show that the composition of mean-variance efficient portfolios is extremely sensitive to return expectations. There exist many approaches to producing better expected return estimates. For example, Jorion (1986) shows that the out-of-sample performance can be improved by applying Bayesian analysis. Black and Litterman (1992) combine 'objective' information in the form of equilibrium asset returns with 'subjective' information which might be provided by experts. For an analytical investigation of expected asset return estimators see Frahm (2011).

The usefulness of quantitative methods of portfolio allocation is vividly discussed in the finance literature. DeMiguel et al. (2009a) argue that the so-called *naive*, *equally-weighted* or '$1/N$' portfolio, where all portfolio weights are equal given a pre-defined set of N assets, is not significantly outperformed by most sophisticated portfolio optimization approaches, which they have taken into consideration. Frahm et al. (2011) emphasize the importance of multiple tests when comparing different investment strategies and show that it is usually not possible to find significant results in favor of the naive approach or any other trivial or non-trivial investment strategy by the use of empirical data.

Traditionally, the estimation of expected asset returns is accomplished by using fundamental data such as, for instance, balance sheets rather than historical asset returns. By contrast, the estimation of variances and covariances is typically done by historical observations. The reason why these estimates are retrieved from historical data is threefold: (i) For a portfolio of N assets, the number of variances and covariances which have to be estimated is $\binom{N+1}{2}$; (ii) As already mentioned, it is commonly believed that the impact of estimation errors due to variances and covariances is less serious, compared to the misspecification of expected returns; (iii) The analytical treatment of (co-)variances is typically considered as being harder than dealing with expected returns.

A relatively new branch of portfolio optimization deals with *minimum-variance portfolios*, which aim at minimizing the overall portfolio return variance, without paying attention to the estimation of expected asset returns. A growing stock of literature confirms superior performance of minimum-variance strategies compared to strategies that evolve from an application of the classical mean-variance framework (DeMiguel et al., 2009a,b; Fletcher, 2011; Frahm and Memmel, 2010; Jagannathan and Ma, 2003).

It seems that combining the assets in a way such that the portfolio return variance is minimized is more efficient than desperately trying to estimate expected asset returns and building seemingly efficient but, actually, highly inefficient portfolios. Put another way, it is mainly the effect of diversification which contributes to the performance of a portfolio strategy. Even though this perception is as old as the hills, in practical applications diversification is often managed by applying ad-hoc techniques, such as using constraints for the portfolio weights or other heuristics.

Surprisingly, there is only a small amount of work on measuring the portfolio diversification effect. While a qualitative definition can be found in Meucci (2009), who describes a portfolio as 'well diversified' if it is 'not heavily exposed to individual shocks', we will use an implicit definition given by the Capital Asset Pricing Model, developed by Sharpe (1966), Lintner (1965), and Mossin (1966).

The following questions are addressed in this:

(i) How can a quantitative measure for the diversification of portfolios of risky assets be defined in a way that is consistent with the qualitative, common-sense definition? Which parameters should such a measure depend upon?
(ii) What are the existing approaches towards the measurement of diversification?
(iii) In the empirical section, can we confirm reliability of our measure when it is applied to portfolios of S&P 500 stocks?
(iv) In connection to (iii), does our measure meet with the intuition that a portfolio containing a large number of stocks is better-diversified than one which is concentrated on a few assets only?
(v) In terms of our measure, does the common belief that the naive portfolio is 'well diversified' really hold true?

Section 13.2 provides the framework of our analysis, a review on statistical properties of minimum-variance as well as constant portfolios. In Section 13.3 we introduce our measure of diversification. This section also contains the finite-sample and the asymptotic properties of our estimator for diversification. Section 13.4 summarizes some statistical tests regarding the portfolio return variance of a single portfolio and the difference of two portfolio return variances. The empirical part of this work can be found in Section 13.5, and Section 13.6 concludes our findings.

13.2 Preliminaries

In our framework, the vector of asset returns R of N risky assets is assumed to follow a N-variate normal distribution with mean vector $\mu \in \mathbb{R}^N$ and positive definite covariance matrix $\Sigma \in \mathbb{R}^{N \times N}$, viz

$$R \sim \mathcal{N}_N(\mu, \Sigma).$$

Let the entries of the covariance matrix Σ be denoted by σ_{ij} for $i,j = 1,\ldots,N$ and $\sigma_i^2 = \sigma_{ii}$ for $i = 1,\ldots,N$.

Given a finite sample $R_1,\ldots,R_T$ of independent copies of R, the unbiased sample covariance matrix corresponds to

$$\widehat{\Sigma} = \frac{1}{T-1}\sum_{t=1}^{T}(R_t - \hat{\mu})(R_t - \hat{\mu})' \sim \frac{\mathcal{W}_N(\Sigma, T-1)}{T-1}, \tag{13.1}$$

where $\mathcal{W}_N(\Sigma, T-1)$ denotes a n-dimensional central Wishart distribution with scale matrix Σ and $T-1$ degrees of freedom.

A vector $v = (v_1,\ldots,v_N) \in \mathbb{R}^N$ is supposed to be a *column* vector, whereas v' represents a *row* vector. Furthermore, $\mathbf{1}$ denotes a column vector of ones, and a portfolio weight vector $w = (w_1,\ldots,w_N) \in \mathbb{R}^N$, or a *portfolio* for short, describes the fractions of wealth invested into the assets $1,\dots,N$, respectively. Since R is a random vector, the portfolio return, $w'R$, is a random variable and its variance reads $\sigma_w^2 := \mathrm{Var}(w'R) = w'\Sigma w$. The covariance matrix Σ is unknown to the investor and may be estimated from the given return data $R_1,\dots,R_T$ via replacing Σ by its sample counterpart (13.1).

13.2.1 Estimating the variance of a constant portfolio

With the sample covariance matrix estimator given by (13.1), the finite-sample distribution of the sample counterpart $\hat{\sigma}_w^2$ of σ_w^2 can be obtained by applying some well-known theorems for the Wishart distribution (see, for example, Muirhead, 1982, ch. 3). It turns out that

$$\hat{\sigma}_w^2 = w'\widehat{\Sigma}\,w \sim \sigma_w^2\,\frac{\chi_{T-1}^2}{T-1}\,.$$

Thus, in the context of normally distributed asset returns, $\hat{\sigma}_w^2$ is an unbiased estimator of σ_w^2, and its variance amounts to

$$\mathrm{Var}(\hat{\sigma}_w^2) = \mathrm{Var}\left(\sigma_w^2\,\frac{\chi_{T-1}^2}{T-1}\right) = \frac{\sigma_w^4}{(T-1)^2}\,\mathrm{Var}(\chi_{T-1}^2) = \frac{2\sigma_w^4}{(T-1)}\,.$$

Hence, $\hat{\sigma}_w^2$ is an unbiased and consistent estimator of σ_w^2.

13.2.2 Estimating the global minimum variance

As mentioned in the introduction, minimum-variance portfolios have started to gain more attention in recent publications. A special portfolio in this context is the *global minimum-variance portfolio* (GMVP), which aims at minimizing the portfolio return variance under the budget constraint only. It is denoted by w_{MV} and defined as

$$w_{\mathrm{MV}} = \arg\min_{w} w'\Sigma w \qquad \text{s.t. } w'\mathbf{1} = 1\,. \tag{13.2}$$

The analytical solution to (13.2) takes the form

$$w_{\mathrm{MV}} = \frac{\Sigma^{-1}\mathbf{1}}{\mathbf{1}'\Sigma^{-1}\mathbf{1}},$$

which leads to the variance

$$\sigma^2 = w_{\mathrm{MV}}'\,\Sigma\,w_{\mathrm{MV}} = \frac{1}{\mathbf{1}'\Sigma^{-1}\mathbf{1}}$$

of the GMVP return. The distribution for the moment estimator of the GMVP return variance, denoted by $\hat{\sigma}^2$, is

$$\hat{\sigma}^2 = \frac{1}{\mathbf{1}'\widehat{\Sigma}^{-1}\mathbf{1}} \sim \sigma^2\,\frac{\chi_{T-N}^2}{T-1}, \tag{13.3}$$

so that

$$\mathrm{E}(\hat{\sigma}^2) = \sigma^2 \frac{\mathrm{E}(\chi^2_{T-N})}{T-1} = \frac{T-N}{T-1}\sigma^2 \approx \left(1 - \frac{N}{T}\right)\sigma^2. \tag{13.4}$$

In the following, $Q := T/N$ is said to be the *effective sample size*. Given an estimate $\hat{\sigma}^2$ of the return variance of the GMVP, it follows that

$$\mathrm{E}\left(\frac{\hat{\sigma}^2}{\sigma^2}\right) \approx 1 - \frac{1}{Q}, \qquad Q > 1.$$

This means $\hat{\sigma}^2$ underestimates the true global minimum variance σ^2. The estimator $\hat{\sigma}^2$ is consistent only if $T/N \to \infty$. For example, when a medium-sized GMVP with $N = 20$ assets is estimated from $T = 60$ monthly return data, the true variance can be expected to be about 50 percent above its estimate.

Figure 13.1 demonstrates the importance of taking into account the effective sample size. With 60 months of return data at hand, denoted by $R_1, \ldots, R_{60}$, the estimation of Σ and w_{MV} is accomplished for various portfolio sizes N. In 25 repetitions, the estimated variance $\hat{\sigma}^2$ as well as its bias-corrected version

$$\hat{\sigma}^{2*} = \frac{Q}{Q-1} \cdot \hat{\sigma}^2$$

are calculated and averaged.

The given confidence interval indicates a large variability of the variance estimators. For $N = 15$, the average bias-corrected variance estimate amounts 1.4 percent on an annual basis, while the confidence interval on the level of 95 percent allows for values between 0.9 percent and 2.4 percent. With respect to the annualized portfolio return standard deviation or volatility, the given confidence interval allows for values between 9.6 percent and 15.8 percent.

There exist different contributions towards how to measure the degree of diversification in an existing portfolio of N risky assets. However, there are different concepts of diversification, and our first aim is to motivate our understanding of diversification. When saying that a portfolio is 'well diversified', one could expect the portfolio return to be immune against shocks created by a single or a few assets. In turn, this does not mean that the return shall not be subject to any fluctuations. As – by its very nature – the universe of risky assets is exposed to price fluctuations, up and downturns in the market will affect its value. As such, the task is to find some sensible benchmark which separates the level of variation induced by idiosyncratic shocks, defined as shocks generated by single assets, from the level of variation that is induced by the market as a whole and thus unavoidable.

In this context, it is also important to clarify what data a measure of diversification should depend upon. Given the portfolio w of N risky assets, we

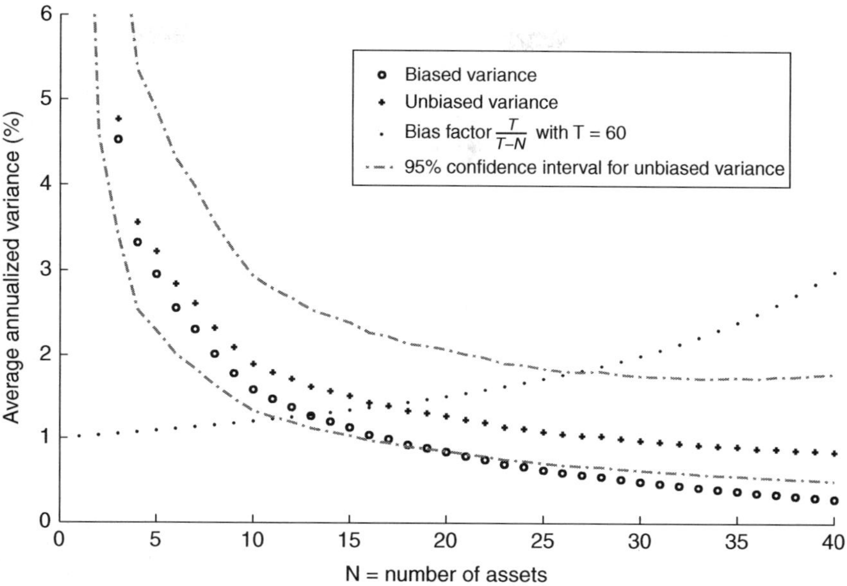

Figure 13.1 Biased and unbiased variance estimates

Notes: Biased and unbiased variance estimates of the *N*-asset GMVP. 60 monthly observations of the excess returns of *N* assets are available, with the assets being randomly selected from the pool of S&P 500 constituents in 2009. As *N* grows from 1 to 40, the bias of the variance estimate can be seen to sharply increase, as indicated by the dotted line. While the estimated GMVP's variance $\hat{\sigma}^2$ decreases with growing *N*, it falls below the 95 percent confidence interval for the true variance, σ^2, for $N > 20$ assets.

believe that a reliable measurement of the degree of diversification can only be achieved by incorporating the linear dependence structure among the assets. Thus, not only must w be taken into account, but also the information of how the portfolio constituents interact. This is done by evaluating the covariance matrix Σ of R.

Nevertheless, not all previous contributions towards diversification measurement are based on the above considerations. Indeed, the existing measures reveal a very different perception of what diversification is or should be. Approaches to diversification, which we have found in the literature, are given by:

(i) counting the number of assets (Evans and Archer, 1968; Fisher and Lorie, 1970);
(ii) using information theory (Bera and Park, 2008; Bouchaud et al., 1997; Woerheide and Persson, 1993);

(iii) calculating measures of concentration or disparity (Woerheide and Persson, 1993);
(iv) measures based on principal components (Partovi and Caputo, 2004; Rudin and Morgan, 2006); and
(v) bringing principal components and information theory together (Meucci, 2009).

13.3 A new measure of diversification

13.3.1 Theoretical considerations

According to the Capital Asset Pricing Model or Arbitrage Pricing Theory the total variance of a portfolio return can be decomposed into a systematic and an unsystematic part. In this chapter we consider the variance of the GMVP as the systematic risk of the given asset universe, since there is no other portfolio with lower return variance. Hence, the residual part of the return variance of some portfolio w is considered as 'unsystematic' and our measure of diversification corresponds to the ratio between the systematic risk (on the market) and the total risk of the given portfolio, that is,

$$\mathcal{D}(w) := \frac{\text{smallest possible variance on the market}}{\text{actual variance of } w}$$

$$= \frac{\text{variance of the GMVP}}{\text{actual variance of } w} = \frac{1/(\mathbf{1}'\Sigma^{-1}\mathbf{1})}{w'\Sigma w}.$$

We believe that $\mathcal{D}$ is a natural measure, as it yields the ratio of non-diversifiable risk to the total risk of the portfolio return. In practice, the portfolio selection process is often a combination of qualitative and quantitative analyses, resulting in portfolios that are subject to investor-specific constraints such as weight restrictions or even legal constraints. For portfolios constructed in this manner, the information of how much removable risk is still contained when compared to the GMVP, which satisfies the budget constraint only, might be valuable to the investor.

It is noteworthy, though, that at this stage, the measure $\mathcal{D}$ is a theoretical construct. This is because the covariance matrix Σ is unknown to the investor. Estimating the parameter Σ introduces estimation error. In contrast to previous studies on diversification, we explicitly account for the estimation error. Since there are no restrictions for the portfolio weights, except that they must sum up to one, the weights are allowed to be negative. Thus it should be noted that the GMVP might also have negative portfolio weights. A possible extension of $\mathcal{D}$, which includes convex portfolio weight constraints and allows for *strategies* but not only fixed portfolios, can be found in Frahm (2012).

For practical purposes, using a constrained minimum-variance portfolio (CMVP) as a benchmark might be even more interesting than using the unrestricted version, as short-selling constraints, for example, are a natural restriction for the private investor as well as for mutual funds. After the last financial crisis, some Euroland countries even consider short-selling constraints for all market participants. In Section 13.5 we make use of the short-selling constraint. So we define the diversification measure

$$\mathcal{D}^{+}(w) = \frac{\text{variance of the CMVP}}{\text{actual variance of } w}. \tag{13.5}$$

Since the variance of the CMVP cannot be smaller than the variance of the GMVP, it holds that $\mathcal{D}^{+}(w) \geq \mathcal{D}(w)$.

13.3.2 Statistical properties

Estimation error is a prominent phenomenon in modern research on portfolio theory, mostly in connection with the expected returns of the assets. Chopra and Ziemba (1993) find that errors in estimating the means are up to four times more harmful than errors in estimating the variances, and up to ten times more harmful than estimation errors in covariances. More recent research also reveals that variances estimated from historical observations might contain large estimation errors (Jagannathan and Ma, 2003; Ledoit and Wolf, 2003; Pafka and Kondor, 2003). In Section 13.2.2 it has been shown that the basic level of return variation can be drastically underestimated by the estimator $\hat{\sigma}^2$ for the return variance of the GMVP. It is worth emphasizing that this phenomenon still holds if the number T of observations and the number N of assets grow to infinity such that $T/N \to q < \infty$. The reliability of the variance estimator crucially depends on the effective sample size $Q = T/N$. Thus, a detailed examination of the measure $\mathcal{D}$ with regard to its susceptibility to estimation error is necessary.

The estimator for $\mathcal{D}(w)$ is defined by

$$\widehat{\mathcal{D}}(w) = \frac{\hat{\sigma}^2}{\hat{\sigma}_w^2} = \frac{1/(\mathbf{1}'\widehat{\Sigma}^{-1}\mathbf{1})}{w'\widehat{\Sigma}w}. \tag{13.6}$$

The same definition holds with respect to the constrained measure of diversification, that is, $\mathcal{D}^{+}(w)$, as defined by (13.5).

Following Frahm and Memmel (2010, Theorem 9), it turns out that

$$\widehat{\mathcal{D}}(w) \sim \left\{1 + \frac{N-1}{T-N} F_{N-1,T-N}(\lambda)\right\}^{-1}, \tag{13.7}$$

where $F_{\nu_1,\nu_2}(\lambda)$ denotes a noncentral F-distribution with noncentrality parameter λ, ν_1 numerator and ν_2 denominator degrees of freedom. The noncentrality parameter is given by

$$\lambda = \{\mathcal{D}^{-1}(w) - 1\}\, \chi^2_{T-1},$$

which is a stochastic quantity in the present context. More precisely,

$$F_{N-1,T-N}(\lambda) = \frac{\chi^2_{N-1}(\lambda)/(N-1)}{\chi^2_{T-N}/(T-N)},$$

where $\chi^2_{N-1}(\lambda)$ has a noncentral χ^2-distribution conditional on λ and $\chi^2_{N-1}(\lambda)$ and χ^2_{T-N} are conditionally independent.

For analyzing the asymptotic properties of $\widehat{\mathcal{D}}(w)$ recall that

$$\widehat{\mathcal{D}}(w) = \frac{\hat{\sigma}^2}{\hat{\sigma}^2_w} = \frac{\sigma^2}{\sigma^2_w}\frac{\chi^2_{T-N}/(T-1)}{\chi^2_{T-1}/(T-1)} = \mathcal{D}(w)\,\frac{\chi^2_{T-N}}{\chi^2_{T-1}}.$$

This means $\widehat{\mathcal{D}}(w)$ is a consistent estimator for $\mathcal{D}(w)$ as $T \to \infty$, given a constant number of assets. Interestingly, this does not hold if $N \to \infty$ such that $T/N \to q$, where $1 \le q < \infty$. In that case $\widehat{\mathcal{D}}(w)$ tends to $(1-q^{-1})\mathcal{D}(w)$ but the modified estimator

$$\widehat{\mathcal{D}}^*(w) = \frac{\widehat{\mathcal{D}}(w)}{1-Q^{-1}}, \qquad Q = \frac{T}{N},$$

is asymptotically unbiased even in the high-dimensional case.

13.4 Testing for variance and diversification

13.4.1 Variance tests

In the following we will give an overview of hypothesis tests for variances. Let $0 < \alpha < 0.5$ be any significance level, for example $\alpha = 0.01, 0.05$ or 0.10. It is assumed that the investor has historical return data of length T at hand, from which he estimates the covariance matrix Σ. Moreover, the historical return data $R_1,\ldots,R_T$ are assumed to stem from a multivariate normal distribution.

13.4.1.1 Testing the variance of a single portfolio

Consider the hypotheses

$$H_0 : \sigma^2_w \ge \tau^2 \qquad \text{vs.} \qquad H_1 : \sigma^2_w < \tau^2.$$

The finite-sample test statistic for this problem is

$$S_w := (T-1)\,\frac{\hat{\sigma}^2_w}{\tau^2} \sim \chi^2_{T-1}.$$

Thus, H_0 can be rejected whenever $S_w < F^{-1}_{\chi^2_{T-1}}(\alpha)$.

Now consider the hypotheses

$$H_0 : \sigma^2 \ge \tau^2 \qquad \text{vs.} \qquad H_1 : \sigma^2 < \tau^2,$$

where σ^2 denotes the variance of the GMVP. The finite-sample test statistic now reads

$$S := (T-1)\frac{\hat{\sigma}^2}{\tau^2} \sim \chi^2_{T-N}.$$

The null hypothesis is rejected whenever $S < F^{-1}_{\chi^2_{T-N}}(\alpha)$. Note that N, (the number of assets) plays a crucial role when testing the global minimum variance.

13.4.1.2 *Testing the difference of two variances*

Now let v and w be two arbitrary portfolios of N assets satisfying the budget constraint and consider the hypotheses

$$H_0 : \sigma_v^2 \geq \sigma_w^2 \qquad \text{vs.} \qquad H_1 : \sigma_v^2 < \sigma_w^2,$$

where σ_v^2 and σ_w^2 denote the variances of the portfolios v and w, respectively. Zhang (1998) and Memmel (2004, p. 140) give the test statistic for the variance difference,

$$t_{T-2} = \sqrt{\frac{T-2}{4}}\,\frac{\hat{\sigma}_v^2 - \hat{\sigma}_w^2}{\sqrt{\hat{\sigma}_v^2\hat{\sigma}_w^2 - \hat{\sigma}_{v,w}^2}}.$$

Here $\hat{\sigma}_v^2$ and $\hat{\sigma}_w^2$ are the sample variances of the portfolio returns of v and w, $\hat{\sigma}_{v,w}$ is the sample covariance between both returns, and t_{T-2} denotes Student's t-distribution with $T-2$ degrees of freedom. Thus, H_0 can be rejected whenever $t_{T-2} < F^{-1}_{t_{T-2}}(\alpha)$.

Another interesting question might be whether – in terms of variance – it is sufficient to hold a portfolio w of N assets or better to search for the GMVP. Consider the hypotheses

$$H_0 : \sigma^2 = \sigma_w^2 \qquad \text{vs.} \qquad H_1 : \sigma^2 < \sigma_w^2. \tag{13.8}$$

The corresponding finite-sample test statistic (Memmel, 2004, p. 94) reads

$$F_{N-1,T-N} = \frac{T-N}{N-1}\left(\frac{\hat{\sigma}_w^2}{\hat{\sigma}^2} - 1\right) = \frac{T-N}{N-1}\left(\widehat{\mathcal{D}}^{-1}(w) - 1\right),$$

so that H_0 can be rejected whenever the F-statistic is greater than $F^{-1}_{F_{N-1,T-N}}(1-\alpha)$.

13.4.2 The diversification test

With the finite sample distribution (13.7) of our diversification measure $\mathcal{D}$ at hand, it is possible to test whether some portfolio w attains a certain degree of diversification. For $\delta \in \,]0,1]$, the hypotheses are given by

$$H_0 : \mathcal{D}(w) < \delta \qquad \text{vs.} \qquad H_1 : \mathcal{D}(w) \geq \delta. \tag{13.9}$$

The critical values for this test can be approximated numerically. This is done by applying a Monte Carlo simulation of

$$\left\{1+\frac{N-1}{T-N}F_{N-1,T-N}(\lambda)\right\}^{-1} \qquad \text{with} \qquad \lambda=(\delta^{-1}-1)\,\chi^2_{T-1}\,.$$

Note that for $\delta = 1$ the diversification test is equivalent to the test (13.8) for the variance difference between the GMVP and the portfolio w.

13.5 Empirical study

The portfolio $w_{\mathrm{N}} = \mathbf{1}/N$, where equal fractions of wealth are allocated to each of the N assets, is said to be the *naive* or *equally-weighted portfolio*. This section gives empirical results for the levels of variance measured in equally-weighted as well as minimum-variance portfolios. We consider a broad basis of S&P 500 constituents, which have been obtained from the CRSP database. For each year between 1965 and 2009, all constituents that had a continuous return history of 120 months were downloaded, yielding a maximal number N of assets between 335 (in 1965) and 461 (in 1983). After retrieving the data from CRSP, the monthly asset returns were converted into excess returns using the 3-month treasury bills for the corresponding months.

Despite these large numbers of available assets, one must keep in mind that estimation of the covariance matrix becomes meaningless for practical purposes, once the number of assets exceeds the number of monthly observations of returns. Even for the case $T > N$ but $T/N \ll \infty$, the variance estimated for the GMVP turns out to be highly unreliable (see Section 13.2).

13.5.1 Evaluation of the naive portfolio

The return variance σ^2_{N} of the naive portfolio reads

$$\sigma^2_{\mathrm{N}} = \frac{\mathbf{1}'\Sigma\,\mathbf{1}}{N^2} = \alpha_N\,\frac{N-1}{N} + \beta_N\,N^{-1}$$

where

$$\alpha_N := \frac{1}{N(N-1)}\sum_{i=1}^{N}\sum_{j\neq i}^{N}\sigma_{ij} \qquad \text{and} \qquad \beta_N := \frac{1}{N}\sum_{i=1}^{N}\sigma_i^2$$

denote the average variances and covariances of the asset returns, respectively. Hence, if $\alpha_N \to \alpha$ and $\beta_N \to \beta$ with $N \to \infty$, it holds that $\sigma^2_{\mathrm{N}} \to \alpha$. This means for a growing number N of portfolio constituents, the impact of their individual variances vanishes, and the overall portfolio variance becomes the average of the constituents' covariances.

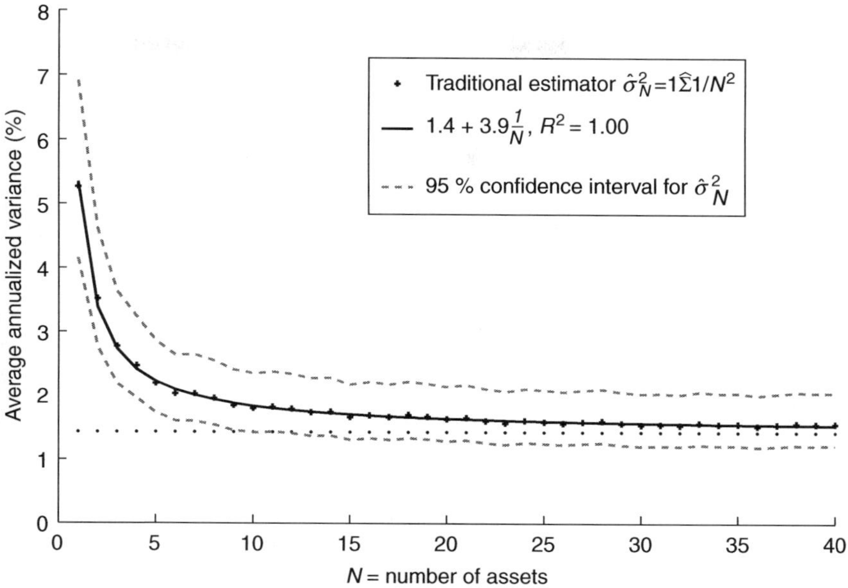

Figure 13.2 Variances of naive portfolios in 1965

Notes: Average return variance of naive portfolios vs. the number N of assets. In line with the theory, the average variance seems to decrease by the rate N^{-1} towards some basic level of variance. S&P 500 constituents from 1965 are used to randomly build equally-weighted portfolios of size N, for N between 1 and 40.

Figures 13.2 and 13.3 show the average variances of naive portfolios as a function of N, with N ranging between 1 and 40. For each end of the years between 1965 and 2009, and for each N between 1 and 40, a total number of 100 naive portfolios are constructed. The constituents of each of these portfolios are randomly drawn (without replacement) from the S&P 500 stocks of the respective year. The average variance $\overline{\sigma}^2_{\mathrm{N}}$ for each period is calculated by the average of the 100 sample variances of the naive portfolios. The data used for the variance estimation consists of 120 monthly excess returns. Afterwards, a linear-regression model of the form

$$\overline{\sigma}^2_{\mathrm{N}} = \alpha + \beta N^{-1} + \epsilon$$

is fitted to the data for each period. Both figures show that, on average, the linear-regression model for the return variance of naive portfolios provides a good fit.

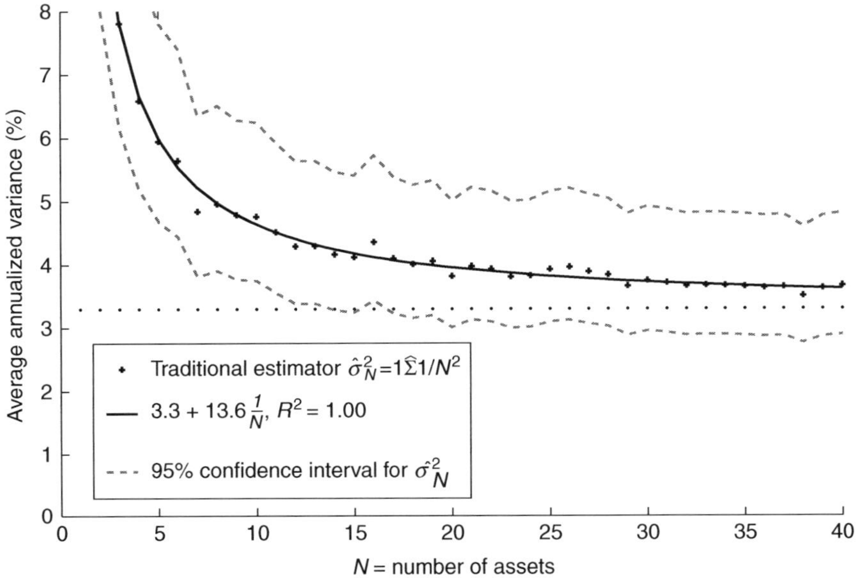

Figure 13.3 Variances of naive portfolios in 2009

Notes: Average return variance of naive portfolios vs. the number N of assets. In line with the theory, the average variance seems to decrease by the rate N^{-1} towards some basic level of variance. S&P 500 constituents from 2009 are used to randomly build equally-weighted portfolios of size N, for N between 1 and 40.

13.5.2 Evaluation of the global minimum-variance portfolio

It can be expected that the average estimated variance of the GMVP decreases with the number of assets, even though, as pointed out by equation 13.4, the estimated variance is heavily biased, especially when the effective sample size $Q = T/N$ is small (see also Figure 13.1). Thus, the gap between the average estimated return variance of the N-asset GMVP and its unbiased counterpart increases for growing N.

Comparing the periods 1965 and 2009, as carried out in Figures 13.4 and 13.5, the basic variance levels are different. While in 1965, a 40-asset GMVP had an average variance of 0.75 percent, the 2009 unbiased estimate is about 1.2 percent. Finally, Figure 13.6 contains the average variances of the 40-asset naive portfolios and Figure 13.7 the corresponding unbiased estimates of the 40-asset GMVP variance for all years between 1965 and 2009.

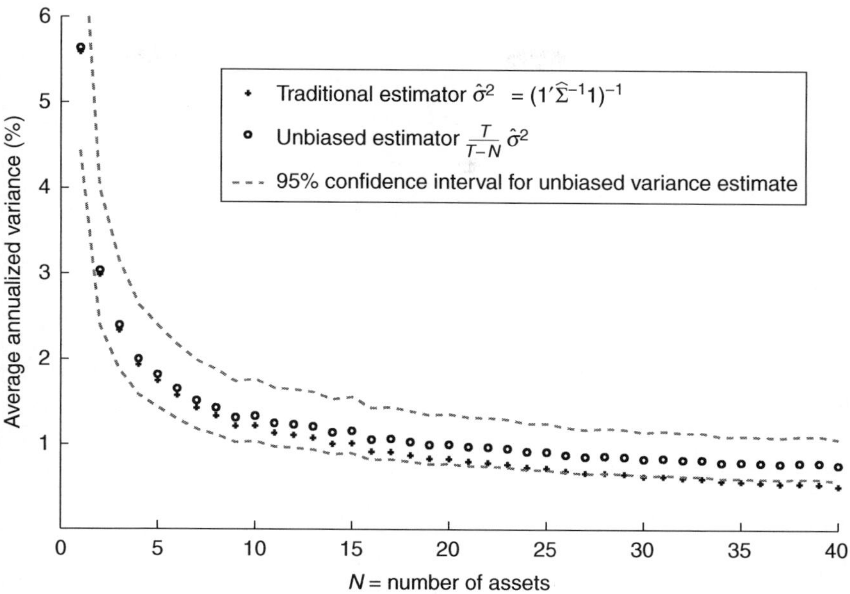

Figure 13.4 Variances of global minimum-variance portfolios in 1965

Notes: Average return variance of N-asset GMVPs vs. the number N of assets in 1965. The average variance seems to decrease towards some relatively low level of variance. The growing discrepancy between the variance estimates for higher N stems from the bias that depends crucially on the portfolio size N.

13.5.3 How well are naive portfolios diversified?

Figure 13.8 shows the average values of $\widehat{\mathcal{D}}(\mathbf{1}/i)$, that is, the degree of diversification of the naive i-asset portfolio as i increases from 1 to 20. The diversification measure is calculated with respect to a universe of 20 assets. In spite of the general perception that a naive portfolio with many constituents is well diversified, it is apparent that, even for 20 assets, about 70 percent of the total return variation is due to unsystematic risk. It can be observed also that a portfolio which is concentrated on a few assets only has an inferior diversification than a portfolio spread among a large number of assets.

In Section 13.3 it was already mentioned that the minimum-variance portfolio can be restricted to non-negative portfolio weights. This is a common restriction to private investors and mutual fund managers, and as such, leads to a more realistic 'benchmark'. The minimum-variance portfolio under the short-selling constraint leads to a return variance which is greater than the return variance of the GMVP and so Figure 13.8 reveals that $\mathcal{D}^{+}(\mathbf{1}/i) > \mathcal{D}(\mathbf{1}/i)$. Nevertheless, even with this modification, the naive portfolio still contains a relatively large amount of unsystematic risk. Another interesting fact is

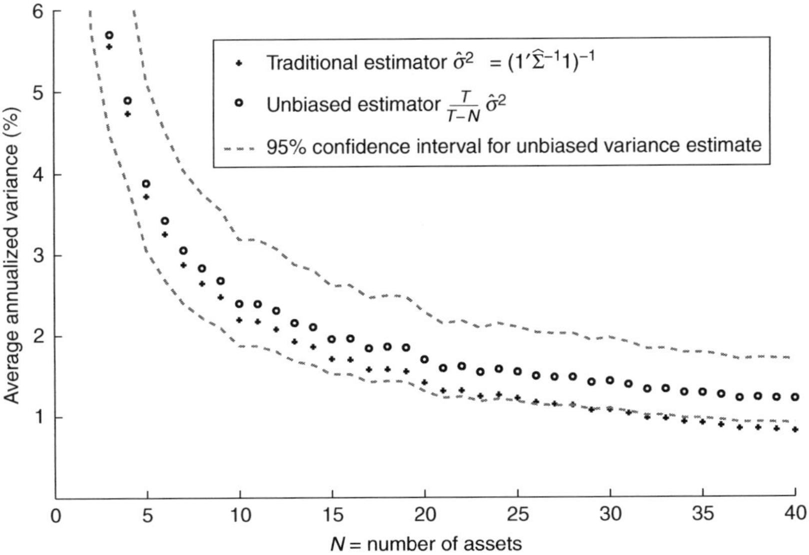

Figure 13.5 Variances of global minimum-variance portfolios in 2009

Notes: Average return variance of N-asset GMVPs vs. the number N of assets in 2009. The average variance seems to decrease towards some relatively low level of variance. The growing discrepancy between the variance estimates for higher N stems from the bias that depends crucially on the portfolio size N.

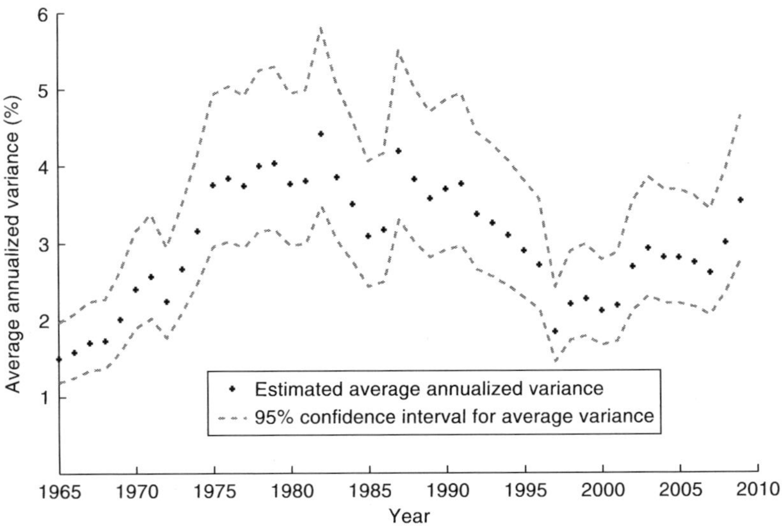

Figure 13.6 Average variance of 40-asset naive portfolios

Notes: Average return variance of 40-asset naive portfolios over the last five decades. The estimates are obtained by using 120 months of excess return data for each year. For example, the variance estimate for 1965 is calculated on the basis of excess returns from January 1956 to December 1965.

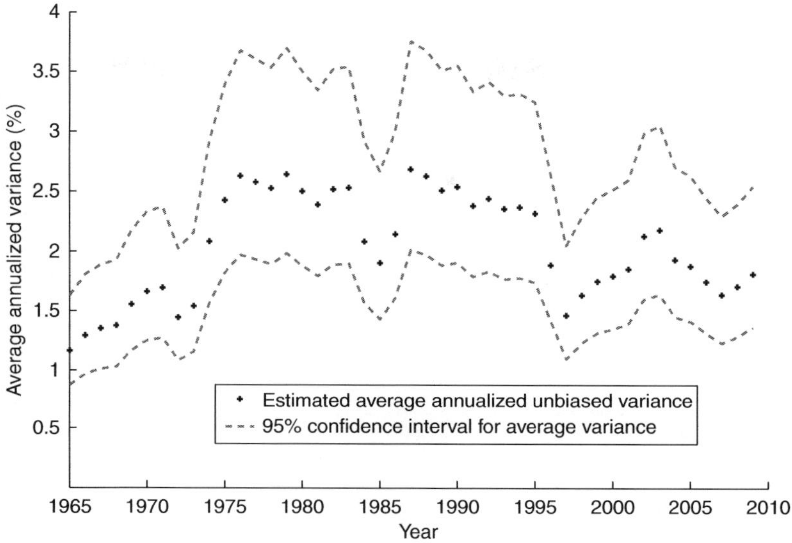

Figure 13.7 Average variance of 40-asset global minimum-variance portfolios

Notes: Average return variance of 40-asset GMVPs over the last five decades. The estimates are obtained by using 120 months of excess return data for each year. For example, the variance estimate for 1965 is calculated on the basis of excess returns from January 1956 to December 1965.

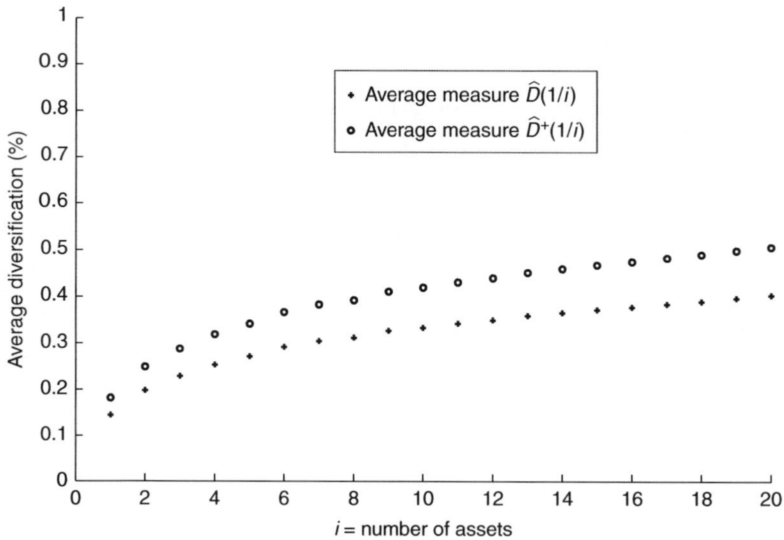

Figure 13.8 Diversification of equally-weighted portfolios in 2009

Notes: Average diversification of an i-asset naive portfolio. It relates the return variance of a 20-asset minimum variance portfolio to the return variance of an i-asset naive portfolio. Underlying data are 120 monthly excess returns from randomly chosen S&P 500 constituents in 2009.

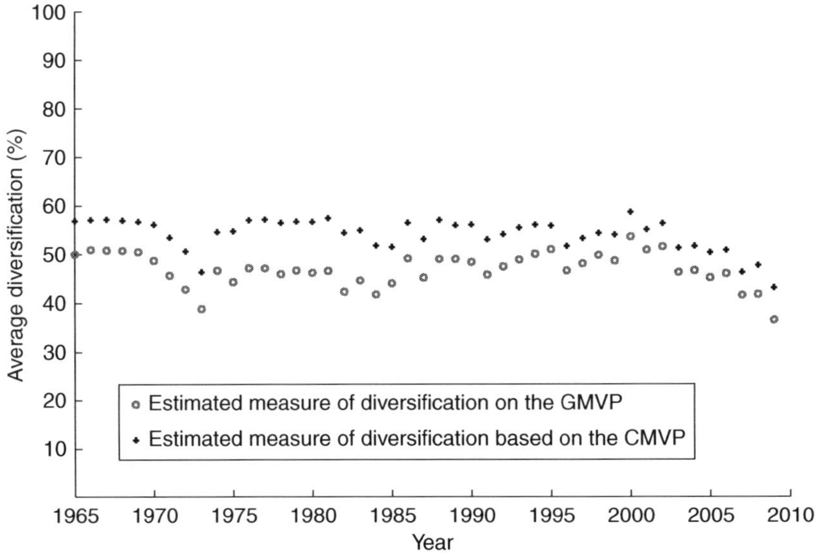

Figure 13.9 Diversification of equally-weighted portfolios from 1965 to 2009

Notes: Average diversification of a 20-asset naive portfolio for each year between 1965 and 2009. It relates the return variance of a 20-asset GMVP to the return variance of a 20-asset naive portfolio. To obtain an average value, this procedure is repeated 100 times. Underlying data are 120 monthly excess returns from randomly chosen S&P 500 constituents in each year in range.

shown in Figure 13.9. The average value of diversification lies between 30 percent and 50 per cent, with a sharp decline in recent years.

13.6 Conclusion

The focus of quantitative portfolio optimization has shifted away from the traditional sample-based mean-variance approach. Especially, the estimation of expected returns is left to analysts who generate qualitative forecasts based on fundamental data rather than historical returns. By contrast, the empirical measurement of the variance of asset returns remains of great interest to the finance industry. In recent years, minimum-variance portfolios have gained attraction not only from the academic, but also from the practical point of view.

The fact that there is only a small amount of work available about how to measure the diversification effect, which is the basic tenet of Markowitz's work, is surprising. We introduced a measure of diversification which relates the systematic risk of a portfolio to its total risk. Its finite-sample properties as well as asymptotic properties have been discussed. Different tests for the variance of single portfolios as well as the variance difference between two portfolios have been presented. The given results are exact in finite samples and useful when analyzing the portfolio return variance, the difference or even the ratio of portfolio return variances.

Our empirical study reconfirms the validity of former empirical studies on the change of regimes of overall market volatility. The basis for the empirical part is provided by monthly data of the S&P 500 constituents from the last five decades. Nevertheless, our study shows that naive portfolios contain a relatively large amount of unsystematic risk which is not diversified away. This result holds even if diversification is related to the minimum-variance portfolio with short-selling constraints. Hence, it can be concluded that taking variances and covariances of asset returns into account still leads to a superior result compared to the equally-weighted portfolio. This statement, of course, implicitly assumes that variance minimization is the main goal of the investor.

References

Bera, A. K. and Park, S. Y. (2008). Optimal portfolio diversification using maximum entropy. *Econometric Reviews*, 27(4–6): 484–512.

Best, M. J. and Grauer, R. R. (1991). On the sensitivity of mean-variance-efficient portfolios to changes in asset means: some analytical and computational results. *The Review of Financial Studies*, 4(2): 315–42.

Black, F. and Litterman, R. (1992). Global portfolio optimization. *Financial Analysts Journal*, 48: 28–43.

Bouchaud, J.-P., Potters, M., and Aguilar, J.-P. (1997). Missing information and asset allocation. `http://econpapers.repec.org/RePEc:sfi:sfiwpa:500045`.

Chopra, V. K. and Ziemba, W. T. (1993). The effect of errors in means, variances, and covariances on optimal portfolio choice. *The Journal of Portfolio Management*, 19(2): 6–11.

DeMiguel, V., Garlappi, L., Nogales, F. J., and Uppal, R. (2009a). A generalized approach to portfolio optimization: improving performance by constraining portfolio norms. *Management Science*, 55(5): 798–12.

DeMiguel, V., Garlappi, L., and Uppal, R. (2009b). Optimal versus naive diversification: how inefficient is the $1/N$ portfolio strategy? *The Review of Financial Studies*, 22(5): 1915–53.

Evans, J. L. and Archer, S. H. (1968). Diversification and the reduction of dispersion: an empirical analysis. *The Journal of Finance*, 23(5): 761–7.

Fisher, L. and Lorie, J. H. (1970). Some studies of variability of returns on investments in common stocks. *The Journal of Business*, 43(2): 99–134.

Fletcher, J. (2011). Do optimal diversification strategies outperform the $1/N$ strategy in U.K. stock returns? *International Review of Financial Analysis*, 20: 375–85.

Frahm, G. (2011). The determinants of the risk functions of estimators for expected asset returns. Technical report, University of Cologne.

Frahm, G. (2012). Capital allocation under risk and uncertainty. Technical report, Helmut Schmidt University.

Frahm, G. and Memmel, C. (2010). Dominating estimators for minimum-variance portfolios. *Journal of Econometrics*, 159: 289–302.
Frahm, G., Wickern, T., and Wiechers, C. (2011). Multiple tests for the performance of different investment strategies. *Advances in Statistical Analysis*, 96: 343–83.
Jagannathan, R. and Ma, T. (2003). Risk reduction in large portfolios: why imposing the wrong constraints helps. *The Journal of Finance*, 58(4): 1651–84.
Jorion, P. (1986). Bayes-Stein estimation for portfolio analysis. *Journal of Financial and Quantitative Analysis*, 21(3): 279–92.
Klein, R. W. and Bawa, V. S. (1976). The effect of estimation risk on optimal portfolio choice. *Journal of Financial Econometrics*, 3: 215–31.
Ledoit, O. and Wolf, M. (2003). Improved estimation of the covariance matrix of stock returns with an application to portfolio selection. *Journal of Empirical Finance*, 10(5): 603–21.
Lintner, J. (1965). The valuation of risky assets and the selection of risky investments in stock portfolios and capital budgets. *The Review of Economics and Statistics*, 47(1): 13–37.
Markowitz, H. M. (1952). Portfolio selection. *The Journal of Finance*, 7(1): 77–91.
Memmel, C. (2004). *Schï£¡tzrisiken in der Portfoliotheorie*. PhD thesis, University of Cologne.
Meucci, A. (2009). Managing diversification. *Risk*, 22(5): 74–9.
Mossin, J. (1966). Equilibrium in a capital asset market. *Econometrica*, 34(4): 768–83.
Muirhead, R. J. (1982). *Aspects of Multivariate Analysis*. Wiley Series in Probability and Mathematical Statistics, New York.
Pafka, S. and Kondor, I. (2003). Noisy covariance matrices and portfolio optimization II. *Physica A*, 319: 487–94.
Partovi, M. H. and Caputo, M. (2004). Principal portfolios: recasting the efficient frontier. *Economics Bulletin*, 7(3): 1–10.
Rudin, A. M. and Morgan, J. S. (2006). A portfolio diversification index. *The Journal of Portfolio Management*, 32(2): 81–9.
Sharpe, W. F. (1966). Mutual fund performance. *The Journal of Business*, 39(1): 119–38.
Woerheide, W. and Persson, D. (1993). An index of portfolio diversification. *Financial Services Review*, 2: 73–85.
Zhang, S. (1998). Fourteen homogeneity of variance tests: when and how to use them. Anual Meeting of the American Educational Research Association (San Diego, CA, April 13–17).

14
Hedge Fund Portfolio Allocation with Higher Moments and MVG Models

Asmerilda Hitaj and Lorenzo Mercuri

14.1 Introduction

The well-known mean-variance model, see Markowitz (1952), despite its popularity and simplicity, is not able to capture the stylized facts of asset returns such as asymmetry and fat tails, which have an impact on portfolio selection, particularly when hedge funds are included.

For this reason, several researchers have proposed advances to the traditional mean variance model in order to include higher moments in the portfolio optimization task. For example, Athayde and Flores (2002) constructed the efficient frontier considering mean-variance-skewness-kurtosis. Alternatively, other authors proposed to approximate the asset return distribution using Gram-Charlier expansion (introduced in finance by Jarrow and Rudd (1982) and applied in portfolio allocation by Berkelaar et al. (2004)), Edgeworth series or Hermite polynomials (see Desmoulins-Lebeault (2006)), while Jondeau et al. (2007) used the Taylor expansion of the expected utility function truncated at the fourth order.

In these approaches, a crucial issue is the estimation of moments and comoments. As observed in Meucci (2005) two alternative methods can be applied. The first one is based on a non-parametric estimation (for instance, sample moments and comoments, constant correlation, see Elton and Gruber (1973), or shrinkage approaches, see Ledoit and Wolf (2003) and Hitaj et al. (2012)). The second is a parametric one where a joint asset return distribution is assumed. In the last case, the simplest assumption is the multivariate normal, which is consistent with the mean-variance model proposed by Markowitz. Recently, as happened for option pricing, the extension to the multivariate case of the Lévy distribution seems to be a natural way to replace the multivariate normal in portfolio allocation (see Barndorff-Nielsen (1997) for normal inverse Gaussian, Madan and Seneta (1990) for variance gamma, Blæ sild (1981) for generalized hyperbolic distribution).

In this chapter, we conduct an empirical analysis on a hedge fund portfolio allocation assuming Multivariate Variance Gamma (MVG henceforth) distribution for returns. The univariate Variance Gamma (VG) distribution can be generalized to a multivariate one in different ways. We consider the MVG with a common mixing density (see Madan and Seneta (1990) for the symmetric case and Cont and Tankov (2003) for generalization), the MVG proposed by Semeraro (2008) and the one proposed by Wang (2009). The first MVG model is characterized by the sharing of the same common mixing density that does not allow independence between assets. To overcome this limit, Semeraro proposed a new MVG model, which is a mixture of independent multivariate normals where the mixing random variable is a multivariate Gamma distribution. In this model the dependence structure is built through a multivariate mixing random vector. As observed in Wang (2009), the Semeraro model, once the marginal distributions are fixed, has only one free parameter that captures the dependence between returns. For this reason, exploiting the summation property of the VG, Wang proposed a MVG model with a more flexible dependence structure.

When dealing with portfolio allocation problem, we need a feasible estimation procedure. The direct optimization of the joint likelihood function has two main limits: the multivariate density does not have a simple formula and the number of parameters increases with the increasing of assets in the portfolio. For these reasons, in the empirical analysis, we use a two-step estimation procedure.

- The parameters that control the marginal distributions have been estimated, for each time series, using the EM algorithm proposed in Loregian et al. (2011).
- The remaining parameters are obtained minimizing the mean squared error between the empirical and theoretical covariance matrices.

This chapter is organized as follows: in Section 14.2, after a brief review of the Jondeau–Rockinger approach, we describe the main features of the three MVG models. In particular, we deeply analyze the covariance structure in the bivariate case. Section 14.3 is dedicated to the empirical analysis based on a portfolio composed of ten hedge funds indexes taken from Hedge Fund Research and conclusions.

14.2 Overview

14.2.1 Portfolio allocation with higher moments

The aim of an investor with a given utility function, $u(x)$, is to maximize the expected utility. This problem, in a static period, can be written as:

$$\begin{cases} \max\limits_{w_i} E[u(\sum_{i=1}^{N} w_i X_i)] \\ s.t. \\ \quad \sum_{i=1}^{N} w_i = 1 \\ \quad lb \leq w_i \leq ub \text{ for } i = 1, \dots, N, \end{cases} \tag{14.1}$$

where w_i is the weight associated to the *ith* asset, N is the number of assets in the portfolio, *lb* and *ub* are the lower and upper bounds[1] respectively.

Following the Jondeau–Rockinger approach, a natural way to introduce higher moments in equation (14.1) is to expand the utility function through Taylor series. The corresponding expected utility, under mild conditions, becomes:

$$E[u(W)] = \sum_{j=0}^{+\infty} u^{(j)}(E[X]) \frac{E[(X - E(X))^j]}{j}, \tag{14.2}$$

where $u^{(j)}(x)$ is the *jth* derivative of the utility function.

Assuming an investor with CARA utility and using the fourth order Taylor approximation, equation (14.1) can be written as:

$$\begin{cases} \max_{w_i} \; -e^{-\lambda\mu_p}\left[1 + \frac{\lambda^2}{2}\sigma_p^2 - \frac{\lambda^3}{6}s_p^3 + \frac{\lambda^4}{24}k_p^4\right] \\ s.t \;\; \sum_{i=1}^{N} w_i = 1 \\ 0 \le w_i \le 1, \end{cases} \tag{14.3}$$

where μ_p, σ_p^2, s_p^3, k_p^4 are respectively the mean, variance, skewness and kurtosis of the portfolio, calculated as:

$$\mu_p = \sum_{i=1}^{N} \mu_i w_i' = \mu\, w'$$

$$\sigma_p^2 = w\, M_2\;\; w'$$

$$s_p^3 = w\, M_3\; (w' \otimes w')$$

$$k_p^4 = w\, M_4\; (w' \otimes w' \otimes w'),$$

where M_2, M_3 and M_4 are the tensors matrices for covariance, coskewness and cokurtosis, respectively (see Jondeau and Rockinger (2006) for a definition of the tensors matrices).

In practice, to solve equation (14.3), the estimation of moments and comoments is crucial. For this reason, we find optimal weights using both sample estimators as well as those obtained assuming MVG distribution of returns. In the following, once the univariate VG has been introduced, we discuss the characteristics of each MVG model.

14.2.2 Univariate Variance Gamma distribution

The VG random variable is a normal variance mean mixture with Gamma mixing density defined as:

$$X := \mu_0 + \theta V + \sigma\sqrt{V}Z$$

with μ_0, $\theta \in \mathbf{R}$, $\sigma \in [0,\infty[$, $Z \sim \mathbf{N}(0,1)$ and $V \sim \Gamma(\alpha,1)$ independent[2] from Z. The VG density can be written in terms of the modified Bessel function of the third kind $K_n(x)$ as follows:

$$f(x) = \frac{\sqrt{2}\left(\frac{|x-\mu|}{\sqrt{\theta^2+2\sigma^2}}\right)^{\alpha-0.5}}{\sqrt{\pi}\sigma\Gamma(\alpha)} \exp\left(\frac{(x-\mu)\theta}{\sigma^2}\right) K_{\alpha-0.5}\left(\frac{|x-\mu|\sqrt{\theta^2+2\sigma^2}}{\sigma^2}\right).$$

As shown in Loregian et al. (2011), this density is well approximated by a finite mixture of normals and a simple historical estimation procedure can be implemented through the EM algorithm.

It is well known that VG distribution is able to capture skewness and kurtosis of returns. In particular if $\theta = 0$ the distribution is symmetric around μ_0 and it is possible to show that the asymmetry has the same sign of θ. The kurtosis is always greater than 3 and is a decreasing function of α. Moreover we obtain, as the limit case, the standard normal if we choose $\sigma = 1$, $\theta = 0$ and $\alpha \to +\infty$.

14.2.3 Multivariate Variance Gamma with common mixing density

The VG with a common mixing density (Model 1 henceforth) is a random vector X defined as:

$$X = \mu + \theta\ V + \sqrt{V}\ \Sigma^{1/2}\ Z$$

where $Z \sim N(0, I_N)$ is composed by N i.i.d standard normals, $V \sim \Gamma(\alpha,1)$ is a univariate Gamma independent of Z, $\mu \in R^N$, $\theta \in R^N$, and $\Sigma^{1/2}$ is a lower triangular matrix:

$$\Sigma_{ij}^{1/2} = \begin{cases} a_{ij} & \text{if } i \geq j \\ 0 & \text{otherwise.} \end{cases}$$

The total number of parameters is $\frac{N^2+5N+2}{2}$.

The main features of this model are as follows.

- The marginal distribution of each single component is a univariate VG.
- The sharing of the same parameter α does not allow independence between assets.
- The sign of covariance[3] depends on the values of θ_i and σ_{ij} for $i,j = 1,\ldots,N$.

In the following we discuss all the possible combinations between θ_i and σ_{ij}:

$$\begin{array}{lll}
\theta_i < 0\,,\,\theta_j < 0\ \ \&\ \sigma_{ij} > 0 \Rightarrow cov(X_i,X_j) > 0 & & \text{(a)} \\
\theta_i < 0\,,\,\theta_j < 0\ \ \&\ \sigma_{ij} < 0\ \& & \left\{\begin{array}{l} \theta_i\,\theta_j > |\sigma_{ij}| \Rightarrow cov(X_i,X_j) > 0 \\ \theta_i\,\theta_j < |\sigma_{ij}| \Rightarrow cov(X_i,X_j) < 0 \end{array}\right. & \begin{array}{l}\text{(b)}\\ \text{(c)}\end{array} \\
\theta_i < 0\,,\,\theta_j > 0\ \ \&\ \sigma_{ij} < 0 \Rightarrow cov(X_i,X_j) < 0 & & \text{(d)} \\
\theta_i < 0\,,\,\theta_j > 0\ \ \&\ \sigma_{ij} > 0\ \& & \left\{\begin{array}{l} |\theta_i\,\theta_j| > \sigma_{ij} \Rightarrow cov(X_i,X_j) < 0 \\ |\theta_i\,\theta_j| < \sigma_{ij} \Rightarrow cov(X_i,X_j) > 0 \end{array}\right. & \begin{array}{l}\text{(e)}\\ \text{(f)}\end{array} \\
\theta_i > 0, \theta_j > 0\ \ \&\ \sigma_{ij} > 0 \Rightarrow cov(X_i,X_j) > 0 & & \text{(g)} \\
\theta_i > 0, \theta_j > 0\ \ \&\ \sigma_{ij} < 0\ \& & \left\{\begin{array}{l} \theta_i\,\theta_j > |\sigma_{ij}| \Rightarrow cov(X_i,X_j) > 0 \\ \theta_i\,\theta_j < |\sigma_{ij}| \Rightarrow cov(X_i,X_j) < 0 \end{array}\right. & \begin{array}{l}\text{(h)}\\ \text{(i)}\end{array}
\end{array} \tag{14.4}$$

where $\sigma_{ij} = \sum_{h=1}^{min(i,j)} a_{i,h}a_{j,h}$.

According to the stylized facts, the distribution of an asset return is characterized by negative skewness, this means that $\theta_i < 0$. From a theoretical point of view, the variance of a portfolio decreases when its components are negatively correlated; this implies a restriction on the value of σ_{ij}, $|\sigma_{ij}| > \theta_i\,\theta_j$ (case 14.4.c), which can be seen as a limit of the model in describing the dependence structure.

The shape of the joint densities and the corresponding isolines are reported in Figures 14.1, 14.2 and 14.3 for different combinations of parameters.

We observe that, when $\theta_i = 0$ and $\theta_j = 0$, the covariance and σ_{ij} have the same sign. In the other cases the orientation of the isolines is consistent with the relations in equation (14.4). Moreover, the sign of θ_i, θ_j also determines the position of the densities with respect to the point (μ_i, μ_j).

14.2.4 Semeraro model

The Semeraro model is a mixture of independent multivariate normals in which the mixing variable is a Multivariate Gamma random vector such that the *ith* component is defined as:

$$G_i = Y_i + a_i Z$$

for $i = 1,\ldots,N$ and $a_i \geq 0$ where $Y_i \sim \Gamma(l_i, m_i)$ and $Z \sim \Gamma(n,k)$. The random vector X is a MVG model if each component is given by:

$$X_i = \mu_i + \theta_i G_i + \sigma_i \sqrt{G_i} W_i$$

where $W_1 \ldots W_N$ are independent standard normals.

To ensure the VG marginal distribution for each X_i, we need G_i to be a Gamma random variable. This is possible under two alternative constraints:

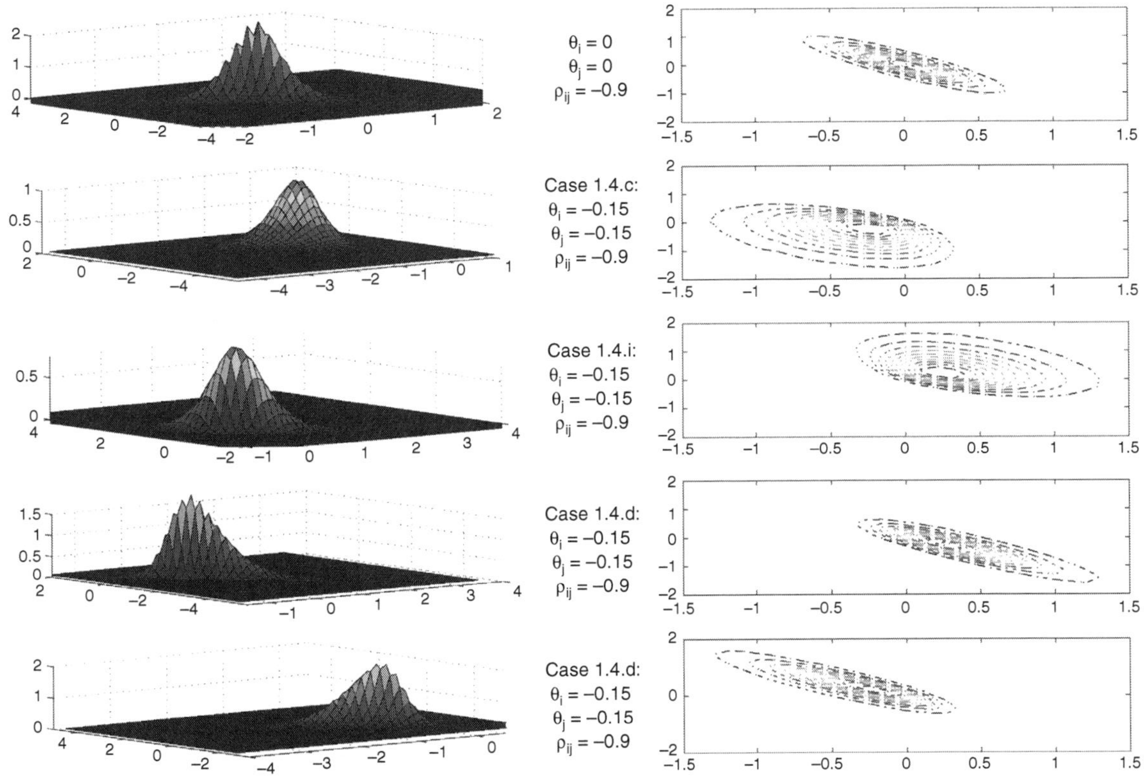

Figure 14.1 Joint densities and corresponding isolines combination 1. Behavior of the joint densities and the corresponding isolines varying the values of θ_i, θ_j, and fixing $\rho_{ij} = \frac{\sigma_{ij}}{\sqrt{\sigma_{ii}}\sqrt{\sigma_{jj}}} = -0.9$, $\mu_i = 0$, $\mu_j = 0$, $\sigma_i = 0.04$, $\sigma_j = 0.09$ and $\alpha = 3$

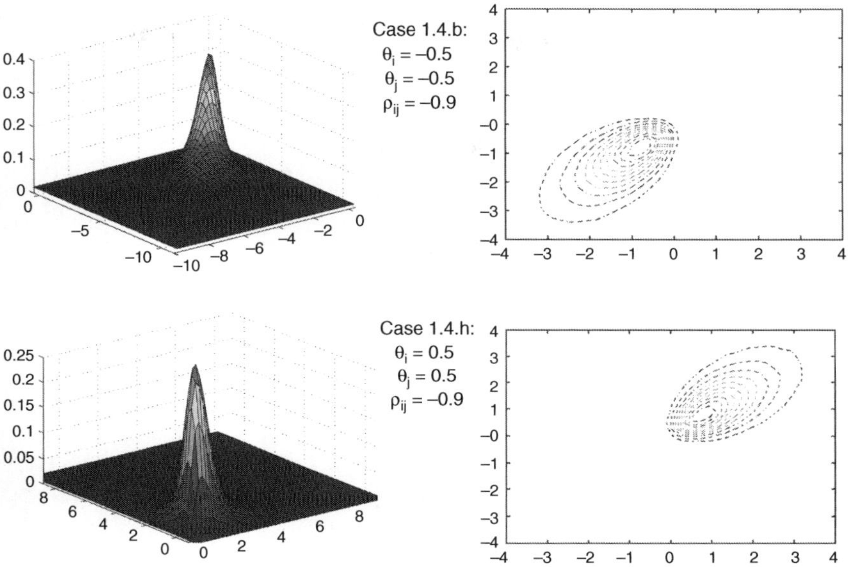

Figure 14.2 Joint densities and corresponding isolines combination 2. Behavior of the joint densities and the corresponding isolines varying the values of θ_i, θ_j, and fixing $\rho_{ij} = -0.9$, $\mu_i = 0$, $\mu_j = 0$, $\sigma_i = 0.04$, $\sigma_j = 0.09$ and $\alpha = 3$

$a_i = 0$ that corresponds to the independence case, or $a_i = k/m_i > 0$ which derives from the summation property of two independent Gamma with the same scale parameter. The main advantage of this model is its parsimony, indeed the number of parameters, $5N + 2$, increases linearly with respect to the number of assets.

As in the first model, in the following, we discuss the sign of covariance in the bivariate case which depends only on θ_i and θ_j:

$$\begin{aligned}
&\theta_i > 0, \theta_j > 0 \Rightarrow cov(X_i\ X_j) > 0 \quad &(a)\\
&\theta_i < 0, \theta_j < 0 \Rightarrow cov(X_i\ X_j) > 0 \quad &(b)\\
&\theta_i \gtrless 0, \theta_j \lessgtr 0 \Rightarrow cov(X_i\ X_j) < 0 \quad &(c,d).
\end{aligned} \tag{14.5}$$

Even if the Semeraro model is more parsimonious than Model 1, its ability in capturing the dependence structure is very limited. For instance, from equation (14.5) we observe that, if the skewness of both components is negative, we will never have a negative covariance. This can be observed even in Figure 14.4 where we report densities and isolines for different combination of θ_i and θ_j.

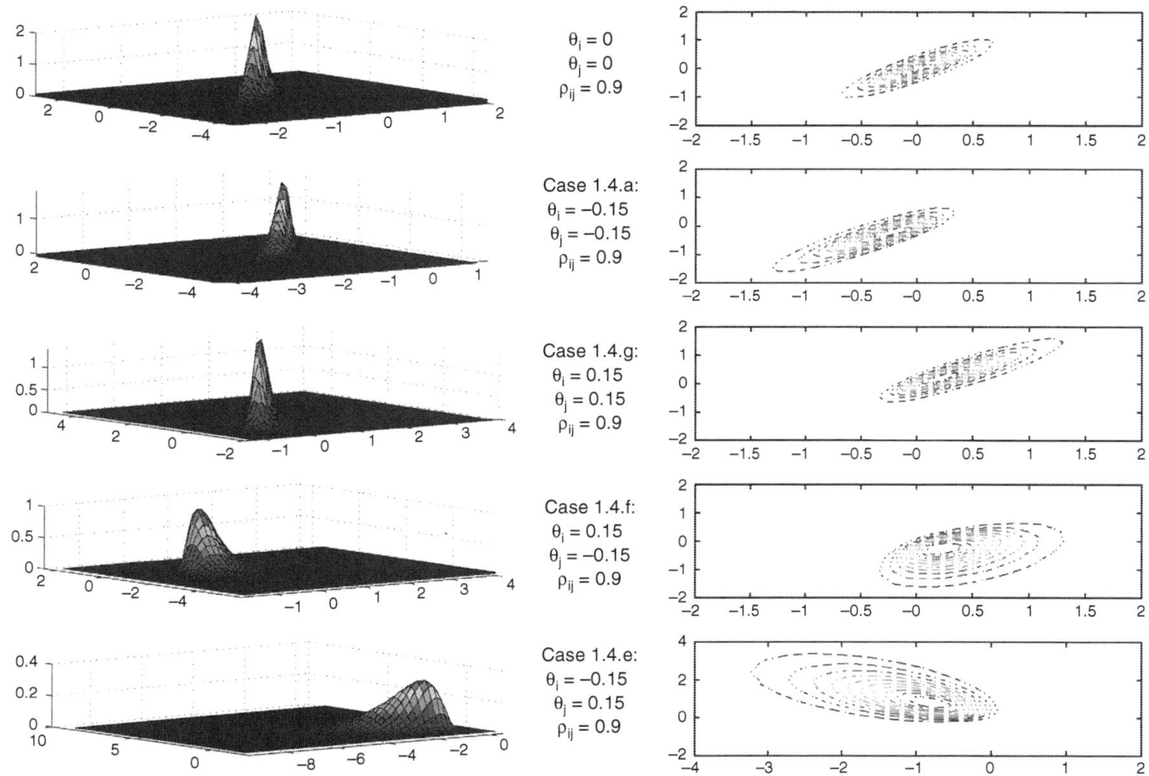

Figure 14.3 Joint densities and corresponding isolines combination 3. Behavior of the joint densities and the corresponding isolines varying the values of θ_i, θ_j, and fixing $\rho_{ij} = 0.9$, $\mu_i = 0$, $\mu_j = 0$, $\sigma_{ii} = 0.04$, $\sigma_{jj} = 0.09$ and $\alpha = 3$

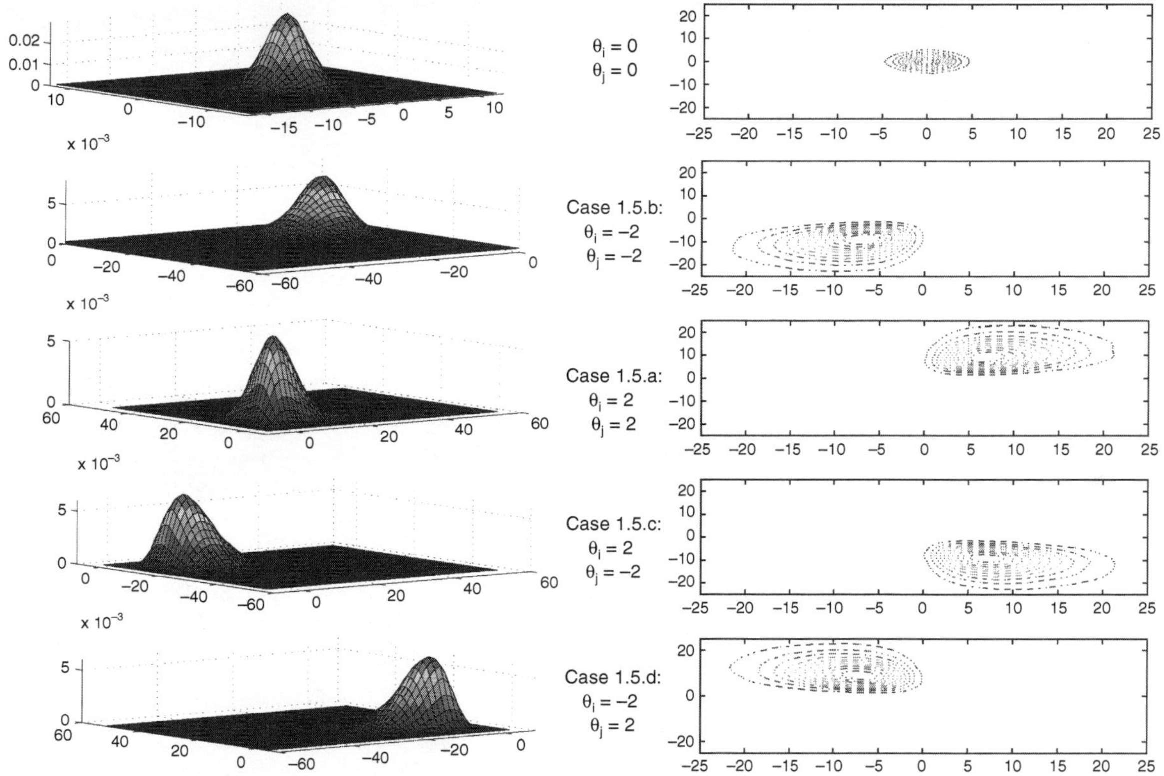

Figure 14.4 Joint densities and corresponding isolines combination 4. Behavior of the joint densities and the corresponding isolines varying the values of θ_i, θ_j, and fixing $\mu_i = 0$, $\mu_j = 0$, $\sigma_i = 1$, $\sigma_j = 1$, $l_i = 2.5$, $l_j = 4.5$, $a_i = 1.3$, $a_j = 1$, $n = 1.3$ and $k = 1$

14.2.5 Wang model

Taking into account the limit of Semeraro's model, Wang proposed a new MVG model exploiting the summation property of two independent VG. A vector X follows the Wang distribution if each component can be expressed as:

$$X_i = \mu_{i0} + A_i + Y_i \quad \forall i = 1, \ldots, N$$

where Y_i, Y_j and A_i are independent for $i, j = 1, .., N$ $(i \neq j)$ and are defined as:

$$Y_i = \theta_i\ G_i + \sigma_{G_i} \sqrt{G_i} W_i^Y$$

$$A_i = \theta_i\ V + \sqrt{V} D_i$$

where $D_i = \sum_{h=1}^{i} a_{ih}\ W_h^A$. $W_i^Y \sim N(0,1)$, $W_i^A \sim N(0,1)$, $V \sim \Gamma\left(\alpha_V, 1\right)$ and $G_i \sim \Gamma\left(\alpha_{G_i}, 1\right)$ are independent from each other. We note that the Wang model is the sum of Model 1 with a random vector Y, whose components are independent VG. To ensure that X_i is VG distributed, we require $\sigma_{G_i}^2 = \sum_{h=1}^{i} a_{ih}^2$, (see Wang, 2009). In total we have $\frac{N^2+7N+2}{2}$ parameters.

Even if the discussion on the sign of the covariance is the same as in Model 1, we note that the limit related to the sharing of the same mixing density is overcome.

To implement the approach in Jondeau and Rockinger (2006) for portfolio allocation, the moments and comoments have been derived recently by Hitaj and Mercuri (2012), for each MVG model. Moreover, they derived the closed form formula for the CARA expected utility using the moment generating function. These results are necessary for our empirical analysis.

14.3 Empirical analysis

We have considered a dataset composed of ten hedge funds indexes taken from Hedge Fund Research. These indexes are: 'Distressed Restructuring', 'Merger Arbitrage', 'Equity Market Neutral', 'Equal Weighted Strategies', 'Equity Hedge', 'Event Driven', 'Global Hedge Fund', 'Macro/CTA', 'Relative Value Arbitrage', 'FI-Convertible Arbitrage'. We have chosen these indexes since they have the longest time series. The returns are daily observed from 1 April 2003 to 3 October 2011. In total, for each index, we have 2145 observations.

To have an idea of the ability of the univariate VG distribution in capturing skewness and fat tails, we have selected the last year of observations and, in Figure 14.5, we report the empirical, the estimated VG and estimated normal densities for each component of the portfolio.

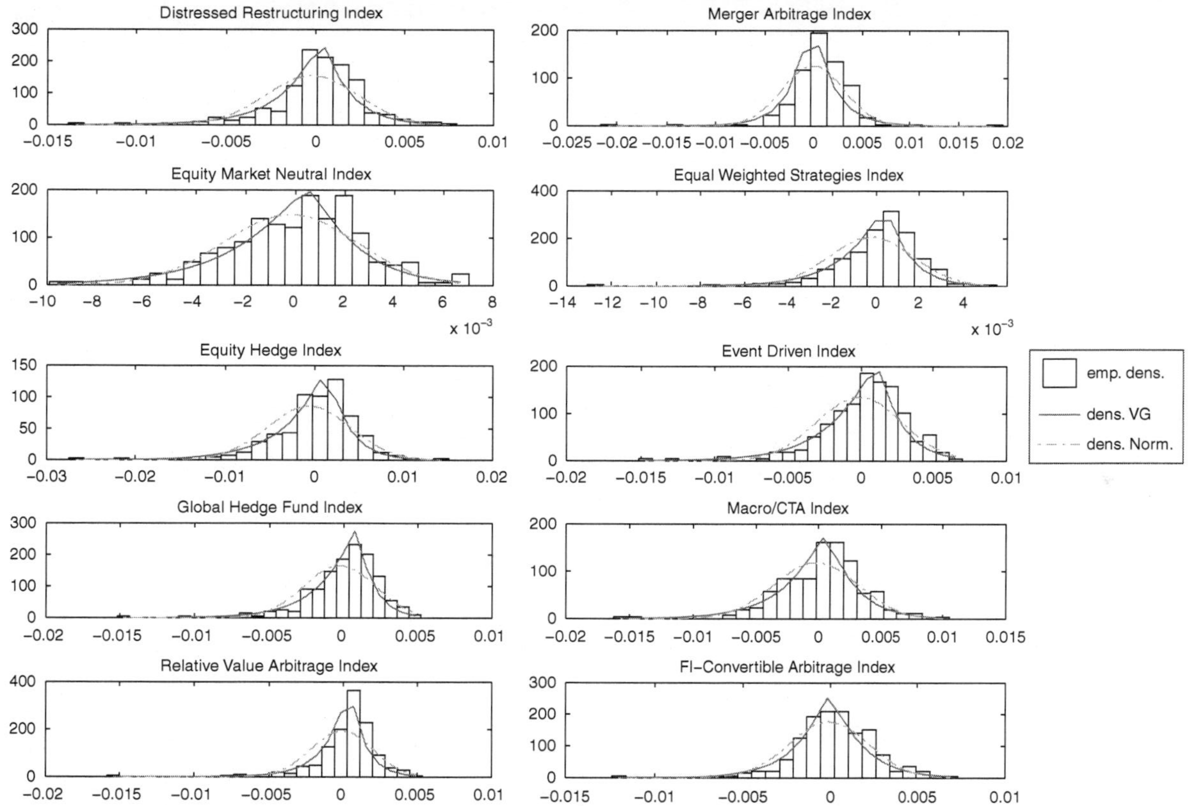

Figure 14.5 Estimated VG, estimated normal and empirical densities

The VG density seems to better describe the empirical distribution since it is more leptokurtic and asymmetric compared to the normal one. This is confirmed in Table 14.1, where the last two columns report the mean square error (MSE) between the empirical and the theoretical cumulative distributions for normal and VG respectively. In general, the lowest MSE is obtained using the VG distribution.

For portfolio allocation, we have used a rolling window strategy of six months in-sample and two months out-of-sample, meaning that, once we have estimated the parameters, we compute, for the in-sample windows, moments and comoments for each MVG model. We consider an investor with CARA utility function and different levels of risk aversion[4] λ. We use both the Jondeau–Rockinger approach with two and four moments and the analytical expected utility to find the in-sample optimal weights, which are kept constant until a new rebalance takes place. We compute the out-of-sample portfolio returns and use the monetary utility gain (MUG),[5] proposed by Ang and Bekaert (2002), to compare the pairwise portfolios obtained with different approaches.

We summarize the results obtained in Tables 14.2, 14.3 and 14.4. In particular, Table 14.2 compares, in terms of MUG, each MVG model with the well-known sample approach and the four moments versus two moments. Table 14.3 gives us an idea of the improvement, with respect to the analytical expected utility, when *4th* order Taylor expansion is used instead of *2nd* order. Table 14.4 reports, for each MVG model, the percentage of cases (in total 57) where the MUG is positive.

Table 14.1 General statistics for each index in the last year of observations

Statistics for each index						
Index	Annual mean	Annual std	Skew	Kurt	MSE N	MSE VG
Distressed Restructuring	−0.001	0.041	−3.222	47.162	0.016	0.001
Merger Arbitrage	0.047	0.049	1.450	61.739	0.017	0.005
Equity Market Neutral	−0.003	0.044	−0.193	19.277	0.035	0.019
Equal Weighted Strategies	0.014	0.031	−1.735	17.021	0.024	0.028
Equity Hedge	0.003	0.069	−0.832	8.309	0.007	0.001
Event Driven	0.036	0.050	−1.176	14.894	0.026	0.001
Global Hedge Fund	0.015	0.040	−1.283	11.554	0.060	0.003
Macro/CTA	0.017	0.070	−1.016	9.542	0.018	0.002
Relative Value Arbitrage	0.017	0.047	−1.646	36.185	0.056	0.001

Table 14.2 Percentage annual MUG for different levels of risk

	MVG vs. Sample MV			MVG vs. Sample MVSK			MVG MVSK vs. MVG MV			Sample MVSK vs. Sample MV
lambda	Model 1	Semeraro	Wang	Model 1	Semeraro	Wang	Model 1	Semeraro	Wang	Sample
4.25	−0.017	0.067	0.104	−0.029	0.061	0.085	−0.000	0.000	−0.007	0.012
7.75	0.129	0.042	0.105	0.123	0.036	0.099	0.001	−0.001	0.000	0.007
11.25	0.087	−0.095	0.076	0.083	−0.109	0.069	0.011	−0.000	0.008	0.014
14.75	0.124	−0.149	0.121	0.117	−0.162	0.111	0.004	−0.002	0.001	0.011

Notes: The column labeled 'MVG vs sample MV' presents the MUG obtained when we consider one of the MVG models vs. the sample approach in *2nd* order expansion for expected utility. The column labeled 'MVG vs. sample MVSK' reports the MUG obtained when we use one of the MVG models versus the sample approach in 4*th* order expansion for expected utility. The column labeled 'MVG MVSK vs. MVG MV' reports the MUG obtained when we use 4*th* order versus 2*nd* order expansion for expected utility using one of the MVG models. The column labeled 'sample MVSK vs sample MV' reports the MUG obtained when we use 4*th* order versus 2*nd* order expansion for expected utility using the sample approach.

Table 14.3 Percentage annual analytical MUG for different levels of risk

	MVG analytical vs. MVG MV			MVG analytical vs. MVG MVSK		
lambda	Model 1	Semeraro	Wang	Model 1	Semeraro	Wang
4.25	−0.00045	0.00049	−0.00072	0.00000	0.00015	0.00640
7.75	0.00087	−0.00062	−0.00034	−0.00002	0.00005	−0.00053
11.25	0.01131	−0.00022	0.00937	0.00034	0.00001	0.00105
14.75	0.00440	−0.00246	0.00280	0.00018	−0.00020	0.00188

Notes: For each MVG model, this table indicates the MUG obtained using the analytical versus *2nd* ('MVG analytical vs. MV') and *4th* ('MVG analytical vs. MVSK') order expansion for expected utility.

Table 14.4 Total percentage of positive MUG.

	MVG vs. sample MV	MVG vs. sample MVSK	MVG MVSK vs. MVG MV
Model 1	0.842	0.842	0.772
Semeraro	0.579	0.561	0.263
Wang	1.000	1.000	0.860

Notes: For each MVG model, this table reports the percentage of positive MUG on all λ.

Considering the results in the column labeled 'MVG vs. sample MV' (Table 14.2), the MUG is almost always positive for each MVG model. In particular, the Wang model always has positive MUG (Table 14.4). These results suggest that using a MVG model is an improvement over using the sample mean-variance approach. These conclusions are valid even when we compare a MVG model versus sample with four moments (see column labeled 'MVG vs sample MVSK' in Tables 14.2 and 14.4). We can conclude that the parametric approach seems to be preferred to the non parametric one.

The remaining question is to understand whether it is better, under the MVG assumption, to approximate the expected utility using the *2nd* or the *4th* order Taylor expansion. To analyze this question we consider the results in the column labeled 'MVG MVSK vs. MVG MV' (Tables 14.2 and 14.4) which suggest that the *4th* order approximation of the utility function generates better results than the *2nd* order one for Model 1 and Wang. In the Semeraro case, we have an unexpected result since the MUG is almost always negative. A possible explanation could be the fact that, as discussed above, the Semeraro model has a more limited ability in capturing the dependence structure between assets.

We conclude this chapter by analyzing the goodness of the approximation based on two or four moments versus analytical expected utility (Table 14.3). As expected, for each MVG model, adding moments in portfolio allocation approximates the true problem better. Indeed, the MUG is almost always closer to zero when four moments are considered instead of two.

Notes

1. In the empirical analysis we choose $lb = 10^{-4}$ and $ub = 0.7$.
2. We decide to use the same parametrization as in Loregian et al. (2011) which is equivalent to that in Madan and Seneta (1990).
3. The explicit formulae for moments and comoments have been derived by Hitaj and Mercuri (2012).
4. Here, λ ranges from 1 to 15 with a step of 0.25; in total we have 57 cases.
5. Let a and b be two different methodologies. The MUG is obtained by solving the following equation with respect to W_a:

$$\frac{1}{T}\sum_{t=1}^{T} -e^{-\lambda(1+r_t^b)} = \frac{1}{T}\sum_{t=1}^{T} -e^{-\lambda W_a(1+r_t^a)},$$

   where r_t^a and r_t^b are the portfolio returns obtained using a and b, respectively. The percentage MUG of b with respect to a is given by $MUG = (W_a - 1) * 100$. If $MUG > 0$ we prefer b instead of a and vice-versa when $MUG < 0$.

References

Ang, A. and Bekaert, G. (2002). International asset allocation with regime shifts. *Review of Financial Studies*, 15(4): 1137–87.

Athayde, G. and Flores, R. G. (2002). The portfolio frontier with higher moments: the undiscovered country. Computing in Economics and Finance 209, Society for Computational Economics.

Barndorff-Nielsen, O. E. (1997). Normal inverse Gaussian distributions and stochastic volatility modelling. *Scandinavian Journal of Statistics*, 24(1): 1–13.

Berkelaar, A. B., Kouwenberg, R., and Post, T. (2004). Optimal portfolio choice under loss aversion. *The Review of Economics and Statistics*, 86(4): 973–87.

Blæ sild, P. (1981). The two-dimensional hyperbolic distribution and related distributions, with an application to johannsen's bean data. *Biometrika*, 68(1): 251–63.

Cont, R. and Tankov, P. (2003). *Financial Modelling with Jump Processes*. Chapman & Hall/CRC Financial Mathematics Series.

Desmoulins-Lebeault, F. (2006). Gram-charlier expansions and portfolio selection in non-gaussian universes. In Jurczenko, J. F. and Maillet, B. B., editors, *Multi-Moment Asset Allocation and Pricing Model*, 79–112. John Wiley & Sons.

Elton, E. J. and Gruber, M. J. (1973). Estimating the dependence structure of share prices-implications for portfolio selection. *Journal of Finance*, 28(5): 1203–32.

Hitaj, A., Martellini, L., and Zambruno, G. (2013). Optimal hedge fund allocation with improved estimates for coskewness and cokurtosis parameters. *The Journal of Alternative Investments*, 14(3): 6–16.

Hitaj, A. and Mercuri, L. (2013). Portfolio allocation using multivariate variance gamma. *Financial Markets and Portfolio Management*, 27(1): 65–99.

Jarrow, R. and Rudd, A. (1982). Approximate option valuation for arbitrary stochastic processes. *Journal of Financial Economics*, 10(3): 347–69.

Jondeau, E., Poon, S.-H., and Rockinger, M. (2007). *Financial Modeling under Non-gaussian Distributions*. Springer Finance, Springer.

Jondeau, E. and Rockinger, M. (2006). Optimal portfolio allocation under higher moments. *European Financial Management*, 12(01): 29–55.

Ledoit, O. and Wolf, M. (2003). Improved estimation of the covariance matrix of stock returns with an application to portfolio selection. *Journal of Empirical Finance*, 10(5): 603–21.

Loregian, A., Mercuri, L., and Rroji, E. (2011). Approximation of the variance gamma model with a finite mixture of normals. *Statistics & Probability Letters*, 82(2): 217–24.

Madan, D. B. and Seneta, E. (1990). The variance-gamma (v. g.) model for share market returns. *Journal of Business*, 63(4): 511–24.

Markowitz, H. (1952). Portfolio selection. *The Journal of Finance*, 7(1): 77–91.

Meucci, A. (2005). *Risk and Asset Allocation*. Springer Finance, Springer.

Semeraro, P. (2008). A multivariate variance gamma model for financial applications. *International Journal of Theoretical and Applied Finance (IJTAF)*, 11(01): 1–18.

Wang, J. (2009). *The Multivariate Variance Gamma Process and Its Applications in Multi-asset Option Pricing*. PhD thesis, Faculty of the Graduate School of the University of Maryland.

15
The Statistics of the Maximum Drawdown in Financial Time Series

Alessandro Casati and Serge Tabachnik

15.1 Introduction

The maximum drawdown (MDD) in financial time series plays an important role in investment management and has been widely studied in the literature. MDD is associated with standards of performance measures such as Calmar or Sterling ratios. Various forms of portfolio optimization based on MDD have been considered (see for example A. Chekhlov and Zabarankin (2005)). In addition, Leal and de Melo Mendes (2005) have proposed a coherent risk measure possessing the properties required by Artzner et al., (1999) similar to the conditional value-at-risk: the maximum drawdown-at-risk $MDaR_{\alpha}$, which is just a quantile with exceedance probability α of the distribution of the maximum drawdown. Despite the widespread use of maximum drawdown among practitioners, financial economists have not paid much attention to this concept. It provides an alternative or complement to the other commonly used risk measures such as value-at-risk, which is still used extensively by the industry and regulatory standards for the calculation of risk capital in banking and insurance despite its well-known shortcomings. The evaluation of both MDD's expectation value and its probability density function (pdf) is of importance for various practical applications, especially when building a robust framework for risk management and capital allocation. This chapter is motivated by the need to gain insights into the statistical properties of the MDD for stochastic processes that, set aside from the academic example of the Brownian motion, are possibly closer to the stylized facts that characterize the real financial time series (see Rosario N. Mantegna, 2000; Cont, 2001; Bouchaud and Potters, 2003).

To our knowledge, analytical expressions of the distribution function of the MDD and of its expectation value have been derived in the limit of a Brownian motion with drift in Ismail et al. (2004a,b); however, these formula involve an infinite sum of integrals that requires a numerical estimate. Alternatively, a method based on the numerical solution of a PDE for computing the expected MDD in the Black-Scholes framework has been proposed in Pospisil and Vecer (2009). Here, a Monte Carlo code is proposed as a versatile tool to explore the higher-order statistics available through the pdf of the MDD in cases that are hardly analytically treatable. In particular, some relevant deviations with respect to the Brownian motion model are analyzed in order to quantify their impact on the statistics of the MDD: the increments of the underlying stochastic process (returns/log-returns) are not independent and present excess kurtosis (heavy tailed) and/or non zero skewness. The chapter is organized as follows. Section 15.2 examines arithmetic processes driven by independent and identically distributed (iid) random variables. The case of Brownian motion with drift provides the framework where the Monte Carlo simulations are presented and validated against the analytical predictions. Section 15.3 analyzes the MDD statistics for stochastic processes following a geometric model with iid increments. Section 15.4 removes the iid ansatz: a general autoregressive model is introduced for the conditional mean and volatility of the innovations. The statistics of the MDD are numerically evaluated when varying the parameters that control the correlation, the symmetry and the tails of the increments distribution. In Section 15.5, a parametric study is performed on the expectation value of the MDD as a function of a number of parameters of practical interest. Section 15.6 presents a comparison between the predictions of the MDD statistics and the historical time series for different asset classes. Finally, Section 15.7 reports the conclusions of this analysis.

15.2 Brownian motion with drift

The value of a portfolio S_t is here assumed to follow the SDE

$$dS_t = \mu dt + \sigma dW_t \tag{15.1}$$

where W_t is a Wiener process, $0 \leq t \leq T$ and both the mean μ and the volatility σ are finite and constant. The MDD is defined as

$$\text{MDD}_T = \max_{0 \leq t \leq T} D_t \qquad \text{with} \qquad D_t = \max_{0 \leq x \leq t} S_x - S_t, \tag{15.2}$$

D_t is the drawdown from the previous maximum value at time t. The behavior of the statistics of the MDD in this framework has been studied in Ismail et al. (2004a). An infinite series representation of its distribution function is derived in the case of zero, negative and positive drift, and formulas for the expectation values for the MDD are given. In the limit of $T \to \infty$, it is found that the T dependence of $E(\text{MDD})$ is logarithmic for $\mu > 0$, square root for $\mu = 0$ and linear for $\mu < 0$. Nevertheless, explicit analytical relations cannot be immediately derived: it is required to numerically evaluate special integral functions in the case of $E(\text{MDD})$, while the infinite series representation of the MDD distribution function involves the solution of particular eigenvalue conditions.

Here we prefer to employ a numerical simulation in order to compute the pdf of the MDD distribution function using a Monte Carlo scheme. One of the main advantages of this approach is the possibility to extend this method to different models for the underlying stochastic process. The Monte Carlo code simulates the discretized version of equation (15.1) using the Euler scheme

$$S_{i+1} = S_i + \mu\Delta t + \sigma\sqrt{\Delta t}X_i, \qquad (15.3)$$

where X_i are iid pseudo-random variables with normal distribution $\mathcal{N}(0,1)$, that is satisfying $E(X_i) = 0$ and $Var(X_i) = 1$; $\Delta t = T/N$, where T is the time in years and N is the number of time steps in the series. Here and in the remainder of this chapter the average return μ and volatility σ are expressed as annualized values. The code is employed to compute the MDD defined by equation (15.2). In order to verify the goodness of this numerical approach, the code is tested against the analytical predictions of the expectation value of the MDD derived in Ismail et al. (2004a). One of the goals of this verification is to reproduce the transition from the logarithmic to the square root and the linear scaling for $T \to \infty$ when changing the drift from $\mu > 0$ to $\mu = 0$ and $\mu < 0$ respectively.

The parameters of this test case are: $\mu = -0.1,\ 0, +0.1,\ \sigma = 0.2$ and $T = 1$ d, 1 m, 6 m, 1 y, 5y, 10 y, 30 y (1 year is considered as being composed of 260 working days). The series that are simulated contain $N = 2 \cdot 10^4$ time steps and each simulation considers the statistics of $M = 4 \cdot 10^4$ samples. The estimator of the expectation value of the MDD is the mean of the MDD samples generated by the code. Figure 15.1 summarizes the numerical estimates in comparison with the analytical predictions derived in Ismail et al. (2004a). The simulations are able to reproduce the analytical expectations for $\mu < 0$, $\mu = 0$ and $\mu > 0$ very well, with a relative error on $E(\text{MDD})$ which always stays below 1 per cent. Recalling the definition of equation (15.2), the MDD is derived from the drawdown process D_t. The latter is itself a Brownian motion reflected in its maximum; a rigorous justification of this statement can be found in Karatzas and Shreve (1997, p. 210) and Graversen and Shiryaev (2000). Hence, if one is interested in the distribution function of the maxima of D_t (the MDD), the extreme value theory (see Reiss and Thomas, 2007; Coles, 2004) provides some powerful insights. Thanks to the Fisher-Tippett theorem, it is expected that the distribution function of the MDD converges to a generalized extreme value distribution (GEV), whose

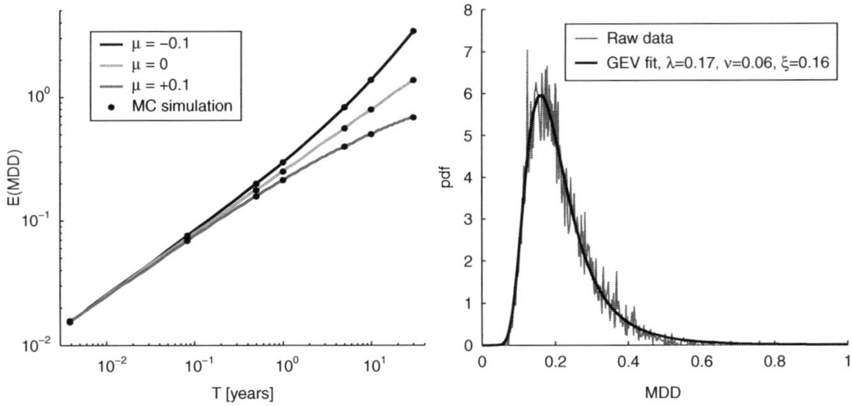

Figure 15.1 Numerical estimates of MDD

Notes: On the left: $E(\text{MDD})$ vs T, analytical expectations compared with the numerical results from the Monte Carlo simulations. On the right: pdf of the MDD obtained by the Monte Carlo simulation fitted to a GEV distribution ($\mu = 0.1$, $\sigma = 0.2$, $T = 1$ y).

density is

$$H_\xi(x) = \begin{cases} \dfrac{1}{\nu}\left(1+\xi\dfrac{x-\lambda}{\nu}\right)^{-\frac{1+\xi}{\xi}} \exp\left[-\left(1+\xi\dfrac{x-\lambda}{\nu}\right)^{-\frac{1}{\xi}}\right] & \xi \neq 0 \\ \dfrac{1}{\nu}e^{-\frac{x-\lambda}{\nu}} \exp\left[-\exp\left(-\dfrac{x-\lambda}{\nu}\right)\right] & \xi = 0 \end{cases} \tag{15.4}$$

where $1+\xi\frac{x-\lambda}{\nu} > 0$; ξ is the shape parameter that controls the tail behavior of the distribution. For completeness, the first two moments of the GEV density are:

$$E(x) = \lambda + \frac{\nu}{\xi}(g_1 - 1) \qquad Var(x) = \frac{\nu^2}{\xi^2}\left(g_2 - g_1^2\right) \tag{15.5}$$

where $g_k = \Gamma(1-k\xi)$, $\Gamma(x)$ being the Gamma function.

The expectation of recovering the GEV density is well verified by the Monte Carlo simulations when computing the pdf of the MDD samples; the raw numerical results can in fact be fitted to the analytical expression (15.4). A nonlinear least squares fitting method is applied: λ, ν, ξ are the free parameters that are computed by the regression, obtaining a typical coefficient of determination $R^2 > 0.96$ for all the cases presented in this chapter. An example of the application of this procedure is shown in Figure 15.1.

A good test for the code is also to sample the iid random variables (rvs) X_i appearing in equation (15.3) from a non normal distribution. We still require that $E(X_i) = 0$ and $Var(X_i) = 1$, but their skewness and kurtosis can take arbitrary values. In the continuous limit of $N \to \infty$ ($t = N\Delta t$) and in the case of zero drift $\mu = 0$, the P. Lévy's martingale characterization of Brownian motion theorem (1997, p. 156) establishes that S_t will still be a Brownian motion. In the more general case of $\mu \neq 0$, as suggested by the central limit theorem, the process S_t will be a semimartingale, that is again a Brownian motion with drift with marginal distribution $\mathcal{N}\left(\mu t, \sigma^2 t\right)$. The skewness and the kurtosis are here defined as:

$$\text{Skewness}\,(X) = E\left[\left(\frac{X-\mu}{\sigma}\right)^3\right] \qquad \text{Kurtosis}\,(X) = E\left[\left(\frac{X-\mu}{\sigma}\right)^4\right] - 3. \tag{15.6}$$

On the other hand, the drawdown process $D_n = \max_{0 \leq j \leq n} S_j - S_n$ is a reflected random walk whose marginal distribution is the same as that of $-\min_{0 \leq j \leq n} S_j$. This result, as well other theorems for this kind of reflected process, is formally treated in Doney et al. (2009); Karatzas and Shreve (1997, p. 210, 418) discusses in detail the reflected Brownian motion. As S_j is a discrete Brownian motion with drift, its marginal distribution is $\mathcal{N}\left(\mu j \Delta t, \sigma^2 j \Delta t\right)$. Therefore, provided that X_i are iid rvs with finite mean and variance and regardless of their moments higher than the second, the MDD for the arithmetic process described by equation (15.3) on the time horizon T converges in the continuous limit of $N \to \infty$ to the statistics obtained in the case of the Brownian motion with drift, in terms of both density and expectation value.

Within the Monte Carlo approach already introduced, the iid pseudo-random variables X_i of equation (15.3) can be sampled from a distribution whose third and fourth moments are non vanishing; the coefficients μ and σ and the first two moments are instead not modified. The code generates the iid sequence X_i from a Pearson type IV distribution satisfying the prescriptions $E\left(X_i\right) = 0$, $Var\left(X_i\right) = 1$, Skewness $\left(X_i\right) = s$ and Kurtosis $\left(X_i\right) = k$, where s and k can be arbitrarily prescribed. Some brief details around the Pearson family of distributions are reported in Appendix.

As expected, despite varying the skewness and the kurtosis of the underlying iid random variables, the statistics of the MDD computed by the Monte Carlo simulations systematically recovers the case of the Brownian motion with drift for a given set of μ, σ and T.

15.3 Geometric process driven by iid increments

It is well known that, instead of the arithmetic model treated in the previous section, geometric processes are more appropriate to describe the financial time series. In terms of SDE, equation (15.1) will then be modified in the following way:

$$\frac{dS_t}{S_t} = \mu dt + \sigma dW_t. \tag{15.7}$$

The latter equation describes a geometric Brownian motion. The natural extension of the definition of the maximum drawdown for a geometric model takes the form:

$$\text{MDD}_T = \max_{0 \le t \le T} D_t \qquad \text{with} \qquad D_t = \frac{1}{\max_{0 \le x \le t} S_x} \left(\max_{0 \le x \le t} S_x - S_t \right). \tag{15.8}$$

The MDD is then the maximum loss relative to the previous peak; consequently, both the relations $0 \le D_t < 1$ and $0 \le \text{MDD}_T < 1$ hold.

Itô's calculus is a powerful instrument to handle the dynamics of equation (15.7); it is in fact possible to write $S_t = \exp(\tilde{X}_t)$, along with the SDE:

$$d\tilde{X}_t = \left(\mu - \frac{1}{2}\sigma^2 \right) dt + \sigma dW_t. \tag{15.9}$$

Thanks to this result, the geometric Brownian motion (15.7) can be effectively treated through an arithmetic model for the process $\tilde{X}_t$ with an adjusted drift $\tilde{\mu} = \mu - \frac{1}{2}\sigma^2$. For the same reason, the analytical results of Ismail et al. (2004a) concerning the expectation value and the distribution function of the MDD, can be immediately extended to the case of a geometric Brownian motion according to the new definition of equation (15.8).

At this point it is interesting to consider

$$\frac{dS_t}{S_t} = \mu dt + \sigma dP_t \tag{15.10}$$

where P_t is a process formed by the sum of iid random variables sampled from a non normal distribution, with the assumptions $E(P_t) = 0$ and $Var(P_t) = 1$, but with arbitrary skewness and kurtosis. In the light of the previously cited Lévy's martingale characterization theorem, P_t is a Brownian motion (it is however important to note that it is not possible to derive a direct generalization of Itô's formula for any arbitrary distribution of the log-increments; this point is treated in detail in Kleinert (2009), where it is shown that only a weaker formula for the expectation value of such a process can be obtained). Itô's formula applies here if we can still write $S_t = f(\tilde{X}_t)$, where f is a C^2 function and the process $\tilde{X}_t$ is a semimartingale (Karatzas and Shreve (1997, p. 149). It is easy to prove that the choice $f(x) = \exp(x)$ and

$$d\tilde{X}_t = \left(\mu - \frac{1}{2}\sigma^2 \right) dt + \sigma dP_t \tag{15.11}$$

fulfills these requirements; $\exp(x)$ is in fact a C^2 function and the process $\tilde{X}_t$ is a semimartingale, since it can be decomposed into a local martingale and a drift term of finite variation. Therefore, Itô's calculus prescribes that S_t is a semimartingale too and that the statistical dynamics of equation (15.10) is equivalent to the SDE (15.11), with $S_t = \exp(\tilde{X}_t)$. Consequently if the process P_t is driven by iid increments sampled from a non normal distribution satisfying the previous requirements, we can expect that the Euler discrete version of equation (15.10) will recover the discretization of equation (15.11) with $S_t = \exp(\tilde{X}_t)$ when using a big enough number of discretization points N.

The latter statement has been numerically verified, evaluating the relative error between the two different approaches as a function of N. In particular, the simulations of a geometric process have been performed in two different ways: S_i^{direct} through the direct discretization of (15.10) and S_i^{Ito} obtained by discretizing equation (15.11) using Itô's formula, where $i = 1 \ldots N$. In both cases the iid random variables are sampled from a Pearson type IV distribution with $\mu = 0.1$, $\sigma = 0.2$, Skewness $= -1.5$ and Kurtosis $= 7$. The normalized relative error defined as $\text{Error} = \sqrt{\sum_{i=1}^{N}\left(S_i^{\text{Ito}} - S_i^{\text{direct}}\right)^2} / \sqrt{\sum_{i=1}^{N}\left(S_i^{\text{direct}}\right)^2}$ is finally found to follow the law: $\text{Error} \propto 1/\sqrt{N}$.

As there is a formal proof that in the continuous limit and under the previous hypotheses the geometric process (15.10) is equivalent to the arithmetic one (15.11), the same argument as in the previous section can be applied for inferring the statistics of the MDD. In particular, the moments higher than the second of the iid rvs that compose the Brownian motion P_t do not affect the statistics of the MDD defined in (15.8) for the geometric process (15.10).

This statement can also be recovered by the Monte Carlo simulations. The discrete version of equation (15.10) used here is the Euler scheme

$$S_{i+1} = S_i\left(1 + \mu\Delta t + \sigma\sqrt{\Delta t}X_i\right). \tag{15.12}$$

As before, X_i is a sequence of iid pseudo-random variables from a Pearson type IV distribution whose first two moments satisfy $E(X_i) = 0$ and $Var(X_i) = 1$ ($\Delta t = T/N$). The case of sampling from the standard normal distribution $\mathcal{N}(0,1)$ is recovered when all the higher moments are vanishing.

The pdf of the MDD for the geometric model (15.12) has been computed exploring the following parametric space: $\mu = [-0.1, 0, +0.1]$, $\sigma = [0.1, 0.2]$, $s = [-1.3, 0]$, $k = [0, 5]$, $T = [1\text{ d}, 1\text{ y}, 10\text{ y}]$. As expected, for any set of μ, σ and T, no difference has been found when changing the skewness and/or the kurtosis of the underlying X_i. Obviously, as the whole pdf of the MDD does not vary, $E(\text{MDD})$ remains the same.

15.4 Autoregressive process

In order to get a deviation from the MDD statistics of the Brownian motion with drift it is necessary to relax the strong hypothesis of iid rvs for the increments (log-returns). In this section this is done using an autoregressive model Bollerslev (1986) for the time series. In particular we consider the following AR(1)-GARCH(1,1) model:

$$Y_i = \mu_i + \epsilon_i \tag{15.13}$$

$$\epsilon_i = \sigma_i Z_i \tag{15.14}$$

$$Z_i \equiv \text{iid rvs} \qquad \text{with} \qquad E\left(Z_i\right) = 0 \qquad Var\left(Z_i\right) = 1 \tag{15.15}$$

for $i = 0, 1, 2, \ldots, N$ $(\Delta t = T/N)$, together with the prescriptions for the conditional mean and volatility

$$\mu_i = c + \phi\left(Y_{i-1} - c\right) \tag{15.16}$$

$$\sigma_i^2 = \alpha_0 + \alpha_1 \epsilon_{i-1}^2 + \beta_1 \sigma_{i-1}^2 \tag{15.17}$$

with $\alpha_0, \alpha_1, \beta_1 > 0$, $\alpha_1 + \beta_1 < 1$ and $|\phi| < 1$. The moments of Z_i higher than the second are explicitly not fixed here, since the skewness and the kurtosis will be varied in the following. The model is defined by the five parameters $c, \phi, \alpha_0, \alpha_1, \beta_1$.

The AR(1)-GARCH(1,1) series Y_i is considered as a sequence of log-returns; therefore, to reconstruct the portfolio value trajectory we use the discrete geometric model

$$S_{i+1} = S_i\left(1 + Y_i\right). \tag{15.18}$$

There is a clear analogy between the latter formulation and the previous geometric model (15.12) driven by iid innovations. To make a direct parallelism between them it is useful to preserve the unconditional mean μ and volatility σ over the time interval $T = N\Delta t$; this is done by fixing the parameters α_0 and c of the AR(1)-GARCH(1,1) series according to

$$\alpha_0 = \sigma^2 \Delta t (1 - \alpha_1 - \beta_1) \tag{15.19}$$

$$c = \mu \Delta t. \tag{15.20}$$

Therefore, for a given set of unconditional μ and σ on the time horizon T, the prescriptions (15.19)–(15.20) guarantee that the autoregressive model (equations (15.13)–(15.18)) is completely specified by the three coefficients α_1, β_1, ϕ and comparable with the iid innovations driven model (15.12). The goal is in fact to evaluate how the MDD distribution is affected passing from one model to the other one. Ultimately, if Z_i has the same distribution of X_i

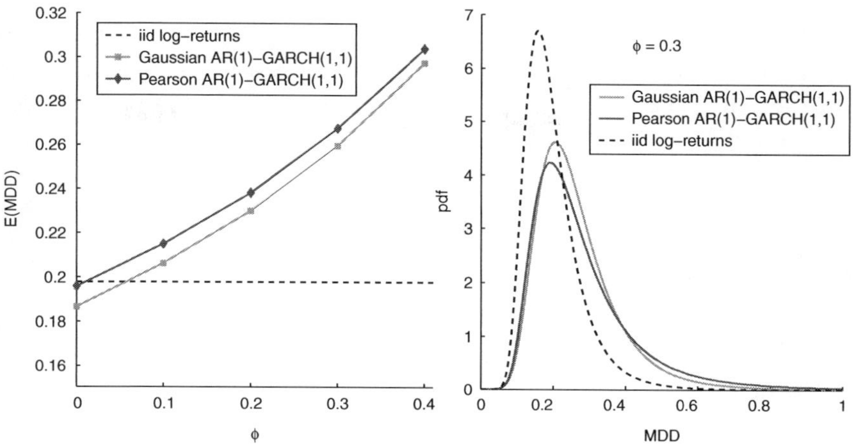

Figure 15.2 Unconditional $\mu = 0.1$, $\sigma = 0.2$, $T = 1$ y

Notes: Left plot: $E(\text{MDD})$ vs. ϕ computed by the Monte Carlo code considering the AR(1)-GARCH(1,1) model and sampling the iid Z_i from $\mathcal{N}(0,1)$ or from a Pearson type IV distribution with $s = -1$ and $k = 0$. Right plot: comparison of the MDD pdf fitted with a GEV at fixed $\phi = 0.3$.

appearing in equation (15.12) and $\alpha_1 = \beta_1 = \phi = 0$, the two models describe exactly the same statistical dynamics.

This autocorrelated geometric process is used to study the statistics of the MDD when changing the coefficient ϕ that controls the serial correlation of the log-returns. In this case we have fixed the following parameters: $\alpha_1 = 0.0897$ and $\beta_1 = 0.9061$ (these values come from the best fit of the daily log-returns of the S&P 500 between 16 May 1995 and 29 April 2003 to a GARCH(1,1) model Starica (2004)), the unconditional mean $\mu = 0.1$, the unconditional standard deviation $\sigma = 0.2$ and the time horizon $T = 1$ y. The Monte Carlo simulations are run sampling the iid Z_i either from $\mathcal{N}(0,1)$ or from a Pearson type IV distribution with $s = -1$ and $k = 0$. The kurtosis of the Pearson distribution has not been increased since the previous parameters of the AR(1)-GARCH(1,1) model already imply a high kurtosis; in particular the skewness implied by the model for the series of log-returns is 0 in the first case and ≈ -1.7 in the second, while the kurtosis is ≈ 12 in both cases. These results are summarized in Figure 15.2. The serial correlation has quite a strong impact on the expected MDD, while it appears that the skewness added in the series of log-returns increases the $E(\text{MDD})$ at maximum by 5 percent with respect to the Gaussian AR(1)-GARCH(1,1) expectation. The analysis of this kind of autoregressive model still deserves further attention in the future.

15.5 Parametric studies

Another possible application of the Monte Carlo simulations presented in the previous sections is to study how the statistics of the MDD are related to a number of parameters of interest. Here the following dependencies are explored when dealing either with iid or autocorrelated log-returns:

1. $\frac{\text{E(MDD)}}{\sigma}$ vs T;
2. $\frac{\text{E(MDD)}}{\sigma}$ vs $\frac{\mu}{\sigma}$, μ/σ being the Sharpe ratio where the risk-free rate is set to 0;
3. $\frac{\mu T}{\text{E(MDD)}}$ vs $\frac{\mu}{\sigma}$, (the Calmar ratio vs. the Sharpe ratio).

The first case is summarized in the left plot of Figure 15.3, considering the time horizons $T = 1$ d, 1 w, 1 m, 6 m, 1 y. We use the unconditional mean and volatility $\mu = 0.1$ and $\sigma = 0.2$. The AR(1)-GARCH(1,1) model of the previous section is applied to generate skewed log-returns (Z_i are sampled from a Pearson distribution with $s = -1$); $\alpha_1 = 0.0897$ and $\beta_1 = 0.9061$ as before, and $\phi = 0.3$.

The results of the dependence of $E(\text{MDD})/\sigma$ on the Sharpe ratio are reported in the central plot of Figure 15.3. The time horizon is $T = 1$ y and the change in the Sharpe ratio is obtained fixing the unconditional $\sigma = 0.15$ while varying the unconditional mean of the log-returns. The parameters for the AR(1)-GARCH(1,1) are the same as before. As is clear from the figure, the Monte Carlo simulations find that the expected MDD for the autocorrelated process decays more slowly with μ/σ with respect to the case of iid innovations.

Finally, the right plot of Figure 15.3, refers to the dependence of the Calmar ratio on the Sharpe ratio for the same parameters of the previous figure. The picture highlights how the risk adjusted returns are lower when the underlying series of log-returns presents positive autocorrelation and negative skewness.

Coming back to the basic hypothesis of iid log-returns with finite and constant mean and volatility described in Section 15.3, despite the simplicity of such a framework it is still of practical interest to derive a heuristic approximation for the behavior of $E(\text{MDD})$ as a function of μ, σ and T. A simple approach could be to assume that this function can be written in terms of a power law,

$$E(\text{MDD}) = f(\mu, \sigma, T) \approx C_0 \mu^{C_1} \sigma^{C_2} T^{C_3}. \tag{15.21}$$

In this framework the function $f(\mu, \sigma, T)$ has an analytical expression Ismail et al. (2004a), but the actual value is obtained through numerically computed functions. On the other hand it is possible to apply a multivariate linear regression to fit the expected MDD to the power law equation (15.21).

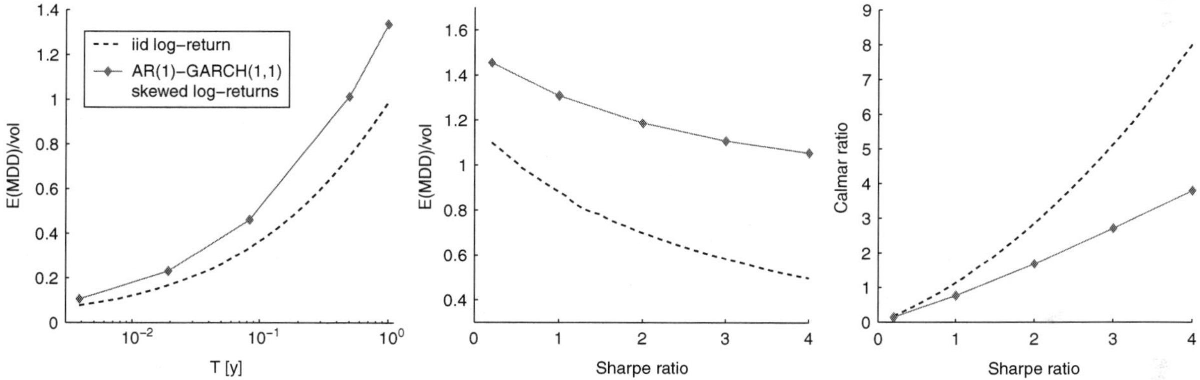

Figure 15.3 MDD related performance figures obtained when considering the underlying log-returns either as iid or as a AR(1)-GARCH(1,1) series with non zero skewness.

Notes: The unconditional $\mu = 0.1$ and $\sigma(\text{vol}) = 0.2$ are kept fixed in both cases; the AR(1)-GARCH(1,1) parameters are $\alpha_1 = 0.0897$, $\beta_1 = 0.9061$, $\phi = 0.3$. On the left: $E(\text{MDD})/\sigma$ vs. T. In the center: $E(\text{MDD})/\sigma$ vs. the Sharpe ratio μ/σ at $T = 1$ y. On the right: Calmar ratio $\mu T/E(\text{MDD})$ vs. the Sharpe ratio μ/σ at $T = 1$ y.

Here we focus the attention on the regime of $\mu > 0$. Using the parametric space $[0.02 < \mu < 0.1]$, $[0.05 < \sigma < 0.2]$, $[1\ \text{d} < T < 6\ \text{m}]$ a linear regression has been performed on the analytical predictions, obtaining the following estimates for the coefficients of equation (15.21):

$$C_0 = 1.0305 \qquad c_1 = -0.0431 \qquad c_2 = 1.0416 \qquad c_3 = 0.4704. \tag{15.22}$$

The mean of the error between the power law with coefficients (15.22) and the analytical results is $3.75 \cdot 10^{-4}$ while the error standard deviation is 0.028. In principle a similar approach can be applied for the case of autoregressive processes, but this would require the creation of a large database of results computed by the Monte Carlo simulations.

15.6 Comparison against historical financial time series

For the purposes of the comparison against the historical financial data, the model for the underlying time series S_t is the following GARCH(1,1) model:

$$S_{t+1} = S_t(1 + Y_t) \tag{15.23}$$

$$Y_t = k + \epsilon_t \tag{15.24}$$

$$\epsilon_t = \sigma_t Z_t \tag{15.25}$$

$$\sigma_t^2 = \alpha_0 + \alpha_1 \epsilon_{t-1}^2 + \beta_1 \sigma_{t-1}^2 \tag{15.26}$$

where Z_t are iid random variables sampled from a Student's T distribution with ν degrees of freedom and unitary variance; the drift k is a constant, $\alpha_0, \alpha_1, \beta_1 > 0$ and $\alpha_1 + \beta_1 < 1$. With respect to the model previously described in Section 15.4 by equations (15.13)–(15.18), here we consider a vanishing autocorrelation of the increments and a less generic distribution for the innovations (Student's T instead of Pearson type IV); despite this simplification the latter model is able to fit the historical series of daily returns analyzed here reasonably well, as will be shown in the following.

The Monte Carlo code is used to evaluate the distribution function of the maximum drawdown MDD_T on the time horizon T. The simulations presented in this section consider the statistics of $M = 1 \cdot 10^6$ MDD samples, each one obtained from a time series composed by $N = 50 \cdot 10^3$ steps. The numerical predictions are compared against six historical financial time series (the data source is Yahoo!Finance), namely the S&P 500 index, CAC40 index, Credit Suisse stock, IBM stock, US Dollar/Japanese Yen spot, US treasury 30-years yield. The analysis is composed by the following steps.

1. The historical data at daily frequency have been considered on a eight year period, namely from 1 January 2002 to 31 December 2009 (nearly 2000 points). The log-returns of the closing prices are used to perform

Table 15.1 Parameters obtained from a maximum likelihood fit to the GARCH(1,1) model with student's T innovations described by equations (15.23)–(15.26).

Instrument	k	α_0	α_1	β_1	ν	LLK
S&P500	4.89E-4	5.46E-7	0.0676	0.9298	9.90	6365.83
CAC40	6.49E-4	1.33E-6	0.0858	0.9091	11.97	6110.21
CS	6.95E-4	3.17E-6	0.0833	0.9151	6.85	4896.05
IBM	2.76E-4	1.65E-6	0.0591	0.9341	5.96	5828.22
USD/JPY	-1.29E-5	3.83E-7	0.0389	0.9534	6.14	7543.11
US 30y	-1.86E-4	5.83E-7	0.0404	0.9561	12.79	6204.93

Notes: LLK is the log-likelihood value obtained from the fit.

a maximum likelihood fit to a GARCH(1,1) model with Student's T distributed innovations (see the above equations).

2. The parameters computed by the best fit are used to run the Monte Carlo code. The simulation evaluates the statistics of the MDD_T, providing in particular the expectation value, 95 percent and 99 percent confidence intervals for the maximum drawdown.
3. *In-sample* test: The code results are compared to the historical MDD_T (the latter is calculated using high and low intra-day prices) observed within the time interval used for the fit of point 1. Four reference time horizons are considered: 10 days, 40 days, 1 year and 8 years.
4. *Out-of-sample* test: Using the same fit parameters obtained at point 1, the code is tested against the historical MDD in the period between 1 Jan 2010 and 15 Mar 2010. The time horizons considered here are: 10, 20 and 40 days.

Table 15.1 summarizes the results from the maximum likelihood fit to a GARCH(1,1) model with Student's T innovations on the previous time series.

The plots of Figure 15.4 firstly report two examples of the *in-sample* comparison between the numerical expectations and the historical maximum drawdown observed between 1 Jan 2002 and 31 Dec 2009. Secondly, using the parameters of Table 15.1 obtained on the training dataset, the *out-of-sample* estimates of the Monte Carlo code are presented for the period between 1 Jan 2010 and 15 Mar 2010.

In conclusion, the Monte Carlo code has been used to evaluate a total number of 42 MDD observations (24 in the 1 Jan 2002 to 31 Dec 2009 period and 18 in the 1 Jan 2010 to 15 Mar 2010 period). Hence the expected number of violations from the model is 2.1 when working with 95 percent CI, and 0.42 when working with 99 percent CI. The present analysis reported three violations from the 95 percent CI and no violations from the 99 per cent CI.

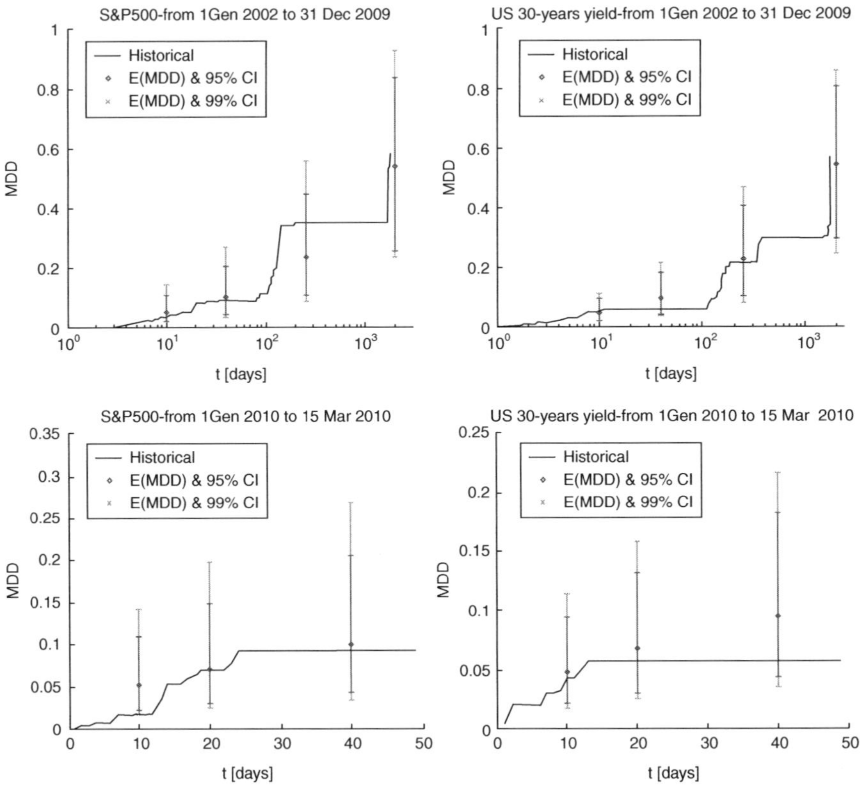

Figure 15.4 On the top: time evolution of the MDD of the historical S&P 500 and US 30-years yield series between 1 Jan 2002 and 31 Dec 2009 compared with the *in-sample* expectation values and their confidence intervals computed by the Monte Carlo code. On the bottom: time evolution of the MDD of the historical S&P 500 and US 30-years yield series between 1 Jan 2010 and 15 Mar 2010 compared with the *out-of-sample* expectation value and their confidence intervals computed by the Monte Carlo code

15.7 Conclusions

The analytical predictions for the expectation value of the maximum drawdown in the case of a Brownian motion with drift are very well recovered by the Monte Carlo code presented here. The numerical simulations also allow us to consistently recover the MDD distribution function in terms of a generalized extreme value distribution.

In the continuous limit of the discretized version of a geometric stochastic process, the MDD statistics are shown to be unaffected by the moments higher than the second that characterize the distribution of the underlying increments, provided that they are iid. This result is consistent with the expectations from the central limit theorem and Itô's formula, and it is recovered by the Monte Carlo code.

When relaxing the iid constraint for the increments of the process and considering an autoregressive AR(1)-GARCH(1,1) model, the MDD statistics are strongly affected; in the cases examined here, the expectation value of the MDD increases roughly linearly with the serial correlation coefficient. In the case of both the geometric Brownian motion and the autoregressive stochastic process, some parametric studies have been performed in order to derive the heuristic behavior of the MDD expected value as a function of time, mean return, volatility and Sharpe ratio.

Finally, under the hypothesis of a GARCH(1,1) process driven by Student's T distributed innovations, the MDD statistics predicted by the Monte Carlo code has been compared to the events observed in different historical financial time series. The relevance of this comparison relies not only on the MDD expectation value but most of all on its confidence interval (at 95 per cent and 99 per cent), available through the MDD distribution function derived from the simulation. Both the *in-sample* and the *out-of-sample* tests show a good match between the numerical expectations and the historical data.

Appendix: Some Details on the Pearson Distributions

The Pearson family of distributions Pearson (1895) is particularly well suited to generating random variables with arbitrary skewness and kurtosis. Seven distribution types are in fact encompassed in the Pearson system; particular members of that family are normal, beta, gamma, Student's T, F, inverse Gaussian and Pareto distributions. The general probability density function $p(x)$ of a Pearson distribution is defined through the differential equation

$$\frac{d\log p(x)}{dx} = \frac{x-\alpha}{a_0 + a_1 x + a_2 x^2}. \tag{A1}$$

The normal distribution is for example recovered for $a_1 = a_2 = 0$.

For our purposes, the Pearson type IV distribution is of particular importance and some of its properties will be briefly recalled here. When $a_1 \neq 0$ and $a_2 \neq 0$, the roots of the denominator of equation (A1) are in general the complex quantities $b \pm ia$. The density of the Pearson type IV distribution can be written as

$$p(x) \propto \left(1 + \frac{x^2}{a^2}\right)^{-m} \exp\left[\delta \arctan\left(\frac{x}{a}\right)\right] \tag{A2}$$

where $m = -\frac{1}{2}a_2$ and $\delta = (b-a)/aa_2$. Equation (A2) is an asymmetric leptokurtic density function. Denoting the skewness by s and the kurtosis by k

(in the context of this appendix only, the kurtosis is defined as the fourth standardized moment, that is $k = 3$ for the normal distribution), the following relations between the parameters of the Pearson type IV distribution (A2) and s and k can be derived:

$$r = \left[\frac{6\left(k - s^2 - 1\right)}{2k - 3s^2 - 6} \right] \quad \text{with} \quad r = 2m - 2 \tag{A3}$$

$$\delta = \frac{r(r-2)s}{\sqrt{16(r-1) - s^2(r-2)^2}} \tag{A4}$$

$$a = \sqrt{\frac{\mu_2}{16}\left[16(r-1) - s^2(r-2)^2\right]} \tag{A5}$$

where μ_2 is the second central moment. The parameters α, a_0, a_1, a_2 appearing in the differential equation (A1) can then be determined by fixing the first four moments of the distribution.

The Pearson family of distributions is hence used in this chapter in order to generate a sequence of iid random variables given a set of mean μ, standard deviation σ, skewness s and kurtosis k for the underlying density.

References

P. Artzner, F. Delbaen, J. E. and Heath, D. (1999). Coherent Measures of Risk. *Mathematical Finance*, 9: 203–28.

Bollerslev, T. (1986). Generalized Autoregressive Conditional Heteroskedasticity. *Journal of Econometrics*, 31: 307–27.

Bouchaud, J.-P. and Potters, M. (2003). *Theory of Financial Risk and Derivative Pricing: From Statistical Physics to Risk Management.* (Cambridge University Press: Cambridge, 2nd edition).

A. Chekholov, S. Uryasev, S. U. and Zabarankin, M. (2005). Drawdown Measure in Portfolio Optimization. *International Journal of Theoretical and Applied Finance*, 8: 1–46.

Coles, S. (2004). *An Introduction to Statistical Modeling of Extreme Values* (Springer: London).

Cont, R. (2001). Empirical Properties of Asset Returns: Stylized Facts and Statistical Issues. *Quantitative Financei*, 1: 223–36.

Doney, R., Maller, R., and Savov, M. (2009). Renewal Theorems and Stability for the Reflected Process. *Stochastic Processes and their Applications*, 119: 270–97.

Graversen, S. E. and Shiryaev, A. (2000). An Extension of P. Lévy's Distributional Properties to the Case of a Brownian Motion with Drift. *Bernoulli*, 6: 615–20.

Ismail et al., M.-M. (2004a). On the Maximum Drawdown of a Brownian Motion. *Journal of Applied Probability*, 41: 147–61.

Ismail et al., M.-M. (2004b). Maximum Drawdown. *Risk Magazine*, 17: 99–102.

Karatzas, I. and Shreve, S. E. (1997). *Brownian Motion and Stochastic Calculus*. (Springer: New York, 2nd edition).

Kleinert, H. (2009). Path Integrals in Quantum Mechanics, Statistics, Polymer Physics, and Financial Markets. *Path Integrals in Quantum Mechanics, Statistics, Polymer Physics, and Financial Markets* (World Scientific: Singapore, 5th edition).

Leal, R. P. C. and de Melo Mendes, B. V. (2005). Maximum Drawdown: Models and Application. *Journal of Alternative Investments*, 7: 83–91.

Pearson, K. (1895). Contributions to the Mathematical Theory of Evolution. II. Skew Variation in Homogeneous Material. *Philosophical Transactions of the Royal Society of London*, 186: 343–414.

Pospisil, L. and Vecer, J. (2009). PDE Methods for the Maximum Drawdown. *Journal of Computational Finance*, 12: 59–76.

Reiss, R.-D. and Thomas, M. (2007). *Statistical Analysis of Extreme Values*. (Birkenhauser: Basel 3rd edition).

Rosario N. Mantegna, H. E. S. (2000). *An Introduction to Econophysics: Correlations and Complexity in Finance* (Cambridge University Press: Cambridge).

Starica, C. (2004). Is Garch(1,1) as Good a Model as the Nobel Prize Accolades Would Imply? *Econometrics 0411015*, EconWPA.

16

On the Effectiveness of Dynamic Stock Index Portfolio Hedging: Evidence from Emerging Markets Futures

Mohammad S. Hasan and Taufiq Choudhry

16.1 Introduction

Since the introduction of financial derivatives markets in developed countries during the 1970s and 1980s, and the later development in emerging markets during the 1990s, there has been much interest over the last three decades towards the modeling and forecasting of the optimal hedge ratios (OHR) and alternative hedging strategies applied to the commodity and financial futures.[1] It is now well known that derivatives markets perform useful functions of price discovery, hedging, speculation and risk-sharing (see Working, 1953; Johnson, 1960; Silber, 1985 and Fortune, 1989). Hedgers use these markets as a means to avoid the market risk associated with adverse price change in the related cash markets. Speculators take positions in derivative instruments in the hope that subsequent price movements will generate profits. Overall, investors are given the choice of altering their asset portfolios between cash and derivatives markets.

This chapter investigates the behavior of dynamic hedge ratios in three emerging stock markets, using alternative variants of GARCH models, and compares the hedging effectiveness of optimal hedge ratios across those models. In derivates markets, a hedge is performed by taking simultaneous positions in cash and futures markets, which result in the offset of any loss sustained from an adverse price movement by a favorable price movement. The hedge ratio is simply the number of futures contracts needed to minimize the exposure of a unit worth position in the cash market.[2] Careful selection of derivatives contracts is conditional upon the accuracy of OHR estimates and volatility forecasting techniques.

Empirical estimation and testing procedures in previous studies have developed and progressed, broadly using two econometric methods: (1) the single equation regression-based model and (2) the system-based estimation method.[3] The traditional regression-based approach includes ordinary least squares (OLS), rolling-window, expanding-window, discounted least squares, and exponentially weighted least squares methods.[4] The system-based estimation method is founded upon autoregressive conditional heteroskedastic (ARCH) and generalized autoregressive conditional heteroskedastic (GARCH) specifications, where the hedging models account for the time dependence in variances as well as covariances of portfolios of cash and futures returns. In the post GARCH era, GARCH modeling techniques are quite dominant in the empirical modeling given the fact that financial asset returns exhibit nonlinearity, time-varying heteroskedasticity, volatility clusters and non-normality.

Given the plethora of literature, there is a gap in the current research strand. Most previous studies confined their attention to more developed and mature financial markets and exchanges. Quite surprisingly, there has been little research to examine the behavior of time-varying hedge ratios for emerging markets.[5] Emerging equity markets now account for more than one-fifth of global equity market capitalization. The burgeoning size of the markets have been supported by a growing domestic investor base, including domestic institutional investors and increased financial integration with rest of the world (Bailey, 2010). Foreign investors can participate in emerging markets by investing in American depositary receipts (ADRs), country fund, or direct participation in the local market. Bekaert and Harvey (2000) in a study based on thirty emerging economies found that average real economic growth increases between 1 percent and 2 percent per annum after a financial liberalization. They contended that a reduction in the cost of capital and an improvement in growth opportunities are the most obvious channels through which financial liberalization can increase the diversification benefits offered by international asset portfolios.

Bailey (2010) noted that emerging markets equity prices have experienced a much larger swing over recent years than equity prices in advanced economies. Alexander and Barbosa (2007) contended that minimum variance (MV) hedging provides superior out-of-sample performance compared to naive hedges in less developed markets, where the advanced communication and active trading in exchange traded funds (ETFs) are at an early stage of development.

Given the topical nature of the issue and paucity of research, this chapter investigates the behavior of dynamic hedge ratios in three emerging stock markets, using alternative variants of GARCH models, and compares the hedging effectiveness of optimal hedge ratios across those models. More specifically, using daily data of the stock spot and futures markets of Brazil, Hungary and South Africa within the framework of bivariate standard GARCH, GARCH-BEKK, GARCH-ECM, GARCH-X, and asymmetric GARCH-GJR models, we estimate the time-varying hedge ratios and compare their hedging performances. Our markets are chosen for three main reasons. First, the three markets are located in different parts of the world: South America, Eastern Europe and Africa. Second, the markets of all three countries have data for a reasonably long period of time. Third, the FTSE group classified Brazil, Hungary and South Africa as advanced emerging markets as they represent upper or lower middle income gross national income (GNI) countries with advanced market structure or high GNI countries with lesser developed market infrastructure. Our analysis has contributed to the existing literature in the following ways. First, we have estimated the time-varying hedge ratios using a longer time span and frequency of data. Second, we have evaluated the hedging performance using two non-overlapping out-of-sample forecasts to ameliorate sampling effect and to obtain more robust results. Third, we have investigated the hedging effectiveness using two distinct frameworks of utility evaluations: (a) the mean-variance and (b) the exponential utility approaches. Fourth, we have computed the minimum capital risk requirement (MCRR) using those hedge ratios to ascertain the superiority of alternative hedging strategy that holds the capital adequacy requirement of the fund at a minimum level. Given that hedge ratios of various portfolios are predictable, an investor always prefers a portfolio with a lower financial capital to reach the maximum risk reduction.

The chapter is organized as follows. Section 16.2 describes and discusses the optimal hedge ratio and the five GARCH models. The data and preliminary diagnostics are described in Section 16.3. Sections 16.4 to 16.6 offer the empirical results based upon estimating conventional and dynamic hedging models and the final section offers a summary and conclusion.

16.2 Estimation of optimal hedge ratios and the GARCH models

16.2.1 The hedge ratio

Johnson's (1960) risk minimizing hedge ratio h^* is defined as:

$$h* = -\frac{\sigma_{c,f}}{\sigma_f^2} = -\frac{\text{cov}(Rc, Rf)}{\text{var}(Rf)} \tag{16.1}$$

where R_c and R_f denote return on spot and future indices. The optimal hedge ratio (OHR) is then computed as the slope coefficient of the following regression:

$$R_{ct} = \alpha + \beta R_{ft} + \varepsilon_t \tag{16.2}$$

where ε_t is an error term.[6] If $\beta = 0$ it implies unhedged position; $\beta = 1$ signifies a fully hedged position; and $\beta < 1$ implies a partial hedge.

It is now well known in the literature that the conventional hedging model has shortcomings. As the distribution of futures and spot prices are changing through time, h^*, which is expressed as the ratio of covariance between futures returns and cash returns and variance of futures returns, moves randomly through time (see for example Cecchetti et al., 1988; Baillie and Myers, 1991 and Kroner and Sultan, 1993). Therefore, equation (16.1) should be modified as:

$$h_T^* = \frac{cov(R_{T+1}^c, R_{T+1t}^f \text{I}\Omega T)}{var(R_{T+1}^f \text{I}\Omega_T)}. \tag{16.3}$$

In equation (16.3), conditional moments are changing as the information set, Ω_T, is updated; consequently, the number of futures contracts held and the optimal hedge ratio will also change through time – hence the t subscripts of h_T^*. Under the condition of time-varying distribution, the bivariate GARCH model is utilized to estimate the time-varying hedge ratios to approximate the dynamic hedging strategies.

16.2.2 Bivariate GARCH model

The time-varying hedge ratios are estimated from five variants of bivariate GARCH models: standard GARCH, GARCH-ECM, GARCH-BEKK, GARCH-GJR and GARCH-X. The following bivariate GARCH(p,q) model is applied to returns from the stock cash and futures markets:

$$y_t = \mu + \varepsilon_t \tag{16.4}$$

$$\varepsilon_t / \Omega_{t-1} \sim N(0, H_t) \tag{16.5}$$

$$vech(H_t) = C + \sum_{i=1}^{p} A_i vech(\varepsilon_{t-i})^2 + \sum_{j=1}^{q} B_j vech(H_{t-j}), \tag{16.6}$$

where $y_t = (r_t^c, r_t^f)$ is a (2×1) vector containing stock returns from the cash and futures markets, H_t is a (2×2) conditional covariance matrix, C is (3×1) parameter vector of constants, A_i and B_j are (3×3) parameter matrices, and vech is the column stacking operator that stacks the lower triangular portion of a symmetric matrix

To make the estimation amenable, Engle and Kroner (1995) have suggested various restrictions to be imposed on the parameters of the A_i and B_j matrices. A parsimonious representation may be achieved by imposing a diagonal restriction on the parameter matrices so that each variance and covariance element depends only on its own past values and prediction errors. The following equations represent a diagonal vech bivariate GARCH(1,1) conditional variance equation(s):

$$H_{11,t} = C_1 + A_{11}(\varepsilon_{1,t-1})^2 + B_{11}(H_{11,t-1}) \tag{16.7a}$$

$$H_{12,t} = C_2 + A_{22}(\varepsilon_{1,t-1}, \varepsilon_{2,t-1}) + B_{22}(H_{12,t-1}) \tag{16.7b}$$

$$H_{22} = C_3 + A_{33}(\varepsilon_{2,t-1})^2 + B_{33}(H_{22,t-1}). \tag{16.7c}$$

In the bivariate GARCH(1,1) model, the diagonal vech parameterization involves nine conditional variance parameters.

Using the bivariate GARCH model, the time-varying hedge ratio can be computed as:

$$h_t^* = \hat{H}_{12,t}/\hat{H}_{22,t}, \tag{16.8}$$

where $\hat{H}_{12,t}$ is the estimated conditional covariance between the cash and futures returns, and $\hat{H}_{22,t}$ is the estimated conditional variance of futures returns. Since the conditional covariance is time-varying the optimal hedge would be time-varying too.

1. GARCH-ECM model

When the bivariate GARCH model incorporates the error correction term in the mean equation, it becomes the GARCH-ECM model which is presented as:

$$y_t = \mu + \delta(u_{t-1}) + \varepsilon_t, \tag{16.9}$$

where u_{t-1} denotes the lagged error correction term, retrieved from the cointegration regression. Therefore, a bivariate GARCH-ECM model will be employed to account for the long-run relationship and basis risk (see Kroner and Sultan, 1993). Equation (16.8) still represents the hedge ratio.

16.3 Bivariate GARCH-BEKK model

In the BEKK model as suggested by Engle and Kroner (1995), the conditional covariance matrix is parameterized to:

$$vech(H_t) = C'C + \sum_{k=1}^{k}\sum_{i=1}^{p} A'_{ki}\varepsilon_{t-i}\varepsilon'_{t-1}A_{ki} + \sum_{k=1}^{k}\sum_{j=1}^{q} B'_{kj}H_{t-j}B_{kj}. \tag{16.10}$$

Equations (16.4) and (5) also apply to the BEKK model and are defined as above. In equation (16.10), A_{ki}, $i = 1,\ldots,q$, $k = 1,\ldots,k$, and $B_{kj}j = 1,\ldots,q$, $k = 1,..,k$ are both $N \times N$ matrices. The GARCH-BEKK model is sufficiently general that it guarantees the conditional covariance matrix, H_t, to be positive definite, and renders significant parameter reduction in the estimation. For example, a bivariate BEKK GARCH(1,1) parameterization requires estimation of only eleven parameters in the conditional variance-covariance structure. The time-varying hedge ratio from the BEKK model is again represented by equation (16.8).

16.3.1 Bivariate GARCH-GJR model

Along with the leptokurtic distribution of stock returns data, empirical research has shown a negative correlation between current returns and future volatility (Black, 1976; Christie, 1982). This negative effect of current returns on future variance is sometimes called the leverage effect (Bollerslev et al., 1992). Glosten et al. (1993) provide a modification to the GARCH model that allows positive and negative innovations to returns to have different impact on conditional variance.[7] Glosten et al. (1993) suggest that the asymmetry effect can also be captured simply by incorporating a dummy variable in the original GARCH:

$$\sigma_t^2 = \alpha_0 + \alpha u_{t-1}^2 + \gamma u_{t-1}^2 I_{t-1} + \beta \sigma_{t-1}^2, \tag{16.11}$$

where $I_{t-1} = 1$ if $u_{t-1} > 0$; otherwise $I_{t-1} = 0$. Thus, the ARCH coefficient in a GARCH-GJR model switches between $\alpha + \gamma$ andα, depending on whether the lagged error term is positive or negative. The time-varying hedge ratio based on the GARCH-GJR model is also expressed as in equation (16.8).

16.3.2 Bivariate GARCH-X model

The GARCH-X model is an extension of the GARCH-ECM model as it incorporates the square of the error correction term in the conditional covariance matrix. In the GARCH-X model, conditional heteroskedasticity may be modeled as a function of the lagged squared error correction term, in addition to the ARMA terms in the variance/covariance equations:

$$vech(H_t) = C + \sum_{i=1}^{p} A_i vech(\varepsilon_{t-i})^2 + \sum_{j=1}^{q} B_j vech(H_{t-j}) + \sum_{k=1}^{k} D_k vech(u_{t-1})^2. \tag{16.12}$$

A significant positive effect may imply that the further the series deviate from each other in the short run, the harder they are to predict. The hedge ratio again is presented by equation (16.8).

It is hypothesized that time-varying hedge ratios would be different across different variants of GARCH models. Therefore, the next question arises: which one is more effective? As stated earlier in this chapter we apply all the above methods to estimate the hedge ratio, and compare their effectiveness. We also compare the hedging performance of dynamic hedging strategies with traditional hedging methods.

16.3.3 Data and diagnostics

The models are estimated using daily data spanning from December 1999 to December 2009 on stock indices and their counterpart futures contracts from Brazil, Hungary and South Africa. Empirical evaluation of hedging performance using daily data has tremendous value for money managers, who adjust their portfolio as often as daily (Figlewski, 1986). Stock index futures contracts, in particular, offer opportunities for unbundling the market and non-market components of risk and return to investment banks, security houses, fund managers and individual investors. For example, stock index futures are routinely used in program trading and index arbitrage to achieve portfolio insurance; or for arbitrage purposes by exploiting the relationship between the cash value of the index and the futures on the index. Fund managers use them to alter, temporarily, the systematic risk of a portfolio without having to buy or sell its constituent stock.

The Bovespa index is a total return index weighted by traded volume and is comprised of the most liquid stocks traded in the Sao Paulo Stock Exchange, Brazil. The Sao Paulo Stock Exchange (Bovespa) and the Brazilian Mercantile and Futures Exchanges (BM&F) merged on 8 May 2008, creating BM&FBOVESPA. There are 450 companies traded at Bovespa as of 30 April 2008.[8] The BUX index is the official capitalization-weighted index of the blue-chip shares listed on the Budapest Stock Exchange (BSE).[9] Its futures and option products are available in the BSE derivatives section. The Johannesburg Stock Exchange (JSE) acquired the South African Futures Exchanges (SAFEX) in 2001 and became the leader in both equities and equity and agricultural derivatives trading in the South African Market. The FTSE/JSE 40 index consists of the largest 40 South African companies ranked by full market value in the FTSE/JSE All-Share index.[10] All futures price indices are continuous series.[11] The data are collected from Datastream International. To avoid the sample effect and overlapping issue, two out-of-sample periods are considered, including one 1-year period (2007) and one 2-year period (2008 to 2009). All models are estimated for the periods 1999–2006 and 1999–2007, and the estimated parameters are applied for forecasting hedge ratios over the horizons of 2007 and 2008–9.

Descriptive statistics relating to the distribution of return indices are presented in Table 16.1. These statistics are: mean, standard deviation, variance, a measure of skewness, a measure of excess kurtosis (normal value is 3), the Jarque-Bera statistics, and unit root test results of cash and future price indices. The table also presents higher order autocorrelation Q, and ARCH effects in the returns indices series. The values of the skewness statistics indicate that the density function is negatively skewed for both cash and future return indices for all markets. The values of the excess kurtosis statistic are more than 2 for all countries, which suggest that the density function for each country has a fat tail. The values of the Jarque-Bera statistic are high, suggesting the return indices are not normally distributed. Judged by the skewness, excess kurtosis and Jarque-Bera statistics, it can be inferred that the return indices exhibit 'fat-tails' in all markets. The data series have also been checked for stationarity using the Elliott-Rothenberg-Stock Dickey-Fuller generalized least squares (DF-GLS) unit root test. The DF-GLS test results indicate that each of the return indices series has no unit root. Tests for autocorrelation in the first moments using the Q(20) statistic indicate

Table 16.1 Descriptive statistics of stock spot and futures indices return

Statistics	Brazil		Hungary		South Africa	
	Cash return	Future return	Cash return	Future return	Cash return	Future return
Mean	.000584	.000573	.000451	.000446	.000365	.000358
Variance	.000631	.000768	.000368	.000362	.0003136	.0003485
Std. dev.	.025130	.027715	.019206	.019046	.017710	.018670
Skewness	−.265225	−.190646	−.328944	−.293191	−.309725	−.81671
Kurtosis	6.92300	5.84232	10.7273	11.6078	7.38807	12.4973
Jarque-Bera	1703.60	894.03	6538.17	8092.09	2134.91	10095.46
Stationarity: t_μ	−8.557[a]	−10.215[a]	−5.675[a]	−4.190[a]	−5.5801[a]	−6.758[a]
t_τ	−13.599[a]	−15.205[a]	−10.293[a]	−7.988[a]	−10.127[a]	−11.50[a]
ARCH(1)	51.96	61.43	172.60	144.35	672.34	582.08
Q(20)	64.81	41.03	112.08	93.32	34.40	28.82

Notes: t_μ and t_τ are the Elliot-Rothenberg-Stock DF-GLS unit root test statistics with allowance for a constant and trend, respectively. The 5 percent critical values of t_μ and t_τ are −1.948 and −3.190 (see Elliot, Rothenberg and Stock, 1996, table 1). [a] implies significance at 1% level.

that none is present in any of the indices. Finally, tests for ARCH using Engle's (1982) LM statistic generally support the hypothesis of time-varying variances.

16.4 Empirical results

In this section we formally evaluate the effectiveness of conventional and time-varying regression results of cash returns and future returns (equation (16.2)) for all three countries, obtained by using the Cochrane-Orcutt method. Here, daily spot changes in the index are regressed on daily changes in the nearby index futures contract. Table 16.2 presents the results. Parameter estimates of the future returns in equation (16.2) represent the constant minimum variance hedge ratio (*t*-stats in parentheses). In all cases, the coefficient attached to the future returns variable is positive and highly significant. The hedge ratio is found to be less than unity in all cases. The largest coefficient is found in the case of Hungary (0.9089) and lowest for Brazil (0.8516). This statistic indicates that a substantial portion of variability in the cash market is hedged using the futures instruments. A higher value of R^2 indicates a higher level of hedging effectiveness by a constant hedge ratio. The South African result indicates the highest R^2 (0.830) and Hungary the lowest (0.775).

The static bivariate regression method of the OHR suffers from several potential limitations, in particular the omission of the basis (error correction term) as a determinant of the hedge ratio and accounting for time dependence in risk. Therefore, in the next step, we have estimated alternative variants of GARCH models to accommodate time dependence in the variance/covariance and error correction term. The standard GARCH, GARCH-BEKK and GARCH-GJR, are estimated without the error correction term in the mean equation. GARCH-ECM incorporates the error correction term in the mean equation whereas the GARCH-X model incorporates the error correction term in both the mean and variance equations. For reasons

Table 16.2 Bivariate regression results of the constant minimum hedge ratio model

Country	Constant	Future's returns	Diagnostic	F-test
Brazil	.0000945 (.6090)	0.8516 (117.08)	R^2 =.811 DW= 2.214	5623.68
Hungary	.0000474 (.3494)	0.9089 (103.16)	R^2 =.775 DW= 2.180	4509.32
South Africa	.0000453 (.452468)	0.8911 (125.367)	R^2 =.830 DW= 2.237	6405.56

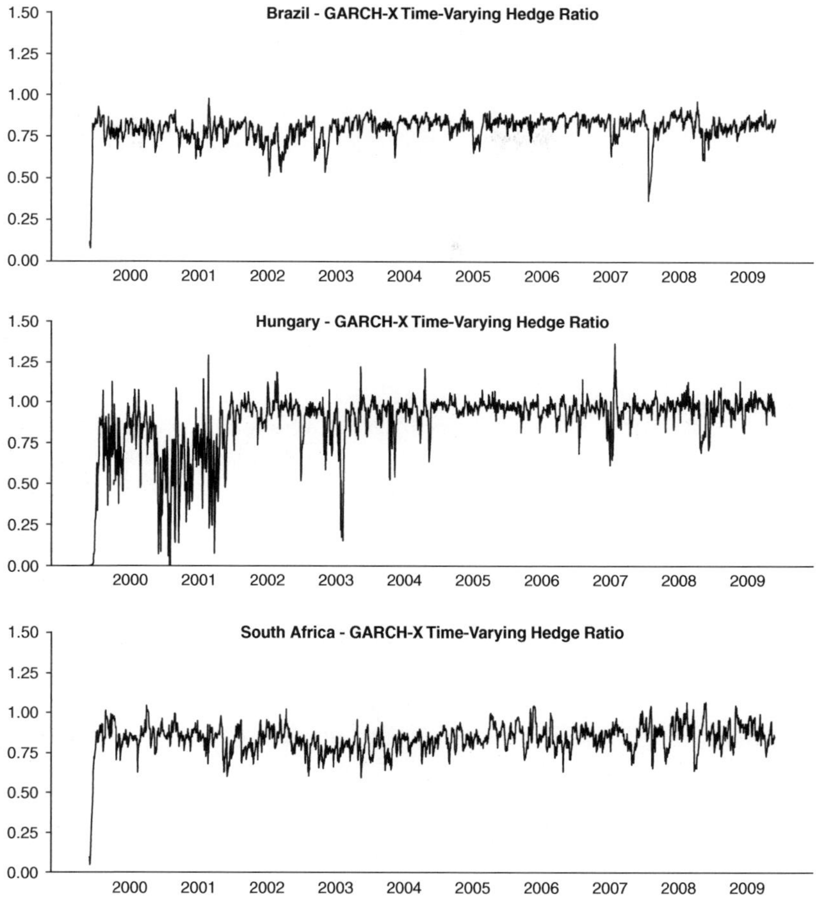

Figure 16.1 GARCH-X time-varying hedge ratios

of economy and brevity, we are not reporting the results obtained from various GARCH models; however, they are available upon request from the authors.

Figure 16.1 shows the dynamic hedge ratio estimated by means of the GARCH-X model for all three markets. Graphs of other hedge ratios are not provided to conserve space but are available on request. It is evident that the hedge ratios are time-varying in each case, suggesting that a time-invariant OHR may be ineffective for financial risk management. Visual inspection shows that the time-varying hedge ratios are well behaved and stationary in all cases. We further test for stationarity of the estimated hedge ratios. Results are not reported here to conserve space. The unit test results indicate that the dynamic hedge ratios are mean reverting, signifying that the effect of a shock to the hedge ratios would eventually die out. We also find that the hedge ratios follow AR(1) process. The result shows that hedge ratios associated with all variants of GARCH models for Brazil, Hungary and South Africa are positively serially correlated, which suggests that if a hedge ratio is large this week, it is expected to remain large next week in the absence of a new shock (Kroner and Sultan, 1993).

16.4.1 In-Sample Variance Reduction

There are four hedging strategies for within-sample and out-of-sample period hedge ratio comparison: no hedge, naive hedge, the conventional minimum variance hedge and conditional hedge. Within the conditional hedge, five different GARCH models are applied to estimate five different hedge ratios for each market. In case of no hedge, the investor takes no position in the futures market to offset market risk in the cash market. In the case of naive hedge, the hedger takes a position in both markets by the same amount but in opposite directions. It is assumed that both spot and future prices are perfectly correlated and tend to move together by the same proportion. However, it would be difficult to achieve a perfect hedge position using a naive hedge strategy, as the basis between future and spot prices is time-varying (Yang and Lai, 2009). The conventional minimum variance hedge ratio is estimated using OLS. Finally, the conditional hedge is based on the time-varying hedge ratios obtained using the different GARCH modeling technique.

Comparison between the effectiveness of different hedge ratios is made by constructing portfolios implied by the computed ratios, and the change in the variance of these portfolios indicates the hedging effectiveness of the hedge ratios. The portfolios are constructed as $(R_t^c - h_t^* R_t^f)$, where R_t^c is the log difference of the cash (spot) prices, R_t^f is the log difference of the futures prices, and h_t^* is the estimated optimal hedge ratio.[12] The variance of these constructed portfolios is estimated and compared. For example, for comparison between the GARCH and GARCH-X-based portfolios, the change in variance is calculated as $(\mathrm{Var}_{GARCH} - \mathrm{Var}_{GARCHX})/\mathrm{Var}_{GARCH}$. Comparison is also provided between the five time-varying hedge ratio oriented portfolios and an unhedged portfolio.

First, we examine the within-sample risk reduction performance of these models as documented in Table 16.3A. The results show that in the case of Brazil, excepting GARCH-BEKK, the dynamic conditional variance hedging model performs better when compared to no hedge, naive hedge and conventional OLS hedging strategies. In the case of Hungary, with the exception of the standard GARCH method, the conditional hedging models outperform the no hedge, naive hedge and conventional OLS hedging strategies.

Table 16.3A Portfolio variance reduction

Parameter	Brazil	Hungary	South Africa
In-sample variance			
No hedge	0.000632	0.000369	0.000314
Naive hedge	0.000166	0.000097	0.000072
OLS hedge	0.000138	0.000092	0.000065
GARCH hedge	0.000136	0.000094	0.000064
GARCH-BEKK hedge	0.000145	0.000083	0.000063
GARCH-GJR hedge	0.000135	0.000083	0.000065
GARCH-ECM hedge	0.000135	0.000086	0.000063
GARCH-X hedge	0.000134	0.000083	0.000062
Percentage in-sample variance reduction of GARCH-X hedge compared to:			
No hedge	78.79	77.50	80.25
Naive hedge	19.27	14.43	13.88
OLS hedge	2.89	9.78	4.61
GARCH hedge	1.47	11.70	3.12
GARCH-BEKK hedge	7.58	0.0	1.58
GARCH-GJR hedge	0.74	0.0	4.61
GARCH-ECM hedge	0.74	3.48	1.58
Sample observations	2609	2609	2609

Table 16.3B Portfolio variance reduction

Parameter	Brazil	Hungary	South Africa
Out-of-sample variance 2006			
No hedge	0.000412	0.000305	0.000342
Naive hedge	0.000086	0.000015	0.000053
OLS hedge	0.000078	0.000015	0.000052
GARCH hedge	0.000081	0.000040	0.000048
GARCH-BEKK hedge	0.000074	0.000041	0.000048
GARCH-GJR hedge	0.000074	0.000041	0.000048
GARCH-ECM hedge	0.000072	0.000041	0.000047
GARCH-X hedge	0.000625	0.000041	0.000047
Percentage out-of-sample variance reduction of GARCH-ECM hedge compared to:			
No hedge	86.52	86.55	86.25
Naive hedge	16.27	−173.33	11.72
OLS hedge	7.69	−173.33	9.61
GARCH hedge	11.11	−2.5	2.08
GARCH-BEKK hedge	2.70	0.0	2.08
GARCH-GJR hedge	2.70	0.0	4.08
GARCH-X hedge	88.46	0.0	0.0
Sample observations	261	261	261

Table 16.3C Portfolio variance reduction

Parameter	Brazil	Hungary	South Africa
Out-of-sample variance 2007–9			
No hedge	0.001056	0.000914	0.000705
Naive hedge	0.000203	0.000071	0.000150
OLS hedge	0.000185	0.000069	0.000139
GARCH hedge	0.000226	0.000072	0.000142
GARCH-BEKK hedge	0.000349	0.000131	0.000258
GARCH-GJR hedge	0.000230	0.000073	0.000149
GARCH-ECM hedge	0.000225	0.000071	0.000143
GARCH-X hedge	0.000260	0.000071	0.000140
Percentage out-of-sample variance reduction of OLS hedge compared to:			
No hedge	82.48	92.45	80.28
Naive hedge	8.86	2.81	7.33
GARCH hedge	18.14	4.16	2.11
GARCH-BEKK hedge	46.99	47.32	46.12
GARCH-GJR hedge	19.56	5.47	6.71
GARCH-ECM hedge	17.77	2.81	2.79
GARCH-X hedge	40.54	2.81	.71
Sample observations	524	524	524

In the case of South Africa, all principal variants of the dynamic hedging models outperform the no hedge, naive hedge and conventional OLS hedging methods. The GARCH-X variant exhibits the lowest risk reduction across hedging strategies and among dynamic hedging models. Overall, the GARCH-X hedged portfolios show the strongest results among the GARCH class models in Brazil, Hungary and South Africa. The result is consistent with Choudhry (2009) and Yang et al. (2001) who claim that cointegration between cash and futures prices should be incorporated into hedging decisions.

Overall, it is indicative of the superiority of conditional models over traditional models in all three cases. We compute the percentage in-sample variance reduction of the GARCH-X model compared with a given benchmark model in the cases of Brazil, Hungary and South Africa. The GARCH-X contributes to 78.79 percent, 77.50 percent and 80.25 percent portfolio variance reduction in Brazil, Hungary and South Africa, compared with a no hedge strategy. The relative risk reduction of GARCH-X ranges from 9.78 percent (Hungary) to 2.89 percent (Brazil) compared with the traditional OLS method. For Brazil, Hungary and South Africa, conditional dynamic hedging models uniformly outperform no hedge, naive hedge and conventional OLS hedging strategies in most cases. Therefore, we see relative superiority of conditional hedging models over traditional models varying across countries and models.

16.4.2 Out-of-sample variance reduction

Baillie and Myers (1991) contend that the more reliable measure of hedging effectiveness is indicated by a comparison of hedged portfolio variance performance using hedge ratios in the out-of-sample periods estimated by different methods. Therefore, we compare the hedging effectiveness of the different methods during two different non-overlapping out-of-sample time periods: from December 2006 to December 2007 (one year), and from December 2007 to December 2009 (two years). Two different lengths of out-of-sample periods are applied to check whether changing the length has any significant effect on the hedging effectiveness of the hedge ratios. Two different lengths are also applied to avoid the sampling effect and overlapping effect. All versions of the GARCH are estimated for the period 1999 to 2005 first, and then the estimated parameters are applied to forecast hedge ratios recursively over the one-year out-of-sample time period. Similarly, the GARCH models are estimated over the period 1999 to 2006 and the estimated parameters are used to recursively forecast hedge ratios over the two year out-of-sample time period.

Table 16.3B shows the variance of the shorter out-of-sample and percentage change in variance (December 2006 to December 2007). Among the GARCH models, portfolios based on both GARCH-ECM and GARCH-X perform best in the case of South Africa. In addition, GARCH-ECM performs best in the case of Brazil, while the standard GARCH outperforms other competing GARCH models in the case of Hungary. In the case of Hungary, a portfolio based on naive and OLS hedges outperforms models from the GARCH family, which indicates that the relative effectiveness of hedging performance may also be viewed as a period-specific phenomenon.

Table 16.3C demonstrates the variance of the longer out-of-sample and percentage change in variance from December 2007 to December 2009. The results show that the out-of-sample portfolio based on OLS hedge outperforms all principal variants of GARCH models. Among the GARCH models, GARCH-ECM based hedging strategy provides the lowest variance for Brazil and Hungary. The GARCH-X based portfolio again provides lowest variance for Hungary and South Africa. The GARCH-BEKK does worst within the GARCH family across all countries. All principal variants of GARCH models significantly outperform the unhedged portfolio for all countries.

Changing the length of the out-of-sample period does affect the performance of the hedge ratios over the different time horizons. Models from the GARCH family exhibit superior risk reduction ability in the shorter forecast horizon, while in the longer forecast horizon, the traditional OLS based strategy offers better results. The shorter out-of-sample results of GARCH-X and GARCH-ECM demonstrate similar performance to the within-sample period results.

16.5 Evaluation of hedging performance using utility functions

The reductions in the variance are quite small in the large majority of in-sample tests, but this is expected given that daily data has been applied. Sephton (1993) also indicates small changes in the portfolio variance while applying daily data. As Kroner and Sultan (1993) contend, small size improvements in portfolio risk do not imply that the economic viability of the proposed strategy is questionable. The GARCH based portfolio should be applied if it makes the investor's utility greater than the reduction in the return caused by the transaction cost incurred. Therefore, we have investigated the economic significance of the time-varying hedge ratio within the utilitarian framework using two distinct approaches: (i) the mean-variance utility function, and (ii) the exponential utility function.

The mean-variance utility function is augmented by the transaction cost:

$$EU(R_{ct} - h_t^* R_{ft}) = E(R_{ct} - h^* R_{ft}) - Q - \psi var(R_{ct} - h_t^* R_{ft}) \tag{16.13}$$

where Q signifies the transaction cost to attenuate the utility level. Following Kroner and Sultan (1993), we assume the expected return to the hedged portfolio to be zero and the value of the coefficient of risk tolerance (ψ) to be 4. Therefore, the average utility from hedging in a given trading day is $-Q - 4var(R_{ct} - h_t^* R_{ft})$. In this chapter we assume a typical round-trip cost of 0.005 percent.[13] The results are reported in Table 16.4. The entries in the column MV show that GARCH-X dominates other hedging strategies in the cases of Brazil and South Africa when hedging performance is validated by the evaluation of the utility function. In the case of Hungary, GARCH-X, GARCH-GJR and GARCH-BEKK dominate the average utility obtained from other competing models. The entries in the column ΔMV demonstrate the utility gains in the GARCH class models with respect to the OLS based hedging strategy. For example, the utility gain for the GARCH-X model with respect to OLS in South Africa is 4.83 percent. Since the typical round trip costs are assumed to be 0.01 percent and 0.005 percent, hedgers would benefit from using a GARCH-X based hedging strategy.

The mean-variance rule and the minimum-variance hedge ratio are designed to select portfolios which are expected to yield the lowest risk for a given expected return. Therefore, the choice of optimal hedge ratio focuses on the first two moments of the asset return distribution, and hedging effectiveness is measured by the proportional reduction in variance of portfolio return. An alternative measure of hedging performance in recent research has underscored the role of skewness and kurtosis of portfolio returns.[14] As Alexander and Barbosa (2008) contend, the hedging performance evaluation based on the proportional variance reduction does not incorporate the effect of variance reduction on skewness and kurtosis. The minimum variance hedged portfolios are designed to have very low return volatility, but

Table 16.4 In-sample hedging performance using utility function

Brazil	Mean Return	Volatility	Skewness	Kurtosis	MV	ΔMV	CE	AIR
Unhedged	.000584	.000632	−.265377	.3.932837	−.002526		−.008827	.0232175
Naïve	.000011	.000166	−.405880	7.571522	−.000664		−.0091675	.0008527
OLS.	.000096	.000138	−.29910	8.899971	−.000552		−.008831	.008159
BGARCH	.000152	.000136	−.078536	3.093069	−.000544	1.47%	−.0066035	−.0130375
GARCHBEKK	.000134	.000145	−.012879	9.805696	−.00056	−7.14%	−.0064015	.0111474
GARCH-GJR	.000177	.000135	−.120565	8.673932	−.00054	2.22%	**−.0055452**	**.001468**
GARCH-ECM	.000150	.000135	−.014031	9.635468	−.00054	2.22%	−.0062855	.0128959
GARCH-X	.000132	.000134	−.104709	9.043601	**−.000536**	2.98%	−.0068631	.0113903[a]
Hungary								
Unhedged	.000451	.000369	−.329133	7.744448	−.001476		−.008065	.023468
Naïve	.000005	.000097	−.175039	10.209868	−.00386		−.0084774	.0005078
OLS	.000045	.000092	−.170527	9.535788	−.000366		−.0080544	.0046996
BGARCH	.000086	.000094	.927819	18.154873	−.000376	−2.65%	**−.0020805**	**.0088636**
GARCHBEKK	−.000012	.000083	−.104207	9.363221	**−.000332**	10.24%	−.0071764	−.0013204
GARCH-GJR	.000068	.000083	.227332	10.838703	**−.000332**	10.24%	−.0093647	.0074566
GARCH-ECM	.000062	.000086	.357862	12.573307	−.000344	6.39%	−.0044067	.0066931
GARCH-X	.000049	.000083	.174819	10.646401	**−.000332**	10.24	−.50715	.005393
South Africa								
Unhedged	.000365	.000314	−.309904	4.398800	−.001256		−.0057661	.0205896
Naïve	.000007	.000072	−.770829	24.773522	−.000286		−.0241595	.0008245
OLS	.000046	.000065	−1.247927	23.701249	−.00026		−.0283916	.005718
BGARCH	.000026	.000064	−.865242	23.207712	−.000256	1.56%	−.024106	**.0032372**
GARCHBEKK	.000063	.000063	−1.109909	19.305432	−.0002542	3.17%	−.0240747	.0079091
GARCH-GJR	.000042	.000065	−.858401	23.022565	−.00026	0.0	**−.0238963**	.0052236
GARCH-ECM	.000038	.000063	−1.090196	21.515735	−.000252	3.17%	−.0252292	.0047837
GARCH-X	.000048	.000062	−1.170550	22.241463	**−.000248**	4.83%	−.026633	.0060612

a high kurtosis indicates that the hedge can be spectacularly wrong on just a few days and a negative skewness indicates that it would be losing rather than making money.

Therefore, the second measure of hedging effectiveness, which accounts for both skewness and kurtosis, is derived from the following certainty equivalent (CE) exponential utility function:[15]

$$U(p) = -\psi \exp(-p/\psi) \tag{16.14}$$

where p signifies wealth. The exponential function has the property U(p) = E[U(p)]. Using a Taylor expansion of U(p) around the mean value and taking the expectation operator up to the fourth term, and after suitable transformation, the certainty equivalent utility function may be approximated as:

$$CE = \mu - \frac{\sigma^2}{2\psi} + \frac{\phi}{6\psi^2} - \frac{\kappa}{24\psi^3}, \tag{16.15}$$

where the third and fourth moments $\phi = E[(p-\mu)^3]$ and $\kappa = E[(p-\mu)^4]$ signify skewness and kurtosis, respectively. Equation (16.15) indicates that when $\psi > 0$, there is an aversion to risk associated with increasing variance, negative skewness and increasing kurtosis.

Formulation (16.15) also suggests an alternative measure of hedging performance known as the adjusted information ratio (AIR):[16]

$$AIR = IR + \left(\frac{\hat{\phi}}{6}\right) IR^2 + \left(\frac{\hat{\kappa}}{24}\right) IR^3, \tag{16.16}$$

where *IR* refers to the ordinary information ratio measured as the ratio of mean return to the volatility of return, $\hat{\varphi}$ denotes the estimated sample skewness and $\hat{\kappa}$ signifies excess kurtosis.

The results are reported in Table 16.4. The entries in the columns CE and AIR show CE utility and AIR associated with different hedging strategies. The bold numbers indicate the maximum (minimum) (dis)utility and AIR. Results show that portfolios based on GARCH-GJR yield minimum disutility in the cases of Brazil and South Africa, and standard bivariate GARCH hedge produces minimum disutility for Hungary.[17] Judged by the AIR, the best results are produced by GARCH-GJR for Brazil, and standard GARCH for Hungary and South Africa. Overall, the results suggest that hedging models based on the GARCH family improve investors' expected utility and adjusted information ratio. However, this method does not consider the issues of transaction cost and portfolio rebalancing.

16.6 Hedging effectiveness minimum capital risk requirement

Given that hedge ratios of various portfolios obtained from GARCH models are predictable, fund managers always prefer a portfolio with a lower financial capital. Over the past twenty years, financial institutions have been using economic models to identify and measure various market risks using a variety of procedures and set aside a provision of capital for potential losses. One popular approach is the calculation of Value at Risk (VaR) using in-house economic models to estimate the Minimum Capital Risk Requirements (MCRR). In this section, we are evaluating hedging effectiveness by estimating and comparing MCRR for portfolio returns obtained under alternative hedging models.

The VaR is a statistical measure of expected maximum loss on the value of the trading position of the asset portfolio taken by an institution which is exposed to market risk. For expository convenience, we denote the value of the portfolio by R; the VaR can be derived from the probability distribution of the future portfolio as the worst possible realization, signified as $R*$ such that the probability of a value lower than $R*$ is:

$$P(R \leq R^*) = \int_{-\infty}^{R*} f(R)dR = 1 - c \tag{16.17}$$

where (1−c) represents the probability of a lower-tail event, (5 percent for over 95 percent confidence level). Following Brooks et al. (2002), we define $R*$ in relation to a benchmark portfolio position such that:

$$R^* = R_1 - R_0, \tag{16.18}$$

where R_0 signifies the initial position; R_1 denotes lowest simulated value of the portfolio in case of a long futures position or the highest simulated value of the portfolio in the case of a short hedge position. The maximum expected loss as a proportion of initial value of the portfolio will depend on the probability distribution of $R*/R_0$. Based on the assumption of lognormal distribution of asset price, the next step is to find the fifth quantile of $In(R_1/R_0)$:

$$\frac{In(^{R1}/_{R0}) - \mu}{\sigma} = \pm\alpha, \tag{16.19}$$

where α is the fifth quantile from a standard normal distribution, μ is the mean of $In(R_1/R_0)$ and σ is the standard deviation of $\text{In}(R_1/R_0)$. Cross-multiplying, taking the exponential, and after certain manipulation:

$$R^* = R_0 \pm [1 - Exponential(\pm\alpha\sigma) + \mu]. \tag{16.20}$$

We calculate the MCRR for 1-day, 10-day, 20-day, 30-day, 60-day and 90-day investment horizons, by simulating densities of portfolio returns

Table 16.5A MCRR estimates GARCH hedging models for Brazil

Days	Unhedged	Naive hedge	GARCH	GARH-ECM	GARCH-X	GARCH-BEKK	GARCH-GJR
A. Long cash and short futures							
1	0.030127	0.011330	0.010685	0.010728	0.010296	0.010726	0.010351
10	0.092068	0.046223	0.040604	0.038261	0.064022	0.042824	0.038518
20	0.134681	0.073942	0.063107	0.062626	0.062375	0.063967	0.064396
30	0.158912	0.095756	0.083200	0.082893	0.081551	0.087861	0.081674
60	0.240787	0.152774	0.130018	0.126651	0.128270	0.132880	0.123011
90	0.301764	0.182374	0.163027	0.158671	0.211389	0.166908	0.159372
B. Short cash and long futures							
1	0.036057	0.010795	0.010502	0.010390	0.010674	0.010572	0.010539
10	0.104269	0.046071	0.046590	0.047968	0.047193	0.044969	0.045916
20	0.153170	0.074474	0.072975	0.076716	0.073131	0.073867	0.074752
30	0.0192423	0.095396	0.099643	0.099720	0.098710	0.094199	0.096791
60	0.273952	0.150904	0.149848	0.153163	0.0154694	0.149197	0.147856
90	0.348227	0.194399	0.193195	0.197081	0.197259	0.196861	0.196182

Table 16.5B MCRR estimates GARCH hedging models for Hungary

Days	Unhedged	Naive hedge	GARCH	GARH-ECM	GARCH-X	GARCH-BEKK	GARCH-GJR
A. Long cash and short futures							
1	0.033938	0.008124	0.008256	0.008034	0.008417	0.008328	0.008005
10	0.096883	0.028563	0.028420	0.027747	0.029987	0.027735	0.028502
20	0.143301	0.043710	0.043187	0.043803	0.043343	0.042153	0.042669
30	0.165359	0.055722	0.054607	0.057916	0.057741	0.057904	0.054302
60	0.217735	0.089288	0.087281	0.087085	0.089946	0.083514	0.095994
90	0.260593	0.115549	0.124108	0.121115	0.124929	0.118854	0123209
B. Short cash and long futures							
1	0.034723	0.008119	0.009096	0.008642	0.008466	0.008707	0.008885
10	0.097830	0.029483	0.031817	0.031238	0.030115	0.030233	0.032050
20	0.135547	0.046116	0.048175	0.46841	0.045496	0.046776	0.049669
30	0.164239	0.061085	0.062250	0.062664	0.058278	0.062311	0.0621159
60	0.212531	0.102806	0.105144	0.099312	0.094186	0.097457	0.102962
90	0.250543	0.140030	0.140368	0.136270	0.13311	0.144506	0139674

Table 16.5C MCRR estimates GARCH hedging models for South Africa

Days	Unhedged	Naive hedge	GARCH	GARH-ECM	GARCH-X	GARCH-BEKK	GARCH-GJR
A. Long cash and short futures							
1	0.020279	0.010681	0.010162	0.009648	0.010036	0.009734	0.010085
10	0.063090	0.035301	0.032887	0.032269	0.033408	0.032948	0.032410
20	0.086588	0.052092	0.049051	0.048081	0.049432	0.047820	0.048279
30	0.110532	0.067130	0.063233	0.059478	0.061162	0.061042	0.058690
60	0.162780	0.099207	0.092207	0.089644	0.092513	0.088046	0.093135
90	0.201144	0.126094	0.115262	0.113074	0.115919	0.112555	0.115816
180							
B. Short cash and long futures							
1	0.021384	0.009912	0.009754	0.009917	0.084722	0.009525	0.009567
10	0.067591	0.035442	0.034202	0.034967	0.036630	0.034759	0.034423
20	0.095726	0.051243	0.052560	0.054154	0.053920	0.052255	0.050945
30	0.118965	0.068646	0.068140	0.071186	0.069517	0.066483	0.065499
60	0.175321	0.104439	0.103164	0.107182	0.105303	0.100665	0.101719
90	0.216240	0.127144	0.133376	0.130843	0132596	0.124859	0.127776

using Efron's (1982) bootstrapping methodology, which is based on a multivariate GARCH(1,1) model.[18] The Monte Carlo simulation procedure used 10,000 simulated paths of portfolio returns based on a GARCH(1,1) model to generate an empirical distribution of the maximum loss.

Table 16.5A presents the MCRR estimates based on the data of Brazil obtained from the alternative hedging models. The top panel of Table 16.5A presents MCRR for a short hedge (long cash and short futures) and the lower panel of Table 16.5A shows the results for a long hedge (short cash and long futures). The results show that for short hedge, GARCH-X outperforms competing models at 1-day, 20-day and 30-day forecast horizons, while GARCH-ECM outperforms competitors in two cases (10-day and 90-day forecast horizons). GARCH-GJR outperforms only at the 60-day investment horizon. For long hedge, GARCH-BEKK performs better at 10-day and 30-day forecast horizons, while the standard GARCH outperforms competing models at 20-day and 90-day forecast horizons. GARCH-GJR outperforms other competing models only at a 60-day investment horizon. The long hedge positions appear to require slightly more capital than comparative short hedge positions over most forecast horizons. Table 16.5B presents the MCRR estimates for the market of Hungary. For short hedge, GARCH-BEKK outperforms competing models at 20-day and 60-day forecast horizons, while GARCH-GJR outperforms competing models at 1-day and 30-day forecast horizons. Standard GARCH and naive hedge outperform other competing models only in one case each, (10-day and 90-day forecast horizons, respectively). For long hedge, the naive hedge outperforms other competing models in four cases (1-day, 10-day, 20-day, and 30-day forecast horizons). GARCH-ECM and GARCH-X outperform other competing models at 60-day and 90-day forecast horizons, respectively. Table 16.5C presents the MCRR estimates for the South African market. The results show that for short hedge, GARCH-ECM performs best among the GARCH class of models in most cases, followed by GARCH-BEKK and GARCH-GJR. For long hedge, each of the GARCH-GJR and GARCH-BEKK outperform competing models in two cases (20-day, 30-day, 60-day and 90-day forecast horizons); GARCH-X outperforms only at a 1-day forecast horizon and standard GARCH performs best at a 10-day investment horizon. When we compare results across Tables 16.5A, 16.5B and 16.5C, it is evident that the position in the South African market requires less capital under both short and long hedge conditions relative to positions in the markets of Brazil and Hungary. These comparative results suggest that the position in the South African market is slightly less risky than positions in the markets for Brazil and Hungary.

16.7 Conclusion

It is a well-documented claim in the futures market literature that the optimal hedge ratio should be time-varying and not constant. Lately, different versions of the GARCH models have been applied to estimate time-varying hedge ratios for different futures markets. This chapter investigates the hedging effectiveness of GARCH estimated time-varying hedge ratios in three emerging futures markets: Brazil, Hungary and South Africa. The time-varying hedge ratios are estimated by means of five different types of GARCH models: the standard bivariate GARCH, GARCH-BEKK, GARCH-ECM, GARCH-X, and asymmetric GARCH-GJR. The GARCH-X and the GARCH-ECM are unique among the GARCH models in taking into consideration the effects of the short-run deviations from a long-run relationship between the cash and the futures price indices on the hedge ratio. The long-run relationship between the price indices is estimated by the Engle-Granger cointegration method. The hedging effectiveness is estimated and compared by checking the variance of the portfolios created using these estimated hedge ratios. The lower the variance of the portfolio, the higher the hedging effectiveness of the hedge ratio. This chapter is unique in the sense that it investigates hedge ratio effectiveness in emerging stock markets.

The empirical tests are conducted by applying daily data. The effectiveness of the hedge ratio is investigated by comparing the within-sample period (December 1999–2009) and out-of-sample period performance of the different hedge ratios for two periods, December 2007 to 2009 (two years) and December 2006 to 2007 (one year). The two different lengths of out-of-sample periods are applied to investigate the effect of changing the period length on the hedging effectiveness of the hedge ratios. The two different periods are also applied to avoid sample effect and overlapping issues.

What do our results show? Results from within-sample show that, overall, the GARCH-X hedged portfolios show the strongest results among the GARCH class models in Brazil, Hungary and South Africa. In the shorter out-of-sample period among the GARCH models, portfolios based on both GARCH-ECM and GARCH-X perform best in the case of South Africa. In addition, GARCH-ECM performs best in the case of Brazil, while the standard GARCH outperforms other competing GARCH models in the case of Hungary. In the case of Hungary, portfolios based on naive and OLS hedges outperform models from the GARCH family, which indicates that the relative effectiveness of hedging performance may also be viewed as a period-specific phenomenon. The longer out-of-sample period results show that the out-of-sample portfolio based on OLS hedge outperforms all principal variants of GARCH models. Among the GARCH models, the GARCH-ECM based hedging strategy provides the lowest variance for Brazil and Hungary. The GARCH-X based portfolio again provides the lowest variance for Hungary and South Africa. The GARCH-BEKK does worst within the GARCH family across all countries. All variants of GARCH models significantly outperform the unhedged portfolio for all countries.

The inconsistent performance of the GARCH models ratios may be attributed to the complexity of the model (Baillie and Myers, 1991). With any GARCH method, the hedge portfolio has to be rebalanced frequently. In this chapter, the time-varying GARCH hedge ratio changed every day. The trade-off between the risk reduction and the transaction cost will determine the practicality of the GARCH hedging method.

The GARCH based portfolio should be applied if it makes the investor's utility greater than the reduction in the return caused by the transaction cost incurred. Therefore, this chapter investigates the economic significance of the time-varying hedge ratio within the utilitarian framework using two distinct approaches: (i) the mean-variance utility function, and (ii) the exponential utility function. Results show that the GARCH-X dominates other hedging strategies in the cases of Brazil and South Africa when hedging performance is validated by the evaluation of the mean-variance utility function. Finally, we have computed the MCRR using the estimated hedge ratios to ascertain the superiority of alternative hedging strategy. Results show that the forecasting superiority of the model depends upon the market under study and the length of forecast horizon.

Results in this chapter advocate further research in this field. Further research may be conducted using different frequencies of the data, different methods of estimation, time period or type of futures markets, for example.

Notes

1. Important events, regimes and episodes in the financial markets, such as the financial market volatility of the 1970s and 1980s, the stock market crash of 1987, the booming growth of the equity market during 1995–2000 followed by the severe downturn in the equity market during the new millennium years of 2001–8, and the recent global financial crisis of 2008, have further rekindled this research thrust and aspiration.
2. Therefore, an investor holding a long position in the cash market should short h units of futures contracts, where h would be the hedge ratio.
3. Kofman and McGlenchy (2005) furnished a succinct discussion on the development and progression of both the static and the various dynamic hedging models.
4. Apart from the static OLS method, all other variants of the single-equation based methodology are known as the early version of the dynamic hedging models.
5. However, studies of Alexander and Barbosa (2007) and Lai et al. (2009) are exceptions.
6. The OLS estimation of the hedge ratio from equation (16.2) is based on the assumption of time-invariant asset distributions suggested by Ederington (1979), and Anderson and Danthine (1980).
7. There is more than one GARCH model available that is able to capture the asymmetric effect in volatility. According to Engle and Ng (1993), the Glosten et al. (1993) model is the best at parsimoniously capturing this asymmetric effect.
8. The BM&FBOVESPA is a Sao Paulo-based stock and futures exchange which is the fourth largest exchange in the Americas in terms of market capitalization, behind the New York Stock Exchange, NASDAQ, and the Toronto Stock Exchange. It is also the tenth largest exchange in the world in terms of market capitalization.

9. The Budapest Commodity Exchange (BCE) and the Budapest Stock Exchange (BSE) merged on October 2005, which made the BSE one of the main derivatives centers in Central Europe. The BSE played a significant role in the privatization of many leading Hungarian companies. BSE was one of the first in the world which started to use free-float capitalization weighting instead of the traditional market capitalization weighting in October 1999.
10. South Africa became the second emerging market to trade index futures when All Share futures were launched on 30 April 1990 in JSE and SAFEX (Smith and Rogers, 2006).
11. The continuous series is a perpetual series of futures prices. It starts at the nearest contract month, which forms the first values for the continuous series, either until the contract reaches its expiry date or until the first business day of the actual contract month. At this point, the next trading contract month is taken.
12. In the case of the constant ratio the time subscript does not exist.
13. Moon et al. (2009) reported that a typical round-trip cost is around 0.00072 percent of KOSTAR future contract value in the Korean market. Yang and Lai (2009) noted that the transaction cost ranges between 0.005 percent and 0.01 percent in the major global exchanges which are trading financial contracts of DJIA, S&P500, NASDAQ100, FTSE100, CAC40, DAX30 and Nikkei225. Rossi and Zucca (2002) noted a transaction cost of 0.0015 percent in the Italian bond market.
14. For example, see Alexander and Barbosa (2008), Cremers et al. (2004), and Harvey et al. (2004).
15. This part is drawn from Alexander and Barbosa (2008).
16. For example, see Alexander and Barbosa (2008).
17. Note that in the case of no hedge, the portfolio consists of a long position in the cash market. This strategy is able to achieve significant positive return in-sample, but with a large variability of portfolio return. As Brooks et al. (2002) contend, any alternative hedging strategies will not generate returns that are significantly different from zero either in-sample or out-of-sample. However, they yield significantly less return variability than unhedged positions. Therefore, we have not compared no hedge strategy with the alternative hedging strategies.
18. Interested readers are referred to Brooks et al.(2002), and Jorion (2007) for a detailed discussion.

References

Alexander, C. and Barbosa, A. (2007). Effectiveness of Minimum-Variance Hedging: The Impact of Electronic Trading and Exchange-Traded Funds. *Journal of Portfolio Management*, 33, 46–59.

Alexander, C. and Barbosa, A. (2008). Hedging Index Exchange Traded Funds. *Journal of Banking and Finance*, 32, 326–37.

Anderson, R. W. and Danthine, J. P. (1980). Hedging and Joint Production: Theory and Illustrations. *Journal of Finance*, 35, 489–97.

Bailey. O. (2010) Developments in Emerging Markets. *Reserve Bank of Australia Bulletin*, December Quarter 2010.

Baillie, R. and Myers, R. (1991). Bivariate GARCH Estimates of the Optimal Commodity Futures Hedge. *Journal of Applied Econometrics*, 6, 109–24.

Bekaert, G. and Harvey, C. R. (2000). Foreign Speculators and Emerging Equity Markets. *Journal of Finance*, LX, 565–613.

Black, F. (1976). Studies of Stock Market Volatility Changes. *Proceedings of the American Statistical Association, Business and Economics Statistics Section*, 177–81.

Bollerslev, T., Chou, R. and Kroner, K. (1992). ARCH Modeling in Finance. *Journal of Econometrics*, 52, 5–59.

Brooks, C., Henry, O. T. and Persand, G. (2002). The Effects of Asymmetries in Optimal Hedge Ratios. *Journal of Business*, 75, 333–52.

Cecchetti, S. G., Cumby, R. E. and Figlewski, S. (1988). Estimation of Optimal Futures Hedge. *Review of Economics and Statistics*, 70, 623–30.

Choudhry, T. (2009). Short-Run Deviations and Time-Varying Hedge Ratios: Evidence from Agricultural Futures Markets. *International Review of Financial Analysis*, 18, 58–65.

Christie, A. (1982). The Stochastic Behavior of Common Stock Variances: Value, Leverage and Interest Rate Effects. *Journal of Financial Economics*, 10, 407–32.

Cremers, J. H., Kritzman, M. and Page, S. (2004). Portfolio Formation with the Higher Moments and Plausible Utility. Revere Street Working Paper Series, *Financial Economics*, 272–12.

Ederington, L. (1979). The Hedging Performance of the New Futures Markets. *Journal of Finance*, 34, 157–170.

Efron, B. (1982). *Jacknife, the Bootstrape, and Other Resampling Plans*. Society for Industrial and Applied Mathematics, Philadelphia.

Elliot, G., Rothenberg, T. J. and Stock, J. H. (1996). Efficient Tests for an Autoregressive Unit Root. *Econometrica*, 64, 813–36.

Engle, R. F. (1982) Autoregressive Conditional Heteroscedasticity with Estimates of the Variance of United Kingdom Inflation. *Econometrica*, 50 (4), 987–1007.

Engle, R. F. and Kroner, K. (1995). Multivariate Simultaneous Generalized ARCH. *Econometric Theory*, 11, 122–50.

Engle, R. F. and Ng, V. (1993). Measuring and Testing the Impact of News on Volatility. *Journal of Finance*, 48, 1749–78.

Figlewski, S. (1986). *Hedging with Financial Futures for Institutional Investors*. Ballinger Publishing: Cambridge, MA.

Fortune, P. (1989). An Assessment of Financial Market Volatility: Bills, Bonds, and Stocks. *New England Economic Review*, November/December, 13–28.

Glosten, L. R., Jagannathan, R. and Runkle, D. E. (1993). On the Relation between the Expected Value and the Volatility of the Nominal Excess Return on Stocks. *Journal of Finance*, 48, 1779–801.

Harvey, C., Liechty, J., Liechty, M. and Muller, P. (2004). Portfolio Selection with Higher Moments. Working Papers 70, Fuqua School of Business, Duke University.

Johnson, L. (1960). The Theory of Hedging and Speculation in Commodity Futures. *Review of Economic Studies*, 27, 139–51.

Jorion, P. (2007). *Value at Risk: The New Benchmark for Managing Financial Risk*. McGraw-Hill: New York.

Kofman, P. and McGlenchy, P. (2005). Structurally Sound Dynamic Index Futures Hedging. *Journal of Futures Markets*, 25, 1173–202.

Kroner, K. F. and Sultan, J. (1993). Time-Varying Distributions and Dynamic Hedging with Foreign Currency Futures. *Journal of Financial and Quantitative Analysis*, 28, 535–51.

Lai, Y., Chen, C. W. S. and Gerlach, R. (2009). Optimal Dynamic Hedging via Copula-Threshold-GARCH Models. *Mathematics and Computers in Simulation*, 79, 2609–24.

Moon, G. H., Yu, W. C. and Hong, C. H. (2009). Dynamic Hedging Performance with the Evaluation of Multivariate GARCH Models: Evidence from KOSTAR Index Futures. *Applied Economics Letters*, 16, 913–9.
Rossi, E. and Zucca, C. (2002). Hedging Interest Rate Risk with Multivariate GARCH. *Applied Financial Economics*, 12, 241–51.
Sephton, P. (1993). Optimal Hedge Ratios at the Winnipeg Commodity Exchange. *Canadian Journal of Economics*, 26, 175–93.
Silber, W. (1985). The Economic Role of Financial Futures, in Peck, A. E. (ed.) *Futures Markets: Their Economic Role*. American Enterprise Institute for Public Policy Research.
Smith, G. and Rogers, G. (2006). Variance Ratio Tests of the Random Walk Hypothesis for South African Stock Futures. *South African Journal of Economics*, 74, 410–21.
Working, H. (1953). Futures Trading and Hedging. *American Economic Review*, 43, 314–43.
Yang, J., Bessler, D. and Leatham, D. (2001). Asset Storability and Price Discovery in Commodity Futures Markets: A New Look. *Journal of Futures Markets*, 21, 279–300.
Yang, M. J. and Lai, Y. C. (2009). An Out-of-Sample Comparative Analysis of Hedging Performance of Stock Index Futures: Dynamic versus Static Hedging. *Applied Financial Economics*, 19, 1059–72.

17

An Optimal Timing Approach to Option Portfolio Risk Management

Tim Leung and Peng Liu

17.1 Introduction

Options are widely used as a tool for investment and risk management. In a liquid market, investors have the flexibility to trade options prior to their expiration dates. This is especially important for investors with an existing option position as they can control risk exposure through timing the option trades. For effective option based portfolio management, it is imperative for any investor to determine *when* to liquidate an option to the market at its trading price. Prior to expiration, the investor can always sell the option immediately, or wait for a potentially better future opportunity. This chapter studies the optimal timing to liquidate an option position to the market.

From the perspective of any particular investor, the market price of an option may not reflect her market view or agree with her valuation of different sources of risks. Therefore, the optimal liquidation timing naturally depends on both the investor's subjective probability measure as well as the market risk-neutral pricing measure. The option payoff and the performance of the underlying stock will also play a crucial role. In addition, we examine the sensitivity of the investor's trading strategy on model parameters.

In this chapter, we identify the situations where holding the option through expiration is optimal, under both a complete diffusion market and an incomplete stochastic volatility market (see Proposition 1). In addition, we analyze several cases with non-trivial optimal liquidation strategies, with numerical examples of liquidating a straddle and a butterfly. We also compare the liquidation timing between different option positions, for example call versus bull spread. The investor's optimal timing can be characterized by a liquidation boundary which represents the critical stock price upon which the investor should sell the option to the market. We also examine the sensitivity of the optimal liquidation value with respect to the drift of the underlying stock. In the stochastic volatility model, we show the connection between the investor's liquidation timing and the option payoff and model parameters. We also derive a variational inequality from which the optimal liquidation strategy can be solved.

In a related study, Leung and Ludkovski (2011) analyzed the optimal timing to buy equity European and American options under a stochastic volatility model and a defaultable stock model through the concept of delayed purchase premium. Leung and Liu (2012) studied the optimal liquidation of defaultable securities in a general intensity-based credit risk model. In both papers, the investor is assumed to value derivatives under some risk-neutral pricing measure that may differ from the market. In contrast, the current article addresses the option portfolio risk management problem from the investor's subjective measure. Leung and Ludkovski (2012) incorporated the investor's risk preferences and applied an exponential utility indifference approach for the optimal timing to purchase derivatives in incomplete markets. Finally, Peskir and co-authors proposed a series of new exotic early-exercisable derivatives called British options (see, for example, Peskir and Samee (2011) and Peskir et al. (2010)), whereby the payoff is the expected terminal payoff assuming that the true drift of the stock price equals a pre-specified contract drift.

The rest of the chapter is organized as follows. In Section 17.2, we formulate the problem of optimally selling an option in a general market setting. In Section 17.3, we analyze the option liquidation problem in a complete market. In particular, we find the conditions whereby holding the option through expiration is optimal. We also numerically compute the early liquidation timing for two option positions: a long straddle and a long butterfly. In Section 17.4, we incorporate stochastic volatility to the model.

17.2 Problem formulation

We start with a probability space $(\Omega, \mathcal{G}, \mathbb{P})$, where $\mathbb{P}$ is the historical or subjective measure. The market consists of a risky liquid stock S and a money market account with a constant interest rate $r \geq 0$. We denote $\mathbb{G} = (\mathcal{G}_t)_{0 \leq t \leq T}$ as the filtration generated by the stock price S. Consider a liquidly traded option with terminal payoff $F(S_T)$ on expiration date T. The market price of the option is given by the conditional expectation under the market's risk-neutral pricing measure $\mathbb{Q}$:

$$C_t = \boldsymbol{E}^{\mathbb{Q}}\{e^{-r(T-t)}F(S_T)|\mathcal{G}_t\}. \tag{17.1}$$

If an investor buys the option at time t and holds it through expiration, then her expected return is given by

$$R_t := \boldsymbol{E}^{\mathbb{P}}\{e^{-r(T-t)}F(S_T)|\mathcal{G}_t\} - C_t. \tag{17.2}$$

However, the investor also has the flexibility to liquidate the option to the market prior to expiration. By selecting the optimal liquidation time, a higher expected return can be achieved. As time progresses, the investor can decide to liquidate immediately or wait to sell the option later. Hence, the investor's maximal expected discounted liquidation value is given by

$$V_t = \operatorname*{ess\,sup}_{t \le \tau \le T} \boldsymbol{E}^{\mathbb{P}}\{e^{-r(\tau-t)} C_\tau \,|\, \mathcal{G}_t\}. \tag{17.3}$$

Here, the ess sup in (17.3) is taken over all $\mathcal{G}$-stopping times $\tau \in [t, T]$.

To quantify the additional value from optimal timing to sell, as opposed to immediate liquidation, we define the optimal liquidation premium by

$$L_t := V_t - C_t = \operatorname*{ess\,sup}_{t \le \tau \le T} \boldsymbol{E}^{\mathbb{P}}\{e^{-r(\tau-t)} C_\tau \,|\, \mathcal{G}_t\} - C_t. \tag{17.4}$$

The optimal liquidation premium L can be interpreted as the expected return from a buy-and-sell strategy. Using standard optimal stopping theory, the optimal liquidation time τ^* is given by

$$\begin{aligned} \tau_t^* &= \inf\{t \le u \le T : V_u = C_u\} \\ &= \inf\{t \le u \le T : L_u = 0\}, \end{aligned} \tag{17.5}$$

where the second equality follows from the definition of L in (17.4). In other words, it is optimal for the investor to sell the option as soon as the optimal liquidation premium L vanishes. Intuitively, this means there is no more value for waiting further to liquidate.

Our framework can be readily applied to the *reverse* problem of shorting an option position at time t and buying it back at time τ. This amounts to changing the ess sup to ess inf in V. In a related study, Leung and Ludkovski (2011) examined the optimal purchase problem of equity options under the investor's risk-neutral pricing measure.

17.3 Optimal liquidation in a complete market

Now let us consider the optimal liquidation problem within a complete Markovian financial market. The asset price S is assumed to follow the SDE

$$dS_t = \mu(t, S_t) S_t \, dt + \sigma(t, S_t) S_t \, dW_t, \tag{17.6}$$

where $\mu(t,s)$ and $\sigma(t,s)$ are deterministic functions, and W is a standard Brownian motion under the subjective measure $\mathbb{P}$. The general price dynamics in (17.6) include many well-known complete market models, including local stochastic volatility models (for example, the CEV model) as well as the geometric Brownian motion.

We assume that any market-traded option is priced under a unique risk-neutral pricing measure $\mathbb{Q}$. For an option with terminal payoff $F(S_T)$ at time

T, the associated option price function $C(t,s)$ is given by the conditional expectation

$$C(t,s) = \boldsymbol{E}^{\mathbb{Q}}_{t,s}\{e^{-r(T-t)}F(S_T)\},$$

where the conditional expectation $\boldsymbol{E}^{\mathbb{Q}}_{t,s}\{\cdot\}$ (given $S_t = s$) is taken under the unique risk-neutral pricing measure $\mathbb{Q}$. The price function is the solution to the PDE

$$-rC + C_t + rsC_s + \frac{\sigma^2(t,s)s^2}{2}C_{ss} = 0, \quad (t,s) \in [0,T) \times \mathbb{R}_+, \tag{17.7}$$

with terminal condition $C(T,s) = F(s)$ for $s \in \mathbb{R}_+$. Here, the subscripts indicate partial derivatives. As is well known, the market price $C(t,s)$ does not depend on the drift μ.

If the investor buys and holds the option through expiration, then the expected return is

$$R(t,s) := \boldsymbol{E}^{\mathbb{P}}_{t,s}\{e^{-r(T-t)}F(S_T)\} - C(t,s). \tag{17.8}$$

On the other hand, if the investor selects the optimal time to sell the option to the market, then her maximal expected profit is given by

$$\begin{aligned} L(t,s) &= \sup_{t \le \tau \le T} \boldsymbol{E}^{\mathbb{P}}_{t,s}\{e^{-r(\tau-t)}C(\tau,S_\tau)\} - C(t,s) \\ &= \sup_{t \le \tau \le T} \boldsymbol{E}^{\mathbb{P}}_{t,s}\Big\{\int_t^\tau e^{-r(u-t)}(-rC + C_t + \mu(u,S_u)S_uC_s + \frac{\sigma^2(u,S_u)S_u^2}{2}C_{ss})du\Big\} \\ &= \sup_{t \le \tau \le T} \boldsymbol{E}^{\mathbb{P}}_{t,s}\{\int_t^\tau e^{-r(u-t)}(\mu(u,S_u) - r)S_uC_s\,du\}, \end{aligned} \tag{17.9}$$

where the last equality follows from the PDE (17.7). According to (17.4), the representation (17.9) is the investor's optimal liquidation premium. Of course, this formulation assumes that the market trading price is indeed given by $C(t,S_t)$ over time $t \in [0,T]$. Under the current complete market model, this is a self-consistent assumption.

Suppose the investor seeks to maximize the expected return through selecting the optimal time to sell the option. We observe that if the integrand in (17.9) is positive (resp. negative) a.s., then it is optimal to pick the largest (resp. smallest) stopping time possible, namely, $\tau = T$ (resp. $\tau = t$). In the case with $\tau = t$ (buy and sell at the same time), we can interpret this as not buying the option at all. Furthermore, for the most common European-style options, that is, puts and calls, the partial derivative (Delta) C_s would take a constant sign. This fact leads to the following result.

Proposition 1 *It is optimal to hold the option till T if*
(i) $\mu(t,s) \ge r$ and $C_s(t,s) \ge 0$ $\forall (t,s) \in [0,T] \times \mathbb{R}_+$, or
(ii) $\mu(t,s) \le r$ and $C_s(t,s) \le 0$ $\forall (t,s) \in [0,T] \times \mathbb{R}_+$.

Applying the first case to call options, this means that one should buy and hold a call (with any strike) till T when the perceived drift μ dominates the risk-free rate r. Similar arguments apply for the second case with puts since they have a negative Delta. This is consistent with the intuition that a bullish investor ($\mu \geq r$) would buy a call, while a bearish investor would buy a put ($\mu \leq r$). Finally, we remark that when $(\mu(t,s) - r)C_s(t,s)$ is not of constant sign, then a non-trivial timing strategy could result. In Proposition 1, the only information required about $\mu(t,s)$ is that $\mu(t,s) \lesseqgtr r$, rather than its exact specification.

In general, the investor's liquidation strategy can be determined by numerically solving the optimal stopping problem:

$$L(t,s) = \sup_{t \leq \tau \leq T} \boldsymbol{E}^{\mathbb{P}} \left\{ \int_t^{\tau} e^{-r(u-t)} G(u,S_u)\, du \,|\, S_t = s \right\}, \tag{17.10}$$

where

$$G(t,s) = (\mu(t,s) - r) s C_s(t,s) \tag{17.11}$$

is called the *drift function*. As we can see from Proposition 1, the sign of the drift function G plays a crucial role in determining the optimal liquidation timing. Indeed, both scenarios in Proposition 1 correspond to the case where $G \geq 0\ \forall (t,s) \in [0,T] \times \mathbb{R}_+$. Then, it follows immediately from (17.10) that the choice of the largest stopping time T is optimal. Similarly, if it turns out that $G \leq 0\ \forall (t,s) \in [0,T] \times \mathbb{R}_+$, then it is optimal for the option holder to sell the option immediately.

The drift function also allows investors to compare liquidation time of two different option positions. For instance, if the drift function of an option A dominates that of another option B, that is, $G^A(t,s) \geq G^B(t,s), \forall (t,s) \in [0,T] \times \mathbb{R}_+$, then $L^A(t,s) \geq L^B(t,s), \forall (t,s) \in [0,T] \times \mathbb{R}_+$. To see this, denote by τ_B^* the optimal liquidation time for $L^B(t,s)$, then we have

$$\begin{aligned} L^A(t,s) &\geq \boldsymbol{E}^{\mathbb{P}}_{t,s} \left\{ \int_t^{\tau_B^*} e^{-r(u-t)} G^A(u,S_u)\, du \right\} \geq \boldsymbol{E}^{\mathbb{P}}_{t,s} \left\{ \int_t^{\tau_B^*} e^{-r(u-t)} G^B(u,S_u)\, du \right\} \\ &= L^B(t,s). \end{aligned}$$

In turn, we can conclude from (17.5) that the optimal liquidation time for option A is always later than that for B.

Example 2 *(Call versus Bull Spread)*

We consider a European call option with strike price K, and a European bull spread with payoff $(S_T - K)^+ - (S_T - \bar{K})^+$ for $K < \bar{K}$. If $\mu(t,s) \geq r, \forall (t,s) \in [0,T] \times \mathbb{R}_+$, the drift function of a European call option is always positive. Consequently, the drift function of the European call option always dominates that of the European bull spread, whose lower strike price coincides with the strike price of call *option. Hence, the optimal liquidation time of the European call option is always later than that of the European bull spread.*

When the optimal liquidation strategy is non-trivial, we look for the numerical solution to the variational inequality for $L(t,s)$:

$$\min\Big(-L_t-\mu(t,s)sL_s-\frac{\sigma^2(t,s)s^2}{2}L_{ss}+rL-G,\ L\Big)=0, \tag{17.12}$$

for $(t,s)\in[0,T)\times\mathbb{R}_+$, with boundary condition $L(T,s)=0$. The investor's optimal timing is characterized by the sell region $\mathcal{S}$ and delay region $\mathcal{D}$, namely,

$$\mathcal{S}=\{(t,s)\in[0,T]\times\mathbb{R}_+:\ L(t,s)=0\}, \tag{17.13}$$

$$\mathcal{D}=\{(t,s)\in[0,T]\times\mathbb{R}_+:\ L(t,s)>0\}. \tag{17.14}$$

We proceed to analyze the non-trivial optimal liquidation strategies for a long straddle and a long butterfly position. In the following, we assume that the underlying stock satisfies SDE in (17.6) such that $\mu(t,s)=\mu$ and $\sigma(t,s)=\sigma$ for constants μ and σ. This allows for explicit computation of the market price of the option positions. We will extend our analysis to a general stochastic volatility model in Section 17.4.

17.3.1 Optimal liquidation of a long straddle

We consider an investor holding a long straddle position, which will make profit if the stock price moves a long way from the strike price in either direction. Precisely, a long straddle is a combination of a call and a put written on the same underlying S with the same maturity T and strike price K, and its payoff is

$$F^{STD}(S_T):=(S_T-K)^++(K-S_T)^+.$$

The market price of a long straddle, denoted by C^{STD}, is simply the sum of the respective Black-Scholes call and put prices

$$C^{STD}(t,s;K,T)=c_{BS}(t,s;K,T)+p_{BS}(t,s;K,T),$$

where $c_{BS}(t,s;K,T)$ and $p_{BS}(t,s;K,T)$ are the Black-Scholes price formulas for a call and a put with strike K and maturity T, respectively. The payoff and price function of a long straddle are shown in Figure 17.1.

The drift function of a long straddle is important to determine the optimal liquidation strategy. Using (17.11), we compute the drift function explicitly by

$$\begin{aligned}G^{STD}(t,s)&=(\mu-r)sC_s^{STD}(t,s)\\&=(\mu-r)s(2\Phi(d_1)-1),\end{aligned} \tag{17.15}$$

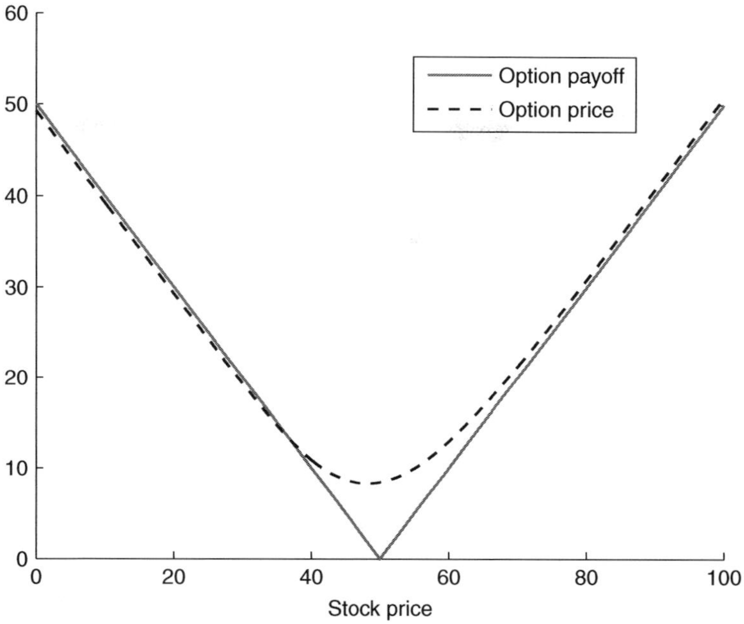

Figure 17.1 The payoff and market price of a long straddle over the underlying stock price

Notes: We take $T = 0.5$, $t = 0$, $r = 0.03$, $\sigma = 0.3$, $K = 50$.

where $\Phi(x)$ is the standard normal cumulative distribution function and

$$d_1 := \frac{\log(\frac{s}{K}) + (r + \frac{1}{2}\sigma^2)(T - t)}{\sigma\sqrt{T - t}}. \tag{17.16}$$

In addition, we observe the limiting behavior for C_s^{STD}:

$$\lim_{s\to 0} C_s^{STD}(t,s) = -1, \qquad \lim_{s\to\infty} C_s^{STD}(t,s) = 1. \tag{17.17}$$

Following the definition in (17.9), we denote L^{STD} as the optimal liquidation premium of a long straddle, and recall that G^{STD} is the associated drift function in (17.11). We first consider the case where $\mu > r$. It follows from (17.17) that $G^{STD}(t,s) > 0$ when the stock price s is very high, and $G^{STD}(t,s) < 0$ when s is close to zero. Indeed, if the current stock price is sufficiently large, then $C_s^{STD}(t,s) \approx 1$ and thus $G^{STD}(t,s) > 0$. In this case, it is clear that $L^{STD} = 0$ does not solve (17.12) and therefore, $L^{STD} > 0$. As a result, the investor will tend to hold onto the option as $s \to +\infty$. Similarly, if $\mu < r$, we have $G^{STD}(t,s) > 0$ when the stock price s is close to zero and therefore $L^{STD}(t,s) > 0$. Hence, it is optimal to delay liquidation as $s \to 0$.

As time approaches maturity T, we have the limits:

$$\lim_{t\to T} d_1 = +\infty, \quad \lim_{t\to T} 2\Phi(d_1) - 1 = 1, \qquad \text{if } s > K,$$
$$\lim_{t\to T} d_1 = -\infty, \quad \lim_{t\to T} 2\Phi(d_1) - 1 = -1, \quad \text{if } s < K.$$

From these limits and (17.15), G^{STD} is discontinuous at $s = K$ on the expiration date. Precisely, if $\mu > r$, $\lim_{t\to T} G^{STD}(t,s) > 0$ for $s > K$ and it is optimal for the investor to hold on position. When $s < K$, we have $\lim_{t\to T} G^{STD}(t,s) < 0$. If the stock starts with price $s < K$ at t very close to T, then the probability that $S_u < K$, and thus, the probability that $G^{STD}(u, S_u) < 0$, for $u \in [t,T]$ is very close to 1. Consequently, it is optimal to sell immediately. As a result, the optimal liquidation boundary converges to strike price at maturity T.

To obtain numerical solutions, we employ the standard fully implicit PSOR algorithm to solve L^{STD} through its variational inequality in (17.12) over a uniform finite grid of time and stock price with Neumann boundary conditions. Since the drift parameter μ is difficult to estimate in practice, it is useful to study the sensitivity of the liquidation strategy on the parameter μ. The left panel of Figure 17.2 corresponds to the case $\mu < r$. The optimal liquidation strategy is to sell as soon as the stock price reaches an upper boundary. The right panel of Figure 17.2 corresponds to the case $\mu > r$, where the sell region and delay region are reversed when compared to the case with $\mu < r$.

17.3.2 Optimal liquidation of a long butterfly

Next, we consider a long butterfly that allows the investor to make profit if the future volatility is lower than the implied volatility. A long butterfly strategy consists of a long position of call with strike price K_1, a short position of two calls with strike price K_2, and a long position of one call with strike price K_3 such that $K_1 < K_2 < K_3$. The payoff of a long butterfly is given by

$$F^{BTF}(S_T) := (S_T - K_1)^+ + (S_T - K_3)^+ - 2(S_T - K_2)^+.$$

The market price of a long butterfly, denoted by C^{BTF}, is given by

$$C^{BTF}(t,s) = c_{BS}(t,s;K_1,T) + c_{BS}(t,s;K_3,T) - 2c_{BS}(t,s;K_2,T).$$

The payoff and price function of a long butterfly for fixed K_1, K_2, K_3 are shown in Figure 17.3.

The drift function for a long butterfly is given by

$$\begin{aligned} G^{BTF}(t,s) &= (\mu - r)sC_s^{BTF}(t,s) \\ &= (\mu - r)s(\Phi(d_1^1) + \Phi(d_1^3) - 2\Phi(d_1^2)), \end{aligned} \tag{17.18}$$

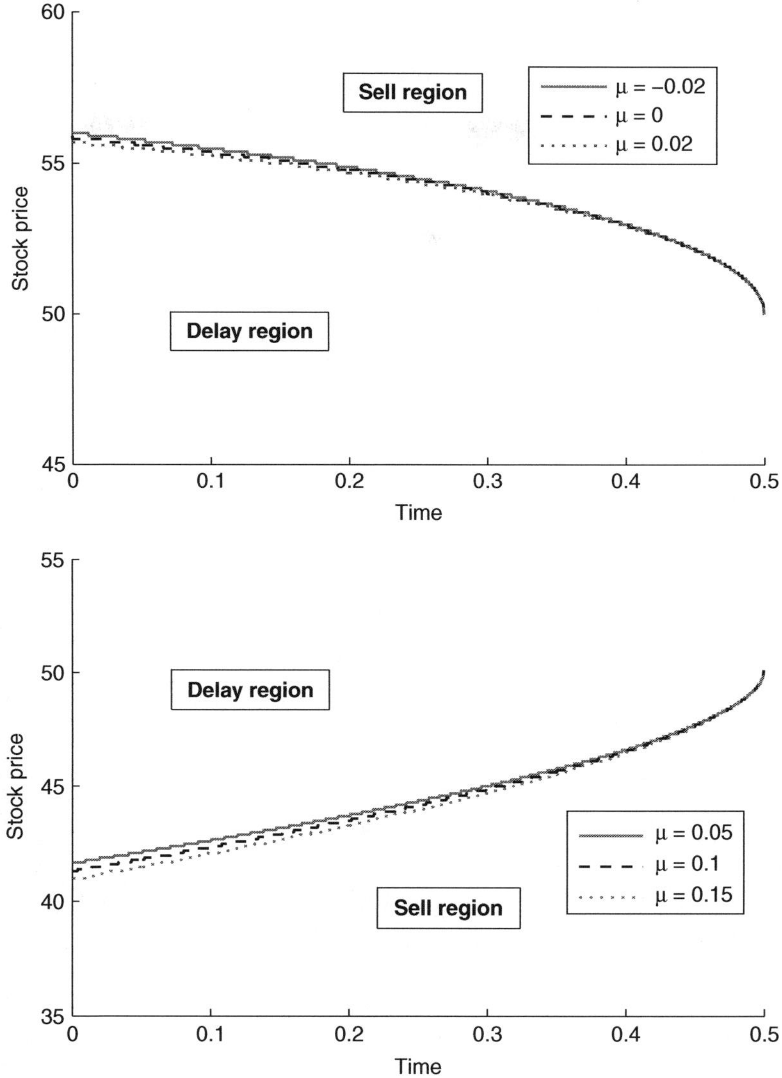

Figure 17.2 The liquidation boundaries of a long straddle over different values of μ

Notes: We take $T = 0.5$, $t = 0$, $r = 0.03$, $\sigma = 0.3$, $K = 50$. *Left panel*: The liquidation boundaries decrease as time progresses and converge to K at maturity T for $\mu = -0.02$, 0, 0.02. *Right panel*: The liquidation boundaries increase with time and converge to K at maturity T for $\mu = 0.05, 0.1, 0.15$.

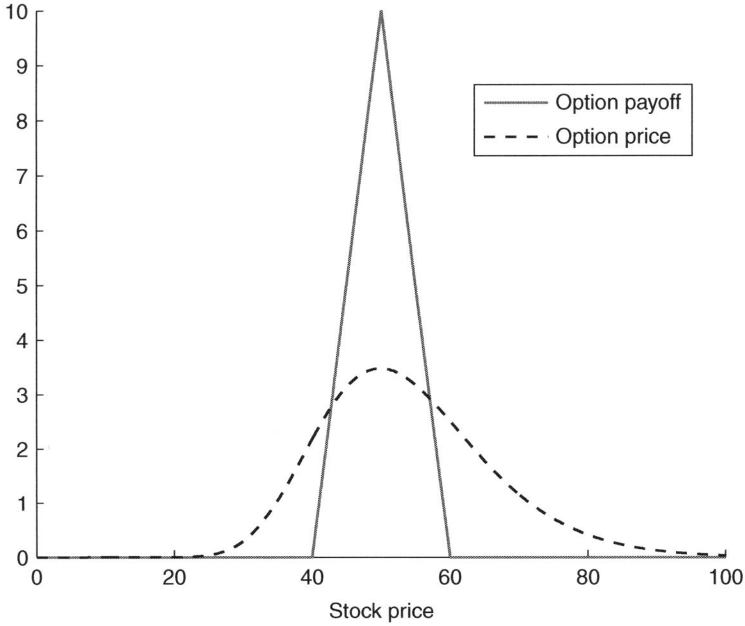

Figure 17.3 Payoff and market price of a long butterfly over stock price
Notes: We take $T = 0.5$, $t = 0$, $r = 0.03$, $\sigma = 0.3$, and $K_1 = 40$, $K_2 = 50$, $K_3 = 60$.

where

$$d_1^i = \frac{\log(\frac{s}{K_i}) + (r + \frac{1}{2}\sigma^2)(T-t)}{\sigma\sqrt{T-t}}, \quad i = 1,2,3. \tag{17.19}$$

In contrast with the case of long straddle, if $\mu > r$, $G^{BTF}(t,s) > 0$ when the stock price s is close to zero and therefore $L^{BTF}(t,s) > 0$. As a result, the investor will tend to hold onto the option as $s \to 0$. If $\mu < r$, we have $G^{STD}(t,s) > 0$ when the stock price s is very high, and hence it is optimal for the investor to delay liquidation as $s \to \infty$.

We consider a numerical example for the optimal liquidation of a long butterfly over different μ. The left panel of Figure 17.4 corresponds to the case $\mu < r$. The optimal liquidation strategy is to sell immediately when the stock price is sufficiently small and hold when the stock price is sufficiently large, which is opposite to the case of a long straddle. The right panel corresponds to the case $\mu > r$, where the sell region and delay region are reversed when compared to the left panel.

We apply the sensitivity analysis to the drift parameter μ to examine its influence on the optimal liquidation strategy. In Table 17.1, we compute in the left column the optimal liquidation premium at time 0 with the initial

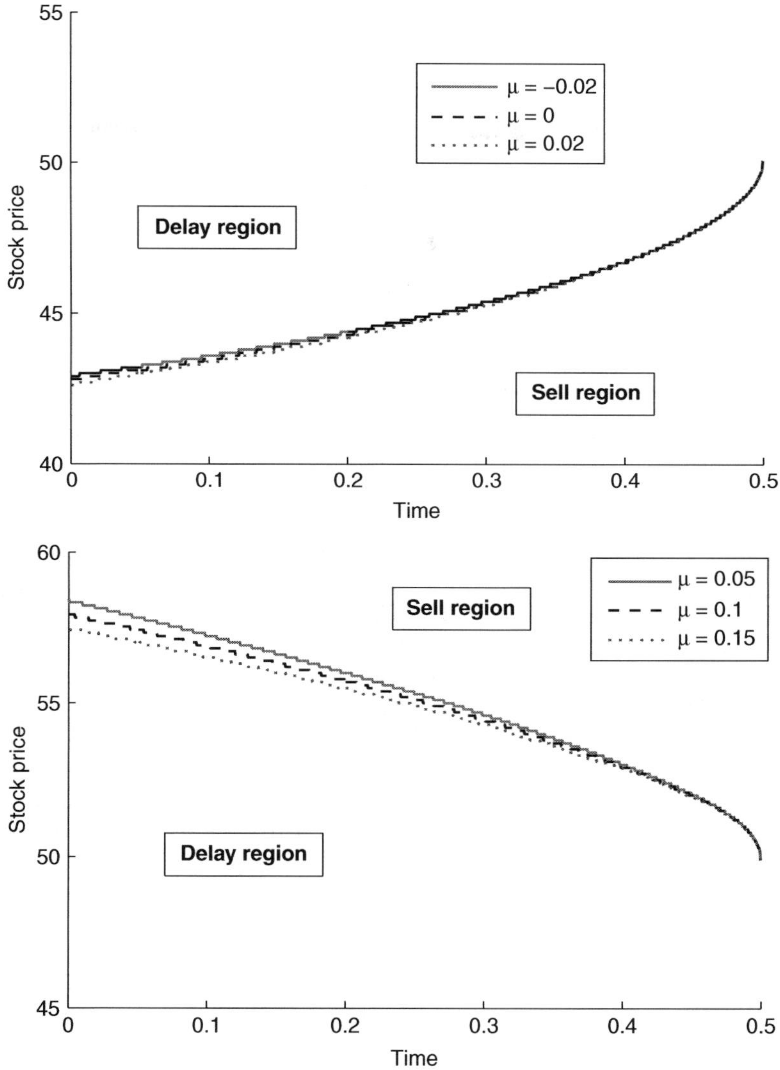

Figure 17.4 The liquidation boundaries of a long butterfly over different values of μ

Notes: We take $T = 0.5$, $t = 0$, $r = 0.03$, $\sigma = 0.3$, and $K_1 = 40$, $K_2 = 50$, $K_3 = 60$. *Left panel*: The liquidation boundaries increase and converge to K_2 at maturity T for $\mu = -0.02, 0, 0.02$. *Right panel*: The liquidation boundaries decrease and converge to K_2 for $\mu = 0.05, 0.1, 0.15$.

Table 17.1 The optimal liquidation premium (left column) and the expected return (right column) from holding the option till T, that is, $R(t,s)$ in (17.8), for a long straddle and long butterfly at time 0 for different values of drift μ

	Straddle		Butterfly	
	$L^{STD}(0,K)$	$R^{STD}(0,K)$	$L^{BTF}(0,K_2)$	$R^{BTF}(0,K_2)$
$\mu=15\%$	1.0832	0.7728	0.1916	−0.1252
$\mu=10\%$	0.5733	0.3646	0.1252	−0.0449
$\mu=5\%$	0.1479	0.0798	0.0397	−0.0046
$\mu=0\%$	0.0909	−0.0838	0.0610	−0.0056
$\mu=-5\%$	0.2763	−0.1297	0.1465	−0.0479

Notes: We take $T=0.5$, $t=0$, $r=0.03$, $\sigma=0.3$, and initial stock price $S_0=50$. The strike price for the long straddle is $K=50$, and the strike prices for the long butterfly are given by $K_1=40$, $K_2=50$, $K_3=60$.

stock price equal to the strike price over different values of μ for a long straddle and a long butterfly. We also compute in the right column the expected return if the position is held until maturity T, that is $R(t,s)$ in (17.8), as a benchmark.

As seen in Table 17.1, the parameter μ has a significant impact on the optimal liquidation value, even though it does not influence the optimal boundary much (see Figure 17.4). We recall from (17.11) that μ controls the sign of G. This is consistent with the result that the sell region and delay region are reversed when we switch from the case $\mu<r$ to $\mu>r$ for a long straddle and a long butterfly in Figures 17.2 and 17.4. Also, we observe from (17.10) and (17.11) that μ scales the optimal liquidation premium L. When $\mu>r$, a higher value of μ implies a higher optimal liquidation premium, which is reflected in Table 17.1. Thirdly, μ affects the $\mathbb{P}$-dynamics of stock price, and hence influences both the liquidation boundary and the optimal liquidation value. In addition, we observe from Table 17.1 that the expected return from optimal liquidation (left column) is significantly greater than the simple strategy of selling at maturity T (right column) for a wide range of μ.

17.4 Optimal liquidation in incomplete markets: an outlook

A natural extension of our analysis is to study the optimal liquidation problem in incomplete markets. To this end, we give an overview under a general Markovian stochastic volatility model (see for example Romano and Touzi

(1997) and Fouque et al. (2000)):

$$dS_t = S_t(\mu(t,Y_t)\,dt + \sigma(Y_t)\,dW_t), \tag{17.20}$$

$$dY_t = b(t,Y_t)\,dt + c(t,Y_t)(\rho dW_t + \hat{\rho} d\hat{W}_t). \tag{17.21}$$

Here, W and $\hat{W}$ are two independent standard Brownian motions, $\rho \in (-1,1)$ and $\hat{\rho} = \sqrt{1-\rho^2}$. The set of pricing measures $\{\mathbb{Q}^\phi\}_\phi$ is parameterized by the *volatility risk premium* process ϕ, where each measure $\mathbb{Q}^\phi$ is defined by

$$\frac{d\mathbb{Q}^\phi}{d\mathbb{P}} = \exp\left(-\frac{1}{2}\int_0^T \left(\kappa^2(s,Y_s) + \phi_s^2\right) ds - \int_0^T \kappa(s,Y_s)\,dW_s - \int_0^T \phi_s\, d\hat{W}_s\right), \tag{17.22}$$

where $\kappa(t,y) = \frac{\mu(t,y)-r}{\sigma(y)}$ is the bounded Sharpe ratio of S.

The observed market option prices reflect a volatility risk premium $(\phi_t^*)_{0\le t\le T}$. Under the market's risk-neutral pricing measure $\mathbb{Q}^* \equiv \mathbb{Q}^{\phi^*}$, the market price of a European option with terminal payoff $F(S_T)$ is given by

$$C(t,s,y) = \boldsymbol{E}^{\mathbb{Q}^*}\left\{e^{-r(T-t)}F(S_T)\,|S_t = s, Y_t = y\right\}.$$

The investor selects the optimal liquidation time to maximize the expected discounted market option price. As introduced in (17.4), the optimal liquidation premium is

$$L(t,s,y) = \sup_{t\le\tau\le T} \boldsymbol{E}^{\mathbb{P}}\{e^{-r(\tau-t)}C(\tau,S_\tau,Y_\tau)\,|S_t = s, Y_t = y\} - C(t,s,y). \tag{17.23}$$

With stochastic volatility, the liquidation strategy for puts and calls may now be non-trivial. This leads to the analytical and numerical studies of the variational inequality satisfied by $L(t,s,y)$. The resulting optimal liquidation strategy will naturally require the investor to continuously monitor, not only the stock price S, but also the volatility level Y.

References

Fouque, J.-P., Papanicolaou, G., and Sircar, R. (2000). *Derivatives in Financial Markets with Stochastic Volatility*. Cambridge University Press.

Leung, T. and Liu, P. (2012). Risk premia and optimal liquidation of credit derivatives. *International Journal of Theoretical and Applied Finance*, 15(8): 1–34.

Leung, T. and Ludkovski, M. (2011). Optimal timing to purchase options. *SIAM Journal on Financial Mathematics*, 2(1): 768–793.

Leung, T. and Ludkovski, M. (2012). Accounting for risk aversion in derivatives purchase timing. *Mathematics & Financial Economics*, 6(4): 363–386.

Peskir, G., Glover, K., and Samee, F. (2010). The British Asian option. *Sequential Analysis*, 29(3): 311–327.
Peskir, G. and Samee, F. (2011). The British put option. *Applied Mathematical Finance*, 18: 537–563.
Romano, M. and Touzi, N. (1997). Contingent claims and market completeness in a stochastic volatility model. *Mathematical Finance*, 7(4): 399–410.

Index

Printed and bound by CPI Group (UK) Ltd, Croydon, CR0 4YY